CONTENTS

GUIDELINE DEVELOPMENT GROUP MEMBERSHIP

Professor Nicol Ferrier (Chair, Guideline Development Group)
Professor of Psychiatry and Head of School of Neurology,
Neurobiology and Psychiatry, University of Newcastle upon Tyne

Mr Stephen Pilling (Facilitator, Guideline Development Group)
Joint Director, National Collaborating Centre for Mental Health
Director, Centre for Outcomes Research and Effectiveness
Consultant Clinical Psychologist, Camden and Islington Mental Health and
Social Care Trust

Mr Stephen Bazire
Director, Pharmacy Services, Norfolk and Waveney Mental Health Partnership
NHS Trust

Dr Roger Beer
Consultant Psychiatrist, Gwent Healthcare NHS Trust

Dr Tamsin Black
Consultant Clinical Psychologist, The Coborn Adolescent Service, East London
and the City Mental Health NHS Trust

Ms Ellen Boddington
Research Assistant, The National Collaborating Centre for Mental Health

Ms Rachel Burbeck
Systematic Reviewer, The National Collaborating Centre for Mental Health

Ms Julie Charles
Service User Representative

Ms Josephine Foggo
Project Manager (2004–2005), The National Collaborating Centre for Mental
Health

Dr Peter Haddad
Consultant in Community Psychiatry, Bolton, Salford and Trafford Mental Health
NHS Trust
Honorary Senior Lecturer, University of Manchester

Ms Alison Hunter
Project Manager (2003–2004), The National Collaborating Centre for
Mental Health

Professor Dominic Lam
Professor of Clinical Psychology, University of Hull

Dr Clare Lamb
Consultant Child and Adolescent Psychiatrist, North Wales Adolescent Service,
Conwy and Denbighshire NHS Trust

Mr Tim McDougall
Nurse Consultant, Pine Lodge Young People's Centre, Chester

Dr Ifigeneia Mavranezouli
Health Economist, The National Collaborating Centre for Mental Health

Professor Richard Morriss
Professor of Psychiatry and Community Health, University of Nottingham
and Nottinghamshire Healthcare Trust, Queen's Medical Centre,
Nottingham

Dr Catherine Pettinari
Project Manager (2004, 2005–2006), The National Collaborating Centre
for Mental Health

Ms Sarah Stockton
Information Scientist, The National Collaborating Centre for Mental Health

Dr Clare Taylor
Editor, The National Collaborating Centre for Mental Health

Professor Nigel Wellman
Professor of Mental Health Nursing, Thames Valley University
Honorary Consultant Nurse, Berkshire Healthcare NHS Trust

Mr Robert Westhead
Service User Representative

Ms Marilyn Wilson
Occupational Therapist, Community Mental Health Team, Essex

Mr Stephen Yorke
Carer Representative

7

ACKNOWLEDGEMENTS

The bipolar disorder Guideline Development Group (GDG) and review team at the National Collaborating Centre for Mental Health (NCCMH) would like to thank the following people:

Those who acted as advisers on specialist topics or have contributed to the process by reviewing drafts of the guideline:
   Robert Baldwin
   David Osborn
   Lucy Robinson

Participants in the consensus conference on the diagnosis of bipolar disorder in children and adolescents:
   Speakers
   David Coghill
   Chris Hollis
   Guy Goodwin, Conference Chair
   Anthony James
   Catrien Reichart
   Eric Taylor
   Stan Kutcher
   Reviewers
   Ellen Leibenluft
   Willem Nolen

Speakers in the consensus conference on the pharmacological management of mental disorders in pregnancy and lactating women:
   Elizabeth McDonald
   David Chadwick
   Patricia McElhatton
   Patrick O'Brien

Researchers contacted for information on unpublished or soon to be published studies:
   RA Kowatch
   Mick Power
   Thomas Meyer
   Jan Scott
   Greg Simon

Project management (from December 2005):
   Liz Costigan

1. EXECUTIVE SUMMARY

KEY PRIORITIES FOR IMPLEMENTATION

The following recommendations have been identified as recommendations for implementation.

Treating bipolar disorder with drugs

- Valproate should not be prescribed routinely for women of child-bearing potential. If no effective alternative to valproate can be identified, adequate contraception should be used, and the risks of taking valproate during pregnancy should be explained.
- Lithium, olanzapine or valproate*[1] should be considered for long-term treatment of bipolar disorder. The choice should depend on:
  - response to previous treatments
  - the relative risk, and known precipitants, of manic versus depressive relapse
  - physical risk factors, particularly renal disease, obesity and diabetes
  - the patient's preference and history of adherence
  - gender (valproate should not be prescribed for women of child-bearing potential)
  - a brief assessment of cognitive state (such as the Mini-Mental State Examination) if appropriate, for example, for older people.
- If the patient has frequent relapses, or symptoms continue to cause functional impairment, switching to an alternative monotherapy or adding a second prophylactic agent (lithium, olanzapine, valproate*) should be considered. Clinical state, side effects and, where relevant, blood levels should be monitored closely. Possible combinations are lithium with valproate*, lithium with olanzapine, and valproate* with olanzapine. The reasons for the choice and the discussion with the patient of the potential benefits and risks should be documented.
- If a trial of a combination of prophylactic agents proves ineffective, the following should be considered:
  - consulting with, or referring the patient to, a clinician with expertise in the drug treatment of bipolar disorder
  - prescribing lamotrigine* (especially if the patient has bipolar II disorder) or carbamazepine.

---

[1]In this guideline, drug names are marked with an asterisk if they do not have a UK marketing authorisation for the indication in question at the time of publication. Prescribers should check each drug's summary of product characteristics (SPC) for current licensed indications.

- If a patient is taking an antidepressant at the onset of an acute manic episode, the antidepressant should be stopped. This may be done abruptly or gradually, depending on the patient's current clinical need and previous experience of discontinuation/withdrawal symptoms, and the risk of discontinuation/withdrawal symptoms of the antidepressant in question.
- After successful treatment for an acute depressive episode, patients should not routinely continue on antidepressant treatment long-term, because there is no evidence that this reduces relapse rates, and it may be associated with increased risk of switching to mania.

Monitoring physical health

- People with bipolar disorder should have an annual physical health review, normally in primary care, to ensure that the following are assessed each year:
  - lipid levels, including cholesterol in all patients over 40 even if there is no other indication of risk
  - plasma glucose levels
  - weight
  - smoking status and alcohol use
  - blood pressure.

Diagnosing bipolar disorder in adolescents

- When diagnosing bipolar I disorder in adolescents the same criteria should be used as for adults except that:
  - mania must be present
  - euphoria must be present most days, most of the time (for at least 7 days)
  - irritability can be helpful in making a diagnosis if it is episodic, severe, results in impaired function and is out of keeping or not in character; however, it should not be a core diagnostic criterion.

1.1   GENERAL RECOMMENDATIONS FOR THE CARE OF PEOPLE WITH BIPOLAR DISORDER

1.1.1   All patients

1.1.1.1   Healthcare professionals should establish and maintain collaborative relationships with patients and their families and carers (within the normal bounds of confidentiality), be respectful of the patient's knowledge and experience of the illness, and provide relevant information (including written information) at every stage of assessment, diagnosis and treatment (including the proper use and likely side-effect profile of medication).

1.1.1.2   Patients, family and carers should be informed of self-help and support groups and be encouraged to take part in them, particularly at initial diagnosis, and regularly after that. Such groups may provide information on early warning signs, treatment and side effects, and support in time of crisis.

1.1.1.3   Healthcare professionals should aim to develop a therapeutic relationship with all patients with bipolar disorder, and advise them on careful and regular self-monitoring of symptoms (including triggers and early warning signs), lifestyle (including sleep hygiene and work patterns) and coping strategies.

1.1.1.4   Advance statements (directives) covering both mental and physical healthcare should be developed collaboratively by people with bipolar disorder and healthcare professionals, especially by people who have severe manic or depressive episodes or who have been treated under the Mental Health Act. These should be documented in care plans, and copies given to the person with bipolar disorder, and to his or her care coordinator and GP.

1.1.1.5   Healthcare professionals should encourage patients to involve their families and carers in assessment and treatment plans if appropriate, and make themselves accessible to family members and carers in times of crisis. The needs of patients' family members or carers should be taken into account, including:
- the impact of the disorder on relationships
- the welfare of dependent children, siblings and vulnerable adults
- the regular assessment of carers' physical, social and mental health needs.

1.1.2   Special groups

1.1.2.1   People with bipolar disorder who have learning difficulties should receive the same care as others, taking into account the risk of interactions with any other medication they are prescribed.

1.1.2.2   People with bipolar disorder and comorbid personality disorder should receive the same care as others with bipolar disorder, because the presence of a personality disorder does not preclude the delivery of effective treatments for bipolar disorder.

1.1.2.3   For people with bipolar disorder and comorbid harmful drug and/or alcohol use, a psychosocial intervention targeted at the drug and/or alcohol use (for example, psychoeducation and motivational enhancement) should be considered. This should normally be delivered by general mental health services, working with specialist substance use services where appropriate.

1.1.2.4   Local services should have a robust protocol for transferring patients from services for adults of working age to those for older people (usually those older than 65 years). This should include agreement about the clinical parameters to take into account (for example, medical comorbidity or cognitive deterioration) and what to do if the patient is no longer in contact with services for adults of working age. Referral or re-referral should be based on the needs of the patient first, rather than simply their chronological age.

1.1.2.5 When treating older people with bipolar disorder, healthcare professionals should:
- be aware of the need to use medication at lower doses
- be alert to the increased risk of drug interactions when prescribing psychotropic medication to older adults
- ensure that medical comorbidities have been recognised and addressed.

1.2   THE ASSESSMENT, RECOGNITION AND DIAGNOSIS OF BIPOLAR DISORDER IN ADULTS

1.2.1   Recognising bipolar disorder in primary care

New or suspected presentations of bipolar disorder

1.2.1.1 Primary care clinicians should normally refer patients with suspected bipolar disorder for a specialist mental health assessment and development of a care plan, if either of the following are present:
- periods of overactive, disinhibited behaviour lasting at least 4 days with or without periods of depression, or
- three or more recurrent depressive episodes in the context of a history of overactive, disinhibited behaviour.

1.2.1.2 Primary care clinicians should urgently refer patients with mania or severe depression, and who are a danger to themselves or other people, to specialist mental health services.

1.2.1.3 Primary care clinicians should ask about hypomanic symptoms when assessing a patient with depression and overactive, disinhibited behaviour.

Existing bipolar disorder in primary care

1.2.1.4 When a patient with existing bipolar disorder registers with a practice, the GP should consider referring them for assessment by specialist mental health services and, if appropriate, development of a care plan.

1.2.1.5 When a patient with bipolar disorder is managed solely in primary care, an urgent referral to secondary care services should be made:
- if there is an acute exacerbation of symptoms, in particular the development of mania or severe depression
- if there is an increase in the degree of risk, or change in the nature of risk, to self or others.

1.2.1.6 When a patient with bipolar disorder is managed solely in primary care, a review by secondary care services or increased contact in primary care should be considered if:
- the patient's functioning declines significantly or their condition responds poorly to treatment
- treatment adherence is a problem

- comorbid alcohol and/or drug misuse is suspected
- the patient is considering stopping prophylactic medication after a period of relatively stable mood.

1.2.2 Assessment of bipolar disorder in secondary care

1.2.2.1 When assessing suspected bipolar disorder healthcare professionals should:
- take a full history including family history, a review of all previous episodes and any symptoms between episodes
- assess the patient's symptom profile, triggers to previous episodes, social and personal functioning, comorbidities including substance misuse and anxiety, risk, physical health, and current psychosocial stressors
- obtain where possible, and within the bounds of confidentiality, a corroborative history from a family member or carer
- consider using formal criteria, including self-rating scales such as the Mood Disorder Questionnaire[2].

1.2.2.2 When considering a diagnosis of bipolar disorder healthcare professionals should take into account that:
- more pronounced psychotic symptoms, increased suicidal ideation, drug misuse, or more disturbed behaviour may be symptoms of a later presentation of bipolar disorder and not of a schizophrenia-spectrum disorder – this may be particularly important when assessing patients from black and minority ethnic groups who may have difficulty accessing services
- drug and/or alcohol misuse may induce manic-like symptoms – in inpatient settings, if there is evidence of misuse, wait 7 days before confirming a diagnosis of bipolar disorder
- symptoms may be due to underlying organic conditions, such as hypothyroidism, cerebrovascular insults and other neurological disorders (for example, dementia), particularly in people with late-onset bipolar disorder (older than 40 years).

1.2.2.3 Before diagnosing rapid-cycling bipolar disorder, healthcare professionals should check alternative explanations for the symptoms including problems such as thyroid disease, antidepressant-induced switching, suboptimal medication regimes, the effects of lithium withdrawal, and erratic compliance. They should also consider asking the patient and/or carer to assess mood and behaviour for at least a year.

1.2.2.4 When assessing people with suspected bipolar disorder and/or personality disorder healthcare professionals should:
- during initial assessment, consider a diagnosis of bipolar disorder before a diagnosis of personality disorder in a person with mood swings and functional impairment

---

[2]Hirschfeld, R.M., Williams, J.B., Spitzer, R.L., *et al*. (2001) Development and validation of a screening instrument for bipolar spectrum disorder: the Mood Disorder Questionnaire. *American Journal of Psychiatry, 158,* 1743–1744.

- during treatment, ensure the patient has had adequate treatment to stabilise symptoms before considering a diagnosis of comorbid personality disorder.

1.2.3 Assessment of risk in primary and secondary care

1.2.3.1 A risk assessment should be undertaken when:
- bipolar disorder is first diagnosed
- a person with bipolar disorder undergoes significant change in mental state or personal circumstances
- a person with bipolar disorder is discharged from or is on leave from inpatient care.

1.2.4 Crisis and risk management plans

1.2.4.1 If a patient is at risk of suicide, exploitation or severe self-neglect, is a significant risk to others (including neglect of dependents), or has a history of recurrent admissions, particularly compulsory admissions, a crisis plan should be developed in collaboration with the patient, covering:
- a list of identified or potential personal, social or environmental triggers, and early warning symptoms of relapse
- a protocol for increasing the dose of medication or taking additional medication (which may be given to the patient in advance) for patients who are at risk of rapid onset of mania and for whom clear early warning signs can be identified – protocols should be monitored regularly, and are not a substitute for an urgent review
- how primary and secondary healthcare services have agreed to respond to any identified increase in risk, for example by increased contact
- how the patient (and where appropriate their carer) can access help, and the names of healthcare professionals in primary and secondary care who have responsibilities in the crisis plan.

1.2.4.2 A limited quantity of psychotropic medication should be prescribed for patients during periods of high risk of suicide.

1.3 TREATMENT SETTING AND PATHWAYS TO CARE

1.3.1 Continuity of care for people with bipolar disorder

1.3.1.1 People with bipolar disorder (including those with sub-threshold symptoms), whether managed in primary or secondary care, should have continuity of care, and see the same healthcare professionals regularly, where possible, to improve long-term outcomes.

1.3.2   Models of service provision

Service provision in primary and secondary care

1.3.2.1   Primary and secondary care organisations should consider establishing integrated care programmes for people with bipolar disorder. These should include:
- regular reviews in primary and secondary care of mental state, and personal and social functioning, to ensure that symptoms (including sub-threshold symptoms) are treated if they significantly impair social functioning
- clear protocols for the delivery and monitoring of pharmacological, psychosocial and psychological interventions
- clear agreements between healthcare professionals on their responsibilities for assessment, monitoring and treatment
- written treatment plans that promote the principles of self-management, and are shared with the patient and, where appropriate, with families and carers.

1.3.2.2   All GP practices should include people with a diagnosis of bipolar disorder in their case register of people with severe mental illness.

1.3.2.3   Primary care teams should consider providing telephone support to patients with bipolar disorder, by appropriately trained staff using clear protocols, in particular for monitoring medication regimes.

Specialist mental health services

1.3.2.4   Referral to a community mental health team should be considered for people with bipolar disorder who:
- have problems in engaging with, and maintaining regular contact with services such as outpatient care
- experience frequent relapses, poor symptom control, continuing functional impairment, or comorbid anxiety disorders
- are at risk of suicide, or harm to self or others, including self-neglect or exploitation
- have problems adhering to medication regimes or with chronic alcohol and/or drug misuse.

1.3.2.5   Crisis resolution and home treatment teams (which should have prompt access to existing care plans) should be considered for people with bipolar disorder to:
- manage crises at home or in the community
- support early discharge from hospital.

1.3.2.6   When delivering crisis care at home, particular attention should be given to managing risk, monitoring behavioural disturbance (particularly during episodes of mania), and the burden on family and carers.

1.3.2.7   Early intervention services for people with psychosis should be available to people with bipolar disorder and should provide specialist expertise in diagnosis, and pharmacological, psychological, social, occupational and educational interventions.

1.3.2.8 Assertive community treatment should be considered for people with bipolar disorder, particularly those who make high use of inpatient services and those who engage poorly with other services and so experience frequent relapse and/or social breakdown.

1.3.2.9 Admission to an inpatient unit should be considered for patients with bipolar disorder at significant risk of harm. The unit should provide facilities for containment within a supportive, low-stimulation environment, including access to a psychiatric intensive care unit. The inpatient service should seek to provide an emotionally warm, safe, culturally sensitive and supportive environment, with high levels of positive engagement between staff and patients.

1.3.2.10 Acute day hospitals should be considered, as an alternative to inpatient care and to facilitate early discharge from inpatient care.

1.3.2.11 Mental health services, in partnership with social care providers and other local stakeholders should consider providing:
- vocational rehabilitation – specifically, individual supported placements, for people with bipolar disorder who want help returning to work or gaining employment
- support to return to or engage with education or other structured, purposeful activities.

1.3.2.12 Enhanced multiprofessional outpatient clinics, such as lithium clinics, should be considered for patients who would benefit from close monitoring, and/or have a physical health risk such as renal damage, and have a record of regular attendance without the need for outreach services.

1.3.2.13 Trusts providing specialist mental health services should ensure that all clinicians have access to specialist advice from designated experienced clinicians on managing bipolar disorder in adults (and, where appropriate, separately for children and adolescents), and on referral to tertiary centres.

1.4 THE TREATMENT AND MANAGEMENT OF BIPOLAR DISORDER

1.4.1 General recommendations

1.4.1.1 Healthcare professionals should fully involve patients in decisions about their treatment and care, and determine treatment plans in collaboration with the patient, carefully considering the experience and outcome of previous treatment(s) together with patient preference.

1.4.1.2 Contraception, and the risks of pregnancy (including the risks of relapse, damage to the fetus, and the risks associated with stopping or changing medication) should be discussed with all women of child-bearing potential, regardless of whether they are planning a pregnancy. They should be encouraged to discuss pregnancy plans with their doctor.

1.4.1.3   People experiencing a manic episode, or severe depressive symptoms, should normally be seen again within a week of their first assessment, and then regularly at appropriate intervals, for example, every 2–4 weeks in the first 3 months and less often after that, if response is good.

1.4.2   The management of acute episodes: mania and hypomania

General advice

1.4.2.1   To help reduce the negative consequences of manic symptoms, healthcare professionals should consider advising patients to avoid excessive stimulation, to engage in calming activities, to delay important decisions, and to establish a structured routine (including a regular sleep pattern) in which the level of activity is reduced.

1.4.2.2   If a patient is taking an antidepressant at the onset of an acute manic episode, the antidepressant should be stopped. This may be done abruptly or gradually, depending on the patient's current clinical need and previous experience of discontinuation/withdrawal symptoms, and the risk of discontinuation/withdrawal symptoms of the antidepressant in question.

Drug treatment for acute mania for people not taking antimanic medication

1.4.2.3   If a patient develops acute mania when not taking antimanic medication, treatment options include starting an antipsychotic, valproate or lithium. When making the choice, prescribers should take into account preferences for future prophylactic use, the side-effect profile, and consider:
- prescribing an antipsychotic if there are severe manic symptoms or marked behavioural disturbance as part of the syndrome of mania
- prescribing valproate or lithium if symptoms have responded to these drugs before, and the person has shown good compliance
- avoiding valproate in women of child-bearing potential
- using lithium only if symptoms are not severe because it has a slower onset of action than antipsychotics and valproate.

1.4.2.4   In the initial management of acute behavioural disturbance or agitation, the short-term use of a benzodiazepine (such as lorazepam*) should be considered in addition to the antimanic agent.

1.4.2.5   If treating acute mania with antipsychotics, olanzapine, quetiapine or risperidone should normally be used, and the following should be taken into account:
- individual risk factors for side effects (such as the risk of diabetes)
- the need to initiate treatment at the lower end of the therapeutic dose range recommended in the summary of product characteristics and titrate according to response

- that if an antipsychotic proves ineffective, augmenting it with valproate or lithium should be considered
- that older people are at greater risk of sudden onset of depressive symptoms after recovery from a manic episode.

1.4.2.6 Carbamazepine* should not be routinely used for treating acute mania, and gabapentin*, lamotrigine* and topiramate* are not recommended.

Drug treatment of acute mania for people taking antimanic medication

1.4.2.7 If a patient already taking an antipsychotic experiences a manic episode, the dose should be checked and increased if necessary. If there are no signs of improvement, the addition of lithium or valproate should be considered.

1.4.2.8 If a patient already taking lithium experiences a manic episode, plasma lithium levels should be checked. If levels are suboptimal (that is, below 0.8 mmol per litre), the dose should normally be increased to a maximum blood level of 1.0 mmol per litre. If the response is not adequate, augmenting lithium with an antipsychotic should be considered.

1.4.2.9 If a patient already taking valproate* experiences a manic episode, the dose should be increased until:
- symptoms start to improve, or
- side effects limit further dose increase.

If there are no signs of improvement, the addition of olanzapine, quetiapine, or risperidone should be considered. Patients on doses higher than 45 mg per kilogram should be monitored carefully.

1.4.2.10 For patients who present with severe mania when already taking lithium or valproate*, adding an antipsychotic should be considered at the same time as gradually increasing the dose of lithium or valproate.

1.4.2.11 For patients who present with mania when already taking carbamazepine, the dose should not routinely be increased. Adding an antipsychotic should be considered, depending on the severity of mania and the current dose of carbamazepine. Interactions with other medication are common with carbamazepine, and doses should be adjusted as necessary.

1.4.3 The management of acute episodes: depressive symptoms

Treatment of depressive symptoms
Patients not taking antimanic medication

1.4.3.1 A patient who is prescribed antidepressant medication should also be prescribed an antimanic drug. The choice of antimanic drug should be compatible with decisions about future prophylactic treatment, the likely side effects and whether the patient is a woman of child-bearing potential.

1.4.3.2   When initiating antidepressant treatment for a patient who is not already taking antimanic medication, prescribers should explain the risks of switching to mania and the benefits of taking an adjunctive antimanic agent. People who are not willing to take antimanic medication, should be monitored carefully. Anti-depressant treatment should begin at a low dose and be increased gradually if necessary.

Patients taking antimanic medication

1.4.3.3   If a person has an acute depressive episode when taking antimanic medication, prescribers should first check they are taking the antimanic agent at the appropriate dose and adjust the dose if necessary.

Patients with mild depressive symptoms

1.4.3.4   For patients with acute mild depressive symptoms, a further assessment should be arranged, normally within 2 weeks ('watchful waiting') if:
● previous episodes of mild depression have not developed into chronic or more severe depression in this patient, or
● the patient is judged not to be at significant risk of developing a more severe depression.
If the patient is judged to be at significant risk of worsening or on review continues to be unwell, they should be managed as for moderate/severe depression particularly if functional impairment is evident.

Patients with moderate or severe depressive symptoms

1.4.3.5   For patients with moderate or severe depressive symptoms, prescribers should normally consider:
● prescribing an SSRI antidepressant (but not paroxetine in pregnant women), because these are less likely than tricyclic antidepressants to be associated with switching, or
● adding quetiapine, if the patient is already taking antimanic medication that is not an antipsychotic

1.4.3.6   If a trial of drug treatment at an adequate dose and with adequate compliance does not produce a significant improvement for moderate depressive symptoms, a structured psychological treatment should be considered. This should focus on depressive symptoms, problem solving, promoting social functioning, and education about medication.

Antidepressant treatment and risk monitoring

1.4.3.7   Antidepressants should be avoided for patients with depressive symptoms who have:
● rapid-cycling bipolar disorder
● a recent hypomanic episode

- recent functionally impairing rapid mood fluctuations.

Instead, consider increasing the dose of the antimanic agent or the addition of a second antimanic agent (including lamotrigine*).

1.4.3.8 Patients' concerns about taking antidepressants should be addressed. For example, they should be advised that craving and tolerance do not occur, and that taking medication should not be seen as a sign of weakness.

1.4.3.9 When antidepressant treatment is started, patients should be told about:

- the possibility of manic or hypomanic switching
- the delay in onset of effect, and the gradual and fluctuating nature of improvement
- the need to take medication as prescribed and the risk of discontinuation/withdrawal symptoms
- the need to monitor for signs of akathisia, suicidal ideation (normally anyone under 30 should be reviewed within 1 week of initiation of treatment), and increased anxiety and agitation (particularly in the initial stages of treatment)
- the need to seek help promptly if these side effects are distressing.

1.4.3.10 If a patient with bipolar disorder develops marked and/or prolonged akathisia or agitation while taking an antidepressant, the use of the drug should be reviewed urgently.

1.4.3.11 Care should be taken when prescribing SSRIs to people – particularly older people – taking other medication that can cause intestinal bleeding, such as non-steroidal anti-inflammatory drugs. The use of a gastroprotective drug may be considered.

Stopping antidepressants after an acute depressive episode

1.4.3.12 When a patient is in remission from depressive symptoms (or symptoms have been significantly less severe for 8 weeks), stopping the antidepressant medication should be considered, to minimise the risks of switching to mania and increased rapid cycling. The dose of antidepressant should be gradually reduced over several weeks, while maintaining the antimanic medication. Particular care is needed with paroxetine and venlafaxine because they are associated with a higher risk of discontinuation/withdrawal symptoms.

Treatments not recommended for routine use

1.4.3.13 The following treatments should not be routinely used for acute depressive episodes in people with bipolar disorder:

- lamotrigine* as a single, first-line agent in bipolar I disorder
- transcranial magnetic stimulation*.

Treatment resistance and psychotic symptoms

Incomplete response to the treatment for acute depression

1.4.3.14   When a patient's depressive symptoms do not fully respond to an antidepressant, the patient should be reassessed for evidence of substance
misuse, psychosocial stressors, physical health problems, comorbid disorders, such as anxiety or severe obsessional symptoms, and inadequate
adherence to medication. Prescribers should then consider:
- increasing the dose of the antidepressant within 'British national
formulary' ('BNF') limits
- individual psychological therapy focused on depressive symptoms
- switching to an alternative antidepressant (for example, mirtazapine or
venlafaxine)
- adding quetiapine* or olanzapine if the patient is not already taking one
of these, or
- adding lithium if the patient is not already taking it.

1.4.3.15   If a patient's depressive symptoms have failed to respond to at least three
courses of treatment for depression of adequate dose and duration, seeking
the advice of, or referral to, a clinician with a specialist interest in treating
bipolar disorder should be considered.

Concurrent depressive and psychotic symptoms

1.4.3.16   For patients with a diagnosis of bipolar disorder experiencing concurrent
depressive and psychotic symptoms, prescribers should consider augmenting the current treatment plan with antipsychotic medication, such as olanzapine, quetiapine, or risperidone, or the use of electroconvulsive therapy
(see section 1.4.6) if the depressive illness is severe.

Persistent depressive symptoms

1.4.3.17   For patients with persistent depressive symptoms and no history of recent
rapid cycling, including those who have declined an antidepressant, structured psychological therapy may be considered. This should focus on
depressive symptoms, problem solving, improving social functioning, and
further discussion of medication concordance.

Additional advice

1.4.3.18   Patients with depressive symptoms should be advised about techniques
such as a structured exercise programme, activity scheduling, engaging in
both pleasurable and goal-directed activities, ensuring adequate diet and
sleep, and seeking appropriate social support, and given increased monitoring and formal support.

1.4.4   The management of acute mixed episodes

1.4.4.1   Prescribers should consider treating patients with an acute mixed episode as if they had an acute manic episode, and avoid prescribing an antidepressant.

1.4.4.2   Prescribers should monitor patients with an acute mixed episode closely (at least weekly), particularly for suicide risk.

1.4.5   The management of an acute episode in rapid-cycling bipolar disorder

1.4.5.1   Acute episodes in patients with rapid-cycling bipolar disorder should normally be managed in secondary mental health services. Treatment should be as for manic and depressive episodes, but in addition healthcare professionals should do the following.
- Review the patient's previous treatments for bipolar disorder, and consider a further trial of any that were inadequately delivered or adhered to.
- Focus on optimising long-term treatment rather than on treating individual episodes and symptoms; trials of medication should usually last at least 6 months.
- Adopt a psychoeducational approach and encourage patients to keep a regular mood diary to monitor changes in severity and frequency of symptoms, and the impact of interventions.

1.4.6   The use of ECT in severe manic and depressive episodes

1.4.6.1   Electroconvulsive therapy (ECT) is recommended only to achieve rapid and short-term improvement of severe symptoms after an adequate trial of other treatment options has proven ineffective and/or when the condition is considered to be potentially life-threatening, in individuals with:
- severe depressive illness
- catatonia
- a prolonged or severe manic episode.[3]

1.4.6.2   The decision as to whether ECT is clinically indicated should be based on a documented assessment of the risks and potential benefits to the individual, including:
- the risks associated with the anaesthetic

---

[3]This recommendation is from *NICE Technology Appraisal 59*, and has been incorporated into this guideline in line with NICE procedures for the development of guidelines.

- current comorbidities
- anticipated adverse events, particularly cognitive impairment
- the risks of not having treatment.[3]

1.4.6.3   When using ECT to treat bipolar disorder, prescribers should consider:
- stopping or reducing lithium or benzodiazepines before giving ECT
- monitoring the length of fits carefully if the patient is taking anticonvulsants.
- monitoring mental state carefully for evidence of switching to the opposite pole.

1.4.7   The prevention and management of behavioural disturbance

1.4.7.1   If a patient with bipolar disorder exhibits seriously disturbed behaviour, or is judged to be at risk of doing so, healthcare professionals should:
- place the patient in the least stimulating and confrontational, and most supportive environment available
- review the patient's safety and physical status, including hydration levels, and take appropriate action
- consider using distraction techniques and diverting the patient's energy into less risky or more productive activities to prevent or reduce behavioural disturbance.

Drug treatment of severe behavioural disturbance

This section on the drug treatment of severe behavioural disturbance should be read in conjunction with the NICE clinical guideline on the short-term management of disturbed/violent behaviour in inpatient psychiatric settings and emergency departments.

1.4.7.2   Severe behavioural disturbance in people with bipolar disorder should normally be treated first with oral medication, such as lorazepam* or an antipsychotic, or a combination of an antipsychotic and a benzodiazepine. Risperidone and olanzapine are available in orodispersible formulations that are easier for patients to take and are more difficult to spit out.

1.4.7.3   If a severely disturbed patient with bipolar disorder cannot be effectively managed with oral medication and rapid tranquilisation is needed, intramuscular olanzapine (10 mg), lorazepam* (2 mg) or haloperidol (2–10 mg) should be considered, wherever possible as a single agent. When making the choice of drug, prescribers should take into account:
- that olanzapine and lorazepam* are preferable to haloperidol because of the risk of movement disorders (particularly dystonia and akathisia) with haloperidol
- that olanzapine and benzodiazepines should not be given intramuscularly within 1 hour of each other

- that repeat intramuscular doses can be given up to 20 mg per day (olan-zapine), or 4 mg per day (lorazepam*) or 18 mg per day (haloperidol) – the total daily dose including concurrent oral medication should not normally exceed 'BNF' limits
- the patient's previous response and tolerability, their current regular medication, and the availability of flumazenil.

1.4.7.4 Intravenous preparations of any psychotropic drug, intramuscular diazepam*, intramuscular chlorpromazine, paraldehyde* and zuclopenthixol acetate are not recommended for routine use for managing behavioural disturbances in people with bipolar disorder.

1.5 THE LONG-TERM MANAGEMENT OF BIPOLAR DISORDER

1.5.1 Drug treatment after recovery from an acute episode

1.5.1.1 Prescribers should consider starting long-term treatment for bipolar disorder:
- after a manic episode that was associated with significant risk and adverse consequences
- when a patient with bipolar I disorder has had two or more acute episodes
- when a patient with bipolar II disorder has significant functional impairment, is at significant risk of suicide or has frequent episodes.

1.5.1.2 Lithium, olanzapine or valproate* should be considered for long-term treatment of bipolar disorder. The choice should depend on:
- response to previous treatments
- the relative risk, and known precipitants, of manic versus depressive relapse
- physical risk factors, particularly renal disease, obesity and diabetes
- the patient's preference and history of adherence
- gender (valproate* should not be prescribed for women of child-bearing potential)
- a brief assessment of cognitive state (such as the Mini-Mental State Examination) if appropriate, for example, for older people.

1.5.1.3 If the patient has frequent relapses, or symptoms continue to cause functional impairment, switching to an alternative monotherapy or adding a second prophylactic agent (lithium, olanzapine, valproate*) should be considered. Clinical state, side effects and, where relevant, blood levels should be monitored closely. Possible combinations are lithium with valproate*, lithium with olanzapine*, and valproate with olanzapine*.

The reasons for the choice and the discussion with the patient of the potential benefits and risks should be documented.

1.5.1.4   If a trial of a combination of prophylactic agents proves ineffective, the following should be considered:
- consulting with, or referring the patient to, a clinician with expertise in the drug treatment of bipolar disorder
- prescribing lamotrigine* (especially if the patient has bipolar II disorder) or carbamazepine.

1.5.1.5   Long-term drug treatment should normally continue for at least 2 years after an episode of bipolar disorder, and up to 5 years if the person has risk factors for relapse, such as a history of frequent relapses or severe psychotic episodes, comorbid substance misuse, ongoing stressful life events, or poor social support. This should be discussed with the patient and there should be regular reviews. Patients who wish to stop medication early should be encouraged to discuss this with their psychiatrist.

1.5.1.6   If, after careful discussion, a patient with bipolar disorder declines long-term medication, they should still be offered regular contact and reassessment with primary or secondary care services.

1.5.1.7   Long-acting intramuscular injections of antipsychotics ('depots') are not recommended for routine use in bipolar disorder. They may be considered for people who were treated successfully for mania with oral antipsychotics, but have had a relapse because of poor adherence.

After an acute depressive episode

1.5.1.8   After successful treatment for an acute depressive episode, patients should not normally continue on antidepressant treatment long-term because there is no evidence that this reduces relapse rates, and it may be associated with increased risk of switching to mania.

Treatment for chronic and recurrent depressive symptoms

1.5.1.9   The following treatments should be considered, in discussion with the patient, for people who have an established diagnosis of bipolar disorder and chronic or recurrent depressive symptoms, but who are not taking prophylactic medication and have not had a recent manic/hypomanic episode:
- long-term treatment with SSRIs at the minimum therapeutic dose in combination with prophylactic medication
- cognitive behavioural therapy (16–20 sessions) in combination with prophylactic medication
- quetiapine*, or
- lamotrigine*.

1.5.1.10   For patients with bipolar II disorder with recurrent depression, lamotrigine*
alone should be considered for long-term treatment

1.5.2   Long-term management of rapid cycling

1.5.2.1   For the long-term management of rapid-cycling bipolar disorder
prescribers should:
- consider as first-line treatment a combination of lithium and
valproate*
- consider lithium monotherapy as second-line treatment; for patients
already taking lithium consider increasing the dose
- avoid the use of an antidepressant, except on advice from a specialist in
bipolar disorder
- consider combinations of lithium or valproate* with lamotrigine*,
especially in bipolar II disorder
- check thyroid function every 6 months together with levels of thyroid
antibodies if clinically indicated, for example, by the thyroid function
tests.

1.5.3   Comorbid anxiety disorders

1.5.3.1   For patients with significant comorbid anxiety disorders, psychological
treatment focused on anxiety or treatment with a drug such as an atypical
antipsychotic should be considered.

1.5.4   Promoting a healthy lifestyle and relapse prevention

1.5.4.1   Patients with bipolar disorder should be given advice (including written
information) on:
- the importance of good sleep hygiene and a regular lifestyle
- the risks of shift work, night flying and flying across time zones, and
routinely working excessively long hours, particularly for patients with
a history of relapse related to poor sleep hygiene or irregular lifestyle
- ways to monitor their own physical and mental state.

1.5.4.2   People with bipolar disorder should be given additional support after
significant life events, such as loss of job or a close bereavement. This
should include increased monitoring of mood and general well-being, and
encouraging the patient to discuss difficulties with family and friends.

1.5.4.3   Healthcare professionals, in collaboration with patients, should develop a
plan to identify the symptoms and indicators of a potential exacerbation of
the disorder, and how to respond (including both psychosocial and pharmacological interventions).

1.5.5 Psychological therapy after recovery from an acute episode

1.5.5.1 Individual structured psychological interventions should be considered for people with bipolar disorder who are relatively stable, but may be experiencing mild to moderate affective symptoms. The therapy should be in addition to prophylactic medication, should normally be at least 16 sessions (over 6–9 months) and should:
- include psychoeducation about the illness, and the importance of regular daily routine and sleep and concordance with medication
- include monitoring mood, detection of early warnings and strategies to prevent progression into full-blown episodes
- enhance general coping strategies.

1.5.5.2 Structured psychological interventions should be delivered by people who are competent to do this and have experience of patients with bipolar disorder.

1.5.5.3 Healthcare professionals should consider offering a focused family intervention to people with bipolar disorder in regular contact with their families, if a focus for the intervention can be agreed. The intervention should take place over 6–9 months, and cover psychoeducation about the illness, ways to improve communication and problem solving.

1.5.6 Psychosocial support

1.5.6.1 Healthcare professionals should consider offering befriending to people who would benefit from additional social support, particularly those with chronic depressive symptoms. Befriending should be in addition to drug and psychological treatments, and should be by trained volunteers providing, typically, at least weekly contact for between 2 and 6 months.

1.6 THE PHYSICAL CARE OF PEOPLE WITH BIPOLAR DISORDER

See Appendix 21 for a list of physical monitoring tests.

1.6.1 Initial physical assessment

1.6.1.1 As soon as practicable after initial presentation of a patient with bipolar disorder, healthcare professionals should:
- establish the patient's smoking status and alcohol use
- perform thyroid, liver and renal function tests, blood pressure, and measure full blood count, blood glucose, lipid profile

- measure weight and height
- consider EEG, CT scan or MRI scan if an organic aetiology or a relevant comorbidity is suspected
- consider drug screening, chest X-ray and ECG if suggested by the history or clinical picture.

1.6.2 Initiating, monitoring and stopping drug treatments

The long-term use of antipsychotics

Initiating antipsychotics

1.6.2.1 When initiating long-term treatment of bipolar disorder with antipsychotics, weight and height, plasma glucose and lipids should be measured in all patients, and an ECG arranged for patients with risk factors for cardiovascular disease or risk factors for it. Prolactin levels should be measured when initiating risperidone* in patients with low libido, sexual dysfunction, menstrual abnormalities, gynaecomastia or galactorrhea.

1.6.2.2 When initiating quetiapine*, the dose should be titrated gradually (in line with the summary of product characteristics), to help maintain normal blood pressure.

Monitoring antipsychotics

1.6.2.3 Patients taking antipsychotics should have their weight checked every 3 months for the first year, and more often if they gain weight rapidly. Plasma glucose and lipids (preferably fasting levels) should be measured 3 months after the start of treatment (and within 1 month if taking olanzapine), and more often if there is evidence of elevated levels. In patients taking risperidone*, prolactin levels should be measured if symptoms of raised prolactin develop; these include low libido, sexual dysfunction, menstrual abnormalities, gynaecomastia and galactorrhea.

Stopping antipsychotics

1.6.2.4 If a patient with bipolar disorder is stopping antipsychotic medication, the antipsychotic:
- should be stopped gradually over at least 4 weeks if the patient is continuing with other medication
- should be stopped over a period of up to 3 months if the patient is not continuing with other medication, or has a history of manic relapse.

Risks associated with the use of antipsychotics

1.6.2.5 Healthcare professionals should discuss with patients the risk of weight gain, and be aware of the possibility of worsening existing diabetes, malignant neuroleptic syndrome and diabetic ketoacidosis with the use of antipsychotic medication; particular caution is needed when treating patients with mania.

The long-term use of lithium

Initiating lithium

1.6.2.6 Lithium should not be initiated routinely in primary care for the treatment of bipolar disorder.

1.6.2.7 When initiating lithium as long-term treatment, prescribers should:
- advise patients that erratic compliance or rapid discontinuation may increase the risk of manic relapse
- measure height and weight, and arrange tests for urea and electrolytes and serum creatinine, and thyroid function
- arrange an ECG for patients with cardiovascular disease or risk factors for it
- arrange a full blood count if clinically indicated
- establish a shared-care protocol with the patient's GP for prescribing and monitoring lithium and checking for adverse effects
- be aware that patients should take lithium for at least 6 months to establish its effectiveness as a long-term treatment.

1.6.2.8 Serum lithium levels should be checked 1 week after starting and 1 week after every dose change, and until the levels are stable. The aim should be to maintain serum lithium levels between 0.6 and 0.8 mmol per litre in people being prescribed it for the first time.

1.6.2.9 For people who have relapsed previously while taking lithium or who still have sub-threshold symptoms with functional impairment while receiving lithium, a trial of at least 6 months with serum lithium levels between 0.8 and 1.0 mmol per litre should be considered.

Monitoring lithium

1.6.2.10 For patients with bipolar disorder on lithium treatment, prescribers should do the following.
- Monitor serum lithium levels normally every 3 months.
- Monitor older adults carefully for symptoms of lithium toxicity, because they may develop high serum levels of lithium at doses in the normal range, and lithium toxicity is possible at moderate serum lithium levels.
- Monitor weight, especially in patients with rapid weight gain.
- Undertake more frequent tests if there is evidence of clinical deterioration, abnormal results, a change in sodium intake, or symptoms suggesting abnormal renal or thyroid function such as unexplained fatigue, or other risk factors, for example, if the patient is starting medication such as ACE inhibitors, non-steroidal anti-inflammatory drugs, or diuretics.

- Arrange thyroid and renal function tests every 6 months, and more often if there is evidence of impaired renal function.
- Initiate closer monitoring of lithium dose and blood serum levels if urea and creatinine levels become elevated, and assess the rate of deterioration of renal function. The decision whether to continue lithium depends on clinical efficacy, and degree of renal impairment; prescribers should consider seeking advice from a renal specialist and a clinician with expertise in the management of bipolar disorder on this.
- Monitor for symptoms of neurotoxicity, including paraesthesia, ataxia, tremor and cognitive impairment, which can occur at therapeutic levels.

Stopping lithium

1.6.2.11 Lithium should be stopped gradually over at least 4 weeks, and preferably over a period of up to 3 months, particularly if the patient has a history of manic relapse (even if they have been started on another antimanic agent).

1.6.2.12 When lithium treatment is stopped or is about to be stopped abruptly, prescribers should consider changing to monotherapy with an atypical antipsychotic or valproate*, and then monitor closely for early signs of mania and depression.

Risks associated with the use of lithium

1.6.2.13 Patients taking lithium should be warned not to take over-the-counter non-steroidal anti-inflammatory drugs. Prescribing non-steroidal anti-inflammatory drugs for such patients should be avoided if possible, and if they are prescribed the patient should be closely monitored.

1.6.2.14 Patients taking lithium should be advised to:
- seek medical attention if they develop diarrhoea and/or vomiting
- ensure they maintain their fluid intake, particularly after sweating (for example, after exercise, in hot climates, or if they have a fever), if they are immobile for long periods or – in the case of older people – develop a chest infection or pneumonia
- consider stopping lithium for up to 7 days if they become acutely and severely ill with a metabolic or respiratory disturbance from whatever cause.

The long-term use of valproate

Initiating valproate

1.6.2.15 Valproate should not be routinely initiated in primary care for the treatment of bipolar disorder.

1.6.2.16 When initiating valproate* as long-term treatment, patients should have their height and weight measured, and have a full blood count and liver function tests.

1.6.2.17   Valproate* should not be prescribed routinely for women of child-bearing potential. If no effective alternative to valproate can be identified, adequate contraception should be used, and the risks of taking valproate during pregnancy should be explained.

1.6.2.18   Valproate* should not be prescribed for young women with bipolar disorder who are younger than 18 years because of the risk of polycystic ovary syndrome and unplanned pregnancy in this age group.

Monitoring valproate*

1.6.2.19   Routine measurement of valproate* blood levels is not recommended unless there is evidence of ineffectiveness, poor adherence or toxicity.

1.6.2.20   Liver function tests and a full blood count should be done after 6 months' treatment with valproate*, and weight should be monitored in patients who gain weight rapidly.

Stopping valproate*

1.6.2.21   When stopping valproate* in patients with bipolar disorder, the dose should be reduced gradually over at least 4 weeks to minimise the risk of destabilisation.

Risks associated with the use of valproate*

1.6.2.22   Patients on valproate*, and their carers, should be advised how to recognise the signs and symptoms of blood and liver disorders and to seek immediate medical help if these develop. If abnormal liver function or blood dyscrasia is detected the drug should be stopped immediately.

1.6.2.23   When prescribing valproate*, prescribers should be aware of:
- its interactions with other anticonvulsants
- the need for more careful monitoring of sedation, tremor and gait disturbance in older people.

Lamotrigine

Initiating lamotrigine

1.6.2.24   Lamotrigine should not be routinely initiated in primary care for the treatment of bipolar disorder.

1.6.2.25   The dose of lamotrigine* should be titrated gradually to minimise the risk of skin rashes, including Stevens–Johnson syndrome. Titration should be slower in patients also taking valproate.

1.6.2.26   When offering lamotrigine* to women taking oral contraceptives, prescribers should explain that the drug may decrease the effectiveness of the contraceptive and discuss alternative methods of contraception. If a woman taking lamotrigine* stops taking an oral contraceptive, the dose of lamotrigine* may need to be reduced by up to 50%.

Monitoring lamotrigine

1.6.2.27   Routine monitoring of blood levels of lamotrigine* is not needed.

Stopping lamotrigine

1.6.2.28   When stopping lamotrigine*, the dose should be reduced gradually over at least 4 weeks to minimise the risk of destabilisation.

Risks associated with the use of lamotrigine

1.6.2.29   Patients taking lamotrigine* should be advised, particularly when starting the drug, to seek medical attention urgently if a rash develops. The drug should be stopped unless it is clear that the rash is not related to the use of lamotrigine*. If an appointment cannot be arranged within a few days or if the rash is worsening, the patient should be advised to stop the drug and then restart if lamotrigine* is not implicated in the development of the rash.

Carbamazepine

Initiating carbamazepine

1.6.2.30   Carbamazepine should be used for the long-term treatment of bipolar disorder only after consulting a specialist.

1.6.2.31   The dose of carbamazepine should be increased gradually to reduce the risk of ataxia.

1.6.2.32   When initiating carmabazepine as long-term treatment, patients should have their height and weight measured, and have a full blood count and liver function tests.

Monitoring carbamazepine

1.6.2.33   Plasma levels of carbamazepine should be measured every 6 months to exclude toxicity, because therapeutic levels and toxic levels are close.

1.6.2.34   Liver function tests and a full blood count should be repeated after 6 months' treatment with carbamazepine, and weight should be monitored in patients who gain weight rapidly.

1.6.2.35   Blood urea and electrolytes should be measured every 6 months after starting treatment with carbamazepine to check for hyponatraemia.

1.6.2.36   Possible interactions of carbamazepine with other drugs, including oral contraceptives, should be monitored closely, particularly if the patient starts a new medication.

Stopping carbamazepine

1.6.2.37   The dose of carbamazepine should be reduced gradually over at least 4 weeks to minimise the risk of destabilisation.

Risks associated with the use of carbamazepine

1.6.2.38   When prescribing carbamazepine for patients taking concomitant medications – for example, people older than 65 years and people with multiple physical problems – prescribers should be aware that carbamazepine has a greater potential for drug interactions than other drugs used to treat bipolar disorder.

Annual review of physical health

1.6.2.39   People with bipolar disorder should have an annual physical health review, normally in primary care, to ensure that the following are assessed each year:
- lipid levels, including cholesterol in all patients over 40 even if there is no other indication of risk
- plasma glucose levels
- weight
- smoking status and alcohol use
- blood pressure.

1.6.2.40   The results of the annual review should be given to the person, and to healthcare professionals in primary and secondary care (including whether the person refused any tests). A clear agreement should be made about responsibility for treating any problems.

1.6.3   Weight gain management

1.6.3.1   If a person gains weight during treatment their medication should be reviewed, and the following considered:
- dietary advice and support from primary care and mental health services
- advising regular aerobic exercise
- referral to mental health services for specific programmes to manage weight gain
- referral to a dietitian if the person has complex comorbidities (for example, coeliac disease).

1.6.3.2   Drug treatments such as high-dose antidepressants, sibutramine, or topiramate* are not recommended to promote weight loss.

1.7   WOMEN WITH BIPOLAR DISORDER WHO ARE PLANNING A PREGNANCY, PREGNANT OR BREASTFEEDING

1.7.1   General principles of management for women

1.7.1.1   The absolute and relative risks of problems associated with both treating and not treating the bipolar disorder during pregnancy should be discussed with women.

1.7.1.2   More frequent contact by specialist mental health services (including, where appropriate, specialist perinatal mental health services), working closely with maternity services, should be considered for pregnant women with bipolar disorder, because of the increased risk of relapse during pregnancy and the postnatal period.

1.7.1.3   A written plan for managing a woman's bipolar disorder during the pregnancy, delivery and postnatal period should be developed as soon as possible. This should be developed with the patient and significant others, and shared with her obstetrician, midwife, GP and health visitor. All medical decisions should be recorded in all versions of the patient's notes. Information about her medication should be included in the birth plan and notes for postnatal care.

1.7.1.4   If a pregnant woman with bipolar disorder is stable on an antipsychotic and likely to relapse without medication, she should be maintained on the antipsychotic, and monitored for weight gain and diabetes.

1.7.1.5   The following drugs should not be routinely prescribed for pregnant women with bipolar disorder:
● valproate – because of risk to the fetus and subsequent child development
● carbamazepine – because of its limited efficacy and risk of harm to the fetus
● lithium – because risk of harm to the fetus, such as cardiac problems
● lamotrigine* – because of the risk of harm to the fetus
● paroxetine – because of the risk of cardiovascular malformations in the fetus
● long-term treatment with benzodiazepines – because of risks during pregnancy and the immediate postnatal period, such as cleft palate and floppy baby syndrome.

1.7.2   Women planning a pregnancy

1.7.2.1   Women with bipolar disorder who are considering pregnancy should normally be advised to stop taking valproate, carbamazepine, lithium and lamotrigine*, and alternative prophylactic drugs (such as an antipsychotic) should be considered.

1.7.2.2   Women taking antipsychotics who are planning a pregnancy should be advised that the raised prolactin levels associated with some antipsychotics reduce the chances of conception. If prolactin levels are raised, an alternative drug should be considered.

1.7.2.3   If a woman who needs antimanic medication plans to become pregnant, a low-dose typical or atypical antipsychotic should be considered, because they are of least known risk.

1.7.2.4   If a woman taking lithium plans to become pregnant, the following options should be considered:

- if the patient is well and not at high risk of relapse – gradually stopping lithium
- if the patient is not well or is at high risk of relapse:
  - switching gradually to an antipsychotic, or
  - stopping lithium and restarting it in the second trimester if the woman is not planning to breastfeed and her symptoms have responded better to lithium than to other drugs in the past, or
  - continuing with lithium, after full discussion of the risks, while trying to conceive and throughout the pregnancy, if manic episodes have complicated the woman's previous pregnancies, and her symptoms have responded well to lithium.

1.7.2.5 If a woman remains on lithium during pregnancy, serum lithium levels should be monitored every 4 weeks, then weekly from the 36th week, and less than 24 hours after childbirth. The dose should be adjusted to keep serum levels within the therapeutic range. The woman should maintain adequate fluid intake.

1.7.2.6 If a woman planning a pregnancy becomes depressed after stopping prophylactic medication, psychological therapy (CBT) should be offered in preference to an antidepressant because of the risk of switching associated with antidepressants. If an antidepressant is used, it should usually be an SSRI (but not paroxetine because of the risk of cardiovascular malformations in the fetus) and the woman should be monitored closely.

1.7.3 Women with an unplanned pregnancy

1.7.3.1 If a woman with bipolar disorder has an unplanned pregnancy:
- the pregnancy should be confirmed as quickly as possible
- the woman should be advised to stop taking valproate, carbamazepine and lamotrigine*
- if the pregnancy is confirmed in the first trimester, and the woman is stable, lithium should be stopped gradually over 4 weeks, and the woman informed that this may not remove the risk of cardiac defects in the fetus
- if the woman remains on lithium during pregnancy serum lithium levels should be checked every 4 weeks, then weekly from the 36th week, and less than 24 hours after childbirth; the dose should be adjusted to keep serum levels within the therapeutic range, and the woman should maintain adequate fluid intake
- an antipsychotic should be offered as prophylactic medication
- offer appropriate screening and counselling about the continuation of the pregnancy, the need for additional monitoring and the risks to the fetus if the woman stays on medication.

1.7.3.2   If a woman with bipolar disorder continues with an unplanned pregnancy, the newborn baby should have a full paediatric assessment, and social and medical help should be provided for the mother and child.

1.7.4   Pregnant women with acute mania or depression

Acute mania

1.7.4.1   If a pregnant women who is not taking medication develops acute mania, an atypical or a typical antipsychotic should be considered. The dose should be kept as low as possible and the woman monitored carefully.

1.7.4.2   If a pregnant woman develops acute mania while taking prophylactic medication, prescribers should:
●   check the dose of the prophylactic agent and adherence
●   increase the dose if the woman is taking an antipsychotic, or consider changing to an antipsychotic if she is not
●   if there is no response to changes in dose or drug and the patient has severe mania, consider the use of ECT, lithium and, rarely, valproate.

1.7.4.3   If there is no alternative to valproate the woman should be informed of the increased risk to the fetus and the child's intellectual development. The lowest possible effective dose should be used and augmenting it with additional antimanic medication (but not carbamazepine*) considered. The maximum dosage should be 1 gram per day, in divided doses and in the slow-release form, with 5 mg/day folic acid.

Depressive symptoms

1.7.4.4   For mild depressive symptoms in pregnant women with bipolar disorder the following should be considered:
●   self-help approaches such as guided self-help and computerised CBT
●   brief psychological interventions
●   antidepressant medication.

1.7.4.5   For moderate to severe depressive symptoms in pregnant women with bipolar disorder the following should be considered:
●   psychological treatment (CBT) for moderate depression
●   combined medication and structured psychological interventions for severe depression.

1.7.4.6   For moderate to severe depressive symptoms in pregnant women with bipolar disorder, quetiapine* alone or SSRIs (but not paroxetine) in combination with prophylactic medication should be preferred because SSRIs are less likely to be associated with switching than the tricyclic antidepressants.

Monitor closely for signs of switching and stop the SSRI if patients start to develop manic or hypomanic symptoms.

1.7.4.7 Women who are prescribed an antidepressant during pregnancy should be informed of the potential, but predominantly short-lived, adverse effects of antidepressants on the neonate.

1.7.5 Care in the perinatal period

1.7.5.1 Women taking lithium should deliver in hospital, and be monitored during labour by the obstetric medical team, in addition to usual midwife care. Monitoring should include fluid balance, because of the risk of dehydration and lithium toxicity.

1.7.5.2 After delivery, if a woman with bipolar disorder who is not on medication is at high risk of developing an acute episode, prescribers should consider establishing or reinstating medication as soon as the patient is medically stable (once the fluid balance is established).

1.7.5.3 If a woman maintained on lithium is at high risk of a manic relapse in the immediate postnatal period, augmenting treatment with an antipsychotic should be considered.

1.7.5.4 If a woman with bipolar disorder develops severe manic or psychotic symptoms and behavioural disturbance in the intrapartum period rapid tranquillisation with an antipsychotic should be considered in preferenceto a benzodiazepine because of the risk of floppy baby syndrome. Treatment should be in collaboration with an anaesthetist.

1.7.6 Breastfeeding

1.7.6.1 Women with bipolar disorder who are taking psychotropic medication and wish to breastfeed should:
  ● have advice on the risks and benefits of breastfeeding
  ● be advised not to breastfeed if taking lithium, benzodiazepines or lamotrigine*, and offered a prophylactic agent that can be used when breastfeeding – an antipsychotic should be the first choice (but not clozapine*)
  ● be prescribed an SSRI if an antidepressant is used (but not fluoxetine or citalopram).

1.7.7 Care of the infant

1.7.7.1 Babies whose mothers took psychotropic drugs during pregnancy should be monitored in the first few weeks for adverse drug effects, drug toxicity or withdrawal (for example, floppy baby syndrome, irritability, constant crying, shivering, tremor, restlessness, increased tone, feeding and sleeping difficulties and rarely seizures). If the mother was prescribed antidepressants in the last trimester, such symptoms may be a serotonergic toxicity syndrome rather than withdrawal, and the neonate should be monitored carefully.

1.8   CHILDREN AND ADOLESCENTS WITH BIPOLAR DISORDER

1.8.1   Special considerations

1.8.1.1   Healthcare professionals working in specialist services with children and adolescents with bipolar disorder should:
- be familiar with local and national guidelines on confidentiality and the rights of the child
- ensure appropriate consent is obtained, considering the adolescent's understanding (including Gillick competence), parental consent and responsibilities, child protection matters, and the use of the Mental Health Act and of the Children Act (1989).

1.8.1.2   When planning the care of children and adolescents with bipolar disorder, healthcare professionals should consider:
- stressors and vulnerabilities in their social, educational and family environments, including the quality of interpersonal relationships
- the impact of any comorbidities, such as attention deficit hyperactivity disorder (ADHD) and anxiety disorders
- the impact of the disorder on their social inclusion and education
- their vulnerability to exploitation, for example, as a result of disinhibited behaviour.

1.8.1.3   Parents or carers (and possibly other family members) should be involved in developing care plans so that they can give informed consent, support the psychological goals of treatment, and help to ensure treatment adherence.

1.8.1.4   Children and adolescents should be offered separate individual appointments with a healthcare professional in addition to joint meetings with their family members or carers.

1.8.2   Diagnosing bipolar I disorder in prepubescent children

1.8.2.1   When diagnosing bipolar I disorder in prepubescent children the same criteria should be used as in adults except that:
- mania must be present
- euphoria must be present most days, most of the time (for a period of 7 days)
- irritability is not a core diagnostic criterion.

1.8.2.2   Bipolar I disorder should not be diagnosed solely on the basis of a major depressive episode in a child with a family history of bipolar disorder. However, children with a history of depression and a family history of bipolar disorder should be carefully followed up.

1.8.3   Diagnosing bipolar I disorder in adolescents

1.8.3.1   When diagnosing bipolar I disorder in adolescents the same criteria should be used as for adults except that:
- mania must be present
- euphoria must be present most days, most of the time (for at least 7 days)
- irritability can be helpful in making a diagnosis if it is episodic, severe, results in impaired function and is out of keeping or not in character; however, it should not be a core diagnostic criterion.

1.8.3.2   Bipolar I disorder should not be diagnosed solely on the basis of a major depressive episode in an adolescent with a family history of bipolar disorder. However, adolescents with a history of depression and a family history of bipolar disorder should be carefully followed up.

1.8.4   Diagnosing bipolar I disorder in older or developmentally advanced adolescents

1.8.4.1   In older or developmentally advanced adolescents, the criteria for establishing a diagnosis of bipolar I disorder in adults should be used.

1.8.5   Bipolar II disorder in both children and adolescents

1.8.5.1   Bipolar II disorder should not normally be diagnosed in children or adolescents because the diagnostic criteria are not well-enough established for routine use.

1.8.5.2   In older or developmentally advanced adolescents, the criteria for diagnosing bipolar II disorder in adults should be used.

1.8.6   Differential diagnosis for children and adolescents

1.8.6.1   The presence of clear-cut episodes of unduly elated mood, inappropriate and impairing grandiosity, and cycles of mood should be used to distinguish bipolar I disorder from attention deficit hyperactivity disorder (ADHD) and conduct disorder.

1.8.6.2   The presence of mood cycles should be used to distinguish bipolar disorder from schizophrenia.

1.8.6.3   Before diagnosing bipolar I disorder in a child or adolescent, other possible explanations for the behaviour and symptoms should be considered, including:

- sexual, emotional and physical abuse if they show disinhibition, hyper-vigilance or hypersexuality
- the possibility of drug and/or alcohol misuse as a cause of mania-like symptoms; consider a diagnosis of bipolar disorder only after 7 days of abstinence
- previously undiagnosed learning difficulties
- organic causes such as excited confusional states in children with epilepsy, and akathisia resulting from neuroleptic medication.

1.8.7   Children and adolescents with learning difficulties

1.8.7.1   When diagnosing bipolar I disorder in a child or adolescent with learning difficulties, the same criteria as are applied to children and adolescents without learning difficulties should be used.

1.8.8   Children and adolescents with sub-threshold symptoms of bipolar disorder

1.8.8.1   If it is not possible to make a diagnosis in a child or adolescent with sub-threshold symptoms of bipolar disorder, they should be carefully followed up.

1.8.9   Assessment methods for children and adolescents

1.8.9.1   The diagnosis of bipolar disorder in children and adolescents should be made by a clinician with specialist training in child and adolescent mental health.

1.8.9.2   Assessment should include:
- a detailed mental state examination based on an individual interview with the child
- a medical evaluation to exclude organic causes
- further neuropsychological and neurological evaluation as appropriate
- a detailed account of the presenting problem from the child, parents or carers, and other significant adults such as teachers
- a detailed developmental and neurodevelopmental history, including birth history, speech and language development, behaviour problems, attachment behaviour and any history of abuse.

1.8.9.3   A specialist diagnostic instrument such as the WASH-U-KSADS may be used; scales completed by parents or carers such as the Child Behaviour Checklist, Conners' Abbreviated Rating Scale, Parent Young Mania Rating Scale and Parent General Behaviour Inventory may also be used. These should not replace a full clinical interview.

1.8.9.4   In severely mentally ill children and adolescents with psychotic symptoms, a diagnosis should be attempted as early as practical, and should be subject to regular specialist review.

1.8.10   Drug treatment of acute mania in children and adolescents

1.8.10.1   When prescribing medication for children or adolescents with an acute manic episode, the recommendations for adults with bipolar disorder should be followed except drugs should be initiated at lower doses. In addition, at initial presentation:
- height and weight should be checked (and monitored regularly afterwards – for example, monthly for 6 months then every 6 months)
- prolactin levels should be measured
- when considering an antipsychotic, the risk of increased prolactin levels with risperidone* and weight gain with olanzapine* should be considered
- where there is an inadequate response to an antipsychotic, adding lithium or valproate* should be considered. Valproate should normally be avoided in girls and young women because of risks during pregnancy and because of the risk of polycystic ovary syndrome.

1.8.11   Drug and psychological treatments of depression in children and adolescents

1.8.11.1   Children and adolescents with bipolar disorder experiencing mild depressive symptoms assessed as not requiring immediate treatment should be monitored weekly and offered additional support, for example at home and in school.

1.8.11.2   Children or adolescents with depressive symptoms needing treatment should normally be treated by specialist clinicians (based in at least Tier 3 services[5]). Treatment should be as for adults with bipolar disorder except that a structured psychological therapy aimed at treating depression should be considered in addition to prophylactic medication.

1.8.11.3   If there has been no response to psychological therapy for depression combined with prophylactic medication after 4 weeks, prescribers should consider:
- adding fluoxetine* starting at 10 mg per day, and increasing to 20 mg per day if needed

---

[5]Specialised child and adolescent mental health services for severe, complex or persistent disorders. Staff include child and adolescent psychiatrists, clinical psychologists, nurses and child and adolescent psychotherapists.

- using an alternative SSRI (sertraline* or citalopram*) if there is no response to fluoxetine after an adequate trial.

  If there is still no response advice should be sought from a specialist in affective disorders.

1.8.11.4 For developmentally advanced adolescents with depressive symptoms, the recommendations on managing depression in adults with bipolar disorder should be followed.

1.8.12 Long-term treatment of children and adolescents

1.8.12.1 Long-term management of children or adolescents with bipolar disorder should normally be by specialist clinicians (based in at least Tier 3 services). Treatment should be as for adults with bipolar disorder except that:

- an atypical antipsychotic that is associated with lower weight gain and non-elevation of prolactin levels should be the first-line prophylactic agent
- lithium should be considered as the second-line prophylactic agent in female patients and valproate or lithium as the second-line prophylactic agent in male patients
- parents and carers should be given support to help the patient maintain a regular lifestyle
- the school or college should be given advice (with permission of the patient and those with parental responsibility) on managing the patient's bipolar disorder.

1.8.13 Inpatient services for children and adolescents

1.8.13.1 Admission as an inpatient or day patient, or more intensive community treatment, should be considered for children and adolescents at risk of suicide or other serous harm. Such care should be provided in specialist units, designed specifically for children and adolescents and able to support their educational, social and personal needs.

1.8.13.2 Severe behavioural disturbance in children and adolescents with bipolar disorder should be managed as for adults, except that rapid tranquillisation with haloperidol* is not recommended because of the increased risk of extrapyramidal side effects in this age group.

1.9 RESEARCH RECOMMENDATIONS

The Guideline Development Group has made the following recommendations for research, on the basis of its review of the evidence. The Group regards these recommendations as important research areas that might contribute to improved NICE guidance and patient care in the future.

1.9.1 Treatments for patients in partial remission from depressive symptoms in bipolar disorder

A randomised controlled trial should be conducted to investigate the efficacy and cost effectiveness of an adding an antidepressant (SSRI) to an existing antimanic agent for patients with bipolar disorder in partial remission from a depressive episode. The trial would ideally recruit from both primary and secondary care and outcome measures would include time to recovery from depression, time to prevention of the next episode, social functioning with a 2-year follow-up period.

Why this is important

The treatment of severe mental illness is a key priority in the National Service Framework for mental health, and depression of all kinds is a major cause of long-term disability and unemployment. People with bipolar disorder suffer more depressive episodes than manic episodes. Partial remission from symptoms is common, so successful treatment would greatly improve functioning and quality of life. But there is little evidence on which to base recommendations for treatment of bipolar depression, and none on treatment after partial remission.

1.9.2 Treatments for depression in bipolar disorder and their risks

A sequenced set of randomised controlled trials should be undertaken to investigate the efficacy and cost-effectiveness of antidepressants, in the presence of an antimanic medication, in treating bipolar depression. The studies should address the different stages of depression (acute, continuation and maintenance) and also evaluate the risks, particularly switching to mania and cycle acceleration, associated with antidepressant treatment. Patients with bipolar I and II disorder should be recruited. Outcome measures would include time to recovery from depression, time to prevention of the next episode and social functioning.

Why this is important

People with bipolar disorder suffer more depressive episodes than manic episodes. Depression is the major cause of suicide and the rate of suicide is very high among patients with bipolar disorder (10–15%). Therefore successful treatment would greatly improve functioning and quality of life. There is little evidence on the treatment of bipolar depression, particularly in different phases of the illness.

Reducing depression could contribute to meeting the national targets to reduce suicide in bipolar disorder, and to reduce depression as a major cause of long-term disability and unemployment.

1.9.3 Choice of prophylactic medication

A randomised placebo-controlled trial should be undertaken to assess the efficacy and cost effectiveness of adding an atypical antipsychotic to existing prophylactic medication (either lithium or valproate) in bipolar I disorder and bipolar II disorder. The primary outcome measure at 2 years would be time to the next bipolar episode requiring treatment, and an important secondary outcome measure would be social functioning. The trial should be adequately powered to investigate tolerability differences and other potential harms such as weight gain and diabetes.

Why this is important

The treatment of severe mental illness is a key priority in the National Service Framework for mental health. Episodes of mania and depression are a significant cause of long-term disability and unemployment. There is insufficient evidence about the use of antipsychotics in the prophylaxis of bipolar disorder treatment, particularly in bipolar II disorder. The results of further research would allow more specific recommendations to be made.

1.9.4 Prophylaxis in children and adolescents

A randomised placebo-controlled trial should be undertaken to assess the efficacy and cost effectiveness of an atypical antipsychotic plus antimanic agent versus antimanic agent alone in children and adolescents in remission from bipolar disorder. The primary outcome measure at 2 years would be time to the next bipolar episode requiring treatment, and an important secondary outcome measure would be social functioning. The trial should also be adequately powered to investigate tolerability differences and other potential harms such as weight gain and diabetes.

Why this is important

Inadequate treatment of psychosis in young people is associated with poor long-term outcomes, including increased risk of suicide. But there is very little evidence of any quality on the drug treatment of bipolar disorder in children and young people. The answer to this question would allow more specific recommendations about the treatment of this group, and would help address standard 9 of the children's National Service Framework.

1.9.5   Configuration of services

A randomised controlled trial should be undertaken to compare the effectiveness of collaborative care for adolescents and adults with bipolar I or bipolar II disorder with treatment as usual in primary and secondary care.

Why this is important

There is very little evidence on effective configuration of services to suit the needs of people with bipolar disorder. The answer to this question would allow more specific recommendations on this topic, and so reduce morbidity.

2.   INTRODUCTION

This guideline has been developed to advise on the treatment and management of bipolar disorder. The guideline recommendations have been developed by a multidisciplinary team of healthcare professionals, patients and guideline methodologists after careful consideration of the best available evidence. It is intended that the guidelines will be useful to clinicians and service commissioners in providing and planning high quality care for those with bipolar disorder while also emphasising the importance of the experience of care for patients and carers.

2.1   NATIONAL GUIDELINES

2.1.1   What are clinical practice guidelines?

Clinical practice guidelines are 'systematically developed statements that assist clinicians and patients in making decisions about appropriate treatment for specific conditions' (NHS Executive, 1996). They are derived from the best available research evidence, using predetermined and systematic methods to identify and evaluate all the evidence relating to the specific condition in question. Where evidence is lacking, the guidelines will incorporate statements and recommendations based upon the consensus statements developed by the Guideline Development Group (GDG).

Clinical guidelines are intended to improve the process and outcomes of healthcare in a number of different ways. Clinical guidelines can:

- provide up-to-date evidence-based recommendations for the management of conditions and disorders by healthcare professionals
- be used as the basis-to-set standards to assess the practice of healthcare professionals
- form the basis for education and training of healthcare professionals
- assist patients and carers in making informed decisions about their treatment and care
- improve communication between healthcare professionals, patients and carers
- help identify priority areas for further research.

2.1.2   Uses and limitations of clinical guidelines

Guidelines are not a substitute for professional knowledge and clinical judgement. They can be limited in their usefulness and applicability by a number of different factors: the availability of high quality research evidence, the quality of the methodology used in the development of the guideline, the generalisability of research findings and the uniqueness of individual patients.

Although the quality of research in bipolar disorder is variable, the methodology used here reflects current international understanding on the appropriate practice for guideline development (AGREE: Appraisal of Guidelines for Research and Evaluation Instrument; www.agreecollaboration.org), ensuring the collection and selection of the best research evidence available and the systematic generation of treatment recommendations applicable to the majority of patients and situations. However, there will always be some patients for whom clinical guideline recommendations are not appropriate and situations in which the recommendations are not readily applicable. This guideline does not, therefore, override the individual responsibility of healthcare professionals to make appropriate decisions in the circumstances of the individual patient, in consultation with the patient and/or carer.

In addition to the clinical evidence, cost-effectiveness information, where available, is taken into account in the generation of statements and recommendations of the clinical guidelines. While national guidelines are concerned with clinical and cost effectiveness, issues of affordability and implementation costs are to be determined by the NHS.

In using guidelines, it is important to remember that the absence of empirical evidence for the effectiveness of a particular intervention is not the same as evidence for ineffectiveness. In addition, of particular relevance in mental health, evidence-based treatments are often delivered within the context of an overall treatment programme including a range of activities, the purpose of which may be to help engage the patient, and provide an appropriate context for the delivery of specific interventions. It is important to maintain and enhance the service context in which these interventions are delivered, otherwise the specific benefits of effective interventions will be lost. Indeed, the importance of organising care, so as to support and encourage a good therapeutic relationship, is at times as important as the specific treatments offered.

2.1.3 Why develop national guidelines?

The National Institute for Health and Clinical Excellence (NICE) was established as a Special Health Authority for England and Wales in 1999, with a remit to provide a single source of authoritative and reliable guidance for patients, professionals and the public. NICE guidance aims to improve standards of care, to diminish unacceptable variations in the provision and quality of care across the NHS and to ensure that the health service is patient-centred. All guidance is developed in a transparent and collaborative manner using the best available evidence and involving all relevant stakeholders.

NICE generates guidance in a number of different ways, two of which are relevant here. First, national guidance is produced by the Technology Appraisal Committee to give robust advice about a particular treatment, intervention, procedure or other health technology. Second, NICE commissions the production of national clinical practice guidelines focused upon the overall treatment and management of a specific condition. To enable this latter development, NICE established seven National Collaborating Centres in conjunction with a range of professional organisations involved in healthcare.

2.1.4   The National Collaborating Centre for Mental Health

This guideline has been commissioned by NICE and developed within the National Collaborating Centre for Mental Health (NCCMH). The NCCMH is led by a partnership between the Royal College of Psychiatrists' training and research unit (College Training and Research Unit) and the British Psychological Society's equivalent unit (Centre for Outcomes Research and Effectiveness).

2.1.5   From national guidelines to local protocols

Once a national guideline has been published and disseminated, local healthcare groups will be expected to produce a plan and identify resources for implementation, along with appropriate timetables. Subsequently, a multidisciplinary group involving commissioners of healthcare, primary care and specialist mental health professionals, patients and carers should undertake the translation of the implementation plan into local protocols. The nature and pace of the local plan will reflect local health care needs and the nature of existing services; full implementation may take a considerable time, especially where substantial training needs are identified.

2.1.6   Auditing the implementation of guidelines

This guideline identifies key areas of clinical practice and service delivery for local and national audit. Although the generation of audit standards is an important and necessary step in the implementation of this guidance, a more broadly based implementation strategy should be developed. Nevertheless, it should be noted that the Healthcare Commission will monitor the extent to which Primary Care Trusts (PCTs), trusts responsible for mental health and social care and Health Authorities have implemented these guidelines.

2.2   THE NATIONAL BIPOLAR DISORDER GUIDELINE

2.2.1   Who has developed this guideline?

The GDG was convened by the NCCMH and supported by funding from NICE. The GDG consisted of people with bipolar disorder and a carer and professionals from psychiatry, clinical psychology, nursing and occupational therapy.

Staff from the NCCMH provided leadership and support throughout the process of guideline development, undertaking systematic searches, information retrieval, appraisal and systematic review of the evidence. Members of the GDG received training in the process of guideline development. The National Guidelines Support and Research Unit, also established by NICE, provided advice and assistance regarding aspects of the guideline development process.

All members of the group made formal declarations of interest at the outset, updated at every GDG meeting. GDG members met a total of 17 times throughout the process of guideline development. For ease of evidence identification and analysis, some members of the GDG became topic leads, covering identifiable treatment approaches. The NCCMH technical team supported group members, with additional expert advice from special advisers where necessary. All statements and recommendations in this guideline have been generated and agreed by the whole GDG.

2.2.2   For whom is this guideline intended?

This guideline will be of relevance to adults and children of all ages who experience bipolar disorder.

The guideline covers the care provided by primary, secondary and other healthcare professionals who have direct contact with, and make decisions concerning the care of, bipolar disorder sufferers.

Although this guideline will briefly address the issue of diagnosis, it will not make evidence-based recommendations or refer to evidence regarding diagnosis, primary prevention or assessment. In sum, this guideline is intended for use by:

- professional groups who share in the treatment and care of people with bipolar disorder, including psychiatrists, clinical psychologists, mental health nurses, community psychiatric nurses (CPNs), other community nurses, social workers, counsellors, practice nurses, occupational therapists, pharmacists, general practitioners and others
- professionals in other health and non-health sectors who may have direct contact with or are involved in the provision of health and other public services for those diagnosed with bipolar disorder. These may include A&E staff, paramedical staff, prison doctors, the police and professionals who work in the criminal justice and education sectors
- those with responsibility for planning services for people with bipolar disorder and their carers, including directors of public health, NHS trust managers and managers in primary care trusts.

2.2.3   Specific aims of this guideline

The guideline makes recommendations for pharmacological treatments and the use of psychological and service-level interventions. Specifically it aims to:

- evaluate the role of specific pharmacological agents in the treatment and management of bipolar disorder
- evaluate the role of specific psychological interventions in the treatment and management of bipolar disorder
- evaluate the role of specific service delivery systems and service-level interventions in the management of bipolar disorder

- integrate the above to provide best practice advice on the care of individuals with bipolar disorder through the different phases of illness, including the initiation of treatment, the treatment of acute episodes and the promotion of recovery
- consider economic aspects of various treatments for bipolar disorder.

The guideline does not cover treatments that are not normally available on the NHS.

2.2.4   Other versions of this guideline

There are other versions of *Bipolar Disorder: The Management of Bipolar Disorder in Adults, Children and Young People, in Primary and Secondary Care*, including:

- the NICE guideline, which is a shorter version of this guideline, containing the key recommendations and all other recommendations
- the Quick Reference Guide, which is a summary of the main recommendations in the NICE guideline
- the Information for the Public, which describes the guidance using non-technical language. It is written chiefly for patients, but may also be useful for family members, advocates, or those who care for people with bipolar disorder.

3. METHODS USED TO DEVELOP THIS GUIDELINE

3.1 OVERVIEW

The development of this guideline drew upon methods outlined by NICE (*Guideline Development Methods: Information for National Collaborating Centres and Guideline Developers*[6]). The GDG, with support from the NCCMH staff, undertook the development of a patient-centred, evidence-based guideline. There are six basic steps in the process of developing a guideline:

- Define the scope, which sets the parameters of the guideline and provides a focus and steer for the development work
- Define clinical questions considered important for practitioners and service users
- Develop criteria for evidence searching and search for evidence
- Design validated protocols for systematic review and apply to evidence recovered by search
- Synthesise and (meta-) analyse data retrieved, guided by the clinical questions, and produce evidence profiles
- Answer clinical questions with evidence-based recommendations for clinical practice.

The clinical practice recommendations made by the GDG are therefore derived from the most up-to-date and robust evidence base for the clinical and cost-effectiveness of the treatments and services used in the treatment and management of bipolar disorder. In addition, to ensure a service user and carer focus, the concerns of service users and carers regarding clinical practice have been highlighted and addressed by good practice points and recommendations agreed by the whole GDG. The evidence-based recommendations and good practice points are the core of this guideline.

3.2 THE SCOPE

Guideline topics are selected by the Department of Health and the Welsh Assembly Government, which identify the main areas to be covered by the guideline in a specific remit (see *The Guideline Development Process – An Overview for Stakeholders, the Public and the NHS*[7]). The remit for this guideline was translated into a scope document by staff at the NCCMH.

---

[6]Available from www.nice.org.uk
[7]Available from: www.nice.org.

The purpose of the scope is to:

- provide an overview of what the guideline will include and exclude
- identify the key aspects of care that must be included
- set the boundaries of the development work and provide a clear framework to enable work to stay within the priorities agreed by NICE and the NCCMH and the remit from the Department of Health/Welsh Assembly Government
- inform the development of the clinical questions and search strategy
- inform professionals and the public about the expected content of the guideline
- keep the guideline to a reasonable size to ensure that its development can be carried out within an 18-month period.

The draft scope was subject to consultation with stakeholders over a week-long period. During the consultation period, the scope was posted on the NICE website (www.nice.org.uk) and comments were invited from stakeholder organisations and the Guideline Review Panel (GRP). Further information about the GRP can be found on the NICE website. The NCCMH and NICE reviewed the scope in light of comments received and the revised scope was signed off by the GRP.

3.3   THE GUIDELINE DEVELOPMENT GROUP

The GDG consisted of service users, a carer and professionals and academic experts in adult, child and adolescent psychiatry and clinical psychology, nursing, occupational therapy and general practice. The guideline development process was supported by staff from the NCCMH, who undertook the clinical and health economics literature searches, reviewed and presented the evidence to the GDG, managed the process and contributed to drafting the guideline.

3.3.1   Guideline Development Group meetings

Seventeen GDG meetings were held between March 2004 and March 2006. During each day-long GDG meeting, in a plenary session, clinical and key questions and clinical and economic evidence were reviewed and assessed and recommendations formulated. At each meeting, all GDG members declared any potential conflict of interest, and service user and carer concerns were routinely discussed as part of a standing agenda.

3.3.2   Topic groups

The GDG divided its workload along clinically relevant lines to simplify the guideline development process, with GDG members forming smaller topic groups to undertake work in specific areas. Topic group 1 covered questions relating to service delivery; topic group 2 covered pharmacological and other physical treatments; and topic group 3 covered psychological therapies and early warning signs. These groups were designed to manage the large volume of evidence appraisal efficiently before presenting it to the GDG as a whole. Each topic group was chaired by a GDG member with expert knowledge of the topic area. Topic groups refined the key questions, drew up clinical definitions of treatment interventions, reviewed and prepared the evidence with NCCMH staff before presenting it to the GDG as a whole and helped the GDG to identify further expertise in the topic. Topic group leaders reported the status of the group's work as part of the standing agenda. They also introduced and led the GDG discussion of the evidence review for that topic and assisted the GDG chair in drafting that section of the guideline relevant to the work of each topic group.

3.3.3   Consensus conferences

Two consensus conferences were held during guideline development. The first addressed the diagnosis of bipolar disorder in children and adolescents; the second, held in collaboration with the GDG developing the NICE guideline for ante- and post-natal mental health, discussed the use of psychotropic medication before, during and after pregnancy. In each, experts from outside the GDG were invited to give presentations and to comment on draft position statements (see chapters 4 and 9, and appendices 19 and 20). Invited experts, additional attendees and external peer reviewers are listed in Appendix 2.

3.3.4   Service users and carers

The GDG included two service users and a carer. They contributed as full GDG members to writing the clinical questions, helping to ensure that the evidence addressed their views and preferences, highlighting sensitive issues and terminology relevant to the guideline and bringing service-user research to the attention of the GDG. In drafting the guideline, they contributed significantly to the writing of Chapter 5 on service user and carer experiences and developed recommendations from the service user and carer perspective.

3.3.5   Special advisors

Special advisors, who had specific expertise in one or more aspects of treatment and management relevant to the guideline, assisted the GDG, commenting on specific aspects of the developing guideline and making presentations to the GDG. Appendix 2 lists those who agreed to act as special advisors.

3.3.6   National and international experts

National and international experts in the area under review were identified through the literature search and through the experience of the GDG members. These experts were contacted to recommend unpublished or soon-to-be published studies in order to ensure up-to-date evidence was included in the development of the guideline. They informed the group about completed trials at the prepublication stage, systematic reviews in the process of being published, studies relating to the cost-effectiveness of treatment and trial data if the GDG could be provided with full access to the complete trial report. Appendix 2 lists researchers who were contacted.

3.4   CLINICAL QUESTIONS

Clinical questions were used to guide the identification and interrogation of the evidence base. The questions were developed using a modified nominal group technique. Before the first GDG meeting, draft questions were prepared by NCCMH staff based on the scope and an overview of existing guidelines, and modified during a meeting with the guideline chair. They were then discussed by the GDG at their first two meetings and amended to draw up a final list. The PICO (patient, intervention, comparison and outcome) framework was used to help formulate questions about interventions. This structured approach divides each question into four components: the patients (the population under study); the interventions (what is being done; or test/risk factor); the comparisons (other main treatment options); and the outcomes (the measures of how effective the interventions have been; or what is being predicted/prevented). Appendix 5 lists the clinical questions.

To help facilitate the literature review, a note was made of the best study design type to answer each question. There are four main types of clinical questions of relevance to NICE guidelines. These are listed in Text Box 1. For each type of question, the best primary study design varies, where 'best' is interpreted as 'least likely to give

Text box 1: Best study design to answer each type of question

Type of question	Best primary study design
Effectiveness or other impact of an intervention	Randomised controlled trial (RCT): other studies that may be considered in the absence of an RCT are the following: internally/externally controlled before and after trial, interrupted time series
Accuracy of information (for example, risk factor, test, prediction rule)	Comparing the information against a valid gold standard in a randomised trial or inception cohort study
Rates (of disease, patient experience, rare side effects)	Cohort, registry, cross-sectional study
Costs	Naturalistic prospective cost study

misleading answers to the question'. However, in all cases, a well conducted systematic review of the appropriate type of study is always likely to yield a better answer
than a single study.

Deciding on the best design type to answer a specific clinical or public health
question does not mean that studies of different design types addressing the same
question were discarded.

3.5   SYSTEMATIC CLINICAL LITERATURE REVIEW

The aim of the clinical literature review was to systematically identify and synthesise
relevant evidence from the literature in order to answer the specific clinical questions
developed by the GDG. Thus, clinical practice recommendations are evidence-based,
where possible and, if evidence was not available, informal consensus methods were
used (see section 2.5.6) and the need for future research was specified.

3.5.1   Methodology

A step-wise, hierarchical approach was taken to locating and presenting evidence to
the GDG. The NCCMH developed this process based on methods set out in the
*Guideline Development Methods: Information for National Collaborating Centres
and Guideline Developers*[8] and after considering recommendations from a range of
other sources. These included:

- Centre for Clinical Policy and Practice of the New South Wales Health
  Department (Australia)
- Clinical Evidence Online
- Cochrane Collaboration
- New Zealand Guidelines Group
- NHS Centre for Reviews and Dissemination
- Oxford Centre for Evidence-Based Medicine
- Scottish Intercollegiate Guidelines Network (SIGN)
- United States Agency for Healthcare Research and Quality
- Oxford Systematic Review Development Programme
- GRADE Working Group.

3.5.2   The review process

After the scope was finalised, a more extensive search for systematic reviews and
published guidelines was undertaken. Existing reviews and relevant guidelines were
used for reference to aid the development process.

---

[8]Available from www.nice.org.uk

The GDG decided which questions were likely to have a good evidence base and which questions were likely to have little or no directly relevant evidence. For questions that were unlikely to have a good evidence base, a brief descriptive review was initially undertaken by a member of the GDG (see section 3.5.6). For questions with a good evidence base, the review process depended on the type of clinical question.

Outcomes were also discussed by the GDG and a list drawn up for reference, together with lists of clinical assessment tools and rating scales (Appendix 11).

Searches for evidence were updated every 6 months with the final search 8 weeks before the first consultation. After this last point, studies were included only if they were judged by the GDG to be exceptional (for example, the evidence was likely to change a recommendation).

For clinical questions related to interventions, the initial evidence base was formed from well-conducted RCTs that addressed at least one of the clinical questions (the review process is illustrated in Flowchart 1). Although there are a number of difficulties with the use of RCTs in the evaluation of interventions in mental health, the RCT remains the most important method for establishing treatment efficacy (this is discussed in more detail in appropriate clinical evidence chapters). For other clinical questions, searches were for the appropriate study design (see above).

All searches were based on the standard mental health related bibliographic databases (EMBASE, MEDLINE, PsycINFO, CINAHL). At the beginning of the development process, a search for all RCTs relevant to the treatment and management of bipolar disorder was undertaken (updated as above). Question-specific searches for other clinical questions were undertaken during the development process. In addition, where appropriate, systematic reviews undertaken for other mental health guidelines were updated with newly published trials.

After the initial search results were scanned liberally to exclude obviously irrelevant papers, the review team used a purpose-built 'study information' database to manage all reviewed studies, regardless of whether they met inclusion criteria. For questions relating to interventions without good quality evidence (after the initial search), a decision was made by the GDG about whether to undertake question-specific searches for non-RCT evidence in bipolar disorder or for RCTs in mixed mental health populations, or whether to adopt a consensus process (see Section 3.5.6). Future updates of this guideline will be able to update and extend the usable evidence base starting from the evidence collected, synthesised and analysed for this guideline.

In addition, searches were made of the reference lists of relevant systematic reviews and all included studies, as well as the evidence submitted by stakeholders. Known experts in the field (see Appendix 2), based both on the references identified in early steps and on advice from GDG members, were contacted for trials in the process of being published (the conditions for accepting unpublished evidence are described later in this section). In addition, the tables of contents of appropriate journals were checked monthly for relevant studies.

Flowchart 1: Guideline review process

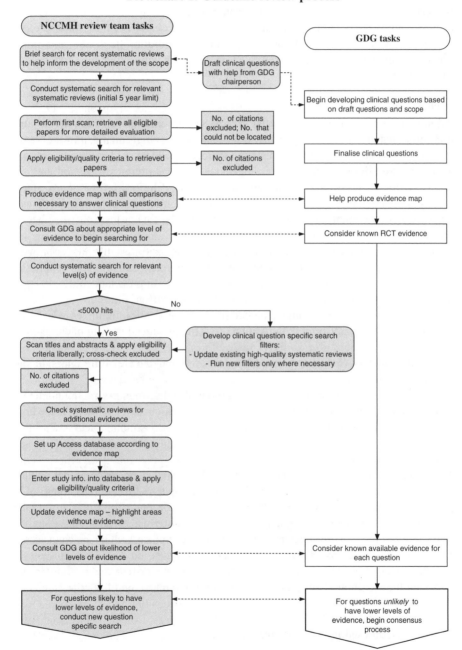

Search filters

Search filters developed by the review team consisted of a combination of subject heading and free-text phrases. Specific filters were developed for the guideline topic and, where necessary, for each clinical question. In addition, the review team used filters developed for systematic reviews, RCTs and other appropriate research designs (Appendix 6).

Study selection

All primary-level studies included after the first scan of citations were acquired in full and re-evaluated for eligibility at the time they were being entered into the study information database. Appendix 7 lists the standard inclusion and exclusion criteria. More specific eligibility criteria were developed for each clinical question and are described in the relevant clinical evidence chapters. Eligible primary-level study papers were critically appraised for methodological quality (see Appendix 7 and Appendix 8). The eligibility of each study was confirmed by at least one member of the appropriate topic group.

For some clinical questions, it was necessary to prioritise the evidence with respect to the UK context (that is external validity). To make this process explicit, the GDG took into account the following factors when assessing the evidence:

● Participant factors (for example, age, stage and severity of illness)
● Provider factors (for example, model fidelity, the conditions under which the intervention was performed, the availability of experienced staff to undertake the procedure)
● Cultural factors (for example, differences in standard care, differences in the welfare system).

It was the responsibility of each topic group to decide which prioritisation factors were relevant to each clinical question in light of the UK context and then decide how they should modify their recommendations.

Unpublished evidence

The GDG used a number of criteria when deciding whether or not to accept unpublished data. First, the evidence must be accompanied by a trial report containing sufficient detail to assess the quality of the data properly. Second, the evidence must be submitted with the understanding that data from the study and a summary of the study's characteristics will be published in the full guideline. Therefore, the GDG did not accept evidence submitted as commercial in confidence. However, the GDG recognised that unpublished evidence submitted by investigators might later be retracted by those investigators if the inclusion of such data would jeopardise publication of their research.

3.5.3   Synthesising the evidence

Outcome data were extracted from all eligible studies meeting the quality criteria using a standardised form (see Appendix 9). Where possible, meta-analysis was used to synthesise the evidence using Review Manager 4.3.7 (Cochrane Collaboration,

2004). If necessary, re-analyses of the data or sub-analyses were used to answer clinical questions not addressed in the original studies or reviews.

For a given outcome (continuous and dichotomous), where more than 50% of the number randomised to any group was not accounted for[9] by trial authors, the data were excluded from the review because of the risk of bias. However, where possible, dichotomous efficacy outcomes were calculated on an intention-to-treat basis (that is a 'once-randomised-always-analyse' basis). This assumes that those participants who ceased to engage in the study – from whatever group – had an unfavourable outcome. This meant that the 50% rule was not applied to dichotomous outcomes where there was good evidence that those participants who ceased to engage in the study were likely to have an unfavourable outcome (in this case, early withdrawals were included in both the numerator and denominator). Adverse effects were entered into Review Manager as reported by the study authors because it was usually not possible to determine if early withdrawals had an unfavourable outcome. For the outcome 'leaving the study early for any reason', the denominator was the number randomised.

The number needed to treat – benefit (NNTB) or the number needed to treat – harm (NNTH) was reported for each outcome where the baseline risk (i.e. control group event rate) was similar across studies. In addition, NNTs calculated at follow-up were only reported where the length of follow-up was similar across studies. When the length of follow-up or baseline risk varies (especially with low risk), the NNT is a poor summary of the treatment effect (Deeks, 2002). Risk differences (RD) were calculated for outcomes with low event rates, such as death.

The meta-analysis of survival data, such as time to any mood episode, was based on log hazard ratios and standard errors. Since individual patient data were not available in included studies, hazard ratios and standard errors calculated from a Cox proportional hazard model were extracted. Where necessary, standard errors were calculated from confidence intervals (CIs) or p-value according to standard formulae (for example, Cochrane Reviewers' Handbook 4.2.2). Data were summarised using the generic inverse variance method using Review Manager 4.2.7 (Cochrane Collaboration, 2004).

Included/excluded studies tables, generated automatically from the study information database, were used to summarise general information about each study (see Appendix 22). Where meta-analysis was not appropriate and/or possible, the reported results from each primary-level study were also presented in the study characteristics table (and included, where appropriate, in a narrative review).

Consultation was used to overcome difficulties with coding. Data from studies included in existing systematic reviews were extracted independently by one reviewer and cross-checked with the existing data set. Where possible, two independent reviewers extracted data from new studies. Where double data extraction was not possible, data extracted by one reviewer was checked by the second reviewer. Disagreements were resolved with discussion. Where consensus could not be reached, a third reviewer resolved the disagreement. Masked assessment (that is blind to the journal from which the article comes, the authors, the institution and the

---

[9]'Accounted for' in this context means using an appropriate method for dealing with missing data (for example LOCF or a regression technique).

magnitude of the effect) was not used since it is unclear that doing so reduces bias (Jadad *et al.*, 1996; Berlin, 2001).

3.5.4   Presenting the data to the GDG

Summary characteristics tables and, where appropriate, forest plots generated with Review Manager, were presented to the GDG, in order to prepare an evidence profile for each review and to develop recommendations.

Evidence profile tables
An evidence profile table was used to summarise both the quality of the evidence and the results of the evidence synthesis (see Table 1 for an example of an evidence profile table). Each table included details about the quality assessment of each outcome: number of studies, limitations to the quality of included studies, information about the consistency of the evidence (see below for how consistency was measured), directness of the evidence (that is, how closely the outcome measures, interventions and participants match those of interest) and other modifying factors (for example, effect sizes with wide CIs would be described as imprecise data). Each evidence profile also included a summary of the findings: number of patients included in each group, an estimate of the magnitude of the effect, the clinical significance of the effect (see section 3.5.5 for how this was determined), quality of the evidence and the importance of the evidence. The quality of the evidence was based on the quality assessment components (study design, limitations to study quality, consistency, directness and any other modifying factors) and graded using the following definitions:

- **High** = Further research is very unlikely to change our confidence in the estimate of the effect.
- **Moderate** = Further research is likely to have an important impact on our confidence in the estimate of the effect and may change the estimate.
- **Low** = Further research is very likely to have an important impact on our confidence in the estimate of the effect and is likely to change the estimate.
- **Very low** = Any estimate of effect is very uncertain.

For further information about the process and the rationale of producing an evidence profile table, see GRADE (2004).

Forest plots
Each forest plot displayed the effect size and CI for each study as well as the overall summary statistic. The graphs were organised so that the display of data in the area to the left of the 'line of no effect' indicated a 'favourable' outcome for the treatment in question. Dichotomous outcomes were presented as relative risks (RR) with the associated 95% CI (for an example, see Figure 1). A relative risk (or risk ratio) is the ratio of the treatment event rate to the control event rate. An RR of 1 indicates no difference between treatment and control. In Figure 1, the overall RR of 0.73 indicates that the event rate (that is, non-remission rate) associated with intervention A is about three quarters of that with the control intervention or, in other words, the relative risk reduction is 27%.

Table 1: Example evidence profile table

	Quality assessment				Summary of findings					
					No. of patients		Effect			
No. of studies	**Quality of included studies**	**Consistency**	**Directness**	**Other modifying factors**	**CBT**	**Waitlist**	**Effect size**	**Likelihood of clinically important effect**	**Overall quality**	**Importance**
Carbamazepine vs placebo										
Efficacy										
Mania: change score at endpoint (manic only)										
Weisler 2004 Weisler 2005	Randomisation not clear (−1)	None	Acute mania	Strong effect (+1)	134	146	WMD = −6.87 (−9.24, −4.49)	Very likely (favouring carbamazepine)	Moderate	Critical
Acceptability/tolerability										
Leaving treatment early for any reason										
Weisler 2004 Weisler 2005	Randomisation not clear (−1)	Significant heterogeneity (−1): random effects model used	Acute mania	None	134	146	RR (random effects) = 0.79 (0.59, 1.06)	Likely (favouring carbamazepine)	Low	Critical

Figure 1: Example of a forest plot displaying dichotomous data

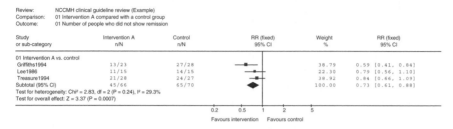

The CI shows with 95% certainty the range within which the true treatment effect should lie and can be used to determine statistical significance. If the CI does not cross the 'line of no effect', the effect is statistically significant.

Continuous outcomes were analysed as weighted mean differences (WMD) or as standardised mean differences (SMD) when different measures were used in different studies to estimate the same underlying effect (for an example, see Figure 2). If provided, intention-to-treat data, using a method such as 'last observation carried forward', were preferred over data from completers.

To check for consistency between studies, both the I^2 test of heterogeneity and a visual inspection of the forest plots were used. The I^2 statistic describes the proportion of total variation in study estimates that is due to heterogeneity (Higgins & Thompson, 2002). An I^2 of less than 30% was taken to indicate mild heterogeneity and a fixed effects model was used to synthesise the results. An I^2 of more than 50% was taken as notable heterogeneity. In this case, an attempt was made to explain the variation (for example, outliers were removed from the analysis or sub-analyses were conducted to examine the possibility of moderators). If studies with heterogeneous results were found to be comparable, a random effects model was used to summarise the results (DerSimonian & Laird, 1986). In the random effects analysis, heterogeneity is accounted for both in the width of CIs and in the estimate of the treatment effect. With decreasing heterogeneity the random effects approach moves asymptotically towards a fixed effects model. An I^2 of 30 to 50% was taken to indicate moderate heterogeneity. In this case, both the chi-squared test of heterogeneity and a visual inspection of the forest plot were used to decide between a fixed and random effects model.

Figure 2: Example of a forest plot displaying continuous data

Review:	NCCMH clinical guideline review (Example)
Comparison:	01 Intervention A compared with a control group
Outcome:	03 Mean frequency (endpoint)

Study or sub-category	N	Intervention A Mean (SD)	N	Control Mean (SD)	SMD (fixed) 95% CI	Weight %	SMD (fixed) 95% CI
01 Intervention A vs. control							
Freeman1988	32	1.30(3.40)	20	3.70(3.60)		25.91	-0.68 [-1.25, -0.10]
Griffiths1994	20	1.25(1.45)	22	4.14(2.21)		17.83	-1.50 [-2.20, -0.81]
Lee1986	14	3.70(4.00)	14	10.10(17.50)		15.08	-0.49 [-1.24, 0.26]
Treasure1994	28	44.23(27.04)	24	61.40(24.97)		27.28	-0.65 [-1.21, -0.09]
Wolf1992	15	5.30(5.10)	11	7.10(4.60)		13.90	-0.36 [-1.14, 0.43]
Subtotal (95% CI)	109		91			100.00	-0.74 [-1.04, -0.45]
Test for heterogeneity: Chi² = 6.13, df = 4 (P = 0.19), I² = 34.8%							
Test for overall effect: Z = 4.98 (P < 0.00001)							

-4 -2 0 2 4
Favours intervention   Favours control

To explore the possibility that the results entered into each meta-analysis suffered from publication bias, data from included studies were entered, where there was sufficient data, into a funnel plot. Asymmetry of the plot was taken to indicate possible publication bias and investigated further.

Forest plots included lines for studies that were believed to contain eligible data even if the data were missing from the analysis in the published study. An estimate of the proportion of eligible data that were missing (because some studies did not include all relevant outcomes) was calculated for each analysis. All forest plots are in Appendix 24.

3.5.5   Forming the clinical summaries and recommendations

The evidence profile table relating to a particular clinical question was completed (together with a summary evidence table based on critical outcomes for ease of reference) in Appendix 23. Finally, the systematic reviewer in conjunction with the topic group lead produced a clinical summary.

In order to facilitate consistency in generating and drafting the clinical summaries, a decision tree was used to help determine, for each comparison, the likelihood of the effect being clinically significant (see Figure 3). The decision tree was designed to be used as one step in the interpretation of the evidence (primarily to separate clinically important from clinically negligible effects) and was not designed to replace clinical judgement. For each comparison, the GDG defined *a priori* a clinically significant threshold, taking into account both the comparison group and the outcome.

As shown in Figure 3, the review team first classified the point estimate of the effect as clinically significant or not. For example, if an RR of 0.75 was considered to be the threshold, then a point estimate of 0.73 (as can be seen in Figure 1), would meet the criteria for clinical significance.

Where the point estimate of the effect exceeded the threshold, a further consideration was made about the precision of the evidence by examining the range of estimates defined by the CI. Where the effect size was judged clinically significant for the full range of plausible estimates, the result was described as *very likely to be clinically significant* (that is, CS1). In situations where the CI included clinically unimportant values, but the point estimate was both clinically and statistically significant, the result was described as *likely to be clinically significant* (that is, CS2). However, if the CI crossed the line of no effect (that is, the result was not statistically significant), the result was described as *inconclusive* (that is, CS4).

Where the point estimate did not meet the criteria for clinical significance and the CI completely excluded clinically significant values, the result was described as *unlikely to be clinically significant* (that is, CS3). Alternatively, if the CI included both clinically significant and clinically unimportant values, the result was described as *inconclusive* (that is, CS4). In all cases described as inconclusive, the GDG used clinical judgement to interpret the results.

Figure 3: Decision tree for helping to judge the likelihood of clinical significance

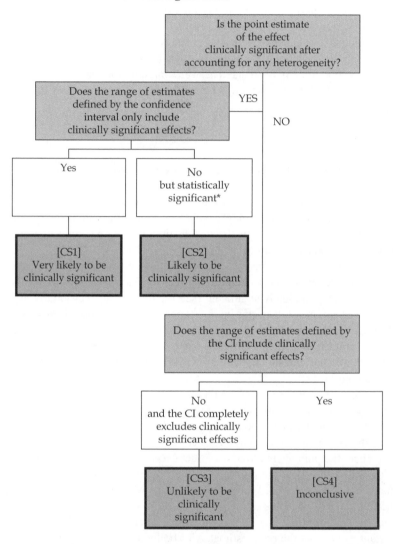

*Efficacy outcomes with large effect sizes and very wide confidence intervals should be interpreted with caution and should be described as inconclusive (CS4), especially if there is only one small study.

Once the evidence profile tables and clinical summaries were finalised and agreed by the GDG, the associated recommendations were produced, taking into account the trade-off between the benefits and risks as well as other important factors. These included economic considerations, values of the GDG and society, and the GDG's awareness of practical issues (Eccles *et al.*, 1998).

3.5.6 Method used to answer a clinical question in the absence of appropriately designed, high-quality research

In the absence of level I evidence (or a level that is appropriate to the question), or where the GDG were of the opinion (on the basis of previous searches or their knowledge of the literature) that there was unlikely to be such evidence, either an informal or formal consensus process was adopted. This process focused on those questions that the GDG considered a priority.

Informal consensus
The starting point for the process of informal consensus was that a member of the topic group identified, with help from the systematic reviewer, a narrative review that most directly addressed the clinical question. Where this was not possible, a brief review of the recent literature was initiated.

This existing narrative review or new review was used as a basis for beginning an iterative process to identify lower levels of evidence relevant to the clinical question and to lead to written statements for the guideline. The process involved a number of steps:

- A description of what is known about the issues concerning the clinical question was written by one of the topic group members.
- Evidence from the existing review or new review was then presented in narrative form to the GDG and further comments were sought about the evidence and its perceived relevance to the clinical question.
- Based on the feedback from the GDG, additional information was sought and added to the information collected. This may include studies that did not directly address the clinical question but were thought to contain relevant data.
- If, during the course of preparing the report, a significant body of primary-level studies (of appropriate design to answer the question) were identified, a full systematic review was conducted.
- At this time, subject possibly to further reviews of the evidence, a series of statements that directly addressed the clinical question were developed.
- Following this, on occasions and as deemed appropriate by the development group, the report was then sent to appointed experts outside of the GDG for peer review and comment. The information from this process was then fed back to the GDG for further discussion of the statements.
- Recommendations were then developed.
- After this final stage of comment, the statements and recommendations were again reviewed and agreed upon by the GDG.

3.6 HEALTH ECONOMICS REVIEW STRATEGIES

The aim of the health economics review was to contribute to the guideline's development by providing evidence on the economic burden of bipolar disorder as well as on the relative cost-effectiveness of different treatment options covered in the guideline. Where available, relevant evidence was collected and assessed in order to help the decision-making process.

This process was based on a preliminary analysis of the clinical evidence and had two stages:
- Identification of the areas with likely major cost impacts within the scope of the guideline.
- Systematic review of existing data on the economic burden of bipolar disorder and cost-effectiveness evidence of different treatment options for bipolar disorder.

In addition, in areas with likely major resource implications where relevant data did not already exist, a primary economic analysis based on decision-analytic economic modelling was undertaken alongside the guideline development process, in order to provide cost-effectiveness evidence and assist decision making.

3.6.1   Key economic issues

The following economic issues relating to the epidemiology and the management of bipolar disorder were identified by the GDG in collaboration with the health economist as primary key issues that should be considered in the guideline:
- The global economic burden of bipolar disorder with specific reference to the UK.
- Comparative cost-effectiveness between pharmacological, psychological and physical interventions for the treatment of patients with bipolar disorder either stabilised or experiencing an acute episode.
- Comparative cost-effectiveness between different types of service provision appropriate for the management of patients with bipolar disorder.

3.6.2   Systematic literature review

A systematic review of the health economic evidence was conducted. The aim of the review was threefold:
- To identify publications providing information on the economic burden of bipolar disorder relevant to the UK context.
- To identify existing economic evaluations of pharmacological, psychological and physical treatment interventions, as well as of appropriate forms of service configuration, for the management of patients with bipolar disorder, that could be transferable to the UK patient population and healthcare setting.
- To identify studies reporting health state utility data transferable to the UK population to facilitate a possible cost-utility modelling process.

Although no attempt was made to review systematically studies with only resource use or cost data, relevant UK-based information was extracted for future modelling exercises if it was considered appropriate.

3.6.3   Search strategy

For the systematic review of economic evidence on bipolar disorder, the standard mental health-related bibliographic databases (EMBASE, MEDLINE, CINAHL, PsychINFO, HTA) were searched. For these databases, a health economics search filter adapted from the Centre for Reviews and Dissemination (CRD) at the

University of York was used in combination with a general filter for bipolar disorder. The subject filter employed a combination of free-text terms and medical subject headings, with subject headings having been exploded. Additional searches were performed in specific health economic databases (NHS EED, OHE HEED). HTA and NHS EED databases were accessed via the Cochrane Library, using the general filter for bipolar disorder. OHE HEED was searched using a shorter, database-specific strategy. Initial searches were performed between November 2004 and February 2005. The searches were updated regularly, with the final search between 6 and 8 weeks before the first consultation.

In order to identify economic evidence on different types of service configurations appropriate for patients with bipolar disorder, further searches were carried out between July and September 2005 in the same electronic databases. In this case, a similar methodology was applied, but a service configuration-focused filter was used. Search strategies used for the health economics systematic review are included in Appendix 6.

In parallel to searches of electronic databases, reference lists of eligible studies and relevant reviews were searched by hand, and experts in the field of bipolar disorder and mental health economics were contacted in order to identify additional relevant published and unpublished studies. Studies included in the clinical evidence review were also screened for economic evidence.

3.6.4 Review process

The database searches for general health economic evidence for bipolar disorder resulted in 211 potentially eligible references. The service configuration-focused searches resulted in 140 studies considered to be potentially relevant. A further 12 possibly eligible references were found by hand-searching. Full texts of all potentially eligible studies (including those for which relevance/eligibility was not clear from the abstract) were obtained. These publications were then assessed against a set of standard inclusion criteria by the health economist and papers eligible for inclusion as economic evaluations were subsequently assessed for internal validity. The quality assessment was based on the 35-point checklist used by the *British Medical Journal* to assist referees in appraising full economic analyses (Drummond & Jefferson, 1996) (Appendix 12).

3.6.5 Selection criteria

The following inclusion criteria were applied to select studies identified by the economic searches for further analysis:
- No restriction was placed on language or publication status of the papers.
- Studies published between 1985 and 2005 were included. This date restriction was imposed in order to obtain data relevant to current healthcare settings and costs.
- Only studies from Organisation for Economic Co-operation and Development (OECD) countries were included, as the aim of the review was to identify

economic information transferable to the UK context. For the systematic review on the cost-effectiveness of different types of service configuration, only studies conducted in the UK were considered, as it was believed that resource use associated with various types of service provision was likely to differ significantly between the UK and other OECD countries.

- Selection criteria based on types of clinical conditions and patients were identical to the clinical literature review (see Appendix 7).
- Studies were included provided that sufficient details regarding methods and results were available to enable the methodological quality of the study to be assessed and provided that the study's data and results were extractable.

Additional selection criteria were applied in the case of economic evaluations:

- Only full economic evaluations that compared two or more options and considered both costs and consequences (that is, cost-minimisation analysis, cost-consequences analysis, cost-effectiveness analysis, cost-utility analysis, or cost-benefit analysis) were included in the review.
- Economic studies were considered only if they utilised clinical evidence derived from a meta-analysis, a well-conducted literature review, an RCT, a quasi-experimental trial or a cohort study.

3.6.6   Data extraction

Data were extracted by the health economist using an economic data extraction form (Appendix 13). Masked assessment, whereby data extractors are blind to the details of journal, authors, etc., was not undertaken.

3.6.7   Presentation of the results

The economic evidence identified by the health economics systematic review is summarised in the respective chapters of the guideline, following presentation of the clinical evidence. The characteristics and results of all economic studies included in the review are provided in the form of evidence tables in Appendix 14. Results of additional economic modelling undertaken alongside the guideline development process are also presented in the relevant chapters.

3.7   STAKEHOLDER CONTRIBUTIONS

Professionals, service users and companies have contributed to and commented on the guideline at key stages in its development. Stakeholders for this guideline include:

- Service user/carer stakeholders: the national service user and carer organisations that represent people whose care is described in this guideline
- Professional stakeholders: the national organisations that represent healthcare professionals who are providing services to service users

- Commercial stakeholders: the companies that manufacture medicines used in the treatment of bipolar disorder
- Primary Care Trusts and Mental Health Trusts
- Department of Health and Welsh Assembly Government.

Stakeholders have been involved in the guideline's development at the following points:
- Commenting on the initial scope of the guideline and attending a briefing meeting held by NICE
- Contributing lists of evidence to the GDG
- Commenting on the first and second drafts of the guideline.

3.8   VALIDATION OF THIS GUIDELINE

Registered stakeholders had two opportunities to comment on the draft guideline, which was posted on the NICE website during the consultation periods. The GRP also reviewed the guideline and checked that stakeholders' comments had been addressed.

Following the final consultation period, the GDG finalised the recommendations and the NCCMH produced the final documents. These were then submitted to NICE. NICE then formally approved the guideline and issued its guidance to the NHS in England and Wales.

4.   BIPOLAR DISORDER AND ITS DIAGNOSIS

4.1   THE DISORDER

4.1.1   Overview

The concept of bipolar disorder grew out of Emil Kraepelin's classification of manic depressive insanity, which was postulated around the end of the 19th century. However, descriptions of frenetic activity associated with the manic state can be found in the writings of Hippocrates and as far back as the ancient Egyptians. In 1957 Leonhard coined the term 'bipolar' for those patients with depression who also experienced mania. In 1966 Angst and Perris independently demonstrated that unipolar depression and bipolar disorder could be differentiated in terms of clinical presentation, evolution, family history and therapeutic response. Their ideas stood the test of time and became assimilated in both the two main modern systems of classification for the diagnosis of mental disorder: the Diagnostic and Statistical Manual of Mental Disorders (DSM) published by the American Psychiatric Association and the International Classification of Disease (ICD) published by the World Health Organization. In 1980 the name bipolar disorder was adopted to replace the older term manic depression, which was tightly associated with psychosis. It became recognised that not all patients who experience mania and depression become psychotic and therefore psychosis should not be required for a diagnosis. In this modern conceptualisation, bipolar disorder is a cyclical mood disorder involving periods of profound disruption to mood and behaviour interspersed with periods of more or less full recovery. The key feature of bipolar disorder is the experience of hypomania or mania – grandiose and expansive affect associated with increased drive and decreased sleep, which ultimately can culminate in psychosis and exhaustion if left untreated. There is some heterogeneity between the major diagnostic classification systems in the criteria for bipolar disorder (see Section 4.4 below). ICD-10 requires two discrete mood episodes, at least one of which must be manic. In DSM-IV a single episode of mania or a single episode of hypomania plus a single major depressive episode would warrant a diagnosis of bipolar disorder.

The bipolar spectrum
Far from being a discrete diagnostic entity, there is increasing recognition of a spectrum of bipolar disorders that ranges from marked and severe mood disturbance into milder mood variations that become difficult to distinguish from normal mood fluctuation. In terms of classification, in DSM-IV a distinction is drawn between bipolar I disorder, in which the patient suffers full-blown manic episodes (most commonly interspersed with episodes of major depression), and bipolar II disorder, in which the

patient experiences depressive episodes and less severe manic symptoms, classed as hypomanic episodes (it must be noted that ICD-10 does not include bipolar II disorder). Cyclothymia is a condition in which the patient has recurrent hypomanic episodes and subclinical episodes of depression. The depressive episodes do not reach sufficient severity or duration to merit a diagnosis of a major depressive episode, but mood disturbance is a continuing problem for the patient and interferes with everyday functioning. 'Softer' forms of bipolar disorder have been proposed, including recurrent depressive episodes with a hyperthymic temperament and a family history of bipolar disorder (Akiskal *et al.*, 2000), or recurrent depression with antidepressant-induced mania. However, these are not currently part of official diagnostic classifications. There are problems with establishing satisfactory inter-rater reliability in the assessments of the 'softer' end of the bipolar spectrum. The clinical utility of these proposed diagnoses has yet to be established and there is currently no indication whether treatment is necessary or effective.

4.1.2   Symptoms and presentation

Depression
Although mania or hypomania are the defining characteristics of bipolar disorder, throughout the course of the illness depressive symptoms are more common than manic symptoms. Patients with bipolar disorder spend a substantial proportion of time suffering from syndromal or sub-syndromal depressive symptoms. The outcome of a 12-year prospective longitudinal study, in which 146 patients with bipolar I disorder completed weekly mood ratings, reported that depressive symptoms were three times more common than manic or hypomanic symptoms (Judd *et al.*, 2002). Patients spent 32% of weeks with symptoms of depression. In a separate study of 86 patients with bipolar II disorder this proportion was much higher at 50% (Judd *et al.*, 2003). A similar study by the Stanley Foundation Bipolar Network monitored 258 bipolar patients (three quarters of whom had bipolar I disorder) for a year using the National Institute for Mental Health (NIMH) Life Chart Method (LCM). On average, patients spent 33% of the time depressed and a large proportion (>60%) suffered four or more mood episodes in a year (Post *et al.*, 2003). However, the proportion of time spent depressed did not differ between bipolar I and II patients. To date, such studies have all been conducted on adults and it is not clear whether these observations extend to children or adolescents with bipolar disorder.

Major depressive episodes in bipolar disorder are similar to those experienced in unipolar major depression. Patients suffer depressed mood and experience profound loss of interest in activities, coupled with other symptoms such as fatigue, weight loss or gain, difficulty sleeping or staying awake, psychomotor slowing, feelings of worthlessness, excessive guilt and suicidal thoughts or actions. For patients presenting with a first episode of depression, it may not be possible to distinguish between those who will go on to suffer recurrent unipolar depression and those who will develop bipolar disorder. However, evidence suggests there may be subtle differences between bipolar and unipolar depression. In particular, depression in the course of bipolar disorder may be more likely to show signs of psychomotor retardation, to have melancholic features (such as feelings of worthlessness and marked anhedonia), to show features of atypical depression (such as hypersomnia and weight gain) (Mitchell & Mahli, 2004) and to show psychotic features – especially in young people (Strober & Carlson, 1982). Patients experiencing a first episode of depression who display these features and have a family history of bipolar disorder may be at increased risk of developing bipolar disorder.

Sub-syndromal depressive symptoms are common in patients with bipolar disorder (especially those with bipolar II disorder) and are often associated with significant interpersonal or occupational disability. The management of these chronic, low-grade depressive symptoms is therefore of major importance, but is also a substantial treatment challenge.

Vignette of a patient with sub-syndromal depression

Unfortunately, living with bipolar disorder isn't always simply a case of being either well or ill – there can be an awful lot of grey in between. It can be very difficult to work out what is 'normal' mood and what isn't.

Diagnosed with rapid-cycling bipolar I aged 19, by 23 I was on a combination of lithium and carbamazepine, which seemed to work for me. However, at some point the following year, in agreement with my psychiatrist, I cut back on my medication. I now know that this resulted in a slow and imperceptible slide into depression. At the time, I just thought I was going through a difficult patch because I was stuck at home convalescing with severe back pain.

It seems unbelievable now, but looking back it appears I remained in this mild to moderate depressed state for about 6 years. I wasn't going up and down because the drugs stopped the cycling, so I didn't realise I was ill. I assumed I was well because I was still taking what I thought was the best possible combination of medication for me.

I was desperately unhappy. Small things like going to the shops and talking to people – even my girlfriend – left me wracked with anxiety. I just came to think I was miserable by nature. I was regularly in contact with several general practitioners (GPs) and psychiatrists over this time, but none identified that I was experiencing sub-syndromal symptoms.

I think there were three reasons for this. My symptoms weren't full-blown major depression – mostly I wasn't suicidal – and I was able to hold down a job and a relationship, so on the surface I appeared to be functioning. Also, my psychiatrists seemed to rely on my judgement as to my health and perhaps would have made treatment recommendations if I'd complained bitterly about feeling depressed. Unfortunately, without having a recent benchmark of experiencing 'normal' mood to compare against, I didn't realise I was depressed. However, there were lots of things which in hindsight were tell-tale signs that I wasn't well.

Continued

Vignette of a patient with subsyndromal depression (*Continued*)

I developed lots of physical aches and pains. My back pain got steadily worse, and I developed neck pain and mysterious tingles in the arms and legs. It later became apparent that these physical problems resulted from muscular trigger points all over my body caused by the depression.

I was so anxious that I could barely speak to anyone without stuttering. My speech became such a problem, I even started seeing a psychologist, which didn't address the real problem.

As the years passed, I felt more and more unhappy. I felt hopeless about the future and decided that life was not worth living. My attempt to take my life finally prompted my psychiatrist into taking some action, and he prescribed mirtazapine. This was a revelation. It immediately sent me into psychotic rapid cycling, but at the same time it dawned on me that I had in fact been unknowingly depressed for ages. I could now tell that my mood, even though it was still up and down, was 'on average', much better than it had been.

I was put on lamotrigine instead of the carbamazepine and then, when that failed to lift my baseline mood, quetiapine. As my mood improved and stabilised over the following months, my physical symptoms of depression – the aches and pains – began to drop away. The easing of my physical symptoms was perhaps the best objective indicator for me that my mood was stabilising at a 'normal' level. Without those outward signs of improvement, it was hard to gauge what 'normal' mood was. I fear that many patients are in the same predicament I was. Psychiatrists must always be vigilant for sub-syndromal symptoms – they ruin lives.

The risk of suicide is greatly elevated during depressive episodes. Approximately 17% of patients with bipolar I disorder and 24% of patients with bipolar II disorder attempt suicide during the course of their illness (Rihmer & Kiss, 2002). Most suicide attempts and most completed suicides occur in the depressed phase of the illness and patients with bipolar II disorder are at especially high risk (Baldessarini *et al.*, 2003a). Annually around 0.4% of patients with bipolar disorder will die by suicide, which is vastly greater than the international population average of 0.017% (Baldessarini & Tondo, 2003). The standardised mortality ratio (SMR) for suicide in bipolar disorder is estimated to be 15 for men and 22.4 for women (Osby *et al.*, 2001).

Mania and hypomania

The longitudinal study of bipolar symptomatology mentioned above reported that patients with bipolar I disorder suffered syndromal or sub-syndromal manic or hypomanic symptoms approximately 9% of the time over 12 years (Judd *et al.*, 2002). For patients with bipolar II disorder, approximately 1% of weeks were spent hypomanic (Judd *et al.*, 2003). Similarly, the 1-year prospective follow-up study conducted by the Stanley Foundation Bipolar Network reported that on average patients experienced syndromal manic symptoms approximately 10% of the time (Post *et al.*, 2003).

However, there was no significant difference in the proportion of time spent with manic symptoms between patients with bipolar I or II disorder. In the majority of cases, individuals with bipolar disorder will experience both manic and depressive episodes throughout the course of their illness, although one epidemiological survey identified a sub-population of approximately 20% who had never experienced a depressive episode (Kessler *et al.*, 1997). For those who have both depressive and manic episodes, the evidence above indicates that mania is much less common than depression in those with bipolar disorder. However, the extreme behaviours associated with it can be devastating and patients with mania often require hospitalisation to minimise harm to themselves or others.

Patients in the acute manic phase exhibit expansive, grandiose affect, which may be predominantly euphoric or irritable. Although dysphoric mood is more frequently associated with depressive episodes, factor analytic studies of symptoms in patients with pure mania suggest dysphoric mood (such as depression, guilt and anxiety) can be prominent in some manic patients (Cassidy *et al.*, 1998; Cassidy & Carroll, 2001).

The clinical presentation of mania is marked by several features, which can lead to significant impairment to functioning (see also the vignette below). These may include inflated self-esteem and disinhibition, for example, over-familiar or fractious and outspoken behaviour. To the observer, an individual with mania may appear inappropriately dressed, unkempt or dishevelled. The person may have an urge to talk incessantly and their speech may be pressured, faster or louder than usual and difficult for others to interrupt. In severe forms of mania, flight of ideas can render speech incoherent and impossible to understand. The patient may find that racing thoughts or ideas can be difficult to piece together into a coherent whole. Patients often describe increased productivity and creativity during the early stages of mania which may feel satisfying and rewarding. However, as the episode worsens severe distractibility, restlessness, and difficulty concentrating can render the completion of tasks impossible. Patients often experience a decreased need for sleep and begin sleeping less without feeling tired. After prolonged periods with little or no sleep the individual can become physically exhausted with no desire to rest. The person may find it hard to stay still or remain seated and other forms of psychomotor restlessness may be apparent, such as excessive use of gestures or fidgeting. Appetite may also increase, although food intake does not always increase to compensate. There might be an increase in impulsive risk-taking behaviour with a high potential for negative consequences. Libido may rise, with increased interest in sexual activity, which may culminate in risky sexual practices. In severe cases individuals may develop psychotic symptoms such as grandiose delusions and mood-congruent hallucinations – for example, the voice of God sending messages of special purpose. Alternatively, persecutory delusions may develop, but are usually consistent with a general grandiose theme such as the belief that others are actively trying to thwart the person's plans or remove their power. Insight is lost in mania – the individual is unaware that their behaviour is abnormal and does not consider him or herself to be in need of treatment. Clinical interventions may be seen as attempts to undermine the person's esteem and power and could provoke or worsen irritability even in patients who are predominantly euphoric.

All the features reported in mania – except psychotic symptoms – can also occur in hypomania to a less severe extent. Generally insight is preserved, although the person may not feel in need of help. Increased productivity and decreased need for sleep can be experienced as a positive enhancement of everyday functioning. Hypomania is accompanied by a change in functioning that is not characteristic of the person when non-depressed and the change is noticed by others, but it is not associated with marked impairment in social or occupational function. According to the DSM-IV diagnostic criteria, symptoms must last at least 4 days to merit the diagnosis of a hypomanic episode. However, there is considerable debate about how long hypomanic symptoms should be present to merit a diagnosis of bipolar II disorder (see Section 4.4.2 below).

Vignette of a patient with mania

I first fell ill with rapid-cycling bipolar disorder at the age of 19. At first, when manic, I felt 'on top of the world', much more sociable than normal and very active and self-confident. I'd have an 'up' of about 9 days, followed by a 'down' for the same period. The same pattern would repeat itself with my mood swings becoming more and more extreme each time. Within a few months, I was experiencing full-blown psychosis. When manic, I was euphoric. Everything was in overdrive. I would only sleep for an hour or two a night. I craved stimulation, whether it was smoking, even though I'm a non-smoker, driving fast or listening to more and much louder music than was normal for me.

As I entered a manic cycle, my thoughts would start to race. I'd develop delusions of grandeur. Suddenly everything seemed to revolve around me and I was the most important thing in the world. The most extreme manifestation of this was the religious delusions I experienced when psychotic. Despite not having a Christian upbringing, I came to secretly believe I was some sort of manifestation of Jesus Christ on a God-given mission. Wherever I looked I saw 'the face of God' staring out at me. For a while, I was haunted by light switches turn with the screw either side of the switch representing the eyes and nose of a face.

And then, as sure as night follows day, everything would come crashing down after about 9 days and I would plunge into a deep depression, in bed 18 hours a day. My thoughts became painfully sluggish and grossly distorted in a negative way. I felt suicidal and haunted by irrational self-doubt such as the belief I was certain to end up homeless or that people thought I was a paedophile because I was standing outside a school.

Mixed states

In a full-blown mixed episode, criteria are met for a depressive episode and a manic episode nearly every day for at least 1 week (American Psychiatric Association, 1994). However, a mixture of manic and depressed symptoms may occur without reaching full diagnostic criteria. For example, a patient may have racing thoughts, agitation, overactivity and flight of ideas, but feel worthless, guilty and suicidal. The

75

patients with bipolar I disorder who took part in the 12-year longitudinal study mentioned previously spent an average 6% of weeks in a mixed or cycling state (where polarity of episode was changing and symptoms of both were present) (Judd *et al.*, 2002). For patients with bipolar II disorder the proportion was just over 2% (Judd *et al.*, 2003). It is estimated that approximately two thirds of patients will suffer a mixed episode at some point in their illness (Mackin & Young, 2005). A study of 441 patients with bipolar disorder reported that subclinical mixed episodes are common – with 70% of those in a depressed episode showing clinically significant signs of hypomania and 94% of those with mania or hypomania showing significant depressive symptoms (Bauer *et al.*, 2005). Sub-threshold mixed episodes were more than twice as prevalent as threshold mixed episodes. The combination of morbid, depressed affect with overactivity and racing thoughts makes mixed states a particularly dangerous time for people with bipolar disorder.

Cycle frequency
There is a large amount of variation in how often patients suffer mood episodes and no criteria exist to define 'normal' cycle frequency. Some patients have discrete episodes that occur rarely (for example, no more than one episode per year) with full recovery in between, others experience episodes more often, and some may fail to fully recover between episodes. A subset of patients suffers from rapid-cycling bipolar disorder, which is defined as the experience of at least four syndromal depressive, manic, hypomanic or mixed episodes within a 12-month period. Ultra-rapid and ultra-ultra-rapid (or ultradian) cycling variants have also been identified, in which mood fluctuates markedly from week to week or even within the course of a single day (Kramlinger & Post, 1996). Whether the differentiation of subtypes of rapid cycling is of clinical significance is currently not known. A review of the last 30 years of research on rapid versus non-rapid cycling indicated differences in illness course and prognosis (Mackin & Young, 2004) and reports suggest the distinction is of value as a course modifier (Maj *et al.*, 1994; Maj *et al.*, 1999). Patients with a rapid cycling illness course tend to be more treatment resistant, suffer a greater burden of depressive episodes and have a higher incidence of substance misuse. A recent study in a sample of 456 bipolar probands identified 91 (20%) patients with a rapid cycling illness who, in comparison to those without rapid cycling, suffered more severe mood symptoms and a greater degree of functional impairment (Schneck *et al.*, 2004). Further data from this cohort suggests rapid cycling is not more common in females than males (Baldassano *et al.*, 2005) as had been indicated by previous studies in smaller samples.

4.2   INCIDENCE AND PREVALENCE

Community-based epidemiological studies consistently report the lifetime prevalence of bipolar I disorder to be approximately 1% (based on DSM-III-R, or DSM-IV criteria). A review of epidemiological surveys in six non-European countries reported that the lifetime rate of bipolar I disorder ranged from 0.3% to 1.5% (Weissman *et al.*, 1996).

Rates reported in European studies have varied more widely from 0.1% to 2.4% (Faravelli *et al.*, 1990; Pini *et al.*, 2005; Szadoczky *et al.*, 1998; ten Have *et al.*, 2002; Regeer *et al.*, 2004). A recent study in Australia reported a lifetime prevalence of 2.5% (Goldney *et al.*, 2005). Estimates of the lifetime prevalence of bipolar II disorder vary more widely due to differences in diagnostic practices both over time and geography. One early American study estimated the lifetime risk of bipolar II disorder to be approximately 0.6% (Weissman & Myers, 1978), whereas more recent studies have suggested a lifetime prevalence of between 5.5%–10.9% for more broadly-defined bipolar II disorder (Angst, 1998; Angst *et al.*, 2003). European studies have produced more conservative prevalence estimates of between 0.2%–2.0% (Faravelli, *et al.*, 1990; Szadoczky, *et al.*, 1998).

Age at onset

Bipolar disorder has a fairly early age of onset, with the first episode usually occurring before the age of 30. In the review of epidemiological surveys mentioned previously, the mean age at onset reported by each of the six studies ranged from 17.1–29 years, with a peak in onset rate occurring between the ages of 15 and 19 years (Weissman *et al.*, 1996). A large retrospective study of patients with bipolar disorder reported that there was an average 8 years' delay from a patient's first recollected mood episode to receiving a diagnosis of bipolar disorder (Mantere *et al.*, 2004). Affective or functional changes occurring prior to the development of bipolar disorder have not been studied systematically. One study provided some evidence of prodromal mood disturbance in patients who went on to develop bipolar disorder, but could not distinguish between patients who went on to develop a different psychiatric disorder (Thompson *et al.*, 2003). In a longitudinal study, the presence of an anxiety disorder in adolescence predicted an increased risk of bipolar disorder in early adulthood (Johnson *et al.*, 2000), suggesting early psychopathology other than mood disturbance may predict later bipolar disorder. While most episodes of bipolar disorder first present by 30 years of age, it can present later in life. Late onset bipolar disorder is characterised by a reduced family history of psychiatric disorder, greater medical comorbidities and a greater incidence of subsequent neurological problems. Late onset bipolar disorder may also show a greater latency between the initial depressive episode and subsequent manic episode.

Gender

Bipolar I disorder occurs approximately equally in both sexes (Lloyd *et al.*, 2005). The symptom profile may differ between men and women; there is some evidence that women tend to experience more episodes of mixed or dysphoric mania than men (Arnold *et al.*, 2000). There is disputed evidence that bipolar II disorder is more common in females than males. Recent data from a large sample of patients with bipolar disorder found a significantly higher incidence of bipolar II disorder in women (29.0%) than men (15.3%) (Baldassano *et al.*, 2005). In a general population survey using DSM-III-R criteria (which require a minimum of 4 days of hypomanic symptoms for a hypomanic episode) there was no reported gender difference in the prevalence of bipolar II disorder (Szadoczky *et al.*, 1998). However, a population

77

study using broader criteria for bipolar II disorder not requiring this minimum duration found a 1-year prevalence rate for hypomania of 7.4% in females and only 2.7% in males (Angst *et al.*, 2003).

For some women, the experience of psychosis in the postnatal period may be the first indicator of bipolar illness. In one study of a well-characterised sample of mothers with bipolar affective puerperal psychosis, almost two thirds went on to experience a non-puerperal mood episode (Robertson *et al.*, 2005). The risk of puerperal psychosis in future pregnancies was also significant with 57% of those who had further children experiencing another episode postnatally. Likewise, for those with an established illness, childbirth brings an increased risk of puerperal psychosis (Chaudron & Pies, 2003) and represents a substantial clinical challenge.

Ethnic minorities

There is evidence of an increased incidence of bipolar disorder in people from black and minority ethnic groups. The recent Aesop Study (Lloyd *et al.*, 2005), which examined the incidence of bipolar disorder in three cities in the UK, reported a higher incidence amongst black and minority ethic groups than in a comparable white population and this finding is consistent with other UK-based studies (Leff *et al.*, 1976; Van Oss *et al.*, 1996). The evidence for the increased incidence of bipolar disorder in minority ethnic groups is similar to that for schizophrenia. In addition to the increased prevalence of bipolar disorder in black and minority ethnic groups there is also evidence of differences in the manner of presentation. Kennedy and colleagues (2004) in an epidemiological study of first presentations of bipolar disorder in the UK which compared African and Afro-Caribbean groups with white Europeans suggested that the former were more likely to present with a first episode of mania (13.5% versus 6%). The African and Afro-Caribbean groups were also more likely to present with severe psychotic symptoms when first presenting with mania. A study in the United States looking at the experience of African Americans with bipolar disorder (Kupfer *et al.*, 2005) reported that Afro-Caribbeans were more likely to be hospitalised than Caucasians (9.8% versus 4.4%) and have a higher rate of attempted suicide (64% versus 49%). Another American study, from the Veterans' Health Administration System (Kilbourne *et al.*, 2005) looked at the clinical presentations of people from minority ethnic groups with bipolar disorder. Again, this confirmed a picture of increased number of psychotic episodes (37% versus 30%) along with increased use of cocaine or alcohol misuse. They also reported that people from black and minority ethnic groups were more likely to be formally admitted to hospital.

The mechanisms underlying the increased prevalence and increased rates of mania and drug misuse amongst black and minority ethnic patients presenting to services with bipolar disorder are not well understood, although it has been suggested that social exclusion and lack of social support may be important factors (Bentall, 2004; Leff, 2001). However, it is possible that many of the features described above may be associated with later presentation of the disorder resulting, in part, from the difficulties that people from black and minority ethnic groups have in accessing services. Kennedy and colleagues (2004), also raised the possibility that the nature of the problems on initial presentation may contribute to greater diagnostic difficulties and the possibility that people from black and minority ethnic groups may be seen as suffering from schizoaffective or other schizophrenia spectrum disorders rather than bipolar disorder.

Although there is now reasonable evidence to show an increased incidence and a difference in the style of presentation of people from black and minority ethnic groups to services, there is little evidence on the outcomes of treatment interventions. An important conclusion to be drawn from the evidence is that services ought to be more available and accessible. This may present a particular challenge for first-episode psychosis services currently being developed in the English healthcare system (Department of Health 2002). More immediately, the evidence suggests that clinicians responsible for the assessment and provision of services for people with serious mental illness should be aware of the increased incidence of bipolar disorder in black and minority ethnic groups and also that the presentation is more likely to be accompanied by mania, possible psychotic symptoms and associated suicidal behaviour.

Treatment of people with learning difficulties with bipolar disorder
Findings indicate that people with intellectual disability are at high risk of developing comorbid serious mental illness, including bipolar disorder. However, dual diagnosis is often overlooked due to difficulties associated with establishing a diagnosis of a mental disorder in people with an intellectual disability, a problem which is heightened when the individual's capacity to participate in a clinical assessment is limited (White *et al.*, 2005). For example, until relatively recently, it was considered that Down's syndrome precluded a diagnosis of mania, or gave rise to an atypical presentation (Cooper & Collacot, 1993). However, this has been shown not to be the case and the clinical features of mania are noted to be similar to those previously described in individuals with learning difficulties due to other causes. However, it has been suggested that rapid-cycling bipolar disorder in people with learning difficulties may differ from non-learning difficulty populations in terms of a relative preponderance of males and a potentially different response to medication (Vanstraelen & Tyrer, 1999). Given the uncertainty around treatment options, the most important point is that the disorder is appropriately recognised in the learning difficulty population and treated effectively.

Clinical practice recommendation

4.2.1.1   People with bipolar disorder who have learning difficulties should receive the same care as others, taking into account the risk of interactions with any other medication they are prescribed.

Rapid cycling
Estimates of the prevalence of rapid cycling within bipolar I and II disorders have ranged from 13–56% depending on the definition of rapid cycling used, but most studies suggest approximately 20% (Mackin & Young, 2004). Although previous studies suggested a strong association between rapid cycling and female gender, reporting that more than two thirds of those with a rapid cycling illness were women

(Bauer *et al.*, 1994; Schneck *et al.*, 2004), a more recent large study reported an equal prevalence in both sexes (Baldassano *et al.*, 2005). The index episode tends to be depression in those with a rapid cycling course and the clinical picture is dominated by depressive symptoms and episodes (Calabrese *et al.*, 2001). As such, several studies have documented that rapid cycling is more common in bipolar II disorder. However, recent investigations in large samples followed longitudinally for several years have suggested it is equally prevalent in bipolar I and II disorders (Kupka *et al.*, 2005; Schneck *et al.*, 2004). In general, rapid cycling is associated with an earlier age of onset, greater severity of symptoms and treatment resistance (Coryell *et al.*, 2003).

4.3 AETIOLOGY

Despite its long history, little is known about what causes bipolar disorder. Explanations in terms of psychosocial factors were mainstream in the 19th century, but recent research has concentrated on identifying possible biological underpinnings of the disorder including genetic components, neurohormonal abnormalities and structural brain differences. There has also been some recent but scanty revival of interest in psychosocial research, including life events and social rhythm (Malkoff-Schwartz *et al.*, 1998), and behavioural activation system (Depue *et al.*, 1987). However, currently there is no overarching explanation and the heterogeneous clinical presentation of bipolar disorder suggests that a number of different mechanisms are involved.

4.3.1 Genetics

Affective disorders often cluster in families, indicating that they may have a heritable basis. Evidence from a number of different sources has identified a high heritable component to bipolar disorder, suggesting a potentially large genetic contribution to the illness. However, the inheritance pattern is not simple and is not consistent with a single gene model of bipolar disorder. Instead it is likely that many genes are involved that convey susceptibility to a spectrum of psychiatric illnesses. There may also be genes that reduce the risk of developing bipolar disorder. No specific genes have been identified, but several areas of the genome are being investigated.

Familial inheritance studies
Family studies report that first-degree relatives of an individual with bipolar disorder face a lifetime risk of developing the illness that is five to ten times greater than the general population (Craddock & Jones 2001). However, they also face approximately double the risk of developing unipolar major depression, suggesting the two disorders may share some degree of genetic susceptibility.

Studies in monozygotic and dizygotic twins where at least one twin is affected by bipolar disorder provide further support for genetic transmission. Monozygotic co-twins of bipolar probands face a 40–70% risk of developing bipolar disorder and the concordance rate of approximately 60% is markedly higher than that for dizygotic twins (Craddock & Jones, 1999). The difference in concordance rates between monozygotic and dizygotic twins can be used to estimate the size of the genetic contribution to the illness. The largest twin study investigating heritability to date reported a heritability estimate of 85%, suggesting almost all of the variance in diagnosis of bipolar disorder was accounted for by genetic factors (McGuffin *et al.*, 2003). However, the concordance rate for monozygotic twins is not 100%, which leaves room for environmental influences. McGuffin and colleagues (2003) found that non-shared environmental influences accounted for the remaining 15% of variance and the influence of shared family environment was negligible.

Linkage studies
Attempts to identify candidate genes using families with multiple cases of bipolar disorder have suggested several potential areas of interest including 4p16, 12q23–q24, 16p13, 21q22 and Xq24–q26 (Craddock & Jones, 2001). More recently McQueen and colleagues (2005) reported on the combined analysis of 11 linkage studies (comprising 5179 individuals from 1067 families) and established significant linkage on chromosomes 6q and 8q. Using a sibling pair genome-wide scan approach, Lambert and colleagues (2005) have confirmed evidence of linkage between bipolar disorder and the chromosomal region 6q16–q21 but also showed linkage at 4q12–q21, an area of interest on the genome reported by Craddock and Jones (2001). As can be seen, studies to date have identified broad areas of the genome rather than specific genes; therefore much work remains before this research can have clinical utility.

Association studies
Using groups of unrelated individuals with bipolar disorder and appropriately matched control groups, association studies have attempted to identify genes that occur more commonly in affected individuals than unaffected individuals. This method has identified the gene for catechol-O-methyl transferase (COMT), an enzyme involved in the breakdown of catecholamines, as a potential course-modifier in bipolar disorder (Craddock & Jones, 2001). In patients with bipolar disorder, those with the low-activity version of the gene are significantly more likely to have rapid-cycling bipolar disorder. However, the gene itself occurs equally often in people with and without bipolar disorder, therefore it is not a candidate susceptibility gene.

Increasing evidence suggests an overlap in genetic susceptibility across the classification systems that separated psychotic disorders into schizophrenia and bipolar disorder with association findings at several loci (Craddock *et al.*, 2005). Identification of susceptibility genes may have a major impact on our understanding of pathophysiology and lead to changes in classification and perhaps management.

4.3.2   Neurohormonal abnormalities

Much attention recently has focussed on the role of the endocrine system in mood disorders. Interest has centred on two biological systems: the hypothalamic-pituitary-adrenal (HPA) axis, one of the major hormonal systems activated during stress, and the hypothalamic-pituitary-thyroid (HPT) axis.

HPA axis dysfunction

In response to stress, neurons in the hypothalamus secrete the chemical messenger corticotropin-releasing hormone (CRH) to the anterior pituitary gland to stimulate the production of adrenocorticotropic hormone (ACTH) which in turn stimulates the adrenal glands to produce cortisol. Cortisol influences immune system function, has a potent anti-inflammatory action and is a major regulator of the physiological stress response. Importantly, it provides negative feedback to the hypothalamus which shuts down the stress response and eventually returns cortisol to normal, pre-stress levels. One of the most consistent findings in depression (especially psychotic depression) is a marked elevation in cortisol levels, which is suggestive of a dysfunctional HPA axis. More sensitive tests of HPA axis function have been developed in which the response of the system to a pharmacological challenge is measured. If the negative feedback system is functioning normally, cortisol production should be suppressed in response to a drug which blocks the corticosteroid receptors in the hypothalamus. A number of studies have reported abnormalities in this system in patients with bipolar disorder which are consistent with reduced HPA axis feedback (Rybakowski & Twanrdowska, 1999; Schmider *et al.*, 1995; Watson *et al.*, 2004). Chronically elevated levels of cortisol can have deleterious consequences, including effects on mood and memory. Interestingly, signs of HPA axis dysfunction have been observed in all stages of bipolar illness, including during remission. Such dysfunction could underlie susceptibility to future episodes and account for the often chronic course of bipolar disorder.

HPT axis and rapid cycling

The HPT axis is also of interest in bipolar disorder, particularly in the genesis of rapid cycling. Abnormalities of thyroid function are noted in patients with depression and mania. Subclinical hypothyroidism is seen in a significant proportion of patients with treatment-resistant depression. Along with evidence of mild hypothyroidism, patients in the manic state may show reduced responsiveness of the pituitary gland to the chemical messenger thyrotropin-releasing hormone which stimulates activity of the thyroid gland. Approximately 25% of patients with rapid-cycling bipolar disorder have evidence of hypothyroidism, which contrasts with only 2–5% of depressed patients in general (Muller, 2002). Since thyroid hormones have profound effects on mood and behaviour, dysfunction in the HPT axis could explain some of the presenting symptoms of patients with bipolar disorder.

4.3.3 Structural brain differences

In comparison with work on schizophrenia, there have been relatively few studies investigating structural brain differences in patients with bipolar disorder and findings have been contradictory. A major review of neuroanatomical studies in bipolar disorder reported some evidence of enlarged ventricles and abnormalities in the frontal and temporal lobes in at least a sub-population of patients (Bearden *et al.*, 2005). An excess of white matter lesions has also been reported (Altshuler, 1995) and one study reported that the number of white matter lesions correlated negatively with functional outcome (Moore *et al.*, 2001). Although the hope in identifying a neuroanatomical profile of bipolar disorder is to develop an understanding of neurodevelopmental or genetic contributions to the illness, it is currently unknown whether differences are the cause or consequence of affective disorder. Interestingly, neuroimaging in the unaffected first-degree relatives of bipolar probands has identified grey matter deficits that correlated with the degree of genetic risk of developing the disorder (McDonald *et al.*, 2004). This suggests that structural brain differences are present before illness onset. However, it is yet to be understood how or whether these differences contribute to observed symptoms.

4.3.4 Psychosocial influences

Although much recent research has focussed on biological factors, a number of psychosocial factors have also been identified that may be relevant to understanding the development and progression of bipolar disorder or a particular individual's presentation. Antecedent factors, such as childhood maltreatment, may act as predisposing factors for developing the disorder, whereas concurrent factors such as social class, social support and self-esteem may act as course modifiers or precipitants for episodes.

A potential role for psychosocial stressors in both the aetiology and exacerbation of acute episodes has been identified in bipolar disorder. Prolonged psychosocial stressors during childhood, such as neglect or abuse, are associated with HPA axis dysfunction in later life which may result in hypersensitivity to stress. In future years such dysregulation may predispose an individual to affective disturbance, and those who develop bipolar disorder may experience an earlier age at onset, increased rates of self-harm and psychotic symptoms. Likewise, acutely stressful life situations and hostility or criticism in a family may trigger episodes in those with an established illness. In turn, illness in itself is stressful which may lead to further destabilisation, creating the possibility of a self-perpetuating cycle. The degree of negative emotionality expressed by close family members (termed 'expressed emotion') has been shown to predict future depressive episodes in patients with bipolar disorder (Yan *et al.*, 2004) and levels of depressive and manic symptoms (Kim & Miklowitz, 2004; Miklowitz *et al.*, 2005). The high prevalence of bipolar disorder in ethnic minority groups, as demonstrated in recent studies in the UK (Lloyd *et al.*, 2005), may relate to the psychosocial stressors of social isolation and lack of social support often experienced by these groups (Bentall, 2004; Leff, 2001).

Traumatic experiences in childhood have been associated with an adverse course of bipolar disorder and the development of comorbid post-traumatic stress disorder (PTSD) in adult life (Goldberg & Garno, 2005). Retrospective studies have shown an association between a history of childhood abuse and an earlier age at illness onset, increased comorbid substance misuse disorders, increased axis I and II comorbidities, and a rapid cycling course (Leverich *et al.*, 2002; Garno *et al.*, 2005). It is estimated that 16% of patients with bipolar disorder also have PTSD, the development of which is associated with greater exposure to trauma, higher levels of neuroticism, lower social support and lower social class (Otto *et al.*, 2004). A study of the impact of childhood abuse on the illness course of adult male patients with bipolar disorder found that those who reported both sexual and physical abuse had higher rates of current PTSD and lifetime alcohol misuse disorders, a poorer level of social functioning, a greater number of lifetime depressive episodes and an increased likelihood of at least one suicide attempt (Brown *et al.*, in press).

Theories of the psychology of bipolar disorder have identified factors such as self-esteem and explanatory style that may contribute to mood symptoms. The manic defence hypothesis explains the appearance of symptoms of mania as an attempt to avoid the negative and ego-destroying thought patterns associated with depression and anxiety. The ascent into feelings of omnipotence and triumph are thought to over-compensate for feelings of worthlessness and underlying depression which are seen as the backdrop to the manic syndrome. This formulation suggests there is a degree of fragility to the manic state and evidence of negative self-concept or thinking styles should be evident in both patients with mania and remitted patients. There is evidence that patients with bipolar disorder have a negative self-concept, highly variable self-esteem and increased drive even during the remitted state (Winters & Neale, 1985; Lyon *et al.*, 1999; Bentall *et al.*, in press). Studies using implicit or disguised measures of explanatory style have found that remitted patients tend to attribute negative outcomes to themselves, but positive outcomes to others – a thinking style typical of patients with depression (Winters & Neale, 1985; Lyon *et al.*, 1999). However, this may be better understood as chronic low-grade depression due either to the debilitating aspects of the illness or due to the physiological processes outlined above rather than as the underlying fuel for mania. Nonetheless, psychological theories of bipolar disorder may help observers understand some of the ideas and beliefs held by those suffering from mania.

4.4   DIAGNOSIS OF ADULTS

4.4.1   Criteria for diagnosis

Both the DSM-IV and ICD-10 outline diagnostic criteria for bipolar disorder; however the two criteria sets are not identical. Crucial differences centre on the number of episodes required for a diagnosis and the distinction between bipolar I and II disorders.

DSM-IV
Full criteria for manic, hypomanic, depressed and mixed episodes are outlined in Box 1.

DSM-IV recognises a spectrum of bipolar disorders consisting of bipolar I disorder, bipolar II disorder and cyclothymia. A diagnosis of bipolar I disorder requires the

Box 1: DSM-IV criteria for a manic episode
(American Psychiatric Association, 1994, p. 332)

A. A distinct period of abnormally and persistently elevated, expansive or irritable mood, lasting at least 1 week (or any duration if hospitalisation is necessary).

B. During the period of mood disturbance, three (or more) of the following symptoms have persisted (four if the mood is only irritable) and have been present to a significant degree:

 1. inflated self-esteem or grandiosity
 2. decreased need for sleep (e.g., feels rested after only 3 hours of sleep)
 3. more talkative than usual or pressure to keep talking
 4. flight of ideas or subjective experience that thoughts are racing
 5. distractibility (i.e., attention too easily drawn to unimportant or irrelevant external stimuli)
 6. increase in goal-directed activity (either socially, at work or school, or sexually) or psychomotor agitation
 7. excessive involvement in pleasurable activities that have a high potential for painful consequences (e.g., engaging in unrestrained buying sprees, sexual indiscretions, or foolish business investments)

---

experience of at least one manic or mixed episode. Frequently, people with bipolar disorder will have experienced one or more depressed episodes, but this is not required for a diagnosis. The type of current or most recent mood episode can be specified as hypomanic, manic, depressed or mixed. The severity of the episode should be classified as mild, moderate, severe without psychotic features, severe with psychotic features, in partial remission, in full remission, with catatonic features or with postnatal onset.

A diagnosis of bipolar II disorder requires the experience of at least one major depressive episode and at least one hypomanic episode. Any history of manic or mixed episodes rules out a diagnosis of bipolar II disorder. Mood specifiers are the same as for bipolar I disorder.

Cyclothymia describes a chronic disturbance of mood consisting of a number of periods of depression and hypomania. Depressive symptoms must not meet full severity or duration criteria for a major depressive episode: however, hypomanic symptoms may meet full criteria for a hypomanic episode. The fluctuating mood should have lasted at least 2 years (1 year in children and adolescents) and must be the source of significant functional impairment.

ICD-10
Full criteria for manic, hypomanic, depressed and mixed episodes are outlined in Box 2.

A diagnosis of bipolar affective disorder requires the experience of at least two mood episodes, one of which must be manic or hypomanic. Unlike DSM-IV, a single

Box 2: ICD-10 criteria for a manic episode
(World Health Organization, 1992)

F30. Manic episode

All the subdivisions of this category should be used only for a single episode. Hypomanic or manic episodes in individuals who have had one or more previous affective episodes (depressive, hypomanic, manic, or mixed) should be coded as bipolar affective disorder (F31.-)

Includes: bipolar disorder, single manic episode

F30.0 Hypomania

A disorder characterised by a persistent mild elevation of mood, increases energy and activity and usually marked feelings of well being and both physical and mental efficiency. Increase sociability, talkativeness. Over familiarity, increases sexual energy, and a decreased need for sleep are often present but not to the extent that they lead to severe disruption of work or result in social rejection. Irritability, conceit and boorish behaviour may take the place of the more usual euphoric sociability. The disturbances of mood and behaviour are not accompanied by hallucinations or delusions.

F30.1 Mania without psychotic symptoms

Mood is elevated out of keeping with the patient's circumstances and may vary from carefree joviality to almost uncontrollable excitement. Elation is accompanied by increased energy, resulting in overactivity, pressure of speech and a decreased need for sleep. Attention cannot be sustained, and there is often marked distractibility. Self-esteem is often inflated with grandiose ideas and overconfidence. Loss of normal social inhibitions may result in behaviour that is reckless, foolhardy or inappropriate to the circumstances, and out of character.

F30.2 Mania with psychotic symptoms

In addition to the clinical picture described in F30.1, delusions (usually grandiose) or hallucinations (usually of voices speaking directly to the patient) are present, or the excitement, excessive motor activity and flight of ideas are so extreme that the subject is incomprehensible or inaccessible to ordinary communication.

Mania with:
- mood-congruent psychotic symptoms
- mood-incongruent psychotic symptoms

Manic stupor

F30.8 Other manic episodes

F30.9 Manic episode, unspecified

Includes: Mania NOS [not otherwise specified]

episode of mania does not merit a diagnosis of bipolar disorder until another mood episode (of any type) is experienced. Episodes can be specified as hypomanic, manic without psychotic symptoms, manic with psychotic symptoms, mild or moderate depression, severe depression without psychotic symptoms, severe depression with psychotic symptoms, mixed or in remission. ICD-10 does not include bipolar II disorder as a separate diagnostic entity.

4.4.2   Diagnostic issues

Hypomania
A matter of considerable and ongoing debate in bipolar disorder is the definition of hypomania. In both DSM-IV and ICD-10 the diagnosis of a hypomanic episode requires symptoms of hypomania to last for at least 4 days, which was reduced from the 7 days required by earlier versions. Those who have hypomanic symptoms lasting between 1 and 3 days can be diagnosed with 'bipolar disorder not otherwise specified'. However, short-lived periods of hypomania may go unnoticed (especially if their absence from official diagnostic nomenclature means they are not enquired about), yet still be an indicator of bipolar illness. A longitudinal prospective study of a community cohort of individuals at high risk of developing psychopathology identified no differences between those who experienced hypomanic symptoms for fewer than 4 days versus those who had episodes of 4 days or longer with respect to the number of hypomanic symptoms experienced, previous diagnosis or treatment of depression and family history of depression (Angst *et al.*, 2003). In a similar vein, the same study concluded that the core feature of hypomania should be overactivity rather than mood change, as hypomanic episodes often occur without associated elation or grandiosity. Reducing the length criterion for hypomanic episodes would increase lifetime prevalence estimates of bipolar II disorder to approximately 11%, but arguably would identify more unipolar depressed patients with subtle signs of bipolarity. There are problems with establishing satisfactory inter-rater reliability in these assessments and the clinical utility of such a diagnostic change in terms of treatment outcome has yet to be established.

Diagnostic uncertainty
Diagnostic uncertainty in the early stages of bipolar disorder – especially after the first episode – is common. Where bipolar disorder is suspected, a provisional diagnosis can be made and the individual should be monitored appropriately for further signs of mood disturbance and the provisional diagnosis updated as necessary.

Clinical practice recommendations

Assessment in primary care
4.4.2.1   Primary care clinicians should ask about hypomanic symptoms when assessing a patient with depression and overactive, disinhibited behaviour.

4.4.2.2   Primary care clinicians should normally refer patients with suspected bipolar disorder for a specialist mental health assessment and development of a care plan, if either of the following are present:
- periods of overactive, disinhibited behaviour lasting at least 4 days with or without periods of depression, or
- three or more recurrent depressive episodes in the context of a history of overactive, disinhibited behaviour.

4.4.2.3   Primary care clinicians should urgently refer patients with mania or severe depression who are a danger to themselves or other people, to specialist mental health services.

4.4.2.4   When a patient with existing bipolar disorder registers with a practice, the GP should consider referring them for assessment by specialist mental health services and, if appropriate, development of a care plan.

4.4.2.5   When a patient with bipolar disorder is managed solely in primary care, an urgent referral to secondary care services should be made:
- if there is an acute exacerbation of symptoms, in particular the development of mania or severe depression
- if there is an increase in the degree of risk, or change in the nature of risk, to self or others.

4.4.2.6   When a patient with bipolar disorder is managed solely in primary care, a review by secondary care services or increased contact in primary care should be considered if:
- the patient's functioning declines significantly or their condition responds poorly to treatment
- treatment adherence is a problem
- comorbid alcohol and/or drug misuse is suspected
- the patient is considering stopping prophylactic medication after a period of relatively stable mood.

Assessment in secondary care

4.4.2.7   When assessing suspected bipolar disorder healthcare professionals should:
- take a full history including family history, a review of all previous episodes and any symptoms between episodes
- assess the patient's symptom profile, triggers to previous episodes, social and personal functioning, comorbidities including substance misuse and anxiety, risk, physical health, and current psychosocial stressors
- obtain where possible, and within the bounds of confidentiality, a corroborative history from a family member or carer
- consider using formal criteria, including self-rating scales such as the Mood Disorder Questionnaire (MDQ).[10]

---

[10]Hirschfeld, R.M., Williams, J.B., Spitzer, R.L., *et al.* (2001) Development and validation of a screening instrument for bipolar spectrum disorder: the Mood Disorder Questionnaire. *American Journal of Psychiatry, 158.* 1743–1744.

4.4.2.8   Before diagnosing rapid-cycling bipolar disorder, healthcare professionals should check alternative explanations for the symptoms including problems such as thyroid disease, antidepressant-induced switching, suboptimal medication regimes, the effects of lithium withdrawal, and erratic compliance. They should also consider asking the patient and/or carer to assess mood and behaviour for at least a year.

Special considerations for older people in secondary care

4.4.2.9   Local services should have a robust protocol for transferring patients from services for adults of working age to those for older people (usually those older than 65 years). This should include agreement about the clinical parameters to take into account (for example, medical comorbidity or cognitive deterioration) and what to do if the patient is no longer in contact with services for adults of working age. Referral or re-referral should be based on the needs of the patient first, rather than simply their chronological age.

4.4.3   Distinguishing bipolar disorder from other diagnoses

The manic stage of bipolar disorder may resemble other conditions and care should be taken during assessment to rule out other possible diagnoses.

Cyclothymia
Careful attention to illness history and duration of episodes is necessary to differentiate bipolar II disorder from cyclothymia. Both disorders are associated with hypomanic episodes, but in cyclothymia depressive symptoms are less severe and do not meet full severity or duration criteria for a diagnosis of a depressive episode. In practice, it may be very difficult to differentiate the two disorders without monitoring the condition for a long period of time and gathering information from other sources such as family members.

Schizophrenia and schizoaffective disorder
In the acute stages mania resembles schizophrenia. Between one tenth and one fifth of manic patients exhibit classic signs of schizophrenia and both disorders can involve severe psychotic symptoms such as thought disorder, delusions and hallucinations. Typically however, the delusions and hallucinations in mania are less stable than those in schizophrenia, the content of them is usually congruent or in keeping with the mood of the patient and auditory hallucinations may be in the second rather than the third person. Sometimes the content of delusions and hallucinations is mood incongruent and auditory hallucinations are in the third person like schizophrenia. Bipolar disorder is more likely if the individual has previously experienced episodes of depression, hypomania or mania, or has a family history of bipolar disorder. Individuals with predominately psychotic symptoms who also suffer affective

disturbance may be more appropriately diagnosed with schizoaffective disorder, although this may be difficult to distinguish from a severe form of bipolar disorder. The diagnosis of bipolar disorder should be employed when there are clear-cut episodes of mania and depression, and there are no psychotic symptoms lasting for more than 2 weeks before or after the symptoms of a mood episode have resolved. The diagnosis of schizoaffective disorder should be used when there is at least one episode when psychotic symptoms dominate the clinical picture and mood symptoms are fleeting, or the psychotic symptoms persist for more than 2 weeks without the presence of any mood symptoms.

Substance misuse

Manic-like symptoms can be the result of using stimulant drugs such as cocaine, khat, ecstasy or amphetamine. Typically, symptoms dissipate within 7 days after the substance is withdrawn, whereas manic symptoms last much longer. Since substance misuse is a common comorbidity in bipolar disorder (see Section 4.4.5), differentiating mania from the effects of substance misuse can be problematic. The clinician must pay close attention to the severity and duration of symptoms to differentiate between a manic episode and the effects of substance use. A clear history of stimulant drug use preceding any manic symptoms with no previous history of manic, hypomanic or mixed episodes not preceded by stimulant drug use could point to this episode being drug induced. However, the clinician must ensure a positive diagnosis is made fully informed by the severity and duration of the presenting symptoms and be aware of the possibility that this episode may be the first presentation of bipolar disorder triggered by use of drugs. Urine screening may be necessary to rule out the use of illicit substances.

Organic brain syndromes

Certain types of organic pathology can present with disinhibited, manic-like behaviour. Progressive frontal lobe dementia, cerebrovascular insult, encephalitis, epilepsy, demyelinating white matter lesions, such as those seen in multiple sclerosis and HIV infection, and space-occupying lesions can all produce affective disturbance that may be difficult to differentiate from a non-organic mood disorder. In patients with a late-onset disorder who have shown no previous signs of affective illness, the possibility of organic pathology should be fully investigated. Thorough cognitive assessment may indicate cognitive disturbances consistent with an organic disorder. Family history of affective disorder, dementia, cerebral tumour or medical illnesses that increase the risk of cerebrovascular events may jointly inform a diagnosis. Organic pathology should be investigated in patients who have developed the illness only after suffering a significant head injury.

Metabolic disorders

Occasionally hyperthyroidism, Cushing's disease, Addison's disease, vitamin B12 deficiency and dialysis can cause manic symptoms. In all these instances, the medical problem must precede the onset of the manic symptoms which resolve within a week or so of the effective treatment of the underlying medical disorder.

Iatrogenic causes

Medications such as corticosteroids (especially in high doses), L-Dopa, and prescribed stimulants (such as methylphenidate) can cause manic-like symptoms. Antidepressants can cause a switch to mania in some patients and those predisposed to bipolar disorder. Close attention to the time course of the development of affective symptoms could indicate whether prescribed medications were a precipitant.

Clinical practice recommendation

4.4.3.1   When considering a diagnosis of bipolar disorder healthcare professionals should take into account that:
- more pronounced psychotic symptoms, increased suicidal ideation, drug misuse or more disturbed behaviour may be symptoms of a later presentation of bipolar disorder and not of a schizophrenia-spectrum disorder – this may be particularly important when assessing patients from black and minority ethnic groups who may have difficulty accessing services
- drug and/or alcohol misuse may induce manic-like symptoms – in inpatient settings, if there is evidence of misuse, wait 7 days before confirming a diagnosis of bipolar disorder
- symptoms may be due to underlying organic conditions, such as hypothyroidism, cerebrovascular insults and other neurological disorders (for example, dementia), particularly in people with late-onset bipolar disorder (older than 40 years).

4.4.4   Assessment methods

Screening

The Mood Disorder Questionnaire (MDQ) is a brief, easy-to-use, self-report form, which has been validated against the structured clinical interview for DSM-IV (SCID) – see below (Hirschfeld *et al.*, 2000). It has shown good sensitivity and specificity in a clinical population but in a general population sample, while the specificity remained high, the sensitivity was low (Hirschfeld *et al.*, 2003a).

Diagnosis

The most widely used and validated instrument for generating a DSM-IV Axis I diagnosis is the SCID which also generates diagnoses on the other DSM-IV axes. The structured interview includes six modules, which cover a wide range of possible different disorders, and the SCID is thus comprehensive and its validity in clinical samples is high. The reliability is lowest in patients whose symptoms are less well defined (Baldassano, 2005). ICD diagnoses must be generated by a semi-structured interview, none of which has been validated, so clinical experience and judgement are essential.

Monitoring

The Life Chart Method (LCM) is the most widely used and researched and has recently been developed further by the creation of an electronic version. While it has been developed for professionals, it can be used by patients and can be very useful as a therapeutic tool (Denicoff *et al.*, 2000). Another instrument suitable for bipolar disorder is the Altman Self-Rating Mania Scale (Altman *et al.*, 1997). However, most self-report scales are not very specific and are less sensitive to detecting problems with cognition and functional impairment.

4.4.5 Comorbidity

Comorbidity is the norm rather than the exception in bipolar disorder. A study of 288 patients with bipolar disorder found 65% had suffered from at least one other (axis I) disorder at some point in their lifetime and one third had at least one current comorbid (axis I) diagnosis (McElroy *et al.*, 2001). However, care should always be taken when diagnosing comorbid illnesses. A diagnosis should only be made on the basis of symptoms present during euthymic periods or once bipolar disorder symptoms are well managed.

Anxiety and substance misuse disorders

The most common comorbid axis I disorders are anxiety and substance misuse disorders, both of which occur in approximately 30–50% of patients with bipolar disorder. Those who have comorbidities tend to have had an earlier age at onset and are more likely to experience cycle acceleration and suffer a more severe illness and self-harm than those without. In those with concurrent substance misuse, it may be difficult to distinguish symptoms and effects of the illness from the effects of the misused substance. Likewise, causality may be difficult to establish: substance misuse may play a role in the aetiology of affective disturbance, be an attempt at self-medication, or substances may simply be used for social and recreational reasons. In general, substance misuse is approximately twice as common in men with bipolar disorder as women. However, rates of substance misuse disorders are four to seven times higher in women with bipolar disorder than rates derived from community samples (Krishnan, 2005).

Personality disorders

Personality disorders are sometimes diagnosed alongside bipolar disorder, although the comorbidity rate varies drastically depending on which measurement instrument is used. Based on strict DSM-IV criteria for axis II disorders, one study reported a comorbidity rate of 38% in euthymic patients with bipolar disorder (Kay *et al.*, 1999). However, previous studies have reported rates as high as 89% using other assessment instruments and assessing patients while they are acutely affectively ill (Turley *et al.*, 1992). Diagnosis of personality disorder must never be made just on current behaviour alone and requires a longitudinal history from an informant who has known the patient when they have not had affective symptoms, preferably since the patient was an adolescent or younger. Cluster B (dramatic and emotional) and C (anxious and fearful) disorders are the most common personality disorder comorbidities in patients with bipolar disorder. Borderline personality disorder, the hallmark of which is affective instability due to markedly reactive mood, shares some features in common with bipolar disorder, particularly with the ultra-rapid cycling variant. Borderline personality disorder is a relatively common comorbidity in those with bipolar disorder and some argue it belongs on the bipolar spectrum (Deltito *et al.*, 2001).

Patients with bipolar disorder and comorbid substance misuse disorders tend to have a higher rate of personality disorder comorbidity than those without substance misuse difficulties. Comorbid personality disorder may also affect outcome in patients with bipolar disorder, for example increasing the severity of residual mood symptoms during remission periods.

Clinical practice recommendation

4.4.5.1 When assessing people with suspected bipolar disorder and/or personality disorder healthcare professionals should:
- during initial assessment, consider a diagnosis of bipolar disorder before a diagnosis of personality disorder in a person with mood swings and functional impairment
- during treatment, ensure the patient has had adequate treatment to stabilise symptoms before considering a diagnosis of comorbid personality disorder.

4.4.6   Risk assessment

Self-harm is more common in bipolar disorder than in most other psychiatric disorders and is comparable to that found in other mood and psychotic disorders. Psychological autopsy studies suggest that suicides occur when depression is underdiagnosed and undertreated, especially in bipolar II disorder, and when there is no long-term maintenance treatment. Suicide may occur with little warning, especially in patients with bipolar disorder comorbid with other impulse control disorders such as substance misuse, borderline personality disorder and eating disorder. The rapid switch from mania or hypomania to depression may also be a particular risk for suicide. Risk assessments are carried out in the same way as in other patient groups but healthcare professionals should be aware that mental state and suicide risk can change quickly. Immediate action is required if a patient with bipolar disorder is assessed to be at high or immediate risk of suicide, such as those with a definite plan or persistent suicidal ideation. Similarly, the disinhibited, changeable and impulsive nature of patients with bipolar disorder, particularly in a manic or a mixed state, means that healthcare professionals should exercise caution when there is a risk of harm to others through violent or reckless behaviour.

Clinical practice recommendations

Assessment of risk in primary and secondary care

4.4.6.1 A risk assessment should be undertaken when:
- bipolar disorder is first diagnosed
- a person with bipolar disorder undergoes significant change in mental state or personal circumstances
- a patient with bipolar disorder is discharged from or is on leave from inpatient care.

Crisis and risk management plans

4.4.6.2 If a patient is at risk of suicide, exploitation or severe self-neglect, is a significant risk to others (including neglect of dependents), or has a history of recurrent admissions, particularly compulsory admissions, a crisis plan should be developed in collaboration with the patient covering:
- a list of identified or potential personal, social or environmental triggers, and early warning symptoms of relapse
- a protocol for increasing the dose of medication or taking additional medication (which may be given to the patient in advance) for patients who are at risk of rapid onset of mania and for whom clear early warning signs can be identified – protocols should be monitored regularly, and are not a substitute for an urgent review
- how primary and secondary healthcare services have agreed to respond to any identified increase in risk, for example by increased contact
- how the patient (and where appropriate their carer) can access help, and the names of healthcare professionals in primary and secondary care who have responsibilities in the crisis plan.

4.4.6.3 A limited quantity of psychotropic medication should be prescribed for patients during periods of high risk of suicide.

4.5   DIAGNOSIS OF CHILDREN AND ADOLESCENTS

The diagnosis for bipolar disorder in children and adolescents is an area of considerable difficulty and some controversy (Biederman *et al.*, 2000). In light of this, the GDG convened a consensus conference to draw on the experience of national and international experts in the area. A fuller account of the outcome of the consensus conference is provided in Appendix 19. What follows is a brief summary of the issues and the outcomes and recommendations of the consensus conference.

The peak age for onset of bipolar disorder is in later adolescence and early adult life. However, a significant number of adults with bipolar disorder, perhaps up to 20%, have experienced initial symptoms before the age of 19 (Harrington, 1994). Lewinsohn and colleagues (1995) estimated a point prevalence figure for adolescence of around 1%. However, the number of pre-pubertal children presenting with bipolar disorder is very small. In a large study in Oregon in the United States (Lewinsohn *et al.*, 1993, 2003) researchers were able to identify only three cases of pre-pubertal bipolar disorder. The typical presentation of bipolar disorder in children and adolescents, particularly those with earlier onset, is that depressive disorder presents first. Children and adolescents with bipolar disorder tend to have a disorder with longer duration of episode, increased mixed presentation and a higher incidence of rapid cycling than in late-onset bipolar disorder.

One considerable problem that the consensus conference faced was the different presentations of symptoms in children, adolescents and adults. Features such as grandiosity and involvement in pleasure and activities vary considerably as a function of age and developmental level, therefore what is pathological in an adult might not be appropriately described as such in a child. A further complication is that for many children with serious mental disorder there is also considerable evidence of comorbidity and co-presentation with symptoms such as those with attention deficit hyperactivity disorder (ADHD), and indeed their subsequent management and medication, can make the diagnostic challenge even more difficult.

After a careful consideration of the current evidence for the diagnosis of bipolar I and bipolar II disorder in children and adolescents, the consensus conference concluded that it was possible and appropriate to diagnose bipolar I disorder in both children and adolescents, although accepted it was a very rare disorder in the former group. However, the consensus conference did not feel, given the present level of evidence, that it was appropriate at this stage to reach a diagnosis of bipolar II disorder in a child or adolescent. A possible exception to this is in older and developmentally well-advanced adolescents where the use of the standard adult diagnostic criteria may be appropriate.

However, in accepting that the diagnosis of bipolar I disorder can be present in children and adolescents, the consensus conference made a number of suggestions for the refinement of the diagnosis. Specifically, the conference took the view that for a diagnosis of bipolar I disorder to be established in a pre-pubescent child mania must be present, euphoria must be present for most days most of the time for 7 days and, although irritability may be a symptom, it should not be a core diagnostic criterion. For adolescents, the conference took the view that in order to establish a diagnosis of bipolar I disorder mania must be present, as must euphoria over a 7-day period. Irritability should not be a core diagnostic criterion, but its presentation if episodic in nature and if it results could be important in helping establishing a diagnosis of bipolar I disorder.

The consensus conference also felt that the diagnosis of bipolar disorder in a young person presenting solely with a depressive episode, but in the context of a family history of bipolar, should not itself warrant a diagnosis of bipolar I disorder. The conference also commented on common comorbidities and important differential diagnoses, appropriate assessment methods and the management of special groups (see Appendix 19).

4.5.1 Clinical practice recommendations

Diagnosing bipolar disorder 1 in prepubescent children
4.5.1.1   When diagnosing bipolar I disorder in prepubescent children the same criteria should be used as in adults except that:
- mania must be present
- euphoria must be present most days, most of the time (for a period of 7 days)
- irritability is not a core diagnostic criterion.

4.5.1.2   Bipolar I disorder should not be diagnosed solely on the basis of a major depressive episode in a child with a family history of bipolar disorder. However, children with a history of depression and a family history of bipolar disorder should be carefully followed up.

Diagnosing bipolar I disorder in adolescents

4.5.1.3   When diagnosing bipolar I disorder in adolescents the same criteria should be used as for adults except that:
- mania must be present
- euphoria must be present most days, most of the time (for at least 7 days)
- irritability can be helpful in making a diagnosis if it is episodic, severe, results in impaired function and is out of keeping or not in character; however, it should not be a core diagnostic criterion.

4.5.1.4   Bipolar I disorder should not be diagnosed solely on the basis of a major depressive episode in an adolescent with a family history of bipolar disorder. However, adolescents with a history of depression and a family history of bipolar disorder should be carefully followed up.

Diagnosing bipolar I disorder in older or developmentally advanced adolescents

4.5.1.5   In older or developmentally advanced adolescents, the criteria for establishing a diagnosis of bipolar I disorder in adults should be used.

Bipolar II disorder in both children and adolescents

4.5.1.6   Bipolar II disorder should not normally be diagnosed in children or adolescents because the diagnostic criteria are not well-enough established for routine use.

4.5.1.7   In older or developmentally advanced adolescents, the criteria for diagnosing bipolar II disorder in adults should be used.

Differential diagnosis for both children and adolescents

4.5.1.8   The presence of clear-cut episodes of unduly elated mood, inappropriate and impairing grandiosity, and cycles of mood should be used to distinguish bipolar I disorder from attention deficit hyperactivity disorder (ADHD) and conduct disorder.

4.5.1.9   The presence of mood cycles should be used to distinguish bipolar disorder from schizophrenia.

4.5.1.10   Before diagnosing bipolar I disorder in a child or adolescent, other possible explanations for the behaviour and symptoms should be considered, including:

- sexual, emotional and physical abuse if they show disinhibition, hypervigilance or hypersexuality
- the possibility of drug and/or alcohol misuse as a cause of mania-like symptoms; consider a diagnosis of bipolar disorder only after 7 days of abstinence
- previously undiagnosed learning difficulties
- organic causes such as excited confusional states in children with epilepsy, and akathisia resulting from neuroleptic medication.

Children and adolescents with learning difficulties

4.5.1.11   When diagnosing bipolar I disorder in a child or adolescent with learning difficulties, the same criteria as are applied to children and adolescents without learning difficulties should be used.

Children and adolescents with sub-threshold symptoms of bipolar disorder

4.5.1.12   If it is not possible to make a diagnosis in a child or adolescent with sub-threshold symptoms of bipolar disorder, they should be carefully followed up.

Assessment methods for children and adolescents

4.5.1.13   The diagnosis of bipolar disorder in children and adolescents should be made by a clinician with specialist training in child and adolescent mental health.

4.5.1.14   Assessment should include:

- a detailed mental state examination based on an individual interview with the child
- a medical evaluation to exclude organic causes
- further neuropsychological and neurological evaluation as appropriate
- a detailed account of the presenting problem from the child, parents or carers and other significant adults such as teachers
- a detailed developmental and neurodevelopmental history, including birth history, speech and language development, behaviour problems, attachment behaviour and any history of abuse.

4.5.1.15   A specialist diagnostic instrument such as the WASH-U-KSADS may be used; scales completed by parents or carers such as the Child Behaviour Checklist, Conners' Abbreviated Rating Scale, Parent Young Mania Rating

Scale and Parent General Behaviour Inventory may also be used. These should not replace a full clinical interview.

4.5.1.16 In severely mentally ill children and adolescents with psychotic symptoms, a diagnosis should be attempted as early as practical, and should be subject to regular specialist review.

4.6   COURSE AND PROGNOSIS

For most patients bipolar disorder is chronic and recurrent. There is a large variation between individuals in the number of episodes experienced, but the average is ten (Mackin & Young, 2005). Episodes of mania and depression tend to cluster together, so typically patients may experience a number of illness episodes together followed by a more quiescent period and then another cluster of episodes. This pattern with hypomanic and depressive episodes is especially common in bipolar II disorder. The risk of recurrence in the 12 months after a mood episode is especially high (50% in 1 year, 75% at 4 years, and afterwards 10% per year) compared with other psychiatric disorders. Furthermore, compared with unipolar depression, bipolar disorder is much more changeable in severity of the mood episode. In those with a recurrent illness pattern, the length of euthymia between episodes may shorten over time suggesting increased frequency of episodes (Kessing *et al.*, 2004b). The length of episodes remains fairly constant for an individual over time, although later episodes may begin more abruptly.

The all-cause SMR is elevated in patients with bipolar disorder relative to the general population. Bipolar disorder is associated with a higher burden of physical illnesses such as diabetes and heart disease and the SMR for premature deaths from natural causes is estimated at 1.9 for males and 2.1 for females (Osby *et al.*, 2001). The SMR for suicide is much higher at approximately 15 for males and 22.4 for females (Osby *et al.*, 2001), with the greatest risk of suicide attempts occurring during depressed or mixed episodes.

4.6.1   Early warning signs

Early detection in bipolar disorder is important for instigating an appropriate management regime with the aim of improving ultimate outcome and minimising harm caused by repeated episodes. Individuals are often able to identify precipitating changes in mood and/or behaviour that indicate the early stages of an episode because each episode starts with a similar pattern of symptoms that is idiosyncratic and typical for that individual. There is greater consistency from episode to episode of mania over time than episode to episode of depression. Relapse signatures can be helpful indicators to individuals themselves, family members, close friends, or clinicians that increased support may be necessary to prevent escalation into a full episode. Identifying particular stressors that are associated with relapse, such as specific psychosocial stressors or events associated with circadian rhythm disturbance, can help individuals learn ways of reducing the risk of triggering episodes. Although triggering events may be identified before some episodes, others will have no obvious trigger. Great care must be given to history taking to establish whether triggering events such as sleep disruption or life stress preceded the mood episode, or were the symptoms or consequences of it.

4.6.2   Neuropsychological function

A number of recent studies have demonstrated that many patients with bipolar disorder have significant psychological impairments characterised by a combination of declarative memory deficits as well as changes in executive functions such as attention, planning and working memory (Ferrier & Thompson, 2003). These impairments can occur when the patient is depressed or manic but can also persist into euthymia (Thompson *et al.*, 2005). This latter observation together with evidence of similar impairments in first degree relatives suggest that these deficits may be trait markers of bipolar disorder. These neuropsychological impairments may relate to structural changes in the brain (see Section 4.3.3) or to some other unknown psychological or biological process. The impairments worsen as the illness progresses and are particularly associated with the number of manic episodes (Robinson & Ferrier, 2006). The impact of these impairments on rehabilitation, engagement in therapy, compliance and quality of life is uncertain but likely to be significant.

4.6.3   Drug/alcohol outcomes

As mentioned above, substance misuse is common in patients with bipolar disorder and impacts negatively on illness outcome. Mixed episodes and rapid cycling mania are more common in patients with comorbid substance misuse, as are medical disorders, suicide and suicide attempts (Krishnan, 2005; Potash *et al.*, 2000). Generally, substance misuse destabilises the illness, increases the time taken to recover and/or triggers relapse.

4.6.4   Switching

Longitudinal studies suggest somewhere between 0–46% of people presenting with major depressive disorder will experience a manic or hypomanic episode and merit rediagnosis with bipolar disorder. One study followed 74 patients prospectively for 15 years from their first episode of depression and documented subsequent episodes of mania or hypomania. It was found that 19% of patients went on to experience a full-blown manic episode and a further 27% had at least one hypomanic episode (Goldberg *et al.*, 2001). Those who presented with psychotic depression were significantly more likely to go on to develop bipolar disorder.

4.6.5   Late-onset bipolar disorder

Mania or hypomania that first appears in later life (after 40 years of age) usually follows many years of repeated episodes of unipolar depression or is secondary to other factors such as steroid medication, infection, neuroendocrine disturbance or neurological problems. However, only 15% of cases of bipolar disorder presenting for the first time to mental health services are precipitated by a medical problem. Late-onset bipolar disorder is less likely to be associated with a family history of the disorder than if it is earlier-onset. The prognosis for late-life depression is generally poor due to a high mortality rate. The majority of the increased mortality rate is accounted for by a greater burden of physical illness, especially cardiovascular and cerebrovascular disease, rather than suicide. The SMR for cardiovascular death may be twice that of the general population but appears to be reduced if patients adhere to long-term medication.

4.7   THE TREATMENT AND MANAGEMENT OF BIPOLAR DISORDER IN THE NHS

4.7.1   History of service provision for adults

Bipolar disorder has struggled to establish itself as a separate diagnostic entity from both unipolar depressive disorder (Angst, 1966; Perris, 1966) and schizophrenia. Traditionally, provision of services for people with bipolar disorder has been through general outpatient and inpatient services of secondary mental health services. The only special service provision for service users with bipolar disorder has been the lithium clinic (Fieve, 1975), typically run by a psychiatrist and a nurse in hospital outpatient departments. Although lithium can be effective, it can also be toxic (Cookson *et al.*, 2002) (the side-effects are discussed in Chapter 8), so lithium clinics were seen as a way of ensuring safe regular monitoring and review of people with bipolar disorder who take lithium as a maintenance treatment. In the 1980s and 1990s lithium clinics were almost universal in British mental health services but they became less popular as mental health services developed a more community, rather than hospital, focus and alternatives to lithium became available.

By the late 1990s, the care of people with bipolar disorder in contact with secondary care services was largely provided by psychiatric outpatient and inpatient services. Only 50% of people with bipolar disorder who had an acute episode of mania or depression were in contact with a community mental health team (CMHT) (Perry *et al.*, 1999). The dominant model of care in England was the care programme approach (CPA) from mental health services or care management from social services, models that addressed the needs of service users with more severe mental illness. Sometimes people with bipolar disorder who had been admitted involuntarily under the 1983 Mental Health Act were soon discharged from the caseloads of CMHTs and the CPA because they seemed to be less needy of continuing support than other patients. The high risk of recurrence of bipolar episodes within 12 months of a manic episode (Tohen *et al.*, 1990) was not recognised. Once discharged from the CPA, people with bipolar disorder would receive only outpatient appointments with a psychiatrist no longer working in a lithium clinic. Apart from via the psychiatrist, general practitioner or emergency department, there was limited access to crisis support and, once a patient was discharged from a CMHT, arrangements to be seen again by the CMHT might take weeks. Few patients with bipolar disorder were treated in day hospitals or lived in supported accommodation. There was little provision of psychoeducation.

As a result of the paucity of care from secondary mental health services, service users accessed self-help, support and education about bipolar disorder from service user groups, particularly MDF The BiPolar Organisation (Shepherd & Hill, 1996). Since the publication of the National Service Framework for Mental Health, a raft of new service developments have been introduced to mental health services in England (Department of Health, 1999b). None of these is specifically targeted at bipolar disorder but may have had an impact on provision of services to service users with bipolar disorder in England. The same service changes have not been implemented in Wales, where services are only now implementing the CPA.

4.7.2   Service needs of adults with bipolar disorder

Recent community surveys reveal that around 25% of people with bipolar disorder have never sought help from health services (ten Have *et al.*, 2002). Those that have sought help may not receive a correct diagnosis of bipolar disorder for at least 6 years from the first appearance of symptoms (Morselli *et al.*, 2003). Service users with bipolar disorder have identified a range of difficulties in accessing services that meet their needs (Highet *et al.*, 2004):

- lack of awareness and understanding about bipolar disorder in the community leading to delays in seeking medical assessment
- the burden of illness is exacerbated by difficulties obtaining an accurate diagnosis and optimal treatment
- inappropriate crisis management
- difficulties accessing hospital care
- inappropriate exclusion of carers and families from management decisions
- frequent discontinuities of medical and psychological care.

In Britain, the needs of people with bipolar disorder have largely been regarded as similar to the needs of other service users with serious mental illness (Department of Health, 1999a). Four features of bipolar disorder have been identified that distinguish the service needs of service users with bipolar disorder from other service users (Morriss *et al.*, 2002):

- Most service users with bipolar disorder have the potential to return to normal function with optimal treatment, but with suboptimal treatment have a poor long-term outcome and become a burden to families and society (Simon & Unutzer, 1999; Ogilvie *et al.*, 2005).
- Optimal treatment of bipolar disorder is challenging and requires long-term commitment from health services.

● Bipolar disorder is characterised by high rates of episodic recurrence (after a manic episode, it is typically 50% recurrence within 12 months; Tohen *et al.*, 1990) with high rates of disabling mood symptoms between recurrences (Judd *et al.*, 2002) and suicide attempts (Jamison, 2000).

● Relatives of service users with bipolar disorder are not only subject to the usual stresses of caring but are also at a particularly high risk of developing bipolar disorder or unipolar depressive disorder themselves (McGuffin & Katz, 1989).

There have been few models of service provision specifically for bipolar disorder in the United Kingdom or anywhere else in the world. If such service provision were to be developed, then it should reinforce the strategies that service users with bipolar disorder already adopt to stay well. These include acceptance of the diagnosis or the problems presented by the disorder if the patient does not accept the diagnosis, education about the condition, identifying both triggers and early warning signs of mania and depression, having adequate amounts of sleep, managing stress, taking medication and using support networks and crisis resolution (Russell & Browne, 2005).

4.7.3   Service needs of children and adolescents

The process of care and provision of treatment for children and adolescents should take account of the four-tier model of child and adolescent mental health services (CAMHS) organisation and delivery (NHS Health Advisory Service, 1995). This is consistent both with the current organisation of CAMHS in England and Wales and with the National Service Framework (NSF) for children and adolescents across both jurisdictions.

Interventions for children and adolescents with bipolar disorder will usually be provided by specialist CAMHS (tiers 2/3 and 4), but children and adolescents also require help from non-specialist health, social work and education services (referred to as tier 1). Services may have tiers that are structural, functional or both, that is, some specialist CAMHS have a combined tier 2 and 3 service with single referral point, others may provide tier 2 as a stand-alone service.

Tier 1 services include those that have direct contact with children and adolescents for primary reasons other than mental health. These include general practitioners, health visitors, paediatricians, social workers, teachers, youth workers and juvenile justice workers. They are the first point of contact with the child/adolescent presenting with mental health problems. At this level, an important role is to detect those at high risk for bipolar disorder and those who are presenting with depression or mania.

Tier 2 CAMHS are provided by specialist trained mental health professionals, working primarily in a community-based setting alongside tier 1 workers. This facilitates consultation to tier 1 workers, prompt assessment of children within the tier 1 setting and the identification of young people requiring referral to more specialist services. Tier 2 professionals are usually closely linked or embedded in tier 3 services, thereby facilitating timely access to the specialist CAMHS.

Tier 3 services comprise multidisciplinary teams of specialist CAMHS professionals working in (secondary care) specialist CAMHS facilities. They should provide specialist co-ordinated assessments and treatments, including a full range of appropriate psychological and pharmacological interventions. Children and adolescents presenting with mania, mixed affective states or moderate to severe depression should be assessed by tier 3 specialist CAMHS. Outreach services should be available to those young people who, as result of their presentation, are unable to access the clinic base of the tier 3 service and to young people who require outreach work as part of an outpatient treatment plan. There may also be a role for early intervention services (EIS) for first-episode psychosis, which is described in Chapter 6.

Tier 4 services are highly specialised tertiary CAMHS in inpatient, day patient or outpatient settings for children and adolescents with severe and/or complex problems requiring a combination or intensity of interventions that cannot be provided by tier 3 CAMHS. In general, referral to tier 4 comes only from tier 3 CAMHS professionals.

A child or adolescent presenting with possible bipolar disorder will usually require assessment and treatment by tier 4 services. Following tier 4 intervention, young people are discharged back to tier 3 CAMHS or outreach services.

4.7.4   Issues of consent for children and adolescents

When admitting a child or adolescent to inpatient care, it is desirable to do so with the informed consent of both the patient and his or her parents, not least because the success of any treatment approach significantly depends on the development of a positive therapeutic alliance involving the child or adolescent, the family and the inpatient team. However, there will be times when the professionals consider admission to be necessary, but either the child or adolescent, or the family, do not consent.

If a person under 18 years of age refuses treatment, but the parent (or guardian) believes strongly that treatment is desirable, then the child or adolescent's wishes may be overruled. However, an adolescent has the right to consent to treatment without involving the consent of parents after his or her 16th birthday, or younger, if deemed 'Gillick competent'. Clinicians need to be mindful of whether a child or adolescent is subject to an order under the Children Act (1989). In most cases, the use of the Mental Health Act (1983) should be considered as it includes safeguards such as involvement of other professionals, a time limit and a straightforward procedure for appeals and regular reviews.

Those professionals involved in assessing children or young people for possible inpatient admission (tier 4 CAMHS staff) should be specifically trained in issues of consent and capacity, the use of current mental health legislation and the use of child care legislation as it applies to this group of patients.

4.8   THE ECONOMIC COST OF BIPOLAR DISORDER

Bipolar disorder is a relatively rare affective disorder when compared with unipolar depression, with a lifetime prevalence estimated at approximately 1%. Despite its low lifetime risk, bipolar disorder was ranked by the World Health Organization (WHO)

103

as the 22nd leading cause of worldwide burden among all diseases in 1990, expressed in disability adjusted life years (DALYs), and the sixth leading cause of DALYs at ages 15–44 years. When separate estimates were made for years of life lost and years lived with disability among all diseases, bipolar disorder was ranked as the sixth leading cause of disability worldwide (Murray & Lopez, 1996).

A recent study estimated the annual cost of bipolar disorder in the UK (Das Gupta & Guest, 2002). The study adopted a societal perspective and evaluated direct health service (NHS) costs of managing bipolar disorder, non-healthcare costs borne by other statutory agencies such as social care authorities and the criminal justice system, and indirect costs to society, related to productivity losses due to unemployment, absenteeism from work and premature mortality resulting from suicide. Cost estimates were based on national statistics data published by the Department of Health and a 0.5% prevalence of bipolar disorder in the UK, translating into 297,000 people with the condition.

The total annual societal cost of bipolar disorder was estimated at £2.055 billion in 1999/2000 prices, consisting of £199 million (10% of total costs) incurred by NHS resource use, £86 million (4%) associated with non-healthcare resource use and £1.77 billion (86%) related to productivity losses. Regarding costs borne by healthcare resource use, £14.9 million (7% of health service costs) was associated with management of bipolar disorder in primary care including drug prescriptions, £69.4 million (35% of health service costs) resulted from inpatient episodes, £57.9 million (29% of health service costs) was borne by day hospital, outpatient and ward attendances, £53.2 million (27% of health service costs) was attributed to community heath service resource use, and the rest (£3.4 million – 2% of health service costs) was related to other services, such as high-security hospital authorities and ambulance transport.

Indirect costs represented by far the most important driver of total costs associated with bipolar disorder. The largest amount of these was attributed to unemployment: an excess of 76,500 people annually were considered to be unemployed as a result of having bipolar disorder, bearing a financial burden of productivity losses approximating £1.51 billion per year (that is, 85% of total indirect costs). Other indirect costs due to absenteeism from work and suicide were estimated at £152 million and £109 million per year respectively.

Similar studies, estimating total costs attributable to bipolar disorder from a societal perspective, have also been conducted in Germany (Runge & Grunze, 2004), the Netherlands (Hakkaart-van Roijen *et al.*, 2004) and the US (Begley *et al.*, 2001; Wyatt & Henter, 1995). Runge & Grunze estimated the total annual cost of bipolar disorder in Germany at €5.8 billion in 2002 prices, of which 98% was associated with productivity losses. In the Netherlands, the respective total annual cost was reported to reach approximately US$1.8 billion, also in 2002 prices, based on an estimated prevalence of bipolar disorder equal to 5.2%. Indirect costs were found to be high in this study too, reaching 75% of total costs.

In the US, Wyatt & Henter calculated the total annual cost of bipolar disorder in 1991 using a lifetime prevalence of bipolar disorder equal to 1.3% (that is, 2,500,000 people diagnosed with the disease at some point during their lives). The total annual cost reached US$45.2 billion, consisting of US$7.6 billion direct costs (mainly health service costs but also costs related to the criminal system, research on bipolar disorder, and so on), and US$37.6 billion indirect costs, which amounted to 83% of total costs.

Begley and colleagues (2001) adopted a different methodology in order to calculate costs attributable to bipolar disorder; based on the incidence rate of the condition, they estimated the lifetime cost of bipolar disorder for all new cases affected by the disease in 1998. The study took into account the fact that only a small number of cases (assumed at 20% per year) would be diagnosed and treated for the disease, whereas the remaining undiagnosed cases would still incur health service costs, but their treatment would not be specific to bipolar disorder. Besides the above costs, estimates included comorbidity costs from alcohol and substance misuse, as well as indirect costs associated with excess unemployment, reduced earnings due to disability and suicide. The lifetime cost of new cases affected by the disease in the US in 1998 was estimated to be as high as US$24 billion, of which US$13.3 billion (55%) referred to medical costs; indirect costs reached US$10.7 billion, equalling 45% of total costs, a proportion significantly lower than that reported in other studies. This divergence was attributed by the authors to differences in the methodology used and in categories of indirect costs included.

In addition to studies adopting a societal perspective, other studies aimed at estimating direct healthcare costs only. An Australian study (Sanderson *et al.*, 2003) estimated the total annual cost of routine treatment for bipolar disorder in Australia at AUS$60.9 million, in 1997/98 prices, based on the results of a national mental health survey. By applying optimal treatment (as achieved by operationalising detailed clinical practice guidelines and expert reviews), the total annual direct medical cost was expected to rise up to AUS$108.4 million.

In France, de Zelicourt and colleagues (2003) estimated the total annual inpatient cost of treating manic episodes at FRF8.8 billion, converted to €1.3 billion (1999 values), reflecting an annual number of 265,000 manic episodes, 63% of which led to hospitalisation. Estimation of cost was based on a prevalence-based top-down approach, using a number of assumptions combined with data from various sources. Using a different methodology, Olié & Lévy (2002) reported a 3-month cost following hospitalisation for a manic episode at €22,297 per case admitted (1999 prices), of which 98.6% accounted for inpatient care. In this case, the analysis was based on case record data derived from 137 patient files.

A significant number of studies undertaken in the US analysed the financial burden of bipolar disorder from the perspective of a third-party payer, such as Medicaid (a public insurance plan for the poor and disabled), or a private insurer, practically paid by the employer. Bipolar disorder was found to be among the most costly mental diseases from an employer's point of view (Goetzel *et al.*, 2000 & 2003; Peele *et al.*, 1998 & 2003). Employees with bipolar disorder were found to incur significantly higher absence costs (related to sick leave, short- and long-term disabilities as well as workers' compensation) compared with employees with other mental disorders, and demonstrated an annual productivity level approximately 20% lower than that of the latter (Kleinman *et al.*, 2005). Regarding direct treatment costs, these were mainly driven by high hospitalisation rates, resulting in substantial inpatient resource use (Bryant-Comstock *et al.*, 2002; Hu & Rush, 1995; Peele *et al.*, 2003; Simon & Unützer, 1999; Stender *et al.*, 2002). Comorbidity of bipolar disorder with other mental disorders and medical conditions was an additional factor contributing to high treatment costs associated with the disease (Peele *et al.*, 2003). Moreover, management of unrecognised/misdiagnosed cases of bipolar disorder characterised by overuse of antidepressants and underuse of potentially effective medications was frequently observed in the US, adding to the total cost of treatment (Birnbaum *et al.*, 2003; Li *et al.*, 2002; Matza *et al.*, 2005; Shi *et al.*, 2004).

Goetzel and colleagues (2000, 2003) found that bipolar disorder was associated with a lower cost per case compared with schizophrenia; however, because a significantly higher number of employees (dependents also included) were affected by bipolar disorder rather than schizophrenia, the total costs to the insurance plans associated with bipolar disorder were approximately 25 times higher compared with costs incurred by employees with schizophrenia. Furthermore, the costs to the employers associated with management of patients with bipolar disorder were almost four times higher than the respective costs incurred by patients with unipolar depression, despite the similar numbers of employees affected by the two disorders, as the cost of a case with bipolar disorder was higher than that of a case with depression. Consequently, it can be inferred that bipolar disorder, despite its rather low lifetime prevalence, can be a relatively common condition within the population under employment, and a significant financial burden to the payers of health services and absenteeism/disability compensations (such as private insurance plans in the US and the public sector in the UK).

The above review demonstrates the major economic burden that bipolar disorder places on the healthcare system and, more substantially, due to productivity losses, to society as a whole. Apart from financial implications, bipolar disorder is associated with a significant psychological burden not only to patients themselves, but also to family and carers (Dore & Romans, 2001; Perlick *et al.*, 1999). Efficient use of available healthcare resources is required to maximise the health benefit for patients suffering from bipolar disorder and, at the same time, reduce the financial and psychological burden to society.

5. SERVICE USER AND CARER EXPERIENCE OF BIPOLAR DISORDER

5.1 INTRODUCTION

This chapter is based around the first-hand experience of people with bipolar disorder, family members and carers. It aims to relate Chapter 4 and the chapters on treatment and process and provision of care to a service user and carer context. The experiences are presented in three ways: by testimonies (both full and excerpted), by excerpts from interviews and from a survey conducted by MDF The BiPolar Organisation, formerly the Manic Depression Fellowship (MDF) (2004). The views represented here are illustrative only and are not intended to be representative of the experience of all people with bipolar disorder and their carers.

The writers of the testimonies were contacted primarily through MDF The BiPolar Organisation and through other service user and carer organisations and asked to write about their experiences of diagnosis, experience of treatment, relationship with psychiatrists or other healthcare professionals, continuity of care, experience of crisis, and self-help and support groups. Some of the questions they were asked to consider within these categories emanate from themes outlined in the qualitative study of 49 people with bipolar disorder by Highet and colleagues (2004).

The service user representative on the GDG also conducted short interviews with people with bipolar disorder on the specific themes above. Short extracts from MDF The BiPolar Organisation survey (2004) have also been used with permission.

5.2 TESTIMONIES FROM SERVICES USERS

5.2.1 Testimony 1: Robert

As a schoolboy (I am now 32), I was very successful academically, popular and sporty, but I'd always been a bit of a worrier. Looking back, I think I first experienced symptoms of bipolar disorder in the sixth form at my grammar school, withdrawing socially and experiencing bouts of feeling low, sometimes bursting into tears for no apparent reason.

I first fell seriously ill while travelling in south-east Asia on a year off between school and university, aged 19. I'd been feeling lonely and low for some time. Although I feel sure I would have fallen ill sooner or later anyway, my first high appeared to have been triggered by me rather stupidly swallowing a lump of cannabis before boarding a flight from Goa to Delhi in India. I arrived a paranoid wreck. Over the next few days my mood improved and all of a sudden I was the life and soul of the party and was having a great time with the friends I was travelling with.

A pattern quickly established itself. I'd be up for 8 to 10 days and then down for 8 to 10 days, as regular as clockwork. With each cycle my mood swings became more and more extreme. When down, I was catatonic and barely able to string two words together; speaking to my travelling companions became an ordeal. When high I would be charming, full of energy and enthusiasm, touring India in high spirits.

While in a depressed phase, miserable and bewildered as to what was happening, I managed to gather the wherewithal to book a flight home after 6 months abroad. By the time I arrived back at Heathrow to be met by my parents, I was as high as a kite. My parents were dumbstruck. I was talking ten to the dozen and told them I only needed 2 hours' sleep a night.

As weeks went by without treatment, my mood swings became even more extreme. When manic, I started spouting poetry spontaneously, talking gibberish, sleeping around and charging about the country in a state of euphoria.

The thing about mania that I've always found hardest to deal with afterwards, notwithstanding the shame and embarrassment, was the religious delusions. Despite not having had a Christian upbringing, when seriously manic I read religious significance into anything and everything. Where other people with mania might think they're Tony Blair or a multi-millionaire, I was on a divine mission, seeing God personified in a black dog and the eyes of a cat. At one point God seemed to 'stare' back at me when I just glanced at the pavement.

Eventually I was sectioned and forcibly sedated – the week I was due to start at university. It was a very damaging experience. I felt betrayed by my family, who were at their wits end and wanted me to have hospital treatment. As I saw it the only advantage of being in hospital was that I was prescribed a mood stabiliser, lithium. I don't think I would have hurt myself or anyone else. I spent my time on the ward dancing around thinking I was the Dalai Lama and painting wildly. I felt very angry about detention. I think it really should be a last resort when all else has failed.

After a week or so, my mood had flattened out and I was released as if I'd make a full recovery. I went straight into a severe depression and the cycling continued for some months.

My start at university was deferred by a year. It wasn't until the end of my second year that my mix of medication was eventually got right. The lithium and carbamazepine stopped the cycling fairly early on. But it took my psychiatrist 2 years to raise the dosage of the lithium to 800 mg, which alleviated my persistently low mood. In retrospect that was 2 years too long.

I graduated from university and then trained and qualified as a journalist a year later. At some point, in agreement with my psychiatrist, I cut back on my medication. I now know that this resulted in a slow and imperceptible slide into depression. At the time, I just thought I was going through a difficult patch because I was stuck at home convalescing with severe back pain.

It seems unbelievable now, but looking back it appears I remained in this mild to moderate depressed state for about 6 years. My mood was stable. I wasn't cycling because of the lithium and carbamazepine, so I didn't realise I was ill. I assumed I was well because I was on what I thought was the optimum combination of medication for me. I just came to think I was miserable by nature.

Over this time, I developed lots of physical problems. My back pain got worse and I developed neck pain and mysterious tingles in the arms and legs. It later became apparent that these physical problems resulted from muscular trigger points all over my body caused by the depression. Somehow I managed to hold down two jobs working in journalism for 5 years despite being desperately unhappy. But then I took a high-pressure job in London. I hated it and my mood worsened. I felt hopeless about the future and decided that life was not worth living – a reasonable conclusion to draw after feeling so awful for years.

I survived a massive lithium overdose. My suicide attempt finally prompted my psychiatrist into taking some action and he prescribed mirtazapine. This was a revelation. It immediately sent me into psychotic rapid cycling again, but at the same time it dawned on me that I had in fact been unknowingly depressed for ages. I now could tell that my mood, even though it was still up and down like a yo-yo, was 'on average' much better than it had been. As my mood improved, my physical symptoms of depression – the aches and pains – began to drop away as if by miracle.

Again it took more than a year to stabilise my mood at a 'normal' level for me. I first tried lamotrigine with lithium and then quetiapine with lithium instead. The quetiapine was very effective.

I was very angry with my psychiatrist, who had failed to recognise that I was suffering from depressive symptoms over such a long period of time. He just told me, rather unhelpfully, that I needed to 'love myself more'. To be fair, several previous psychiatrists I'd seen over the years had also missed the signs of depression – perhaps because I was coping, holding down a job and in a relationship. I hadn't even recognised I was depressed myself. But I do wish my psychiatrists had been more aggressive and pro-active in my treatment. It might have saved me from wasting 6 years of my life.

I am now married with a baby boy and starting a new job; I feel a lot better. I'm still prone to the occasional drop in mood and I still get anxious easily. Another characteristic I attribute to the illness is my appalling memory. Lots of people complain of a bad memory, but mine is significantly worse than anyone else's I know. It limits my ability to do my job properly and I'm considering coming off lithium to see if that helps.

For me, the most important thing about my treatment is having a good relationship with a psychiatrist in whom you have confidence – someone who will take a full history, listen to what you have to say and then lay out all the options with all the pros and cons. Being available on the phone in a crisis is also much appreciated.

5.2.2   Testimony 2: Jane

I first became depressed and suicidal in 1980 at the age of 17 (I am now 42). I had a bout of glandular fever and had just done my A levels. I didn't feel that I could talk to my parents because my grandmother had a long-term mental illness. I had heard how miserable all this was and I very much felt that I was letting the side down by getting ill too. However, my parents persuaded me to go to my GP who called them anyway and suggested that I might have bipolar disorder (this idea fell by the wayside). I was referred to a psychiatrist at the hospital who diagnosed depression. He wanted to admit me but I refused, so I ended up in a day hospital that consisted almost entirely of confused older patients.

Against everyone's advice I went to university that autumn. I was taking a tricyclic antidepressant, lorazepam and some kind of sleeping pill and spent most of my first year getting almost no sleep, drinking heavily, partying wildly, sleeping around and for several weeks not eating because I'd convince myself that I didn't need any food. I was seeing a consultant psychiatrist and a GP but just told them I was fine. At some point I stopped taking the pills. As the year went on I became depressed again, which as before I tried to conceal. I painted my face with green eye shadow and was convinced I was invisible. I couldn't study anymore because the words swam around on the page. Finally, I took a handful of sleeping pills mixed with alcohol, and then screamed because I'd forgotten to write a note. Then I threw up. The next time I saw the psychiatrist I told him that I was depressed and he admitted me to hospital for about a month and put me back on the medication. Conditions on the psychiatric ward were terrible, but I was allowed to go to the university to take my exams.

Over the next 16 years I got depressed again a few times. On one occasion I went to a place that offered free counselling for about 6 months, which I don't think helped me get over the depression any quicker, but helped me survive it. On another occasion I went to the doctor but she said that I wasn't depressed, just having a hard time coping with two young children.

In the summer of 1997 I got depressed again quite quickly. One weekend after a row with my husband I got really hyper in a very unpleasant sort of way, couldn't sit still, was very angry, drove at 100 mph and was hallucinating. In October I was suicidal to the point of making plans and went to see my GP. She was extremely sympathetic and prescribed paroxetine, which made me feel a bit better, but things never got back to normal. I did an online manic depression test, scored high and laughingly dismissed the result. In April 1998 things got steadily weirder. I couldn't stop mentally singing songs, couldn't think straight and was obsessively sending emails. I read messages into everything: clouds, road signs and so on. At a social event I was mesmerised by a flashing light, couldn't sit still, saw a mushroom cloud which I thought foretold a death in the family and thought the pavement was blue. I didn't tell anyone. By now I was almost certain I had bipolar disorder, but I hoped it would go away.

Things got scary. Crows were following me. There was a TV camera in my head. Both of these were organised by a malevolent Celtic goddess who was trying to compel me to kill myself. I couldn't think straight at all, couldn't concentrate. I was turning into a bird, I was turning into the phoenix, the phoenix could save the world, the phoenix could save the world by burning to death, the phoenix could save the world through the internet, the phoenix was poisoning the world through the internet and needed to cut her hands off so she couldn't type any more. At this point I admitted that I really did have to seek help. The doctor I saw was very calm, soothing and practical, and told me I was hypomanic and should go to hospital. I was told I would only be assessed, but I was admitted for a couple of weeks. I was given medication (without any discussion) and told that I had bipolar disorder. I was confused a lot of the time, particularly about which doctor was in charge of me. They put me on carba-mazepine, haloperidol and, for the first few days, zopiclone. I did lots of painting, wrote pages of complete gobbledy-gook, and co-operated pretty well.

For the next couple of years I kept getting a few days of hypomania here or there, and then bouts of sudden and severe depression for which I was hospitalised (another six admissions varying from 2–6 weeks). I always resisted going into hospital but never quite got sectioned. I didn't always get on well with the staff at the hospital; some of them made me feel like a nuisance and some of them didn't do their jobs properly (for example, nurses supposedly on observation slept in front of the TV at night). The student nurses were often the most helpful and sympathetic. The ward was usually disorganised and I found it very stressful waiting for hours to see a doctor, missing activities or even meals because I was worried I would miss them. I was also angry that there were no occupational therapists on any of my admissions from 1998 onwards.

By now I had a different psychiatrist, with whom I got on very well, and a CPN who was fantastic and reliable. I stayed on the haloperidol, but after a while they tried tapering off the carbamazepine and started me on several other drugs (lithium and paroxetine) which made me worse. In the end I was given a high dose of lamotrigine and since then I have been out of hospital for about 4 years. Eventually I stopped taking the haloperidol because even at a very low dose it made me feel dopey.

During this period I also attended a self-management course run by my GP, had cognitive behavioural therapy (CBT) for 6 months as part of a trial and, on the advice of my psychiatrist, started going to the local self-help group (MDF The BiPolar Organisation). The course and CBT were quite good at helping me to identify when I was getting ill, the CBT helped me improve relationships with my family, and through MDF The BiPolar Organisation I was able to meet other people who'd been through the same experience. Neither the course nor the CBT helped me stay out of hospital at the time, but these days I am much better at dealing with the odd up or down day, and I wonder if without them I would still be spiralling out of control.

At the present time I am not seeing a psychiatrist or a CPN, which I am not very happy about. They didn't even tell my GP they were discharging me. I feel that no one is keeping an eye on me except for the physical check from the practice nurse once a year. I was discharged on 1000 mg carbamazepine and 500 mg lamotrigine per day, but I've had a lot of trouble with side effects, particularly double vision and dizzi-ness. My GP recently tried slow-release carbamazepine, which also helped and I've cut down the dose by 200 mg per day. Very occasionally if I get very anxious or panicky I take a clonazepam or haloperidol tablet.

I had to give up work during the period of repeated admissions, partly because my concentration was affected and partly because the pressure of having to be well enough for work and not coping made me stressed and depressed. I think giving up work and the exercise and fresh air involved in taking on an allotment have helped me a great deal (although I still have real problems with concentration and memory that considerably impair my daily life). I am also involved with MDF The BiPolar Organisation as a treasurer and feel that that is a good safety net.

Over the years, with so many admissions and illnesses, it has been a huge strain on my husband who would become very anxious. Now, however, he no longer panics if I seem a bit low. In recent years I have been quite open about my illness with my children and it doesn't seem to worry them. These days I am mostly stable and free from physical side effects.

5.2.3   Testimony 3: James

I first became aware that I possibly had a mental disorder in my last year at university, aged 20/21 (I am now 32), when I had serious problems sleeping; it was the start of some strange behaviour, such as thinking that I could talk with birds and that I was infested with fleas. I would have times of great enthusiasm, but would also have awful times when I wouldn't know what to do with myself. After a few nights of not sleeping at all, I saw a doctor and was given temazepam.

At university I visited a different doctor and was given another sleeping tablet and encouraged to see a counsellor, which I did on one occasion. I felt quite embarrassed to be going but it was good to talk. Coming to the end of university was a difficult time. I was in a state of indecision about my future and my parents were moving away. I felt rudderless and depressed, and was punching walls. Over the next few years a stable, but rather boring, job got me back on a more regular path but my depression and intermittent insomnia continued. When I was aged about 26/27, I was sent to see a consultant psychiatrist, but she concluded that the depression was not severe enough to need treatment. I wasn't receiving any treatment for my insomnia at this time either. I have generally been able to present myself well to doctors and put a brave face on my problems.

I got married and trained to become a teacher when I was aged 27, but I still coped with regular insomnia and depression for another 3 years. My week would have a regular pattern: on Monday I would have to leave work as soon as the school day ended as I was tired and depressed. On Tuesday I would really get into things, work late and then not be able to sleep till about 3 or 4 in the morning sometimes. During the rest of the week I was in a bit of a fog of tiredness, but I would generally leave on Friday enthused by things. Saturday afternoon was the lowest point of the week.

After seeing a poster at the doctor's describing the signs of depression, and feeling that I experienced nearly all of the signs, I mentioned this to the doctor and he prescribed an antidepressant (escitalopram). Apart from completely losing my sex drive, I was able to function well on this medication and was successful at work. It helped me sleep and I felt that I was on a more even keel. I stayed on this medication for 3–4 months.

While going through a difficult period in my marriage, I began to have mood swings. It was at this time that I read a book about bipolar disorder and thought it sounded like what I was experiencing, although I seemed to be rapid cycling. I saw a locum who put me back on escitalopram. I asked for an appointment with a psychiatrist, and had to wait 4 or 5 weeks for this. The appointment with the psychiatrist was very thorough and we discussed the possibility of bipolar disorder; the consultant said that I possibly had bipolar 3.[11]

After this, sleep became a problem again so the doctor stopped the escitalopram and put me on lamotrigine and zopiclone. (I stated my concern at stopping the escitalopram suddenly as I had to do it gradually last time, and it was only after he had received a letter from the psychiatrist that I was advised to stop the escitalopram gradually.) The first night on the change of medication was rather disconcerting. After taking the zopiclone I got ataxia and my wife had to help me upstairs. I also thought that I was getting visual disturbances. I was told that I could take zopiclone every other night, but on the night that I didn't take it, I couldn't sleep. I was concerned that I was getting a rash, and I was also having spotting on my eyes. I called NHS Direct, who in the end suggested that I go into hospital. The doctor checked my eyes and couldn't see anything wrong, so I went to see my GP the next day. I was feeling in a bit of a state, exhausted from the night before and a bit at sea with the drugs that I was taking. My GP suggested that I go back to the hospital.

At the hospital I was interviewed by the charge nurse but no discussion was had with me about the effects of the medication I had taken. I was feeling very anxious and angry with the GP, who I felt had started all these problems off earlier in the week with the bad advice about stopping the escitalopram. I was then given a medical by a senior house officer (SHO), who asked me if I thought that I had any special powers. I replied that I was a Christian, which seemed to be significant to the SHO. (I feel much closer to God when I am feeling a bit elated.) I also told the SHO that the previous night I had felt a conviction that this day might be my last. This was tied up with my religious feelings.

In the end I was put on a section 5.4 under the Mental Health Act because I had tried to leave the hospital to stop my wife driving home. (I was worried that she might have an accident.) I then had an interview with the nurse and another doctor, but I was concerned because my rights were not discussed with me and I was not informed what being under section meant until the next morning. I was trying to write things down so that I had a record of the meetings and of what was being said. I asked to see my uncle, who is a doctor, but this was refused. At one point I said to the charge nurse that I felt that he was trying to wind me up and he said that he was.

I was eventually given 1 mg of lorazepam which made me feel much calmer. I was held over the weekend and met the consultant on the Monday. There was a large group of people who I hadn't met before, consisting of at least one nurse, a student, two consultants and a phlebotomist. The consultant told me about the various possible treatments with medication and I read about them. She was keen to get me on an antipsychotic, which was hard for me to accept. I was feeling defensive and hard done by, and was not convinced at the time that I was psychotic. She felt that I was not co-operating with my medication so put me on a section 2 under the Mental Health Act. This was very distressing, so I contacted a mental health solicitor. At this point

---

[11]Not recognised in DSM-IV or ICD-10.

I had my first panic attack. (I had several more of these over the next few months.) The solicitor began to arrange for a mental health tribunal, but after a few days I was taken off the section. I stayed in hospital for 2 weeks in all. The consultant said that I was possibly suffering from bipolar II and I was put on lamotrigine for several months and olanzapine. Looking back, I realise that I was a bit psychotic and that this was my second psychotic experience, with my first occurring at the end of university.

After 3 weeks at home, I went back to work but was concerned about losing my job. I stopped the mood stabiliser, which made me feel I was in a permanent fug, and started escitalopram again, which allowed me to perform a lot better. I also have olanzapine when I am feeling high and zoplicone. I still have bad days, but on the whole I am functioning well and feeling happy for the majority of the time. My relationship with my consultant was not good to start with but is better now. I seem to be able to influence decisions about my medication, but I would have more confidence in her if she was more confident with her treatment. I get on very well with the nurse who comes and visits me every few weeks. She has given me some good advice and has helped me have more confidence in myself. But while it is helpful to have regular contact with someone, it is not a talking therapy, which I think would have been beneficial. (I am on a waiting list to see a psychologist.)

5.2.4 Testimony 4: Helen

While living in France I had two 'breakdowns' in my early thirties (I am now 43). I was told by a French psychiatrist that I would always be vulnerable, 'like a vase that had cracked' but was offered no diagnosis or explanation of how this might have happened or how I might try to make some sense of this experience, and offered no hope outside medication. I was sectioned on three occasions and, after an unnecessarily protracted period in a French asylum, my father had to come to get me out.

I returned to England and was diagnosed with bipolar disorder. With help from the plain commonsense approach of a locum psychiatrist, I felt that my hope of recovery could begin and I attempted to come to terms with what I now understood to be two manic episodes with psychotic features. I was enabled in this by England's more forward-looking, client-centred, recovery-based approach in the community that offered hope, empowerment and support.

I would describe psychosis as like a waking dream and reality that merge, slowly leaving reality behind as you enter an increasingly frightening new 'reality' of seeing things and people that aren't there and hearing voices that don't exist telling you to do increasingly irrational, dangerous and injurious things. All this is tinged with ever-growing paranoia. As the psychosis takes hold, combined with a manic mood swing, it is possible not to feel hunger, not to need sleep, not even to feel pain, as the body is whipped up to maximum motor output. The mind is racing at top speed, making impossible connections between events; the heightened euphoric emotions all combine together to direct some deluded 'mission'. The ultimate height of mania is the adoption of a persona; mine tended towards the good ones: Mother Earth and God's daughter as the second coming of Christ.

Having a diagnosis was supremely important. Despite the horrors of psychosis, it is more frightening not being told what the illness is and to live with the fear of something you know nothing about happening again, and for it to actually happen again. My psychiatrist could offer little practical help other than to mention MDF The BiPolar Organisation. I joined one of their local self-help groups and followed their self-management training course some years later. During this 6-week course, I learned how to recognise and cope with 'episodes'. I learned there were others like me with the same illness and that people with bipolar disorder were actually quite talented, intelligent, empathic individuals who had much to offer society.

My psychiatrist discussed drug maintenance with mood stabilisers with me at length, although it was not until some 3 years after my second episode that I was given a 6-week psychological therapy which helped me to become more assertive in relationships.

I am sorry to say that the treatment I needed was not on offer. I felt that I needed a therapy that would teach me the skills and encourage me to rebuild my life, my 'self' which had been shattered by my experiences. Rather than go through years of expensive private counselling, I took a degree in psychology, determined to improve my understanding, and I worked for MDF The BiPolar Organisation co-ordinating their research into their self-management training programme. I realised that, like me, people with bipolar disorder were much more than their illness and hence needed a more holistic, comprehensive approach to training than simple mood recognition and management. I started to create my own lifestyle development training programme for people with bipolar disorder based on my research. The training offers insight into the condition and a hopeful recovery approach that is attainable, but sadly such holistic therapies are still not available.

My relationship with my psychiatrist has been excellent. I could not have wished for a more supportive, person-centred, empathic individual to encourage me in my understanding and later research of this disorder. He did not specify the exact type of bipolar disorder that I had but was happy to discuss it with me when I asked if it was bipolar I (he confirmed that it was). I did not, however, find the initial rare visits from the CPN and social worker supportive; I thought that they limited me to more cautious objectives that they were able to monitor. After a few visits of this nature, I told them I would telephone them if they were ever needed. Now discharged from secondary services, I am reluctant to rely on primary care which is not, I feel, equipped to deal with mental health issues. My relationship with my GP is limited to e-mailing requests for repeat prescriptions for carbamazepine (200 mg/day).

Since being diagnosed, I consider I have come a long way. I believe that although mood swings will come and go – I have experienced only minor short-lasting bouts which have been successfully self-managed since my last episode over 8 years ago – there is the real possibility of growth. My recent work, as chair of a charity enabling mental health service users to put forward their views in order to shape services, has allowed me to encourage others to hope for a greater recovery and to take a greater part in how they would wish to be treated.

5.2.5   Testimony 5: Patrick

I was told that that I had bipolar disorder about 6 weeks after my life had fallen apart. My marriage had ended abruptly and I believed that I had lost my wife, my two sons and my home for good. My confidence and self-esteem had collapsed, I couldn't stop crying and I could scarcely perform at work.

Yet the diagnosis was in part a relief. It confirmed the conclusion I had myself reached about 3 months earlier after looking at a Mind leaflet and thinking that the symptoms of bipolar disorder matched my experience exactly. I was 43 years old and realised that I had suffered what I came to recognise as recurrent, severe depression from the age of 7. There was a social and family history to all this: my mother suffered from recurrent depression all her life, my father was discharged from the army having suffered battle shock (from which it took him years to partially get over) and my brother has also been diagnosed with bipolar disorder. My early life was an emotional cauldron, involving several hospital admissions (including a period in isolation) before I was five years old.

I was compulsorily admitted to hospital with mania on two occasions during my late twenties. Those were the peaks of episodes that occurred over 4 years, with depression following each winter/early spring. Those great fluctuations of mood started whilst I was still in the army. I was doing very well in my chosen career, but the sudden onset of mood swings (which I could not have named then) left me bewildered. I would feel alternately omnipotent or worthless, focused and achieving or directionless and riddled with self-doubt. I bought myself out of the army when I felt everyone had given up on me (which I know was not the case). No one suggested I should consult a doctor and it never occurred to me – I had no idea that what I was experiencing was an illness or had a name.

I joined the ambulance service and feel sure that the experiences I had in this emotionally challenging field of work, coupled with the disturbed sleep pattern of the shift worker and the other frustrations of my life (including difficulty forming relationships with women) ate away at my stability. I first saw a psychiatrist during this time. He did not put a name to my condition, though he did prescribe chlorpromazine hydrochloride and offered me inpatient treatment to examine me more closely. Working for the ambulance service, I did not feel I could 'come out' in this way and declined the offer. Nor did I connect myself with the occasional manic patient on a section that I helped to transport to psychiatric hospitals.

I experienced full mania for the first time during my first summer as a student after recovery from a deep depression, a lack of sleep and a real sense of social dislocation and lack of direction. I came to believe I was at one with the universe, colours took on a new vividness, I could see the meaning of life in a pond and I argued fiercely and incoherently with anyone who contradicted me. Again no one suggested I should see a doctor and I sought no help. Gradually the condition eased.

At the end of my student days, I was taken to a psychiatric hospital by police. I had taken refuge in a police station because I was convinced the IRA wanted to kill me. Once in a cell I stripped naked and dissolved into incoherence. This was the culmination of several weeks of self-neglect, little sleep, hunger and over-use of alcohol following final exams. On the night I was taken into hospital I was terrified, making connections between everything I saw (in particular wires which I found everywhere), completely disinhibited and exhausted. Looking back, I am grateful that I was admitted as it put a stop to a steep decline in my life that could have ended in a far worse place.

Although my enforced hospitalisation served its purpose, providing safety and stabilising my mood, it was an awful experience. I was completely disoriented at first, received some physical and verbal abuse from one nurse and had no sense of having a defined problem to be treated nor of there being an end in sight. I was just required to fit into an institutionalised regime and submit to someone else's idea of what was good for me. I was discharged after a month suffering from the side effects of haloperidol without any idea that the shuffling and drooling *were* side effects. The delusions had gone; the psychiatrist told me that I was not mentally ill, but I was left with physical symptoms that were embarrassing, frightening and incomprehensible. Fortunately my brother was able to intervene on my behalf and the problems eased.

A year later I was back in hospital briefly. This time I thought I was in the 19th century (I was studying history by then at another university). Medication-induced sleep rapidly re-oriented me and I was able to continue my studies. No one, least of all me, connected the episodes. I was moving around from place to place and each occurrence seemed to me to be because of 'stress' or self-neglect. At the end of my studies I started a job as a social worker. At my medical I avoided the truth about my condition because no one had given it a name; even after I had the diagnosis I still did not disclose it. But I lived with the fear that people could 'tell'.

Marrying and having children brought some stability to my life, although I continued to experience periodic lows and quite often pressure of speech and flight of ideas. I frequently flew into rages and resorted to alcohol to dampen down the feeling of going high. However, I am sure regular sleep and hours after years of chaotic student life, shift work and deprivation of sleep in the army, made a difference in keeping mania at bay. But after a period of intense effort and responsibility at work, I was overwhelmed with pressures and life at home was unbearable for everybody. My marriage ended and I consulted my doctor, as I was no longer able to cope at work.

My GP was excellent. She listened, amidst my tears, to my whole story. I immediately felt the sense of someone professionally standing with me and she arranged for an emergency psychiatric consultation. I was given the diagnosis but only after directly asking the registrar who had just told me, without explaining why, that I might have to take lithium for the rest of my life. Within weeks I started the lithium treatment and began to learn about bipolar disorder. MDF The BiPolar Organisation has been, for me, the most important source of learning about the condition and its management, helping me to develop a sense of control over my symptoms. At local meetings I have met people with similar experiences who have become real friends. We benefit from mutual support and contact. Sometimes when people feel ashamed after a manic episode the group provides a non-judgemental place to begin to pick up the pieces. I have benefited personally from a self-management programme run by MDF The BiPolar Organisation, which teaches a variety of proven self-help methods for coping with the condition.

Initially after diagnosis I was discharged from hospital care and felt that I had been cast off with no NHS support. (Without MDF The BiPolar Organisation I would have felt alone, as I had no one else to talk to about living with a major mental health problem.) My GP, however, was very good in getting me re-connected with hospital services. At first, I saw a different doctor every time I went, all of whom saw medication as the only treatment option (one of the drugs reduced me to a zombie-like state), but my psychiatrists have been excellent in recent years.

My GP also helped by obscuring the real reasons for occasional absences from work on certificates, whilst encouraging me to think about ill-health retirement. Eventually, I came under the care of a consultant. I was usually angry when I saw him but gradually I came to appreciate him and to see retirement as a way of escaping an intolerable work situation. My doctors proved to be right and life has improved considerably since leaving full-time work. My consultant continues to be the anchor in the management of my condition and being on my GP's practice register also gives me a feeling of security.

During a particularly low time I was helped by a CPN using cognitive behavioural techniques. This helped at the time and also during other periods when I had negative thoughts or setbacks. It is now a very long time since I have suffered from full-blown mania. Occasionally, when facing severe stress I have 'heard' the odd voice, noticed how certain lights appear unusually bright, or thought that a crow landing near me has significance. So far I have been able to catch myself and dismiss such thoughts.

It is my experience that services have changed for the better over the years and I feel well supported by the NHS and MDF The BiPolar Organisation. I know this is not always the case for others, particularly the undiagnosed sufferers of bipolar disorder who are in the majority. I am concerned that my sons may inherit the disorder, but I hope they will not have to wait 22 years for a diagnosis.

5.2.6 Summary of themes and concerns

Diagnosis

People with bipolar disorder have reported that it has taken them years, sometimes decades to get a formal diagnosis of bipolar disorder and consequently to receive appropriate care (Highet *et al.*, 2004). This problem is one that occurs in both primary care and specialist mental health services (Highet *et al.*, 2004). For some people, getting a diagnosis and treatment can be made more difficult by the stigma associated with mental illness. It took Eileen, now aged 50, more than 20 years to get a diagnosis of bipolar disorder:

> *'I was 42 before I was diagnosed. I first became aware I was suffering severe mood swings as a young child. I can only ever remember being either very happy*

or very sad. When low I wished I'd never been born. My dad had also always suffered severe mood swings throughout my childhood and spent long spells in hospital, but I was told it was for treatment for a 'heart attack'. My parents felt such shame about his mental illness they never told me about it, and they never told me their suspicions about my illness. It was only when I broke the news about my diagnosis more than 20 years later that they said they 'had always known'. I felt quite angry really that they'd never said something earlier. If I had been diagnosed earlier I would have got the right treatment earlier'. (Interview)

Without an accurate diagnosis, people may receive treatment that can be insufficient or harmful. It may be the case that symptoms of depression – for which patients are much more likely to seek treatment – will be recognised, but symptoms of hypomania may be missed or not initially detected by healthcare professionals when taking a patient's history. After making a suicide attempt at 15, Eileen saw a succession of GPs:

'Over the next 27 years, they all treated me for depression, prescribing me more than a dozen different antidepressants. As far as I can tell they did nothing to stabilise my mood swings. None of the GPs ever recognised that my high moods in between the lows were symptomatic of bipolar disorder. It was only when my GP referred me to a CPN after a particularly bad bout of feeling suicidal that the CPN immediately picked up on the highs and said she thought I had bipolar disorder. She referred me onto a consultant psychiatrist who made the diagnosis. He prescribed mood stabilisers and my moods have been a lot more stable ever since. I only wish I'd got the diagnosis 20 years earlier'. (Interview)

The cyclical nature of the illness, whereby symptoms – and consequently the patient's judgement – changes from day to day, week to week and month to month, makes diagnosis much more difficult. For example, a patient who makes an appointment to see a psychiatrist when depressed and desperate for treatment may feel very different when attending the appointment several weeks later. By then, s/he might have switched into a hypomanic state. Suddenly, the patient is wildly optimistic – life is seen through extremely rose-tinted glasses. The bouts of depression are forgotten and the patient convinces him/herself s/he has made a full recovery. In fact, s/he tells the psychiatrist, s/he wasn't really all that depressed at all, s/he was just perhaps 'a bit down in the dumps'. Full of confidence, s/he sounds very convincing to the doctor. Persuaded by the patient's account of his/her recovery, the psychiatrist fails to probe sufficiently into the patient's current state of mind to establish whether his/her mood is normal or high. He makes an appointment for 3 months' time. If the psychiatrist has not seen the patient on a previous occasion, it makes it much more difficult to judge what is his/her normal mood.

But even when a person sees a GP or a psychiatrist while in a depressed phase, the testimonies reveal that professionals might not be able to recognise bipolar disorder. First episodes of bipolar disorder can be very difficult for patients to recognise. Moderate to mild symptoms can be easily misinterpreted as simply being in either a 'really good' or a 'really bad' mood. People with bipolar disorder can labour under the illusion that they are 'just moody' for years. They may struggle to understand what is happening to them, but are likely to try to interpret their moods in the same way that everyone does – simply in terms of life events making them happy or sad – and struggle on.

Often it is only when the highs are sufficiently extreme (for example with symptoms like delusions or extreme pressure of speech) that friends and family can be panicked into seeking medical help and the symptoms become unmistakable to healthcare professionals. The symptoms of depression, which are usually not as obviously noticeable as mania, can more easily pass ignored by those around the sufferer. Too often, it is only when a desperate act like a suicide attempt has been made that those close to someone with bipolar disorder recognise the need for help.

In order to address some of these issues, there needs to be greater public and professional awareness of and understanding about bipolar disorder. Because healthcare professionals, in particular GPs, sometimes fail to diagnose the condition, they should be aware that people who have symptoms of depression may have experienced mania. The patient may need encouragement to talk about his/her symptoms, which can be achieved through sensitive questioning (family members and carers may also need to be asked about symptoms and behaviour within the bounds of confidentiality).

Experience of treatment and care
When contact is made with services, healthcare professionals should encourage patients to keep their appointments and ensure that first contact is positive. To promote more effective communication between doctor and patient, doctors should have cultural competence so that they can work effectively within diverse communities.

The testimonies and surveys (Morselli & Elgie, 2003) demonstrate that people with bipolar disorder require healthcare professionals to provide full and clear information about the condition and about the treatment options, ideally in written form (for example, booklets or newsletters) or video (Kupfer *et al.*, 2002). In providing this information, the social, cultural and educational background of the patient (and carer) need to be taken into consideration.

The testimonies and surveys (Morselli & Elgie, 2003) also emphasise the importance of a trusting, open and respectful working relationship between themselves and the professional. What is valued in a professional is someone who will undertake a thorough assessment, listen attentively to the patient's description of his or her symptoms, and to their carers, and who will clearly explain the treatment options and the risks and benefits. Patients nowadays expect to be treated as an equal partner, no longer the passive recipients of treatment, but as experts in their own condition (Morselli & Elgie, 2003), unlike the individual who felt that '*my psychiatrist and other professionals tend to decide what is best for me, rather than listening to my thoughts and feelings*' (MDF The BiPolar Organisation survey). This will necessitate that patients are fully involved in decisions about their treatment and care, and that their preferences for a particular treatment, or their decision not to have an intervention, is taken into consideration by the professional when the treatment plan is prepared.

Highet and colleagues (2004) report that patients experience a restricted range of treatment, both in primary and secondary care, mostly limited to medication. MDF

The BiPolar Organisation also report that 'a very high number of people still do not have access to a psychologist' (MDF The BiPolar Organisation survey, 2004). After a psychotic episode, Linda (aged 34) *'pushed for some counselling but was made to feel like I was asking for a pot of gold by the hospital psychiatrist'*. But counselling *'helped me come to terms with what I'd been through and also my counsellor suggested I go on some courses (anxiety management, relaxation and problem solving), which were held at the local outpatients centre and were all really helpful'* (extract from testimony). Cynthia says that she benefited from group CBT (run specifically for people with bipolar disorder) and a self-management course because she gained knowledge about her condition, felt less isolated and learned about strategies to help her to cope with both mania and depression:

> *'During my last manic episode I did not, as before, develop psychosis and was able to maintain more control over my treatment and avoid admission to hospital. I was able to put some of what I had learnt from the self-management course into practice. I was also more responsive to professionals and to agreeing to an increase in medication. Once I started to feel better I began to understand what had triggered the high (stress) and how it had built up over several months. I had not had this degree of insight before'* (extract from testimony).

Regarding medication, patients highlight the need for full discussion about dose and side effects. Sally (aged 51), a university lecturer, says that her psychiatrist *'listens to me and takes my view into account. I told him how my last psychiatrist put me on 20 mg olanzapine and turned me into a zombie. One time I fell asleep while in a lecture I was so tired, and two of my students reported me to my head of department. My new psychiatrist listened to what I told him about my experiences and he put me on just 5 mg which has been fine'* (extract from testimony).

Continuity of care and crisis management

It has been suggested that people with bipolar disorder and depression are more likely than those with disorders such as schizophrenia to receive disorganised and poorly coordinated care (Hickie, 2000).

Highet and colleagues (2004) reported that 'current crisis management practices were considered to contribute to negative perceptions and stigma' and they identified a need for 'prompt and improved access to crisis care during the early phases of acute relapse'. Sally has a crisis team but on one occasion could not access anybody to come out and assess her: *'the result was that I left home in my car in a manic state and had a fortunately minor accident some hours later, 100 miles away'* (extract from testimony). On another occasion she made four telephone calls to her team but was nevertheless sectioned the next day. She feels that *'everything should be done to avoid hospital: the staff there are generally not interested and offer virtually no psychological support. The experience is traumatic and one's stay tends to be prolonged. The crisis team should play a role here in preventing this'* (extract from testimony).

Due to the episodic nature of the condition, however, people with bipolar disorder should be able to access care and treatment when they need it, particularly during a crisis. Cynthia benefited by a supportive CPN with whom she drew up a relapse prevention plan and who *'worked intensively with me to avoid admission to hospital and offered almost daily support at home'*. Similarly Linda agreed an action plan with her psychiatrist should she relapse:

> *'This includes having a supply of medication at home (to start taking when I get ill), having telephone numbers for people I can contact in an emergency and making an appointment with my psychiatrist. He also suggested getting into a regular sleep routine and advised me about the best time of day to exercise'* (extract from testimony).

Self-help and support groups

MDF The BiPolar Organisation reports that it has 142 self-help groups in England and Wales and estimates that on average about 50 or 60 people a year attend each group meeting. Members report that they tend to find out about groups through word-of-mouth or through their own research, rather than through their GP or psychiatrist.

Some patients report that it is only in self-help groups that they can find people who can really empathise. The simple fact of knowing that they are not alone, and that others have the condition, is in itself comforting and helpful. They report that it is very therapeutic to talk to other people who have had similar experiences, for example, psychotic delusions.

The groups are also a very good way of pooling knowledge about drug treatment and local services and form a good support network on which many people rely. Some groups organise speakers and experts to come and talk to members about the condition.

5.3   TESTIMONIES FROM FAMILY MEMBERS/CARERS

5.3.1   Testimony 1: Stuart

My wife's crisis occurred in 1996 when she began talking about suicide. In retrospect, I believe the trigger for the illness was a sequence of events. Within a relatively short period of time four of our friends were diagnosed with cancer, and within 6–8 months most of them had died. My wife's father and a number of her closer aunts and uncles all passed away, and then she took on a fairly stressful short-term job that demanded a lot of her time and increasing responsibility. It was during this time that we moved house and her sleep patterns and behaviour began to change. She seemed to become more dependent and needed constant attention. Sleep became non-existent and she was constantly on the go but achieving nothing; as a family we were worn out. At the time we were not really able to understand what was happening and it took us a long time to realise what we were dealing with. The psychiatrist who came to the house to see her made what seemed to me to be a snap diagnosis of hypomania; the only treatment my wife was given at this time was a minimal dose of chloral hydrate (1/4 ml, three times a day). At this time my wife had been running around all day and all night for almost a fortnight. We were all sleep deprived and unable to deal with the situation, but there was no further help.

It was not until we moved to North Wales and my wife actually made an attempt on her life that we got help. May 2000 was a very difficult time; her GP thought initially that she was menopausal and treated her for that. We had told him about her recent behaviour and problems, but she presented fairly well to him and he did not take mental illness into account. My wife then went to one of his satellite surgeries; by that time she was hypomanic so he gave her some mild tranquilisers.

Shortly after this my wife took a number of paracetamol tablets. She was then admitted to the local A&E department where she was transferred to the psychiatric unit. She was in the unit for about a month, during which time I went away for a holiday to get some rest. The week I returned, the hospital discharged my wife and sent her home, even though there was no one in the house; she was sitting in the dark as I walked through the door.

The major problem following the initial admission was that the psychiatrists insisted my wife was well when she was not. The initial diagnoses were anxiety state and depression, then a form of bipolar disorder, and eventually a schizoaffective disorder primarily because of her very odd thoughts such as body displacement. She thought that her head was in the next street, that her limbs were attached to places they shouldn't be, that she had to move her nerves out of the way before she could sit down and that her mouth did not belong to her. The latter caused all sorts of problems and stops her eating sometimes.

In all it took over 4 years and a number of admissions before a diagnosis of schizoaffective disorder was made. By this time the family was totally exhausted. The effect of all this on the family was to make us all less tolerant of each other and of my wife. It is my experience that healthcare professionals do not think of involving the family in treatment plans or even in communicating basic information: we are usually told to sit outside, to wait and then to go home. I have had to find most of the information about my wife's illness on the internet. (It is also an excellent research tool to help find out about side effects of medication.) I was not given any information about self-help or support groups.

The lack of any help from the professionals and the inability of social services to do anything, especially when it came to assessing carers, was annoying. It took 3 years after we arrived in North Wales to find Hafal (who are contracted by local authorities throughout Wales to look after carers for the severely mentally ill); it was only then that I had a carer's assessment. This enabled me to be in touch with others who had similar problems and made me realise that I had to take care of my needs if I was going to stay the course with my wife.

There were continual admissions over the next few years, which meant that the family did not have time to recover properly. The consequence of this is that we have all become unable to cope when my wife is at home. My wife doesn't talk but shouts and she settles only for short times. If we are out at a restaurant she is liable to do anything on the spur of the moment. If she wants something she will get up and get it not waiting for staff to help her; when she's finished she gets up and walks out. She has not settled in the residential home where she is recovering either, and the social worker is now looking for a new placement for her. By the time I take her back to the residential home I am exhausted and the rest of the family are wound up.

Relationships between my son and daughter and their mother are strained most of the time. It takes a long time for a family to recover, some never do, and I can understand why divorce is seen as a way out. I sometimes wonder what I feel for her as she is not the woman I married; this illness can devastate a person, depending on the form it takes and the treatment received, especially the speed and consistency of care given.

Although at this point in time my wife has not been in hospital for a year, she has had an increase in medication as she was showing signs of becoming ill again; she is very difficult to manage when she's like this because she listens to no one and just does her own thing regardless of others. Her current package of medication is olanzapine, valproate and lorazepam, but she doesn't think they are doing any good. No psychological treatment has been offered at all. I feel that it has been a very long process to get to any real level of wellness.

5.3.2   Testimony 2: Leela

I am a carer of my husband whom I married in June 1968 in an arranged marriage in the South Asian tradition. My husband was in his late thirties when we first met. It would not be wrong to say that I hardly knew him. As I got to know him better I realised that while he was gentle, kind, generous and helpful, he had difficulties in coping with work and was sometimes short-tempered.

My husband visited the UK in 1972 to do his law exams and it was here that we realised that there was something seriously wrong with him. He was insecure, irritable and lonely, his sleep was erratic and he would wander around London aimlessly. When he came home he seemed back to normal. I followed my husband to the UK the following year, but our son died soon after. My husband could not cope with this traumatic turn of events and drifted from one low-level job to another. I began to notice his restless and sleepless nights, his increased drinking and non-stop smoking. He began to live in a world of fantasy, imagining being offered jobs in top-ranking firms and also planning various business ventures beyond his ability. There were long periods of normalcy and we coped, but when there was a crisis he would 'collapse'. Eventually, one collapse resulted in him resigning from his job.

Our GP prescribed my husband diazepam and some sleeping tablets, but he soon became dependent on these and would throw tantrums when the doctor tried to prescribe fewer tablets. By 1980, his condition was worsening: he was becoming increasingly argumentative and I would hesitate to go anywhere with him. We arranged to see a consultant psychiatrist privately who diagnosed bipolar disorder. I also got a shock to learn from the consultant that my husband had told him that he had had mental health problems since his early teens, a fact that had been concealed from me by him and his family. Looking back, it is amazing that the GP did not consider my husband ill enough to be referred to a specialist.

My husband was referred to our local hospital in 1980 and was treated there till 1994. The consultant at the hospital, who was an authority on bipolar disorder, confirmed the diagnosis and prescribed lithium and chlorpromazine. The chlorpromazine caused problems, including Parkinsonian symptoms such as a tremor. My husband was seen as an outpatient by the consultant only twice, which meant that there was no chance of developing a good relationship with any one of the doctors, who were of varying ability and seniority, or for any doctor to understand his problem fully and monitor his progress (although his lithium levels were checked). Even though my husband was hospitalised on two occasions (the first when he was under observation and the second when his behaviour was becoming unpredictable), the nature of my husband's condition was not explained to me and the effects of chlorpromazine not made clear. My husband often presented a façade of normalcy but the turmoil was there beneath. I recall his doctor once saying he had to 'peel off layer by layer' to understand the problem.

At the age of 65 my husband was transferred to the older adult services at another hospital. He was reluctant to attend until the consultant personally phoned him and he agreed to see him. The consultant seemed very young to us, but the meeting was a positive experience and my husband became co-operative and trusting. This was so different from the experience at the previous hospital. We both felt at ease and confident of being in his care, and almost every time we attended an outpatient appointment, the same consultant saw us.

The entire culture in this hospital was different from that of the first hospital. It felt more home-like and focused on the needs of a particular age group, with every attempt made to meet their needs. Most of the staff were accessible when there was a crisis. For about 5 years my husband was relatively stable, with episodes occurring only a couple of times a year. A CPN was assigned to him who reported back to his consultant weekly. Chlorpromazine was discontinued and other drugs tried and discarded as side effects emerged. Any change was explained to us. My husband is now on lithium, lamotrigine and quetiapine.

My husband was stable until 1998/99, when his behaviour started becoming increasingly unpredictable. In the end he was sectioned after a series of events following his decision to return to his home country, even though he was not fit to travel; this included trying to jump out of a moving car. He was first admitted to a private hospital as there were no NHS beds available. Here I was unable to speak to the doctor for some days and when I did he said my husband was well and ready for discharge. Fortunately my husband's consultant transferred him back to his own hospital. Here the ward doctor was experienced, accessible and reassuring and worked closely with the consultant. I felt a sense of relief that my husband was in safe hands. On discharge, arrangements were made for attendance at the day hospital, where the standard of patient care was also high.

The months that followed saw him in and out of this ward and followed up in the day hospital. Until recently I could contact the duty doctor in the night or during long weekends in times of crisis and obtain adequate advice. Sadly this has now changed. We are now put through to a nurse manager who usually advises us to take the patient to A&E (which is not appropriate for an agitated patient) or to wait till the end of the holiday break.

125

During these many years, my husband had long spells of stability when we lived as a normal family. But since 1999 he has been more ill than well. The severity appeared to be less, but the frequency of the episodes increased. With advancing age, I myself began to find it difficult to take care of him. I could not protect him from himself, especially in the nights when he used to walk around the house restlessly, sometimes wandering out of the house, leaving the door open. His incessant smoking and the tremors were a fire hazard and he was also constantly falling down, sometimes unconscious. Taking care of him at home seemed no longer possible and we were compelled to look at the option of a nursing home. It was a traumatic and emotional decision to make but there seemed little alternative. The hospital supported me in finding a suitable nursing home, where my husband has been for the last 6 months. He has had several episodes, but to my relief he is still in the care of his own consultant who visits this nursing home.

Bipolar disorder has stalked our lives for 33 years. During this time, my husband found it impossible to find work at the level he was accustomed to or operate in his own field effectively. This made him really frustrated, which in turn led to episodes of varying levels of intensity. Sometimes I found life impossible and threw myself into my own job which I loved. But I was saddened to see my husband's confidence crumbling and that he was angry and sad that he was not the breadwinner and resented my success in my own profession. The entire fabric of our marriage was eroding till there was hardly any 'marriage' left at all. I was compelled to play down any formal recognition of my work and concealed from friends and relatives the nature of his illness because of the social stigma (I told them that he was a heavier drinker than he really was). I was always, however, frank with his doctors.

I did not recognise that I, as a main carer, needed help, though I often felt helpless and lonely in a new country with few friends or relatives to go to for comfort and advice. It was only when my husband was seriously ill at the second hospital that I noticed medical staff showing concern for my own health, although at the time I wondered why. I was referred to a consultant to whom I was able to relate, and a CPN was assigned to me. I was sent to a psychologist for eight sessions of CBT but the psychologist was still a student who seemed to be going through textbook procedures. I found that short sessions with my doctor, in which I was able to open up to a sympathetic professional, were much more useful, together with the citalopram she prescribed. At the first hospital I felt I was an onlooker and I sometimes even felt a touch of condescension in their manner: Would I understand what all this was about? Did I even understand the English language? But at the second hospital, I found myself being drawn into the process of my husband's treatment. The consultant would explain to me why he was prescribing the particular medication and the possible side effects. I felt more of an active participant in my husband's treatment.

This encouraged me to read about bipolar disorder and I joined MDF The BiPolar Organisation. My husband's consultant also invited me to be a consumer representative on one of his research projects which led to an interest in Consumers in NHS Research (now called INVOLVE). I was also directed to organisations where I could volunteer in my retirement and encouraged to take on positions of responsibility so that I would regain my diminishing confidence.

5.3.3 Summary of themes and concerns

Impact on families and carers

Bipolar disorder can take a terrible toll on those who care for people with the condition and other family members. Most carers are partners, not parents (Hill *et al.*, 1998), and the high rate of divorce among couples in which one spouse has bipolar disorder is a reflection of the emotional damage the illness can have on long-term relationships (MDF The BiPolar Organisation survey, 2004).

Both the highs and lows of the illness can be devastating for families and friends, as can the transition from a depressive phase to a manic phase. Mania, and the uncharacteristic behaviour it results in, can be particularly difficult for loved ones to cope with. Excessive spending, infidelity, offensive, abusive or domineering behaviour and talking incoherently are just a few of the symptoms of mania that can cause distress to carers. It can be particularly upsetting when a person becomes manic for the first time because their behaviour can appear inexplicable to family and friends. What can seem like the relentless patterns of the illness put relationships under strain, especially if the normal course of life (including sleep patterns) is disrupted.

Depression takes a toll in a different way. The patient can seem 'cut off' from their family and friends, isolated in their own misery. Their loss of interest and any enthusiasm in life makes it hard to get on with life as normal. Interestingly, partners who responded to a survey conducted in 2004 by MDF The BiPolar Organisation reported that they found the depressive phase of the illness more difficult to cope with than mania. Depressive episodes were felt to be more time-consuming, upsetting and disruptive to family life and caused partners more feelings of guilt and worry (MDF The BiPolar Organisation survey, 2004). Family members and carers may also live with the fear that their relative or friend will attempt suicide. During depressive episodes carers said they felt less able to talk to their partner about how they were being affected by the illness. This difficulty in sharing their worries and concerns with their partners when they were depressed affected their ability to cope with the situation.

Involvement of families and carers in the patients' care and treatment

Partners, parents and other carers can often feel excluded from the care and treatment of the patient. Highet and colleagues (2004) report that families and carers were 'ignored or not actively included in management decisions'. The effect of leaving the family out at the early stage of the illness can create a barrier that takes a lot of hard work to break down. A mother of a 28-year-old daughter who killed herself in 2000 said that she was never included in her daughter's care by her NHS psychiatrist: '*I only ever managed to speak to my daughter's psychiatrist in passing and was never invited to attend one of her appointments*' (interview). Her daughter's suicide followed an episode of severe depression that had lasted 4 months after treatment for mania. Her diagnosis was never properly explained to the family and she was never told that she was at risk of suicide:

> '*Two months before she killed herself, my daughter told me that suicide was not an option for her. I learned later that she spoke to her psychiatrist of suicide*

every week but she never confided in me. I am totally convinced that if we had been kept informed about our daughter's mental condition that we could have prevented her from killing herself. It was a terrible lapse in communication between us, our daughter and the medical services. Carers need to be informed what the patient's condition is and they need to have the condition and the dangers explained to them by psychiatrists' (interview).

In situations such as this, questions of patient consent and confidentiality need to be considered, but it may be necessary for healthcare professionals to encourage patients, where appropriate, to involve their families and carers in assessments and treatment plans. Young patients may have particular concerns about their parents attending appointments and healthcare professionals should be trained in issues of consent and capacity in this age group.

In a survey (1998) conducted by MDF The BiPolar Organisation, carers said that they would like to have 'their role in helping to manage the illness recognised by professionals' (Hill *et al.*, 1998). Indeed families and carers of people with bipolar disorder have a very significant role to play in the management of the patient's condition because they can help the patient to recognise the onset of symptoms and cope with crises. It is important that this is taken into account by healthcare professionals because information that the carer can provide about symptoms and behaviour might help to reduce hospital admission in the long term. Taking note of carer experience also helps carers to come to terms with their relative's or friend's illness, reduces the risk of the carer feeling alienated and also keeps the lines of communication open between professionals and the family.

A survey (1998) conducted by MDF The BiPolar Organisation reported that respondents ranked receiving information and education about the condition amongst the greatest needs of carers and family members. In order for families and carers to fully support the patient, it is essential that as well as the patient they are also given comprehensive and clear information about the course of bipolar disorder and the treatments available (Hill *et al.*, 1998).

Support for families and carers
If patients are to be cared for in the community effectively, then the role of the carers is paramount. This means good access to services and support, especially out of hours. Carers need to be alert to changes in the patient and be able to take practical steps immediately. For this, the carer must be well informed of the nature of the illness, the medication and side effects (see above) and know what to do and whom to contact in case of emergency. It is also important that healthcare professionals are accessible in times of crisis because both patients and carers can be anxious when they seek help and advice. There should be a transparent management plan, which is shared with the patient and carer, and a healthcare professional should be accessible during long weekends and holidays to give advice on the phone.

Due to the episodic nature of the condition, family members and carers require ongoing support, but carers who responded to a survey conducted by MDF The BiPolar Organisation reported they felt their needs were largely overlooked (MDF

The BiPolar Organisation survey, 2004). Because of the burden of care, family members and carers can suffer from stress, anxiety and depression (Hill *et al.*, 1998):

> *'Since my wife was diagnosed with bipolar disorder 8 years ago the pressure of caring for her has led to me losing my job and becoming ill myself with reactive depression ... if appropriate care services had been in place I would probably still be in work' (MDF The BiPolar Organisation survey, 2004).*

It is important therefore that the individual needs of family members and carers are recognised and met accordingly. Healthcare professionals should ensure that if the patient's condition is chronic or moderate to severe that they offer family members/carers an assessment of their social, occupational and mental health needs. They should also be informed of local self-help and support groups and encouraged to attend, because partners attending local support groups report a number of benefits. They said they felt less negative about the illness, had fewer feelings of worry and guilt, and felt positive about their relationship with the patient. Partners who attend groups also report a greater understanding of bipolar disorder and are more proactive about seeking out this information. They report less disruption of family relationships as a result of their partner's illness and experience less worry about the future (MDF The BiPolar Organisation survey, 2004). As with patients, carers put a high value on meeting other people who had shared the same experience (Hill *et al.*, 1998).

5.4   RECOMMENDATIONS

5.4.1   People with bipolar disorder

5.4.5.1   Healthcare professionals should fully involve patients in decisions about their treatment and care, and determine treatment plans in collaboration with the patient, carefully considering the experience and outcome of previous treatment(s) together with patient preference.

5.4.5.2   Advance statements (directives) covering both mental and physical healthcare should be developed collaboratively by people with bipolar disorder and healthcare professionals, especially by people who have severe manic or depressive episodes or who have been treated under the Mental Health Act. These should be documented in care plans, and copies given to the person with bipolar disorder, and to his or her care coordinator and GP.

5.4.2   Families and carers

5.4.2.1   Healthcare professionals should encourage patients to involve their families and carers in assessment and treatment plans if appropriate and make themselves accessible to family members and carers in times of crisis. The needs of patients' family members or carers should be taken into account including:

- the impact of the disorder on relationships
- the welfare of dependent children, siblings and vulnerable adults
- the regular assessment of carers' physical, social and mental health needs.

6. THE PROCESS OF CARE AND PROVISION OF SERVICES IN THE MANAGEMENT OF BIPOLAR DISORDER – GENERAL CARE

6.1 INTRODUCTION

Currently there is no specialist comprehensive service for people with bipolar disorder in England and Wales. The needs of people with bipolar disorder are met by a variety of services because people with bipolar disorder require different types of service from primary and secondary care services depending on their phase of illness, age, function and recent history of illness. On the one hand, acutely ill people with bipolar disorder may require emergency, inpatient, crisis resolution, assertive outreach, day hospital or CMHT care from secondary care mental health services. On the other hand, people who have largely recovered may be accessing vocational rehabilitation and case management services from secondary care or self-help and voluntary services complemented by primary care with no involvement of secondary care mental health services. Overall, people with bipolar disorder value services that provide an accurate diagnosis of the disorder and phase of illness, optimal treatment and crisis management, continuity of medical and psychological care, and involvement of patients, carers and families in decisions about the management of the patient's care/symptoms (Highet *et al.*, 2004). These requirements are the most important principles of care and should be followed in each service setting. This and the following chapter will therefore review the evidence base for service provision that is currently available to service users with all types of serious mental illness in England and Wales, as well as those targeted specifically at people with bipolar disorder. Where it is possible to review data on outcome in service users with bipolar disorder or predominantly bipolar disorder, the evidence will be presented. In each section, the particular service needs of patients with bipolar disorder and gaps in provision will be highlighted.

6.1.1 Interface between primary and secondary care

Primary care provides a necessary and valuable service for people with bipolar disorder because many of them never consult secondary care mental health services or have been discharged from secondary care services (ten Have *et al.*, 2002). Also there is an important role for shared care in those who do access secondary mental health care. It has been estimated that up to three-quarters of people with bipolar disorder do not receive optimal care for bipolar disorder and a quarter of people with bipolar disorder never consult primary or secondary care specifically for their mood-related problems (ten Have *et al.*, 2002).

Improved knowledge concerning bipolar disorder is required in primary care if patients are going to be assessed and managed more quickly and effectively. Changes to the contract of general practitioners from April 2006 will provide an incentive to assess the presence of both unipolar and bipolar depression. The extent to which knowledge about bipolar disorder needs to be improved in primary care is arguable. Around a third of all attenders in primary care with depressive symptoms could be diagnosed with bipolar I disorder, bipolar II disorder or bipolar spectrum disorder (Manning *et al.*, 1997). Bipolar disorder is associated with a high attendance rate in primary care, providing ample opportunity for detection; overall, 10 per cent of patients had a lifetime diagnosis of bipolar disorder but only half received a diagnosis of current depression and none received a diagnosis of bipolar disorder from their general practitioner (Das *et al.*, 2005).

There is no convincing evidence that the recognition and management of bipolar spectrum disorder would confer any advantage to patients in terms of clinical outcome over the recognition and management of unipolar depressive disorder. However, the recognition in primary care and secondary mental healthcare of bipolar II disorder among patients who are traditionally diagnosed as having recurrent unipolar depressive disorder may be important. For example, the suicide rate among people with lifetime bipolar II disorder may be at least four times the rate for unipolar depressive disorder (Rihmer *et al.*, 1990).

In both primary care and secondary mental healthcare a high index of suspicion is required to recognise the possibility that a person with depression may have bipolar disorder. Many patients experience long delays in both the diagnosis of bipolar disorder and the start of appropriate treatment for bipolar disorder, with an average of 8 years from initial presentation to secondary care mental health services (Baldessarini *et al.*, 2003b; Mantere *et al.*, 2004). In one national survey, 70% of people with bipolar disorder were initially misdiagnosed, usually with unipolar depression, although inevitably half of all cases of bipolar disorder initially present with depressive episodes and the diagnosis of bipolar disorder is not possible until a further episode of hypomania, mania or a mixed affective episode. On average they consulted four doctors before receiving a correct diagnosis of bipolar disorder, while one third waited over 10 years for the correct diagnosis (Hirschfeld *et al.*, 2003b). Predictors of a bipolar disorder diagnosis among patients presenting initially with depression are antidepressant-induced hypomania, family history of bipolar disorder (especially if there are multiple family members involved from multiple generations), greater acuteness and severity of depression in bipolar I disorder, a more protracted course with shorter well periods in bipolar II disorder, depression with hypersomnia and psychomotor retardation or psychotic features or mood lability, postnatal onset, or onset before the age of 25 years (Akiskal *et al.*, 1983; Akiskal *et al.*, 1995). Hypomania can be difficult to differentiate from a period of normal improved mood in patients with recurrent depression and from disturbed behaviour due to other causes. Often manic episodes were misdiagnosed as psychotic disorders, reactions to stress or adjustment disorders, or mental or behavioural disorders due to psychoactive substance use, especially in young and female patients (Kessing, 2005). If general practitioners have a high index of suspicion of bipolar disorder in patients with recurrent depression, secondary care mental health services can play a useful role in the diagnosis of bipolar disorder when such patients are referred. Failure to diagnose bipolar I or bipolar II disorder may lead to switches from depression to mania, hypomania or rapid-cycling mood states.

There are three particular roles for primary care in the assessment and management of patients with bipolar disorder in secondary care. These are looking after carers and managing physical healthcare and the lifestyles of people with bipolar disorder.

Caregivers of people with bipolar disorder who suffer with depression and anxiety are high users of primary care (Perlick *et al.*, 2005). People with bipolar disorder have high rates of physical morbidity and a doubling of the mortality rate from cardiovascular causes compared with the general population (Osby *et al.*, 2001; Angst *et al.*, 2002). The mortality rate for both suicide and medical causes is especially high among those not receiving medication beyond the acute episode for their bipolar disorder (Angst *et al.*, 2005). Obesity, diabetes mellitus and other cardiovascular risk factors require monitoring because of their high prevalence in bipolar disorder (Kilbourne *et al.*, 2004; Beyer *et al.*, 2005), as do thyroid, renal and cardiac function in patients with bipolar disorder taking lithium; other health checks are required for people taking other psychotropic medication. Primary care could play a key role in assessing and managing the physical healthcare needs of patients with bipolar disorder, whether they are taking psychotropic medication such as lithium or not. The recently negotiated contracts for practices have set targets for lithium monitoring and the creation of registers of people with serious mental illness (including bipolar disorder) as well as targets for reducing risk factors for cardiovascular disease in the population registered with the practice. Primary care could offer to people with bipolar disorder a number of health promotion services that may particularly help them and may be routinely available locally in primary care such as smoking cessation, healthy eating, weight loss, sexual health, medication use, substance use and sleep improvement programmes.

Clinical practice recommendations
A schedule of physical monitoring tests covering the annual check is in Appendix 21.

6.1.1.1   People with bipolar disorder should have an annual physical health review, normally in primary care, to ensure that the following are assessed each year:
● lipid levels, including cholesterol in all patients over 40 even if there is no other indication of risk
● plasma glucose levels
● weight
● smoking status and alcohol use
● blood pressure.

6.1.1.2   The results of the annual review should be given to the person, and to healthcare professionals in primary and secondary care (including whether the person refused any tests). A clear agreement should be made about responsibility for treating any problems.

In principle, there is no reason why the stepped care and the chronic care models for recurrent depressive disorder developed for primary care (Katon *et al.*, 1995; Katon *et al.*, 1996; Simon *et al.*, 2000; Wells *et al.*, 2000) could not be applied to the management of bipolar disorder in primary care as well. Stepped care seeks to identify the least restrictive and least costly intervention that will be effective for the problems with which an individual presents (Davison *et al.*, 2000). The chronic care model, widely used for diabetes and asthma, requires the systematic follow-up of all patients across the primary care-secondary care interface. The high recurrence rate for bipolar disorder and use of long-term medication, with the potential for adverse effects on both mental and physical health, necessitates such a systematic approach to follow-up for bipolar disorder in primary care. Approaches that have enhanced care for people with mood disorders (primarily depression) in primary care have included additional staff who facilitate medication uptake (Katon *et al.*, 1995; Simon *et al.*, 2000), provide or facilitate referral to psychological therapies (Schulberg *et al.*, 1996; Ward *et al.*, 2000) or both (Katon *et al.*, 1996; Wells *et al.*, 2000). More recently, a wider role as care co-ordinator, liaising with the GP, providing educational materials to the patient, providing informal support to the patient and promoting the take up and adherence to medication has been advocated (Katon *et al.*, 1995; Katon *et al.*, 1996; Simon *et al.*, 2000; Wells *et al.*, 2000).

Some specific versions of the chronic care model have been developed for patients with bipolar disorder (Bauer *et al.*, 2001; Simon *et al.*, 2002; Suppes *et al.*, 2003). These models of care can be employed in secondary care or across the primary care-secondary care interface. The models tend to share the following features:

- development of a collaborative treatment plan
- easy access to a single primary mental healthcare manager (usually a nurse) to provide continuity of care
- access to a structured patient or family psychoeducation programme
- algorithm-based medication recommendations for the prescribing doctor

In addition there may be monthly telephone monitoring of patients with feedback to doctors and outreach care in the patient's home (Simon *et al.*, 2002).

There are issues concerning which additional health professional might provide enhanced care to patients with mood disorders, and also the training requirements for primary care. Traditionally, practice education does not give much emphasis to the assessment and management of people with bipolar disorder. Primary care nurses have multiple and increasing demands on their time while many are also disinterested in working with patients on their mental disorders (Nolan *et al.*, 1999). The appointment of new graduate primary care mental health workers may facilitate enhanced care to patients with mood disorders but their role within the primary care team will need to be clarified and competencies developed (Department of Health, 2000; Department of Health, 2003). Some general practitioners are also setting up specialist mood disorder clinics within primary care (Kendrick, 2000). There are also gateway workers from the CMHT linking with practices that might provide a role in assessing and monitoring the care of people with bipolar disorder as well as co-ordinate care across the primary-secondary care interface.

6.1.2   Emergency care services for people with bipolar disorder

Sometimes people with bipolar disorder report inadequate or inappropriate crisis management (Highet *et al.*, 2004). To some extent the use of emergency care by people with bipolar disorder may reflect the lack of access to continuity of care that addresses their needs (Bauer *et al.*, 1997). The need for urgent emergency psychiatric care in people with bipolar disorder who are at risk of harming themselves or others is reflected in a high proportion of the use of emergency detentions from the community under Section 4 of the Mental Health Act, employed when the clinical situation cannot wait for the process by which Sections 2 or 3 of the Mental Health Act are completed (Webber & Huxley, 2004). The use of these sections was especially high in non-white patients with bipolar disorder and those lacking community support. Black patients with bipolar disorder have higher rates of emergency psychiatric inpatient admission and suicide rates than Caucasians (Kupfer *et al.*, 2005). The use of emergency services by people with bipolar disorder is much more common in young adults than older age groups (Depp *et al.*, 2005). Patients with mania, mixed affective episodes or severe depression will require emergency care, sometimes accessed through ambulance, police, accident and emergency, primary care or crisis team services. In these clinical situations, risks to the patient include (Morriss, 2003):

● suicide (depression, irritability and agitation seen in mania as well as depression)
● risks due to misjudgement and recklessness, (for example, driving recklessly over the speed limit and not obeying traffic signals)
● impulsive acts (Michaelis *et al.*, 2004; Swann *et al.*, 2004)
● other people reacting aggressively to the disinhibited behaviour of a patient with mania
● reckless behaviour involving health risks because of sexual indiscretion, including the risks of contracting hepatitis B, hepatitis C and human immunodeficiency virus
● self-neglect, dehydration and poor nutritional state
● the medical effects of self-harm
● overspending or irresponsible spending of personal finances.

Risks to others include (Morriss, 2003):

● irritability leading to aggression and violence
● abandonment, neglect or mistreatment of dependent, vulnerable people usually cared for by the patient (for example, babies, children, the disabled, the elderly)
● neglect or mistreatment of others at work
● reckless and disinhibited behaviour in high-risk situations for example, reckless driving, operating machinery
● reckless behaviour in those who pose medical risks to other people (for example, sexual indiscretion in a person carrying hepatitis B, hepatitis C or HIV)
● overspending or irresponsible spending of family or organisational finances.

6.1.3   Self-management

Self-management is a term that gives the person with a long-term health problem the information and skills to help them actively manage some or all of the key aspects of their disorder (Palmer and Scott, 2003). Individuals gain confidence from their capacity to make informed choices about the treatments and lifestyle they wish to adopt to manage their health and well-being. When people with severe mental illness, including bipolar disorder, organise themselves to run services for themselves, there can be improvements in social function, partly mediated by the use of more problem–centred coping strategies by people with serious mental illness to improve their social functioning (Yanos *et al.*, 2001). However, there are also potential dangers in giving a person with bipolar disorder too much responsibility for their state of health, at a time when they are not well enough, not mature enough or do not know enough about their illness. A person with bipolar disorder may also develop unrealistic expectations of what they can achieve through their own efforts or underestimate the seriousness of their condition, leading to non-adherence to medication or other risky behaviour (Weinstein, 1982). The principles of self-management in bipolar disorder are embodied in the current NHS expert patient programme. This programme, which is not condition-specific, and covers all types of chronic disease, calls for the NHS to recruit and involve 'expert patients' who have successfully managed their condition. (Department of Health, 2001).

There is a tradition of self-management in bipolar disorder in the United Kingdom and in other countries such as the United States, the Netherlands and Australia. Typically, self-management would employ the use of mood monitoring, such as the use of mood diaries and identifying relapse signatures for the onset of manic or depressive episodes coupled with relapse prevention strategies (Chapter 11). MDF The BiPolar Organisation was formed in 1983 with the aim of promoting self-help and to provide a network of support for people with bipolar disorder and their carers in the United Kingdom. Their self-management training programme was devised by consulting both people with experience of managing their bipolar disorder and professional experts in the condition. The programme has been widely used and is similar in content to psychoeducation programmes for bipolar disorder with demonstrated efficacy (Perry *et al.*, 1999; Colom *et al.*, 2003a,b). However, MDF The BiPolar Organisation's self-management training programme, or similar self-management programmes for bipolar disorder, have not yet been evaluated in any published research. Extensions of MDF The BiPolar Organisation's self-management programme have included a greater use of information technology to promote self-management by the *beyondblue* movement in Australia, and the concept of the person with bipolar disorder as a co-manager or partner with the health professional in the collaborative practice model in the United States (Bauer, 2001).

6.1.4   Collaborative care and joint crisis planning

Collaborative care between the person with bipolar disorder and their care co-ordinator, or health professional organising the person's care, should be the aim of treatment (Bauer, 2001). However, a person with bipolar disorder has a high likelihood of entering a mental state such as mania or severe depression when they no longer have the capacity to make decisions about their care. The person with bipolar disorder may issue an advance statement about the care that they would like to receive. Advance statements by people with serious mental illness including bipolar disorder were ineffective in reducing compulsory admissions to inpatient care, probably because they were not agreed in advance with the treatment team, who may not have felt obliged to follow them (Papageorgiou *et al.*, 2002). In contrast, a joint crisis plan agreed collaboratively by the person with serious mental illness, including bipolar disorder, with their care co-ordinator and psychiatrist reduced the number of compulsory admissions and time spent under compulsory admission (Henderson *et al.*, 2004). The joint crisis plan should contain contact information in an emergency, details of mental and physical illnesses, treatments, indicators for relapse and advance statements for preferences for care in the event of future relapse. In many ways the results of this study confirm the findings of a trial teaching people with bipolar disorder to recognise early signs of mania and seek help early from a provider of the person's choice (Perry *et al.*, 1999). In the latter study, the number of episodes of mania rather than compulsory admission was reduced. However, admissions for mania are often compulsory.

6.1.5   Continuity of care

Continuity of medical and psychological care for people with bipolar disorder is a clearly expressed need by patients and their carers (Morselli *et al.*, 2003; Highet *et al.*, 2004). In the chronic care model for the optimal management of any medical or psychiatric illness, five elements of care need to be integrated:
1. the use of evidence-based planned care as outlined in the rest of this guideline
2. definition of provider roles within an overall monitored system of healthcare (monitored and managed at either primary or secondary care level)
3. patient and carer self-management supported and enhanced by health providers
4. systematically obtained clinical information on the patient
5. provision of decision support by more specialist care providers to less specialist care providers, including if necessary assessment and management by more specialist care providers for a period of time (Wagner *et al.*, 1996; Wagner, 2000).

There are differences between the care of a person with bipolar disorder and a person with some other chronic recurrent physical and mental health condition using the chronic care model: firstly bipolar disorder can be highly changeable in terms of mental state and the speed with which care plans may need to be changed and specialist or emergency services are provided; secondly the person's mental state, insight and maturity may mean that for a period of time a person may not be able to practice self-management, and decisions about care may have to be made on behalf of the patient by a healthcare provider in consultation with a carer (but still informing the person with bipolar disorder of the decision and the reasons for the decision).

At times the provision of most of the care for a person with bipolar disorder who is relatively might well be provided largely at a primary care level, as with most people with recurrent unipolar depressive disorders. Under the chronic care model, the person with bipolar disorder would need regular review in primary care and access to maintenance treatment for bipolar disorder; if necessary, decision support should be available to primary care from secondary care mental health services without the patient's care being taken over at a secondary care level. Such an approach has been shown to be cost effective for unipolar depression (von Korff *et al.*, 1998) and could be applied to well people with bipolar disorder, which is a more recurrent disorder (Paykel *et al.*, 2005). A person with a more unstable history of bipolar disorder will probably have their care organised and monitored at a secondary care level but it may still involve primary care in a specific defined role, as well as a number of different agencies within mental health services or external agencies, such as those providing employment, housing and social care provision.

Clinical practice recommendation

6.1.5.1   People with bipolar disorder (including those with sub-threshold symptoms), whether managed in primary or secondary care, should have continuity of care, and see the same healthcare professionals regularly, where possible, to improve long-term outcomes.

Research recommendation

Configuration of services

6.1.5.2   A randomised controlled trial should be undertaken to compare the effectiveness of collaborative care for adolescents and adults with bipolar I or bipolar II disorder with treatment as usual in primary and secondary care.

Why this is important

There is very little evidence on effective configuration of services to suit the needs of people with bipolar disorder. The answer to this question would allow more specific recommendations on this topic, and so reduce morbidity.

6.1.6   Interfaces between the NHS and the voluntary sector

In England and Wales the voluntary sector has come to play a very significant role in the life of many individuals with bipolar disorder and/or their carers. Varying from locality to locality, voluntary sector organisations provide a wide range of services including bed-based services, through day care and drop-in centres to employment services, peer support and telephone help and crisis lines. It is clear from user and carer feedback that these services are valued by many people with bipolar disorders and/or their carers, although the effectiveness of these services is seriously under-researched.

Voluntary sector provision is rather varied and patchy and its development has often been hampered by problems in securing stable recurrent funding. The most prominent voluntary sector organisations providing services to the bipolar population are MDF The BiPolar Organisation and Mind (the National Association for Mental Health) in England or Hafal (formerly the National Schizophrenia Fellowship) in Wales. MDF The BiPolar Organisation have been running a self-management programme for people with bipolar disorder for some years and also run a self-management programme specifically aimed at young people who have bipolar disorder or who are experiencing extreme mood swings. MDF The BiPolar Organisation provides an extensive network of self-help groups across England and Wales and also offers legal advice and insurance services.

Nationally, one of the directions of current mental health policy is to increase the choice of service provision available to people experiencing mental health problems. The voluntary sector clearly has a role to play in providing alternatives to statutory sector provision, although organisations such as Mind have become increasingly active as service providers, and in a number of areas receive health and/or social care funding to provide day care, residential and other services.

Close co-operation and liaison between health commissioners and both statutory and voluntary service providers is essential to ensure that services develop in ways which are sustainable while providing people with bipolar disorder and their carers with genuine choice. Services provided by statutory and voluntary sector organisations need to become genuinely complementary, comprehensive and non-overlapping if the diverse needs of this population are to be met and duplication and waste avoided.

6.1.7   Interfaces between primary, secondary and tertiary care

The care of people with bipolar disorder can produce many diagnostic, assessment and management challenges (Morriss *et al.*, 2002). Moreover, bipolar disorder has a frequently changing course of illness (Judd *et al.*, 2002) so problems such as antidepressant or antipsychotic drug-induced mood switching can sometimes have dramatic effects. The literature on bipolar disorder has expanded particularly quickly over recent years (Clement *et al.*, 2003), with many new developments in relation to the diagnosis, assessment and management of bipolar disorder. As a result there is a demand for seeking second opinions from psychiatrists or other mental health professionals who have both specialist knowledge and practical experience in the diagnosis, assessment and management of bipolar disorder. This form of decision support is an important principle in the stepped care or the chronic disease management model. The availability of such expertise can improve the confidence of front-line secondary care mental health and primary care services in addressing the needs of people with bipolar disorder.

The development of specialist expertise in the diagnosis, assessment and management of bipolar disorder has been haphazard in England and Wales, largely reflecting the interests of academic departments of psychiatry, clinical psychology, pharmacy and nursing. Some areas of England and Wales are provided for but others have very little access to specialist expertise in bipolar disorder. Where such expertise exists, it is usually in the form of outpatient consultation in NHS centres rather than comprehensive multidisciplinary services, but there are exceptions.

There are a number of potential problems with tertiary care services when they are the only providers of care to people with bipolar disorder living many miles from the service. Bipolar disorder is a chronic mental disorder requiring continuity of both mental and physical healthcare, often from a variety of health and other service providers, and crisis services that can intervene quickly and provide outreach into the continuity. Therefore people with bipolar disorder who access specialist tertiary care services should retain their service provision from secondary care mental health and primary care services at a level commensurate with their current needs.

Clinical practice recommendation

6.1.7.1   Trusts providing specialist mental health services should ensure that all clinicians should have access to specialist advice from designated experienced clinicians on managing bipolar disorder in adults (and, where appropriate, separately for children and adolescents), and on referral to tertiary centres.

6.1.8   Inpatient environment

Acute admission wards serve people experiencing a wide variety of mental health problems as well as bipolar disorder and often have to manage high levels of distress, need and disturbance. Admission should provide safety for actively suicidal, behaviourally disturbed or vulnerable individuals. Admission to hospital can also offer a valuable opportunity for systematic and collaborative multidisciplinary assessment and care-planning, as well as an opportunity for the expert review of pharmacological and other treatments. All inpatient units should seek to provide a safe, culturally competent and supportive environment. This environment should offer patients a structured day, incorporating groups and activities which seek to reduce distress and enhance coping skills as well as also providing appropriate opportunities for recreation and relaxation. Ward programmes, or programmes accessible to inpatients, should incorporate psychoeducation; techniques for enhancing coping strategies, managing anxiety, anger and self-harm; techniques for coping with specific symptoms such as hearing voices and managing medication; as well as other opportunities to engage in other structured activities. Additional to such programmes it is also essential that all inpatients receive regular individual attention from staff. These one-to-one sessions should incorporate a focus on techniques for managing distress, assisting the patient to envisage and work towards achieving solutions to their current problems and to enhancing their coping strategies, as well as providing ongoing psychological support. Effective inpatient care should also embrace the patient's family, carers and friends and ensure that both the patient and the inpatient care team remain in close contact with other professionals and agencies involved in his/her ongoing care.

Patients with bipolar depression may experience a wide-range of problems including profound anergia, psychomotor retardation, marked social withdrawal and self-neglect. These patients need regular skilled nursing input at a number of different levels. At the most basic level, the fluid balance of patients with profound depression may need to be monitored and considerable nursing time and input may be necessary to ensure that they maintain an adequate intake of food and fluids. While depressed, these patients may need time, assistance and gentle support and encouragement to maintain their basic hygiene and self-care. These patients should receive regular one-to-one attention from staff who should employ techniques such as activity scheduling to help them structure their day and gradually increase their activity levels. Staff should assist patients to set realistic and attainable goals that will gradually increase in scope as the patient recovers. Staff should give praise and encouragement for the attainment of goals and avoid dwelling on any temporary failures or setbacks.

Many patients experiencing bipolar depression will have been admitted to hospital because they have become actively suicidal. These patients require high levels of support and monitoring to ensure their safety. It is common for suicide risk to rise in the early stages of recovery from severe depression. Patients recovering from bipolar depression may additionally experience symptoms of pressure of thought and sudden bursts of energy while still feeling profoundly pessimistic. Patients commencing treatment of any kind need to be warned of this risk and advised that this temporary phase will pass and that they will experience relief from their distress within a few days or weeks. Staff need to monitor patients closely for signs of increasing activation so that they can provide patients in the early stages of recovery with increased support and should also maintain increased surveillance of these patients in order to detect and forestall any suicidal acts that they may plan.

Patients with mania are particularly sensitive to high levels of noise, activity and disturbance in inpatient units. This sensitivity, coupled with their increased energy, drive and disinhibition means that they are particularly likely to come into conflict with staff and other patients. Skilled nursing is essential in managing these patients. Their energies can often be diverted into harmless or productive activities. The timely use of distraction, humour and de-escalation techniques will avoid many incidents and reduce the risk of these patients becoming involved in conflict on the ward and thus experiencing restraint, seclusion or rapid tranquillisation.

The administration of high doses of medication to control disturbed behaviour can expose these patients to increased risk of side effects and harm. Aversive experiences with medication in acute phases of illness may reduce long-term adherence to prescribed maintenance medication regimes. With bipolar disorder as with all long-term disorders, it is particularly important to reduce these aversive experiences to an absolute minimum by ensuring that all reasonable options have been exhausted before administering medication against a patient's wishes. Skilled nursing care should ensure that patients with mania are managed in a calming, emotionally warm and supportive environment.

The presence of several behaviourally disturbed patients on a ward at the same time increases the risk of violent incidents occurring and may lead to an exacerbation of symptoms in patients experiencing manic episodes. If a patient with mania appears to be failing to respond to treatment on an acute admission ward, consideration should be given to transferring that patient to a supportive lower stimulus environment such as that often provided by a psychiatric intensive care unit (PICU).

It is common practice for patients recovering from major mental disorders to return home in a staged manner, beginning with very brief periods of home leave, which extend to overnight leave from the ward and then to weekend and longer periods of leave as the patient's recovery progresses. A particular challenge with patients with bipolar disorder is that a percentage of these patients will switch from appearing euthymic or mildly depressed into mania or from appearing euthymic or mildly elevated in mood into depression and this mood switching may take place over a short period of time, perhaps over one or two days. This potential for switching with its concomitant risks means that it is essential that patients with bipolar disorder are closely monitored when they begin to extend their periods of leave from the ward. Monitoring of leave can be accomplished in a number of ways, including telephone contact from the ward, home visits by ward staff, or home visits from CMHT members or home treatment team members. Alternatively, patients on leave can be asked to make brief visits to the ward to meet their keyworker for assessment and support. Whatever system of monitoring is put in place, a degree of co-ordination of services will be required and systems need to be established to identify and react to mood switching and provide patients with appropriate care and support.

Clinical practice recommendation

6.1.8.1   Admission to an inpatient unit should be considered for patients with bipolar disorder at significant risk of harm. The unit should provide facilities for containment within a supportive, low-stimulation environment, including access to a psychiatric intensive care unit. The inpatient service should seek to provide an emotionally warm, safe, culturally sensitive and supportive environment, with high levels of positive engagement between staff and patients.

6.2   OVERVIEW OF CLINICAL EVIDENCE REVIEW

6.2.1   Evidence search

Many of the reviews in this and the following chapter are based on systematic literature reviews of RCTs and update those undertaken for other guidelines. Since few RCTs in this topic area have been undertaken in patients with bipolar disorder, the reviews assess service-level interventions for people with serious mental illness, usually including a small percentage of patients with bipolar disorder. Table 2 lists databases searched.

Table 2: Databases searched and inclusion/exclusion criteria for clinical effectiveness of service-level interventions

Electronic databases	MEDLINE, EMBASE, PsycINFO, CINAHL searched from inception to between February 2005 – May 2005
Update searches	September 2005
Study design	RCT
Patient population	Serious mental illness
Interventions	Service-level interventions
Outcomes	See various reviews
Exclusion criteria	See appendices

6.2.2 Presenting the evidence

Systematic reviews of the evidence are based on the searches described above, supplemented with additional narrative as necessary. Relevant characteristics of all included studies are in Appendix 22, together with a list of excluded studies with reasons for exclusion. These are presented for each topic covered in this chapter. To aid readability, summaries of the study characteristics are included below, followed by a summary of the evidence profile, which can be seen in full in Appendix 23. In all of these, studies are referred to by a study ID (primary author in capital letters and year of study publication, except where a study is *in press* or only submitted for publication, then a date is not used).

Based on the GRADE methodology outlined in Chapter 3, the quality of the evidence is summarised in the evidence profiles and summary of the evidence profiles as follows:

High = Further research is very unlikely to change our confidence in the estimate of the effect;

Moderate = Further research is likely to have an important impact on our confidence in the estimate of the effect and may change the estimate;

Low = Further research is very likely to have an important impact on our confidence in the estimate of the effect and is likely to change the estimate;

Very low = Any estimate of effect is very uncertain.

6.3 OVERVIEW OF HEALTH ECONOMICS REVIEW

The systematic economic literature search focused on studies conducted in the UK, so as to evaluate the cost effectiveness of different forms of service provision specifically in the UK healthcare system. References, characteristics and results of all studies included in the review are provided in the health economics evidence tables in Appendix 14.

6.4 COMMUNITY MENTAL HEALTH TEAMS (CMHTs)

6.4.1 Introduction

One of the earliest service developments in community-based care was that of the community mental health team (CMHT) (Merson *et al.*, 1992). CMHTs are multidisciplinary teams comprising all the main professions involved in mental health including nursing, occupational therapy, psychiatry, psychology and social work. Having developed in a relatively pragmatic way, CMHTs have become the mainstay of community-based mental health work in developed countries (Bouras *et al.*, 1986; Bennett & Freeman, 1991), as well as in many developing nations (Pierides, 1994; Slade *et al.*, 1995; Isaac, 1996).

Surveys of people with bipolar disorder have sometimes found that they often do not have access to CMHTs, with ongoing care outside acute bipolar episodes provided by psychiatrists and general practitioners (Perry *et al.*, 1999; MDF The BiPolar Organisation, 2001). People with bipolar disorder can appear to be quite capable compared with other people with serious mental illness so they may be in contact with CMHTs for relatively short periods after inpatient admission. Unfortunately, patients with bipolar disorder with a history of admission in the last year have a 50% chance of acute bipolar episodes in the next 12 months (Tohen *et al.*, 1990). Having been discharged from the CMHT, a person would need to be re-referred, therefore they may not be able to access help from the CMHT in time to prevent a further deterioration in their mental state (Morriss, 2004).

6.4.2 Definition

The GDG employed the definitions used in the Cochrane review of the effects of CMHT management compared with non-team community management for people with serious mental health problems (Tyrer *et al.*, 2002).

- CMHTs involved 'management of care from a multidisciplinary, community-based team (that is, more than a single person designated to work within a team)'.
- 'Standard' or 'usual care' must be stated to be the normal care in the area concerned, non-team community care, outpatient care, admission to hospital (where acutely ill people were diverted from admission and allocated CMHT or inpatient care), or day hospital.

The review specifically focused upon CMHT management and therefore excluded studies which involved any additional method of management in the CMHT.

6.4.3 Studies considered for review

This review updates that undertaken for the NICE schizophrenia guideline (NCCMH, 2002) which was based on the Cochrane review by Tyrer and colleagues (2002). This review included five studies of CMHTs, three undertaken in London (1992; 1993; 1998), one from Australia (1981) and one from Canada (1979). One of these five studies was excluded on the grounds of inadequate allocation concealment (BURNS1993) and two further studies were excluded as they were primarily studies of crisis intervention teams rather than CMHTs (FENTON1979; HOULT1981). The update search undertaken for the schizophrenia guideline found one additional study (GATER1997) for which there was no extractable data and that for the present guideline found another (SELLWOOD1999).

Excluded studies with reasons for exclusion can be seen in Appendix 22.

Important characteristics of the included studies are in Table 3, with fuller details of studies in Appendix 22.

Clinical summary
There is little evidence that CMHTs have advantages or disadvantages over other means of organising care for people with bipolar disorder. However, they have

Table 3: Summary of study characteristics for CMHTs in the management of bipolar disorder

	Versus standard inpatient care	Versus standard care	Versus CMHT and intensive case management (ICM)	Versus hospital outpatient rehabilitation
No. participants	*100*	*155*	*84*	*65*
Study ID	MERSON 1992	TYRER 1998	MALM2001	SELLWOOD 1999
Diagnosis	38% schiz-ophrenia; 32% mood disorders; 35% severe neurosis; 5% other	56% schiz-ophrenia; 13% bipolar; 16% depres-sion; 16% other	100% schiz-ophrenia and related disorders	100% schiz-ophrenia and related disorders
Intervention	Usually outpatient departments, occasional home visits.	Care plans and reviews organised from hospital base.	Assertive case management, outreach and crisis services, social network resource group.	Outpatient follow-up by consultant psychiatrist every 2–3 months, plus support from CPN, day hospital, OT and outpatient psychology.
Mean age (years)	32	Not given	38	40
Setting	UK	UK	Sweden	UK
Follow-up	3 months	12 months	24 months	9 months

become an acceptable and almost universally available way of organising community care, and have the potential to co-ordinate and integrate care effectively, including the provision of other community-based services for people with bipolar disorder. They may be useful when there is a need for community-based monitoring of the mental state in people who relapse frequently, represent a significant degree of risk, have complex needs or show residual impairment. An overview of the results is provided in Table 4 with the full evidence profile in Appendix 23.

Table 4: Summary evidence profile for CMHTs in the management of bipolar disorder

	Versus standard inpatient care	**Versus standard care**	**Versus CMHT and ICM**	**Versus hospital outpatient rehabilitation**
% Bipolar	Unclear	13% bipolar	0%	0%
Evidence for mental state outcomes (quality)	Inconclusive (no data available)	Inconclusive (no data available)	Inconclusive (low)	Unlikely to be a difference (low)
Evidence for other efficacy outcomes (quality)	Inconclusive (low)	Inconclusive (low)	Inconclusive (low)	CMHTs reduce hospital admission compared with ICM (low)

6.4.4   Health economic evidence

The Cochrane review by Tyrer and colleagues (2002) concluded that CMHT management of patients with severe mental illness was likely to be less costly than standard care. The findings of the economic review in the NICE schizophrenia guideline (NCCMH, 2002) suggested that CMHTs were likely to be equally cost effective compared with standard care. The economic review undertaken for this guideline identified four eligible studies conducted in the UK, all based on RCTs (BURNS1991, GATER1997, MERSON1992, TYRER1998). BURNS1991 compared CMHT with standard community treatment, while the rest compared CMHT and standard hospital care. GATER1997 adopted a societal perspective, whereas the rest of the studies estimated costs related to health and social services.

BURNS1991 and TYRER1998 failed to demonstrate any significant difference in costs or outcomes between CMHTs and standard care. GATER1997 found CMHTs to be significantly more effective than standard hospital-based care in terms of patients' met needs and satisfaction. However, the two services did not significantly differ in costs incurred. MERSON1992 demonstrated that CMHT and standard secondary care resulted in similar clinical outcomes, with CMHT being associated with greater patient satisfaction. Mean costs per patient treated by CMHT were lower compared with respective costs associated with hospital-based care; nevertheless, because the distribution of costs was highly skewed, median cost of treatment was 50% higher in the CMHT group.

The available evidence suggests that there is probably no difference in cost-effectiveness between CMHTs and standard care in the UK.

Clinical practice recommendation

6.4.4.1   Referral to a community mental health team should be considered for people with bipolar disorder who:

- have problems in engaging with, and maintaining regular contact with, services such as outpatient care
- experience frequent relapses, poor symptom control, continuing functional impairment or comorbid anxiety disorders
- are at risk of suicide, or harm to self or others, including self-neglect or exploitation
- have problems adhering to medication regimes or with chronic alcohol and/or drug misuse.

6.5   CASE MANAGEMENT AND EFFECTIVE CARE CO-ORDINATION

6.5.1   Introduction

Many people with serious mental illness such as bipolar disorder have a wide range of needs for health and social care. For most people this will involve family/carers, primary care health workers, secondary mental health services, social services, legal and forensic services, and work and education organisations. Moreover, each service user's health and social care needs will vary, often considerably, over time. For the delivery of variable and often complex treatment and care arrangements in a flexible and well-integrated way, especially when service users live in the commnity outside psychiatric institutions, services need systematic methods of co-ordinating care reliably. Case management was introduced as a means of ensuring that people with serious mental health problems remained in contact with services, and to more effectively co-ordinate the provision of treatment across services and between agencies. The CPA was introduced as a system for the co-ordination and transmission of information between patients and healthcare professionals (Department of Health, 1990). Case management is about the provision of a particular model of care.

Effective care co-ordination (ECC) and care co-ordinators were forms of case management brought in to promote greater teamwork but delivered in a co-ordinated way with a care co-ordinator as a first point of contact for the patient, a person responsible for monitoring and co-ordinating care along the principles of the chronic care model and often practised in assertive outreach teams (AOTs). Thus the care co-ordinator may deliver less care personally than in some forms of case management, would not necessarily have a small caseload, would identify healthcare professionals or other organisations that are best positioned to provide a particular aspect of care and promote greater decision making and self-management by the patient.

Although a key ingredient of case management involves the allocation of a named and known professional to act as a case manager for each service user, whose role is to maintain contact with the service user and to individually arrange and coordinate care across all agencies, numerous models exist including 'brokerage', intensive case management (ICM) and the CPA. Also, studies of case management often use the same term for rather different approaches, sometimes describing assertive community treatment (ACT) or 'home-based' care as case management. Nevertheless, case management, in the form of the CPA, has been formally endorsed as the preferred method of co-ordinating care by the Department of Health (Department of Health, 2002) and all service users with more than one service involved in the delivery of their treatment and care, as is often the case for people with bipolar disorder who have frequently relapsed or remain impaired, are subject to a more intensive version known as 'enhanced CPA'. ICM is used infrequently in people with bipolar disorder under the age of 65 years but much more frequently in people with bipolar disorder after the age of 65 years because of multiple medical, cognitive and social infirmity (Depp *et al.*, 2005).

6.5.2   Definition

Given the variation in models of case management evaluated in the literature, the GDG followed the definition used in a Cochrane review in this area (Marshall *et al.*, 2002): an intervention was considered to be 'case management' if it was described as such in the trial report. In the original review no distinction, for eligibility purposes, was made between 'brokerage', 'intensive', 'clinical' or 'strengths' models. For the purposes of the current review, ICM was defined as a caseload of less than or equal to 15. The UK terms 'care management'and 'care programme approach' were also treated as synonyms for case management. However, the review excluded studies of two types of intervention often loosely classed as 'case management', including assertive community treatment and 'home-based care'. One study was of enhanced case management (ODONNELL1999), which involved case managers endeavouring to work in equal partnership with clients, including drawing up customised recovery plans and focusing on individual strengths and capabilities. Another (RUTTER2004) compared a brokerage model with standard case management.

6.5.3   Review overview

This review updates that undertaken for the NICE schizophrenia guideline (NCCMH, 2002), which had been based on the review by Marshall and colleagues (2002). This review incorporated ten trials of case management published between 1966 and 1997 (CURTIS1992, FORD1995, FRANKLIN1987, JERRELL1995, MACIAS1994, MARSHALL1995, MUIJEN1994, QUINLIVAN1995, SOLOMON1994, TYRER 1995). A further search for trials published since the original review was undertaken for the schizophrenia guideline finding three new trials (BURNS1999, HOLLOWAY 1998, ISSAKIDIS1999). An additional update search for the present guideline using updated search strings found three new trials (BJORKMAN2002, BRUCE2004, RUTTER2004). An overview of the characteristics of included trials is in Table 5.

Clinical summary

The majority of patients in this review had schizophrenia and related disorders. Therefore outcomes tend to be skewed towards those important in schizophrenia and do not include psychiatric symptoms other than overall mental state and depression. Outcomes particularly relevant to case management, such as number losing contact with case manager, are also infrequently reported.

The review found some evidence favouring case management over standard care, but there was insufficient evidence to adequately compare the impact of ICM with standard case management, with outcomes showing little difference between the two, or being inconclusive. In addition, there was only limited evidence favouring enhanced case management over standard case management, and no evidence favouring case management over brokerage case management. There are no RCTs examining the effectiveness of case management delivered using effective care co-ordination compared with other forms of case management. An overview of the results is provided in Table 6, with the full evidence profile in Appendix 23.

6.5.4   Health economic evidence

According to the Cochrane review by Marshall and Lockwood (1998) and the updated economic review in the NICE schizophrenia guideline (NCCMH, 2002), no firm conclusions can be drawn on the cost effectiveness of case management relative to standard care. Compared with ACT or CMHTs, case management appeared to be associated with similar costs. ICM was likely to have comparable cost effectiveness to standard case management.

Six UK-based studies that met the inclusion criteria were identified by the systematic search performed for this guideline (BURNS1999(UK700), FORD1995, FORD2001, MARSHALL1995, MUIJEN1994, RUTTER2004). All studies adopted a public service perspective. Apart from one study with prospective cohort design (FORD2001), all other studies were RCTs.

Two studies compared case management to standard care (MARSHALL1995, MUIJEN1994). Both found no significant differences between interventions in terms of either costs or clinical and social outcomes. However, the studies were characterised by a small patient sample (n = 80 and 82 patients respectively), which did not allow for potential differences in costs to be detected. Another small RCT (n = 77) showed that ICM resulted in similar clinical and social outcomes to those of standard care; however, costs associated with ICM were significantly higher than standard care (FORD1995). All three studies adopted a time horizon of 14–18 months. FORD2001 compared three alternative approaches for a period of 5 years: an ICM programme, an ICM programme switched to standard case management (reduced caseloads) at 18 months and an ICM programme replaced by usual care after 18 months. The study demonstrated that although clinical and social outcomes were similar among the three

Table 5: Summary of study characteristics for case management

	Case management versus standard care	ICM versus standard case management	Enhanced case management versus standard case management	Case management versus brokerage case management
No. studies (No. participants)	*13 RCTs (2333)*	*2 RCTs (781)*	*1 RCT (74**)*	*1 RCT (26)*
Study ID	(1) BJORKMAN2002 (2) BRUCE2004* (3) CURTIS1992 (4) FORD1995 (5) FRANKLIN1987 (6) HOLLOWAY1998 (7) JERRELL1995 (8) MACIAS1994 (9) MARSHALL1995 (10) MUIJEN1994 (11) QUINLIVAN1995 (12) SOLOMON1994 (13) TYRER1995	(1) BURNS1999 (UK700) (2) ISSAKIDIS1999	ODONNELL 1999	RUTTER2004
Diagnosis	(1) 52% schizophrenia; 20% psychotic illness; 28% other (2) 66% major depressive disorder; 44% minor depression	(1) 86% schizophrenia or schizoaffective disorder; 5% bipolar; 8% other	66% schizophrenia; 12% bipolar; 16% schizoaffective disorder; 6%	Severe mental illness

	(3) 45% schizophrenia; 55% other (4) 82% schizophrenia; 18% other (5) 55% schizophrenia; affective disorder; 10% substance use disorder; 13% other (6) 68% schizophrenia/schizoaffective disorder; 26% bipolar; 9% other (7) SMI; unknown (8) 46% schizophrenia; 54% other (9) 74% schizophrenia; 11% mood disorder; 6% personality disorder; 9% other (10) 83% schizophrenia; 17% affective psychosis (11) 68% schizophrenia; 23% bipolar (12) schizophrenia, major affective disorder and other (% not given) (13) 54% schizophrenia; 22% mood disorder; 25% other	(2) 88% schizophrenia; 10% bipolar; 2% other	schizophreniform disorder	
Mean age	36–49, except (2) 60–94	38–42	36	Not given
Number of clients per case manager	(1) 9 (2) 8 (3) 35–40 (4) 10 (5) 30 (6) 8	(1) 12-15 vs 35 (2) up to 10 vs up to 40	Not given	Unclear

Continued

Table 5: (*Continued*)

	Case management versus standard care	ICM versus standard case management	Enhanced case management versus standard case management	Case management versus brokerage case management
No. studies (No. participants)	*13 RCTs (2333)*	*2 RCTs (781)*	*1 RCT (74**)*	*1 RCT (26)*
	(7) 15–18 (8) 20 (9) 10 (10) 8–11 (11) up to 15 (12) 10 (13) not clear			
Setting	(1) Sweden (2) (3) (5) (7) (8) (11) (12) US (4) (6) (9) (10) (13) UK	(1) UK (2) Australia	Australia	UK
Follow-up	12–52 months	1–2 years	1 year	6 months

*Cluster randomised – trial analysed separately
**Total n = 119, but only two groups used in analyses

Table 6: Summary evidence profile for case management in the management of bipolar disorder

	Case management versus standard care	ICM versus standard case management	Enhanced case management versus standard case management	Case management versus brokerage case management
% Bipolar	c.8% bipolar	c.10% bipolar	12% bipolar	Not specified
Mental state outcomes (quality)	Inconclusive (low)	Inconclusive (low)	No relevant outcomes	No relevant outcomes
Other outcomes (quality)	Admitted to hospital favours standard care (moderate) Number of days in hospital favours case management (moderate) Death inconclusive (low) Quality of life (unlikely) Non-compliance favours case management (moderate)	Lost contact with case manager inconclusive (low) Death (suicide or other causes) unlikely (moderate) Admitted to hospital inconclusive (low) Number of days in hospital unlikely (moderate) Non-compliance inconclusive (low) Quality of life unlikely (moderate)	'General disability' favours standard case management (moderate)	Number of days in hospital inconclusive (low)

options over 5 years, costs were significantly higher for the programmes that retained case management services after the 18-month period.

The biggest UK study (n = 667) evaluating cost effectiveness of case management was BURNS1999(UK700), which compared intensive with standard case management over 2 years. The study did not find any significant difference in terms of either costs or the primary outcome (number of days in hospital for psychiatric problems) between the two interventions.

Finally, one study (RUTTER2004) assessed the cost effectiveness of an integrated (internal) model of case management, in which the case manager was a member of the multidisciplinary healthcare team, against a brokerage model, in which the case manager operated externally to the healthcare team. The study, which was conducted on a very small patient sample (n = 26), found no difference in costs and outcomes between the two models of case management.

In conclusion, there is some evidence that, in the short term, case management is equally cost effective compared with standard care in the UK; however its cost effectiveness is likely to decrease in the long-term. There is stronger evidence suggesting that no difference in cost effectiveness exists between intensive and standard case management.

Clinical practice recommendation
There are no specific recommendations for case management in the management of people with bipolar disorder.

6.6 CRISIS RESOLUTION AND HOME TREATMENT TEAMS (CRHTTs)

6.6.1 Introduction

There is a growing interest in attempting to manage acute episodes of serious mental illness in the community, thereby avoiding the stigma and costs associated with hospital admission and providing benefits to patients and service providers. Moreover, from a clinical perspective patients recover at home in the environment in which they will have to function in the community rather than in an inpatient environment that bears little resemblance to normal living conditions. CRHTTs are methods of organising services that aim to avoid admitting acutely ill people to hospital by providing intensive home-based support. However, it is important that staff in these services, patients and carers are realistic about their ability to manage manic episodes, especially when there is little need for sleep or rest, disinhibited, reckless or aggressive behaviour, and there is a need to employ rapid tranquillisation. There are few alternatives to admission to hospital in these circumstances. Many cases of severe bipolar depression could be managed in the community through CRHTTs provided an adequate risk assessment and management plan are devised. CRHTTs need to have access to care plans for bipolar disorder, including those employing early warning interventions, because they may be able to prevent admission for manic or depressive episodes by providing a short period of intense home treatment when the first characteristic symptoms of a manic or depressive episode arise (Morriss, 2004). Even when patients with bipolar disorder are admitted to inpatient units discharge and leave from the inpatient unit may be achieved earlier and more safely through liaison between the inpatient and CRHTTs.

6.6.2   Definition

The GDG adopted the inclusion criteria developed by the Cochrane review (Joy *et al.*, 2002) team for studies of CRHTTs in the management of people with schizophrenia. Crisis intervention for people with serious mental health problems was selected by the GDG for review and further analysis.

Crisis intervention and the comparator treatment were defined as follows:

- **crisis resolution:** any type of crisis-orientated treatment of an acute psychiatric episode by staff with a specific remit to deal with such situations, in and beyond 'office hours'
- **standard care:** the normal care given to those suffering from acute psychiatric episodes in the area concerned. This involved hospital-based treatment for all studies included.

The focus of the review was to examine the effects of CRHTT models for anyone with serious mental illness experiencing an acute episode when compared with the 'standard care' they would normally receive.

6.6.3   Studies considered for review

The Cochrane review of CRHTTs (Joy *et al.*, 2002) included five RCTs. The update search undertaken for the NICE schizophrenia guideline (NCCMH, 2002) found one RCT (FENTON1998) not included in the Cochrane review and suitable for inclusion. The search undertaken for the present guideline found one new study (JOHNSON2005) suitable for inclusion. Excluded studies with reasons for exclusion can be seen in Appendix 22.

Important characteristics of the included studies are in Table 7, with fuller details of studies in Appendix 22.

6.6.4   Outcomes

The following outcomes were extracted following the initial crisis: scores on the Global Assessment Scale (GAS) and Brief Psychiatric Rating Scale (BPRS), plus the number of patients who died, were admitted to hospital, arrested, imprisoned, attempted suicide and were in employment. Scores on the BPRS and the number of patients admitted to hospital were considered critical outcomes. Also, the number leaving the study early for any reason was extracted.

Table 7: Summary of study characteristics for CRHTTs

	Versus standard inpatient care
No. studies (No. participants)	*7 studies (1207)*
Study ID	(1) FENTON1979 (2) FENTON1998 (3) HOULT1981 (4) JOHNSON2005 (5) MUIJEN1992 (6) PASAMANICK1964 (7) STEIN1980
Diagnosis	(1) 41% schizophrenia; 29% manic depressive psychosis; 30% depressive neurosis (2) 55% schizophrenia; 20% bipolar; 3% other (3) 70% schizophrenia or related disorders; 30% other (4) 30% depression; 25% schizophrenia; 13% personality disorders; 10% bipolar; 22% other (5) 53% schizophrenia; 17% mania; 19% depression; 19% other (6) 100% schizophrenia (7) 50% schizophrenia
Mean age (years)	35 – mostly not given
Setting	(1)(2) Canada (3) Australia (4) (5) UK (6) (7) US
Follow-up	6–24 months
Intervention	(1) Home assessment and treatment by multidisciplinary team, 24-hour cover, included pharmacotherapy, psychotherapy and instruction in living skills (2) Counsellors and social workers, formal treatment avoided (3) Multidisciplinary team, 24-hour cover, providing medication, counselling, instruction in living skills, family interventions, support and education (4) Acute 24-hour care (5) Multidisciplinary team, 24-hour cover, instruction in living skills, problem solving, relative support, assistance with finance and housing. (6) Multidisciplinary team, 24-hour cover, patient and carer support, pharmacotherapy (7) Multidisciplinary team, 24-hour cover, patient and carer support, pharmacotherapy, coping skills taught.

Clinical summary

For people with serious mental health problems in an acute crisis, CRHTTs are superior to standard hospital-based care in reducing admissions and shortening stay in hospital; they appear to be more acceptable than hospital-based care for acute crises and are less likely to lose contact with service users. CRHTTs may also have a marginally better effect on some clinical outcomes.

An overview of the results is provided in Table 8 with the full evidence profile in Appendix 23.

**Table 8: Summary evidence profile for CRHTTs in the
management of bipolar disorder**

	CRHTTs
Evidence for efficacy (quality)	CRHTTs are more effective than standard hospital care on some service-use outcomes such as hospitalisation, but clinical outcomes are inconclusive (low)
Evidence for acceptability/ harm (quality)	CRHTTs are more acceptable to patients and appear to reduce death rates (low)

6.6.5   Health economic evidence

Results from the Cochrane review on crisis intervention for people with severe mental illness (Joy *et al.*, 2004) indicated that CRHTTs were likely to be more cost effective than hospital care. The NICE schizophrenia guideline (NCCMH, 2002) suggested that CRHTTs were cost-saving for at least a year compared with standard care, and for at least 6 months compared with hospital-based acute psychiatric treatment, although the cost effectiveness of CHRTTs was significantly reduced in the long term.

Two studies carried out in the UK met the inclusion criteria and were included in this review (JOHNSON2005A, MUIJEN1992). MUIJEN1992, based on a randomized trial design, demonstrated that CRHTTs were significantly more cost effective than standard care, as they were slightly more effective and resulted in cost savings compared with standard care, from the view point of health and social services. However, this cost difference between the two forms of care constantly decreased after 12 months. In effect, in the long term (45 months), there was no difference between CRHTTs and standard care in terms of cost effectiveness. Regarding indirect costs, preliminary analysis suggested that there were no differences between interventions.

JOHNSON2005A used a quasi-experimental design to assess the introduction of a CRHTT in an area with well-established CMHTs. CRHTTs were found to reduce admission rate in the 6 months following crisis and increase patient satisfaction. However, no significant differences emerged in terms of other outcomes such as clinical symptoms, social functioning and quality of life; in addition, although mean health and social service costs per patient were lower after the introduction of the service, this finding did not reach statistical significance.

In conclusion, CRHTTs are likely to be a cost-effective intervention in the UK in the short run. However, in the long term they appear to be similar to standard care in terms of cost effectiveness.

Clinical practice recommendations

6.6.5.1   Crisis resolution and home treatment teams (which should have prompt access to existing care plans) should be considered for people with bipolar disorder to:
- manage crises at home or in the community
- support early discharge from hospital.

6.6.5.2   When delivering crisis care at home, particular attention should be given to managing risk, monitoring behavioural disturbance (particularly during episodes of mania), and the burden on family and carers.

6.7   DAY HOSPITALS

6.7.1   Introduction

The review of day hospitals is divided into day hospitals for acute and non-acute care.

The review updates that undertaken for the NICE schizophrenia guideline (NCCMH, 2002) which was a re-analysis of a Health Technology Assessment (Marshall *et al.*, 2001). No new studies were found. Of the 8 trials of non-acute day hospitals included in the original review, 4 were excluded from the review undertaken for the schizophrenia guideline because more than 80% of the participants had diagnoses other than schizophrenia. Three of these were excluded from the present review for other reasons (BATEMAN1999; DICK1991; PIPER) (see Appendix 22).

Outcomes included scores on the BPRS, burden on relatives (IPD-SBAS) and the GAS, plus the number hospitalised, in employment or died, and the number of days spent in hospital. The number leaving the study early for any reason was also extracted. The number of patients who were hospitalised was considered to be the critical outcome.

6.7.2   Acute day hospitals

Given the substantial costs and high use of inpatient care, the possibility of day hospital treatment programmes acting as an alternative to acute admission gained credence in the early 1960s in United States (Kris, 1965; Herz *et al.*, 1971) and later in Europe (Wiersma *et al.*, 1989) and the UK (Dick *et al.*, 1985; Creed *et al.*, 1990). However, there is no specific evidence that acute day hospitals act as an effective alternative to inpatient admission for either mania or severe depression. In fact RCTs evaluating the effectiveness of acute day hospitals have either excluded patients with mania altogether (Creed *et al.*, 1997) or contain very few patients with a diagnosis of bipolar disorder (Dick *et al.*, 1985; Sledge *et al.*, 1996). Patients with mania may be very difficult to treat in an acute day hospital because of their overactivity, disinhibition and lack of the need to sleep. Acute day hospitals do not provide the round-the-clock support to carers when CRHTTs cannot manage people who are acutely ill with bipolar disorder. Similarly, acute day hospitals may not be a safe alternative to acute inpatient care for patients who are aggressive or disinhibited. Provided these caveats are observed, there may be a role for acute day hospitals as an alternative to admission for people with bipolar disorder, especially in severe depression.

Definition
Acute psychiatric day hospitals were defined by the GDG as units that provided 'diagnostic and treatment services for acutely ill individuals who would otherwise be treated in traditional psychiatric inpatient units'. Thus, trials would only be eligible for inclusion if they compared admission to an acute day hospital with admission to an inpatient unit. Participants were people with acute psychiatric disorders (all diagnoses) who would have been admitted to inpatient care had the acute day hospital not been available. Studies were excluded if they were largely restricted to people who were under 16 or over 65 years of age, or to those with a primary diagnosis of substance misuse and/or organic brain disorder.

Studies considered for review
Important characteristics of the included studies are in Table 9, with fuller details of studies in Appendix 22, which also lists excluded studies with reasons for exclusion.

Clinical summary
Although there is reasonable evidence that acute day hospital care is a viable alternative to inpatient care for other patients with serious mental illness, there is virtually no evidence to support the use of acute day hospital care for mania. The reluctance to include patients with mania in evaluations of acute day hospital reflects the fact that acute daycare is an inadequate replacement for acute inpatient care because of the needs of the patient with mania and their carer for round the clock care. Acute day hospital care is unsuitable for patients displaying aggressive or disinhibited behaviour. Acute day hospital care may be an alternative to acute inpatient care for severe bipolar depression or for the management of rapid-cycling bipolar disorder marked by severe depression and hypomania rather than mania. A summary of the evidence profile is in Table 10, with the full evidence profile in Appendix 23.

Health economic evidence
The evidence provided in the Health Technology Assessment by Marshall and colleagues (2001) and the NICE schizophrenia guideline (NCCMH, 2002) suggested that day hospital care was probably more cost effective than inpatient care for the management of patients with acute psychiatric disorders. On the other hand, there

Table 9: Summary of study characteristics for acute day hospitals in the management of bipolar disorder

	Versus inpatient care
No. of trials (No. participants)	**6 RCTs (808)**
Study ID	(1) CREED1990 (2) CREED1997 (3) DICK1985 (4) HERZ1971 (5) KRIS1965 (6) SLEDGE1996A
Diagnosis	(1) 24% schizophrenia; 51% other; 25% mood disorder – excluded if too ill (2) 38% schizophrenia; 30% mood disorder; 32% other - excluded if too ill (3) 58% depression; 42% other (4) 36% schizophrenia; 64% other (5) 100% psychotic illness (not specified) (6) 39% schizophrenia; 52% mood disorder; 9% other
Mean age	(1) 42 (2) 38 (3) 35 (4) 32 (5) No information (6) 33
Intervention	(1) Staffed by 8 nurses and 3 occupational therapists (2) No details given (3) 2 trained staff + occupational therapist, individual counselling, groups, activities and medication (4) Group orientated, weekdays only (5) Group and milieu orientated, weekday afternoons only (6) Respite programme + 'back up' bed if necessary. (Day hospital is a 20-patient facility with doctors, nurses, social workers, therapists, open 9–3pm Mondays to Fridays. Emphasis on group work, control of symptoms and improvement of daily skills).
Comparison treatment	Standard inpatient care (6) 36 bed unit staffed by doctors, nurses, psychologist and mental health workers, a very active programme.

Continued

Table 9: (*Continued*)

	Versus inpatient care
No. of trials (No. participants)	*6 RCTs (808)*
Setting	(1) (2) (3) UK (4) (5) (6) US
Follow-up	2–24 months

Table 10: Summary evidence profile for acute day hospitals in the management of bipolar disorder

	Versus inpatient care
Evidence for efficacy (quality)	Some evidence that day hospitals are more effective than inpatient care on mixed SMI populations (low), but inconclusive on most outcomes (low)
Evidence for harm (quality)	Inconclusive (low)

was insufficient evidence on the cost-effectiveness of daycare centres relative to outpatient care.

The economic review for this guideline identified one study that met the eligibility criteria (CREED1997). The study compared day hospital care to routine inpatient care for patients with acute psychiatric illness. The economic analysis was conducted alongside a RCT. A broad societal perspective was adopted, including patient and carer expenses as well as productivity losses. The two interventions assessed were shown to result in similar clinical and social outcomes, except that the burden on carers was significantly less in the day hospital group; nevertheless, acute day hospital care was associated with significant cost savings compared with inpatient care (1 year median societal cost per patient £2,880 versus £5,931 respectively, p = 0.001; 1994/95 prices).

The existing evidence suggests that acute day hospital care is likely to be more cost effective than routine inpatient care in the UK.

6.7.3 Non-acute day hospitals

Introduction
There are some people with chronic residual or persistent bipolar depressive episodes punctuated by brief periods of hypomania who may be helped by non-acute day

hospital care providing rehabilitative approaches to improve function, psychotherapy for residual depression or comorbid non-bipolar psychiatric disorder, or to shorten the length of an acute hospital admission for a bipolar depressive episode (Perugi *et al.*, 2002; Kallert *et al.*, 2004). However, surveys of people with bipolar disorder (for example, Morselli *et al.*, 2003) and service data examining contacts of people with bipolar disorder reveal relatively little use of non-acute day hospitals by people with bipolar disorder (Mbaya *et al.*, 1998).

Definition
For this review, and following the review by Marshall and colleagues (2001), the GDG agreed the following definitions for non-acute day hospitals, in so far as they apply to people with serious mental health problems, including people with bipolar disorder:
● daycare centres were defined as 'psychiatric day hospitals offering continuing care to people with severe mental disorders'
● standard outpatient care.

Studies considered for review
Important characteristics of the included studies are in Table 11, with fuller details of studies in Appendix 22, which also lists excluded studies with reasons for exclusion.

Clinical summary
Apart from a relatively small group of people with bipolar disorder with chronic or residual depression with or without other psychiatric disorder such as anxiety disorders, obsessive compulsive disorder or substance misuse, there appears to be little role for non-acute day hospitals in bipolar disorder. When there is a role it is usually for one of three reasons: to provide rehabilitation in people with impaired function, to deliver structured psychotherapy or to maintain contact and monitor patients to shorten the length of an acute admission for bipolar depression. Overall there is little evidence to support the delivery of these treatment approaches in a day hospital as opposed to other forms of community care delivering rehabilitation, psychotherapy or monitoring the patient's mental state. A summary of the evidence profile is in Table 12, with the full profile available in Appendix 23.

Health economic evidence
No evidence on the cost-effectiveness of non-acute day hospital care was identified by the systematic search of the literature.

Table 11: Summary of study characteristics for non-acute day hospitals

	Daycare centres versus outpatient care	Transitional day hospital versus outpatient care
No. studies (No. participants)	*3 RCTs (378)*	*1 RCT (79)*
Study IDs	(1) LINN1979 (2) MELTZOFF1966 (3) WELDON1979 (4) TYRER1979	(1) GLICK1986
Diagnosis	(1) 100% schizophrenia (2) 91% schizophrenia; 4% affective; 6% neurotic (3) 100% schizophrenia (4) 73% depression; 10% anxiety; 17% other	47% schizophrenia; 53% major affective disorder
Mean age	37–41 (4) 16–60	35
Intervention	(1) Employed social workers and physicians and offered: recreational activities, group therapy, counselling, occupational therapy and medication follow-up (2) Individual and group psycho-therapy and medication (3) Group and goal-directed therapy (4) Two different types of day hospital: one specialising in neurotic disorders (well staffed with psychotherapeutic orientation) and the other a standard day hospital (psychiatrists, nurses, occupational and art therapists)	Milieu, family, supportive and group therapy; medication; care management; recreation and dance therapy; discharge planning.
Comparator treatment	(1) OP drug management from same physicians offering medication follow-up in intervention group	OP follow-up involving: group therapy, medication management, 24-hour crisis intervention.

Continued

Table 11: (*Continued*)

	Daycare centres versus outpatient care	**Transitional day hospital versus outpatient care**
No. studies (No. participants)	*3 RCTs (378)*	*1 RCT (79)*
	(2) Standard OP care (3) Psychotherapy-oriented OP care (4) Standard OP care	
Setting	US (4) UK	US
Follow up	3–24 months	12 months

Table 12: Summary evidence profile for non-acute day hospitals

	Daycare centres versus outpatient care	**Transitional day hospital versus outpatient care**
Evidence for efficacy (quality)	Inconclusive (low)	Inconclusive (low)
Evidence for harm (quality)	Inconclusive (low)	Inconclusive (low)

6.7.4   Clinical practice recommendation

6.7.4.1   Acute day hospitals should be considered, as an alternative to inpatient care and to facilitate early discharge from inpatient care.

6.8   SERVICES FOR CHILDREN AND ADOLESCENTS

6.8.1   The process and provision of care

The process of care and provision of treatment for children and adolescents should take account of the four-tier model of CAMHS organisation and delivery (NHS Health Advisory Service, 1995). This is consistent both with the current organisation of CAMHS in England and Wales and with the National Service Framework (NSF) for Children, Young People and Maternity Services (Department of Health, 2004c) across both jurisdictions.

Interventions for children and adolescents with bipolar disorder will usually be provided by CAMHS with expertise in managing psychiatric disorder (tiers 2/3 and 4). However, children and adolescents also require help from non-specialist health, social work and education services, referred to as tier 1 CAMHS. Services may have tiers that are structural, functional or both, that is some CAMHS have a combined tier 2 and 3 service with single referral point, others may provide tier 2 as a stand-alone service.

Tier 1 services include those that have direct contact with children and adolescents for primary reasons other than mental health. These include general practitioners, health visitors, school nurses, paediatricians, social workers, teachers, youth workers and juvenile justice workers. They are the first point of contact with the child/adolescent presenting with mental health problems. At this level, an important role is to detect those at high risk for bipolar disorder and those who are presenting with depression or mania so that these children and adolescents can be referred to specialist CAMHS at tiers 3 or 4.

Tier 2 CAMHS is provided by specialist trained mental health professionals, working primarily in a community-based setting alongside tier 1 workers. This facilitates consultation to tier 1 workers, prompt assessment of children within the tier 1 setting and the identification of young people requiring referral to more specialist services. Tier 2 professionals are usually closely linked or embedded in tier 3 services, thereby facilitating timely access to the specialist CAMHS.

Tier 3 services are multidisciplinary teams of specialist CAMHS professionals working in (secondary care) specialist CAMHS facilities. They should provide specialist co-ordinated assessments and treatments including a full range of appropriate psychological and pharmacological interventions. Children and adolescents presenting with mania, mixed affective states or moderate to severe depression should be assessed by tier 3 specialist CAMHS. Outreach services should be available to those young people who as a result of their presentation are unable to access the clinic base of the tier 3 service and to young people who require outreach work as part of an outpatient treatment plan.

Tier 4 services are highly specialised tertiary CAMHS in inpatient, day patient or outpatient settings for children and adolescents with severe and/or complex problems requiring a combination or intensity of interventions that cannot be provided by tier 3 CAMHS. In general, referral to tier 4 usually comes from tier 3 CAMHS professionals.

A child or adolescent presenting with possible bipolar disorder will usually require assessment and treatment by tier 3 or 4 services. If young people require admission to hospital because they cannot safely be managed in the community, they should usually be discharged back to tier 3 CAMHS or outreach services following tier 4 intervention.

6.8.2 Emergency care services for children and adolescents with bipolar disorder

Young people presenting with mania, mixed affective episodes or severe depression may require emergency care. Children and adolescents under 16 years of age who present to emergency services should be triaged, assessed and treated by appropriately trained children's nurses and doctors in a separate children's area of the emergency department. Triage nurses should be trained in the assessment and early management of mental health problems in young people. The consent of the parent (or other legally responsible adult) should be obtained prior to mental health assessment. In addition, special attention should be paid to issues of confidentiality, the young person's consent (including Gillick competence), child protection, the Children Acts (1989 and 2004) and the use of the Mental Health Act (1983). For this reason, it is important that staff who have contact with children presenting in an emergency have been adequately trained to assess mental capacity in children of different ages and to understand how issues of mental capacity and consent apply to this group. In addition emergency department staff should have access at all times to specialist CAMHS advice about the clinical management of the young person and access to legal advice in relation to assessment and treatment decisions. Out of hours services may be provided by specialist CAMHS or adult mental health, in which case access to specialist CAMHS advice should be the next working day.

Models of care

Variants of the 'stepped care' and 'chronic care' models may be applied to the assessment and treatment of bipolar disorder in children and adolescents. The current organisation of CAMHS function into 4 tiers is effectively a 'stepped care' approach. The higher steps (tiers 3 and 4) involve increasing specialisation and will be required for the assessment and treatment of bipolar disorder in children and adolescents. The 'chronic care' model requiring systematic follow-up of all patients will be required for all children and adolescents diagnosed with bipolar disorder. This will share many of the features outlined in the care of adults with bipolar disorder. However, the child and adolescent with bipolar disorder will usually be living with and dependant on parents/carers, and treatment plans must involve parents/carers as well the young person. Regular appointments should be offered to parents/carers with responsibility for the child or adolescent, and consideration given to the involvement of siblings and other family members in structured psychoeducation programmes. In addition to this, children and adolescents with bipolar disorder should be offered individual appointments with a healthcare professional separate to those with their family members or carers. Liaison with the school, college or other education setting is integral to the successful management of bipolar disorder in children and adolescents. Consent to contact the school/college must be obtained from the young person and the parent/carer with parental responsibility.

In some parts of England the early intervention service (EIS) for first-episode psychosis will have a role in the assessment and treatment of a young person over 14 years old with bipolar disorder. In some cases the EIS will take over the clinical care early in the diagnostic process. In other cases the EIS may work jointly with specialist CAMHS in co-ordinating and providing care and treatment to the young person and his/her family or carers. However, in many areas of England and across Wales, the ongoing care will be carried out by specialist CAMHS (tiers 3 and 4).

6.8.3   Interface between CAMHS and adult services

In the case of children and adolescents with a diagnosis of bipolar disorder, case management should usually remain with specialist CAMHS until the 18th birthday, after which care will usually be transferred to adult mental health services. Increasingly however, some adolescents may be in the care of specialist EIS (with both CAMHS and adult clinicians) where the management of the bipolar disorder may continue beyond the 18th birthday.

Where EIS are not in place, joint protocols need to be in place and agreed by CAMHS and adult mental health services in order to ensure smooth transition of care of adolescents with bipolar disorder from CAMHS to adult services at age 18 years. Handover of care should be discussed with and agreed by the adolescent and family in advance of the 18th birthday. If necessary, case notes from the CAMHS team should be made available to the adult mental health services and with the agreement of the adolescent and his/her family, a handover meeting should be arranged using the CPA. The General Practitioner should be involved and kept informed of the handover process. Consent should be sought from the adolescent to liaise with any other statutory and non-statutory agencies involved in providing care and support. Some of these agencies continue support across the age range into early adulthood and can provide some continuity in the process of transition.

6.8.4   Inpatient treatment

Inpatient treatment will need to be considered in cases of severe depression, mania and mixed affective states when the adolescent presents a significant risk to self or others through suicidal behaviour or reckless acts and/or needs intensive assessment, treatment or supervision not available elsewhere. As in the case of adults, young people with mania or mixed affective episodes have lots of energy and can behave in reckless, disinhibited, aggressive and unpredictable ways. The risk of suicide is high. Alternatives to inpatient treatment include treatment as a day patient or the provision of more intensive community treatment such as assertive outreach or home-based treatment services. The treatment setting will need to take into account the issues of risk as well as the individual and family needs and circumstances in each case.

When inpatient treatment is required for children and adolescents with bipolar disorder, admission should be to age-appropriate facilities which have the capacity to provide education and related activities. The provision of psychiatric inpatient units for children and adolescents within England and Wales is variable (O'Herlihy *et al.*, 2003). There is evidence that in the absence of appropriate provision, some young people are admitted to adult mental health wards or paediatric wards (Gowers *et al.*, 2001). Both the English and Welsh NSF for mental health of adults of working age state the need for clear protocols of care when an adolescent is admitted to an adult ward. The NSF in Wales states that nobody under 18 years should be admitted to an adult ward, but states the need for clear protocols of care if admission is unavoidable. If initial admission to an adult mental health ward is unavoidable, the young person should be transferred to an adolescent inpatient unit at the earliest opportunity. Sometimes admission to an adult ward may be the safest alternative, in which case, in order to ensure child protection, one-to-one nursing care and supervision should be provided.

When inpatient treatment is indicated, professionals need to involve the child or adolescent and their family in the admission and treatment process whenever possible.

Commissioners should ensure that inpatient treatment is available within reasonable travelling distance to enable the involvement of families and maintain social and community links. Inpatient services need to have a range of treatments available including medication, individual and group psychological interventions and family support.

Planning for aftercare arrangements should take place prior to admission or as early as possible during an admission and should be based on the CPA.

It is desirable to admit young people with the informed consent of both the patient and those with parental responsibility, not least because the success of any treatment approach significantly depends on the development of a positive therapeutic alliance between the child, the family and the inpatient team. However, there will be times when the professionals consider admission to be necessary, but either the young person or family do not consent. A child has the right to consent to treatment without involving the consent of parents after the 16th birthday, or younger, if deemed 'Gillick competent.' If a young person below 18 years of age refuses treatment, but the parent (or guardian) believes strongly that treatment is desirable, then the young person's wishes may be overruled. Whilst the use of parental consent to admission and treatment is legal, it is now considered good practice to consider the use of the Mental Health Act 1983 as it includes safeguards such as involvement of other professionals, a time limit and a straightforward procedure for appeals and regular reviews. Alternative legislation under the Children Act 1989 includes using a Care Order (Section 31), a Specific Issue Order (Section 8) or a Wardship Order (section 100).

The professionals involved in assessing children or young people for possible inpatient admission should be specifically trained in issues of consent and capacity, the use of current mental health legislation and the use of childcare legislation as it applies to this group of patients.

6.8.5 Clinical practice recommendations

6.8.5.1 Admission as an inpatient or day patient, or more intensive community treatment, should be considered for children and adolescents at risk of suicide or other serious harm. Such care should be provided in specialist units, designed specifically for children and adolescents and able to support their educational, social and personal needs.

6.8.5.2 Severe behavioural disturbance in children and adolescents with bipolar disorder should be managed as for adults, except that rapid tranquillisation with haloperidol* is not recommended because of the increased risk of extrapyramidal side effects in this age group.

6.8.5.3 Healthcare professionals working in specialist services with children and adolescents with bipolar disorder should:
- be familiar with local and national guidelines on confidentiality and the rights of the child
- ensure appropriate consent is obtained, considering the adolescent's understanding (including Gillick competence), parental consent and responsibilities, child protection matters, and the use of the Mental Health Act and of the Children Act (1989).

7. THE PROCESS OF CARE AND PROVISION OF SERVICES IN THE MANAGEMENT OF BIPOLAR DISORDER – SPECIALIST SERVICES

7.1   INTRODUCTION

The National Service Framework for Mental Health (Department of Health, 1999b) and subsequent NHS plan created a range of new services for people with severe mental illness, namely assertive community treatment/outreach teams, early intervention services (EIS), gateway primary care workers and graduate primary care mental health workers. These services are now found in most parts of England but less frequently in Wales. In addition, NHS Mental Health Trusts have traditionally run lithium clinics and along with other providers, such as the voluntary sector, also run supported employment or pre-vocational employment schemes. With the exception of lithium clinics, these services are not targeted at the specific needs of people with bipolar disorder. However, there are many people with bipolar disorder who might benefit and receive such services. Therefore, this chapter includes reviews of:

- assertive community treatment (ACT)/assertive outreach teams (AOT)
- vocational rehabilitation
- early intervention services (EIS)
- organisational developments
- lithium clinics.

7.1.1   Presenting the evidence

Systematic reviews of the evidence are based on the searches described in Chapter 7, supplemented with additional narrative as necessary. Relevant characteristics of all included studies are in Appendix 22, together with a list of excluded studies with reasons for exclusion. These are presented for each topic covered in this chapter. To aid readability, summaries of the study characteristics are included below, followed by a summary of the evidence profile, which can be seen in full in Appendix 23. In all of these, studies are referred to by a study ID (primary author in capital letters and year of study publication, except where a study is *in press* or only submitted for publication, then a date is not used).

Based on the GRADE methodology outlined in chapter 3, the quality of the evidence is summarised in the evidence profiles and summary of the evidence profiles as follows:

High = Further research is very unlikely to change our confidence in the estimate of the effect;

Moderate = Further research is likely to have an important impact on our confidence in the estimate of the effect and may change the estimate;

Low = Further research is very likely to have an important impact on our confidence in the estimate of the effect and is likely to change the estimate;

Very low = Any estimate of effect is very uncertain.

7.2 ASSERTIVE COMMUNITY TREATMENT (ACT)/ASSERTIVE OUTREACH TEAMS (AOTs)

7.2.1 Introduction

Assertive community treatment (ACT), usually known as assertive outreach teams (AOTs) in the UK, is a method of delivering treatment and care for people with serious mental health problems in the community (Thompson, 1990). First developed in the 1970s as a means of preventing or reducing admission to hospital, the model of care has since been defined and validated, based upon the consensus of an international panel of experts (McGrew *et al.*, 1994; McGrew & Bond, 1995). ACT is now a well-defined model of service delivery with relatively clearly defined aims:
- to keep people with serious mental health problems in contact with services
- to reduce the extent of hospital admissions (and cost)
- to improve outcomes (particularly quality of life and social functioning).

7.2.2 Definition

To evaluate the effects of AOT/ACT, a recent systematic review of ACT (Marshall & Lockwood, 2002) was selected, which identified key elements of ACT, including:
- a multidisciplinary team-based approach to care (usually involving a psychiatrist with dedicated sessions)
- care is exclusively provided for a defined group of people (those with serious mental illness)
- team members share responsibility for clients, so that several members may work with the same client, and members do not have individual caseloads (unlike case management)
- ACT teams attempt to provide all the psychiatric and social care for each client rather than referring on to other agencies
- care is provided at home or in the work place, as far as this is possible
- treatment and care is offered assertively to unco-operative or reluctant service users ('assertive outreach')
- medication concordance is emphasised by ACT teams.

The GDG adopted the definition of ACT used by Marshall and Lockwood (1998), which followed a pragmatic approach based upon the description given in the trial report. For a study to be accepted as ACT, Marshall and Lockwood required that the trial report had to describe the experimental intervention as 'Assertive Community

Treatment, Assertive Case Management or PACT; or as being based on the Madison, Treatment in Community Living, Assertive Community Treatment or Stein and Test models.'

ACT and similar models of care are forms of long-term intervention for those with severe and enduring mental illnesses. Thus, the review did not consider the use of ACT as an alternative to acute hospital admission. The review also excluded studies of 'home-based care', as these were regarded as forms of crisis intervention and are reviewed with CRHTTs below.

7.2.3   Studies considered for review

This review updates that undertaken for the NICE schizophrenia guideline (NCCMH, 2002) which was based on the review by Marshall and Lockwood (1998). The update search undertaken for the schizophrenia guideline located two additional studies (CHANDLER1997; FEKETE1998) and the update search undertaken for the present guideline found a further two (DEKKER2002; DRAKE1998). Studies included had to conform to the definition of ACT given above, and comparator treatments were: standard community care, hospital-based rehabilitation or case management. Inclusion criteria were widened to include populations with serious mental illness since no study included all patients with a diagnosis of bipolar disorder.

Altogether 69 trials were identified from searches of electronic databases, with 23 meeting the eligibility criteria set by the GDG. Excluded studies with reasons for exclusion can be seen in Appendix 22.

Important characteristics of the included studies are in Table 13, with fuller details of studies in Appendix 22.

7.2.4   Clinical summary

Caution is necessary in the interpretation and translation of these findings for application in a UK context since most of the evidence is based on studies undertaken in the US. Also, only 9% of the patients in these studies had a diagnosis of bipolar disorder, and there is no specific evidence that ACT/AOT is more or less effective in bipolar disorder than other types of serious mental illness. When AOT/ACT is targeted on people who tend not to receive services and have little social support or help, such as the homeless, improvements in areas such as quality of life will be from a very low baseline. Generalising such findings to people with much better access to services and/or better social support is problematic. AOT/ACT teams may need to consult with experts in the assessment and management of bipolar disorder for some patients who are not responsive to first or second-line treatments. With these caveats in mind, this review found evidence that, for people with severe mental disorders, ACT, when compared with standard care, is more likely to improve contact with services and decrease the use of hospital services. A summary of the evidence profile is in Table 14, with the full profile available in Appendix 23.

Table 13: Summary of study characteristics for ACT/AOT

	Versus standard care	Versus hospital-based rehabilitation	Versus case management
No. studies (No. participants)	*13 RCTs (2244)*	*4 RCTs (286)*	*6 RCTs (890)*
Study ID	(1) ABERG1995 (2) AUDINI1994 (3) BOND1988 (4) BOND1990 (5) DEKKER2002 (6) FEKETE1998 (7) HAMPTON1992 (8) HERINCKX1997 (9) LEHMAN1997 (10) MORSE1992 (11) QUINLIVAN (12) ROSENHECK1993 (13) TEST1991	(1) CHANDLER1997 (2) DECANGAS1994 (3) LAFAVE1996 (4) MARX1973	(1) BUSH1990 (2) DRAKE1998 (3) ESSOCK1995 (4) JERRELL1995 (5) MORSE1997 (6) QUINLIVAN1995
Diagnosis	(1) 88% schizophrenia; 12% psychotic illness (2) 30% schizophrenia; 70% other (3) 61% schizophrenia; 39% other (4) 37% schizoaffective; 29% schizoaffective; 22% affective disorder; 12% other (5) 100% schizophrenia	(1) 61% schizophrenia; 34% schizo-affective disorder; 5% other (2) SMI (3) 57% schizophrenia; 17% personality disorder (4) 80% schizophrenia; 20% other	(1) 86% schizophrenia; 7% bipolar disorder; 7% personality disorder (2) 54% schizophrenia; 22% schizoaffective disorder; 24% bipolar (all substance use disorder) (3) 67% schizophrenia; 23% other (4) Psychotic illness or affective disorder (n not given)

	(6) 48% schizophrenia; 32% affective disorders; 20% other (7) 42% schizophrenia; 58% other (8) 60% psychotic illness; 40% affective disorders (9) 58% schizophrenia; 27% bipolar; 11% depressive disorder; 18% schizoaffective disorder; 16% other (10) 66% schizophrenia; 15% recurrent depression; 13% bipolar disorder; 12% psychotic illness; 4% other* (11) 23% bipolar; 68% schizophrenia (12) 50% schizophrenia; 16% bipolar; 34% other (13) 74% schizophrenia; 26% schizoaffective disorder.		(5) 68% schizophrenia; 15% depression; 13% bipolar; 12% psychosis (6) 68% schizophrenia; 23% bipolar
Intervention	Case management based	Case management based	Case management based
Comparison	Standard community care (4) provided by a drop-in centre	(2) Standard inpatient care followed by standard community care (3) Standard inpatient or community care	(1) Low-intensity case management (3) High-intensity case management

Continued

173

Table 13: *(Continued)*

	Versus standard care	Versus hospital-based rehabilitation	Versus case management
No. studies (No. participants)	*13 RCTs (2244)*	*4 RCTs (286)*	*6 RCTs (890)*
Mean age (years)	23–40	29–36 or not given	34–41
Setting	Sweden, UK, US, Holland	US, Canada	US
Follow-up	12–36 months	6–24 months	18–36 months
Problems with trial affecting efficacy assessments	(2) Sample recruited from a previous study of ACT (10) problems with randomisation		

*As described in the paper

7.2.5   Health economic evidence

The Cochrane review by Marshall and Lockwood (1998) and the NICE schizophrenia guideline (NCCMH, 2002) reported evidence suggesting that, from a health service perspective, ACT was likely to be cost effective, if correctly targeted on high users of inpatient care. Nevertheless, none of the studies included in the above reviews was conducted in the UK. The economic review undertaken for this guideline identified one study meeting the eligibility criteria that was conducted in the UK (HARRISON-READ2002). The study compared ACT with standard community care; the economic analysis was conducted alongside an RCT and adopted the NHS perspective. No difference was found between the two interventions in terms of costs and outcomes.

There is limited evidence that ACT is likely to be similar to standard community care in terms of cost-effectiveness in the UK.

Table 14: Summary of evidence profile for AOT/ACT

Comparator	Versus standard care	Versus hospital-based rehabilitation	Versus case management
% Bipolar	9% bipolar disorder	0% bipolar disorder	11% bipolar disorder
Evidence for psychiatric outcomes (quality)	AOT/ACT is more effective than standard care on some outcomes (reduced admission, living independently) otherwise evidence is inconclusive or there is unlikely to be a difference	AOT/ACT is more effective than hospital-based rehabilitation on most outcomes (low)	Other than on mean number of days in stable accommodation, there was no difference between AOT/ACT and case management (low)
Evidence for other outcomes (quality)	Fewer people receiving AOT/ACT were lost to follow-up; other outcomes unlikely to be a difference (all low)	Inconclusive (very low)	Fewer people receiving case management lost contact with services (low)

7.2.6 Clinical practice recommendation

7.2.6.1 Assertive community treatment should be considered for people with bipolar disorder, particularly those who make high use of inpatient services and those who engage poorly with other services and so experience frequent relapse and/or social breakdown.

7.3 VOCATIONAL REHABILITATION

7.3.1 Introduction

Surveys from patient organisations show a great discrepancy between the educational achievements of people with bipolar disorder and their employment status (MDF The BiPolar Organisation, 2001; Morselli *et al.*, 2003). Furthermore, work is seen by people with bipolar disorder as an important way of staying well (Russell & Browne, 2005), providing regular structure to the day, normalising everyday life to combat stigma, providing social contact and increasing income. In contrast the persistence of mood symptoms, comorbid personality disorder and poor level of interpersonal social functioning may limit employment opportunities in bipolar disorder (Gitlin *et al.*, 1995; Hammen *et al.*, 2000). A specific issue for people with bipolar disorder is the degree to which they feel able to recognise and prevent or manage acute bipolar episodes because interventions which teach people with bipolar disorder to recognise and manage early symptoms of bipolar disorder have shown improved work performance (Perry *et al.*, 1999; Lam *et al.*, 2003).

7.3.2 Definitions

For this review, the GDG used the following definitions for pre-vocational training, supported employment, modifications of vocational rehabilitation and standard care:

Pre-vocational training: any approach to vocational rehabilitation in which participants were expected to undergo a period of preparation before being encouraged to seek competitive employment. This preparation phase could have involved either work in a sheltered environment (such as a workshop or work unit), or some form of pre-employment training or transitional employment. This included both traditional (sheltered workshop) and clubhouse approaches.

Supported employment: any approach to vocational rehabilitation that attempted to place clients immediately in competitive employment. It was acceptable for supported employment to begin with a short period of preparation, but this had to be of less than 1 month's duration and not involve work placements in a sheltered setting, training, or transitional employment.

Modifications of vocational rehabilitation programmes: defined as either prevocational training or supported employment that had been enhanced by some technique to increase participants' motivation. Typically, such techniques consisted of payment for participation in the programme, or some form of psychological intervention.

Standard care: defined as the usual psychiatric care for participants in the trial, without any specific vocational component. In all trials where an intervention is compared against standard care, unless otherwise stated, clients will have received the intervention in addition to standard care. Thus, for example, in a trial comparing pre-vocational training against standard community care, participants in the pre-vocational training group will also be in receipt of standard community services, such as outpatient appointments.

7.3.3   Review overview

The review was based on that undertaken for the NICE schizophrenia guideline (NCCMH, 2002) which updated an existing Cochrane review (Crowther *et al.*, 2001). There were 18 RCTs in the original review, with two added during this update (Mueser *et al.*, 2001; Lehman *et al.*, 2002), and update searches undertaken for the present guideline adding a further three studies (BEUTLE2005; BRIEN2003; VAUTH2005). All included trials fulfilled the GDG definitions for the different types of vocational rehabilitation. Trials primarily evaluating case management or ACT were excluded. Specific inclusion criteria were age between 16 and 65 years and a diagnosis of severe mental disorder. Trials were excluded if the majority of participants had a learning disability, or if the clients had substance misuse as the primary or sole diagnosis. Trials involving people with substance misuse as a secondary diagnosis to a mental disorder were included. Characteristics of included trials are in Appendix 22, together with excluded trials with reasons for exclusion.

Extracted outcomes include number not in employment, number not in competitive employment, number not participating in the programme, and number admitted to hospital.

7.3.4   Pre-vocational training

Fourteen trials met inclusion criteria, providing comparisons with standard hospital or community care and, in combination with additional treatment, pre-vocational training alone. Summary study characteristics are in Table 15.

Summary of evidence profile for interventions for pre-vocational training
An overview of the results is provided in Table 16, with the full evidence profile in Appendix 23.

7.3.5   Supported employment

Nine trials met inclusion criteria, providing comparisons with standard hospital or community care and, in combination with additional treatment, pre-vocational training alone. Summary study characteristics are in Table 17, with fuller details in Appendix 22.

Table 15: Summary of study characteristics for pre-vocational training

	Versus standard hospital care	Versus standard community care	Versus pre-vocational training
No. trials (No. participants)	*3 RCTs (344)*	*6 RCTs (2241)*	*5 RCTs (561)*
Study ID	(1) BECKER1967 (2) BEUTEL2005 (+hospital care) (3) WALKER1969	(1) BEARD1963 (2) BRIEN2003* (3) DINCIN1982 (4) GRIFFITHS1974 (5) OKPAKU1977 (6) WOLKON1971	(1) BELL1993 (+payment) (2) BLANKERTZ1996 (+psychological intervention) (3) BOND1986 (accelerated versus gradual entry) (4) KLINE1981 (+psychological intervention) (5) VAUTH2005 (+CAST or TSSN)
Diagnosis	(1) 78% schizophrenia; 8% severe neurosis; 14% chronic brain syndrome (2) 38% affective disorder; rest other (not schizophrenia) (3) 50% schizophrenia; 50% not specified	(1) 82% schizophrenia or related; 7% other psychotic illness; 11% major affective disorder; 7% not known (2) 53% psychotic illness; 9% bipolar; 21% depression/anxiety; 12% other; 5% not known (3) 86% schizophrenia or related; 14% other	(1) 100% schizophrenia or related (2) 72% schizophrenia; 25% major affective disorder; 3% other (3) 55% schizophrenia or related; 26% personality disorder; 19% affective disorder (4) 100% schizophrenia or related (5) 100% schizophrenia

	(4) 100% psychotic illness (5) 21% mood disorder; 23% schizophrenia; 33% none; 29% other (6) 88% schizophrenia or related; 12% other	(1) Not given (2) Not given (3) 25 (4) Not given (5) 37 (6) 36	(1) 43 (2) 36 (3) 25 (4) 28 (5) 29
Mean age	(1) 46 (2) 38 (3) Not given		
Setting	Inpatients; US, (2) Germany	All US (1) Psychiatric rehab centre (2) In/outpatients (3) Rehab centre (4) Unclear (5) Mental health centres (6) Social rehab centre	All US except (2) UK (5) Germany (1) General hospital (2) CMHT (3) Rehab unit (4) Psychosocial rehab (5) Inpatients

Notes: *cluster randomised, analysed separately

179

Table 16: Summary of evidence profile for pre-vocational training

	Versus standard hospital care	Versus standard community care	Versus pre-vocational training + psycho-logical intervention or payment
Evidence for critical outcome (employment) (quality)	Pre-vocational training is more effective in ensuring employment than hospital care (although not competitive employment) (low)	Unlikely to be a difference between pre-vocational training and standard community care (low)	Pre-vocational training with payment or psychological treatment or CAST is more effective than pre-vocational training alone (moderate)
Evidence for other outcomes (quality)	Unlikely to be a difference in discharge rates (low)	Pre-vocational training helps reduce hospital admission (very low)	Pre-vocational training with payment helps reduce hospital admission (moderate)

Summary of evidence profile for interventions for supported employment
Combining all forms of supported employment resulted in significant heterogeneity. Therefore, individual support was analysed separately. A summary of the evidence profile is in Table 18, with the full profile in Appendix 23.

7.3.6   Clinical summary

There is evidence from US studies to suggest that supported employment is superior to pre-vocational training programmes in helping people with serious mental health problems gain competitive employment.

Table 17: Summary of study characteristics for supported employment

	Versus standard community care	**Versus pre-vocational training**
No. trials (No. participants)	*2 RCTs (1529)*	*7 RCTs (907)*
Study ID	(1) CHANDLER1996 (2) COOK2005	(1) BOND1995 (2) DRAKE1994* (3) DRAKE1999* (4) GERVEY1994 (5) LEHMAN2002* (6) MCFARLANE2000 (7) MUESER2001*
Diagnosis	(1) 51% schizophrenia and related disorders; 10% bipolar; 39% other (2) 50% schizophrenia; 50% unclear	(1) 66% schizophrenia and related disorders; 11% affective disorders; 14% personality disorders; 9% other (2) 47% schizophrenia and related disorders; 43% mood disorders; 10% other (3) 67% schizophrenia and related disorders; 17% bipolar; 17% depression (4) schizophrenia; paranoid personality disorder, major affective disorder; ADHD; oppositional defiant disorder (% unknown) (5) 75% psychotic disorders; 25% mood disorders (6) 65% schizophrenia and related disorders; 35% mood disorder (7) 52% schizophrenia; 21% schizoaffective disorder; 17% MDD; 5% bipolar; 4% other
Mean age (years)	38 (no info for (1))	33–42

Continued

Table 17: (*Continued*)

	Versus standard community care	**Versus pre-vocational training**
No. trials (No. participants)	*2 RCTs (1529)*	*7 RCTs (907)*
Setting	US (1) Integrated services agency (2) Outpatients	All US; 2 CMHTs, 1 outpatient, others not clear
Length of follow-up	(1) 36 months (2) 24 months	18–24 months

*individual placement and support

Table 18: Summary of evidence profile for supported employment

	Versus standard community care	**Versus pre-vocational training**
Evidence for psychiatric outcomes (quality)	Supported employment, including individual placement and support, is more effective than standard community care (moderate)	Supported employment, including individual placement and support, is more effective than pre-vocational training (moderate)
Evidence for other outcomes (quality)	No data (very low)	No data (very low)

7.3.7   Health economic evidence

Economic evidence on the costs associated with pre-vocational training and supported employment for people with severe mental illness has been rather inconclusive, according to the NICE schizophrenia guideline (NCCMH, 2002). One cross-sectional study conducted in the UK met the inclusion criteria and was included in this economic review (SCHNEIDER1997). The study compared various sheltered work schemes for people with severe mental illness in terms of patients' satisfaction, size of personal social networks developed, and associated health and social service costs. Two of the schemes evaluated involved the sheltered workshop form of pre-vocational training and the clubhouse approach. No statistically significant differences were found in patient satisfaction or size of personal social networks between the schemes.

Sheltered workshops were associated with lower costs compared with the clubhouse approach (mean weekly cost per-patient £273 and £307 respectively, net cost per placement £3,449 and £6,172 respectively); however, no statistical analysis of costs was undertaken in the study.

No firm conclusions can be drawn about the cost-effectiveness of vocational rehabilitation programmes in the UK based on the available evidence.

7.3.8   Clinical practice recommendations

7.3.8.1   Mental health services, in partnership with social care providers and other local stakeholders should consider providing:
- vocational rehabilitation – specifically, individual supported placements – for people with bipolar disorder who want help returning to work or gaining employment
- support to return to or engage with education or other structured, purposeful activities.

7.4   EARLY INTERVE---NTION SERVICES

7.4.1   Introduction

The NHS Plan sets out a clear requirement on mental health services to establish the first elements of an early intervention service (EIS) from April 2004 onwards. Therefore, EIS are currently expected to provide for people aged between 14 and 35 years with a first presentation of psychotic symptoms during the first three years of their illness. Early intervention is a relatively new idea and therefore there are only a few models available to guide service development, for example, Birmingham (Initiative to Reduce the Impact of Schizophrenia, IRIS, 2002) and London (Lambeth Early Onset Service, LEO, Garety and Jolley, 2000) in the UK and Stavanger, Norway (Johannessen *et al.*, 2000) or Melbourne, Australia (National Early Psychosis Project, NEPP, 2002) internationally. Early intervention is primarily concerned with identification and initial treatment. Identification may either be directed at people in the prodromal phase of the illness ('earlier early intervention') or at those who have already developed psychosis ('early intervention'). Intervention with prodromal 'patients'is an interesting but potentially controversial area, which at present is outside the scope of the guideline. The GDG is, however, aware of recent developments in the field that may be reviewed in future versions of the guidelines (for example, McGorry *et al.*, 2002). Early identification of people with psychotic disorders does not, however, fall within the scope of the guidelines. Central to the rationale for this type of early identification is the concept of duration of untreated, psychosis (DUP). A number of researchers have reported that the longer the psychosis goes untreated, the poorer the prognosis (for example, Loebel *et al.*, 1992, McGorry *et al.*, 1996). This finding has led them to argue that new services are required to reduce the length of time people with psychosis remain undiagnosed and untreated.

Moreover they have argued that these services should offer specialised phase-specific treatment to their clients to maximise their chances of recovery.

There is little specific literature on EIS for bipolar disorder but there is plenty of evidence that a significant proportion of patients have a poor functional outcome, high risk of suicide, high prevalence of comorbid diagnoses, long delay until treatment starts and poorer outcome from treatment after the first manic episode (Conus and McGorry, 2002). Therefore, there is every reason to suppose that EIS will be as helpful to young people with first- or second-episode bipolar disorder as other forms of psychosis.

7.4.2 Definitions

EIS are multidisciplinary teams of community-based mental health workers who specifically seek to engage young people with early symptoms of psychotic illness in a range of treatment options so that the DUP is reduced.

7.4.3 Review overview

The review was based on one by Marshall and Lockwood (2003). This had four included studies with a further two being identified though update searches (KUIPERS2004; CRAIG2005 (LEO study)). Extracted outcomes included symptom status, general functioning, admission and leaving treatment early.

7.4.4 Studies considered for review

Six trials met inclusion criteria, providing comparisons with standard hospital or community care and, in combination with additional treatment, EIS alone. Summary study characteristics are in Table 19, with fuller details in Appendix 22.

7.4.5 Clinical summary

There is some evidence that early intervention is effective in people with first-episode psychosis (although very little evidence in people with bipolar disorder) in terms of reducing the loss of young people with psychosis to follow-up and preventing read-mission. The findings are not robust and require replication.

To reduce the DUP, the Scandinavian study (TIPS) design compared a sector with a specialist early detection system against two other sectors that relied on the existing detection and referral system. The enhanced detection system managed to reduce DUP from 1.5 years (mean) to 0.5 years.

There is increasing interest in investigating the possible connections between DUP and prognosis, but this is complicated by issues such as severity of symptoms

Table 19: Summary of study characteristics for EIS

care	Specific prevention intervention versus needs-based intervention	First episode family intervention versus standard care	First episode family intervention + individual intervention versus individual intervention	EIS versus standard
No. studies (No. participants)	1 RCT (59)	2 RCTs (630)	1 RCT (76)	2 RCTs (203)
Study ID	MCGORRY2002	(1) JORGENSEN2000 (OPUS) (2) ZHANG1994	LINSZEN1996	(1) CRAIG2005 (LEO) (2) KIUPERS2004
Diagnosis	At risk of progressing to first-episode psychotic disorder	100% schizophrenia; first episode	55% schizophrenia; 21% schizoaffective disorder; 24% other psychotic disorders All first episode	Schizophrenia or related, first episode (2) 6% bipolar
Mean age	20	(1) 26 (2) 34	21	26–28
Intervention	Low-dose risperidone + CBT	(1) ACT enhanced with family involvement and social skills training, allocated case worker providing support and encouragement	Individual therapy – education about illness, identifying prodromal signs, sources of stress and coping methods	(1) Multidisciplinary team, AOT with extended hours, medication, CBT, family counselling and vocational strategies

Continued

185

Table 19: (*Continued*)

	Specific prevention intervention vs needs-based intervention	First episode family intervention vs standard care	First episode family intervention + individual intervention vs individual intervention	EIS vs standard care
No. studies (*No. participants*)	*1 RCT (59)*	*2 RCTs (630)*	*1 RCT (76)*	*2 RCTs (203)*
		(2) Group sessions every 3 months including discussion of illness management, importance of medication, life events, coping strategies	Family therapy – psychoeducation, communication training, problem solving, role rehearsal and modelling	(2) Medication review and monitoring, vocational and benefits help, information about psychosis, individual therapy for positive symptoms (CBT), family meetings, 24-hour crisis care – low case-load per team (<12) compared with comparator treatment (up to 35)
Setting	US; inpatients	(1) Denmark; in/out patients (2) China	Holland; inpatients	UK; CMHT referrals
Follow-up	12 months	(1) 2 years (2) 18 months	1 and 5 years	(1) 18 months (2) 12 months

and duration thresholds, and also in developing and evaluating means of shortening DUP through early identification and intervention. The rationale for EIS is powerful, both ethically (helping people with serious mental health problems at an early stage to reduce distress and possibly disability) and in terms of choice (service users and carers want help sooner than is usually currently available). However, there are some important questions that are still to be answered such as whether reducing DUP will alter the prognosis for people with psychosis, including bipolar disorder.

A summary of the evidence profile is in Table 20, with full results in Appendix 23.

7.4.6 Health economic evidence

None of the randomised clinical trials included in the Cochrane review by Marshall and Lockwood (2003) on EIS for patients with psychosis reported costs of services. The NICE schizophrenia guideline (NCCMH, 2002) also reported poor evidence on the cost-effectiveness of these services. The systematic search for economic evidence conducted for this guideline failed to identify any relevant economic studies conducted in the UK. Therefore, conclusions on the cost-effectiveness of early interventions in the UK cannot be drawn.

7.4.7 Clinical practice recommendations

7.4.7.1 Early intervention services for people with psychosis should be available to people with bipolar disorder and should provide specialist expertise in diagnosis, and pharmacological, psychological, social, occupational and educational interventions.

7.5 ORGANISATIONAL DEVELOPMENTS

7.5.1 Introduction

Since the late 1980s, there has been a growing interest primarily from North America in the development of systems of care for managing depression. This work has been influenced by organisational developments in healthcare in the United States, such as managed care and health maintenance organisations (Katon *et al.*, 1999), developments in the treatment of depression, the development of stepped care (Davison, 2000), and influences from physical healthcare, for example chronic disease management. A significant factor in driving these developments has been the recognition that, for many people, depression is a chronic and disabling disorder.

A similar process is now taking place in the UK, fuelled in part by the advent of primary care organisations in the NHS. A key challenge in reviewing this literature is the translation of findings from non-UK settings to the NHS in England and Wales.

Table 20: Summary of evidence profile for EIS

	Specific prevention intervention versus needs-based intervention	First-episode family intervention versus standard care	First-episode family intervention + individual intervention versus individual intervention	EIS versus standard care
Evidence for psychiatric outcomes (quality)	Inconclusive (low)	First-episode family intervention more effective than standard care (moderate)	Inconclusive (low)	Inconclusive (low)
Evidence for other outcomes (quality)	No data	First-episode family intervention reduces rehospitalisation compared with standard care (moderate)	No data	Early intervention reduces rehospitalisation compared with standard care (moderate)

Other international developments, for example the development of crisis intervention teams, have also been led by non-UK base services, for example in the United States (Stein & Test, 1980) and Australia (Hoult *et al.*, 1983), although their place in the UK healthcare system is more developed (see the role of crisis services in the National Service Framework, Department of Health, 1999b) than managed care systems for the treatment of depression.

7.5.2   Definitions

- There are many terms used to describe the interventions covered in this section and they are often used interchangeably in this area. For the purposes of the guideline, we identified a series of interventions that we consider to be of most relevance to the NHS. They included telephone support, guideline implementation, development in the roles of mental health specialists and primary care staff, and multifaceted care (where a number of different models are delivered concurrently). These approaches may or may not be provided within the context of a fixed budget (for example, the Health Maintenance Organisation (HMO) in the USA). Other terms subsumed within the definition are: collaborative care, stepped care, enhanced care and integrated care.

7.5.3   Interventions included

- The term 'organisational developments' was used as an umbrella term to cover all interventions considered in this section.
- Multifaceted care – this was defined as any systematic approach to the treatment of mood disorder that combined any standard treatment approach with any of the following approaches to the management of depression: telephone contact, specialist assessment or consultation, professional or paraprofessional role development and guideline implementation.
- Multifaceted care with telephone support – this was defined as an augmentation of a therapeutic intervention designed to improve the effectiveness of the intervention; it usually consisted of a limited number of telephone contacts that had a facilitative and monitoring function.
- Guideline implementation – this was defined as any intervention designed to support the implementation of guideline recommendations.
- Nurse-led care (either primary care or specialist nurses) – this was defined as any intervention which placed a specific role or responsibility on a nurse (either a practice or specialist nurse) for the implementation of whole or part of an intervention.
- Drug therapy management – focused on managing medication plus psychoeducation and follow-up including telephone contact.

7.5.4 Organisational developments: studies considered

Sixteen trials of organisational developments (versus standard care) met the eligibility criteria set by the GDG. Excluded studies with reasons for exclusion can be seen in Appendix 22. Important characteristics of the included studies are in Table 21, with fuller details of studies in Appendix 22.

Clinical summary

The complex nature of many of the interventions covered in this section makes for difficult interpretation. This is exacerbated by the fact that the majority of trials are not in patients with a diagnosis of bipolar disorder, and most of the large well-conducted studies have been undertaken almost exclusively in the US, leading to considerable caution in extrapolating their findings to the UK setting. However, three key findings emerge from the review.

First, multifaceted care has a number of benefits for the treatment and care of mood disorders. Although there was considerable variation in both the nature of the populations covered and the complexity of the interventions, these programmes have a number of shared characteristics that are common to most if not all of the studies. These include a system-based approach to the delivery of care focusing on all levels of the primary care organisation; the use of clear protocols to guide professional practice (for example, medication protocols) and facilitate inter-professional communication; a stepped approach to care; and the development of specific staff roles (for example, depression care managers). There has also been an increasing trend in these studies towards the use of para-professional or non-specialist mental health staff.

Second, there appears to be no support for guideline implementation programmes as single interventions for improving outcomes for people with depression. This finding is consistent with another review (Von Korff & Goldberg, 2001), which recommends a multi-modal (or multifaceted) approach to guideline implementation.

Third, the evidence for an enhanced role for nurses working in primary care in the care of depression in interventions is equivocal. It is possible that this reflects differences among healthcare systems; the results in the US looked better, but this could reflect some other difference than just the characteristics of the healthcare system. One such possibility is that the enhanced nurse interventions in the US appeared to have a more system-based approach and were supported by the protocols that may well play an important part in the success of multifaceted care. Clearly this area needs further research.

An overview of results is provided in Table 22, with further details in Appendix 23.

Table 21: Summary of study characteristics for organisational developments compared with standard care in the management of bipolar disorder

	Multifaceted intervention	Multifaceted intervention with telephone support	Nurse-led care	Drug therapy management	Guideline Implementation
No. trials (No. participants)	*5 RCTs (2829)*	*3 RCTs (1440)*	*3 RCTs (920)*	*1 RCTs (125)*	*4 RCTs (2573)*
Study IDs	(1) ARAYA2003 (2) KATON1996 (3) KATON1999 (4) KATZELNICK 2000 (5) UNUTZER2002	(1) KATON2001 (2) SIMON2000A (3) SIMON2005	(1) BLANCHARD 1995 (2) DIETRICH 2004A (3) MANN1998	FINLEY2003	(1) BAKER2001 (2) ROLLMAN (3) ROST (4) WELLS2000
Diagnosis	Major depression (2) Depression (diagnosis uncertain)	(1) Depression (2) Depression (diagnosis uncertain) (3) 35% bipolar I; 65% bipolar II	(1) (3) Depression (diagnosis uncertain) (2) 79% Major depressive disorder; 2% dysthymia	79% Major depressive disorder; 2% dysthymia	Depression (diagnosis uncertain)
Setting	All US apart from (1) Chile	US	(1) (3) UK (2) US	US	All US apart from (1) UK
Mean age	(1) 43 (2) 44 (3) 46 (4) 45 (5) 71	(1) 45 (2) 46 (3) 44	(1) 75 (2) 42 (3) 18–74	54	41

Continued

191

Table 21: (*Continued*)

	Multifaceted intervention	Multifaceted intervention with telephone support	Nurse-led Care	Drug therapy management	Guideline Implementation
No. trials (No. participants)	5 RCTs (2829)	3 RCTs (1440)	3 RCTs (920)	1 RCTs (125)	4 RCTs (2573)
Length of trial	(1) 6 months + 3 months follow-up (2) 6 months (3) 8 months (4) 1 year (5) 1 year	(1) 1 year (2) 6 months (3) 1 year	(1) 3 months (2) (3) 6 months	6 months	18 months
Intervention	(1) Psychoeducation, monitoring pharmacotherapy (2) Psychoeducation, pharmacotherapy (3) Psychoeducation, pharmacotherapy (4) Psychoeducation, pharmacotherapy (5) Psychoeducation (later life depression), relapse prevention, support	(1) Psychoeducation, relapse prevention, telephone support (2) Monitoring, telephone support (3) Psychoeducation (groups), monitoring, telephone support, pharmacotherapy	(1) Weekly visits for 3 months, intervention negotiated by patient (2) Weekly telephone support, encouraging self-management (3) Regular contact with nurse	Clinical pharmacists monitored medication and provided telephone support	(1) Clinician interviewed to assess obstacles to implementation (2) Clinician received advisory message at each clinic visit (3) Clinician intervention training (4) Clinician training in medication and therapy
Other	(4) Cluster randomised - analysed separately		(2) Cluster randomised – analysed separately; specifically excluded bipolar disorder		All cluster randomised

Table 22: Summary of evidence profile for organisational developments in the management of bipolar disorder

	Multifaceted intervention	Multifaceted intervention with telephone support	Nurse-led care	Drug therapy	Guideline implementation
Evidence for psychiatric outcomes (quality)	More effective than usual care (low)	More effective than usual care (low) (inconclusive (low) for study of bipolar patients)	Unlikely to be any advantage (low)	Inconclusive (very low)	Unlikely to be a difference (very low)
Evidence for other outcomes (quality)	Fewer people leave usual care than multifaceted intervention (moderate)	Inconclusive (low)	Fewer people leave usual care than nurse care (moderate)	No data	Inconclusive (very low)

7.5.5   Clinical practice recommendations

7.5.5.1   All GP practices should include people with a diagnosis of bipolar disorder in their case register of people with severe mental illness.

7.5.5.2   Primary and secondary care organisations should consider establishing integrated care programmes for people with bipolar disorder. These should include:
- regular reviews in primary and secondary care of mental state, and personal and social functioning, to ensure that symptoms (including sub-threshold symptoms) are treated if they significantly impair social functioning
- clear protocols for the delivery and monitoring of pharmacological, psychosocial and psychological interventions
- clear agreements between healthcare professionals on their responsibilities for assessment, monitoring and treatment
- written treatment plans that promote the principles of self-management, and are shared with the patient and, where appropriate, with families and carers.

7.5.5.3   Primary care teams should consider providing telephone support to patients with bipolar disorder, by appropriately trained staff using clear protocols, in particular for monitoring medication regimes.

7.6   LITHIUM CLINICS

Since the late 1960s lithium clinics have been introduced to provide systematic care to people with bipolar disorder who take lithium, in view of its potential toxicity (Bey *et al.*, 1972). Typically the lithium clinic is situated in the psychiatric outpatient department of a local hospital or community mental health centre and is staffed by a psychiatrist with a nurse or other health professional (Ellenberg *et al.*, 1980). Occasionally the lithium clinic is staffed by a pharmacist, utilising pharmacist skills and providing an efficient lithium monitoring service (Courtney *et al.*, 1995). Sometimes the lithium clinic is used for psychoeducation of the patient with bipolar disorder and their carer, with demonstrated improvements in the knowledge about, lithium and the underlying disorder (Cochran, 1984; Peet & Harvey, 1991; van Gent *et al.*, 1991). In the United States, the lithium clinic has been a site for the provision of individual or group psychotherapy (Gitlin & Jamison, 1984).

In the United Kingdom the number of lithium clinics has probably declined for a number of reasons:
1. A psychiatric outpatient service may appear anachronistic in the days of community-focused mental health services.
2. The needs of patients with bipolar disorder, have been assumed to be similar to the needs of patients with schizophrenia and recurrent severe depressive disorder, so services are developed for serious mental illness as a whole.
3. Prophylactic agents other than lithium are being used, although all of them require careful monitoring to prevent harm and produce optimal benefits.

4. Resources have been diverted away from non-mandatory services such as lithium clinics towards the mandatory development of new services such as assertive outreach, early intervention and CRHTTs.

Nevertheless, there is a body of evidence on lithium clinics that suggests they may serve the needs of some patients with bipolar disorder well. For instance compared with patients supervised in general practice, the lithium clinic maintained lower levels of lithium, checked lithium levels and renal function more frequently and more often prescribed lithium at lower doses and several times per day when there was evidence of renal impairment (Masterton *et al.*, 1988). However, services for people with serious mental illness may serve some patients with bipolar disorder better, particularly those who have not done well in lithium clinics such as those with comorbid substance misuse and a history of non-attendance at appointments and poor adherence to medication (Kallner *et al.*, 2000).

Naturalistic studies suggest that patients with bipolar disorder who remain in contact with secondary care lithium clinics may do better than patients with bipolar disorder who do not remain in contact with such services in terms of recurrence rates, function, suicide attempts and mortality both from suicide and all causes (Ahrens *et al.*, 1995; Kallner *et al.*, 2000). It should also be noted that a recent review suggests that long-term lithium treatment is effective in preventing suicide, deliberate self-harm and deaths from all causes compared with placebo or other active treatments (Cipriani *et al.*, 2005). The precise reasons for the improved outcomes are unclear but likely explanations include the effectiveness of lithium as a prophylactic agent, the systematic care and follow-up provided by the clinics and by healthcare professionals with a knowledge and interest in bipolar disorder, the opportunities for psychoeducation about lithium and bipolar disorder, and selection and direction of resources to people with bipolar disorder who have better outcomes.

The availability of efficacious psychological treatments, including psychoeducation, and apparent success of lithium clinics in secondary care services in terms of reducing morbidity and mortality, has encouraged the development of enhanced care based on the chronic care model in secondary care mental health services (Bauer *et al.*, 2001; Simon *et al.*, 2002; Suppes *et al.*, 2003). In secondary care mental health services psychosocial interventions are most likely to be used by patients with bipolar disorder who also have personality disorders, alcohol and drug misuse disorders, anxiety disorders, poorer psychosocial function and are unmarried (Lembke *et al.*, 2004).

7.6.1   Clinical practice recommendation

7.6.1.1   Enhanced multiprofessional outpatient clinics, such as lithium clinics, should be considered for patients who would benefit from close monitoring, and/or have a physical health risk such as renal damage, and have a record of regular attendance without the need for outreach services.

8. THE MEDICAL AND PHARMACOLOGICAL MANAGEMENT OF BIPOLAR DISORDER – PART I

8.1 INTRODUCTION

Effective pharmacological treatment of bipolar disorder requires treatment of depressive and manic/hypomanic episodes together with long-term treatment to prevent future episodes, both syndromal and sub-syndromal. In recent years the importance of long-term treatment (that is, maintenance treatment) has been emphasised by several guidelines. The need for maintenance treatment is supported by the desire to prevent the costs of future episodes, that is, the intangible suffering to patients and their families and the economic burden of direct and indirect costs. In addition maintenance treatment may reduce long-term impairment associated with the bipolar disorder. There is evidence that functional impairment in patients who have recovered from acute episodes and are asymptomatic is related to the number of previous depressive episodes. The tendency for episodes to become more frequent with time also supports the rationale for maintenance treatment.

In the last decade, evidence from RCTs has accumulated regarding the effectiveness of several 'new' agents in the treatment of bipolar disorder. These include valproate (in various forms), lamotrigine and various atypical antipsychotics. The active control arms in several such studies have provided further evidence for the efficacy of 'older' treatments, in particular haloperidol (a conventional antipsychotic) in the treatment of mania and lithium in the prophylaxis of mania.

8.1.1 Methodological issues in RCTs

It is important to acknowledge that the RCT evidence base in bipolar disorder has a number of weaknesses which can be summarised as follows:

- Dominance of industry-sponsored studies: most studies are sponsored by the pharmaceutical industry. Such studies are more likely to report results that favour the sponsor's product than are independent studies. This may reflect publication bias or design bias.
- Restricted entry criteria: RCTs tend to have strict inclusion and exclusion criteria. For example, patients with significant suicidal ideation or drug/alcohol misuse are often excluded. A recent study estimated that only 16% of a consecutive series of patients hospitalised for mania or a mixed episode would qualify to enter a standard placebo-controlled RCT in acute mania (Storosum *et al.*, 2004).

Consequently it is arguable how representative the results are regarding many patients treated in clinical practice.

- Short duration: most RCTs in mania range from 3 to 6 weeks in length. In practice many patients take longer to respond.

- Enriched samples: long-term maintenance studies usually recruit patients in either a depressive phase or manic phase and then randomise those who respond to acute treatment for the maintenance phase of the study. This design inevitably means that the sample is pre-selected for those who are responders to acute treatment. The results cannot therefore be extrapolated to those who start the study drug in a euthymic phase or in an acute illness of the opposite pole.

- Reliance on statistical as opposed to clinically significant outcome measures.

- Many aspects of the treatment of bipolar disorder are 'neglected' by RCTs: there are few or no RCTs to guide clinical practice in many areas. Examples of 'neglected' areas include the treatment of rapid cycling, hypomania and bipolar depression.

8.1.2   Outcomes research in pharmacological therapies for people with bipolar disorder

In the last 10 years there has been a dramatic increase in research in bipolar disorder. Despite this the evidence base remains relatively small and many of the key questions that concern clinicians are addressed inadequately or not at all by the existing research base. For example, there is virtually no RCT data on the treatment of rapid-cycling bipolar disorder, bipolar II disorder or the relative effectiveness of antimanic agents in combination versus monotherapy. Another problem is that the majority of trials deal with the treatment of either mania or major depressive episodes (that is, syndromes seen in bipolar disorder) yet research has clearly demonstrated that subsyndromal symptoms are three times more common than syndromal symptoms during the long-term course of both bipolar I disorder and bipolar II disorder (Judd *et al.*, 2002; Judd *et al.*, 2003).

The issue of the management of resistant mania and depression (that is, episodes that have not responded to first-line treatment) is a common clinical problem but one that is largely ignored by RCTs. The main reason for this neglect is that most RCTs are conducted with the aim of helping a drug gain a licence.

The majority of research has addressed bipolar-I disorder. Trials for mania and bipolar depression are usually short term (3 weeks and up to 10 weeks respectively) and based on changes observed using standard rating scales for example, the Young Mania Rating Scale (YMRS) and the Hamilton Depression Rating Scale. The outcome measures used include the mean change in scores from baseline to end point, response rates and remission rates. Patients entering acute mania trials represent the milder end of the severity spectrum not least because more severely ill patients will be unable to give informed consent. A key issue in trials of treatments for acute mania is that of high attrition rate, with a figure of around 70% not being uncommon in 3-week trials (for example, Zajecka *et al.*, 2002). Another potential concern, relevant to all aspects of bipolar disorder, is publication bias. In industry-sponsored trials, a further bias is that trials may be designed to favour the sponsor's compound. For example the efficacy of most atypical antipsychotics in mania has been supported by RCTs in which the comparator is haloperidol; haloperidol is a potent blocker of dopamine-2 receptors and is associated with a high risk of extrapyramidal symptoms. It is therefore not surprising that such RCTs show a benefit for the atypical in terms of a lower prevalence of extrapyramidal symptoms (EPS). Extrapolating from data in schizophrenia, it is reasonable to assume that if such studies had been repeated with a low-potency low-dose antipsychotic, then there may have been a less marked advantage or no difference at all in terms of the prevalence of EPS.

In acute mania there are a series of trials that assess the effectiveness of various atypical antipsychotics versus (1) a conventional antipsychotic, usually haloperidol; (2) placebo; and (3) the effectiveness of the atypical plus an antimanic agent (valproate or lithium) versus the antimanic agent alone. Trials that assess long-term efficacy in bipolar disorder usually take patients who have responded to treatment for an acute episode (mania or depression) and then randomise them to different long-term treatment options. A key issue in interpreting long-term studies is the relationship between the drug or drugs that were used in the initial acute treatment phase versus the long-term treatment phase, because selecting patients who are known responders can be an issue (so-called 'enriched' samples). A full discussion of issues in research in this area and the state of current research is beyond the scope of this chapter.

8.1.3   Mood stabiliser – a term best avoided

There is confusion over what the term 'mood stabiliser' refers to. Although the term is widely used in clinical practice, there is no universally accepted definition. The most rigorous definition of a mood stabiliser is that it is a drug that treats both poles of bipolar disorder and is protective against a return of both poles (Bauer & Mitchner, 2004). A less stringent criterion is that it is an agent that is effective in treating one pole of the disorder and in preventing a recurrence at that pole but that does not increase the risk of the opposite pole of the illness appearing. Adopting either criterion still leaves open the issues of how one (1) defines effectiveness, that is, what additional benefit above placebo is required to regard a drug as effective and (2) how one distinguishes between acute and maintenance treatment.

It has been argued that the most stringent definition of a mood stabiliser (that is, a drug that has short and long-term efficacy at both poles) is only fulfilled by lithium. However, even with lithium the data relating to efficacy in the treatment of bipolar depression is limited and that which does exist indicates only a modest effect. In contrast there is stronger evidence that lithium is effective in the acute and long-term treatment of mania. If one required evidence from at least two RCTs to indicate a clinically significant benefit in the acute and long-term treatment of both phases of bipolar disorder (that is, efficacy in four separate domains) then no drug would fulfil the criteria for a mood stabiliser. For this reason the less stringent criterion of acute and long-term efficacy and prophylaxis at one pole, without evidence of a worsening of the opposite pole, seems a more clinically useful definition and is the one that is adopted by many professionals.

Even this restricted definition of a mood stabiliser is associated with problems. The term may imply that these drugs cause absolute tranquillity of mood in any setting; in reality RCTs indicate that drugs labelled as mood stabilisers are effective, to varying degrees, in the treatment and prophylaxis of a limited number of affective syndromes in bipolar disorder, with most RCTs being limited to major depression or mania. To extrapolate from this to assume that these drugs are effective in sub-syndromal forms of these syndromes plus other affective states is to go beyond the evidence. For some patients the idea of a mood stabiliser, perceived as a drug that 'flattens' mood, may be off-putting. Another concern is that 'mood stabiliser' becomes a marketing label used by the pharmaceutical industry to promote drugs in bipolar disorder. In this context the term 'mood stabilisers' may lead prescribers to conclude all so-called 'mood stabilisers' have identical properties rather than to question the evidence for each drug in turn.

Valproate, carbamazepine and lithium have traditionally been regarded as mood stabilisers by clinicians and they fulfil the less stringent definition given above. However, so do other agents (most notably olanzapine and lamotrigine) and it is likely that future trials will enable other agents, particularly other atypical antipsychotics, to be subsumed within this definition of a mood stabiliser. Even without this expansion, it is apparent that existing mood stabilisers are a diverse range of drugs in terms of class, chemical structure, pharmacodynamic action and adverse effects. They also differ in the pole where they exert their main effect; the acute and long-term efficacy of lamotrigine is confined to the depressive pole while all other mood stabilisers are predominantly effective in the acute and long-term treatment of mania.

These pharmacological differences, the ambiguous nature of the term and the potential for it to become a marketing label all raise the question of how useful the term 'mood stabiliser' is. Perhaps the best that can be said in support of it is that there is some benefit to a 'shorthand' to refer to drugs with combined acute and long-term efficacy without the risk of worsening the course of the illness. However, given the inherent problems, the guideline avoids the term mood stabiliser and uses instead 'antimanic agent' or 'antimanic medication' to refer to antipsychotics, valproate, carbamazepine and lithium.

8.1.4   Current practice

In the UK, prior to the introduction of the atypical antipsychotics, the mainstay of drug treatment to control manic symptoms was the use of a typical antipsychotic often supplemented with a benzodiazepine. There is now increasing use of atypical antipsychotics and higher-dose valproate salts, particularly since the licensing of valproate (as valproate semisodium) with full dosage information in the summary of product characteristics (Anderson *et al.*, 2004; Lloyd *et al.*, 2003).

Bipolar depression remains a challenging disorder to manage. Studies show a delay of several years between onset of symptoms and diagnosis. The role of antidepressants in the acute treatment of bipolar disorder and in maintenance treatment remains controversial as discussed later in this chapter. A recent survey of prescribing in Greater Manchester, covering the period 2001-2, showed that approximately one third of outpatients seen with bipolar disorder were currently receiving an antidepressant (Anderson *et al.*, 2004) which was significantly higher than in a survey in Newcastle covering the period 2000-2001 (Lloyd *et al.*, 2003). In the Manchester survey, about half of antidepressant prescriptions were for a tricyclic antidepressant (TCA) despite suggestions they are associated with a greater risk of switching to mania than selective serotonin reuptake inhibitors (SSRIs). In the Newcastle survey nearly one third of patients were prescribed two or more prophylactic agents and nearly one fifth lamotrigine. In contrast in the Manchester survey only a quarter of patients received two or more prophylactic agents and there were no patients receiving lamotrigine. The differences between the two surveys may reflect the local availability of a specialist mood disorder service in Newcastle.

In the maintenance phase for relapse prevention, prophylactic medication use has increased and now about 90% of people with bipolar disorder may be on mood stabilisers, although less than a third are as monotherapy. Lithium remains the most commonly prescribed prophylactic agent (about 50%), although there may have been a slight decline in usage, matched by increased use of valproate salts and lamotrigine. Carbamazepine is less popular. Although the evidence base is limited, combinations of prophylactic agents are widely used, perhaps more by tertiary treatment centres.

It should be noted that the treatment of bipolar disorder in the US and UK differs in two main respects. First, at the present time in the US there is less emphasis on the use of antidepressants in treating bipolar depression, with lamotrigine being the favoured treatment. The fact that lamotrigine is licensed for the maintenance treatment of bipolar depression in the US, but not in Britain, may partly explain this difference (lamotrigine was licensed by the US Food and Drug Administration in June 2003). Concerns about the risk of antidepressant-induced switching to mania and cycle acceleration are another reason. The second difference is that over the last decade the US has seen a switch from using lithium to valproate as the prophylactic agent of choice, whereas lithium still remains widely used in Britain. The change in US practice has resulted from concerns about lithium toxicity and long-term side effects, concerns about lithium's effectiveness and increased attention to the risks of rebound mania following abrupt discontinuation.

Some aspects of clinical practice have not been investigated by RCTs. For example clinicians often use combinations of prophylactic agents (including combinations of lithium, valproate and lamotrigine) but there are no published trials addressing the efficacy of these combinations. This is not to say that such combinations are ineffective, indeed there are good reasons to believe that certain combinations are effective. There is a pressing need for large-scale, well-designed RCTs to investigate combination treatments. Two studies of maintenance treatment are currently underway which are investigating the effectiveness of a combination of lithium and divalproex (valproate semisodium) versus other treatments. These studies are the Bipolar Affective Disorder Lithium/Anticonvulsant Comparative Evaluation

(BALANCE) and the Systematic Treatment Enhancement Program for Bipolar Disorder (STEP-BD).

Another important weakness of the existing evidence is that it is almost totally restricted to the treatment of bipolar I disorder. There is very little evidence regarding the treatment of bipolar II disorder and rapid-cycling bipolar disorder.

8.1.5 Issues in the pharmacological management of patients with bipolar disorder

Concordance and compliance

Concordance refers to a process in which a healthcare professional and patient reach a shared agreement about a medication treatment plan. It involves negotiation and reflects an alliance between the two individuals, with the healthcare professional respecting the patient's views. Compliance is a different concept in that it refers to a behaviour, namely whether a patient follows the treatment plan that is agreed with the health professional. Poor compliance may be unintentional (for example a patient forgetting medication) or intentional (for example because a patient believes they do not need medication to keep well or because they are troubled by adverse effects). Clearly compliance is more likely to follow from a consultation that is concordant.

In all chronic conditions, compliance with medication is poor. Research into compliance is hindered by methodological issues; most studies use proxy measures of compliance such as patient reports, pill counts or medicine containers with a microchip in the lid which records how often the bottle is opened. None of these measures indicates that medication was taken as prescribed. In patients with bipolar disorder, compliance can also be assessed by the number of repeat prescriptions requested and by checking blood levels of drugs such as lithium, valproate and carbamazepine. Prescribers usually prefer to use blood levels to assess compliance in clinical practice when they can.

It is generally assumed that better tolerated medications are associated with better rates of compliance. However, studies comparing atypical and conventional antipsychotics show only marginal advantages for the former in terms of compliance. Patients with early signs of hypomania and mania often stop their medication as they feel well and do not realise that they are ill. Also some patients find that hypomanic and manic symptoms are initially pleasurable and so stop medication in order to experience these symptoms. This is particularly likely to occur when patients are suffering from depression or life circumstances and they perceive that, at least initially, hypomania or mania will be a release. Other patients want to experience hypomania as it facilitates creativity, productivity at work and the possible achievement of goals. Although hypomania can have this positive side to it, mania is, by definition, associated with significant impairment of functioning.

Non-compliance often occurs when a patient perceives that the benefits of medication are outweighed by the disadvantages. However, we would argue that in such cases the patient should not stop medication unilaterally but first consult with their doctor. This allows the clinician to understand the patient's experience of medication. It also allows the patient to receive the clinician's views of the benefits and risks of medication, to hear about alternative treatments and ensures that a decision is made in light of the best evidence. Furthermore if medication is stopped it is usually preferable to do so gradually to prevent withdrawal or discontinuation effects, issues that are particularly relevant to antidepressants and lithium.

In some patients with bipolar disorder who would benefit from a long-term antipsychotic, a long-acting intramuscular preparation may aid compliance. However, long-acting injections, like oral tablets, should be chosen as a result of a concordant consultation. Only one atypical antipsychotic is available as a long-acting injection in such a formulation (risperidone); it is licensed for schizophrenia and other psychosis in patients tolerant to oral risperidone. In inpatients in whom compliance is a problem, consideration should be given to the use of medication in liquid formulations or in an oral dispersible formulation. Two atypical antipsychotics (olanzapine and risperidone) are available in oral dispersible formulations.

Advance statements (directives)
The use of advance statements (directives) in bipolar disorder, and psychiatry as a whole, remains low. Advance statements involve ensuring that the patient has a full understanding of the risks and benefits, and the opportunity to weigh them against the risks of the illness, and then making a plan for future care and treatment in light of this knowledge. Lithium should not be started without informed consent from the patient, particularly as early discontinuation can be harmful. Advance directives should be seriously considered after an acute episode, or where one is anticipated. Whilst these can only formally cover medication refusal, they can refer to a patient's preferred drugs. Whilst there is little direct formal evidence for the outcomes from advance statements, they are widely advocated and evidence is emerging of the benefits of the active involvement of patients in decision making about their care (Henderson *et al.*, 2004).

The pharmacological management of older adults with bipolar disorder
Older adults with bipolar disorder (that is those over 65 years) should be treated in the same way as other adults, but with additional consideration being given to pharmacokinetic differences plus comorbidities and co-prescribed medications both of which are more common in this age group. Mania developing for the first time in older adults is associated with a high rate of medical and neurological disease (Tohen *et al.*, 1994; Young & Klerman, 1992) including subcortical lesions. Consequently all patients presenting with first onset of mania in later life should be carefully screening for contributing medical disorders.

In terms of pharmacokinetics, the elderly tend to have a reduced volume of distribution and reduced renal clearance. Consequently older patients usually require lower drug doses than younger patients. They may also be more susceptible to adverse reactions due to increased end-organ sensitivity. For example the elderly are at higher risk of EPS with antipsychotics, postural hypotension and falls with a variety of drugs, and gastro-intestinal bleeding with SSRIs. The tolerability of lithium is also lower in the elderly, who can develop signs of neurotoxicity at plasma concentrations considered 'therapeutic' in the general adult population (Sproule *et al.*, 2000). Those taking valproate may be particularly prone to sedation, tremor or gait disturbance.

Licensed indications

At the date of publication the following drugs have UK marketing authorisation for the treatment of mania: carbamazepine, lithium, olanzapine, quetiapine, risperidone, valproate (as semisodium valproate). Medications which do not have a UK marketing authorisation for the indication recommended at the date of publication are marked with an asterisk in the recommendations (*); the summary of product characteristics for current licensed indications should be checked. No drugs have UK marketing authorisation for the treatment of bipolar depression.

Regarding the use of psychotropic medication in children and adolescents under the age of 18, at the date of publication, the only drug to have a UK marketing authorisation is lithium, which is licensed for use in people aged 12 years and over. However, in 2000, the Royal College of Paediatrics and Child Health issued a policy statement on the use of unlicensed medicines, or the use of licensed medicines for unlicensed applications, in children and adolescents. This states that such use is necessary in paediatric practice and that doctors are legally allowed to prescribe unlicensed medicines where there are no suitable alternatives and where the use is justified by a responsible body of professional opinion.[12]

8.1.6 Clinical practice recommendation

8.1.6.1 When treating older people with bipolar disorder, healthcare professionals should:
- be aware of the need to use medication at lower doses
- be alert to the increased risk of drug interactions when prescribing psychotropic medication to older adults
- ensure that medical comorbidities have been recognised and addressed.

8.1.7 Topics covered

The following topics in the medical and pharmacological management of bipolar disorder are covered in this chapter:
- the treatment and management of acute episodes
- manic, hypomanic and mixed episodes
- economic evidence for treatment of acute mania
- depressed episodes
- acute episodes in the context of rapid cycling
- economic evidence for the use of electroconvulsive therapy (ECT) in all illness phases
- rapid tranquillisation.

---

[12]Joint Royal College of Paediatrics and Child Health/Neonatal and Paediatric Pharmacists Group Standing Committee on Medicines (2000) *The Use of Unlicensed Medicines or Licensed Medicines for Unlicensed Applications in Paediatric Practice - Policy Statement*. London: Royal College of Paediatrics and Child Health.

8.2   OVERVIEW OF CLINICAL EVIDENCE REVIEW

8.2.1   Evidence search

The review team conducted a systematic search for RCTs that assessed the efficacy of pharmacological interventions, transcranial magnetic stimulation and ECT for people with bipolar disorder at all stages of the illness. See Table 23.

Table 23: Databases searched and inclusion/exclusion criteria for clinical effectiveness of pharmacological interventions, transcranial magnetic stimulation and ECT

Electronic databases (searched from inception to date in brackets)	MEDLINE (February 2004), EMBASE (February 2004), PsycINFO (February 2004), CINAHL (February 2004)
Update searches	October 2004; April 2005; September 2005
Study design	RCT
Patient population	See eligibility document (Appendix 7)
Interventions	All pharmacological interventions, transcranial magnetic stimulation, ECT
Outcomes	Efficacy outcomes: remission, symptom levels (mania, depression, psychosis), functional status, relapse (as defined by the study), hospitalisation. Acceptability/tolerability outcomes: discontinuation from treatment for any reason, discontinuation from treatment because of side effects, number of people reporting side effects, number of people reporting specific side effects (weight gain), symptoms levels for EPS and akathisia, death (including suicide), self-harm
Exclusion criteria	See appendices

8.2.2   Additional inclusion criteria

In addition to the general inclusion criteria for studies reviewed in the guideline (see Appendix 7), the GDG set inclusion criteria specific to studies of pharmacological therapy, as follows:

Dose
The GDG set minimum therapeutic doses for study medication in included studies based on the British National Formulary (BNF).

Study length
The GDG set the minimum length of studies of people in an acute phase of illness at 3 weeks.

8.2.3   Presenting the evidence

Systematic reviews of the evidence are based on the searches described above, supplemented with additional narrative as necessary. Relevant characteristics of all included studies are in Appendix 22, together with a list of excluded studies with reasons for exclusion, and full references for both included and excluded studies. These are presented for each topic covered in this chapter. To aid readability, summaries of the study characteristics are included below, followed by the critical outcomes from the evidence profiles, together with a summary of the evidence profile.

In all of these, studies are referred to by a study ID (primary author in capital letters and date of study publication, except where a study is *in press* or only submitted for publication, then a date is not used).

Based on the GRADE methodology outlined in chapter 3, the quality of the evidence is summarised in the evidence profiles and summary of the evidence profiles as follows:
- high = Further research is very unlikely to change our confidence in the estimate of the effect
- moderate = Further research is likely to have an important impact on our confidence in the estimate of the effect and may change the estimate
- low = Further research is very likely to have an important impact on our confidence in the estimate of the effect and is likely to change the estimate
- very low = Any estimate of effect is very uncertain.

8.3   THE PHARMACOLOGICAL TREATMENT OF ACUTE MANIC, HYPOMANIC AND MIXED EPISODES

8.3.1   Introduction

The main aim in treating mania, hypomania and mixed episodes is to achieve rapid control of symptoms. This is particularly important as mania can result in disturbed behaviour that, when extreme, can be a risk to the safety of the patient and others. More commonly mania may cause patients to act in a disinhibited manner and such behaviour may have long-term repercussions for the individual's career and relationships. Mixed states in which manic and depressive symptoms coexist are reported to be associated with an increased risk for suicide. Various drugs possess antimanic efficacy and these are considered in the following sections.

Lithium
Lithium is held to be effective in acute mania but its onset of action is slower than with antipsychotics. In addition practical considerations mean it is not the treatment

of choice in acute mania. For example, prior to starting treatment one needs to establish that baseline renal and thyroid function are normal, but in reality a patient may refuse venepuncture. Furthermore there may be a need to start immediate treatment without waiting for the result of blood tests. Also it is prudent to increase the dose of lithium gradually to minimise the risk of lithium toxicity and this will further increase the time to response.

Lithium is associated with acute and long-term adverse effects and a low therapeutic index. Furthermore abrupt discontinuation can lead to an increased risk of mania and depression over the next few months (that is, 'rebound' mania and depression). This phenomenon has been paid relatively little attention but is potentially one of the most serious drawbacks of lithium particularly in those who adhere poorly to treatment. It has been estimated that lithium needs to be continued for 2 years for the detrimental effects associated with abrupt discontinuation to be balanced by the benefits that accrue from its long-term effect (Goodwin, 1994). The risk of rebound appears to be prevented if lithium is withdrawn gradually and several studies suggest that withdrawal over 2 weeks is sufficient (Baldessarini *et al.*, 1997; Faedda *et al.*, 1993).

Adverse effects of lithium that occur at therapeutic plasma levels include polyuria, polydipsia, tiredness, fine tremor, metallic taste and diarrhoea. Toxic levels of lithium (>1.2 mmol/l) cause a range of symptoms including confusion, myoclonic jerks, cardiac arrhythmias, confusion, ataxia, dysarthria, and, as levels rise, further convulsions, coma and death. The diagnosis of lithium toxicity is made on clinical grounds with laboratory confirmation, but toxicity can sometimes occur despite an apparent normal plasma level. Long-term complications of lithium include thyroid abnormalities (particularly hypothyroidism), chronic renal impairment and diabetes insipidus (Macritchie & Young, 2004). Lithium is also associated with an increased rate of malformations particularly of the cardiovascular system.

Antipsychotics

Prior to the introduction of the atypical antipsychotics, the conventional antipsychotics were the standard treatment for mania despite a relative lack of RCTs to support their use. In recent years several atypical antipsychotics agents have been licensed to treat mania, with RCT data underpinning these decisions. Atypical antipsychotics currently licensed in the UK for the treatment of acute mania are olanzapine, risperidone and quetiapine. A major advantage of the atypical antipsychotics over conventional antipsychotics is the lower risk of EPS though this differential has largely been demonstrated in trials where the comparator is haloperidol, a high-potency conventional antipsychotic that is associated with a relatively high incidence of EPS. Some atypical antipsychotics are prolactin sparing, but others raise serum prolactin levels, which can lead to distressing symptoms, including sexual dysfunction, and may also be associated with long-term health risks, particularly if it leads to secondary hypogonadism. Some atypical antipsychotics, in particular olanzapine, are associated with a high risk of significant increase in body weight ($\geq 7\%$ baseline body weight). Concern has only focused on the potential for metabolic complications with the atypical antipsychotics, though high-quality data on this area is lacking.

Anticonvulsants
Valproate is available in various forms including sodium valproate, valproic acid and valproate semisodium, although only valproate semisodium has UK marketing authorisation for the treatment of manic episodes in the context of bipolar disorder. The active element in all formulations is the valproate ion. The guideline uses the generic term 'valproate' except when describing the agent used in a particular study, when it uses the name used by the study authors. Carbamazepine is licensed for the treatment of patients with bipolar disorder who are intolerant of lithium or in whom lithium is ineffective. A major complication of carbamazepine is that it can lower the plasma level of concurrently prescribed drugs including antipsychotics. Both carbamazepine and valproate are teratogenic, being associated with an increased risk of neural tube defects. In addition pre-natal exposure to valproate may be associated with an increased risk of developmental problems including reduced cognitive performance.

Calcium channel blockers
Calcium channel-blocking drugs (that is, diltiazem, nifedipine, nimodipine, verapamil) are licensed to treat high blood pressure and angina. Occasionally they are prescribed to treat mania. Side effects include headache, hypotension and tenderness of the gums.

Transcranial magnetic stimulation and ECT
ECT remains a valuable treatment for severe depression where there is an urgent need for a rapid response. Examples include a depressed patient with marked psychomotor retardation who is refusing fluids and food and a depressed patient with persistent and severe suicidal intent. There is a smaller body of evidence which indicates the effectiveness of ECT in acute mania. Transcranial magnetic stimulation is a recently introduced treatment but most of the research undertaken so far is limited to unipolar depression.

Benzodiazepines

Benzodiazepines are often used by clinicians, in conjunction with antimanic agents, for symptomatic control of agitation and insomnia. Sleep deprivation can lead to rapid deterioration in manic episodes and so the short-term use of hypnotics to maintain a circadian rhythm is both reasonable and advisable. Problems include the risks of tolerance, withdrawal symptoms and dependence. These risks become greater when use continues beyond 4 weeks. Other problems include sedation, ataxia and an increased risk of falls, particularly in the elderly. Comorbid anxiety disorders, including generalised anxiety disorder, are common in bipolar disorder. Their treatment should follow similar lines to such disorders that occur in isolation with the proviso that antidepressants should be used with caution due to the risks of cycle acceleration and switching to mania.

Combination therapy

The combination of antipsychotics and antimanic medication (especially lithium and valproate) has been shown to be effective in the treatment of mania. However, there may be an increased risk of adverse effects including weight gain (for example, Casey *et al.*, 2003).

8.3.2   Review strategy

Evidence from RCTs was found for the following treatment strategies:

- **lithium**, including lithium compared with placebo and with anticonvulsants and antipsychotics
- **anticonvulsants**, including carbamazepine and valproate semisodium (compared with placebo and other drugs), and gabapentin
- **antipsychotics**, including antipsychotics compared with placebo, lithium, valproate semisodium and haloperidol
- **miscellaneous pharmacological and non-pharmacological physical interventions**, including ECT, transcranial magnetic stimulation and calcium channel blockers

No RCT evidence was found for the use of benzodiazepines in acute mania.

A summary of the evidence for the pharmacological treatment of mania, hypomanic and mixed states in children and adolescents is also provided.

Some trials appear in more than one section where the GDG felt this was appropriate, for example, trials comparing lithium with antipsychotics are included in both sections.

8.3.3   Lithium in the treatment of mania

Studies considered

Twelve trials of lithium in the treatment of mania met inclusion criteria. Excluded studies with reasons for exclusion can be seen in Appendix 22. RCTs published prior to 1973 were not picked up in searches, although several trials published before this date exist. The GDG decided not to include them because of concerns about trial methods and study populations (Schou *et al.*; 1954, Magg, 1963, Goodwin *et al.*, 1969, Stokes *et al.*, 1971).

Included trials compared lithium with placebo, anticonvulsants, antipsychotics and ECT in the treatment of mania. An overview of the included studies is in Table 24, with further details available in Appendix 22. A trial comparing lithium with ECT is considered in section 1.3.6 below.

Table 24: Summary of study characteristics table for lithium in the treatment of mania

Comparator	Placebo	Anticonvulsants	Antipsychotics
No. trials (No. participants)	*3 RCTs* (328)*	*5 RCTs* (544)*	*5 RCTs* (314)*
Study IDs	(1) BOWDEN1994 (2) BOWDEN2005 (3) GELLER1998	(1) BOWDEN1994 (2) FREEMAN1992 (3) ICHIM2000 (4) LERER1987 (5) SMALL1991	(1) BERK1999 (2) BOWDEN2005 (3) GARFINKEL1980 *** (4) SEGAL1998 (5) SHOPSIN1975A ***
Diagnosis	(1) Acute manic episode (2) Acute manic episode with psychotic features (3) Acute manic episode with substance use disorder (<2 months' duration)	All: Acute manic episode	All: Acute manic episode
Setting	Inpatients; US	Inpatients; all US except (3) (South Africa)	Inpatients; all US except (1), (4) (South Africa)

Continued

209

Table 24: (Continued)

Comparator	Placebo	Anticonvulsants	Antipsychotics
No. trials (No. participants)	3 RCTs* (328)	5 RCTs* (544)	5 RCTs* (314)
Baseline data	(1)(3) No relevant baseline data available (2) YMRS mean: lithium 33.3; placebo 34 MADRS mean: lithium 6.3; placebo 6.2	(1)(2)(4) no relevant baseline data available (3) BPRS mean: lithium 46.8; lamotrigine 52.8 MRS mean: lithium 31.6; lamotrigine 34.4 (5) MRS: lithium = 30.3, carbamazepine = 30.9, HRSD: lithium 29.9, carbamazepine +29.4, BPRS: 49.1, carbamazepine 47, GAS: 38.8	(4) BPRS lithium: 17.4 (7.33); haloperidol: 15.2 (7.33) (1) Lithium 46.8; olanzapine 53
Lithium serum levels	(1) 1.5 mmol/l (2) 0.6–1.4 meq/l** (3) 0.9–1.3 meq/l	(1) 1.5 mmol/l (2) 1.5 mmol/l (3) Responders 0.77 (0.21), non-responders 0.71 (0.25) (4) 1–1.4 meq/l	(1) 400 mg bid (serum level not given) (2) 0.6–1.4 meq/l (3) 1.20 (0.2) mmol/l (4) 0.6–1.2 mmol/l

Comparator	Placebo	(5) 0.6–1.5 mmol/l (1) Valproate semisodium (2) Valproate (3) Lamotrigine (4) Carbamazepine (5) Carbamazepine	(5) 2 meq/l (1) Olanzapine (2) Quetiapine (3) Haloperidol (4) Haloperidol (5) Haloperidol or chlorpromazine
Mean age (or range of mean ages)	(1) 39 (2) 40 (3) 16	Where given, 33 to 38	Where given, 30–39
Length of trial	(1) 3 weeks (2) 12 weeks (3) 6 weeks	All 3 weeks except (5) (8 weeks)	3 or 4 weeks

*Number of participants in relevant treatment groups – trials may have additional treatment groups

**Equivalent to mmol/litre

***Acceptability data only

Lithium serum levels are referred to as mmol/litre except where the papers refer to meq/litre. The two measures are equivalent.

Summary of evidence for lithium in the treatment of mania
An overview of the results is provided in Table 25, with the full evidence profile in Appendix 23. Three placebo-controlled trials conducted since 1994 indicate that lithium is effective in acute mania. In addition several older trials support the effectiveness of lithium but were excluded from the analysis due to methodological weaknesses common to many trials of the period. The three placebo-controlled RCTs that were analysed all employed a minimum plasma level of ≥ 0.6 mmol/l. In contrast many UK laboratories quote a lower limit of the therapeutic range of 0.4 to 0.6 mmol/l. There does not appear to be an evidence base to support this as an effective range. In terms of active-comparator trials, one trial indicated that lithium was more effective than valproate and several trials indicated equivalent efficacy to various antipsychotics.

8.3.4   Anticonvulsants in the treatment of mania

Studies considered for review
Seven trials met the eligibility criteria set by the GDG. Excluded studies with reasons for exclusion can be seen in Appendix 22. Excluded trials included a study of topiramate, which meant that no high-quality study of this drug was available.

Included trials looked at carbamazepine, valproate semisodium and gabapentin in the treatment of mania. Placebo-controlled trials were available for carbamazepine and valproate.

An overview of the included studies is in Table 26, with further details available in Appendix 22.

Summary of evidence
An overview of the results is provided in Table 27, with the full evidence profile in Appendix 23. RCTs indicate that carbamazepine is superior to placebo in acute mania. Although valproate semisodium is licensed in the UK and in the USA for the treatment of acute mania, only one placebo-controlled trial of valproate semisodium fulfilled the GDG's criteria. This showed that valproate semisodium is more effective than placebo (moderate quality evidence). Another RCT showed valproate semisodium to be as efficacious as olanzapine, a drug that has been shown to be superior to placebo in two placebo-controlled RCTs. However, valproate semisodium was less efficacious than lithium in another trial (see Table 25). In summary, although the evidence base supporting the efficacy of valproate in mania is relatively small, it appears that valproate is effective in the treatment of mania.

Valproate is available in several formulations including valproate semisodium, sodium valproate and valproic acid. Most trials in bipolar disorder have used valproate semisodium. There has been debate about whether other forms of

Table 25: Summary of evidence profile for lithium in the treatment of mania

Comparator	Placebo	Placebo (for substance misuse)	Anticonvulsants	Antipsychotics
Evidence for efficacy (quality)	Lithium more effective than placebo (moderate)	Lithium more effective than placebo (moderate)	Lithium versus carbamazepine or lamotrigine: data are inconclusive (low). Lithium more effective than valproate (moderate)	Data are inconclusive (low) for efficacy outcomes
Evidence for acceptability/ tolerability (quality)	Data are inconclusive (low) for tolerability/ acceptability outcomes	Data are inconclusive (low) for tolerability/ acceptability outcomes	Lithium versus carbamazepine or lamotrigine: data are inconclusive (low) for tolerability/ acceptability outcomes	Data are inconclusive (low) for tolerability/ acceptability outcomes

Table 26: Summary of study characteristics table for anticonvulsants in the treatment of mania

	Carbamazepine versus placebo	Carbamazepine versus other drugs	Valproate semisodium versus placebo	Valproate semisodium versus other drugs	Gabapentin
No. trials (No. participants)	*2 RCTs (443)*	*1 RCT (54)*	*1 RCT (141)*	*2 RCTs (150)*	*1 RCT (117)*
Study IDs	(1) WEISLER2004 (2) WEISLER2005	LUSZNAT1988*	BOWDEN1994**	(1) DELBELLO2002 *** (2) ZAJECKA2002	PANDE2000
Diagnosis	(1) Bipolar I: 47% manic, 53% mixed (2) Bipolar I: 79% manic, 21% mixed	Manic, % not given; hypomanic % not given	Acute manic episode	(1) Bipolar I: 24% manic, 76% mixed (2) Bipolar I: manic	Bipolar I: 25% mixed, 23% manic, 46% hypomanic, 3% depressed, 3% unspecified
Setting	(1) in/out patients; US (2) in/outpatients; US, India	Inpatients; UK	Inpatients; US	Inpatients; US	Outpatients; US

214

Baseline data	(1) YMRS mean: carbamazepine 27.5; placebo 26 (2) YMRS mean: carbamazepine 28.5; placebo 27.9	None available	None available	None available	YMRS gabapentin 18.4 (7.1); placebo 18.8 (7.3)
Study drug	Carbamazepine	Carbamazepine + neuroleptics	Valproate semisodium	(1) Valproate semisodium + quetiapine (2) Valproate semisodium	Gabapentin (+ lithium or valproate)
Comparator	Placebo	Neuroleptics	Placebo	(1) Valproate semisodium (2) Olanzapine	Placebo (+ lithium or valproate)
Mean age	(1) 37 (2) 38	Not given	39	(1) Range 12–18 (2) 39	39
Trial length	3 weeks	6 weeks + 12 months follow-up	3 weeks	(1) 6 weeks (2) 3 weeks	10 weeks

* Acceptability data only

** Study also has lithium arm which is considered in 8.3.3 Lithium in the treatment of mania, above

*** Study also considered in 8.3.7 The treatment of mania in children and adolescents, below

Table 27: Summary of evidence profile for anticonvulsants in the treatment of mania

	Carbamazepine versus placebo	Carbamazepine versus other drugs	Valproate semisodium versus placebo	Valproate semisodium versus other drugs	Gabapentin
Evidence for efficacy (quality)	Carbamazepine more effective than placebo for those with manic symptoms (high); inconclusive for mixed episodes (low)	(Carbamazepine + neuroleptics versus lithium + neuroleptics) Appropriate efficacy data not available	Valproate semisodium more effective than placebo (moderate)	(versus olanzapine) No difference on mania scores; favours olanzapine on general psychiatric functioning (moderate) (+ quetiapine versus valproate semisodium) Appropriate efficacy data not available	(+ (lithium or valproate) versus placebo + (lithium or valproate)) Inconclusive (low)

Evidence for acceptability/tolerability (quality)				
Carbamazepine more acceptable to patients with mania than placebo (moderate); inconclusive for mixed episodes (low); tolerability: inconclusive (low); more side effects with carbamazepine (low)	Data are inconclusive (low) for tolerability/ acceptability outcomes	Data are inconclusive (low) for tolerability/ acceptability outcomes	(versus olanzapine) no difference on acceptability (moderate); inconclusive on side effects (low) (+ quetiapine versus valproate semisodium) Valproate semisodium alone more acceptable (low) (adolescents only)	(+ (lithium or valproate) versus placebo + (lithium or valproate)) Inconclusive (low); inconclusive on side effects (low)

valproate share the efficacy of valproate semisodium. There are no good pharmacological reasons why there should be a difference in the efficacy of these different compounds since the valproate ion is the active moiety, although there may be slight tolerability differences for valproate semisodium compared with valproic acid and sodium valproate. In previous years this debate was relevant due to the higher cost of valproate semisodium in comparison with sodium valproate and valproic acid. However, recent changes in pricing mean that there is now little difference in the price of these variations. Given the absence of a significant price differential, the licensed status of valproate semisodium, and the fact that most RCTs of valproate in bipolar disorder used valproate semisodium, it is reasonable to regard valproate semisodium as the compound of choice when valproate is required in mania, although the guideline recommendations refer to valproate throughout and none of the salts is licensed for maintenance treatment.

It cannot be assumed that all anticonvulsants are effective in mania as the results of a trial of gabapentin were classified inconclusive. No trial of topiramate met inclusion criteria.

Carbamazepine is more effective than placebo in the treatment of mania. However, carbamazepine, like valproate, is teratogenic. In addition it induces liver enzymes and so increases the breakdown of various co-prescribed drugs, reducing their effectiveness. Well-recognised examples of this include carbamazepine reducing the plasma level and effectiveness of co-prescribed warfarin, the contraceptive pill and various antipsychotics including haloperidol, olanzapine, risperidone and quetiapine. Uncommon but potentially serious adverse effects include blood dyscrasias and skin rashes. Common adverse effects include reversible blurring of vision, dizziness and ataxia, which are dose-related. Due to these side effects it is usual practice to initiate carbamazepine at a low dose and build this up gradually. This and the potential interaction with antipsychotics both reduce the practicality of carbamazepine as a treatment in acute mania hypomania and bipolar depression.

8.3.5   Antipsychotics in the treatment of mania

Studies considered for review
Twenty-four trials met the eligibility criteria set by the GDG. Excluded studies with reasons for exclusion can be seen in Appendix 22. Characteristics of included studies are in Table 28, with further details in Appendix 22.

A trial of an antipsychotic with and without ECT is considered with other ECT trials below (section 8.3.6).

Notes on evidence
Where a placebo-controlled trial compared two antipsychotics (that is, a three-arm trial: antipsychotic A, antipsychotic B, placebo) the data from the following arms were entered into the comparison with placebo: SMULEVICH2005 risperidone, MCINTYRER2005 quetiapine. This means that there are no data for haloperidol presented in this analysis.

Table 28: Summary of study characteristics table for antipsychotics in the treatment of mania

	Versus placebo	Versus placebo (with prophylactic agent)	Versus lithium	Versus valproate semisodium	Versus haloperidol
No. trials (No. participants)	*11 RCTs (2698)*	*7 RCTs (1238) (incs all of 4)*	*5 RCTs (299)*	*1 RCT (120)*	*5 RCTs (867)*
Study IDs	(1) BOWDEN2005* (2) HIRSCHFELD 2004 (3) KECK2003 (4) KECK2003C (5) KHANNA2005 (6) MCINTYRER 2005** (7) POTKIN2005 (8) SACHS2006 (9) SMULEVICH 2005** (10) TOHEN1999A (11) TOHEN2000	(1) GARFINKEL 1980 (2) NAMJOSHI 2004 (3) SACHS2002** (4) SACHS2004 (5) TOHEN2002 (6) YATHAM2003	(1) BERK1999 (2) BOWDEN2005 (3) GARFINKEL 1980*** (4) SEGAL1998 (5) SHOPSIN 1975A***	ZAJECKA2002	(1) MCINTYRER 2005 (2) SHI2002 (3) SHOPSIN1975 (4) SMULEVICH 2005 (5) VIETA2005
Diagnosis	(1) Acute manic episode; 27% with psychotic features	(1) Acute manic episode (2) Bipolar I mixed or manic	Acute manic episode	Bipolar I manic	(1) Acute manic episode (2) Bipolar I 6% mixed, 95%

Continued

Table 28: (*Continued*)

	Versus placebo	Versus placebo (with prophylactic agent)	Versus lithium	Versus valproate semisodium	Versus haloperidol
No. trials (No. participants)	*11 RCTs (2698)*	*7 RCTs (1238) (incs all of 4)*	*5 RCTs (299)*	*1 RCT (120)*	*5 RCTs (867)*
	(2) Bipolar I manic; 43% with psychotic features (3) Bipolar I manic; 33% mixed, 23% rapid cycling (4) Bipolar I 60% mixed (5) Bipolar I manic; 5% mixed, 59% psychotic features (6) Acute manic episode; 42% with psychotic features (7) Bipolar I manic; 40% mixed	(3) Bipolar I 21% mixed, 79% manic (4) Bipolar I manic (5) Bipolar I manic (6) Bipolar 92% manic, 8% mixed			manic, 57% psychotic features (3) Acute manic episode (4) Acute manic episode 33% with psychotic features (5) Bipolar I 89% manic, 11% mixed

Continued

	(1)	(2)	(3)	(4)	(5)
	(8) Acute manic episode 58%; acute mixed 42% (9) Acute manic episode; 33% with psychotic features (10) Bipolar I manic; 17% mixed (11) Bipolar I 43% mixed, 57% manic; 57% with psychotic features			Inpatients; US	(1) Inpatients; South America, Europe, Asia (2) In/out patients; multi-continent (3) Inpatients (4) Inpatients; 10 countries—Europe, Asia (5) US, Japan, Europe
Setting	(1) In/outpatients; US (2) Outpatients; US (3) Inpatients; US (4) Inpatients; US, Brazil (5) Inpatients; India (6) Inpatients; South America, Europe, Asia (7) Inpatients; US, Brazil, Mexico (8) Inpatients; US (9) Inpatients;	(1) Inpatients; Canada (2) Outpatient (3) Inpatients; US (4) In/out patients; US (5) In/out patients; US	(1) Inpatients; South Africa (2) Inpatients; US (3) Inpatients; US (4) Inpatients; South Africa (5) Inpatients		

Table 28: (*Continued*)

	Versus placebo	Versus placebo (with prophylactic agent)	Versus lithium	Versus valproate semisodium	Versus haloperidol
No. trials (No. participants)	*11 RCTs (2698)*	*7 RCTs (1238) (incs all of 4)*	*5 RCTs (299)*	*1 RCT (120)*	*5 RCTs (867)*
	10 countries—Europe/Asia (10) Outpatients; US (11) In/outpatients; US				
Baseline data	(1) YMRS 32–34 (2) YMRS 29 (3) YMRS 28.2–29.7 (4) MRS 26–27 (5) YMRS 37 (6) Not available (7) MRS 12.84–13.18 (8) YMRS 28.5–28.8 (9) Not available (10) Not given (11) YMRS 29.1	(1) Not available (2) YMRS 22 (3) YMRS 28 (4) Not available (5) Not available (6) YMRS 28–29	(1) BPRS 46.8–53 (2) YMRS 32–34 (3) Not available (4) BPRS 15.2–17.4 (5) Not available	None available	(1) Not available (2) YMRS 30–31 (3) Not available (4) Not available (5) YMRS 31

Study drugs	(1) Quetiapine (2) Risperidone (3) Aripiprazole (4) Ziprasidone (5) Risperidone (6) Quetiapine** (7) Ziprasidone (8) Aripiprazole (9) Risperidone** (10) Olanzapine (11) Olanzapine	(1) Haloperidol (2) Olanzapine (3) Haloperidol (4) Quetiapine (5) Olanzapine (6) Risperidone All with prophylactic agent	(1) Olanzapine (2) Quetiapine (3) Haloperidol (4) Haloperidol (5) Haloperidol or chlorpromazine	Valproate semisodium versus olanzapine; olanzapine	(1) Quetiapine (2) Olanzapine (3) Chlorpromazine (4) Risperidone (5) Aripiprazole
Comparator	Placebo	Placebo (+ prophylactic agent)	Lithium	Valproate semisodium	Haloperidol
Adjunctive prophylactic agent	Not applicable	(1) Lithium (2) Lithium or valproate (3) Lithium or valproate (4) Lithium or valproate (5) Lithium or valproate (6) Lithium, valproate or carbamazepine	Not applicable	Not applicable	Not applicable

Continued

223

Table 28: (Continued)

	Versus placebo	Versus placebo (with prophylactic agent)	Versus lithium	Versus valproate semisodium	Versus haloperidol
No. trials (No. participants)	*11 RCTs (2698)*	*7 RCTs (1238) (incs all of 4)*	*5 RCTs (299)*	*1 RCT (120)*	*5 RCTs (867)*
Lithium serum levels	Not applicable	(1) 900 mg/d adjusted according to response (2) Not given (3) 0.6–1.4 meq/l***** (4) 0.7–1.0 meq/l***** (5) Not available (6) Not available	(1) 400 mg bid (serum level not given) (2) 0.6 to 1.4 meq/l***** (3) 1.20 (0.2) mmol/l (4) 0.6–1.2 mmol/l (5) 2 meq/l*****	Not applicable	Not applicable
Mean age	35–43 (4) (10) not given	39–42	30–39	39	40–43 (3) not given
Trial length	3 weeks except (1) (6) 12 weeks (11) 4 weeks	3 weeks**** except (3) 7 weeks	3 or 4 weeks	3 weeks	3 weeks except (1) (5) 12 weeks (2) 7 + 6 week continuation

*Number of participants in relevant treatment groups – trials may have additional treatment groups

**Trials with two antipsychotic arms – see 'study drugs' for data used (data added for dichotomous outcomes where appropriate)

*** Acceptability data only

*****Plus 18-month follow-up – data used in the review of long-term maintenance below

******Equivalent to mmol/litre

Due to heterogeneity, KHANNA2005 was removed from the following analyses as an outlier: mania endpoint scores and leaving the study early for any reason.

Summary of evidence for anipsychotics in the treatment of mania
Note that most studies included a proportion of participants with psychotic features and some also included participants experiencing mixed episodes.

An overview of the results is provided in Table 29, with the full evidence profile in Appendix 23.

RCTs for several atypical antipsychotics indicate superiority over placebo (aripiprazole, olanzapine, quetiapine, risperidone, ziprasidone) and equivalent efficacy to haloperidol (aripiprazole, olanzapine, quetiapine, risperidone, ziprasidone), lithium (olanzapine) and valproate semisodium (olanzapine) in the treatment of mania. The addition of several atypical antipsychotics to either valproate or lithium in patients with partially treated mania has been shown in RCTs to be more effective than continuing treatment with valproate or lithium alone.

8.3.6 Miscellaneous pharmacological and non-pharmacological physical interventions

Studies considered for review
Four trials met the eligibility criteria set by the GDG. Excluded studies with reasons for exclusion can be seen in Appendix 22. Characteristics of included studies are in Table 30, with further details in Appendix 22.

Summary of evidence
An overview of the results is provided in Table 31, with the full evidence profile in Appendix 23. None of the treatments considered (that is, ECT, transcranial magnetic stimulation and calcium channel blockers) was of proven efficacy.

Table 29: Summary of evidence profile for antipsychotics in the treatment of mania

	Versus placebo	Versus placebo (with prophylactic agent)	Versus lithium	Versus valproate semisodium	Versus haloperidol
Evidence for efficacy (quality)	Antipsychotics more effective than placebo (high)	Antipsychotics more effective than placebo (high)	Antipsychotics more effective than lithium (moderate)	Unlikely to be a difference (moderate)	Unlikely to be a difference (moderate)
Evidence for acceptability/ tolerability (quality)	Antipsychotics more acceptable than placebo (moderate), some evidence of side effects (moderate)	Prophylactic agents with or without antipsychotics equally acceptable (high); tolerability data largely inconclusive (low) other than antipsychotics produce EPS and weight gain (moderate)	Acceptability inconclusive (low); tolerability unlikely to be a difference (moderate)	Acceptability: unlikely to be a difference (moderate) Tolerability: data not extractable	Acceptability: unlikely to be a difference (high); Tolerability: antipsychotics more tolerable than haloperidol (high), except on weight gain where haloperidol better than olanzapine (moderate)

Table 30: Summary of study characteristics for miscellaneous pharmacological and non-pharmacological physical interventions in the treatment of mania

	ECT	Transcranial magnetic stimulation (TMS)	Calcium channel blockers
No. trials (No. participants)	*2 RCTs (76)*	*1 RCT (16)*	*1 RCT (32)*
Study IDs	(1) SIKDAR1994 (2) SMALL1988**	GRISARU1998	JANICAK1998
Diagnosis	(1) Mania (2) Bipolar I manic	Manic; 25% with psychotic features	Bipolar I; 94% manic, 6% mixed, 71% psychotic features
Setting	(1) In/outpatients; (2) Inpatients; US	Israel	Inpatients
Baseline data	(1) YMRS 23–25 (2) MRS 19–20	YMRS 23–28	MRS 26–29
Study treatment	(1) ECT + chlorpromazine (2) ECT	TMS: right stimulation	Verapamil
Comparator	(1) Simulated ECT + chlorpromazine (2) Lithium	TMS: left stimulation	Placebo
Lithium serum levels	(1) Not applicable (2) 0.6–1.5 mmol/l (to max 1.2 mmol/l for those taking neuroleptics)	Not applicable	Not applicable
Mean age	(1) Not available (2) 37	33	36
Trial length	(1) 2 weeks (2) 8 weeks	2 weeks	3 weeks

*Number of participants in relevant treatment groups – trials may have additional treatment groups

**Acceptability data only

227

Table 31: Summary of evidence profile for miscellaneous pharmacological and non-pharmacological physical interventions in the treatment of mania

	ECT	Transcranial magnetic stimulation	Calcium channel blockers
Evidence for efficacy (quality)	No evidence versus lithium More effective than an antipsychotic alone (moderate)	No evidence versus placebo; right-hand stimulation more effective than left-hand stimulation (moderate)	Data are inconclusive (low) for efficacy outcomes
Evidence for acceptability/ tolerability (quality)	Data are inconclusive (low) for tolerability/ acceptability outcomes	Data are inconclusive (low) for tolerability/ acceptability outcomes	Data are inconclusive (low) for tolerability/ acceptability outcomes

8.3.7 The treatment of mania in children and adolescents

Lithium in the treatment of mania in children and adolescents

Studies considered
Three RCTs of lithium in the treatment of mania in children and adolescents were considered (GELLER1998, KAFANTARIS2004, KOWATCH2000). KOWATCH2000 is not a double-blind trial, but was included since evidence in this area is scarce. A summary of study characteristics is in Table 32, with further details in Appendix 22.

Summary of evidence for lithium in the treatment of mania
in children and adolescents
An overview of the results is provided in Table 33, with the full evidence profile in Appendix 23. The KAFANTARIS2004 trial is of children and adolescents given lithium for 4 weeks and then randomised to continue or discontinue treatment. In addition, 25% with psychotic features received antipsychotic treatment. The estimated effect size shows little difference in mania scores, although the 95% CIs are wide making this hard to interpret. In the trial of mania with substance use disorder, lithium was superior to placebo. Given the lack of other trials of pharmacotherapy in children and adolescents, it is necessary to cautiously extrapolate from the adult evidence base.

Antipsychotics in the treatment of mania in children and adolescents

Three RCTs of antipsychotics in the treatment of mania in children and adolescents were included, only one of which was a double-blind, fully randomised

**Table 32: Summary of study characteristics for lithium in the treatment
of mania in children and adolescents**

	Lithium versus placebo	Lithium versus other drugs
No. trials (No. participants)	*2 RCTs (65)*	*1 RCT open label (42)*
Study IDs	(1) GELLER1998 (2) KAFANTARIS2004	KOWATCH2000A
Diagnosis	(1) Acute manic episode with substance use disorder (<2 months' duration) (2) Acute manic episode with psychotic features	Bipolar I manic/mixed 53%, Bipolar II manic/mixed 47%
Setting	Inpatients; US (25% of (2) outpatients)	Outpatients; US
Baseline data	No relevant baseline data available	None available
Study treatment	(1) Lithium 0.9–1.3 meq/l* (2) Lithium 0.6–1.2 meq/l*	Lithium 0.8–1.2 meq/l*
Comparator	Placebo	(1) Carbamazepine 7–10 μg/l (2) Valproate semisodium 85–110 μg/l
Mean age	16	11
Trial length	(1) 42 days (2) 14 (after 4-week open treatment with lithium)	42 days

*Equivalent to mmol/litre

trial. A summary of study characteristics is in Table 34, with further details in Appendix 22.

Summary of evidence for antipsychotics in the treatment of mania in children and adolescents

An overview of the results is provided in Table 35 with the full evidence profile in Appendix 23. Data for the use of antipsychotics in the treatment of mania in children and adolescents is sparse and of very low quality. Given this it is necessary to extrapolate cautiously from the adult evidence base.

Table 33: Summary of study characteristics for lithium in the treatment of mania in children and adolescents

Comparator	Lithium versus placebo	Placebo (for substance misuse)	Lithium versus other drugs
Study population	Mean age 15	Mean age 16	Mean age 11
Evidence for efficacy (quality)	Data are inconclusive (low)	Lithium more effective than placebo (moderate)	Versus valproate semisodium and carbamazepine: data not available (very low)
Evidence for acceptability/ tolerability (quality)	Data are not available	Data are inconclusive (low)	Versus valproate semisodium and carbamazepine: data are inconclusive (low)

8.3.8 Clinical summary and practical considerations for the treatment of mania

In terms of pharmacological treatment, acute mania has been more studied than any other aspect of bipolar disorder. Drugs that have been shown to be superior to placebo in acute mania include carbamazepine, valproate, lithium and several atypical antipsychotics including aripiprazole, olanzapine, quetiapine, risperidone and ziprasidone. RCTs are not uniformly positive in acute mania. For example, verapamil, a calcium channel antagonist, was not more effective than placebo (JANICAK1998) and gabapentin in combination with valproate or lithium was not more effective than valproate or lithium alone (PANDE2000).

Given the existence of several efficacious agents in mania, comparative efficacy and tolerability should be considered. In terms of comparative efficacy there are few head-to-head trials of single agents in mania. Most such trials (for example, olanzapine versus lithium, olanzapine versus valproate semisodium, and olanzapine versus haloperidol) do not reveal convincing evidence for differential efficacy or tolerability though an exception is a single trial in which lithium was superior to valproate. In view of this non-RCT data, practical issues need to be considered when choosing between monotherapies for mania.

Carbamazepine
Carbamazepine is not a simple drug to use; side-effects include nausea, blurring of vision and unsteadiness. To minimise these it is necessary to gradually increase the

Table 34: Summary of study characteristics for antipsychotics in the treatment of mania in children and adolescents

	Quetiapine	Lithium + risperidone versus valproate semisodium + risperidone	Risperidone versus olanzapine
No. trials (No. participants)	*1 RCT (30)*	*1 RCT open label (40)*	*1 semi-randomised RCT (31)*
Study IDs	DELBELLO 2002	PAVULURI2004A	BIEDERMAN 2005A
Diagnosis	Bipolar I; 24% manic, 76% mixed	Bipolar I and II manic/mixed (78% ADHD)	Bipolar I manic/mixed, Bipolar II manic/mixed
Setting	Inpatients; US	Outpatients; US	Outpatients; US
Baseline data	None available	YMRS 29–30 CDRS-R 62–71	No relevant baseline data available
Study treatment	Valproate semisodium + quetiapine	Lithium 0.6–1.0 meq/l* + risperidone mean dose 750 mg/d	Risperidone: mean dose 1.4 mg/d
Comparator	Valproate semisodium	Valproate semisodium 50–120µg/ml + risperidone mean dose 750 mg/d	Olanzapine: mean dose 6.3 mg/d
Mean age	Range 12–18	12	5 (range 4–6)
Trial length	6 weeks	26 weeks	8 weeks

*Equivalent to mmol/litre

dose. Carbamazepine can also cause blood dyscrasias and skin rashes and is teratogenic. It reduces the plasma level of many co-prescribed medications, including antipsychotics, by inducing hepatic enzymes. As a result it cannot be recommended as a first-line treatment for acute mania.

**Table 35: Summary of evidence for antipsychotics in the treatment
of mania in children and adolescents**

Comparator	Quetiapine	Lithium + risperidone versus valproate semisodium + risperidone	Risperidone versus olanzapine
Study population	Age 12–18	Mean age 12	Mean age 5 (range 4–6)
Evidence for efficacy (quality)	Appropriate efficacy data not available (very low)	Data on general function is inconclusive (very low); no other data available	Favours risperidone (low)
Evidence for acceptability/ tolerability (quality)	Leaving the study early favours placebo (moderate)	Leaving the study early favours valproate semisodium (low); other data is inconclusive (very low)	Favours risperidone (low)

Lithium

Lithium is associated with a number of problems, including long-term risk of chronic renal impairment and hypothyroidism. Lithium can impair renal function in several ways. It inhibits the effect of antidiuretic hormone on the distal tubule and so impairs water reabsorption. This is relatively common, manifests as polyuria and polydipsia and, when severe, can lead to frank diabetes inspidius which occurs in about 10% of patients on long-term lithium treatment (Bendz & Aurell, 1992). Complications include dehydration and an increased risk of toxicity from drugs with a low therapeutic index including lithium. The effects of lithium on renal concentrating ability are usually reversible on stopping treatment. In a small minority of patients, long-term lithium treatment can lead to a reduction in glomerular filtration and a gradual rise in serum creatinine. This may reflect a chronic interstitial or tubulointerstitial nephropathy which can be irreversible, even on stopping lithium. The exact prevalence of this complication is uncertain but it appears to be the exception rather than the rule and progression to end-stage renal failure appears very rare.

Pre- and regular (every 6 months) post-treatment checks of renal and thyroid function are therefore essential. The low therapeutic index of lithium requires that after treatment is commenced the dose is gradually built up to achieve an effective plasma level. In order to achieve satisfactory plasma levels, plasma levels need to be checked one week after initiation (and after every dose change) then every 3 months. Plasma levels of lithium are increased by several medications including diuretics and non-steroidal anti-inflammatory drugs. Lithium is also teratogenic. It must be withdrawn gradually to minimise the occurrence of rebound mania or depression. All these considerations mean that lithium is a rather impractical agent to commence *de novo* for the treatment of mania. However, in patients whose bipolar illness has previously been controlled by lithium a recurrence of mania associated with a low serum lithium level, perhaps secondary to poor concordance, may be treated by increasing the dose of lithium particularly if symptoms are relatively mild.

Valproate

Valproate is generally well tolerated. More frequent side effects include gastric irritation, nausea, ataxia and tremor. These side effects are often dose related and as the effective dose varies between patients it is usual practice to increase the dose gradually according to clinical response. Plasma level monitoring is not necessary unless there is evidence of ineffectiveness, poor adherence or toxicity, though pre-treatment and post-treatment checks of full blood count and hepatic function are advisable. Valproate can elevate serum levels of carbamazepine and lamotrigine. Its most serious side effects are its association with structural teratogenicity and mental impairment in the newborn when prescribed during pregnancy. Consequently valproate cannot be recommended as a first-line agent in the treatment of mania in women of child-bearing age (unless they are using a highly reliable from of contraception such as an intra-uterine device). In other women and in men valproate can be considered, alongside antipsychotics, as a first-line agent for the treatment of mania.

Polycystic ovary syndrome is characterised by excess androgen levels and ovulatory dysfunction. Several studies have reported a higher prevalence in women with epilepsy and bipolar disorder. Debate has centred on whether this reflect an association with the underlying disorder (that is, epilepsy or bipolar disorder) or the result of antiepileptic drugs, in particular valproate (Rasgon, 2004). Current research is not sufficient to provide a definitive answer but suggests that both pathways may be relevant. In particular a recent small study of reproductive function in women with bipolar disorder found a high rate of menstrual disturbances that in many cases preceded the diagnosis and treatment for the disorder (Rasgon *et al.*, 2005). Furthermore, treatment with valproate was associated with a higher risk of development of menstrual abnormalities than other treatments and valproate was also associated with an increase in testosterone levels over time.

Antipsychotics

Antipsychotics can either be started at a therapeutic antimanic dose on day one of treatment or (in the case of quetiapine and risperidone where titration is necessary to minimise side-effects) rapidly titrated to allow a therapeutic dose to be reached within a few days which is shorter than is the case with titration of lithium and valproate. There is no evidence of teratogenicity with antipsychotics, though one has to be cautious particularly with newly introduced agents such as aripiprazole where experience is more limited. RCTs indicate that the addition of several atypical antipsychotics to pre-existing treatment with either valproate or lithium in patients with partially treated mania is more effective than continuing treatment with valproate or lithium alone. These factors make antipsychotics suitable as first-line treatments for mania.

In choosing between antipsychotics, atypical antipsychotics are preferred to conventional antipsychotics due to the existence of a greater number of supportive RCTs and the lower risk of EPS, at least when the comparator is haloperidol. Several atypical antipsychotics are associated with a low risk of elevation of serum prolactin, another advantage compared with haloperidol. This advantage is not shared by all atypical antipsychotics; both risperidone and amisulpride are commonly associated with elevation of serum prolactin. The atypical antipsychotics licensed for the treatment of mania in the UK are olanzapine, quetiapine and risperidone.

Atypical antipsychotics are not without their drawbacks. All can cause significant weight gain in some patients. The risk is greatest with olanzapine which is associated with about 30% of patients gaining $\geq 7\%$ of body weight in short-term trials (Lieberman *et al.*, 2005). There is also concern about the potential for metabolic disturbance (elevation of serum glucose and lipids) with the atypical antipsychotics. The absolute and relative risk of metabolic disturbance with atypical antipsychotics is unclear due to the lack of long-term RCTs with metabolic data. What metabolic data is available is often not present for all trial participants and sometimes consists of measures that are not ideal for example, non-fasting serum glucose levels when fasting glucose levels are more relevant. Non-prospective data, which has many methodological limitations, suggests that as a class, atypical antipsychotics are associated with a greater risk of diabetes than conventional antipsychotics. Some evidence suggests that within the atypical class the risk of serum glucose elevation (as opposed to frank diabetes) is greater with olanzapine. Olanzapine may also have more potential to elevate serum cholesterol and triglycerides than other atypical antipsychotics.

Despite controversy about the relative risk of metabolic disturbance with different agents, there is a consensus that patients prescribed atypical antipsychotics should have pre- and post-treatment checks of plasma glucose, cholesterol and triglycerides. At the present time, given the limitations of the evidence, it is not possible to make recommendations regarding choice between individual atypical antipsychotics licensed for the treatment of acute mania on the basis of safety and tolerability other than to state that weight gain is more common with olanzapine and raised prolactin is more common with risperidone. Should the uncertainty about the risk of metabolic disturbance with different atypical antipsychotics be resolved and robust evidence emerge of a differential effect, then this situation may change. This would also be the case should evidence emerge of a differential efficacy.

Summary

In summary, for women of child-bearing potential not currently taking medication, the treatment of choice for acute mania is an atypical antipsychotic. In other women or those using a highly reliable form of contraception such as an intra-uterine device, and in men, the treatment of choice is either an atypical antipsychotic or valproate. In a patient with mania already taking lithium (with a suboptimal plasma level) or taking valproate, one can consider increasing the dose of the existing antimanic agent. However if symptoms are severe, such dose increases will often need to be done in conjunction with starting an antipsychotic. For patients already taking lithium or valproate where it is not appropriate to increase the dose, treatment options include adding either lithium or valproate or adding an antipsychotic.

8.4   ECONOMIC EVIDENCE FOR THE TREATMENT OF ACUTE MANIC EPISODES

8.4.1   Review overview

The literature search identified six economic studies that assessed the cost-effectiveness of pharmacological agents for the treatment of acute manic episodes associated with bipolar disorder. Four of the studies (TOHEN1999A; ZAJECKA2002; TOHEN2002A; REVICKI2005) were conducted alongside RCTs, whereas the other two analyses (KECK1996; BRIDLE2004) were based on decision-analytic modelling.

Full references, characteristics and results of all studies included in the economic review are presented in the form of evidence tables in Appendix 14.

8.4.2   Olanzapine versus placebo

One study evaluated the improvements in clinical symptoms and health-related quality of life (HRQOL), as well as direct medical cost implications from a third party payer's perspective (insurance), associated with olanzapine treatment in patients diagnosed with bipolar I disorder experiencing a manic or mixed episode (TOHEN1999A). The study was undertaken in the US. Improvements in clinical symptoms and HRQOL were measured using the YMRS and the Medical Outcomes Study 36-item short-form Health Survey (SF-36) respectively. The time horizon of the study was one year (52 weeks), comprising a 3-week acute phase in which patients were randomised to receive either olanzapine or placebo, followed by a 49-week open-label extension; during the second phase, use of lithium and fluoxetine was permitted for patients experiencing breakthrough symptoms. Direct costs were estimated only for the 49-week open-label extension, and were compared with respective costs incurred over 12 months prior to the study.

In both the acute phase and the open-label extension, olanzapine was associated with overall improvement in clinical and HRQOL outcomes. Compared with costs incurred 12 months prior to the study, olanzapine therapy resulted in monthly savings of almost $900 per patient (1995 prices) during the 49-week open-label extension, largely driven by inpatient cost reductions over that period. The authors concluded that olanzapine had a significant impact on the treatment of mania and could be considered a cost-effective treatment option for use in patients with bipolar I disorder. However, the main drawback of the economic analysis was that it utilised findings of a within-group comparison (before-after study), which may have potentially introduced systematic bias and confounding in the analysis.

8.4.3 Valproate semisodium versus lithium

REVICKI2005 compared the effectiveness and medical costs between valproate semi-sodium and lithium for the treatment of patients with bipolar I disorder hospitalised for an acute manic or mixed episode. The analysis was based on a pragmatic, multi-centre, open-label RCT carried out in the US. The trial was performed under conditions of routine psychiatric care without blinding; patients entering the study continued to receive their usual medical care. Other medications for treating bipolar disorder were administered as clinically necessary, although concurrent treatment with both study medications was strongly avoided, unless clinically required. The time horizon of the analysis was 12 months, comprising an acute phase, extending from randomisation to hospital discharge, and a maintenance phase, starting from the day after discharge and lasting until the total 12-month duration of the trial. The primary clinical outcomes were the mean number of months without DSM-IV level manic or depressive symp-toms, as well as the patient functioning and well-being measured using the Mental Component Summary (MCS) and Physical Component Summary (PCS) of the SF-36. The perspective of the analysis was that of the health service, therefore only direct medical costs were estimated. The results of the analysis demonstrated that there were no significant differences between valproate semisodium and lithium in terms of effec-tiveness and medical costs. Total medical costs per patient were \$28,911 for valproate semisodium and \$30,666 for lithium (p = 0.693, 1997 prices).

KECK1996 assessed the one-year direct medical costs associated with valproate semisodium or lithium monotherapy for the management of patients with bipolar I disorder hospitalised for a manic or mixed episode, or rapid cycling. The study, carried out in the US, was based on a deterministic decision-analytic model. The model incor-porated rates of response to treatment (defined as >50% improvement in clinical symptoms), length of initial hospitalisation, relapse rates and rates of adverse events, and subsequently estimated the total costs incurred over a year of acute and long-term treatment associated with each of the agents compared. Total costs consisted of costs of medication, initial hospitalisation, long-term treatment and treatment of relapses, including laboratory test costs and costs of treating side effects. Initial response rates to treatment were calculated as a weighted mean of response rates reported in studies identified in a literature review; other effectiveness and resource-use parameters were based on published and unpublished data and an expert panel opinion.

The total annual cost per patient was estimated to be \$39,643 for valproate semi-sodium, and \$43,400 for lithium (1994 prices). Overall savings associated with valproate semisodium, despite its higher acquisition costs, were attributed to the lower cost of initial hospitalisation, resulting from a shorter length of stay (14.3 days with valproate semisodium versus 18.4 days with lithium). As expected, cost results were highly sensitive to the length of initial hospitalisation: a 30% increase in the length of stay for valproate semisodium or a 37% decrease in the length of stay for lithium would lead to total costs of treatment being equal for the two drugs. Although no effectiveness measure was explicitly used in the economic analysis, it can be inferred from the base-case results that, since valproate semisodium was associated with a higher response rate compared with lithium (0.59 versus 0.49 respectively), and the two drugs were considered to have equivalent relapse rates (0.56), valproate semisodium was likely to be a more cost-effective option than lithium, as it was associated with lower costs and better outcomes.

8.4.4   Valproate semisodium versus olanzapine

A 12-week, double-blind, multi-centre RCT compared the clinical, HRQOL and economic outcomes of valproate semisodium and olanzapine for the treatment of acute mania in patients with bipolar I disorder (ZAJECKA2002). The study was conducted in the US. Clinical symptoms were measured using the Mania Rating Scale (MRS) from the Schedule for Affective Disorders and Schizophrenia (SADS) Change Version, and the Hamilton Rating Scale for Depression (HRSD). HRQOL was measured using the Quality of Life Enjoyment and Satisfaction Questionnaire (Q-LES-Q) and the number of days with restricted activity. Economic outcomes consisted of direct medical costs and a health service perspective was adopted. The results of the analysis showed that there were no significant differences between the two agents in terms of clinical, HRQOL and economic outcomes over the 12-week period. Valproate semisodium was associated with significantly lower outpatient costs compared with olanzapine; nevertheless, total direct medical costs related to the two agents were similar (valproate semisodium \$13,703 per patient, olanzapine \$15,180 per patient, p = 0.88).

Another study comparing valproate semisodium and olanzapine in terms of direct treatment costs and various clinical outcomes (including YMRS scores, remission rates, median times to remission etc) was also performed in the US (TOHEN2002A). The economic analysis was conducted alongside a 47-week, double-blind, multi-centre RCT. The study population consisted of patients with bipolar I disorder hospitalised for an acute manic or mixed episode and the study adopted a health service perspective. Overall, clinical outcomes were reported to be favouring olanzapine, while total direct medical costs were found to be similar for the two pharmacological agents compared (valproate semisodium \$15,801 per patient, olanzapine \$14,967 per patient, p > 0.05).

8.4.5   Assessment of newer drugs for the treatment of mania (quetiapine, olanzapine, valproate semisodium)

BRIDLE2004 was the only study included in the review that was carried out in the UK; therefore, it is discussed in more detail. The economic analysis was conducted as part of an NHS Health Technology Assessment; the objective of the report was to evaluate the clinical and cost-effectiveness of quetiapine, olanzapine and valproate semisodium in the treatment of mania associated with bipolar disorder. For this purpose a systematic review of the literature was undertaken. Based on the results of the review, the authors concluded that, regarding clinical effectiveness, all three agents were superior to placebo in reducing manic symptoms. In comparison to lithium, no significant differences were found for any of the three drugs in terms of clinical effectiveness. The clinical effectiveness of quetiapine and olanzapine was found to be comparable to that of haloperidol; however, olanzapine resulted in fewer negative outcomes regarding HRQOL relative to haloperidol. All three agents were associated with side effects.

Regarding cost-effectiveness, no safe conclusions could be drawn from the findings of the literature review, due to a number of important limitations characterising already published studies, such as lack of direct comparisons between the drugs under evaluation, as well as differences between the studies regarding the study designs and assumptions used. Moreover, the economic studies included in the review had been carried out in the US; consequently their results referred to a setting that was likely to differ substantially compared with the UK healthcare setting in terms of resource utilisation and costs. Therefore, a new probabilistic economic model was developed, in order to overcome these limitations and assist the decision-making process in the context of the NHS.

The model estimated total medical costs and benefits resulting from treating acute manic episodes associated with bipolar disorder. Effectiveness data were derived from a meta-analysis that incorporated seven of the studies included in the systematic review, based on additional selection criteria. The availability of effectiveness data from the systematic review determined the choice of treatments included in the economic analysis; the following pharmacological agents were thus analysed: quetiapine, olanzapine, valproate semisodium, haloperidol and lithium. The primary measure of benefit used in the economic analysis was the number of responders to treatment; response was defined as ≥50% improvement in patient's manic symptoms, expressed in changes in YMRS scores. The time horizon was equal to 3 weeks in the base-case analysis, to reflect the most commonly reported length of follow-up for which effectiveness data were provided in the clinical trials. Estimated costs, expressed in 2001–2002 prices, included direct medical costs from the NHS perspective; these consisted of hospitalisation and drug-acquisition costs, as well as costs of diagnostic and laboratory tests required for the monitoring of patients. Costs of treating adverse events were not included in the analysis, due to lack of relevant data reported in the literature. However, the authors' opinion was that the majority of adverse events associated with the agents compared were unlikely to have significant resource implications in the 3-week time horizon of the model. Hospitalisation costs were estimated to be the same for all drug treatment options, as all patients were assumed to be hospitalised at the start of the model and to remain hospitalised for the total 3-week period, regardless of response to treatment.

The base-case results of the analysis showed that mean response rates for olanzapine (0.54) and haloperidol (0.52) were higher than for lithium (0.50), quetiapine (0.47), and valproate semisodium (0.45). Haloperidol had the lowest mean total costs per patient (£3,047) in comparison to valproate semisodium (£3,139), olanzapine (£3,161), lithium (£3,162), and quetiapine (£3,165). In terms of cost-effectiveness, lithium, valproate semisodium, and quetiapine were dominated by haloperidol, that is, they were both less effective and more costly, and therefore were excluded from further analysis. Compared with haloperidol, olanzapine was both more effective and more costly, demonstrating an incremental cost-effectiveness ratio (ICER) equal to £7,179 per additional responder. The authors concluded that if decision makers were prepared to pay less than £7,179 per additional responder, then haloperidol was the optimal decision; however, if they were prepared to pay at least £7,179 per additional responder, then olanzapine became the most cost-effective option.

One-way sensitivity analyses were undertaken, to explore whether using alternative model assumptions would have an impact on the base-case results. In terms of dominance, results were robust to the majority of alternative assumptions tested (such as discharge of non-responders at a later time than responders, treatment of non-responders with second and third-line pharmacological therapies, reductions in diagnostic and laboratory costs, inclusion of effectiveness data for patients initially excluded from analysis according to a modified intention-to-treat approach, and inclusion of treatment costs for extrapyramid symptoms due to haloperidol use). The ICER of olanzapine compared with haloperidol ranged between £1,236 (when longer hospitalisation was assumed for non-responders) and £7,165 (when second and third-line treatment was assumed for non-responders, with a low cost estimate used) per additional responder. Base-case results were sensitive only to the entire exclusion of diagnostic and laboratory costs from the analysis, which constituted a rather extreme scenario. In this case lithium became the cheapest option. Valproate semisodium and quetiapine were dominated by both lithium and haloperidol. The ICERs of olanzapine and haloperidol relative to lithium were £7,109 and £103 per additional responder respectively in this scenario.

In order to incorporate the uncertainty within the model related to both cost estimates and response rates, a probabilistic analysis was carried out using Monte Carlo simulation techniques. Instead of mean values, costs and response rates were assigned a range of values based on probability distributions; results were presented in the form of Cost-Effectiveness Acceptability Curves (CEACs), which demonstrated the probability of each agent being the most cost-effective option after taking into account the underlying uncertainty in model input parameters. Probabilities were estimated for a range of potential maximum cost values that the health service was willing to pay in order to achieve an additional unit of benefit (that is, an additional responder). The CEACs demonstrated that, for a willingness to pay (WTP) equal to £20,000 per additional responder, the probabilities of treatments under assessment being cost-effective were: olanzapine 0.44, haloperidol 0.37, lithium 0.16, quetiapine 0.029 and valproate semisodium 0.01. The probability that olanzapine was cost-effective increased as the WTP increased: for a maximum WTP £10,000 per additional responder this probability was 0.42, increasing to 0.45 if the maximum WTP rose to £40,000. At the extreme of a zero value placed on the WTP for an additional responder, haloperidol was proved to be the most cost-effective option (with probability equalling 1).

Although the above analysis was well conducted, it was characterised by a number of limitations, as acknowledged by the authors. The effectiveness rates utilised in the model were based on indirect evidence; this fact may have introduced bias in the analysis. Moreover, systematic searches for all possible comparators were not undertaken, which means that there may have been additional indirect evidence that was not incorporated in the meta-analysis that provided the effectiveness rates for the economic model. In addition, no combination therapies or 2nd and 3rd line treatments were considered in the analysis, due to lack of available data. Finally, the results of the meta-analysis demonstrated that the effectiveness rates were similar between the drugs assessed (as shown by overlapping 95% CIs around mean response rates), which means that their relative cost-effectiveness in practice depended on differences in associated costs only. Cost differences between pharmacological agents were found to be very small (varying between £3,047 and £3,165), and were attributed exclusively to differences in acquisition and monitoring costs, as no evidence was available to suggest a difference in the length of hospital stay relating to each pharmacological treatment examined. However, potential differences between drugs in terms of associated length of hospitalisation may affect significantly their relative cost-effectiveness, as inpatient care is the major driver of total medical costs associated with treatment of acute mania.

In terms of model structure and assumptions used, the short time frame of the analysis limits the value of the results, as potential differences between pharmacological agents in terms of overall length of hospitalisation – beyond the time frame of 3-weeks may strongly affect their relative cost effectiveness. On the other hand, it was assumed that all patients (both responders and non-responders) were hospitalised over the 3-week time frame of the model; if some of the agents are actually associated with lower length of hospital stay for responders, this assumption has underestimated their cost-effectiveness, probably in a significant degree.

Finally, the use of response rates as the primary outcome measure instead of a generic measure of outcome such as Quality Adjusted Life Years (QALYs) due to lack of appropriate data, and the exclusion of costs and quality of life aspects of adverse events from the analysis due to the same reason, were also acknowledged by the authors as further limitations of their analysis.

8.4.6 Summary of economic evidence

Overall, the existing economic evidence suggests that it is likely that there is no significant difference in the relative cost-effectiveness between the various pharmacological agents used for the management of acute manic episodes associated with bipolar disorder. REVICKI2005 concluded that there were no significant differences between valproate semisodium and lithium in terms of effectiveness and costs. KECK1996 stated that valproate semisodium was likely to be a more cost-effective option than lithium; however, the results of this analysis were highly sensitive to the length of initial hospitalisation for the treatment of mania. ZAJECKA2002 and TOHEN2002A demonstrated that valproate semisodium and olanzapine were associated with similar overall treatment costs; the findings of the two studies differed in terms of effectiveness: the first study concluded that the two treatments were equally effective, while the second one reported a higher rate of effectiveness for olanzapine.

The BRIDLE2004 economic analysis, the only one that utilised UK cost data, showed that lithium, valproate semisodium and quetiapine were more costly and less effective than haloperidol. Olanzapine was found to be more effective and more costly than haloperidol, with an ICER equal to £7,179 per additional responder.

However, the results of the meta-analysis conducted as part of the same study suggested that treatments did not differ significantly in terms of clinical effectiveness. Moreover, the differences in total medical costs between the drugs assessed were shown to be very small. This was expected, as hospitalisation costs, the major component of costs associated with the treatment of acute mania, were estimated to be equal for all agents, due to lack of evidence of a differential effect of treatments on the length of hospitalisation following an acute manic episode.

Based on the results of the literature review it can be concluded that if all medications for the treatment of acute mania have a similar effect on the length of hospital stay, then their relative cost-effectiveness is likely to be comparable. Future research, exploring whether pharmacological treatments used for the management of acute mania in patients with bipolar disorder have a differential impact on the length of hospital stay, may determine their relative cost-effectiveness with more certainty.

8.4.7   Clinical practice recommendations for the treatment of acute mania

General advice

8.4.7.1   As soon as practicable after initial presentation of a patient with bipolar disorder, healthcare professionals should:
- establish the patient's smoking status and alcohol use
- perform thyroid, liver and renal function tests, blood pressure, and measure full blood count, blood glucose, lipid profile
- measure weight and height
- consider EEG, CT scan or MRI scan if an organic aetiology or a relevant comorbidity is suspected
- consider drug screening, chest X-ray and ECG if suggested by the history or clinical picture.

8.4.7.2   Contraception, and the risks of pregnancy (including the risks of relapse, damage to the fetus, and the risks associated with stopping or changing medication) should be discussed with all women of child-bearing potential, regardless of whether they are currently planning a pregnancy. They should be encouraged to discuss pregnancy plans with their doctor.

8.4.7.3   To help reduce the negative consequences of manic symptoms, healthcare professionals should consider advising patients to avoid excessive stimulation, to engage in calming activities, to delay important decisions, and to establish a structured routine (including a regular sleep pattern) in which the level of activity is reduced.

8.4.7.4   If a patient is taking an antidepressant at the onset of an acute manic episode, the antidepressant should be stopped. This may be done abruptly or gradually, depending on the patient's current clinical need and previous experience of discontinuation/withdrawal symptoms, and the risk of discontinuation/withdrawal symptoms of the antidepressant in question.

8.4.7.5   People experiencing a manic episode, or severe depressive symptoms, should normally be seen again within a week of their first assessment, and then regularly at appropriate intervals, for example, every 2–4 weeks in the first 3 months and less often after that, if response is good.

Pharmacological management of acute mania for those
not currently taking antimanic medication

8.4.7.6   If a patient develops acute mania when not taking antimanic medication, treatment options include starting an antipsychotic, valproate or lithium. When making the choice, prescribers should take into account preferences for future prophylactic use, the side-effect profile, and consider:
- prescribing an antipsychotic if there are severe manic symptoms or marked behavioural disturbance as part of the syndrome of mania
- prescribing valproate or lithium if symptoms have responded to these drugs before, and the person has shown good compliance
- avoiding valproate in women of child-bearing potential
- using lithium only if symptoms are not severe because it has a slower onset of action than antipsychotics and valproate.

8.4.7.7   In the initial management of acute behavioural disturbance or agitation, the short-term use of a benzodiazepine (such as lorazepam*) should be considered in addition to the antimanic agent.

8.4.7.8   If treating acute mania with antipsychotics, olanzapine, quetiapine or risperidone should normally be used, and the following should be taken into account:
- individual risk factors regarding side effects (such as the risk of diabetes)
- the need to initiate treatment at the lower end of the therapeutic dose range recommended in the summary of product characteristics and titrate according to response
- that if an antipsychotic proves ineffective, augmenting it with valproate or lithium should be considered
- that older people are at greater risk of sudden onset of depressive symptoms after recovery from a manic episode.

8.4.7.9   Carbamazepine* should not be routinely used for treating acute mania, and gabapentin*, lamotrigine*, topiramate* are not recommended.

Pharmacological management of acute mania for those currently taking antimanic
medication

8.4.7.10   If a patient already taking an antipsychotic experiences a manic episode, the dose should be checked and increased if necesssary. If there are no signs of improvement, the addition of lithium or valproate should be considered.

8.4.7.11   If a patient, already taking lithium experiences a manic episode, plasma lithium levels should be checked. If levels are suboptimal (that is, below 0.8 mmol per litre), the dose should normally be increased to a maximum blood level of 1.0 mmol per litre. If the response is not adequate, augmenting lithium with an antipsychotic should be considered.

8.4.7.12   If a patient, already taking valproate* experiences a manic episode, the dose should be increased until:
- symptoms start to improve, or

- side effects limit further dose increase.

  If there are no signs of improvement, the addition of olanzapine, quetiapine, or risperidone should be considered. Patients on doses higher than 45 mg per kilogram should be monitored carefully.

8.4.7.13 For patients who present with severe mania when already taking lithium or valproate*, adding an antipsychotic should be considered at the same time as gradually increasing the dose of lithium or valproate.

8.4.7.14 For patients who present with mania when already taking carbamazepine, the dose should not routinely be increased. Adding an antipsychotic should be considered, depending on the severity of mania and the current dose of carbamazepine. Interactions with other medication are common with carbamazepine, and doses should be adjusted as necessary.

The management of acute mixed episodes

8.4.7.15 Prescribers should consider treating patients with an acute mixed episode as if they had an acute manic episode, and avoid prescribing an antidepressant.

8.4.7.16 Prescribers should monitor patients with an acute mixed episode closely (at least weekly), particularly for suicide risk.

The management of acute manic episodes in children and adolescents

8.4.7.17 When prescribing medication for children or adolescents with an acute manic episode, the recommendations for adults with bipolar disorder should be followed except drugs should be initiated at lower doses. In addition, at initial presentation:
- height and weight should be checked (and monitored regularly afterwards) – for example, monthly for 6 months then every 6 months
- prolactin levels should be measured
- when considering an antipsychotic, the risk of increased prolactin levels with risperidone* and weight gain with olanzapine* should be considered
- where there is an inadequate response to an antipsychotic, adding lithium or valproate* should be considered. Valproate should normally be avoided in girls and young women because of risks during pregnancy and because of the risk of polycystic ovary syndrome.

8.5 THE PHARMACOLOGICAL TREATMENT OF ACUTE EPISODES IN THE CONTEXT OF RAPID CYCLING

8.5.1 Introduction

Rapid cycling occurs in approximately 20% of patients with bipolar disorder. It is usually defined as the occurrence of four or more distinct mood episodes (that is, depression, mania, hypomania or mixed states) within one year. Some patients who would be regarded clinically as rapid cycling may not meet the somewhat arbitrary criteria in a standard diagnostic manual such as DSM-IV. For example in DSM-IV two consecutive mood episodes in the same direction need to be interrupted by 8 weeks of euthymia, or substantial improvement, to qualify towards rapid cycling.

Since rapid cycling was identified by researchers in the 1970s, further subtypes have been recognised including 'ultra rapid cycling' in which episodes last less than 24 hours and 'ultra ultra rapid cycling' in which several switches of mood can occur in a 24-hour period. Rapid cycling is a course specifier rather than a specific type of bipolar disorder i.e. any person with bipolar disorder can develop a rapid cycling pattern but then revert to a non-rapid cycling course. Rapid cycling is more prevalent in bipolar II subtype, and those with thyroid abnormalities (Calabrese *et al.*, 2001; Kupka *et al.*, 2003). Data from a cohort of 456 bipolar probands suggests rapid cycling is not more common in females than males (Baldassano *et al.*, 2005), as had been indicated by previous studies in smaller samples.

Key elements in the treatment of rapid cycling are to eliminate any maintaining factors, particularly substance misuse and antidepressant use. With regard to the treatment of mania in rapid cycling, secondary analyses from several placebo-controlled studies of mania including valproate semisodium, olanzapine, and risperidone (Nemeroff, 2000; Bowden *et al.*, 1994, Sachs *et al.*, 2002) have demonstrated no difference between those with and those without a rapid-cycling course. This suggests that the short-term efficacy of other antimanic agents may not differ according to the cycling status of patients.

The predominant mood state in most rapid-cycling patients is depression. Lamotrigine may be useful in rapid-cycling bipolar disorder. The only RCT in the maintenance treatment of rapid-cycling bipolar disorder (Calabrese *et al.*, 2000) demonstrated that lamotrigine was superior to placebo in time to discontinuation for any reason, and in percentage of patients completing the trial (see Chapter 9).

8.5.2   Clinical practice recommendations

8.5.2.1   Acute episodes in patients with rapid-cycling bipolar disorder should normally be managed in secondary mental health services. Treatment should be as for manic and depressive episodes, but in addition healthcare professionals should do the following.

- Review the patient's previous treatments for bipolar disorder, and consider a further trial of any that were inadequately delivered or adhered to.
- Focus on optimising long-term treatment rather than on treating individual episodes and symptoms; trials of medication should usually last at least 6 months.
- Adopt a psychoeducational approach and encourage patients to keep a regular mood diary to monitor changes in severity and frequency of symptoms, and the impact of interventions.

**8.6   THE PHARMACOLOGICAL TREATMENT OF ACUTE
        DEPRESSED EPISODES**

8.6.1   Introduction

The treatment of bipolar depression has tended to be ignored, with far more interest
focusing on mania. This is paradoxical as the average patient with bipolar disorder
experiences more depressive than manic episodes, on average depressive episodes last
longer than manic ones, the suicide risk is higher in bipolar depression than in mania
and the number of depressive episodes correlates more strongly than the number of
manic episodes with social functioning when patients are in between episodes.

The main aims of the treatment of bipolar depression are resolution of symptoms
and return to a premorbid level of social functioning. What differentiates the treatment of unipolar and bipolar depression is that in the latter one has to ensure that
treatment does not cause switching to mania/hypomania or acceleration of cycling.
There is controversy among guidelines as to what appropriate first-line treatments for
bipolar depression are. The first-line treatments listed in the American Psychiatric
Association bipolar guidelines are lithium and lamotrigine. In contrast there has been
a tradition in Europe to use antidepressants as first-line treatments. The situation has
recently become more complex, with preliminary data indicating that quetiapine, at a
moderate dose, may be an effective treatment for bipolar depression.

8.6.2   The role of antidepressants in bipolar disorder

There are widely differing views on the roles of antidepressants in bipolar disorder. On
one hand, there is the view that antidepressants have significant risks and limited benefits in bipolar disorder and as a result their use should be restricted (for example,
Ghaemi *et al.*, 2003). On the other, there is the view that the risks have been somewhat
exaggerated and that antidepressants have a useful role (for example, Moller &
Grunze, 2000; Altshuler *et al.*, 2004). In more detail these opposing arguments centre
on five issues, though some of these overlap.

The risk of antidepressant-induced switching
Opponents of antidepressants cite high switch rates to mania/hypomania. The opposing argument is that switch rates are fewer with SSRIs than TCAs and can be reduced
further by concomitant use of antimanic medication. The subject of antidepressant-
induced switching to mania/ hypomania is therefore controversial. This largely reflects
the paucity of randomised prospective studies investigating the phenomenon. Most
authorities regard switching as a proven risk, but a minority dispute this and regard
'switching' as representing the natural course of the bipolar disorder. Among those
who accept the reality of antidepressant-induced switching, debate centres on the
magnitude of the risk and to what extent treatment and patient variables influence it.

Estimates of the incidence of switching vary greatly. In a detailed review, Goldberg
and Truman (2003) concluded that in bipolar disorder switch rates associated with antidepressant treatment varied from 20% to 40% and that while mood stabilisers may

reduce the risk they do not totally eradicate it. In contrast, in a recent meta-analysis of 12 RCTs, in which patients with bipolar disorder were randomised to receive an antidepressant or placebo, the switch rate did not differ significantly between the antidepressant and placebo groups (Gijsman *et al.*, 2004). This finding may reflect the fact that 75% of patients were receiving a mood stabiliser which may reduce the risk of switching.

Individual studies differ in their estimates of the degree of protection that antimanic medication offers. A small naturalistic study (Henry *et al.*, 2001) found that mood switches were less frequent in patients receiving lithium (15%, 4/26) than in patients not treated with lithium (44%, 8/18; p = 0.04) but that anticonvulsants did not protect against switching. In contrast, several studies have reported a general protective effect from antimanic agents including carbamazepine and valproate (Boerlin *et al.*, 1998; Bottlender *et al.*, 2001).

Antidepressant-induced switching has been reported in both bipolar I and II disorder and also in children (Briscoe *et al.*, 1995). A pharmacoepidemiological study from the United States, which assessed switching rates in children, adolescents and young adults with an anxiety or non-bipolar mood disorder, concluded that patient age affected the risk of antidepressant-associated manic switching (Martin *et al.*, 2004). In this study, treatment with antidepressants was associated with the highest switch rate among children aged 10 to 14 years.

Other factors reported to be associated with higher risk of switching include a high score on the hyperthymia component of the Semistructured Affective Temperament Interview (p = 0.008) (Henry *et al.*, 2001) and a history of a greater number of past manic episodes (p < 0.023) (Boerlin *et al.*, 1998). Goldberg and Truman (2003) have suggested that a family history of bipolar disorder, a history of previous antidepressant-induced mania and onset of bipolar illness in adolescence or young adulthood may all confer an increased risk. These risk factors can be considered as indicating an increased genetic loading for bipolar disorder and switching.

More controversial is the suggestion by Goldberg and Truman (2003) that exposure to multiple antidepressant trials is associated with a higher switch rate. In other words, antidepressant use may carry a long-term risk in bipolar disorder. However it could be argued that patients with bipolar disorder who have received multiple antidepressant trials are more 'cyclical' than other patients and therefore switching would be more likely to be observed even if there was not a causal relationship with antidepressant use. It is interesting to note that psychiatrists with more interest in bipolar disorder are more cautious about using antidepressant in patients with bipolar disorder (Ghaemi *et al.*, 2003). It is unclear whether female gender is a risk factor for switching (Goldberg & Truman, 2003).

Although antidepressant-induced switching has been reported with all the major antidepressant classes, there is a general consensus that the risk is higher with TCAs than with SSRIs (Calabrese *et al.*, 1999). Peet (1994) calculated the rate of treatment-emergent switch into mania from all available clinical trial data on four SSRIs (fluoxetine, fluvoxamine, paroxetine, sertraline) relative to comparative groups treated with TCAs or placebo. In patients with bipolar disorder a higher switch rate was observed with TCAs (11.2%) than with SSRIs (3.7%) or placebo (4.2%). In contrast in unipolar depressives, the rate of manic switch was less than 1% and differences between drugs and placebo were statistically but not clinically significant. Mania has been reported in association with use of hypericum (St John's wort) (Nierenberg *et al.*, 1999).

Prior to starting an antidepressant, clinicians should warn patients of the risk of antidepressant-induced switching. To minimise the risk, where at all possible, TCAs should be avoided in bipolar disorder and antidepressants only prescribed in conjunction with an antimanic agent.

The risk of antidepressant-induced cycle acceleration

It has been suggested that antidepressants may cause an increase in the cycling rate of bipolar disorder (sometimes referred to as 'mood destabilisation'). This possibility has received less attention than antidepressant-induced switching although, if it occurs, it is potentially a greater problem. Unfortunately, there are no published RCT data to inform the debate. One often-quoted naturalistic study that suggests that TCAs can cause cycle acceleration is Wehr and colleagues (1988). However, this study was based on an atypical group of patients in that they all had treatment-resistant bipolar disorder and were assessed in a specialist mood service. An unpublished randomised study suggests that there may be some increase in affective morbidity in patients with bipolar disorder who remain on antidepressants long term (Ghaemi *et al.*, 2005).

In contrast are the results of a non-randomised 1-year study of long-term antidepressant use, versus early antidepressant discontinuation, after remission of bipolar depression (Altshuler *et al.*, 2004). All subjects continued with ongoing antimanic medication throughout. In this study the risk of depressive relapse was significantly associated with discontinuing antidepressants soon after remission. Furthermore, there was no evidence of manic switching in association with continued antidepressant use. In summary, this study did not show any association with cycle acceleration and suggested a beneficial effect of antidepressant use. The authors argued that maintenance of antidepressant treatment in combination with a mood stabiliser may be warranted in some patients with bipolar disorder. A major weakness of the study is that subjects were not randomised to the antidepressant continuation and discontinuation groups.

The effectiveness of antidepressants in acute depression

Although there is RCT evidence to support the use of antidepressants in the acute treatment of bipolar depression, the data are limited and opponents argue that equally good evidence is available for lamotrigine. However, the beneficial effect of lamotrigine is delayed due to the need to gradually increase the dose in order to reduce the risk of skin rashes.

The effectiveness of antidepressants in prophylaxis of bipolar depression

Proponents of antidepressants have argued that they have a long-term effect in bipolar depression. The Altshuler and colleagues study (2004) supports this view but is potentially flawed as it is non-randomised. Other studies have failed to demonstrate the effectiveness of antidepressants in preventing relapse in patients with bipolar disorder (Ghaemi *et al.*, 2001; Zablotsky *et al.*, 2005). Of particular note is the Zablotsky and colleagues study (2005) which is an interim analysis of patients with bipolar disorder who had recovered from a depressive episode following treatment with a mood stabiliser and an antidepressant who were then randomised to continue or discontinue the antidepressant and then followed up for 1 year. After adjusting for potential confounders, the time that patients remained in remission did not differ significantly between the two groups. This study is the first RCT to assess the efficacy of antidepressants in the prevention of bipolar disorder and suggests that such efficacy is lacking. Further interim data from this same study suggested that in patients with non-rapid-cycling bipolar disorder long-term antidepressant treatment may increase affective morbidity (Ghaemi *et al.*, 2005). The final element relevant to this issue is that opponents of antidepressants argue that there is RCT evidence that lamotrigine can prevent recurrence of bipolar depression and that lithium also has a long-term antidepressant effect, albeit weaker, and that neither lithium nor lamotrigine carry the risks of switching or cycle acceleration that occur with antidepressants.

The effectiveness of antidepressants in reducing suicide

Opponents of antidepressants point out that there is no data to indicate that antidepressants reduce suicide in bipolar disorder but evidence does suggest that lithium can do this. (See next section for further discussion).

The conflicting evidence regarding the long-term effect of antidepressants in bipolar depression contrasts with the situation in unipolar depression. In unipolar depression there is a strong evidence base supporting the routine use of continuation treatment after symptomatic recovery from an acute depressive episode and also supporting the use of maintenance treatment in those with recurrent depression.

8.6.3   LITHIUM AND SUICIDE

Tondo and colleagues (2001) reported studies on lithium treatment in patients with bipolar disorder, major affective disorder and schizoaffective disorder that examined data on suicide rates. Twenty-two studies on a total of 5,647 patients with 33,473 patient years were included. Only three of the studies were randomized. For comparison, data from 13 studies reported suicide rates on patients who were not receiving lithium treatment over a mean period of 5 years. The suicide rate during lithium treatment was significantly less than for those without lithium treatment. Results consistent with a protective effect against suicide were also found when the analysis was restricted to the three randomized trials. The antisuicidal effects of lithium in mood disorders has been recently further supported by two large long-term studies – a retrospective one by Kessing and colleagues (2005) and a prospective one by Angst and colleagues (2005). A naturalistic study by Brodersen and colleagues (2000) reported on the suicide rate in a cohort of patients with mood disorders who were discharged from hospital after commencement of lithium. Over 16 years of follow-up, the SMR for suicide was significantly increased compared with the general population. Within the first 2 years of the study, the suicide rate was higher in those who were non-compliant versus those who were compliant with lithium. However, the suicide SMR was elevated in both the compliant and non-compliant groups indicating that although compliance with lithium reduced the risk of suicide it did not eliminate it. The above data make a strong case for an antisuicidal effect of lithium but cannot separate whether the effect is specific or non-specific (that is, only found because patients who are compliant with long-term lithium are patients who are less likely to die by suicide).

A meta-analysis of 32 RCTs comparing lithium with placebo or other compounds used in long-term treatment for mood disorders provides some support for a specific anti-suicidal effect of lithium (Cipriani *et al.*, 2005). In the 32 trials, 1,389 patients were randomly assigned to receive lithium and 2,069 to receive other compounds. Patients who received lithium were less likely to die by suicide than were patients treated with other compounds. The combined outcome measure of suicide plus self-harm was also lower in patients who received lithium. The authors concluded that lithium is effective in the prevention of suicide and self-harm in patients with mood disorders. However, there were insufficient data to discern whether this effect was also seen in bipolar disorder.

In a narrative review, Muller-Oerlinghausen and colleagues (2005) summarised the evidence for lithium's effects against suicide and suicidal behaviour in affective disorders, concentrating on bipolar disorder. Two interesting questions were raised: is the putative anti-suicidal effect of lithium specific to lithium and does it only occur with improvements in affective symptoms?

In discussing whether the anti-suicidal effect of lithium is shared by other psychotropic agents, the authors cited two trials. Firstly, the Multicenter Study of Affective Psychoses (MAP) (Thies-Flechtner *et al.,* 1996) compared lithium with carbamazepine treatment for 2.5 years in bipolar and schizoaffective patients. There were significantly more suicides and suicide attempts in the carbamazepine group. Secondly, Goodwin and colleagues (2003) conducted a retrospective review of suicide risk in patients on lithium compared with those on valproate and those on carbamazepine. The adjusted suicide risk was 2.7 times higher in valproate treated patients in comparison to that of the lithium group. The study was insufficiently powered to allow similar comparisons with carbamazepine.

In order to determine whether lithium has a specific antisuicidal effect, independent of its effects in episode treatment and prevention, a sub-analysis of data from the International Group for the Study of Lithium-treated Patients (IGSLI) (Ahrens and Muller-Oerlinghausen, 2001) selected patients with recurrent affective disorders and at least one suicide attempt prior to the onset of lithium treatment (a total of 176) and categorised them depending on their response to lithium. A statistically significant reduction in suicide attempts was found in all three groups, even those who were considered to have responded poorly to treatment. Although clearly not conclusive, these data support an independent antisuicidal an effect for lithium.

The weight of all of this evidence underscores the importance of compliance measures particularly early in the course of lithium treatment and a probable long-term benefit not shared by other prophylactic agents. However, specific studies in bipolar disorder are needed to examine how generalisable this effect is and to investigate the role of factors associated with good compliance in the mediation of this effect.

8.6.4   Treatments considered

Studies were found to enable the following treatments to be considered in the treatment of acute depression, both as monotherapy and in combination therapy: antidepressants, antipsychotics, anticonvulsants, and transcranial magnetic stimulation. In addition, a single study of ECT was found (DALY2001), but was excluded.

Antidepressants

As discussed in the previous section, a key issue in the use of antidepressants for bipolar depression is that of inducing switching to mania and the possibility of cycle acceleration. In the UK no antidepressant is specifically licensed for use in bipolar depression.

Lithium

There are no RCTs of lithium monotherapy as treatment for bipolar depression. Several cross-over studies were completed prior to 1980 and it is largely on these that lithium is recommended as a first-line treatment. A practical disadvantage of lithium as an antidepressant is the long delay before an antidepressant effect begins to be seen (usually 6–8 weeks).

8.6.5   Review strategy

Evidence from RCTs was found for the following treatment strategies:
- **Antidepressants**, including antidepressants compared with placebo, another antidepressant an antipsychotic, lithium or valproate semisodium
- **Antipsychotics**, including antipsychotic compared with placebo, and antipsychotic-antidepressant combination
- **Anticonvulsants**, including lamotrigine and valproate semisodium
- **Transcranial magnetic stimulation** compared with sham-transcranial magnetic stimulation.

A summary of the evidence for the pharmacological treatment of depression in children and adolescents is also provided.

There are no RCTs of lithium in the treatment of acute bipolar depression.

8.6.6   Antidepressants in the treatment of acute depression

Studies considered

Nine trials met the eligibility criteria set by the GDG. Excluded studies with reasons for exclusion can be seen in Appendix 22. Efficacy data could not be extracted from three studies (AMSTERDAM2005, COHN1989, HIMMELHOCH1991). Data were therefore available to compare imipramine and paroxetine (in patients maintained on lithium, both high (>0.8 mmol/litre) and low serum levels ($=<0.8$ mmol/litre)) with both placebo and each other, imipramine with moclobemide, and idazoxan[13] with bupropion.[14] In addition, data were available to compare amitriptyline with the antipsychotic l-sulpiride. (A comparison of fluoxetine combined with an antipsychotic against an antipsychotic is considered below.) In most studies, some patients were maintained on lithium. See Table 36 for outline study characteristics and Appendix 22 for more detailed information.

---

[13]Does not have UK marketing authorisation.

[14]Does not have UK marketing authorisation for the treatment of depression.

Table 36: Summary of study characteristics for antidepressants in the treatment of acute depression

	Versus placebo	Versus another antidepressant	Versus an antipsychotic	Versus prophylactic agent
No. trials (No. participants)	*4 RCTs (703)*	*5 RCTs (391)*	*2 RCTs (64)*	*1 RCT (27)*
Study IDs	(1) AMSTERDAM2005 (2) COHN1989 (3) NEMEROFF2001 (4) TOHEN2003 * (5) SILVERSTONE2001	(1) COHN1989 (2) GROSSMAN1999 (3) HIMMELHOCH1991 (4) NEMEROFF2001	(1) AMSTERDAM2005 (2) BOCCHETTA1993	YOUNG2000
Population	US; outpatients (4) 13 countries, in- and outpatients	US; outpatients (apart from (5), New Zealand; outpatients	(1) US; outpatients (2) Italy; outpatients	Canada; outpatients
Diagnosis	(1) Bipolar I – depressed phase 94%; bipolar II – depressed phase 6% (2) (3) Bipolar – depressed phase: at least one manic episode (for (2) or depressed episode) in last five years (4) Bipolar I – depressed phase; psychotic features 12.7%	Bipolar – depressed phase (apart from (3)): bipolar I – depressed phase 43%; bipolar II – depressed phase 57%	(1) Bipolar – depressed phase (2) Bipolar – depressed phase	Bipolar I – depressed phase 41%; bipolar II – depressed phase 59%

Continued

251

Table 36: (Continued)

No. trials (No. participants)	Versus placebo	Versus another antidepressant	Versus an antipsychotic	Versus prophylactic agent
	4 RCTs (703)	*5 RCTs (391)*	*2 RCTs (64)*	*1 RCT (27)*
Study interventions	(1) Fluoxetine**** (2) Fluoxetine 20 mg–80 mg (58% on 80 mg); imipramine 75 mg–300 mg (27% on 225 mg–300 mg) (3) Imipramine 116.7 mg*; paroxetine 32.6 mg* (4) Olanzapine 9.7 mg**; olanzapine 7.4 mg** and fluoxetine 39.3 mg**	(1) Fluoxetine 20 mg–80 mg (58% on 80 mg); imipramine 75 mg–300 mg (27% on 225 mg–300 mg) (2) Idozoxan 240 mg; bupropion 450 mg*** (3) Tranylcypromine 36.8 mg*; imipramine 245.5 mg* (4) Imipramine 116.7 mg*; paroxetine 32.6 mg* (5) Imipramine up to 250 mg; moclobemide up to 750 mg (31% on highest dose)	(1) Fluoxetine, olanzapine**** (2) Amitriptyline 62 mg**; l-sulpiride 55 mg*	Paroxetine 36 mg*
Concurrent lithium	(1) 15% (2) 25% (3) 100%	(1) 25% (2) not clear (3) not given	(1) 15% (2) 100% (maintained at 0.5–1.0 mmol/l)	Second prophylactic agent (lithium 0.9 mmol/l* or valproate)

	(4) None, although benzodiazepine use allowed throughout (actual use not reported)	(4) 100% (5) 47%	On lithium or valproate semisodium for at least 3 months before entering study	semisodium 510 mmol/l*)
Minimum depression score at entry (mean baseline score (SD) or range of means)	(1) HRSD-17 >= 17 (not given) (2) HRSD-21 >= 20 (26–27.7**) (3) HRSD-21 >= 15 (20.38 (3.9) to 21.57 (3.87)) (4) MADRS >= 20	(1) HRSD-21 >= (26–27.7**) (2) HRSD-17 >= 16 (21.3 (4) to 20.8 (3.6)) (3) HRSD >= 15 (22.1 (3.8) to 23.2 (3.6)) (4) HRSD-21 >= 15 (5) HRSD >= 16 (23 (3.8) to 22.5 (3.6))	(1) HRSD-17 >= 17 (not given) (2) HRSD-21 >= 17 (22.1 (5.2) to 23.9 (6.1))	
Mean age	Around 40	Around 40	45*	41*
Length of trial	(1) 8 weeks* (2) 26 weeks* (3) 10 weeks* (4) 8 weeks	(1) 26 weeks* (2) 7 weeks* (3) 6 weeks (4) 10 weeks* (5) 8 weeks	4 weeks*	5 weeks*
Problems with trial	(1) No data available – authors contacted (2) Efficacy data not extractable	(1) and (3) Efficacy data not extractable	(1) No data available – authors contacted	Efficacy data not extractable

Notes: * Also in antipsychotic section below **mean

***used in meta-analysis with TOHEN2003 study since 300 mg is minimum therapeutic dose

An additional study, BOCCHETTA1993 is considered with antidepressants above.

**** 4-arm trial

Table 37: Summary of evidence profile for antidepressants in the treatment of acute depression

	Versus placebo	Versus another antidepressant	Versus an antipsychotic	Versus prophylactic agent
Drugs for which data are available	Paroxetine; imipramine (all patients on lithium); fluoxetine (all on olanzapine)	Imipramine versus moclobemide (50% lithium); idazoxan versus bupropion*; paroxetine versus imipramine (100% lithium)	Amitriptyline versus l-sulpiride (100% lithium); fluoxetine versus olanzapine versus fluoxetine + olanzapine	Paroxetine
Evidence for efficacy (quality)	Antidepressants are more effective than placebo for patients with low serum lithium levels or on olanzapine (moderate)	Moclobemide more effective than imipramine (moderate), otherwise inconclusive (low) or no data (paroxetine versus imipramine)	Data are inconclusive (low) for efficacy outcomes	No data
Evidence for acceptability/ tolerability (including switching) (quality)	Antidepressants more acceptable than placebo (low); tolerability inconclusive (low)	Acceptability inconclusive (low); tolerability unclear (low)	Data are inconclusive (low) for tolerability/ acceptability outcomes	Data are inconclusive (low) for tolerability/ acceptability outcomes

*Idazoxan and bupropion do not have UK marketing authorisation as antidepressants

Summary of evidence for antidepressants in the treatment of acute depression
An overview of the results is provided in Table 37, with the full evidence profile in
Appendix 23.

Clinical summary for antidepressants in the treatment of acute depression
The evidence for the use of antidepressants in bipolar depression is weak. In patients
maintained on lithium, there is no difference in the efficacy of paroxetine
or imipramine on any outcome measure. Both are more efficacious than placebo, but
the difference is neither statistically nor clinically significant. However, when the data
are analysed by lithium serum levels, with >0.8 mmol/litre classified high and
<= 0.8 mmol/litre as low, there is a clinically important advantage for both paroxe-
tine and imipramine compared with placebo in the low-serum group but not for the
high-serum group. Moclobemide is superior to imipramine, although nearly half the
patients in the comparison were taking lithium, which makes the data hard to interpret. In addition, there are concerns regarding the risk of interaction with serotonergic
agents and certain foodstuffs, and these risks are likely to be higher in patients with
bipolar disorder compared with those with unipolar disorder because of the risk of
mixed affective states and mania, which may impair judgement.

There is no significant difference between idazoxan and bupropion on any
outcome measure or between imipramine and tranylcypromine. There is only inconclusive evidence of efficacy, acceptability and tolerability for an antidepressant
compared with an antipsychotic. The study of lithium or valproate semisodium plus
paroxetine versus lithium or valproate semisodium alone does not report extractable
efficacy outcomes. All acceptability and tolerability measures were inconclusive. In a
comparison between amitriptyline and l-supiride, there is no significant difference
between the two. All patients were on lithium in this study.

Based on evidence from trials in unipolar depression (NCCMH, 2004), SSRIs are
the safest treatment for depression because of their increased tolerability and safety
compared with TCAs and monoamine oxidase inhibitors. In addition, in bipolar
depression data suggests a lower risk of switching compared with TCAs.

8.6.7   Antipsychotics in the treatment of acute depression

Studies considered
Three trials met the eligibility criteria set by the GDG. Excluded studies with reasons
for exclusion can be seen in Appendix 22. See Table 38 for outline study characteristics and Appendix 22 for more detailed information.

Summary of evidence
The efficacy data for olanzapine and quetiapine (300 mg and 600 mg) could not
be combined in meta-analysis because of extreme heterogeneity ($I^2 = 91\%$). They
were therefore analysed separately. There was not such difficulty with
tolerability/acceptability data. One study (CALABRESE2005) also included both
patients with bipolar II disorder and those with bipolar I disorder. The data for those
with bipolar I disorder were analysed in a sub-analysis.

Table 38: Summary of study characteristics for antipsychotics in the treatment of acute depression

	Versus placebo	Dose-finding study	Versus another antipsychotic and antidepressant
No. trials (No. participants)	*3 RCTs (1409)*	*1 RCT (542)*	*1 RCT (833)*
Study IDs	(1) AMSTERDAM2005 (2) CALABRESE2005A (3) TOHEN2003	CALABRESE2005A	TOHEN2003
Population	(1) US; outpatients (2) US; outpatients (3) 13 countries; in- and outpatients	US; outpatients	13 countries; in- and outpatients
Diagnosis	(1) Bipolar I – depressed phase 94%; bipolar II – depressed phase 6% (2) Bipolar I – depressed phase 66%; bipolar II – depressed phase 33% 21% rapid cyclers (3) Bipolar I – depressed phase, 12.7% psychotic features	Bipolar I – depressed phase 66%; bipolar II – depressed phase 33% 21% rapid cyclers	Bipolar I – depressed phase, 12.7% psychotic features
Study drugs	(1) Olanzapine (2) Quetiapine 300 mg*** or 600 mg (3) Olanzapine 9.7 mg**	Quetiapine 300 mg and 600 mg	Olanzapine 9.7 mg**; olanzapine 7.4 mg** and fluoxetine 39.3 mg**

Concomitant medication	(1) Lithium allowed (2) Benzodiazepine use allowed in first 3 weeks for insomnia or severe anxiety (3) Benzodiazepines allowed in acute phase	Benzodiazepine use allowed in first 3 weeks	Benzodiazepine use allowed throughout
Minimum depression score at entry	(1) HRSD-17 >= 17 (not given) (2) HRSD-17 >= 20 (24.3 to 24.6) (3) MADRS >= 20 (30.8 (0.70 to 32.6(0.3)))	HRSD-17 >= 20	MADRS >= 20
Mean age (or range of mean ages)	(1) 40 (2) 37 (3) 42	37	42
Length of trial	8 weeks	8 weeks	8 weeks
Study problems	(1) No data available – authors contacted (2) High non-completion rate, particularly in placebo group (61%)		

Notes: **mean

***used in meta-analysis with TOHEN2003 study since 300 mg is minimum therapeutic dose

An additional study BOCCHETTA1993 is considered with antidepressants above.

An overview of the results is provided in Table 39, with the full evidence profile in Appendix 23.

**Table 39: Summary of evidence profile for antipsychotics
in the treatment of acute depression**

	Versus placebo	**Dose-finding study**	**Versus another antipsychotic and antidepressant**
Drugs for which data are available	Olanzapine, quetiapine (300 mg or 600 mg)	Quetiapine (300 mg or 600 mg)	Olanzapine + fluoxetine, olanzapine
Evidence for efficacy (quality)	Quetiapine more effective than placebo (moderate) Limited evidence of efficacy for olanzapine versus placebo (moderate); a sub-analysis of bipolar I patients gave similar results	No difference (moderate)	Combination treatment is more effective than placebo or an antipsychotic alone (moderate)
Evidence for acceptability/ tolerability (including switching) (quality)	Antipsychotics were as acceptable as placebo, but less tolerable, with olanzapine likely to cause weight gain; a sub-analysis of bipolar I patients gave similar results (moderate)	Quetiapine 300 mg was more acceptable and tolerable than quetiapine 600 mg	Combination treatment is more acceptable than placebo or antipsychotic alone, less tolerable than placebo, but more tolerable than antipsychotic alone (moderate). It is more likely to cause weight gain (moderate). Switching is unclear.

Clinical summary

There is some evidence for the use of atypical antipsychotics in acute bipolar depression, although none is licensed in the UK for the treatment of bipolar depression. However, the single study of olanzapine has quality issues, in particular a high attrition rate and apparently different results for different measures of depression. In addition, weight gain was five times more likely to be reported by those taking olanzapine than those on placebo. This is supported by a review of weight gain in patients with schizophrenia taking antipsychotics, which showed mean weight gain after 10 weeks' treatment with olanzapine was more marked than with other antipsychotics, with the exception of clozapine (Allison *et al.*, 1999). Quetiapine was more effective than placebo, although there was no difference between high (600 mg/day) and low (300 mg/day) doses of the drug on efficacy measures. However, people on low-dose quetiapine were less likely to leave treatment early or to leave because of side effects. There was also a high attrition rate from this study.

8.6.8   Anticonvulsants in the treatment of acute depression

Studies considered for review

Three trials met inclusion criteria. See Table 40 for outline study characteristics, and Appendix 22 for more detailed information.

Summary of evidence

An overview of the results is provided in Table 41 with the full evidence profile in Appendix 23.

Clinical summary

Of the two trials of anticonvulsant monotherapy in acute depression in people with bipolar disorder that met the inclusion criteria, one was of lamotrigine and the other valproate semisodium. Neither drug is licensed in the UK for the treatment bipolar depression. The overall risk-benefit ratios in both trials were unclear since in both the acceptability and tolerability data were inconclusive, although there is evidence of efficacy versus placebo for valproate semisodium. In the lamotrigine trial, the risk of switching to mania did not differ significantly between the 50 mg/day, 200 mg/day and placebo groups.

The most serious (but rare) side effect of lamotrigine is Stevens-Johnson syndrome. In early clinical trials in epilepsy the incidence of serious rash was 0.3% in adults and 1% in children (Guberman *et al.*, 1999; Messenheimer *et al.*, 1998). However, the introduction of a slow dose titration reduced the risk of serious rash to 0.01% in adults, which is similar to that seen with other anticonvulsants (Calabrese *et al.*, 1999). Rashes can occur at any point during treatment but are most common early on in treatment and when lamotrigine is co-prescribed with valproate. Particular concern attaches to a rash that is widespread or associated with fever, sore throat or mucosal involvement. Patients prescribed lamotrigine must be advised to see their psychiatrist or GP if any rash appears. If it has any of the features listed previously, lamotrigine must be stopped. Lamotrigine may have limited use in the treatment of acute depression because of its slow dose titration and onset of action.

Table 40: Summary of study characteristics for anticonvulsants in the treatment of depression

	Lamotrigine	Valproate semisodium
No. trials (No. participants)	*1 RCT (195)*	*1 RCT (23)*
Study IDs	CALABRESE1999B	DAVIS 2005
Population	US, UK, France, Australia; outpatients	US; outpatients
Diagnosis	Bipolar I disorder — depressed phase	Bipolar I disorder — depressed phase
Study drug	Lamotrigine 50 mg or 200 mg	Valproate semisodium serum levels 50–100ug/ml
Comparator	Placebo	Placebo
Concomitant medication	None, but randomisation stratified according to intensity of lithium treatment in previous 5 months	Diphenhydramine or hydroxyzaine (25 mg−50 mg/day) as a sedative
Minimum depression score at entry	HRSD-17 >= 18	HRSD-17 >= 18
Mean age (or range of mean ages)	42	41
Length of trial	7 weeks	8 weeks
Study problems		

**Table 41: Summary of evidence profile for anticonvulsants
in the treatment of acute depression**

	Lamotrigine	Valproate semisodium
Drugs for which data are available	Lamotrigine 50 mg and 200 mg versus placebo	Valproate semisodium versus placebo
Evidence for efficacy (quality)	Data are inconclusive (low) for efficacy outcomes	Some evidence of efficacy versus placebo (moderate)
Evidence for acceptability/ tolerability (including switching) (quality)	Data are inconclusive (low) for tolerability/acceptability outcomes	Data are inconclusive (low) for tolerability/acceptability outcomes
Overall risk-benefit ratio	Unclear	Unclear

8.6.9 Transcranial magnetic stimulation in the treatment of acute depression

Studies considered
Two trials were identified from searches of electronic databases, with one meeting inclusion criteria. See Table 42 for a summary of the study characteristics and Appendix 22 for more detailed information.

Summary of evidence
An overview of the results is provided in Table 43, with the full evidence profile in Appendix 23.

Clinical summary
There is no difference in the efficacy of transcranial magnetic stimulation compared with sham transcranial magnetic stimulation on reducing depression symptoms, but participants receiving sham treatment had lower endpoint mania symptom scores. No one left treatment early and the data on side effects are not reported.

Table 42: Summary of study characteristics for transcranial magnetic stimulation in the treatment of depression.

	Versus sham transcranial magnetic stimulation
No. trials (No. participants)	*1 RCT (23)*
Study IDs	NAHAS2003
Population	US Outpatients
Diagnosis	Bipolar I – mixed phase 8% Bipolar I – depressed phase 52% Bipolar II – depressed phase 39%
Comparisons between	Transcranial magnetic stimulation
Concomitant medication	Carbamazepine or valproate (alone or in combination) or benzodiazepines
Minimum depression score are entry	HRSD $>=$ 18 (32.5 (4.3) to 32.8 (7.6))
Mean age (or range of mean ages)	42
Length of trial	10 days

Table 43: Summary of evidence profile for transcranial magnetic stimulation in the treatment of depression

	Transcranial magnetic stimulation (TMS)
Drugs for which data are available	TMS versus sham TMS
Evidence for efficacy (quality)	Data are inconclusive (low) for efficacy outcomes
Evidence for acceptability/tolerability (including switching) (quality)	Unlikely (moderate); some evidence of higher mania scores in TMS group (moderate)

8.6.10   Fatty acids in the treatment of acute depression

Studies considered for review
One trial of omega 3 fatty acids in the treatment of acute depression met inclusion criteria. This compared omega 3 fatty acids with placebo. An overview of the study is in Table 44, with further details available in Appendix 22.

Summary of evidence
Only one trial met inclusion criteria. This shows a significant effect on depression scores for omega 3 fatty acids (at both 1 g and 2 g doses) compared with placebo in patients with moderate depression. The effect on mania scores was hard to judge since the 95% CIs were wide. However, the estimated effect sizes are small, indicating little effect on manic symptoms. Despite this, since the trial is small (around 25 in each arm), there is insufficient evidence to warrant recommending omega 3 at present. An overview of the results is provided in Table 45, with the full evidence profile in Appendix 23.

**Table 44: Study information table for omega 3 fatty acids
in the treatment of acute depression**

	Omega 3
No. trials (No. participants)	1 RCT (75)
Study IDs	FRANGOU2006
Diagnosis	Bipolar I depression 86%; bipolar II depression 14%
Setting	UK; outpatients
Baseline scores	HRSD mean 14.7–15.4 YMRS mean 4.7–6.6
Omega 3 fatty acid dose	Ethyl-eicosapentaenoic acid (EPA) 1 g/d, Ethyl-eicosapentaenoic acid (EPA) 2 g/d
Comparator	Placebo
Mean age	47
Length of trial	12 weeks

**Table 45: Summary evidence profile for omega 3 fatty acids
in the treatment of acute depression**

	Omega 3
Evidence for efficacy (quality)	Omega 3 is more effective than placebo at both 1 mg and 2 mg doses (moderate)
Evidence for acceptability/ tolerability (quality)	Omega 3 does not appear to induce switching (low); 11% more people taking 1 mg/day reported side effects compared with placebo (low); 3% fewer taking 2 mg/day reported side effects compared with placebo

8.6.11 The treatment of treatment-resistant depression

Studies considered for review
One trial (NIERENBERG2006) met the eligibility criteria set by the GDG. There were no excluded studies. See Table 46 for outline study characteristics and Appendix 22 for more detailed information. The trial, which is part of STEP-BD, used equipoise randomisation whereby participants could choose which two of three available study treatments (risperidone, lamotrigine, inositol) they preferred in addition to existing antimanic medication (lithium, valproate or carbamazepine) and antidepressant(s). They were then randomised to one of their chosen acceptable treatments. This created four strata: risperidone versus lamotrigine, risperidone versus inositol, lamotrigine versus inositol. The study is analysed according to these strata. However, three participants were willing to be randomised to any treatment and these data are included twice. Since the number involved was small, data from different strata are combined in meta-analysis.

Summary of evidence for the treatment of treatment-resistant depression
Treatment-resistance depression (that is, no response to treatment in the first 12 weeks of standard or randomised care pathway for bipolar depression or a well-documented failure of at least two antidepressants or an antidepressant plus antimanic agent). All the calculated effect sizes were inconclusive since the 95% CIs were too wide to draw firm conclusions. This is probably because the study lacked power since the randomisation method led to low numbers in each treatment group. However, most effect sizes indicated little difference between treatments, although that for non-responders taking lamotrigine compared with inositol approached both clinical and statistical significance favouring lamotrigine, but that for lamotrigine compared with risperidone did not. Also, that for inositol versus risperidone favoured inositol. Although data for switching to mania/hypomania were available, the number of events was too low to draw firm conclusions. An overview of the results is provided in Table 47, with the full evidence profile in Appendix 23.

Table 46: Summary of study characteristics for treatment-resistant depression

No. trials (No. participants)	*1 RCT (66*)*
Study IDs	NIERENBERG2006 (STEP-BD)
Diagnosis	Bipolar I depression 52%; bipolar II depression 48%
Setting	Outpatients; US
Baseline scores	SUM-D (equivalent to MADRS) median (50% range) 6 (3.5) to 8.6 (4); SUM-M (equivalent to YMRS) 0 (1.3) to 1.5 (1.5)
Study drugs	Lamotrigine (150–250 mg); risperidone (6 mg); inositol (10–25 g)
Concomitant medication	Lithium (0.6–0.9 mmol/l), valproate (45–90 μg/ml) or carbamazepine 4–10 μg/ml) plus antidepressant(s)
Mean age	42
Length of trial	16 weeks
Other factors	Open label and equipoise randomisation

*Study reports data on 69 participants as data from three counted twice due to equipoise randomisation (see Appendix 22)

Table 47: Summary evidence profile for treatment-resistant depression

Evidence for efficacy (quality)	Efficacy data (non-response) are inconclusive (low)
Evidence for acceptability/ tolerability (quality)	Data are inconclusive on all outcomes (low)

8.6.12 Economic evidence for the pharmacological treatment of acute depressive episodes

No economic studies on the cost-effectiveness of pharmacological treatment for acute depressive episodes in patients with bipolar disorder were identified.

8.6.13   Clinical practice recommendations

8.6.13.1   A patient who is prescribed antidepressant medication should also be prescribed an antimanic drug. The choice of antimanic drug should be compatible with decisions about future prophylactic treatment, the likely side effects and whether the patient is a woman of child-bearing potential.

8.6.13.2   When initiating antidepressant treatment for a patient who is not already taking antimanic medication, prescribers should explain the risks of switching to mania and the benefits of taking an adjunctive antimanic agent. People who are not willing to take antimanic medication should be monitored carefully. Treatment should begin at a low dose and be increased gradually if necessary.

8.6.13.3   If a person has an acute depressive episode when taking antimanic medication, prescribers should first check they are taking the antimanic agent at the appropriate dose and adjust the dose if necessary.

8.6.13.4   For patients with acute mild depressive symptoms, a further assessment should be arranged, normally within 2 weeks ('watchful waiting') if:
- previous episodes of mild depression have not developed into chronic or more severe depression in this patient, or
- the patient is judged not to be at significant risk of developing a more severe depression.

If the patient is judged to be at significant risk of worsening or on review continues to be unwell, they should be managed as for moderate or severe depression, particularly if functional impairment is evident.

8.6.13.5   For patients with moderate or severe depressive symptoms, prescribers should normally consider:
- prescribing an SSRI antidepressant (but not paroxetine in pregnant women) because these are less likely than tricyclic antidepressants to be associated with switching, or
- adding quetiapine, if the patient is already taking antimanic medication that is not an antipsychotic

8.6.13.6   If a trial of drug treatment at an adequate dose and with adequate compliance does not produce a significant improvement for moderate depressive symptoms, a structured psychological treatment should be considered. This should focus on depressive symptoms, problem solving, promoting social functioning, and education about medication.

Starting antidepressant treatment and monitoring risk

8.6.13.7   Antidepressants should be avoided for patients with depressive symptoms who have:
- rapid-cycling bipolar disorder
- a recent hypomanic episode
- recent functionally impairing rapid mood fluctuations.

Instead consider increasing the dose of the antimanic agent or the addition of a second antimanic agent (including lamotrigine*).

8.6.13.8 Patients' concerns about taking antidepressants should be addressed. For example, they should be advised that craving and tolerance do not occur, and that taking medication should not be seen as a sign of weakness.

8.6.13.9 When antidepressant treatment is started, patients should be told about:
- the possibility of manic or hypomanic switching
- the delay in onset of effect, and the gradual and fluctuating nature of improvement
- the need to take medication as prescribed and the risk of discontinuation/withdrawal symptoms
- the need to monitor for signs of akathisia, suicidal ideation (normally anyone under 30 should be reviewed within 1 week of initiation of treatment), and increased anxiety and agitation (particularly in the initial stages of treatment)
- the need to seek help promptly if these side effects are distressing.

8.6.13.10 If a patient with bipolar disorder develops marked and/or prolonged akathisia or agitation while taking an antidepressant, the use of the drug should be reviewed urgently.

8.6.13.11 Care should be taken when prescribing SSRIs* to people – particularly older people – taking other medication that can cause intestinal bleeding, such as non-steroidal anti-inflammatory drugs. The use of a gastroprotective drug may be considered.

Stopping antidepressants after the treatment of acute depression

8.6.13.12 When a patient is in remission from depressive symptoms (or symptoms have been significantly less severe for 8 weeks), stopping the antidepressant medication should be considered, to minimise the risk of switching to mania and increased rapid cycling. The dose of antidepresant should be gradually reduced over several weeks, while maintaining the antimanic medication. Particular care is needed when discontinuing paroxetine and venlafaxine because they are associated with a higher risk of discontinuation/withdrawal symptoms.

Additional guidance on specific treatments

8.6.13.13 The following treatments should not be routinely used for acute depressive episodes in people with bipolar disorder:
- lamotrigine* as a single, first-line agent in bipolar I disorder
- transcranial magnetic stimulation*.

Incomplete response to the treatment for acute depression

8.6.13.14 When a patient's depressive symptoms do not fully respond to an antidepressant, the patient should be reassessed for evidence of substance abuse, psychosocial stressors, physical health problems, comorbid disorders, such as anxiety or severe obsessional symptoms, and inadequate adherence to medication. Prescribers should then consider:
- increasing the dose of the antidepressant within 'British national formulary' ('BNF') limits

- individual psychological therapy focused on depressive symptoms
- switching to an alternative antidepressant (for example, mirtazapine or venlafaxine)
- adding quetiapine* or olanzapine if the patient is not already taking one of these, or
- adding lithium if the patient is not already taking it.

Management of treatment-resistant depression in bipolar disorder

8.6.13.15 If a patient's depressive symptoms have failed to respond to at least three courses of treatment for depression of adequate dose and duration, seeking the advice of, or referral to, a clinician with a specialist interest in treating bipolar disorder shold be considered.

Management of concurrent depressive and psychotic symptoms

8.6.13.16 For patients with a diagnosis of bipolar disorder experiencing concurrent depressive and psychotic symptoms, prescribers should consider augmenting the current treatment plan with antipsychotic medication, such as olanzapine, quetiapine, or risperidone, or the use of electroconvulsive therapy if the depressive illness is severe.

Management of persistent depressive symptoms

8.6.13.17 For patients with persistent depressive symptoms and no history of recent rapid cycling, including those who have declined an antidepressant, structured psychological therapy may be considered. This should focus on depressive symptoms, problem solving, improving social functioning, and further discussion of medication concordance.

8.6.14 Research recommendations

Treatments for patients in partial remission from depressive symptoms in bipolar disorder

8.6.14.1 A randomised placebo-controlled trial should be conducted to investigate the efficacy and cost effectiveness of adding an antidepressant (SSRI) to an existing antimanic agent for patients with bipolar disorder in partial remission from a depressive episode. The trial would ideally recruit from both primary and secondary care and outcome measures would include time to recovery from depression, time to prevention of the next episode and social functioning with a 2-year follow-up period.

Why this is important

The treatment of severe mental illness is a key priority in the National Service Framework for mental health, and depression of all kinds is a major cause of long-term disability and unemployment. People with bipolar disorder suffer more depressive episodes than manic ones. Partial remission from symptoms is common, so successful treatment would greatly improve functioning and quality of life. But there is little evidence on which to base recommendations for treatment of bipolar depression, and none on treatment after partial remission.

Treatments for depression in bipolar disorder, and their risks

8.6.14.2   A sequenced set of randomised controlled trials should be undertaken to investigate the efficacy and cost effectiveness of antidepressants, in the presence of an antimanic medication, in treating bipolar depression. The studies should address the different stages of depression (acute, continuation and maintenance) and also evaluate the risks, particularly switching to mania and cycle acceleration, associated with antidepressant treatment. Patients with bipolar I and II disorder should be recruited. Outcome measures would include time to recovery from depression, time to prevention of the next episode and social functioning.

Why this is important

People with bipolar disorder suffer more depressive episodes than manic episodes. Depression is the major cause of suicide and the rate of suicide is very high among patients with bipolar disorder (10–15%). Therefore successful treatment would greatly improve functioning and quality of life. There is little evidence on the treatment of bipolar depression, particularly in different phases of the illness. Reducing depression could contribute to meeting the national targets to reduce suicide in bipolar disorder, and to reduce depression as a major cause of long-term disability and unemployment.

8.6.15   The treatment of acute depression in children and adolescents

There are no studies of the management of acute depression in children and adolescents with bipolar disorder. It is necessary to extrapolate cautiously from the adult database and to refer to the evidence on the treatment of unipolar depression in children and adolescents. The NICE guideline Depression in Children and Young People (NCCMH, 2005) summarises the evidence for the use of antidepressants in under 18 year olds with unipolar depression. Fluoxetine is the only SSRI antidepressant where clinical trials demonstrated that the risk benefit ratio was positive for unipolar depression in young people under 18 years. However, the issue of whether SSRIs are linked to increased suicide risk is unclear. Whilst there is evidence that the rates in those taking SSRIs are no different to those taking TCAs (Jick *et al.*, 2004; Martinez *et al.*, 2005), the risk may also be due to discontinuation of treatment due to adverse events. However, there is evidence of increased risk of non-fatal self-harm in those taking SSRIs under 18 (Martinez *et al.*, 2005). The addition of CBT may reduce this risk. Antidepressants should normally first be prescribed only in conjunction with psychological therapies and the child or adolescent should be monitored for agitation, suicidal ideation and self-harm. If treatment with fluoxetine is unsuccessful or not tolerated because of side effects, consideration should be given to the use of another antidepressant. In the case of children and adolescents, sertraline or citalopram are the recommended second-line treatments. In the UK none of these drugs is licensed for use in under 18 year olds but can be prescribed unlicensed by a specialist practitioner.

8.6.16   Clinical practice recommendations

Depression in children and adolescents

8.6.16.1   Children and adolescents with bipolar disorder experiencing mild depressive symptoms assessed as not requiring immediate treatment should be monitored weekly and offered additional support, for example at home and in school.

8.6.16.2   Children or adolescents with depressive symptoms needing treatment should normally be treated by specialist clinicians (based in at least Tier 3 services). Treatment should be as for adults with bipolar disorder except that a structured psychological therapy aimed at treating depression should be considered in addition to prophylactic medication.

8.6.16.3   If there has been no response to psychological therapy for depression combined with prophylactic medication after 4 weeks, prescribers should consider:

● adding fluoxetine* starting at 10 mg per day, and increasing to 20 mg per day if needed

● using an alternative SSRI (sertraline* or citalopram*) if there is no response to fluoxetine after an adequate trial.

If there is still no response, advice should be sought from a specialist in affective disorders.

8.6.16.4   For developmentally advanced adolescents with depressive symptoms, the recommendations on managing depression in adults with bipolar disorder should be followed.

8.7   ELECTROCONVULSIVE THERAPY (ECT) (ALL ILLNESS PHASES)

8.7.1   Clinical evidence

No study of ECT in acute bipolar depression met inclusion criteria, although there is some evidence for its effectiveness compared with an antipsychotic in acute mania. The recommendations below are adapted from the NICE technology appraisal of ECT (NICE, 2003).

8.7.2   Health economics evidence

A recent NHS Health Technology Assessment (Greenhalgh *et al.*, 2005) aimed at evaluating the clinical and cost effectiveness of ECT for depressive illness, schizophrenia, catatonia and mania. The report failed to identify any economic studies relating to ECT fulfilling the inclusion criteria set for the systematic review. In addition, although decision-analytic models were developed in order to assess the cost effectiveness of ECT for the management of depressive illness and schizophrenia, it was not possible to construct any economic models for either mania or catatonia, due to lack of published data relating to these disease areas.

Only one economic study relating to ECT for the management of acute bipolar episodes was identified and included in the systematic review carried out for this guideline (KUTCHER1995). The study, which was conducted in Canada, compared ECT to standard pharmacological inpatient care for the management of adolescents and young adults (16–22 years old) with treatment-resistant acute bipolar episodes, either manic or depressive, and was based on a retrospective comparative design. The main drawback of the analysis was the method of group assignment, which was based on self-selection: patients eligible for ECT chose whether they wanted to undergo ECT; those agreeing comprised the ECT group, while those denying received standard inpatient care. Costs consisted of hospitalisation costs only; intervention costs were not estimated. Clinical outcomes included improvement in clinical symptoms as measured using the BPRS, length of hospital stay, and rate of side effects in the ECT group. The time horizon of the analysis was the period until hospital discharge.

The analysis demonstrated that both groups were characterised by significant improvement in BPRS scores over time, with the ECT group score at discharge being significantly lower than that of the control group. Side effects of ECT were reported to be generally mild, occurring in 28% of the ECT sessions. The length of hospital stay was shorter for the ECT group, resulting in lower hospitalisation costs compared with the control group ($58,608 versus $143,264 per admission respectively). Overall, ECT appeared to be more cost-effective than standard care; however, the design of the study, which was subject to major selection bias, as well as the estima-tion of hospitalisation costs only and the omission of all other relevant costs from the analysis, limit considerably the scope of it; consequently, no robust conclusions on the cost-effectiveness of ECT can be drawn based on this study.

Full reference, characteristics and results of the above study are presented in the evidence tables for economic studies in Appendix 14.

8.7.3   Clinical practice recommendations

8.7.3.1   Electroconvulsive therapy (ECT) is recommended only to achieve rapid and short-term improvement of severe symptoms after an adequate trial of other treatment options has proven ineffective and/or when the condition is considered to be potentially life-threatening, in individuals with:
   ● severe depressive illness
   ● catatonia
   ● a prolonged or severe manic episode.[15]

---

[15] This recommendation is from NICE *technology appraisal* 59 and has been incorporated into this guide-line in line with NICE procedures for the development of guidelines.

8.7.3.2 The decision as to whether ECT is clinically indicated should be based on a documented assessment of the risks and potential benefits to the individual, including:
- the risks associated with the anaesthetic
- current comorbidities
- anticipated adverse events, particularly cognitive impairment
- the risks of not having treatment.[15]

8.7.3.3 When using ECT to treat bipolar disorder, prescribers should consider:
- stopping or reducing lithium or benzodiazepines before giving ECT
- monitoring the length of fits carefully if the patient is taking anticonvulsants
- monitoring mental state carefully for evidence of switching to the opposite pole.

8.8 THE MANAGEMENT OF ACUTE BEHAVIOURAL DISTURBANCE

8.8.1 Introduction

Acute behavioural disturbances in the context of bipolar disorder typically occur during periods of hospitalisation, but may arise at any time during the course of the illness, as part of an exacerbation. A person may be agitated, aggressive or violent towards others, secondary to psychotic symptoms (for example, grandiose delusions, command hallucinations) or non-psychotic symptoms (for example, high levels of arousal). However, in the Royal College of Psychiatrists' guideline on the management of imminent violence (1998), environmental factors, including overcrowding, lack of privacy, lack of activities and long waiting times to see staff, are identified as playing an important role in increasing the likelihood of aggression or violence. Also, social factors, such as poor communication between patients and staff and weak clinical leadership, may contribute to feelings of frustration and tension amongst all parties. Dealing with these issues in advance may reduce the risk of violence and aggression (Royal College of Psychiatrists, 1998).

The initial response should be to provide structure, reduce stimulation and try to verbally reassure and calm the person (Osser & Sigadel, 2001). Staff need to be trained to anticipate possible violence and to de-escalate the situation at the earliest opportunity. Physical means of restraint or seclusion should be resorted to 'only after the failure of attempts to promote full participation in self-care'. In this context, the use of drugs to control disturbed behaviour (rapid tranquillisation) is often seen as a last resort, for use where appropriate psychological and behavioural approaches have failed or are inappropriate. However, patients who participated in discussion groups on this topic have expressed the view that when they behaved violently, their preference was for medication rather than seclusion or prolonged physical restraint (Royal College of Psychiatrists, 1998).

The aim of drug treatment in such circumstances is to calm the person and reduce the risk of violence and harm, rather than treat the underlying psychiatric condition.

An optimal response would be a reduction in agitation or aggression without sedation, allowing the patient to participate in further assessment and treatment. Ideally, the drug should have a rapid onset of action and a low level of side effects. Psychiatrists, and the multidisciplinary team, who use rapid tranquillisation should be trained in the assessment and management of patients specifically in this context: this should include assessing and managing the risks of drugs (benzodiazepines and antipsychotics), using and maintaining the techniques and equipment needed for cardiopulmonary resuscitation, and prescribing within therapeutic limits and using flumazenil (a benzodiazepine antagonist).

8.8.2   Current practice

In clinical practice in the UK, the most common choice of drug for rapid tranquillisation has been an antipsychotic, such as haloperidol or chlorpromazine, often in combination with a benzodiazepine, such as diazepam or lorazepam (Pilowsky *et al.*, 1992; Cunnane, 1994; Mannion *et al.*, 1997; Simpson & Anderson, 1996). Zuclopenthixol acetate, a short-acting depot antipsychotic, has also been commonly used, although doubts as to its value have recently been raised (Fenton *et al.*, 2000). Previously published guidelines have generally recommended that drug treatment should be administered orally, if the person is willing to accept this (Atakan & Davies, 1997; Kerr & Taylor, 1997; Royal College of Psychiatrists, 1997). Liquid or rapidly dissolving preparations may be particularly useful.

However, current practice is not underpinned by a strong evidence base. There are relatively few controlled studies on which to base prescribing decisions. Further, in studies of drug treatment of acute behavioural disturbance, there may be some doubt about the generalisability of the patient samples, in that many of the individuals who require rapid tranquillisation would be too disturbed to give informed consent to participate. Placebo-controlled studies would be necessary to assess the overall advantage of treatment using the various drug regimens, but such studies are likely to be regarded as unethical given that rapid tranquillisation is usually indicated only after other non-pharmacological approaches have failed. In any event, a major concern in this situation is to minimise the risk of harm to the individual, the staff and others.

8.8.3   Safety considerations in rapid tranquillisation

The benefit of reducing the risk of harm to the individual or others must be balanced against the risk of adverse effects associated with such drug regimens. In a survey of around 100 incidents of rapid tranquillisation, Pilowsky and colleagues (1992) found few adverse events, although those reported were potentially serious cardiovascular and cardiorespiratory events. The cardiovascular effects of antipsychotics in such situations have become a source of growing concern. Osser and Siagdel (2001) recommend that chlorpromazine is avoided because of its greater risk of hypotension. Droperidol, an antipsychotic widely used for rapid tranquillisation, was voluntarily withdrawn in 2001 because of reports of QT prolongation, serious ventricular arrhythmia and sudden death. A change in the rate-corrected QT interval (QTc) on the ECG associated with an antipsychotic may be an indicator of cardio toxicity. An increased risk of QT interval prolongation has been reported with several antipsychotic drugs (Royal College of Psychiatrists, 1997). In a naturalistic study in the UK (Reilly *et al.*, 2000), a prolonged QTc was associated with both thioridazine and droperidol. Partly on the basis that QTc prolongation may be a marker of risk of arrhythmia, the use of thioridazine has been restricted in the UK since the end of 2000 and would not be appropriate for rapid tranquillisation.

Acute EPS, such as akathisia, parkinsonism and dystonia, are commonly observed with intramuscular conventional antipsychotic drugs. Dystonic reactions can be particularly severe and unpleasant (Royal College of Psychiatrists, 1997) and both akathisia and dystonia could exacerbate disturbed behaviour. If an antipsychotic is to be used alone in people at high risk for dystonia, such as males under 35 years of age, long-term antiparkinsonian drug treatment should be considered (Osser & Sigadel, 2001).

Benzodiazepines, although considerably safer, can cause cognitive impairment, behavioural disinhibition, over-sedation and, most seriously, respiratory depression with the administration of high doses (Mendelson, 1992). The benzodiazepine partial antagonist flumazenil can counter these effects, but it is not easy to give in an emergency situation by those inexperienced in its use: flumazenil has a shorter half-life than the majority of benzodiazepines, meaning that repeated doses may be required. It can also induce seizures in people who have been receiving regular benzodiazepines.

8.8.4   Definition and aim of rapid tranquillisation

Rapid tranquillisation means the use of drug treatments to achieve rapid, short-term behavioural control of extreme agitation, aggression and potentially violent behaviour that places the individual or those around them at risk of physical harm (Broadstock, 2001). The term rapid tranquillisation is usually restricted to parenteral forms of medication. The aim of rapid tranquillisation is to achieve sedation sufficient to minimise the risk posed to the person themselves or to others. The individual should be able to respond to spoken messages throughout the period of sedation (Royal College of Psychiatrists, 1998).

8.8.5   Studies considered for review

This review is based on a new systematic search for RCTs of pharmacological agents used in rapid tranquillisation. Since there are very few studies in specific bipolar populations, inclusion criteria allowed studies with people with other severe mental illness. The search was undertaken in May 2005; 30 trials were identified from searches of electronic databases, with five meeting the eligibility criteria set by the GDG. Excluded studies with reasons for exclusion can be seen in Appendix 22.

Important characteristics of the included studies are in Table 48, with fuller details of studies in Appendix 22.

8.8.6   Outcomes

The following outcomes were extracted at 2 and 24 hours after administration of study drugs: scores on the Positive and Negative Symptom Scale (PANSS) excited subscale and total scale, overt aggression scale, agitated behaviour scale, YMRS, and BPRS, plus the number who received benzodiazepines. Scores on the PANSS excited subscale and agitated behaviour scales were considered primary outcomes. Also, the number leaving the study early for any reason and because of side effects were extracted, together with side effects including parkinsonian side effects, akathisia, EPS, dystonia, nausea, vomiting, hyperkinesias [EPS or movement disorders] agitation, somnolence and QTc interval change. Parkinsonian side effects, akathisia, EPS and QTc interval change were also considered primary outcomes.

8.8.7   Clinical summary

Only six studies met inclusion criteria. Of these, only one included 100% bipolar patients (MEEHAN2001), with two others including a proportion of people with bipolar disorder (FOSTER1997, 35%; CURRIER2004, 8%). The majority of people in the dataset had a diagnosis of schizophrenia or related disorders. There was also some uncertainty about the quality of the included trials, with only one (CURRIER2004) describing an adequate randomisation process. The others failed to report how randomisation was carried out. Among other things, these aspects led to downgrading of evidence.

On critical outcomes there was evidence (moderate quality) that IM olanzapine and IM lorazepam are effective in reducing aggressive behaviour compared with placebo, as well as evidence (low quality) for the efficacy of IM haloperidol compared with placebo. There was inconclusive evidence (very low quality) of any difference in efficacy between IM olanzapine (10 mg) and IM haloperidol (7.5 mg), but some evidence that IM olanzapine is more effective than IM lorazepam (moderate quality). There were no critical outcomes reported for IM haloperidol compared with IM lorazepam and the available evidence was graded very low quality. In the one study including oral medication (oral risperidone + oral lorazepam versus IM risperidone + oral lorazepam) (CURRIER2004), there was no difference between the two drug combinations (moderate quality).

Turning to side effects, there was no difference on critical side effects between olanzapine and placebo (low quality evidence), and some evidence that haloperidol

Table 48: Summary of study characteristics for rapid tranquillisation in the management of acute behavioural disturbance

	IM antipsychotic or benzodiazepine versus IM placebo	IM antipsychotic versus IM antipsychotic	IM antipsychotic versus benzodiazepine (versus combination)	Oral antipsychotic + benzodiazepine versus IM antipsychotic + benzodiazepine
No. trials (No. participants)	*3 RCTs (782)*	*2 RCTs (581)*	*2 RCTs (238)*	*1 RCT (162)*
Study IDs	(1) BRIER2002 (2) MEEHAN2001 (3) WRIGHT2001	(1) BRIER2002 (2) WRIGHT2001	(1) FOSTER1997 (2) MEEHAN2001	CURRIER2004
Diagnosis	(1) (3) 100% schizophrenia (2) 100% bipolar manic phase	100% schizophrenia	(1) 65% schizoaffective disorders or psychotic illness; 35% bipolar disorder (2) 100% bipolar manic phase	55% schizoaffective disorders; 8% bipolar; 18% other
Agitation status	(1) PANSS-EC >= 14 (with >= 4 on at least 1 item) (2) Agitation severe enough to be appropriate candidates for receiving injections,	(1) PANSS-EC >= 14 (with >= 4 on at least 1 item) (2) PANSS-EC >= 14 (with >= 4 on at least 1 item)	(1) Judged to be an imminent danger to themselves, required 4-point physical restraints, scored >= 5 on at least 3 items on BPRS and	Patients exhibiting both psychosis and agitation judged by clinicians to require pharmacological intervention

PANSS-EC >= 14 (with >= 4 on at least 1 item) (3) PANSS-EC >= 14 (with >= 4 on at least 1 item)	had score of at least 4 on CGI. (2) Agitation severe enough to be appropriate candidates for receiving injections, PANSS-EC >= 14 (with >= 4 on at least 1 item)		US (24 sites)
Setting (1) Croatia, Italy, Romania, South Africa (2) US, Romania (3) Australia, N America, Europe, S Africa	(1) Croatia, Italy, Romania, South Africa, Australia, N America, Europe, S Africa	(1) US psychiatric emergency service (2) US, Romania	
Study drugs (1) IM olanzapine 10 mg*, IM haloperidol 7.5 mg, placebo (2) IM olanzapine, IM lorazepam, placebo (3) IM olanzapine, IM haloperidol, placebo	(1) IM olanzapine 10 mg, IM haloperidol 7.5 mg, placebo (2) IM olanzapine, IM haloperidol, placebo	(1) Haloperidol or lorazepam (both oral or IM at discretion of clinician) (2) IM olanzapine, IM lorazepam, placebo	Oral risperidone + oral lorazepam IM haloperidol + oral lorazepam
Mean age range 36–40 or not specified	36 or not specified	36–42	38

Notes: *study includes IM olanzapine at other doses, but 10 mg chosen for this review because it is the dose given by the BNF

Table 49: Summary of evidence profile for rapid tranquillisation in the management of acute behavioural disturbance

	IM antipsychotic or benzodiazepine versus IM placebo	IM antipsychotic versus IM antipsychotic	IM antipsychotic versus benzodiazepine (versus combination)	Oral antipsychotic + benzodiazepine versus IM antipsychotic + benzodiazepine
Evidence for efficacy (quality)	Olanzapine (high), haloperidol (moderate) and lorazepam (high) effective versus placebo	Data are inconclusive (low) for efficacy outcomes	Olanzapine more effective than lorazepam (high)	No difference between two combinations (high)
Evidence for side effects (quality)	Olanzapine has most favourable side-effect profile (low)	Olanzapine has most favourable side-effect profile (high)	Relevant side effects not reported	Data are inconclusive (low) for tolerability/ acceptability outcomes

caused more side effects than placebo (low quality evidence). Critical outcomes were not reported by the study comparing lorazepam with placebo. When olanzapine was compared with haloperidol, there was some evidence of a more favourable side-effect profile for olanzapine (moderate quality evidence). Relevant side effects were not reported in the study of olanzapine compared with lorazepam. Evidence was inconclusive (very low quality) for oral risperidone + oral lorazepam versus IM risperidone + oral lorazepam.

An overview of the results is provided in Table 49, with the full evidence profile in Appendix 23.

8.8.8 Clinical recommendations

8.8.8.1 If a patient with bipolar disorder exhibits seriously disturbed behaviour, or is judged to be at risk of doing so, healthcare professionals should:
● place the patient in the least stimulating and confrontational, and most supportive environment available
● review the patient's safety and physical status, including hydration levels, and take appropriate action
● consider using distraction techniques and diverting the patient's energy into less risky or more productive activities to prevent or reduce behavioural disturbance.

Pharmacological management of severe behavioural disturbance in people with bipolar disorder

8.8.8.2 Severe behavioural disturbance in people with bipolar disorder should normally be treated first with oral medication, such as lorazepam* or an antipsychotic, or a combination of an antipsychotic and a benzodiazepine. Risperidone and olanzapine are available in orodispersible formulations that are easier for patients to take and are more difficult to spit out.

8.8.8.3 If a severely disturbed patient with bipolar disorder cannot be effectively managed with oral medication and rapid tranquilisation is needed, intramuscular olanzapine (10 mg), lorazepam* (2 mg) or haloperidol (2–10 mg) should be considered, wherever possible as a single agent. When making the choice of drug, prescribers should take into account:
● that olanzapine or lorazepam* are preferable to haloperidol because of the risk of movement disorders (particularly dystonia and akathisia) with haloperidol
● that olanzapine and benzodiazepines should not be given intramuscularly within 1 hour of each other
● that repeat intramuscular doses can be given up to 20 mg per day (olanzapine), or 4 mg per day (lorazepam*) or 18 mg per day (haloperidol) – total daily dose including concurrent oral medication should not normally exceed 'BNF' limits

- the patient's previous response and tolerability, their current regular medication, and the availability of flumazenil.

8.8.8.4   Intravenous preparations of any psychotropic drug, intramuscular diazepam*, intramuscular chlorpromazine, paraldehyde* and zuclopenthixol acetate are not recommended for routine use for managing behavioural disturbances in people with bipolar disorder.

9. THE MEDICAL AND PHARMACOLOGICAL MANAGEMENT OF BIPOLAR DISORDER – PART II

9.1 INTRODUCTION

The following aspects of the medical and pharmacological management of bipolar disorder are considered in this chapter:
- the long-term treatment of bipolar disorder including health economic evidence
- the discontinuation/withdrawal of medication
- pharmacological issues in the management of women having a baby.

9.2 THE LONG-TERM PHARMACOLOGICAL MANAGEMENT OF BIPOLAR DISORDER

9.2.1 Introduction

Long-term treatment aims to prevent the occurrence of future episodes of bipolar disorder and is important due to the recurrent nature of bipolar disorder. Aspects of long-term treatment include helping patients recognise signs of early relapse, avoiding triggers for episodes and employing pharmacotherapy. The long-term nature of treatment in bipolar disorder makes establishing a positive therapeutic alliance between patient and staff crucial. Patients require long-term medication to prevent a recurrence of both depression and mania. The relative importance of these two aims will be determined by the past history, that is, how many previous depressive and manic episodes have occurred and their severity. Lamotrigine is thought to have a specific effect in reducing the risk of recurrence of bipolar depression. Drugs that are thought predominantly to reduce the occurrence of mania include valproate, lithium and olanzapine, though each of these may also have significant effects in reducing the likelihood of depressive relapse. On average, people with bipolar disorder spend more time suffering from depressive symptoms than from manic symptoms. This is particularly the case in bipolar II disorder in which, in one study (Judd *et al.*, 2003), the ratio of time depressed to hypomanic was 37 to 1 compared with 3 to 1 in bipolar I disorder (Judd *et al.*, 2002). It could therefore be argued that the amelioration of depression is a key aim for most bipolar patients. Tolerability will often be a bigger concern for patients during long-term treatment than during acute treatment.

There are relatively few long-term trials in bipolar disorder. Interpretation of these trials is hindered by different definitions of relapse, inadequate description of the clinical history of participants (for example, whether the sample was liable to manic or depressive relapses) and the fact that some studies do not distinguish between depressive and manic relapses.

9.2.2   Treatments considered

Licensed indications

Lithium and olanzapine have UK marketing authorisation for the prophylaxis of bipolar disorder, and carbamazepine has marketing authorisation for the prophylaxis of bipolar disorder unresponsive to lithium. Medications which do not have a UK marketing authorisation for the indication recommended at the date of publication are marked with an asterisk (*); check the summary of product characteristics for current licensed indications.

Regarding the use of psychotropic medication in children and adolescents under the age of 18, at the date of publication no drugs have a UK marketing authorisation. However, in 2000, the Royal College of Paediatrics and Child Health issued a policy statement on the use of unlicensed medicines, or the use of licensed medicines for unlicensed applications, in children and adolescents. This states that such use is necessary in paediatric practice and that doctors are legally allowed to prescribe unlicensed medicines where there are no suitable alternatives and where the use is justified by a responsible body of professional opinion.[16]

Lithium

Lithium has been used in the treatment of bipolar disorder for over 50 years and has been regarded as the gold standard long-term agent, although lithium salts were first used in the 19th century (Healy, 2002). However, recent research suggests that its effect is mainly confined to prevention of mania. Observational studies suggest that long-term lithium treatment has an anti-suicidal effect in mood disorders (Baldessarini *et al.*, 2003a). Goodwin and colleagues (2003) reported a large naturalistic study that found a 2.7-fold increase in the risk of suicide in patients prescribed valproate semisodium compared with patients prescribed lithium. Such studies cannot help distinguish whether such an effect is non-specific due to the benefit arising from the long-term monitoring provided for patients who remain on lithium, or a specific benefit from the action of lithium. A recent meta-analysis of RCTs showed a benefit of lithium in the prevention of suicide, deliberate self-harm and death from all causes, suggesting the latter mechanism, although it was not possible to assess the impact of the efficacy of lithium compared with comparators in producing this effect (Cipriani *et al.*, 2005).

---

[16]Joint Royal College of Paediatrics and Child Health/Neonatal and Paediatric Pharmacists Group Standing Committee on Medicines (2000) *The Use of Unlicensed Medicines or Licensed Medicines for Unlicensed Applications in Paediatric Practice – Policy Statement*. London: Royal College of Paediatrics and Child Health.

Issues to consider in long-term treatment with lithium include the narrow therapeutic index, the risk of thyroid disorders and chronic renal impairment, and the risk of rebound phenomena. These were discussed in the previous chapter.

Antipsychotics

Conventional antipsychotics have tended to be used in the long-term treatment of bipolar disorder by European psychiatrists. One atypical antipsychotic (olanzapine) is licensed for prevention of relapse in bipolar disorder. Weight gain is a concern with most antipsychotics and particularly olanzapine, which is associated with a higher mean weight increase than other atypical antipsychotics (Allison *et al.*, 1999). With olanzapine, weight tends to reach a plateau after about 9 months of treatment (Kinon *et al.*, 2001).

Recently, there has been increasing concern about the possible metabolic side effects of atypical antipsychotics including elevation of glucose, cholesterol and triglycerides. The US Federal Drugs Agency has regarded hyperglycaemia and risk of diabetes as a class effect of atypical antipsychotics. The issues of whether (i) atypical antipsychotics differ in their propensity to cause metabolic side effects and (ii) the clinical significance of any such differences are both controversial. This reflects a relative lack of long-term RCTs, with metabolic data plus contradictory results in the existing literature. Much of the data is retrospective and has methodological weaknesses that include potential screening bias, failure to thoroughly assess non-pharmacological risk for diabetes and lack of randomisation, which makes it impossible to confidently tease apart drug effects from non-pharmacological effects, such as lifestyle and family history. Within the general population, approximately half of those with abnormal glucose tolerance and diabetes are undiagnosed and this also holds for those with severe psychiatric illness (Subramaniam *et al.*, 2003). Most of the data concerning metabolic abnormalities in those receiving atypical antipsychotics relates to patients with schizophrenia and not bipolar disorder.

Despite these issues, a recent randomised double-blind study of nearly 1500 patients with schizophrenia treated for up to 18 months showed mean elevation of cholesterol, triglycerides and glycosylated haemoglobin were all greater with olanzapine than with several other atypical antipsychotics, though mean elevation of blood sugar did not differ between the groups (Lieberman *et al.*, 2005). The results suggest that metabolic abnormalities are more frequent with olanzapine than with other atypical antipsychotics. However, it seems that all atypical antipsychotics can, in some patients, lead to elevation of glucose and indeed this adverse effect was reported with chlorpromazine in the 1950s. Many guidelines now recommend monitoring of glucose and lipid levels for patients prescribed any antipsychotic and this is the view adopted by this guideline. It is also important to note that many patients with bipolar disorder may be at high risk of developing diabetes mellitus and dyslipidaemias due to aspects of their lifestyle, irrespective of antipsychotic treatment.

Anticonvulsants

Similar issues that apply to short-term treatment also apply to long-term treatment with anticonvulsants (see the previous chapter). In addition there is evidence that weight gain with valproate can continue over an entire 12-month period. In a 47-week maintenance trial 17.9% of patients treated with divalproex gained at least 7% of their body weight (last observation carried forward (LOCF) analysis) (Tohen *et al.*, 2003). Weight gain appeared to be more gradual with divalproex than in the olanzapine comparator group.

Valproate semisodium is licensed for the treatment of mania. Carbamazepine is licensed for the treatment of bipolar patients who are intolerant of lithium or in whom lithium is ineffective. A major complication of carbamazepine is that it can lower the plasma level of concurrently prescribed drugs, including antipsychotics. Both carbamazepine and valproate are teratogenic, being associated with an increased risk of neural tube defects. Sodium valproate is also associated with the development of a range of other major abnormalities including facial dysmorphias and distal digit hypoplasia (Holmes *et al.*, 2001; Morrow *et al.*, 2006; O'Brien & Gilmour-White, 2004). The monotherapy major malformation rate (MMR) for valproate was 5.9% (4.3–8.2), significantly higher than the other commonly used prophylactic agents (carbamazepine 2.3% (1.4–3.7), lamotrigine 2.1% (1.0–4.0)). The risk is thought to be greater in those prescribed >1 g valproate per day versus lower doses (Omtzigt *et al.*, 1992). It is important to note that the neural tube closes at day 30 of gestation which will usually be before a pregnancy has been confirmed; for this reason prevention is essential. In addition, there is evidence that the use of valproate is associated with a significant reduction in cognitive functioning of children born to mothers who used valproate during pregnancy (Adab *et al.*, 2004a, b).

Lamotrigine
Although lamotrigine is generally considered safer in long-term use than other drugs, there are some concerns with its use in pregnant women. Morrow and colleagues (2006) found that whilst the overall rate of malformations in babies of women taking the drug during pregnancy is similar to the background rate (3.2%), there may be a dose–response relationship with the rate rising to 5.4% in those taking >200 mg daily, whilst for those on the lowest dose the rate was 1.3%. The Morrow and colleagues (2006) study is based on those taking drugs to control epilepsy.

Antidepressants
Concerns about cycle acceleration and the long-term efficacy, if any, of antidepressants are of key relevance to the question of how long to continue to prescribe antidepressants.

9.2.3   Review strategy

RCTs were found for the following treatment strategies:
- **Lithium monotherapy**, compared with placebo, an anticonvulsant, an antidepressant or an antipsychotic
- **Lithium in combination** with an antidepressant
- **Lithium at different doses or lithium in different dosing regimens**
- **Other monotherapies** (anticonvulsants, antipsychotics)
- **Antipsychotic** combinations.

A summary of the evidence for the long-term pharmacological treatment of children and adolescents is also provided.

9.2.4   Study design and outcomes

Most studies recruited participants to an open-label acute phase during which they were stabilised on one or both of the study drugs (so called 'enrichment trials'). Euthymic participants were randomised to continue open-label medication or switch to another drug. In some trials patients were switched to the randomised treatment without tapering the acute-phase medication (for example, BOWDEN2000). Both these features are likely to influence outcomes. In DUNNER1976 participants entered the study during a period of 'normal mood'. Participants in TOHEN2003 had participated in a previous double-blind acute-phase study.

The primary outcome extracted was the number of participants relapsing, however defined by the trialists. In order to apply intention-to-treat principles (see Chapter 3) this was extracted as the number not completing the study in sustained remission, where this was given in the papers.

9.2.5   Lithium monotherapy in long-term management

Studies considered for review
Ten trials of lithium monotherapy (versus another monotherapy or placebo) met the eligibility criteria set by the GDG. Excluded studies with reasons for exclusion can be seen in Appendix 22. Lithium serum levels are referred to as mmol/litre except where the papers refer to meq/litre. The two measures are equivalent. See Table 50 for a summary of the study characteristics and Appendix 22 for more detailed information.

Clinical summary
BOWDEN2003 is analysed separately (lithium, lamotrigine, placebo) because the trialists stopped randomising patients to the lithium arm early due to slow recruitment. The trial was also stopped early.

There is evidence that lithium is effective in reducing relapse. The lithium levels in the studies are relatively high (0.8–1.2 mmol/l) compared with those used in current practice (0.5–0.8 mmol/l). Given that most UK laboratories providing testing services cite a level of 0.4 mmol/l as adequate, a reasonable compromise would be 0.6 mmol/l.

With regard to efficacy, there was considerable heterogeneity in the studies comparing lithium with placebo, with the later studies (published in 2000 and 2003, and both including another active treatment group) showing little effect at 12 or 18 months and the earlier studies (published 1973) showing a strong effect at 24 or 30 months. In addition, although it is generally accepted that lithium is more effective in reducing manic relapses than depressed relapses, it was possible to reproduce this finding only with considerable heterogeneity in the dataset. In particular, the BOWDEN2000 study gave different results to the other studies, with a poor result for

Table 50: Summary of study characteristics for lithium monotherapy in long-term treatment

	Versus placebo	Versus an anticonvulsant	Versus an antidepressant	Versus an antipsychotic
No. trials (No. participants)	*5 RCTs (1102)*	*7 RCTs (1154)*	*1 RCT (117)*	*1 RCT (431)*
Study IDs	(1) BOWDEN2000 (2) BOWDEN2003 (3) CALABRESE2003 (4) DUNNER1976 (5) PRIEN1973 (6) STALLONE1973	(1) BOWDEN2000 (2) BOWDEN2003 (3) CALABRESE2003 (4) CALABRESE2005 (5) COXHEAD1992 (6) FINDLING2005 (7) HARTONG2003	PRIEN1984	TOHEN2005
Population	US; outpatients	All US except (7): Holland Participants in (7) lithium-naive	US; in- and outpatients	North America, Europe, South Africa
Diagnosis at entry to study	(1) Bipolar I – manic phase (2) Bipolar I – not in acute episode (3) Bipolar I – depressed phase (4) Bipolar II – 'normal mood'	(1) Bipolar I – manic phase (2) Bipolar I – not in acute episode (3) Bipolar I – depressed phase (4) Bipolar I – unclear, but rapid cycling in	Bipolar – major depressive disorder	Bipolar (recruited during episode for open-label phase: 94% manic, 6% mixed, 26% psychotic features)

Continued

	(5) Bipolar I – recently remitted (6) Bipolar I – not in acute phase	past 12 months (5) Bipolar (patients currently on lithium prophylaxis) (6) Bipolar I (92%)/Bipolar II (8%); 3.3% psychotic features; 58% comorbid ADHD; 50% rapid cycling (7) Bipolar – not in episode when recruited but some randomised when in acute episode (depression or (hypo)mania)	
		Treatment at the discretion of the investigator to control acute symptoms; once controlled; lithium and imipramine at maintenance dose levels (150 mg/day/0.6–0.9 meq/litre***	6–12 weeks, open-label co-treatment with olanzapine (15 mg) and lithium (0.6–1.2 meq/litre***); 4-week double-blind taper of discontinued drug
Acute open-label phase	(1) <= 3 months, treatment at the discretion of investigator (2) (3) 8–16 weeks lamotrigine (>= 100 mg/day) plus any other psychotropic medication required; lamotrigine titrated to achieve around	(1) <= 3 months, treatment at the discretion of investigator (2) (3) 8–16 weeks lamotrigine (>= 100 mg/day) plus any other psychotropic medication required; lamotrigine titrated to achieve	

Table 50: (Continued)

No. trials (No. participants)	Versus placebo	Versus an anticonvulsant	Versus an antidepressant	Versus an antipsychotic
	5 RCTs (1102)	7 RCTs (1154)	1 RCT (117)	1 RCT (431)
	200 mg/day by beginning of randomised trial (4) No open phase (5) No open phase, but patients stabilised on lithium before discharge from hospital 0.5–1.4 meq/litre*** (6) No open phase, but some patients had been receiving prophylactic lithium	around 200 mg/day by beginning of randomised trial (4) 6 months' treatment with lithium + valproate combination (5) No open phase (6) Up to 20 weeks' lithium + valproate combination (7) No open phase, but those randomised when in episode started study regimen when euthymic; totally lifetime treatment with study drugs limited to 6 months		

Bipolar history	(1) (3) depressed tendency; (6) not clear	(1) (3) depressed tendency; (5) manic tendency		3% history of rapid cycling; 93% manic index episode
Serum levels of lithium (mmol/l)	(1) 0.8–1.2 (2) 0.8–1.1 (3) 0.8–1.1 (4) 0.8–1.2 (5) 0.7** (6) 0.8–1.3	(1) 0.8–1.2 (2) 0.8–1.1 (3) 0.8–1.1 (4) 0.92* (5) 0.6–1.0 (6) 0.6–1.2 (7) 0.6–1.0	0.75	0.6–1.2
Comparator drug(s)	Placebo	(1) Valproate 71 µg/ml – 125 µg/ml (2) Lamotrigine 100 mg–400 mg (3) Lamotrigine 200 mg and 400 mg (4) Valproate 77 µg/ml (5) Carbamazepine 35–51 mmol/l (6) Valproate 81.1 mg/ml* (7) Carbamazepine 6 mg/l (1.2)*	Imipramine 132 mg*	Olanzapine mean dose 11.9 mg

Continued

Table 50: (*Continued*)

	Versus placebo	Versus an anticonvulsant	Versus an antidepressant	Versus an antipsychotic
No. trials (No. participants)	*5 RCTs (1102)*	*7 RCTs (1154)*	*1 RCT (117)*	*1 RCT (431)*
Concomitant medication	(1) Lorazepam and haloperidol (2) Short-term chloral hydrate or benzodiazepine (3) Chloral hydrate or benzodiazepine	(1) Lorazepam and haloperidol (2) Short-term chloral hydrate or benzodiazepine (3) Chloral hydrate or benzodiazepine (4) Lorazepam (5) Temazepam (6) Psychostimulants for ADHD (7) Benzodiazepines	None	Benzodiazepines, anticholinergics
Mean age range	39–52	(5) 11 (range 5–17) 31–51	38	42
Length of trial	(1) 52 weeks (2) (3) 18 months (4) 16 months (5) 24 months (6) 30 months*	(1) 7.5 weeks* (2) (3) 18 months (4) 20 months (5) 12 months (6) 76 weeks (7) 2 years*	2 years	52 weeks (including 4-week taper period)

| **Problems with trial affecting efficacy assessments** | (2) Lithium arm closed before end of trial and trial stopped early
(3) Stopped randomising to one of the lamotrigine groups
All studies achieved high lithium doses | (2) Not fully randomised therefore analysed separately
(3) Stopped randomising to one of the lamotrigine groups; also high dose lamotrigine would effect cognitive function
(4) Participants randomised to carbamazepine switched to study drug without titration
(1)(2)(3) Achieved high lithium doses | Participants stabilised on lithium + olanzapine during open-label phase |

Notes: *mean **median, most patients above 0.5*** equivalent to mmol/l lithium compared with placebo, especially in reducing manic relapses. The authors believe this may have been due to possible bias in recruitment, leading to a less ill sample compared with other studies (see Appendix 22).

It was difficult to categorise study populations reliably as either prone to depressive relapse or manic relapse based on the information given by the study authors, so last episode type was noted instead. However, some studies recruited only those recently recovered from a particular episode type, thus making it hard to associate one drug or another with preventing a particular kind of relapse.

Data comparing lithium with lamotrigine show that lithium is more effective against manic relapse, but data are unclear for depressive relapse. However, the BOWDEN2003 trial shows the anticonvulsant to be effective against depression.

It should be noted that the dose of lamotrigine should be increased when prescribed to a woman taking oral contraceptives, or the use of another contraceptive method discussed, since oral contraceptives seem to reduce lamotrigine plasma levels (Sabers *et al.*, 2003). When switching a patient from an oral contraceptive to another form of contraception, the dose of lamotrigine should be reduced.

Data for lithium versus carbamazepine were inconclusive and there was little difference between lithium and valproate.

With regard to antipsychotics compared with lithium in long-term treatment, only one study met inclusion criteria (TOHEN2005). This showed that olanzapine was more effective than lithium in reducing manic relapse, but lithium was more effective against depressive relapse. However, the study stabilised patients on a lithium-olanzapine combination and for 94% the most recent episode was manic. Also, around 26% had psychotic features. This may have favoured olanzapine.

An overview of the results is provided in Table 51, with the full evidence profile in Appendix 23.

Table 51: Summary of evidence profile for lithium monotherapy in long-term treatment

	Versus placebo	Versus an anticonvulsant	Versus an antidepressant	Versus an antipsychotic
Drugs for which data are available/last episode type	Lithium/various last episode types	Lamotrigine/depression, carbamazepine/unclear, valproate semisodium/ manic	Imipramine/unclear	Olanzapine – in patients whose most recent episode is manic
Evidence for efficacy (quality)	Lithium more effective than placebo at reducing manic relapses (moderate) and unlikely to make a difference with regard to depressive relapses (high)	Unlikely to be a difference between lamotrigine and lithium, except on reducing manic relapses where lithium more effective (moderate) Lithium versus carbamazepine is inconclusive (low) Lithium versus valproate semisodium unlikely to be a difference (moderate)	Lithium more effective than imipramine, particularly in reducing manic relapse (moderate); the evidence was inconclusive for depressive relapses (low)	Olanzapine more effective than lithium overall and at reducing manic episodes; lithium more effective at reducing depressive episodes (moderate)

Continued

293

Table 51: (*Continued*)

	Versus placebo	Versus an anticonvulsant	Versus an antidepressant	Versus an antipsychotic
Evidence for acceptability/ tolerability (including switching) (quality)	Placebo better tolerated than lithium on most outcomes (low)	Lamotrigine more tolerable than lithium (moderate), acceptability inconclusive (low) Carbamazepine more acceptable than lithium (moderate) but tolerability inconclusive (low) Lithium more tolerable than valproate on weight gain (moderate), no difference on acceptability (moderate)	Data are inconclusive (low) for acceptability outcomes and not tolerability outcomes were extractable	Olanzapine more acceptable and tolerable than lithium (moderate)

9.2.6   Combination treatment with lithium and an antidepressant in the long-term management of bipolar disorder

Studies considered for review
Two trials met the eligibility criteria set by the GDG and both involved imipramine. Excluded studies with reasons for exclusion can be seen in Appendix 22. A summary of study characteristics is in Table 52, with further details in Appendix 22.

Clinical summary
Adding imipramine to lithium does not appear to reduce relapse compared with lithium monotherapy, although both the combination and lithium monotherapy are more effective than imipramine alone.

An overview of the results is provided in Table 53, with the full evidence profile in Appendix 23.

Table 52: Summary of study characteristic for lithium/imipramine combination versus lithium or imipramine alone in long-term treatment

	With an antidepressant
No. trials (No. participants)	*2 RCTs (192)*
Study IDs	(1) PRIEN1984** (2) QUITKIN1981***
Population	US; outpatients; (2) includes some inpatients
Diagnosis at entry to open-label phase	Bipolar I
Acute open-label medication	Physicians' choice
Serum levels of lithium during maintenance phase (mmol/l)	(1) 0.7 (2) 0.8–1.2
Additional drug	(1) Imipramine 132 mg* (2) Imipramine 100 mg – 150 mg
Concomitant medication	None
Mean age (or range of mean ages)	38
Length of trial	(1) 2 years (2) 5 months
Study problems	None

*mean **3-arm trial: lithium, imipramine, combination ***Lithium + imipramine versus lithium + placebo

Table 53: Summary of evidence profile for lithium augmentation

	With an antidepressant
Most recent episode type	Not clear
Drugs for which data are available	Imipramine
Evidence for efficacy (quality)	Combination treatment has greater efficacy than an antidepressant alone (moderate), but evidence is inconclusive versus lithium alone (low)
Evidence for acceptability/ tolerability (including switching) (quality)	Monotherapy is more tolerable than combination therapy (moderate); evidence for acceptability is inconclusive (low)

9.2.7 Treatment with lithium at different plasma levels or administration patterns in the long-term treatment of bipolar disorder

Studies considered for review
Two trials were identified from searches of electronic databases, both of which met inclusion criteria. Summary characteristics can be seen in Table 54.

Clinical summary
For all relapses there was little difference between standard-level lithium and low-level lithium. However, standard-level lithium was more effective against manic episodes and low-level lithium more effective against depressive episodes. However, participants on low-level lithium were switched without titration, so these results may have been affected by sudden changes in levels in the low-level group.

An overview of the results is provided in Table 55, with the full evidence profile in Appendix 23.

Table 54: Summary of study characteristics for lithium at different plasma levels or administration patterns in long-term treatment

	Lithium at different plasma levels	Lithium every day compared with lithium every other day
No. trials (No. participants)	*1 RCT (94)*	*1 RCT (50)*
Study IDs	GELENBERG1989	JENSEN1995
Population	US; inpatients	Denmark; inpatients
Diagnosis	Bipolar	86% bipolar;14% MDD
Comparisons	1. 'Standard' level: 0.8–1.0 2. 'Low' level: 0.4–0.6	1. 800 mg daily* 2. 1200 mg lithium every other day (serum levels remained the same for all participants; all on lithium before start of study)
Open-label phase	2 months' lithium at standard levels	
Concomitant medication	Not given	5 patients given antipsychotics
Mean age (or range of mean ages)	39	50
Length of trial	2.8 years*	5 months
Study problems	Participants randomised to lower dose not titrated	

Notes: *mean

Table 55: Summary of evidence profile for lithium at different levels or regimens in long-term treatment

	Lithium in different levels	**Lithium every day compared with lithium every other day**
Most recent episode type	Not clear	Not clear
Evidence for efficacy (quality)	Lithium at standard level is more effective than lithium at low dose in reducing manic episodes, whilst low-dose lithium is more effective at reducing depressive episodes (moderate)	Taking a daily dose of lithium is more effective than taking it every other day (moderate)
Evidence for acceptability/ tolerability (including switching) (quality)	Low-level lithium is more acceptable (moderate), but tolerability is inconclusive (low)	Data are inconclusive (low) for acceptability/tolerability outcomes

9.2.8 Treatment with anticonvulsant and antipsychotic monotherapy in long-term treatment

Studies considered for review
Six placebo-controlled trials met inclusion criteria. Summary characteristics can be seen in Table 56, with fuller details in Appendix 22.

Clinical summary
Three drugs in monotherapy are superior to placebo in preventing relapse (lamotrigine, valproate semisodium, olanzapine). However, the result for valproate is not convincing and was categorised as unlikely to be a difference for all relapse types. However, for depressive relapses valproate was more effective than placebo, and lamotrigine was effective in rapid-cycling bipolar disorder.

Olanzapine was effective in reducing manic relapses in olanzapine responders but not depressive relapses. Other than this, the present analysis was unable to ascertain whether particular agents were effective in reducing relapse of a particular type, although it is generally believed that lamotrigine is effective at preventing depressive relapse, whereas olanzapine and valproate semisodium are considered to have an effect on both poles of the illness though they are more effective at preventing mania.

An overview of the results is provided in Table 57, with the full evidence profile in Appendix 23.

Table 56: Summary of characteristics for anticonvulsant and antipsychotic monotherapy in long-term treatment

	Lamotrigine	Valproate semisodium	Olanzapine
No. trials (No. participants)	*3 RCTs (822)*	*2 RCTs (402)*	*1 RCT (361)*
Study IDs	(1) BOWDEN2003 (2) CALABRESE2000 (3) CALABRESE2003	(1) BOWDEN2000 (2) FRANKENBURG2002	TOHEN2006
Population	North America	US; Outpatients	US and Romania; in- and outpatients
Diagnosis	(1) Bipolar I – not in acute episode (2) 70% Bipolar I, 30% Bipolar II; 100% rapid cycling – euthymic or in episode (any type) (3) Bipolar I – depressed phase	(1) Bipolar I – manic phase (2) Bipolar II – with borderline personality disorder	Bipolar I
Acute open-label phase	(1) (3) 8–16 weeks, lamotrigine (>= 100mg/day) plus any other psychotropic medication required; lamotrigine titrated to achieve around 200 mg/day by beginning of randomised trial (2) 6-week titration of lamotrigine to target dose 200 mg/day;	(1) <= 3 months, treatment at the discretion of investigator (2) Not applicable	6–12 weeks' olanzapine flexible dose 5–20 mg Patients unable to tolerate minimum dose discontinued

Continued

299

Table 56: *(Continued)*

	Lamotrigine	Valproate semisodium	Olanzapine
No. trials (No. participants)	*3 RCTs (822)*	*2 RCTs (402)*	*1 RCT (361)*
	concomitant valproate or carbamazepine allowed; between 4 and 8 weeks all meds other than lamotrigine tapered if HRSD <= 14 and MRS <= 12		
Study drugs	(1) Lamotrigine 100 mg–400 mg (2) Lamotrigine 287 mg* (3) Lamotrigine 200 mg and 400 mg	(1) Valproate semisodium – serum levels 71–125 mg/l (2) Valproate semisodium – serum levels 50–100 mg/l	Olanzapine 12.5 mg*
Concomitant medication	(1) Short-term chloral hydrate or benzodiazepine (2) Additional pharmacotherapy for emerging mood symptoms (3) Chloral hydrate or benzodiazepine	(1) Lorazepam and haloperidol if needed (2) None	Anticholinergic medication where permitted

Comparator	Placebo	Placebo	Placebo
Mean age (or range of mean ages)	31–51	26–39	Not given
Length of trial	(1) (3) 18 months (2) 6 months	(1) 1 year (2) 6 months*	1 year
Problems with trial	(1) Not fully randomised therefore analysed separately (3) Stopped randomising to one of the lamotrigine groups; also high-dose lamotrigine would affect cognitive function	(2) Participants recruited via the press	None

Notes: *mean

Table 57: Summary of evidence profile for anticonvulsant and antipsychotic monotherapy in long-term treatment

	Lamotrigine	Valproate semisodium	Olanzapine
Most recent episode type	Depressed (any for rapid cycling)	Manic	Manic
Evidence for efficacy (quality)	Lamotrigine no more effective than placebo (moderate), except for those with rapid cycling bipolar disorder where it is more effective than placebo (moderate)	Valproate semi-sodium is unlikely to be more effective than placebo (moderate). It was effective in educing rdepressive relapse (moderate), but data were inconclusive for manic (low)	Olanzapine is more effective than placebo in reducing manic relapse in olanzapine responders
Evidence for acceptability/ tolerability (including switching) (quality)	Lamotrigine is less acceptable and tolerable than placebo (moderate), except for those with rapid cycling bipolar disorder where data are inconclusive (low); other harm outcomes unclear (low)	Inconclusive (low), other than for weight gain where valproate semisodium is less tolerable than placebo (moderate)	Olanzapine is less tolerable than placebo and may cause weight gain (high)

9.2.9 Antipsychotics in combination with lithium or an anticonvulsant

Studies considered for review
Two trials were identified from searches of electronic databases, with one meeting inclusion criteria. Summary characteristics can be seen in Table 58, with fuller details in Appendix 22.

Clinical summary
The evidence for the long-term use of an antipsychotic in addition to lithium or an anticonvulsant is very limited, particularly since only two trials met inclusion criteria. However, for patients who are still symptomatic following 6 months' treatment, the combination of two antimanic agents (lithium, olanzapine, valproate) could be considered, provided there is close monitoring of the patient's clinical state, any side

Table 58: Summary of study characteristics for antipsychotic in combination with lithium or an anticonvulsant

	Prophylactic agent plus antipsychotic
No. trials (No. participants)	*2 RCTs (381)*
Study IDs	(1) TOHEN2002 (2) ZARATE2004
Population	(1) US, Canada; inpatients/outpatients (2) US; outpatients
Diagnosis at entry to open-label/acute phase	(1) Bipolar I mixed phase 52%; bipolar manic phase 48% (only those achieving remission randomised to long-term phase) (2) Bipolar (manic or mixed phase)
Acute phase	(1) Olanzapine plus lithium or valproate for 6 weeks (2) Perphenazine + lithium, carbamazepine or valproate for 10 weeks (1-week taper for those randomised to discontinue perphenazine)
Serum levels of lithium during maintenance phase (mmol/l)	(1) 0.76*/0.74* (two study groups) (2) 0.6–1.2
Comparisons	(1) Olanzapine 5 mg–10 mg plus lithium or valproate versus lithium or valproate (2) Perphenazine plus lithium or valproate or carbamazepine versus lithium or valproate or carbamazepine
Concomitant medication	(1) Benzodiazepine for up to 14 days, plus anticholinergic therapy for EPS (2) Lorazepam and benztropine mesylate
Mean age (or range of mean ages)	(1) 40 (2) 33–38
Length of trial	(1) 18 months (6-week acute phase reported above) (2) 6 months

*mean

effects and, where relevant, blood levels. Appropriate combinations are lithium and valproate, lithium with olanzapine, or valproate and olanzapine.

An overview of the results is provided in Table 59, with the full evidence profile in Appendix 23.

**Table 59: Summary of evidence profile for antipsychotic augmentation
of prophylactic agents in long-term treatment**

	With an antipsychotic
Most recent episode type	Manic or mixed
Drugs for which data are available	Olanzapine 5 mg–10 mg plus lithium or valproate versus lithium or valproate Perphenazine plus lithium or valproate or carbamazepine versus lithium or valproate or carbamazepine
Evidence for efficacy (quality)	Data are inconclusive (low) for efficacy outcomes
Evidence for acceptability/ tolerability (including switching) (quality)	Antipsychotics more likely to cause weight gain (moderate); other outcomes inconclusive (low)

9.2.10 The long-term management of children and adolescents with bipolar disorder

Studies considered for review
There is one trial already considered of the long-term management of people aged under 18. This is summarised in Table 60.

Summary of evidence for combination treatment
Results for FINDLING2005 are included in the evidence profile for lithium monotherapy. An overview of the results is provided in Table 61.

The only trial of long-term treatment in children or adolescents to meet inclusion criteria showed inconclusive results. Long-term maintenance is key to managing bipolar disorder in this age group. Therefore, treatment should be initiated and monitored by clinicians with expertise in this area and should be based on the findings for adults, bearing in mind particular considerations for the age group; these include the increased sensitivity to the side effects of medication. The use of valproate is not recommended in females (see section on drugs in pregnancy) in which case lithium should be the medication of choice. Lithium is not recommended as a first-line treatment in young males in whom adherence to medication and monitoring may be an issue. Children and adolescents with a diagnosis of bipolar disorder should continue treatment and follow-up within tier 3 or tier 4 CAMHS until the age of transition to adult mental health services.

**Table 60: Summary of study characteristics for long-term management
of children and adolescents**

	Lithium versus an anticonvulsant
No. trials (No. participants)	*1 RCT (60)*
Study IDs	FINDLING2005
Population	US
Diagnosis at entry to open-label phase	Bipolar I (92%)/Bipolar II (8%), 3.3% psychotic features; 58% comorbid ADHD; 50% rapid cycling
Serum levels of lithium during maintenance phase (mmol/l)	0.6–1.2
Study drug	Valproate 81.1 mg/ml*
Concomitant medication	Psychostimulants for ADHD
Mean age (or range of mean ages)	11 (range 5–17)
Length of trial	76 weeks

*mean

**Table 61: Summary of evidence profile for long-term treatment
in children and adolescents**

	Versus an anticonvulsant
Drugs for which data are available	Valproate semisodium
Evidence for efficacy (quality)	Data are inconclusive (low)
Evidence for acceptability/ tolerability (including switching) (quality)	Data are inconclusive (low)

9.3 HEALTH ECONOMICS EVIDENCE IN THE LONG-TERM PHARMACOLOGICAL TREATMENT OF BIPOLAR DISORDER

9.3.1 Economic evidence from the systematic literature review

No evidence on the cost-effectiveness of any pharmacological agents used for the long-term treatment of patients with bipolar disorder was identified.

9.3.2   Economic modelling

Introduction – rationale for economic modelling
The choice of pharmacological treatment used for the long-term maintenance therapy of patients with bipolar disorder was identified by the GDG and the health economist as an area with potential major resource implications. For this reason, and since there was no existing economic evidence to support decision making, a decision-analytic model was developed in order to assess the relative cost-effectiveness of various pharmacological agents considered in the guideline for the long-term treatment of patients with bipolar disorder.

Study population
The study population consisted of patients with bipolar I disorder in a stable state following an acute episode (that is either a sub-acute or a euthymic state). The economic analysis considered patients with bipolar I disorder only, as the vast majority of available effectiveness data required for the development of the model referred to this patient population. Three different patient sub-populations were examined separately: male patients, female patients without child-bearing potential, and female patients with child-bearing potential. This distinction was regarded essential, as the three sub-populations were subject to different risks when receiving long-term medication, as discussed later.

Pharmacological agents examined
The choice of pharmacological agents included in the economic analysis was based on the availability of relevant evidence on clinical effectiveness identified in the systematic literature review. Treatments shown to be clinically effective were further assessed in terms of cost effectiveness. Only the use of pharmacological agents as monotherapy was assessed. The daily dosage of agents was determined according to optimal average dosage used in routine clinical practice (GDG consensus) and was assumed to remain unchanged over time. Titration of dosage following lack of clinical response, development of side effects, or changes in blood concentration levels of medications under evaluation, was not considered in the economic model. The following pharmacological agents were evaluated:
- lithium, at a dosage of 1,000 mg daily
- valproate semisodium, at a dosage of 1,250 mg daily
- olanzapine, at a dosage of 10 mg daily

In addition, the option of no long-term pharmacological treatment (referred to as 'no treatment') was included in the analysis, in order to allow for the active value of long-term pharmacological interventions to be assessed.

Model structure
A decision-analytic Markov model was developed using Microsoft Excel XP. This type of model allowed the assessment of the relative cost-effectiveness of maintenance pharmacological therapies for patients with bipolar I disorder in the longer term, given the cyclical nature of the disease. The time horizon of the analysis

was 5 years, as this was recommended by the GDG as the optimal duration of maintenance therapy for patients at risk of relapse. The model was run in yearly cycles.

According to the model structure, hypothetical cohorts of 1,000 patients with bipolar I disorder received one of the four long-term treatment alternatives assessed and were followed for the 5-year time horizon of the analysis. Within each year, patients either remained in the initial non-acute stable state, they relapsed and experienced an acute manic or depressive episode, or they died as a result of suicide. After remission of the acute episode, patients returned to the initial, sub-acute or euthymic state. The relapse rates and the risk regarding the nature of the acute episode (mania or depression), as well as the risk of suicide, were specific to the kind of pharmacological treatment received. A schematic diagram of the Markov model is provided in Figure 4.

Figure 4: Schematic diagram of the structure of the economic model

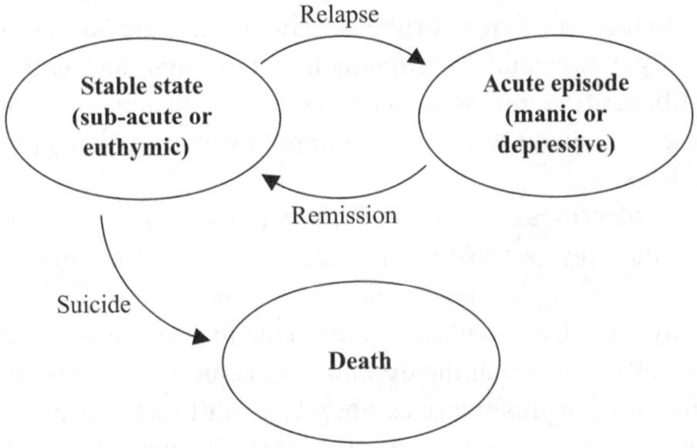

Costs and health benefit measures included in the analysis
The analysis adopted the perspective of the NHS. Health service costs consisted of long-term treatment costs as well as costs associated with the management of acute episodes. It was assumed that patients in a stable state receiving long-term treatment were attended by healthcare professionals on a regular basis. In contrast, stable patients under no maintenance treatment did not have any contact with healthcare professionals until they experienced an acute episode. Once they experienced an acute episode, they too were assumed to be seen by healthcare professionals on a regular basis for the remaining time of the model. All patients receiving long-term medication underwent laboratory blood testing as part of their monitoring, depending on the type of medication received.

Patients developing an acute manic episode were either hospitalised or treated in an outpatient setting by a CRHTT. The majority of patients experiencing acute depression received enhanced outpatient care; the rest were managed in an inpatient setting or by CRTs. All patients in an acute episode received medication for the management of mania or depression, in addition to maintenance medication.

In summary, the following health service cost elements were included in the analysis:

Long-term treatment
- medication
- contact with healthcare professionals
- drug-specific laboratory tests required for patient monitoring.

Management of acute episodes
- hospitalisation, CRTs or enhanced outpatient care
- additional medication.

Costs of treating side effects of long-term medications were not included in the analysis, as data on the rate of side effects of pharmacological treatment requiring healthcare resource utilisation, as well as respective costs, were not possible to identify in the published literature. Omission of costs associated with treatment of side effects is acknowledged as a limitation of the analysis.

Social service costs, such as those related to residential care, were not included in the analysis due to lack of relevant evidence. However, these costs were not believed to vary significantly between the four treatment options assessed. Other societal costs, including social benefit payments, costs associated with legal system services, and productivity losses of patients and carers were not estimated, as they were beyond the scope of the analysis.

Three different measures of health benefit were used in the economic analysis:
1. Number of acute episodes averted by pharmacological treatment relative to no treatment.
2. Number of days free from acute episodes. This measure was selected in order to take into account the fact that the duration of manic episodes is generally shorter than the duration of depressive ones; therefore, a differential preventive effect of a pharmacological agent on manic versus depressive episodes might significantly alter the total length of time over which a patient is in acute episode.
3. Number of Quality Adjusted Life Years (QALYs). QALYs are considered to be the most appropriate generic measure of health benefit that incorporates both gains from reduced mortality and improvements in health-related quality of life (HRQOL). The analysis using QALYs as a measure of outcome is called cost-utility analysis.

Total costs and health benefits associated with each treatment option over 5 years were estimated and combined in order to assess the relative cost-effectiveness between the pharmacological treatment options evaluated.

Cost data

Since no patient-level data in terms of resource use were available, the economic analysis was based on deterministic costing of all treatment options and of all events related to them, including management of acute episodes. Relevant healthcare resource use was estimated and subsequently combined with unit prices to provide costs associated with the various health states incorporated in the economic model. The majority of resource utilisation estimates were based on the GDG expert opinion, owing to lack of research-based evidence.

It was assumed that patients initiating long-term treatment (that is, at the start of the model) were attended by a range of healthcare professionals, including psychiatric consultants and SHOs, GPs, and CPNs. The frequency and duration of contact was determined by the GDG according to optimal clinical practice. If patients remained stable and did not experience an acute episode, their contact with healthcare staff was assumed to be that provided in Table 62.

Estimated healthcare resource utilisation for the management of acute episodes depended on the nature of the episode. The majority of patients with an acute manic episode (80%) were treated as inpatients, with the remaining 20% being treated at an outpatient setting by a CRHTT. Outpatient care predominated management of patients experiencing acute depressive episodes, with 70% of patients receiving enhanced outpatient standard care and 20% being treated by a CRHTT. The remaining 10% of patients with acute depression were assumed to require hospitalisation.

Length of hospitalisation during acute mania and depression were derived from the Hospital Episode Statistics for England, for the year 2003–2004 (Department of Health, 2004a). Duration of CRHTT management for patients with manic and depressive episodes was assumed to be equal to that of the length of hospitalisation for acute mania and depression respectively. After discharge from hospital or completion of CRHTT-led treatment, patients were assumed to contact healthcare professionals following the same pattern as that described for initiation of long-term treatment (frequent contacts at first, with increasing intervals between visits later in time). This pattern was also applied to patients with acute depression receiving enhanced outpatient care, with the first visit taking place on the first day of an acute episode. Resource use estimates related to the management of patients experiencing acute episodes are presented in Table 63.

In order to estimate the total annual cost associated with patients' contact with healthcare professionals following an acute episode, it was assumed that acute episodes occurred in the middle of the year if patients were under pharmacological treatment and at 3 months if patients took no long-term medication. The latter was consistent with the median time to relapse reported in the published literature for

Table 62: Long-term treatment: patients' contact with healthcare professionals

Contact with psychiatric consultants and SHOs: At weeks 1, 2, 4, 6, 10, 14, 22 and every 3 months thereafter; first four visits and one visit at the end of the year with a psychiatric consultant; remaining contact with an SHO. Duration 20 min per visit, with the exception of the first and second visit, lasting 45 and 30 min respectively.
Contact with GPs: At weeks 2, 4, 6 and every 6 weeks thereafter; duration 10 min per visit, with the exception of the first two visits, lasting 20 min each.
Contact with CPNs: Home visits at weeks 1, 2, 4 and every 4 weeks thereafter; duration 30 min per visit.

Table 63: Resource use relating to the management of acute episodes

Type of episode	Type of treatment	Resource use estimate	Source – comments
Manic	Hospitalisation (80%)	Length of stay 4 weeks (28 days); after discharge, initiation of contact with healthcare professionals as described in Table 62	Length of stay derived from Hospital Episode Statistics, England 2004; median length of stay for manic episode (ICD-10: F30); further treatment based on GDG opinion
	CRHTT (20%)	Duration of therapy 4 weeks; after completion of CRHTT management, initiation of contact with other healthcare professionals as described in Table 62	GDG opinion
Depressive	Hospitalisation (10%)	Length of stay 5 weeks (35 days); after discharge, initiation of contact with healthcare professionals as described in Table 62	Length of stay derived from Hospital Episode Statistics, England 2004; median length of stay for bipolar affective disorder (ICD-10: F31); further treatment based on GDG opinion
	CRHTT (20%)	Duration of therapy 5 weeks; after completion of CRHTT management, initiation of contact with other healthcare professionals as described in Table 62	GDG opinion
	Enhanced outpatient care (70%)	Initiation of contact with healthcare professionals as described in Table 62, starting from the first day in episode	GDG opinion

patients receiving placebo, which was similar in the majority of clinical studies. For pharmacological treatments, reported median times to relapse varied considerably across studies and, therefore, the estimate was based on GDG consensus. The above assumptions had no impact on the outcomes of the analysis, as they did not affect the relapse rates and the subsequent development of an acute episode; they were only used in order to estimate the additional amount of healthcare professionals' time consumed within a year, following development and remission of an acute episode.

Patients in a stable state either received one of the pharmacological treatments assessed, that is, lithium 1,000 mg daily, valproate semisodium 1,250 mg daily, or olanzapine 10 mg daily, or underwent no maintenance treatment. Patients in acute manic episodes were administered olanzapine at a dose of 15 mg daily for the total duration of the episode, in addition to continuation of long-term treatment; in the case of patients already treated with olanzapine as maintenance therapy, the long-term dose of 10 mg was adjusted to the level of 15 mg during acute manic episodes. All patients in acute depressive episodes received fluoxetine at a dose of 40 mg for the total duration of the episode in parallel with long-term medication. Patients under no maintenance treatment were treated exactly as those taking long-term medication if they experienced acute episodes; following acute treatment, they were assumed to receive no maintenance medication, even though they initiated contact with health-care professionals on a regular basis and with the same pattern as that described for patients receiving long-term treatment.

During maintenance treatment, patients underwent laboratory blood testing required for monitoring purposes, depending on the type of long-term medication they received. Further laboratory blood tests were undertaken on all patients, irrespective of the type of pharmacological treatment they obtained. The types and frequency of laboratory tests included in the model were in agreement with the guideline clinical recommendations. It was assumed that a practice nurse spent 5 minutes on taking blood samples from patients, each time one or more laboratory tests were carried out. The types and frequency of laboratory tests undertaken are presented in Table 64.

Unit prices were taken from a variety of UK sources, including the BNF 51 (British Medical Association & Royal Pharmaceutical Society of Great Britain, March 2006), the Unit Costs for Health and Social Care 2005 (Curtis & Netten, 2005) and the NHS reference costs 2005 (Department of Health, 2006). Laboratory testing costs were derived from the Newcastle upon Tyne Hospitals NHS trust (personal communication).

Costs were adjusted to year 2006 using the Hospital and Community Health Services (HCHS) pay and prices inflation index (Curtis & Netten, 2005). The inflation index for year 2006 was estimated using the average value of HCHS pay and prices indices of the previous 3 years. Discounting of costs was applied at an annual rate of 3.5%, as recommended by the NICE guidance on technology appraisals (NICE, 2004b). Unit costs utilised in the economic model are presented in Table 65.

Total costs associated with maintenance and acute treatment of patients with bipolar I disorder, as calculated based on the above estimates on resource use and unit costs, are shown in Appendix 15.

Table 64: Types and frequency of laboratory tests required for monitoring of patients under long-term medication

Medication	Laboratory tests	Frequency
Lithium	Serum lithium concentration	3 times over 6 weeks following initiation of treatment; every 3 months thereafter
	Blood urea & electrolytes	At initiation; every 6 months thereafter
	Thyroid function	At initiation; every 6 months thereafter
Valproate semisodium	Full blood count	At initiation & over the first 6 months
	Liver panel	At initiation & over the first 6 months
Olanzapine	Glucose test	At initiation & at 3 months; annually thereafter
	Lipid profile test	At initiation & at 3 months; annually thereafter
Common to all medications	Glucose	Annually

Effectiveness data and other input parameters of the economic model

Effectiveness data used in the economic model were derived from the guideline meta-analysis. Further criteria for selection of clinical studies already included in the guideline systematic review for inclusion in the economic analysis were:

● Relapse rates reported as a primary or secondary clinical outcome.

● Data on relapse rates specific to manic/mixed and depressive episodes extractable; the distinction between manic/mixed and depressive episodes was deemed important for the economic analysis, as a differential effect of an agent on prevention of manic versus depressive episodes was likely to have a strong impact on resource use as well as on associated health benefits (that is, number of days free from acute episode, QALYs gained).

Seven studies met the additional eligibility criteria (BOWDEN2000, BOWDEN2003, CALABRESE2003, PRIEN1973, STALLONE1973, TOHEN2005, TOHEN2006). Data from BOWDEN2003 were analysed separately in the systematic review of clinical evidence due to incomplete randomisation and therefore this study was excluded from the economic analysis.

As expected, none of the six remaining studies made direct comparisons across all treatment options assessed in the economic analysis. Therefore, in order to populate the

Table 65: Cost data utilised in the economic model

Cost element	Unit price (2006)	Source – comments
Medication:		
Long-term Lithium 1,000 mg daily	£0.11	BNF 51
Valproate semisodium 1,250 mg daily	£0.68	
Olanzapine 10 mg daily	£2.84	
Acute mania Olanzapine 15 mg daily	£5.23	
Acute depression Fluoxetine 20 mg daily	£0.09	
Healthcare professionals' time:		
Psychiatric consultant per hour of patient contact	£275	Curtis & Netten, 2005; qualification costs included
SHO per hour worked	£40	
GP per hour of patient contact	£150	
CPN per hour of home visit including travel costs	£88	
Practice nurse per hour of patient contact	£30	
Laboratory tests:		
Full blood count	£2.29	Newcastle upon Tyne Hospitals NHS trust, 2005; personal communication
Liver panel	£3.55	
Blood urea	£0.71	
Electrolytes	£1.42	
Serum lithium concentration	£2.74	
Thyroid function	£15.65	
Glucose test	£0.71	
Lipid profile test	£2.13	
Management of acute episodes:		
Inpatient stay per day	£235	NHS reference costs 2005; inpatient mental health services for acute care
CRHTT per contact	£54	Curtis & Netten, 2005

economic model, indirect comparisons across pharmacological agents were performed by combining efficacy data derived from the six studies. However, it is acknowledged that this may have introduced bias in the analysis, as there were differences between the studies in terms of patient characteristics, definition of manic and depressive episodes, concomitant medication and time horizon. In addition, the studies differed in some aspects of the protocol design. For example, in PRIEN1973 and STALLONE1973 patients experiencing an acute episode remained in the analysis and might have more than one acute episode over the study period; therefore the number of relapses reported in these two studies referred to the number of *events* and not the number of patients experiencing an acute episode. However, the number of patients remaining in remission at the end of the analysis was also provided. In contrast, patients in the remaining four studies were removed from the trials once they experienced an acute episode; consequently, the number of relapses reported in these studies reflected both number of events *and* number of patients having an acute episode within each study time horizon.

Characteristics of the six studies considered in the economic analysis are provided in Appendix 22. The treatments examined in each of the studies and the respective time horizons are shown in Table 66.

Since the vast majority of the studies included placebo in one of the trial arms, relative risks of manic and depressive relapses of all pharmacological treatments versus placebo were used as the basis for indirect comparisons across agents, with the placebo serving as the baseline common comparator. Relative risks were assumed to remain practically stable over time and therefore combination of efficacy data from studies with different time horizons was possible. The TOHEN2005 study was not included in the base-case analysis, as it did not contain a placebo arm. Data from this study were examined separately in a sensitivity analysis, as described below. Where rates of mixed episodes were reported separately, these were combined with rates of manic episodes, as mixed episodes are predominated by manic symptoms.

Table 66: Clinical studies considered in the economic analysis

Study	Comparators	Time horizon
BOWDEN2000	Lithium versus valproate semisodium versus placebo	1 year
CALABRESE2003	Lithium versus lamotrigine* versus placebo	18 months
TOHEN2005	Lithium versus olanzapine	1 year
TOHEN2006	Olanzapine versus placebo	1 year
PRIEN1973	Lithium versus placebo	2 years
STALLONE1973	Lithium versus placebo	28 months

*Data referring to lamotrigine was not considered in the economic analysis

Analysis of efficacy data and subsequent estimation of relative risks was based on an intention-to-treat approach, where patients discontinuing treatment (non-completers) for reasons other than having an acute episode were accounted for as 'bad outcomes', that is they were considered as having a relapse. Relative risks (RR) of relapse specific to manic and depressive episodes with their 95% CIs that were utilised in the economic analysis are presented in Table 67.

The absolute one-year relapse rates of manic and depressive episodes associated with long-term placebo treatment were estimated based on:

● The one-year overall relapse rate for placebo (for any acute episode); this was calculated from studies included in the meta-analysis that had a time horizon of one year and contained a placebo arm (BOWDEN2000; TOHEN2006); only *confirmed* cases of relapse were considered in the estimation of the absolute relapse rate of placebo, that is, non-completers with unknown outcome were not taken into account.

● The findings of a naturalistic study reporting the percentage of the total time patients with bipolar I disorder spent in depressive, manic and mixed states over 14 years (Judd *et al.*, 2002).

● The opinion of the GDG on the duration of manic and depressive episodes.

Details on the calculation of the 1-year absolute relapse rates of manic and depressive episodes during long-term treatment with placebo are provided in Appendix 16.

The overall absolute 1-year relapse rate and the absolute 1-year rates of manic and depressive confirmed episodes estimated for placebo were assumed to apply to the alternative of no treatment included in the analysis.

Absolute 1-year relapse rates of manic and depressive episodes for all pharmacological treatments assessed were estimated by multiplying the relative risks of manic and depressive relapses for each agent derived from the meta-analysis by the absolute

Table 67: Relative risks of relapse to an acute episode (manic/mixed or depressive) of long-term pharmacological agents versus placebo – data utilised in the base-case economic analysis

Pharmacological agent	Type of acute episode	RR	95% CI	Studies combined
Lithium	Manic/mixed	0.62	0.35 to 1.08	BOWDEN2000 CALABRESE2003
	Depressive	0.91	0.77 to 1.08	PRIEN1973 STALLONE1973
Valproate semisodium	Manic/mixed	1.03	0.78 to 1.36	BOWDEN2000
	Depressive	0.53	0.34 to 0.82	
Olanzapine	Manic/mixed	0.58	0.44 to 0.76	TOHEN2006
	Depressive	1.12	0.90 to 1.40	

1-year relapse rates of manic and depressive episodes, respectively, as calculated for placebo. Annual relapse rates of manic and depressive episodes for all treatment options in the following years were extrapolated from the respective 1-year relapse rates, owing to lack of long-term data on efficacy of maintenance treatment.

Estimation of suicide risks
Lithium has been demonstrated to have a strong antisuicidal effect in mood disorders (Cipriani *et al.*, 2005). The risk of suicide associated with lithium was estimated based on a Swiss study of patients with mood disorders who were followed up for a period of 40–44 years (Angst *et al.*, 2005). The study reported SMRs for suicide specific to patients with bipolar disorder; rates were reported separately for patients treated with lithium and those not treated with lithium. The economic model conservatively assumed that reported SMRs for patients not treated with lithium applied, besides patients under no maintenance treatment, to patients treated with olanzapine and valproate semisodium too, since there was no evidence to support an antisuicidal effect of long-term use of these agents on patients with bipolar disorder.

SMRs derived from the Swiss study were then multiplied by age- and gender-specific absolute suicide rates observed in the UK general population in 2000 (Office of National Statistics, 2002), in order to estimate the absolute suicide rates of the study population used in the model. The age-specific suicide rates selected for the analysis were those for the population aged 25–44 years, as the initiation of long-term pharmacological treatment following an acute episode is largely relevant to this age group of patients with bipolar I disorder.

Estimation of QALYs
In order to express clinical outcomes in the form of QALYs, utility weights for health states relating to bipolar disorder were required. Utility weights represent the HRQOL associated with specific health states; they are estimated based on people's preferences and perceptions of quality of life characterising the health states under consideration. A systematic review of the literature identified two studies providing utility weights for health states referring to bipolar disorder (Tsevat *et al.*, 2000; Revicki *et al.*, 2005). Tsevat and colleagues (2000) reported patients' own ratings (valuations) of their current mental and overall health. However, the study did not provide utility weights for distinct health states characterising patients with bipolar disorder and therefore its findings could not be utilised in the economic model.

Revicki and colleagues (2005) reported patients' valuations of various hypothetical bipolar disorder-related health states. Fifty-five hypothetical health states were constructed based on reviews of psychiatric literature and consultation with psychiatrists experienced in treating bipolar disorder. Each health state described bipolar symptom severity, functioning and well-being, as well as side effects related to treatment. Ninety-six well-educated, clinically stable outpatients with bipolar I disorder were asked to value each of the health states using visual analogue scale and standard gamble techniques. The study provided patients' valuations for stable state, inpatient mania, outpatient mania and severe depression, varying with respect to the kind of pharmacological treatment obtained and the presence or absence of side effects. The utility weights for the various health states reported in this study allowed for a cost-utility analysis to be undertaken alongside the cost-effectiveness analysis. However, the study was characterised by important limitations, such as the selected study sample and the small sample sizes used for the valuation of health states (some health states were valued by 7 to 14 patients). Therefore, the results of the cost-utility analysis must be interpreted with caution. In addition, owing to lack of relevant data, the utility weight for moderate depression treated with fluoxetine was taken from another study reporting patients' utility weights for states of unipolar depression (Revicki & Wood, 1998). Consequently, it was assumed that the utility weight of moderate unipolar depression treated with fluoxetine was the same as the utility weight of acute moderate depression in patients with bipolar I disorder treated with fluoxetine plus long-term pharmacological treatment. This assumption constitutes a further limitation of the cost-utility analysis.

Utilities reported in Revicki and colleagues (2005) that were relevant to the economic model structure involved the following health states:

● stable state with or without weight gain; utilities were provided separately for monotherapy with lithium, valproate or olanzapine, as well as for no long-term treatment

● inpatient mania with mild or moderate symptoms/side effects, common to all treatments

● outpatient mania with mild or moderate symptoms/side effects; utilities relevant to the model were those referring to acute treatment with olanzapine and also to acute treatment with olanzapine plus mood stabiliser

● severe depression; one mean value for all treatments was provided.

The only utility derived from Revicki and Wood (1998) was that referring to moderate depression treated with fluoxetine.

Rates of side effects, required in order to estimate QALYs, were based on the results of the systematic review of clinical studies undertaken for the guideline. Rates of weight gain during long-term treatment were based on data provided in BOWDEN2000 and TOHEN2006. Relative risks for each pharmacological treatment compared with placebo were calculated first and were then multiplied by the weighted average 1-year absolute rate of weight gain associated with placebo, to provide absolute rates of weight gain specific to each agent assessed. Regarding rates of moderate symptoms/side effects associated with treatment of acute manic episodes with olanzapine as monotherapy or in combination with another antimanic agent, the absolute rates of EPS reported for the treatment of acute manic episodes with antipsychotics were used as a proxy. The rate of EPS of patients with acute mania treated with an antipsychotic was estimated as a weighted average rate based on data reported in KHAN2005 and VIETA2005. The rate of EPS of patients with acute mania treated with olanzapine plus another antimanic agent was adopted from YATHAM2003.

Discounting

As in the case of costs, discounting of benefits was applied at an annual rate of 3.5% as recommended by NICE guidance on technology appraisals (NICE, 2006).

All effectiveness rates and other input parameters included in the economic model are provided in Table 68.

Table 68: Effectiveness rates and other input parameters included in the model

Input parameter	Baseline value	Source – comments
1-year relapse rates		
		Absolute relapse rates of manic and depressive episodes for pharmacological treatments were estimated by multiplying relative risks for manic and depressive episodes for each agent versus placebo by 1-year absolute manic and depressive relapse rates respectively estimated for placebo; relative risks were derived from a meta-analysis of studies undertaken for the guideline.
Lithium		
Manic episode	0.16	
Depressive episode	0.34	
Valproate semisodium		
Manic episode	0.27	
Depressive episode	0.20	
Olanzapine		1-year relapse rate estimates for placebo specific to mania and depression were based on the overall confirmed relapse rate for placebo derived from studies included in the meta-analysis, after taking into account the estimated proportion between manic and depressive episodes (see below).
Manic episode	0.15	
Depressive episode	0.42	
No treatment		No treatment relapse rates were assumed to equal the respective rates estimated for placebo.
Manic episode	0.26	
Depressive episode	0.37	
Rate of manic versus depressive episodes following treatment with placebo or no treatment	41:59	Estimates based on data from Judd and colleagues (2002) and further GDG opinion on the duration of manic and depressive episodes (see Appendix 16).
Duration of acute episodes		
Manic episodes	9 weeks	GDG consensus
Depressive episodes	13 weeks	

SMRs for suicide		
Lithium treated	5.7	Derived from Angst and colleagues (2005); data referring to patients with bipolar disorder
Non-lithium treated	16.5	
Absolute suicide rates per 100,000 general population, aged 25–44 years		
Men	23.4	Data referring to the UK population in 2000 (Office for National Statistics, 2002)
Women	6.4	
Utility weights		All utility estimates based on Revicki and colleagues (2005), except for the utility weight for moderate depression treated with fluoxetine, taken from Revicki and Wood (1998). Depression treated in hospital assumed to reflect severe depression; depression treated by CRTs or enhanced outpatient care assumed to represent moderate depression.
Stable state		
Lithium – no weight gain	0.71	
Valproate – no weight gain	0.74	
Olanzapine – no weight gain	0.82	
No treatment – no weight gain	0.74	
Decrement owing to weight gain	0.066	
Acute mania		
Mild symptoms/side effects		
Inpatient	0.26	
Outpatient – olanzapine	0.64	
Outpatient – olanzapine + prophylactic agent	0.56	
Moderate symptoms/side effects		
Inpatient	0.23	
Outpatient – olanzapine	0.53	
Outpatient – olanzapine + prophylactic agent	0.53	

Continued

Table 68: (*Continued*)

Input parameter	Baseline value	Source–comments
Acute depression		
Severe depression	0.29	
Moderate depression – fluoxetine	0.63	
Side effect rates		Rates of weight gain for each treatment estimated by multiplying relative risks for each agent versus placebo by one-year absolute rate of weight gain associated with placebo; data based on studies included in the guideline systematic review (BOWDEN2000; TOHEN2006).
Long-term treatment – weight gain		
Lithium	0.07	
Valproate semisodium	0.11	
Olanzapine	0.21	
No treatment	0.04	
Acute mania – moderate side effects		Based on rates of EPS following treatment of acute mania with antipsychotics alone or in combination, reported in studies included in the guideline systematic review (KHAN2005; VIETA2005; YATHAM2003).
Olanzapine + prophylactic agent	0.21	
Olanzapine	0.21	
Discount rate	3.5%	Based on NICE 2006; applied to both costs and benefits

Sensitivity analysis

Apart from the base-case analysis, which utilised the most accurate cost and effectiveness estimates available, a sensitivity analysis was undertaken to investigate the robustness of the results under the uncertainty or variability characterising input parameters of the model: selected input parameters were varied over a range of values and the impact of these variations on the results was explored. Three methods of sensitivity analysis were employed: one-way, threshold, and probabilistic sensitivity analysis.

One-way sensitivity analyses examined whether changes in values of various input parameters and different model assumptions had a significant impact on the results. A big part of these analyses tested to what degree the uncertainty characterising the efficacy data utilised in the model affected the results of the economic analysis. Four cases were investigated:

1. Exclusion of BOWDEN2000 and CALABRESE2003 from the meta-analysis of efficacy data for lithium; this scenario was considered important to test because of the great heterogeneity between these and the other two lithium studies included in the meta-analysis (PRIEN1973 and STALLONE1973).
2. Alternatively, exclusion of PRIEN1973 and STALLONE1973 from the meta-analysis.
3. Direct comparison between olanzapine and lithium using efficacy data from TOHEN2005.
4. Modification of the intension-to-treat analysis by considering patients discontinuing treatment as 'good outcomes' (not relapsing).

In addition to hypotheses investigating uncertainty in efficacy data, the following scenarios were tested:

1. Changes in the rate of manic versus depressive episodes following treatment with placebo or no treatment; two extreme scenarios, 75:25 and 25:75, respectively, were explored (in the base-case scenario this rate was estimated to be 41:59).
2. Changes in the duration of acute episodes of ±25% of the base-case estimates.
3. Changes in the absolute relapse rates of placebo or no treatment; rates of 40% and 86% were explored (the latter was the absolute relapse rate for placebo derived from combining data from BOWDEN2000 and TOHEN2006 if patients discontinuing treatment were considered as bad outcomes, that is, cases of relapse).
4. Extension of the time horizon of the model to 10 years; this scenario aimed at exploring whether the cumulative antisuicidal effect of lithium had an impact on its relative cost effectiveness in the longer term.
5. Reduction in the number and duration of healthcare professional contacts by 25% of the base-case estimate.

Because the utility values for the stable state reported by Revicki and colleagues (2005) clearly favoured olanzapine, a threshold analysis was conducted to identify the value at which the utility weight of olanzapine should fall, or the utility weights of valproate and lithium should rise, in order for the conclusions of the cost-utility analysis, expected to favour olanzapine, to be reversed.

Finally, in a probabilistic sensitivity analysis, conducted using Crystal Ball 7.1 (Decisioneering, Inc), selected parameters of the model were simultaneously varied randomly over a range of values according to appropriate distributions. Relative risks of manic and depressive relapses of all pharmacological agents compared with placebo were varied according to a log-normal distribution. The placebo/no-treatment relapse rate was varied according to binomial distribution. Costs associated with healthcare professional contact and with management of acute episodes were attached a gamma distribution, while utilities were given a range of values based on a beta distribution.

In effect, 10,000 Monte Carlo simulations of the economic model were performed. This analysis, in which some of the most uncertain model parameters were given a distribution of values rather than a point estimate, allowed for the estimation of the entire range of results produced after the uncertainty surrounding these parameters was fully taken into account.

Results
The results of the economic analysis are presented in the form of ICERs, expressing additional cost per additional unit of benefit associated with one treatment option compared with another.

$$ICER = \frac{\text{difference in costs between two treatment options}}{\text{difference in benefit between two treatment options}}$$

$$ICER = \frac{\text{additional costs of one treatment options versus another}}{\text{additional benefit of one treatment options versus another}}$$

The estimation of such a ratio allows consideration of whether the additional benefit is worth the additional cost when choosing one treatment option over another.

In the case of a treatment option being more effective (that is providing greater benefit) and less costly than its comparator, the calculation of such a ratio is not required; the treatment option in question, characterised as the dominant option, is clearly more cost-effective than its comparator (absolute dominance). Extended dominance of an option occurs where the ICER between this option and the next most effective one is higher than the ICER between the preceding most effective option and the option in question.

All treatment options under assessment have been ranked from the most to the least effective. Cases of absolute dominance and extended dominance have been identified and excluded from further analysis. ICERs between the non-dominated treatment options remaining in the analysis have been subsequently calculated.

Results of the economic analysis are presented separately for three sub-populations within the study population: male patients, female patients without child-bearing potential, and female patients with child-bearing potential. This distinction was deemed necessary for two reasons:
● Men are characterised by higher suicide rates than women, and therefore the antisuicidal effect of lithium might be significantly stronger in male patients
● Valproate semisodium was considered inappropriate for the long-term management of women of child-bearing potential because of significant hazards for the

fetus in the case of pregnancy and therefore was excluded from the economic analysis concerning this patient sub-population.

For each patient sub-population, three sub-analyses have been performed, each relating to one of the three measures of health benefit used in the economic analysis. Results of the base-case analysis are provided first, followed by the results of the sensitivity analysis.

Base-case analysis

Men and women without child-bearing potential
Among all treatment options, valproate semisodium resulted in greatest health benefits in terms of 'physical' outcomes (that is number of acute episodes averted relative to no treatment and number of days free from acute episode). Olanzapine was dominated by valproate semisodium and lithium, as it was the most expensive alternative and less effective than the other two pharmacological agents evaluated; consequently it was excluded from further analysis. No treatment was dominated by lithium which was the cheapest option. The ICER of valproate semisodium versus lithium was £17,564 and £16,529 per additional acute episode averted for men and women respectively, or £148 and £104 per additional day free from acute episode achieved for men and women respectively.

In the cost-utility analysis, in which QALYs are used as measure of outcome, olanzapine was shown to be the most effective option, with lithium being the least effective among all options assessed. These results were primarily attributed to the long-term treatment-specific utility weights attached to the stable state: the utility weight for stable state was maximum for olanzapine (0.82) and minimum for lithium (0.71) (Revicki *et al.*, 2005). Valproate semisodium and no treatment were dominated by the rule of extended dominance and therefore were excluded from further analysis. The ICER of olanzapine versus lithium was £11,810/QALY and £11,419/QALY for men and women respectively. This value is within the cost-effectiveness threshold of £20,000/QALY determined by NICE (NICE, 2006).

Women of child-bearing potential
Lithium dominated both olanzapine and no treatment when number of acute episodes averted and number of days free from episode were considered. In the cost-utility analysis, the ICER of olanzapine versus lithium was £11,419/QALY.

Number of suicides averted by lithium
According to the economic model, long-term management of male patients with lithium resulted in 12 suicides averted per 1,000 patients over 5 years compared with any other treatment option, as all other medications had been assumed to be similar to no treatment in terms of anti-suicidal effect. The number of suicides prevented by lithium in 1,000 female patients over 5 years was three. This was explained by the lower suicide risk associated with women in the general population.

Full results of the base-case analysis are presented in Table 69. Results for male patients are also provided in the form of graphs in Appendix 17.

Table 69: Results of the base-case analysis, referring to a hypothetical cohort of 1,000 patients with bipolar I disorder

MALE PATIENTS

Measure of benefit: number of acute episodes averted relative to no treatment and number of days free from acute episode

Treatment option	Episodes averted	Days free from episode	Costs (£)	Cost effectiveness
Valproate	777	1,526,583	15,549,957	**Valproate versus lithium:** £17,564/acute episode averted £148/day free from episode
Lithium	626	1,508,644	12,901,557	
Olanzapine	295	1,467,519	17,346,242	**Dominated** by lithium and valproate
No treatment	0	1,454,833	14,077,425	**Dominated** by lithium

Measure of benefit: number of QALYs gained

Option	QALYs	Costs (£)	Cost-effectiveness
Olanzapine	3,566	17,346,242	**Olanzapine versus lithium: £11,810/QALY**
Valproate	3,265	15,549,957	**Dominated** by extended dominance
No treatment	3,261	14,077,425	**Dominated** by extended dominance
Lithium	3,190	12,901,557	

FEMALE PATIENTS WITHOUT CHILD-BEARING POTENTIAL

Measure of benefit: number of acute episodes averted relative to no treatment and number of days free from acute episode

Treatment option	Episodes averted	Days free from episode	Costs (£)	Cost effectiveness
Valproate	783	1,539,196	15,652,478	Valproate versus lithium: £16,529/acute episode averted £104/day free from episode
Lithium	618	1,512,936	12,930,643	
Olanzapine	297	1,479,644	17,461,106	**Dominated** by lithium and valproate
No treatment	0	1,466,854	14,175,400	**Dominated** by lithium

Measure of benefit: number of QALYs gained

Option	QALYs	Costs (£)		Cost-effectiveness
Olanzapine	3,641	17,461,106		Olanzapine versus lithium: **£11,419/QALY**
Valproate	3,319	15,652,478		**Dominated** by extended dominance
No treatment	3,288	14,175,400		**Dominated** by extended dominance
Lithium	3,194	12,930,643		

Continued

Table 69: (Continued)

FEMALE PATIENTS WITH CHILD-BEARING POTENTIAL

Measure of benefit: number of acute episodes averted relative to no treatment and number of days free from acute episode

Treatment option	Episodes averted	Days free from episode	Costs (£)	Cost effectiveness
Lithium	618	1,512,936	12,930,643	Dominant
Olanzapine	297	1,479,644	17,461,106	Dominated by lithium
No treatment	0	1,466,854	14,175,400	Dominated by lithium

Measure of benefit: number of QALYs gained

Option	QALYs	Costs (£)	Cost-effectiveness	
Olanzapine	3,641	17,461,106	Olanzapine versus lithium: £11,419/QALY	
No treatment	3,288	14,175,400	Dominated by extended dominance	
Lithium	3,194	12,930,643		

One-way sensitivity analysis

A. *Exploring uncertainty characterising efficacy data*

Results were very sensitive to the underlying uncertainty in the efficacy data. Exclusion of BOWDEN2000 and CALABRESE2003 from the meta-analysis strongly favoured lithium when physical outcomes were used as measure of benefit: lithium became the dominant option, as it became the most effective and least costly among all treatment options. In the cost-utility analysis, the ICER of olanzapine versus lithium rose to £18,688 and £17,909/QALY for men and women respectively.

In contrast, exclusion of PRIEN1973 and STALLONE1973 from the meta-analysis reduced the effectiveness of lithium and increased moderately its overall cost. In the majority of sub-analyses (except those involving women of child-bearing potential) lithium was dominated by either absolute (analyses using physical outcomes) or extended (cost-utility analysis) dominance. Regarding women of child-bearing potential (for whom valproate is not an option), olanzapine prevented a higher number of acute episodes compared with lithium, at an additional cost of £27,736 per episode averted. However, lithium remained dominant over olanzapine when days free from episode were used as the measure of benefit. In the cost-utility analysis, lithium became dominated by no treatment. The ICER of olanzapine versus no treatment was approximately £10,700/QALY for both men and women.

In the direct comparison between olanzapine and lithium using efficacy data from TOHEN2005, olanzapine dominated lithium in all sub-analyses for all three sub-populations considered. Finally, when the intension-to-treat analysis treated patients that discontinued treatment as 'good outcomes' (that is assuming they did not relapse after discontinuation), the ranking of treatments in terms of effectiveness was not affected but the base-case ICERs of all sub-analyses were substantially reduced, ranging from 37% reduction in cost/QALY (olanzapine versus lithium) to 77% reduction in cost/acute episode averted (valproate versus lithium, where applicable).

B. *Exploring uncertainty characterising other input parameters*

Changes in the rate of manic versus depressive episodes

Increasing the proportion of manic episodes developed under no treatment so that the rate of manic versus depressive episodes became 75:25 favoured lithium and olanzapine and disfavoured valproate semisodium. Lithium became the dominant option in the sub-analyses where physical outcomes were used as measure of benefit. In the cost-utility analysis, the ICER of olanzapine versus lithium was only slightly affected.

Changing the rate of manic to depressive episodes under no treatment to 25:75 favoured valproate semisodium (for the sub-populations of men and women of no child-bearing potential), while it had a negative impact on the relative cost-effectiveness of lithium and olanzapine. The ICER of valproate versus lithium fell on average at £2,190 per episode averted or £23 per day free from episode for men and women of no child-bearing potential. In the cost-utility analysis there was no extended dominance over no treatment. The average ICER of olanzapine versus no treatment was £16,473/QALY; the average ICER of no treatment versus lithium was £1,665/QALY.

The above results were expected, as efficacy data utilised in the economic model had shown the preferential preventive effect of olanzapine and lithium over manic episodes, and of valproate semisodium over depressive episodes. Therefore, an increase in the proportion of manic episodes over all episodes revealed the antimanic effect of lithium and olanzapine, while predominance of depressive episodes improved the overall effectiveness of valproate semisodium.

Changes in the duration of acute episodes

Varying the duration of acute episodes by 25% did not change the ranking of options by magnitude of benefits; it only affected the values of ICERs. A 25% increase in the duration of acute episodes led to a 20% increase in the cost/acute episode averted and a 7%–16% reduction (depending on the sub-population examined) in the cost/day free from episode of valproate versus lithium. The ICERs estimated in the cost-utility analysis remained practically unaffected.

A 25% decrease in the duration of acute episodes resulted in a 20% decrease in the cost/acute episode averted and a 12%–40% increase (depending on the sub-population examined) in the cost/day free from episode of valproate versus lithium. In the cost-utility analysis no treatment stopped being under extended dominance. The ICER of olanzapine versus no treatment was approximately £12,800/QALY for all patient sub-populations; the ICER of no treatment versus lithium approximated £5,750/QALY for both men and women.

Changes in the absolute rates of no treatment

Reducing the absolute relapse rate of no treatment to 40% favoured no treatment, which became the cheapest option. It also increased the ICERs of valproate versus lithium at £23,196 and £19,639 per acute episode averted or £284 and £129 per day free from episode achieved for men and women of no child-bearing potential respectively. Lithium was more effective than no treatment but at an additional cost of approximately £1,550 per episode averted or £20 per day free from episode. In the cost-utility analysis, lithium was dominated by no treatment; the ICER of olanzapine versus no treatment reached £12,300/QALY for all patient sub-populations.

An absolute relapse rate of no treatment of 86% led to moderate reductions of 8%–22% in the ICERs of valproate semisodium versus lithium concerning physical outcomes and a small increase of 8% in the ICER of olanzapine versus lithium in the cost-utility analysis.

Extension of the time horizon of the analysis to 10 years

The relative cost-effectiveness between treatment options was practically unaffected when the measure of outcome was expressed by the number of acute episodes averted or by QALYs. When the number of days free from acute episode was used as the measure of benefit, the ICER of valproate versus lithium rose significantly for men and equalled £279 per day free from episode. In contrast, this ICER increased only moderately for women of no child-bearing potential, reaching £113 per day free from episode. This is justified by the stronger anti-suicidal effect of lithium on the male patient sub-population over time, as in the general population the suicide rate of men aged 25–40 years is much higher (3.7 times) relative to women of the same age.

Reduction in healthcare professional contact during long-term treatment
Reducing healthcare professional contact during long-term treatment by 25% had practically no impact on the results; cases of dominance remained and the ICERs between non-dominated options changed only very slightly.

The analytic results of one-way sensitivity analysis are provided in Appendix 18.

Threshold analysis
The analysis showed that small changes in the utility values of the stable state were sufficient to alter the base-case results of the cost-utility analysis.

The stable state utility for lithium used in the base-case analysis was 0.71 (Revicki *et al.*, 2005). When this was increased to 0.73 (0.74 for women), lithium dominated no treatment and valproate semisodium; at 0.75 (0.76 for women), the ICER of olanzapine versus lithium exceeded £20,000/QALY, which is the maximum ratio accepted for an intervention to be deemed as an effective use of NHS resources based primarily on its cost effectiveness (NICE, 2006). At a value of 0.81, lithium dominated olanzapine.

The stable state base-case utility for valproate was 0.74. When it was raised to 0.78, valproate was no longer under extended dominance. At 0.80, the ICER of olanzapine versus valproate was above the cost-effectiveness threshold of £20,000/QALY. At 0.82, valproate dominated olanzapine.

Finally, the stable state base-case utility for olanzapine was 0.82. When this fell to 0.78 (0.77 for women), the ICER of olanzapine versus lithium increased beyond the cost-effectiveness threshold. When it fell further to 0.74, olanzapine was dominated by no treatment and valproate; when it reached 0.72 it was dominated by lithium too.

The threshold analysis demonstrated that the results of the cost-utility analysis were greatly dependent on the utility values of the stable state attached to each of the treatment options considered.

Probabilistic sensitivity analysis
Results of probabilistic analysis are provided in the form of CEACs, which demonstrate the probability of each treatment option being cost-effective over a range of potential cost values of WTP in order to achieve an additional unit of benefit.

Analysis for men and women without child-bearing potential
Lithium was the most likely cost-effective option in all sub-analyses for a wide range of WTP, starting from zero to approximately £17,000 per acute episode averted, £150 per day free from episode, or £12,000/QALY. The probability of lithium being the most cost-effective treatment reached its maximum (70%) at a WTP of £2,500 per acute episode averted or £25 per day free from episode; in the cost-utility analysis this probability was maximum (66%) at a zero WTP and decreased as WTP increased.

When physical outcomes were used as measures of benefit, valproate had the highest probability of being the most cost-effective option when WTP was set above £17,000 per acute episode averted or £150 per day free from episode; however, this probability, although constantly increasing with higher values of WTP, reached only 50% at a WTP of £22,500 per acute episode averted or £175 per day free from episode.

In the cost-utility analysis, olanzapine demonstrated the highest probability of being the most cost-effective among treatments for WTP above £12,000/QALY. The probability of olanzapine being cost-effective became higher as WTP increased, reaching 90% at a WTP equalling the cost-effectiveness threshold of £20,000/QALY.

Analysis for women of child-bearing potential

Lithium had the maximum probability of being the most cost-effective option for any value of WTP when physical outcomes were considered. In terms of WTP for an acute episode averted, the highest probability was 85% at a WTP of £7,500 and fell to 81% at a WTP of £25,000. Regarding WTP for a day free from episode, lithium reached its highest probability of being the most cost-effective option (86%) at £100. This probability remained stable as WTP for a day free from episode increased further.

In the cost-utility analysis, lithium showed greatest probability of being the most cost-effective option for a WTP starting from zero and up to approximately £12,000/QALY. Beyond that value, olanzapine was the most likely cost-effective treatment, with a probability of 92% at the cost-effectiveness threshold of £20,000/QALY.

Full results of probabilistic sensitivity analysis in the form of graphs presenting CEACs are provided in Appendix 18.

Limitations of the economic analysis

The economic analysis was undertaken using the best effectiveness and cost data available. Nevertheless, evidence on clinical effectiveness was derived from a limited number of studies (data from five clinical studies were utilised in the base-case analysis). In addition, relative effectiveness of treatment options was based on indirect comparisons between pharmacological agents assessed, and this may have introduced bias in the analysis. Long-term relapse rates were extrapolated from data on relative risks of relapse derived from trials with varying time horizons, between 12 and 28 months. The economic analysis has therefore implicitly assumed that annual relapse rates associated with each treatment are stable over time. This assumption was necessary in order to combine data from studies with different time horizons and due to lack of longer-term efficacy data. However, the efficacy of maintenance treatment may vary over time, and this constitutes a further limitation of the analysis.

Estimates regarding healthcare resource use and other input parameters were based on GDG expert opinion due to lack of research-based data available; as a consequence, results of the analysis are subject to considerable uncertainty surrounding these values. Nonetheless, one-way and probabilistic sensitivity analyses were performed in order to take into account the uncertainty characterising the variables incorporated in the economic model.

Potential harms associated with long-term treatment were generally not considered in the analysis. Some of the side effects associated with pharmacological treatments assessed were implicitly taken into account in the cost-utility analysis, as utility weights varied by medication due to differences between medications in terms of type, severity and frequency of associated side effects. Still, it is not known to what extent longer-term adverse events were captured in the estimation of utility values used in the economic analysis. The costs of treating side effects of long-term medication were also excluded from the analysis owing to lack of relevant data and this omission may have affected the economic results to some extent.

Results of the cost-utility analysis were considerably different from those obtained when physical outcomes were used as measure of benefit. This difference was attributed to the utility weights for the stable state used in the cost-utility analysis, which were significantly higher for olanzapine in comparison to those for other medications. Utility weights used in the model were taken from the only study identified in the literature review that reported utility weights for bipolar disorder-related health states. However, the patient sample that attached valuations onto relevant health states was very small; in addition, it was selected among well-educated, stable outpatients, and therefore it might not be representative of the population of patients with bipolar I disorder. On the other hand, utilities should ideally be based on public and not patient preferences (NICE, 2006).

Overall conclusions from economic analysis

Based on the results of economic analysis, it can be concluded that lithium is likely to be a cost-effective long-term treatment option for patients with bipolar I disorder when WTP for an additional episode averted or an additional day free from episode is below £17,500 and £150 respectively. Above these values, valproate semisodium is likely to be the most cost-effective option for men and women of no child-bearing potential. The cost-effectiveness of valproate semisodium improves when depressive episodes predominate. This can be explained by the high preventive effect valproate semisodium has on depressive episodes, as demonstrated by clinical evidence presented in the guideline.

To the extent that utility weights used in the economic analysis reflect accurately patient preferences on quality of life associated with long-term treatment of bipolar I disorder, olanzapine is highly likely to be the most cost-effective option among all treatments assessed for all patients when the WTP is set at the cost-effectiveness threshold of £20,000/QALY (probability exceeding 90% at this point). This result is almost exclusively attributed to the high utility weight of stable state attached to olanzapine, reflecting a higher overall quality of life associated with long-term use of olanzapine relative to other treatments. The utility weight of stable state is the driver of overall utility experienced by patients with bipolar I disorder, as patients spend most of their time in stable state according to the model structure (over a year patients remain in a stable state for 39 weeks in the case of development of a depressive episode, 43 weeks in the case of development of a manic episode and 52 weeks when no acute episode is experienced).

The above conclusions are subject to a number of limitations, as already discussed. Further research is needed on the long-term effectiveness and adverse events of maintenance treatment for the management of patients with bipolar disorder, as well as on utilities associated with bipolar disorder-related health states, in order to reduce uncertainty characterising treatment outcomes especially in the long term, and to contribute to determining with higher certainty the relative cost effectiveness between medications used for maintenance treatment of patients with bipolar I disorder.

9.4   THE LONG-TERM TREATMENT OF BIPOLAR DISORDER – SUMMARY OF CLINICAL AND HEALTH ECONOMICS EVIDENCE

There is little high-quality evidence for the long-term pharmacological management of bipolar disorder, with evidence of efficacy for only lithium, olanzapine and valproate. The primary economic analysis undertaken for this guideline demonstrated that lithium is likely to be a cost-effective option; however, this conclusion is subject to the great uncertainty characterising efficacy data. On the other hand, olanzapine seems to be more cost effective when issues of overall HRQOL are taken into consideration. In clinical practice, selecting a long-term prophylactic medication should be made on an individual patient basis. Factors that will influence choice include the current medication that the patient is taking, particularly if they have just recovered from manic illness (lithium, olanzapine and valproate are all effective in treating acute mania), the patient's views and experience of tolerability, compliance and potential for pregnancy. Due to concern about withdrawal/rebound effects, lithium is not an ideal drug for those with a history of erratic compliance. Valproate is teratogenic and is also associated with neurodevelomental problems in children whose mothers took valproate in pregnancy, and it should not be routinely prescribed to women of child-bearing potential. Caution should also be exercised in the use of lithium in pregnancy because of its teratogenic properties.

9.5   CLINICAL PRACTICE RECOMMENDATIONS FOR THE LONG-TERM TREATMENT OF BIPOLAR DISORDER

A schedule of physical monitoring tests covering initial assessment and checks to be undertaken on initiation of treatment is in Appendix 21.

9.5.1   Initiating long-term treatment

9.5.1.1   Prescribers should consider starting long-term treatment for bipolar disorder:
- after a manic episode that was associated with significant risk and adverse consequences
- when a patient with bipolar I disorder has had two or more acute episodes
- when a patient with bipolar II disorder has significant functional impairment, is at significant risk of suicide or has frequent episodes.

9.5.1.2   Lithium, olanzapine or valproate* should be considered for long-term treatment of bipolar disorder. The choice should depend on
- response to previous treatments
- the relative risk, and known precipitants, of manic versus depressive relapse

- physical risk factors, particularly renal disease, obesity and diabetes
- the patient's preference and history of adherence
- gender (valproate* should not be prescribed for women of child-bearing potential)
- a brief assessment of cognitive state (such as the Mini-Mental State Examination) if appropriate, for example, for older people.

9.5.1.3   If the patient has frequent relapses, or symptoms continue to cause functional impairment, switching to an alternative montherapy or adding a second prophylactic agent (lithium, olanzapine, valproate*) should be considered. Clinical state, side effects and, where relevant, blood levels should be monitored closely. Possible combinations are lithium with valproate*, lithium with olanzapine*, and valproate with olanzapine*. The reasons for the choice and the discussion with the patient of the potential benefits and risks should be documented.

9.5.1.4   If a trial of a combination of prophylactic agents proves ineffective, the following should be considered:
- consulting with, or referring the patient to, a clinician with expertise in the drug treatment of bipolar disorder
- prescribing lamotrigine* (especially if the patient has bipolar II disorder) or carbamazepine.

9.5.1.5   Long-term drug treatment should normally continue for at least 2 years after an episode of bipolar disorder, and up to 5 years if the person has risk factors for relapse, such as a history of frequent relapses or severe psychotic episodes, comorbid substance misuse, ongoing stressful life events, or poor social support. This should be discussed with the patient and there should be regular reviews. Patients who wish to stop medication early should be encouraged to discuss this with their psychiatrist.

9.5.1.6   If, after careful discussion, a patient with bipolar disorder declines long-term medication, they should still be offered regular contact and reassessment with primary or secondary care services.

9.5.1.7   Long-acting intramuscular injections of antipsychotics ('depots') are not recommended for routine use in bipolar disorder. They may be considered for people who were treated successfully for mania with oral antipsychotics, but have had a relapse because of poor adherence.

9.5.2   The use of antipsychotics in long-term pharmacological treatment

Initiating antipsychotics

9.5.2.1   When initiating long-term treatment of bipolar disorder with antipsychotics, weight and height, plasma glucose and lipids should be measured in all patients, and an ECG arranged for patients with cardiovascular disease or risk factors for it. Prolactin levels should be measured when initiating risperidone* in patients with low libido, sexual dysfunction, menstrual abnormalities, gynaecomastia or galactorrhea.

9.5.2.2   When initiating quetiapine*, the dose should be titrated gradually (in line with the summary of product characteristics), to help maintain normal blood pressure.

Monitoring antipsychotics
9.5.2.3   Patients taking antipsychotics should have their weight checked every 3 months for the first year, and more often if they gain weight rapidly. Plasma glucose and lipids (preferably fasting levels) should be measured 3 months after the start of treatment (and within 1 month if taking olanzapine), and more often if there is evidence of elevated levels. In patients taking risperidone*, prolactin levels should be measured if symptoms of raised prolactin develop; these include low libido, sexual dysfunction, menstrual abnormalities, gynaecomastia and galactorrhea.

Risks associated with the use of antipsychotics
9.5.2.4   Healthcare professionals should discuss with patients the risk of weight gain, and be aware of the possibility of worsening existing diabetes, malignant neuroleptic syndrome and diabetic ketoacidosis with the use of antipsychotic medication; particular caution is needed when treating manic patients.

9.5.3   The use of lithium in long-term pharmacological treatment

Initiating lithium
9.5.3.1   Lithium should not be initiated routinely in primary care for the treatment of bipolar disorder.
9.5.3.2   When initiating lithium as long-term treatment, prescribers should:
   ● advise patients that erratic compliance or rapid discontinuation may increase the risk of manic relapse
   ● measure height and weight, and arrange tests for urea and electrolytes and serum creatinine, and thyroid function
   ● arrange for an ECG for patients with cardiovascular disease or risk factors for it.
   ● arrange a full blood count if clinically indicated
   ● establish a shared-care protocol with the patient's GP for prescribing and monitoring lithium and checking for adverse effects
   ● be aware that patients should take lithium for at least 6 months to establish its effectiveness as a long-term treatment.
9.5.3.3   Serum lithium levels should be checked 1 week after starting and 1 week after every dose change, and until the levels are stable. The aim should be to maintain serum lithium levels between 0.6 and 0.8 mmol per litre in people being prescribed it for the first time.
9.5.3.4   For people who have relapsed previously while taking lithium or who still have sub-threshold symptoms with functional impairment while receiving

lithium, a trial of at least 6 months with serum lithium levels between 0.8 and 1.0 mmol per litre should be considered.

Monitoring lithium

9.5.3.5   For patients with bipolar disorder on lithium treatment, prescribers should do the following:
- Monitor serum lithium levels normally every 3 months.
- Monitor older adults carefully for symptoms of lithium toxicity, because they may develop high serum levels of lithium at doses in the normal range, and lithium toxicity is possible at moderate serum lithium levels.
- Monitor weight, especially in those with rapid weight gain.
- Undertake more frequent tests if there is evidence of clinical deterioration, abnormal results, a change in sodium intake, or symptoms suggesting abnormal renal or thyroid function such as unexplained fatigue, or other risk factors, for example, if the patient is starting medication such as ACE inhibitors, non-steroidal anti-inflammatory drugs, or diuretics.
- Arrange thyroid and renal function tests every 6 months, and more often if there is evidence of impaired renal function.
- Initiate closer monitoring of lithium dose and blood serum levels if urea and creatinine levels become elevated, and assess the rate of deterioration of renal function. The decision whether to continue lithium depends on clinical efficacy, and degree of renal impairment; prescribers should consider seeking advice from a renal specialist and a clinician with expertise in the management of bipolar disorder on this.
- Monitor for symptoms of neurotoxicity, including paraesthesia, ataxia, tremor and cognitive impairment, which can occur at therapeutic levels.

Risks associated with the use of lithium

9.5.3.6   Patients taking lithium should be warned not to take over-the-counter non-steroidal anti-inflammatory drugs. Prescribing non-steroidal anti-inflammatory drugs for such patients should be avoided if possible, and if they are prescribed the patient should be closely monitored.

9.5.3.7   Patients taking lithium should be advised to:
- seek medical attention if they develop diarrhoea and/or vomiting,
- ensure they maintain their fluid intake, particularly after sweating (for example, after exercise, in hot climates, or if they have a fever) if they are immobile for long periods or – in the case of older people – develop a chest infection or pneumonia.
- consider stopping lithium for up to 7 days if they become acutely and severely ill with a metabolic or respiratory disturbance from whatever cause.

9.5.4 The use of valproate in long-term pharmacological treatment

Initiating valproate

9.5.4.1 Valproate should not be routinely initiated in primary care for the treatment of bipolar disorder.

9.5.4.2 When initiating valproate* as long-term treatment, patients should have their height and weight measured, and have a full blood count and liver function tests.

9.5.4.3 Valproate* should not be prescribed routinely for women of child-bearing potential. If no effective alternative to valproate can be identified, adequate contraception should be used, and the risks of taking valproate during pregnancy should be explained.

9.5.4.4 Valproate* should not be prescribed for young women with bipolar disorder who are younger than 18 years because of the risk of polycystic ovary syndrome and unplanned pregnancy in this age group.

Monitoring valproate

9.5.4.5 Routine measurement of valproate* blood levels is not recommended unless there is evidence of ineffectiveness, poor adherence or toxicity.

9.5.4.6 Liver function tests and a full blood count should be done after 6 months' treatment with valproate*, and weight should be monitored in patients who gain weight rapidly.

Risks associated with the use of valproate

9.5.4.7 Patients on valproate*, and their carers, should be advised how to recognise the signs and symptoms of blood or liver disorders and to seek immediate medical help if these develop. If abnormal liver function or blood dyscrasia is detected the drug should be stopped immediately.

9.5.4.8 When prescribing valproate*, prescribers should be aware of:
- its interactions with other anticonvulsants
- the need for more careful monitoring of sedation, tremor and gait disturbance in older people.

9.5.5 Lamotrigine

Initiating lamotrigine

9.5.5.1 Lamotrigine should not be routinely initiated in primary care for the treatment of bipolar disorder.

9.5.5.2 The dose of lamotrigine* should be titrated gradually to minimise the risk of skin rashes, including Stevens–Johnson syndrome. Titration should be slower in patients also taking valproate.

9.5.5.3 When offering lamotrigine* to women taking oral contraceptives, prescribers should explain that the drug may decrease the effectiveness of the contraceptive and discuss alternative methods of contraception. If a woman taking lamotrigine* stops taking an oral contraceptive, the dose of lamotrigine* may need to be reduced by up to 50%.

Monitoring lamotrigine

9.5.5.4   Routine monitoring of blood levels of lamotrigine* is not needed.

Risks associated with the use of lamotrigine

9.5.5.5   Patients taking lamotrigine* should be advised, particularly when starting the drug, to seek medical attention urgently if a rash develops. The drug should be stopped unless it is clear that the rash is not related to the use of lamotrigine*. If an appointment cannot be arranged within a few days or if the rash is worsening, the patient should be advised to stop the drug and then restart if lamotrigine* is not implicated in the development of the rash.

9.5.6   Carbamazepine

Initiating carbamazepine

9.5.6.1   Carbamazepine should be used for the long-term treatment of bipolar disorder only after consulting a specialist.

9.5.6.2   The dose of carbamazepine should be increased gradually to reduce the risk of ataxia.

9.5.6.3   When initiating carbamazepine as long-term treatment, patients should have their height and weight measured, and have a full blood count and liver function tests.

Monitoring carbamazepine

9.5.6.4   Plasma levels of carbamazepine should be measured every 6 months to exclude toxicity, because therapeutic levels and toxic levels are close.

9.5.6.5   Liver function tests and a full blood count should be repeated after 6 months' treatment with carbamazepine, and weight should be monitored in patients who gain weight rapidly.

9.5.6.6   Blood urea and electrolytes should be measured every 6 months after starting treatment with carbamazepine to check for hyponatraemia.

9.5.6.7   Possible interactions of carbamazepine with other drugs, including oral contraceptives, should be monitored closely, particularly if the patient starts a new medication.

Risks associated with the use of carbamazepine

9.5.6.8   When prescribing carbamazepine for patients taking concomitant medications – for example, people older than 65 years and people with multiple physical problems – prescribers should be aware that carbamazepine has a greater potential for drug interactions than other drugs used to treat bipolar disorder.

9.5.7　Additional considerations for long-term treatment following an acute depressive episode

9.5.7.1　After successful treatment for an acute depressive episode, patients should not routinely continue on antidepressant treatment long-term because there is no evidence that this reduces relapse rates, and it may be associated with increased risk of switching to mania.

9.5.8　Treatment for chronic depressive symptoms

9.5.8.1　The following treatments should be considered, in discussion with the patient, for people who have an established diagnosis of bipolar disorder and chronic or recurrent depressive symptoms, but who are not taking prophylactic medication and have not had a recent manic/hypomanic episode:
* long-term treatment with SSRIs at the minimum therapeutic dose in combination with prophylactic medication
* cognitive behavioural therapy (16–20 sessions) in combination with prophylactic medication
* quetiapine*, or
* lamotrigine*.

9.5.8.2　For patients with bipolar II disorder with recurrent depression, lamotrigine* alone should be considered for long-term treatment.

9.5.9　Long-term management of rapid cycling

9.5.9.1　For the long-term management of rapid-cycling bipolar disorder prescribers should:
* consider as first-line treatment a combination of lithium and valproate*
* consider lithium monotherapy as second-line treatment; for patients already taking lithium consider increasing the dose
* avoid the use of an antidepressant, except on advice from a specialist in bipolar disorder
* consider combinations of lithium or valproate* with lamotrigine*, especially in bipolar II disorder
* check thyroid function every 6 months together with levels of thyroid antibodies if clinically indicated, for example, by the thyroid function tests.

9.5.10　Comorbid anxiety disorders

9.5.10.1　For patients with significant comorbid anxiety disorders, psychological treatment focused on anxiety or treatment with a drug such as an atypical antipsychotic should be considered.

9.5.11 Long-term management of bipolar disorder in children and adolescents

9.5.11.1 Long-term management of children or adolescents with bipolar disorder should normally be by specialist clinicians (based in at least Tier 3 level services). Treatment should be as for adults with bipolar disorder except that:

- an atypical antipsychotic that is associated with lower weight gain and non-elevation of prolactin levels should be the first-line prophylactic agent
- lithium should be considered as the second-line prophylactic agent in female patients and valproate or lithium as the second-line prophylactic agent in male patients
- parents and carers should be given support to help the patient maintain a regular lifestyle
- the school or college should be given advice (with permission of the patient and those with parental responsibility) on managing the patient's bipolar disorder.

9.6 RESEARCH RECOMMENDATIONS

9.6.1 Choice of prophylactic medication

A randomised placebo-controlled trial should be undertaken to assess the efficacy and cost-effectiveness of adding an atypical antipsychotic to existing prophylactic medication (either lithium or valproate) in bipolar I disorder and bipolar II disorder. The primary outcome measure at 2 years would be time to the next bipolar episode requiring treatment, and an important secondary outcome measure would be social functioning. The trial should be adequately powered to investigate tolerability differences and other potential harms such as weight gain and diabetes.

Why this is important

The treatment of severe mental illness is a key priority in the National Service Framework for mental health. Episodes of mania and depression are a significant cause of long-term disability and unemployment. There is insufficient evidence about the use of antipsychotics in the prophylaxis of bipolar disorder treatment, particularly in bipolar II disorder. The results of further research would allow more specific recommendations to be made.

9.6.2 Prophylaxis in children and adolescents

A randomised placebo-controlled trial should be undertaken to assess the efficacy and cost-effectiveness of an atypical antipsychotic plus an antimanic agent of a different class versus antimanic agent alone in children and adolescents in remission from bipolar disorder. The primary outcome measure at 2 years would be time to the next bipolar episode requiring treatment, and an important secondary outcome measure would be social functioning. The trial should also be adequately powered to investigate tolerability differences and other potential harms such as weight gain and diabetes.

Why this is important

Inadequate treatment of psychosis in young people is associated with poor long-term outcomes, including increased risk of suicide. But there is very little evidence of any quality on the drug treatment of bipolar disorder in children and young people. The answer to this question would allow more specific recommendations about the treatment of this group, and would help address standard 9 of the children's National Service Framework.

9.7 THE DISCONTINUATION/WITHDRAWAL OF MEDICATION

9.7.1 Introduction

Relapse prevention of bipolar disorder will usually involve long-term management with medication and discontinuation of drugs may be necessary for a variety of reasons, for example, changing drugs, mood switches, adverse reactions and pregnancy. Withdrawal mania is well recognised with lithium (Goodwin, 1994) and sudden stoppage of antidepressants can cause a variety of transient physical and psychological withdrawal or discontinuation symptoms (Haddad, 2001). Withdrawal symptoms, including movement disorders, have been noted with conventional antipsychotics. So, unless unavoidable, adjustments should be carried out gradually. Rapid and mood-reactive changes to a drug regimen ('to chase a mood change') may actually provoke rapid cycling, worsen an acute episode and hence be detrimental to long-term functioning.

9.7.2 Lithium

Sudden stopping of lithium (either deliberate or accidental, including running out of medication) or abrupt changes in lithium plasma levels may cause rebound mania or depression and increase the risk of suicide, and must be avoided. Lithium should be discontinued step-wise over at least 4 weeks, and preferably over a longer period (up to 3 months). It has been estimated that if lithium is stopped abruptly then 2 years of prior treatment are required for the detrimental effects of sudden stoppage, in terms of rebound illness, to be balanced by its prophylactic effects (Goodwin, 1994).

9.7.3 Antidepressants

In rapid cycling or after a mood switch to mania, it will usually be necessary to stop any potentially precipitating or contributory drugs such as antidepressants. This must be balanced against the need to avoid the possibility of adverse discontinuation symptoms (Haddad, 2001). These can include:

Tricyclic antidepressants (TCAs): cholinergic rebound, for example, headache, restlessness, diarrhoea, nausea and vomiting, flu-like symptoms, lethargy, abdominal cramps, sleep disturbance and movement disorders.

Selective serotonin reuptake inhibitors (SSRIs): dizziness, vertigo/light-headedness, nausea, fatigue, headache, sensory disturbance, 'electric shocks' in the head, insomnia, abdominal cramps, chills, flu-like symptoms, increased dreaming, anxiety/agitation and volatility. These are most common with paroxetine but have been reported with other SSRIs (MHRA, 2004).

Fluoxetine has a long half-life and abrupt stopping carries little risk.

Other antidepressants: Venlafaxine may be particularly difficult to discontinue and extra care with dose reduction and monitoring should be carried out. There are no reported significant problems with discontinuation of mirtazapine, moclobemide or reboxetine.

9.7.4 Others

There is little evidence yet for any significant rebound phenomena or withdrawal symptoms in bipolar disorder on discontinuation of carbamazepine, valproate, quetiapine, lamotrigine, risperidone or olanzapine, but it is wise to be careful. Tapered discontinuation over at least 4 weeks would minimise the potential for destabilisation.

9.7.5 Clinical practice recommendations

Stopping lithium

9.7.5.1   Lithium should be stopped gradually over at least 4 weeks, and preferably over a period of up to 3 months, particularly if the patient has a history of manic relapse (even if they have been started on another antimanic agent).

9.7.5.2   When lithium treatment is stopped or is about to be stopped abruptly, prescribers should consider changing to monotherapy with an atypical antipsychotic or valproate*, and then monitor closely for early signs of mania and depression.

Stopping valproate

9.7.5.3   When stopping valproate* in patients with bipolar disorder, the dose should be reduced gradually over at least 4 weeks to minimise the risk of destabilisation.

Stopping lamotrigine

9.7.5.4   When stopping lamotrigine*, the dose should be reduced gradually over at least 4 weeks to minimise the risk of destabilisation.

Stopping carbamazepine

9.7.5.5   The dose of carbamazepine should be reduced gradually over at least 4 weeks to minimise the risk of destabilisation.

Stopping antipsychotics

9.7.5.6   If a patient with bipolar disorder is stopping antipsychotic medication, the antipsychotic:

- should be stopped gradually over at least 4 weeks if the patient is continuing with other medication
- should be stopped over a period of up to 3 months if the patient is not continuing with other medication, or has a history of manic relapse.

9.8   THE PHARMACOLOGICAL MANAGEMENT OF BIPOLAR II DISORDER

9.8.1   Introduction

This section considers studies where more than 50% of participants had a diagnosis of bipolar II disorder. All of these studies also appear in other reviews in this or the previous chapter.

9.8.2   Treatment of acute hypomania in bipolar II disorder

There are no trials of pharmacological treatment of acute hypomania in people with bipolar II disorder that met inclusion criteria.

9.8.3   Treatment of acute depression in bipolar II disorder

Two trials of treatment for acute depression in bipolar II disorder met inclusion criteria. A summary of study characteristics is in Table 70, with fuller details in Appendix 22.

Table 70: Summary of study characteristics of studies for the treatment of depression in bipolar II disorder

	Antidepressant versus another antidepressant	Antidepressant versus prophylactic agent
No. trials (No. participants)	*1 RCT (56)*	*1 RCT (27)*
Study IDs	HIMMELHOCH1991	YOUNG2000
Population	US; outpatients	Canada; outpatients
Diagnosis at entry to study	Bipolar I – depressed phase 43% Bipolar II – depressed phase 57%	Bipolar I – depressed phase 41% Bipolar II – depressed phase 59%
Study drug	Tranylcypromine** 36.8 mg*	Paroxetine 36 mg*
Comparator drug(s)	Imipramine 245.5 mg*	Second prophylactic agent (lithium 0.9 mmol/l* or valproate semisodium 510 mmol/l*)
Concomitant medication	None	On lithium or valproate semisodium for at least 3 months before entering study
Mean age range	Around 39	41*
Length of trial	6 weeks + 10-week follow-up	5 weeks*
Problems with trial affecting efficacy assessments	Efficacy data not extractable	Efficacy data not extractable

Notes: *mean, **Tranylcypromine is not licensed in the UK.

Clinical summary

There are two trials of the pharmacological management of bipolar disorder where more than 50% of participants have a diagnosis of bipolar II disorder. Neither of these had extractable efficacy data and therefore it is not possible to assess the evidence. An overview of results is in Table 71, with the full evidence profile in Appendix 23.

Table 71: Summary of evidence characteristics of studies for the treatment of depression in bipolar II disorder

	Antidepressant versus another antidepressant	Antidepressant versus prophylactic agent
Evidence for efficacy	No data (very low)	No data (very low)
Evidence for acceptability/ tolerability (including switching)	Data are inconclusive (low) for acceptability/tolerability outcomes	Data are inconclusive (low) for acceptability/tolerability outcomes
Overall risk-benefit ratio	Unclear	Unclear

9.8.4   Long-term maintenance in bipolar II disorder

Studies considered

Two studies of long-term maintenance in bipolar II disorder met inclusion criteria. Summary study characteristics are in Table 72 with fuller details in Appendix 22.

Clinical summary

Evidence for the long-term treatment of bipolar II disorder is limited. An overview of the results is provided in Table 73, with the full evidence profile in Appendix 23.

9.8.5   Clinical practice recommendations

Additional recommendations for bipolar II disorder are included in the initiating long-term treatment, recurrent depression and management of rapid cycling sections above.

Table 72: Summary of study characteristics for long-term maintenance in bipolar II disorder

	Lithium versus placebo	**Valproate semisodium versus placebo**
No. trials (No. participants)	*1 RCT (40)*	*1 RCT (30)*
Study IDs	DUNNER1976	FRANKENBURG2002
Population	US; outpatients	US; outpatients
Diagnosis at entry to study	Bipolar II – 'normal mood'	Bipolar II – with borderline personality disorder
Serum levels of lithium (mmol/L)	0.8–1.2	Valproate semisodium – serum levels 50–100 mg/l
Comparator drug(s)	Placebo	Placebo
Concomitant medication	not reported	not reported
Mean age	40	39
Length of trial	16 months	6 months*
Problems with trial affecting efficacy assessments		Participants recruited via the press

*mean

Table 73: Summary of evidence profile for lithium monotherapy in long-term maintenance of bipolar II disorder

	Lithium	Valproate semisodium
Evidence for efficacy (quality)	Data are inconclusive (low) for efficacy outcomes	Data are inconclusive (low) for efficacy outcomes
Evidence for acceptability/ tolerability (including switching) (quality)	Data are inconclusive (low) for acceptability/tolerability outcomes	Data are inconclusive (low) for acceptability/tolerability outcomes

9.9   THE PHARMACOLOGICAL MANAGEMENT OF WOMEN OF CHILD-BEARING POTENTIAL: BEFORE, DURING, AND AFTER PREGNANCY

9.9.1   Introduction

The pharmacological management of women of child-bearing potential is challenging in bipolar disorder. The GDG approached this issue by convening a consensus conference in collaboration with the NICE guideline development group for antenatal and postnatal mental health. A summary of the conference as applied to bipolar disorder is contained in Appendix 20.

The management of bipolar disorder in women of reproductive age is complicated by several issues. These include the following:

- the effect of bipolar illness on conception (mania can lead to sexual disinhibition and unplanned pregnancy)
- the effect of pregnancy and childbirth on the natural course of bipolar disorder (in women with a diagnosis of bipolar disorder there is approximately a 50% chance of an episode of psychosis in the postnatal period (Brockington, 1996; Craddock & Jones, 2001))
- the risk of bipolar disorder in the offspring of parents with the condition (there is a genetic contribution to bipolar disorder and so parents with bipolar disorder are more likely to have a child with bipolar disorder – clinicians often offer to discuss this with patients)
- the effect of medication on fertility (conventional antipsychotics and some atypical antipsychotics (for example, risperidone, amilsulpride) can reduce

fertility by causing hyperprolactinaemia sufficient to cause disruption of the hypothalamic-pituitary-gonadal axis (Haddad & Wieck, 2004), whilst carbamazepine reduces the effectiveness of the oral contraceptive by causing hepatic enzyme induction (Spina *et al.*, 1996)).

Perhaps the most important factor, though, is the potential for medication prescribed during pregnancy to cause adverse obstetric and neonatal outcomes, including teratogenesis. Although most data regarding the adverse effects of antiepileptic drugs have been obtained from studies of women with epilepsy rather than bipolar disorder, these have helped clarify that teratogenicity is related primarily to the drugs rather than the condition. Therefore, these data are likely to be as applicable to their use in patients with bipolar disorder as to those with epilepsy. First trimester use of sodium valproate, carbamazepine and lithium are all associated with an increased risk of major malformation. Teratogenic effects are not as well established with other psychiatric drugs though the risk cannot be totally excluded, for example, the risk of cardiac defects with lithium. Drugs that have been widely used in clinical practice for long periods without teratogenic effects being identified are regarded as safer than more recently introduced drugs. A fuller summary of these risks is contained in Appendix 20.

Drugs may also cause adverse neonatal symptoms. For example, lithium may cause thyroid disorders and conventional antipsychotics may lead to EPS, with benzodiazepines leading to sedation or, with long-term use, withdrawal symptoms. With antidepressants, particularly SSRIs, a range of neonatal symptoms have been reported, including jitteriness, convulsions, crying, poor feeding and hypertonia (Laine *et al.*, 2003). Whether these symptoms represent serotonin toxicity, a withdrawal effect or a combination of both mechanisms remains unclear (Haddad *et al.*, 2005).

In addition, all medications used in bipolar disorder are secreted in breast milk to some degree. Clozapine and lithium are generally regarded as absolute contraindications to breastfeeding due to the risk of agranulocytosis with clozapine and lithium toxicity; lithium is secreted in breast milk at 40% of the maternal serum concentration (American Academy of Paediatrics Committee on drugs, 2000). Occasional reports of adverse neonatal effects, presumably due to transfer of the drug in the milk, have appeared (for example, Kent and Laidlaw, 1995). The most cautious approach is to advise that breast feeding is avoided whenever a psychotropic is prescribed but many authorities regard this as too prescriptive.

Current practice
Central to the effective management of women of child-bearing age is information about the risk of relapse during and after pregnancy and risks to the unborn child. Women need to be provided with information regarding the importance of contraception, including the option of long-term reversible contraception (NICE, 2005b). They also need to be aware of the risk of a puerperal relapse and of a child developing bipolar disorder (about 5% if one parent suffers from bipolar disorder versus

a general population risk of 1%) and of the potential effects of medication on fertility. Those prescribed prolactin-raising antipsychotics need to be aware that fertility may be compromised. Conversely, women who are stopping a prolactin-raising antipsychotic must be informed that this may lead to a return of fertility, otherwise an unplanned pregnancy may result. Women prescribed carbamazapine will need specialist advice as enzyme induction with carbamazepine affects both progesterone only and combined oral contraceptives, as well as some long-acting preparations.

It is vital that women are aware of the potential for medication to cause adverse obstetric and neonatal outcomes, including teratogenesis. Women who are considering conceiving should discuss the matter with their psychiatrist, in particular the issue of medication and maintenance treatment for their bipolar disorder. The advice that is given will depend on the individual's history and circumstances. Various options are available and these include stopping medication prior to trying to conceive and remaining medication free thereafter, stopping medication prior to conception and restarting it either after the first trimester or immediately after birth, remaining on the existing medication throughout the process of conception, pregnancy and birth or switching medication prior to attempting to conceive. Which strategy is chosen will depend on the wishes of the mother and the advice of the medical team, who need to balance the risks of under treating the disorder (for example, relapse) with the risk of harming the unborn child by remaining on medication. The risk of relapse partly depends on the number and severity of past episodes of illness and the degree of support and monitoring that is currently available.

There is strong evidence that folic acid supplements reduce the incidence of neural tube defects (Lumley *et al.*, 2001). As a result, all women planning a pregnancy are advised to take 0.4 mg folic acid per day before conception and during the first 12 weeks of pregnancy. Women with a neural tube defect, or a neural tube defect in a previous child, are advised to take a higher dose of 5 mg per day (BNF). Given the association of valproate and carbamazepine with neural tube defects, and the fact that both drugs interfere with folic acid metabolism, some authorities recommend that women of child-bearing potential prescribed these drugs should receive folic acid supplements. However, to date, no study has demonstrated that prescribing folic acid supplements to women taking anticonvulsants during pregnancy reduces the risk of neural tube defects, and neural tube defects have been reported in the offspring of such women (for example, Duncan *et al.*, 2001). There is a danger that routine folic acid prescribing in this group may incorrectly imply that getting pregnant is safe and that the risk of neural tube defect posed by the anticonvulsant has been counteracted. Given this, and the lack of data, it is unclear whether prescribers should routinely prescribe folic acid to women of child-bearing potential prescribed valproate and carbamazepine. If a woman receiving either of these drugs presents at less than 12 weeks pregnant, it would seem prudent to start folic acid supplementation although, given that the neural tube closes by day 28 after fertilisation, it is debatable whether or not this provides any protection.

Choice of antipsychotics

There has been increasing use of antipsychotics in women with bipolar disorder planning pregnancy and this based on antimanic efficacy and antidepressant properties. There is no evidence of teratogenicity with antipsychotics, though caution is needed with more recently introduced agents due to the limited pharmacovigilance data from women who have conceived while prescribed the drug.

Unplanned pregnancy

Often a pregnancy will be unplanned and healthcare professionals will be faced with a woman who has conceived while taking her existing medication. All major structural teratogenic effects, including neural tube defects occur in the first trimester. Screening for major anomalies should be carried out for all women who receive any anti-epileptic drug or lithium in early pregnancy and all should receive urgent referral to specialist feto-maternal medicine services. Whether existing medication is stopped or switched will depend on the drugs and the risks and benefits perceived in that individual case. If valproate, carbamazepine or lithium have been prescribed in the first trimester, there should be close consultation with the obstetric team who can provide appropriate screening and counselling. Screening for neural tube defects involves maternal serum alpha-fetoprotein estimation (sometimes followed by amniocentesis) and high-resolution ultrasound scanning at weeks 18–23. In the case of lithium, an ultrasound scan can also help identify cardiac anomalies. If congenital defects are identified then the mother should be offered counselling by the obstetric team and a termination of pregnancy is one available option. Psychological support is essential should a woman conceive a child with a malformation, irrespective of whether she decides to continue with the pregnancy or to terminate it. If she continues with the pregnancy, full paediatric assessment of the child is required with appropriate social and medical help being provided for mother and child.

Any child born to a mother prescribed a psychotropic drug up to delivery should be monitored for the development of adverse drug effects in the first week to 10 days after delivery.

If lithium treatment is prescribed during the third trimester or commenced shortly after delivery, close monitoring of the mother's plasma lithium level is required due to changes in the volume of distribution. Serum lithium levels should be monitored every 4 weeks during pregnancy, weekly from the 36th week, and within 24 hours of childbirth, with doses adjusted to maintain appropriate serum levels. Women should maintain an adequate fluid intake because of the risk of lithium toxicity.

Care of the infant

Symptoms including irritability, constant crying, shivering, tremor, restlessness, increased tone, feeding and sleeping difficulties, and, rarely, seizures have been reported in children born to mothers taking SSRIs at delivery. Many of these symptoms are mild and self-limiting. In many cases these symptoms appear casually related to antidepressant exposure though there is debate as to what extent they represent serotonergic toxicity or a withdrawal reaction. Neonates of mothers taking psychotropic drugs during pregnancy should be carefully monitored.

9.9.2   Clinical practice recommendations

General principles of management for women of child-bearing potential and for women with bipolar disorder who are pregnant

9.9.2.1   The absolute and relative risks of problems associated with both treating and not treating the bipolar disorder during pregnancy should be discussed with women.

9.9.2.2   More frequent contact by specialist mental health services (including, where appropriate, specialist perinatal mental health services), working closely with obstetric services, should be considered for pregnant women with bipolar disorder, because of the increased risk of relapse during pregnancy and the postnatal period.

9.9.2.3   A written plan for managing a woman's bipolar disorder during the pregnancy, delivery and postnatal period should be developed as soon as possible. This should be developed with the patient and significant others, and shared with her obstetrician, midwife, GP and health visitor. All medical decisions should be recorded in all versions of the patient's notes. Information about her medication should be included in the birth plan and notes for postnatal care.

9.9.2.4   If a pregnant woman with bipolar disorder is stable on an antipsychotic and likely to relapse without medication, she should be maintained on the antipsychotic, and monitored for weight gain and diabetes.

9.9.2.5   The following drugs should not be routinely prescribed for pregnant women with bipolar disorder:
- valproate – because of risk to the fetus and subsequent child development
- carbamazepine – because of its limited efficacy and risk of harm to the fetus
- lithium – because risk of harm to the fetus, such as cardiac problems
- lamotrigine* – because of the risk of harm to the fetus
- paroxetine – because of the risk of cardiovascular malformations in the fetus
- long-term treatment with benzodiazepines – because of risks during pregnancy and the immediate postnatal period, such as cleft palate and floppy baby syndrome.

Women planning a pregnancy

9.9.2.6   Women with bipolar disorder who are considering pregnancy should normally be advised to stop taking valproate, carbamazepine, lithium and lamotrigine*, and alternative prophylactic drugs (such as an antipsychotic) should be considered.

9.9.2.7 Women taking antipsychotics who are planning a pregnancy should be advised that the raised prolactin levels associated with some antipsychotics reduce the chances of conception. If prolactin levels are raised, an alternative drug should be considered.

9.9.2.8 If a woman who needs antimanic medication plans to become pregnant, a low-dose typical or atypical antipsychotic should be considered, because they are of least known risk.

9.9.2.9 If a woman taking lithium plans to become pregnant, the following options should be considered:
- if the patient is well and not at high risk of relapse – gradually stopping lithium
- If the patient is not well or is at high risk of relapse:
  - switching gradually to an antipsychotic, or
  - stopping lithium and restarting it in the second trimester if the woman is not planning to breastfeed and her symptoms have responded better to lithium than to other drugs in the past, or
  - continuing with lithium, after full discussion of the risks, while trying to conceive and throughout the pregnancy, if manic episodes have complicated the woman's previous pregnancies, and her symptoms have responded well to lithium.

9.9.2.10 If a woman remains on lithium during pregnancy, serum lithium levels should be monitored every 4 weeks, then weekly from the 36th week, and less than 24 hours after childbirth. The dose should be adjusted to keep serum levels within the therapeutic range. The woman should maintain adequate fluid intake.

9.9.2.11 If a woman planning a pregnancy becomes depressed after stopping prophylactic medication, psychological therapy (CBT) should be offered in preference to an antidepressant because of the risk of switching associated with antidepressants. If an antidepressant is used, it should usually be an SSRI (but not paroxetine because of the risk of cardiovascular malformations in the fetus) and the woman should be monitored closely.

Women with an unplanned pregnancy

9.9.2.12 If a woman with bipolar disorder has an unplanned pregnancy:
- the pregnancy should be confirmed as quickly as possible
- the woman should be advised to stop taking valproate, carbamazepine and lamotrigine*
- if the pregnancy is confirmed in the first trimester, and the woman is stable, lithium should be stopped radually over 4 weeks, and the woman informed that this may not remove the risk of cardiac defects in the fetus
- if the woman remains on lithium during pregnancy serum lithium levels should be checked every 4 weeks, then weekly from the 36th week, and

less than 24 hours after childbirth; the dose should be adjusted to keep serum levels within the therapeutic range, and the woman should maintain adequate fluid intake

- an antipsychotic should be offered as prophylactic medication
- offer appropriate screening and counselling about the continuation of the pregnancy, the need for additional monitoring and the risks to the fetus if the woman stays on medication.

9.9.2.13 If a woman with bipolar disorder continues with an unplanned pregnancy, the newborn baby should have a full paediatric assessment, and social and medical help should be provided for the mother and child.

Pregnant women experiencing acute mania or depression

Acute mania

9.9.2.14 If a pregnant women who is not taking medication develops acute mania, an atypical or a typical antipsychotic should be considered. The dose should be kept as low as possible and the woman monitored carefully.

9.9.2.15 If a pregnant woman develops acute mania while taking prophylactic medication, prescribers should:

- check the dose of the prophylactic agent and adherence
- increase the dose if the woman is taking an antipsychotic, or consider changing to an antipsychotic if she is not
- if there is no response to changes in dose or drug and the patient has severe mania, consider the use of ECT, lithium and, rarely, valproate.

9.9.2.16 If there is no alternative to valproate the woman should be informed of the increased risk to the fetus and the child's intellectual development. The lowest possible effective dose should be used and augmenting it with additional antimanic medication (but not carbamazepine*) considered. The maximum dosage should be 1 gram per day, in divided doses and in the slow-release form, with 5 mg/day folic acid.

Depressive symptoms

9.9.2.17 For mild depressive symptoms in pregnant women with bipolar disorder the following should be considered:

- self-help approaches such as guided self-help and computerised CBT
- brief psychological interventions
- antidepressant medication.

9.9.2.18 For moderate to severe depressive symptoms in pregnant women with bipolar disorder the following should be considered:

- psychological treatment (CBT) for moderate depression
- combined medication and structured psychological interventions for severe depression.

9.9.2.19 For moderate to severe depressive symptoms in pregnant women with bipolar disorder, quetiapine* alone or SSRIs (but not paroxetine) in combination with prophylactic medication should be preferred because SSRIs are less likely to be associated with switching than the tricyclic antidepressants. Monitor closely for signs of switching and stop the SSRI if patients start to develop manic or hypomanic symptoms.

9.9.2.20 Women who are prescribed an antidepressant during pregnancy should be informed of the potential, but predominantly short-lived, adverse effects of antidepressants on the neonate.

Care in the perinatal period

9.9.2.21 Women taking lithium should deliver in hospital, and be monitored during labour by the obstetric medical team, in addition to usual midwife care. Monitoring should include fluid balance, because of the risk of dehydration and lithium toxicity.

9.9.2.22 After delivery, if a woman with bipolar disorder who is not on medication is at high risk of developing an acute episode, prescribers should consider establishing or reinstating medication as soon as the patient is medically stable (once the fluid balance is established).

9.9.2.23 If a woman maintained on lithium is at high risk of a manic relapse in the immediate postnatal period, augmenting treatment with an antipsychotic should be considered.

9.9.2.24 If a woman with bipolar disorder develops severe manic or psychotic symptoms and behavioural disturbance in the intrapartum period rapid tranquillisation with an antipsychotic should be considered in preference to a benzodiazepine because of the risk of floppy baby syndrome. Treatment should be in collaboration with an anaesthetist.

Breast feeding

9.9.2.25 Women with bipolar disorder who are taking psychotropic medication and wish to breastfeed should:

- have advice on the risks and benefits of breastfeeding
- be advised not to breastfeed if taking lithium, benzodiazepines or lamotrigine*, and offered a different prophylactic agent that can be used when breastfeeding – an antipsychotic should be the first choice (but not clozapine*)
- be prescribed an SSRI if an antidepressant is used (but not fluoxetine or citalopram).

Care of the infant

9.9.2.26 Babies whose mothers took psychotropic drugs during pregnancy should be monitored in the first few weeks for adverse drug effects, drug toxicity or withdrawal (for example, floppy baby syndrome, irritability, constant crying, shivering, tremor, restlessness, increased tone, feeding and sleeping difficulties and rarely seizures). If the mother was prescribed antidepressants in the last trimester, such symptoms may be a serotonergic toxicity syndrome rather than withdrawal, and the neonate should be monitored carefully.

10. PSYCHOLOGICAL THERAPIES IN THE TREATMENT OF BIPOLAR DISORDER

10.1 INTRODUCTION: HISTORY OF TREATMENT FOR BIPOLAR DISORDER

Treatment for bipolar disorder traditionally has been predominantly pharmacotherapy. However, prophylactic agents such as lithium provide a long-term benefit for only about two thirds of patients with bipolar disorder (Goodwin, 2002; Prien & Potter, 1990). Lamotrigine may have a long-term role in delaying or preventing the recurrence of depressive episodes but lithium, antipsychotics and valproate semisodium remain first-line treatments (Calabrese, *et al.,* 2002). In view of the limitations of pharmacotherapy alone to prevent relapses, there has been an emerging interest in developing psychological treatments specifically designed for bipolar disorder in recent years (Lam, 2002).

One of the first psychological treatments to be offered to people with bipolar disorder was psychoanalytic psychotherapy. There has been a longstanding clinical and theoretical interest in the treatment of bipolar disorder in the field of psychoanalysis. Over the past 70 years a number of case studies have reported treatment outcomes for people with bipolar disorder but there have been no systematic reviews or controlled trials that have evaluated the psychoanalytic treatment of bipolar disorder.

10.2 PRINCIPLES OF PSYCHOLOGICAL TREATMENT

10.2.1 Diathesis-stress model and combined treatment

As for most severe mental disorders, the diathesis-stress model applies to bipolar disorders. Biology predisposes individuals to be vulnerable to bipolar disorders. Yet, stress can both bring on the illness and affect its course. Hence, all randomised controlled psychological treatment studies cited below are combined treatments of medication and psychological therapy.

10.2.2 Aims of psychological intervention

The aims of psychological therapy are the prevention of relapses and the promotion of social functioning. Other aims may include the reduction of mood symptoms and mood fluctuations, promoting good coping skills, the enhancement of medication compliance and promoting communication within the family.

10.2.3   Time of recruitment

Bipolar disorder is a complex illness. Treatments for different phases of the illness are likely to be different. Psychological strategies designed for prevention of relapses may be minimally effective for an acute episode. In fact, strategies designed to target an acute episode may be different. Hence, it is important to be clear whether the goal of intervention is for the acute episode or relapse prevention for patients out of an acute episode. So far, the evidence for efficacy of combined drug and psychological treatment is mainly in relapse prevention for patients who are out of an acute episode (for example, Lam *et al.*, 2003) or very stable patients (for example, Colom *et al.*, 2003a).

10.2.4   Therapists' variables

Psychological treatments for bipolar disorder are complex and require a high level of therapist expertise. These include psychological skills as well as sound knowledge about bipolar disorder and its pharmacological treatment. Such knowledge enables therapists to discuss treatment options intelligently with patients and gain credibility. Furthermore, it enables therapists to detect early stages of a manic relapse and institute strategies to prevent early stages escalating to full-blown episodes. Pharmacological intervention may also need to be instituted for patients with a history of rapid swings into mania. This is made much easier if therapists are familiar with the disorder and its pharmacological management.

10.2.5   Variation in delivery of psychological therapy

Efficacy evidence for psychological therapy in bipolar disorder has come from a variety of sources including individual work (Frank *et al.*, 2005; Lam *et al.*, 2000; Scott *et al.*, 2001; Lam *et al.*, 2003; Scott *et al.*, 2006), group work (Colom *et al.*, 2003a) and family work (Miklowitz *et al.*, 2000). The choice of mode of delivery depends on patients' preference, constraints of local services and patients' mental state. For example, complex psychoeducational groups as conducted by Colom's group should only be considered when patients have been stable for several months.

Psychological treatment approaches specific for bipolar disorder identified by the GDG to have some evidence of treatment efficacy include the following:
- Cognitive behavioural therapy (CBT)
- 'Complex' psychoeducation
- Focused family therapy
- Interpersonal and social rhythm therapy (IPSRT)
- Identifying early warnings and seeking help.

10.2.6   Shared common features

Irrespective of differences in theoretical frameworks and mode of delivery, there are some common features in psychological work in relapse prevention in bipolar disorders. These include:

● Psychoeducation about the illness
● Promoting medication adherence
● Promotion of regular daily routine and sleep
● Monitoring mood, detection of early warnings and strategy to prevent early stages from developing into full-blown episodes
● General coping strategies including problem-solving techniques

10.3   THE EARLY WARNING APPROACH

The interest in studying early warnings of relapse in bipolar disorder is based on the assumption that if patients can detect early warnings, actions may be taken to prevent the development of a full episode. Studies have found that bipolar patients can report early warnings of relapses reliably (Molnar *et al.*, 1988; Lam *et al.*, 2001) and are better at reporting early warnings of mania than early warnings of depression (Lam & Wong, 1997). However, the patterns of early warnings and the length of early warning periods are different for different patients (Smith & Tarrier, 1992; Jackson *et al.*, 2003; Lam & Wong, 2005). Only one study investigated the effect of adaptive coping with early warnings on the course of the illness in bipolar disorder. A cross-sectional study reported that bipolar patients' level of functioning was highly related to how well they coped with the early warning signs (Lam & Wong, 1997). It was also found that adaptive cognitive and behavioural coping strategies for early warnings predicted fewer manic symptoms, good functional outcomes and reduced relapses 18 months later (Lam & Wong, 2001). Common early warning signs of mania include decreased need for sleep, increased activity, being more sociable and racing thoughts, while common early warning signs of depression are loss of interest, not being able to put worries aside and interrupted sleep (Lam *et al.*, 2001).

10.4   OVERVIEW OF CLINICAL REVIEW

10.4.1   Definitions of psychological therapies reviewed

Cognitive behavioural therapies (CBT)
Cognitive behavioural therapies were defined as discrete, time limited, structured psychological interventions derived from the cognitive behavioural model of affective disorders and where the patient:

● works collaboratively with the therapist to identify the types and effects of thoughts, beliefs and interpretations on current symptoms, feelings states and/or problem areas

- develops skills to identify, monitor and then counteract problematic thoughts, beliefs and interpretations related to the target symptoms/problems
- tackles dysfunctional assumptions, which may maintain some high-goal attainment behaviour
- learns a repertoire of coping skills appropriate to the target thoughts, beliefs and/or problem areas.

Family interventions

Family sessions with a specific supportive or treatment function based on systemic, cognitive behavioural or psychoanalytic principles, which must contain at least one of the following:

- psychoeducational intervention
- problem solving/crisis management work
- intervention with the identified patient.

Complex psychoeducation

Complex psychoeducation was defined as any group programme involving an explicitly described educational interaction between the information provider and the patient/carer as the prime focus of the intervention. Patients/carers should be provided with information, support and different management strategies, including:

- illness awareness
- treatment compliance
- early detection of prodromal symptoms and relapse
- lifestyle regularity.

Interpersonal and social rhythm therapy (IPSRT)

IPSRT was defined as discrete, time limited, structured psychological intervention derived from an interpersonal model of affective disorders that focuses on:

- working collaboratively with the therapist to identify the effects of key problematic areas related to interpersonal conflicts, role transitions, grief and loss, and social skills, and their effects on current symptoms, feelings states and/or problems
- seeking to reduce symptoms by learning to cope with or resolve these interpersonal problem areas
- seeking to improve the regularity of daily life in order to minimise relapse.

10.4.2 Evidence search

The review team conducted a new systematic search for RCTs that assessed the efficacy of psychological interventions for people with bipolar disorder, both in an acute illness phase and as long-term treatment for people who have recovered from an acute episode. Databases searched are in Table 74.

Table 74: Databases searched and inclusion/exclusion criteria for clinical effectiveness of psychological interventions.

	Psychological interventions
Electronic databases	All searched from inception: MEDLINE, EMBASE, PsycINFO, CINAHL
Update searches	October 2004, April 2005, September 2005
Study design	RCT
Patient population	Bipolar I or II, regardless of state at time of recruitment
Interventions included	All psychological therapies
Outcomes	Primary outcomes: relapse, not in remission, mean number of days in episode, discontinuation from treatment for any reason Secondary outcomes: symptom levels (mania, depression, psychosis), functional status, hospitalisation
Exclusion criteria	See appendices

10.4.3   Presenting the evidence

Systematic reviews of the evidence are based on the searches described above, supplemented with additional narrative as necessary. Relevant characteristics of all included studies are in Appendix 22, together with a list of excluded studies with reasons for exclusion, and full references for both included and excluded studies. These are presented for each topic covered in this chapter. To aid readability, summaries of the study characteristics are included below, followed by the critical outcomes from the evidence profiles, together with a summary of the evidence profile.

In all of these, studies are referred to by a study ID (primary author in capital letters and date of study publication, except where a study is *in press* or only submitted for publication, then a date is not used).

Based on the GRADE methodology outlined in chapter 3, the quality of the evidence is summarised in the evidence profiles and summary of the evidence profiles as follows:
- high = Further research is very unlikely to change our confidence in the estimate of the effect
- moderate = Further research is likely to have an important impact on our confidence in the estimate of the effect and may change the estimate
- low = Further research is very likely to have an important impact on our confidence in the estimate of the effect and is likely to change the estimate
- very low = Any estimate of effect is very uncertain.

10.4.4   Search results

Twenty-one trials were identified from searches of electronic databases, 11 of which met the eligibility criteria set by the GDG (COCHRAN1984; COLOM2003; COLOM2003A; FRANK1997; LAM2000; LAM2003; MIKLOWITZ2000; PERRY1999; REA2003; SCHMITZ2003; SCOTT2001), and pre-publication copies of a further four trials were sourced directly from known researchers in the field, one of which has been subsequently published (MILLER2004; SCOTT2006; MEYER unpub; BALL, in press). Three of these met inclusion criteria (BALL, in press MILLER2004; SCOTT2006) (see section on CBT below). Excluded studies with reasons for exclusion can be seen in Appendix 22. See tables below for a summary of the characteristics of included studies. Further details are available in Appendix 22.

10.4.5   Review strategy

There are very few studies of psychological therapy in bipolar disorder. In addition, there are no studies of psychological therapy where all participants are in an acute episode, although some studies recruited during acute-phase treatment (for example, REA2003) and others included some acute-phase patients (for example, SCOTT2006). In the main, it was not possible to combine studies using meta-analysis because of heterogeneity in study populations and interventions. Therefore, the review team calculated effect sizes for study outcomes for each study individually (see evidence profiles). The studies are presented below by intervention, with particular issues with individual studies discussed as appropriate.

10.5   OVERVIEW OF HEALTH ECONOMICS REVIEW

The systematic literature search for economic studies identified one study that assessed the cost-effectiveness of CBT combined with pharmacological treatment for long-term maintenance of patients with bipolar disorder (LAM2003). The full reference and characteristics of the study are presented in the evidence tables for economic studies in Appendix 14.

10.6   FAMILY INTERVENTIONS

10.6.1   Clinical studies considered for family interventions

Three studies were of family interventions (REA2003; MIKLOWITZ2000; MILLER unpub) all undertaken in the US. These recruited patients during an acute episode, with treatment starting either whilst the acute phase was still ongoing (MILLER2004, MIKLOWITZ2000) or once participants were stabilised (REA2003). See Table 75.

Table 75: Summary of study characteristics for family interventions (all adjunctive to medication)

	Family intervention versus individual intervention	Family intervention versus crisis management	Family intervention versus multi-family group psychoeducation versus no therapy
No. trials (No. participants)	*1 RCT (53)*	*1 RCT (101)*	*1 RCT (92)*
Study ID	REA2003	MIKLOWITZ2000	MILLER2004
Diagnosis	100% bipolar I manic	51% bipolar I manic 35% bipolar I depressed 15% bipolar mixed	74% bipolar I manic 20% bipolar I depressed 6% bipolar I mixed
Mean age	26	34	39
Bipolar history	40% in first episode	Age at onset (SD): 23.9 (7.5)/25.4 (10.6) Duration of illness (SD): 12.2 (9) years/10.9(9.2)	Age at onset: depression – 19–25; mania – 27–29; previous episodes: depression – 5–10; mania – 4–6
Outcome measures at start of study	Not available	SADS-C total (SD): Treatment – 3.1 (8); control – 2.8 (7)	BRMS (SD): family therapy 21 (11), multi-family therapy 20 (11), no therapy 22 (11) HRSD (SD): 9 (10), 9 (8), 10 (10) GAF (SD): 27 (6), 27 (8), 29 (6)
Length of treatment	1 year (9 months for psychological treatment)	9 months	12 weeks
Length of follow-up	1 year	1 year	2 years

10.6.2   Overview of clinical findings

An evidence profile detailing results from these trials is in Appendix 23, and a summary is provided in Table 76.

The three studies of family interventions provide some evidence of effectiveness of family interventions, although the overall quality is moderate. Patients in all studies were taking prophylactic medication.

REA2003 included a young patient population (average age 26 years), recruited during an acute manic episode (40% in a first episode), with treatment starting once patients were stabilised. There were no details of the randomisation process. For this population, there is evidence that compared with individual interventions, a family intervention resulted in better outcomes as measured by relapse and hospitalisation at 1 year follow-up, although this evidence is of moderate quality. Other outcomes were inconclusive.

MIKLOWITZ2000 included a mix of people with more established morbidity in depressed, acute and mixed illness phases. It is not clear whether treatment started during the acute episode. However, the study provides some evidence of efficacy of family interventions compared with crisis management at follow-up.

MILLER2004 provides evidence of family interventions compared with pharmacotherapy with clinical management or multi-family psychoeducation groups. Evidence was inconclusive compared with multi-family psychoeducation groups. Compared with pharmacotherapy plus clinical management family interventions showed some efficacy, although the overall quality of evidence is low.

Table 76: Summary evidence profile for family interventions

	Family intervention versus individual intervention	Family intervention versus crisis management	Family intervention versus multi-family group psychoeducation
Evidence for efficacy (quality)	Family therapy reduces relapse and hospitalisation at 1 year (moderate)	Family therapy reduces non-remission (moderate)	Efficacy data are inconclusive (low)
Evidence for acceptability/ tolerability (quality)	Other than for leaving treatment early, which was inconclusive (low), there are no acceptability/ tolerability data	Other than for leaving treatment early, which was inconclusive (low), there are no acceptability/ tolerability data	Other than for leaving treatment early, which was inconclusive (low), there are no acceptability/ tolerability data

10.7   PSYCHOEDUCATION

10.7.1   Clinical studies considered for psychoeducation

There were two studies of 'complex' psychoeducation (COLOM2003; COLOM2003A), with one further study classified as psychoeducation (PERRY1999). Only COLOM2003 and COLOM2003A were combined in meta-analysis. All these studies recruited euthymic patients. See Table 77.

Table 77: Summary of study characteristics for psychoeducation (all adjunctive to medication)

	Complex group psychoeducation versus group non-directive support	Psychoeducation + TAU versus TAU
No. trials (No. participants)	*2 RCTs (170)*	*1 RCT (69)*
Study ID	COLOM2003 COLOM2003A	PERRY1999
Diagnosis	85% bipolar I 15% bipolar II	91% bipolar I 9% bipolar II
Mean age	35–44	45
Bipolar history	Euthymic for 6 months. Around nine previous episodes, but recent history not clear. All patients in COLOM2003 had been compliant for past 6 months	Euthymic but vulnerable to relapse
Outcome measures at start of study	No baseline data available	HRSD: CBT 4.1 (3.6); control 3.8 (3.6) BRMS: CBT 0.5 (1.1); control 0.4 (0.6) MC Social Performance: CBT 3.7 (2.6); control: 3.1 (3.0)
Length of treatment	20 weeks	3–6 months
Length of follow-up	2 years	18 months

* Median (Q1, Q3)

10.7.2   Overview of clinical findings

An evidence profile detailing results from these trials is in Appendix 23 and a summary is provided in Table 78.

COLOM2003 and COLOM2003A compared group complex psychoeducation (which included psychoeducation about bipolar disorder, communication enhancement training and problem-solving skills training) with group non-directive support in patients who were euthymic at baseline and, in COLOM2003, had been compliant to medication in the previous 6 months. Both studies were undertaken in a specialist centre in Spain and all participants were maintained on medication. There was a high dropout rate. Group complex psychoeducation was more effective than group non-directive support at 2-year follow-up based on the number relapsed. However, other outcomes were inconclusive and the overall quality of evidence is moderate.

PERRY1999 compared psychoeducation with no additional treatment in euthymic patients maintained on medication and was undertaken in the UK. The intervention focused on helping patients to identify early warning signs. The intervention was effective in helping to prevent relapse into manic episodes, but not depressed episodes. Other primary outcomes were inconclusive. The overall quality of evidence is moderate.

Table 78: Summary evidence profile for psychoeducation

	Complex group psychoeducation versus group non-directive support	**Psychoeducation + TAU versus TAU**
Evidence for efficacy (quality)	Complex group psychoeducation reduces relapse compared with non-directive support (moderate)	Efficacy data are inconclusive (low)
Evidence for acceptability/ tolerability (quality)	Complex group psychoeducation is more acceptable than non-directive support (moderate)	Fewer people left treatment early in the treatment-as-usual group (moderate)

10.8   COGNITIVE BEHAVIOURAL THERAPY (CBT)

10.8.1   Clinical studies considered for CBT

Four studies of CBT (LAM2000, LAM2003, SCOTT2001, SCOTT2006), all undertaken in the UK, met inclusion criteria. The majority of these studies recruited euthymic patients maintained on prophylactic medication, two being of patients liable to relapse (LAM2000, LAM2003) and one study, SCOTT2006, which included a proportion of patients in the acute phase as well as some unmedicated patients. For SCOTT2006, data were obtained from the trial authors that excluded these acute patients. In addition, the GDG secured initial data from an unpublished study undertaken in Germany (MEYER unpub). However, this study was not included in the analyses since the relevant outcomes could not be reliably extracted. An additional study, BALL unpub, was also secured and included in the analysis. A summary of study characteristics of included studies is in Table 79.

10.8.2   Overview of clinical findings

An evidence profile detailing results from these trials is in Appendix 23, and a summary is provided in Table 80.

There were some quality issues in the SCOTT2001 trial (randomisation method not clear, and not clear if assessors blinded). However, there was some evidence of the efficacy of CBT compared with no psychological therapy based on relapse data at follow-up, although there was considerable heterogeneity in the dataset. The SCOTT2006 and LAM2003 studies produced consistently different effect sizes, with LAM2006 producing an effect favouring CBT and the SCOTT2006 result either favouring neither CBT nor treatment as usual, or favouring treatment as usual but with wide 95% CIs leading to a categorisation of inconclusive. This is likely to be due to the different populations in the trials. SCOTT2006 included patients with a history of multiple recurrences, substance use and other psychiatric diagnoses. The trial was removed in sensitivity analyses to reduce or remove heterogeneity.

10.8.3   Health economics evidence

One study assessing the cost-effectiveness of CBT as part of prophylactic treatment for patients with bipolar disorder met the eligibility criteria for inclusion in the systematic review of economic literature (LAM2003). The economic analysis was undertaken alongside an RCT conducted in the UK. The study population consisted of adult patients with bipolar I disorder who experienced frequent relapses despite being prescribed commonly used prophylactic agents. Patients experiencing an acute episode or with high residual symptoms at the beginning of the study were excluded from the trial. CBT comprised an average of 14 sessions over 6 months plus two booster sessions in the following 6 months. CBT was added to standard care, defined as treatment with prophylactic medication at a recommended level combined with regular psychiatric outpatient follow-up. Therefore, the CBT group received CBT added to standard care, whereas the control group received standard care alone. The time frame of the analysis was 30 months overall, with results over the first 12 months of the trial also being analysed. The perspective of the analysis was that of health and social care; estimated costs included costs associated with hospital care (inpatient,

Table 79: Summary of study characteristics for CBT
(all adjunctive to medication)

	CBT versus medication only
No. trials (No. participants)	**5 RCTs (457)**
Study ID	(1) BALL unpub (2) LAM2000 (3) LAM2003 (4) SCOTT2001A (5) SCOTT2006**
Diagnosis	c. 94% bipolar I c. 7% bipolar II
Mean age	39–52
Bipolar history	(1) > = 1 episode in last 18 months; 0–8 depressive episodes; 2–3 manic episodes (2) Euthymic but vulnerable to relapse (No. of previous manic episodes: CBT 7, TAU 8; hypomanic episodes: CBT 1. TAU 0; depressed episodes: CBT 8 TAU 7) (3) Euthymic but vulnerable to relapse (No. previous depressive episodes: 5 for both groups; manic episodes: CBT 6, TAU 4; hypomanic episodes: CBT 1, TAU 0) (4) All = > 1 episode of bipolar in last year (5) (Whole sample) prone to relapse (25%–28% had at least 30 previous episodes; 47% lifetime or current substance misuse/dependence; 33%–41% other psychiatric diagnoses)
Outcome measures at start of study	(1) BDI: CBT 12.88 (7.98), TAU 19.98 (13.23) MRS: CBT 1.92 (4.24), TAU 1.22 (2.83) (2) BDI: CBT 13.54 (10.45), TAU 12.18 (6.01) (3) BDI: CBT 12.8 (9.4), TAU 14.3 (10.7) MRS: CBT 2 (3.2), TAU 1.8 (2.1) (4) BDI: CBT 20.7 (12.1), WLC: 17.0 (14.1); ISS activation: CBT 106.7 (80.6), WLC 95.1 (62.1) (5) (Whole sample) HRSD: CBT 6* (2,14), TAU 8 (3,13); BRMS: CBT 1* (0,3); TAU 2 (0,3)
Length of treatment	Up to 30 weeks
Length of follow-up	Up to 2 years

* median (interquartile range)
** data for patients who were euthymic and taking prophylactic medication at baseline only

Table 80: Summary of evidence profile for CBT in preventing relapse

	CBT (+ TAU) versus TAU
Evidence for efficacy (quality)	CBT is effective in reducing relapse in patients not prone to relapse (moderate)
Evidence for acceptability/ tolerability (quality)	Other than for leaving treatment early, which was inconclusive (low), there are no acceptability/tolerability data

outpatient, day hospital, accident and emergency attendances), mental health services (psychiatrists, psychologists, community mental health nurses, and so on), contact with GPs, social workers, support groups, and residential care. The primary outcome measure of the analysis was the number of days free from acute bipolar episode per patient.

CBT added to standard care was demonstrated to be more effective than standard care alone. Patients in the CBT group spent on average significantly fewer days in acute bipolar episodes compared with the control group over 12 months and also over the whole follow-up period of 30 months. In addition, mean total costs per patient in the CBT group were lower than those in the control group for both periods of time examined, as costs associated with provision of CBT were offset by a reduction in costs of other health and social services. However, this difference in costs between the two groups was not statistically significant (mean total cost per patient over 30 months £10,352 in the CBT group and £11,724 in the control group, 1999/2000 prices).

A probabilistic analysis based on a regression model by applying bootstrapping techniques on the trial results was also carried out. Results were presented in the form of CEACs, which showed the probability of CBT added to standard care being cost-effective for a range of potential values placed on the WTP for an additional day free from bipolar episode. The analysis demonstrated that, even with zero WTP for an additional day free from episode, the probability of CBT being cost-effective was 0.85 for the first 12 months and 0.80 for the whole 30-month study period. At a WTP equal to £10 per additional day free from episode, the probability of CBT being cost-effective rose to 0.90 for the first 12 months and 0.85 for the overall 30-month time frame of the analysis.

Despite the limitations of the study, such as the small study size (n = 103 at randomisation; cost data available for n = 83 subjects at 30 months) and the method of collection of costing data, which was based on self-report and hospital records, the analysis suggests that addition of CBT to standard prophylactic pharmacological treatment is likely to be a cost-effective option in the UK for patients with bipolar I disorder: it is significantly more effective than prophylactic pharmacological treatment alone at no extra total cost.

10.9 PSYCHOLOGICAL THERAPY FOR PEOPLE WITH COMORBID SUBSTANCE USE DISORDER

10.9.1 Studies considered for review

There was one study of psychological therapy for people with comorbid substance use disorder (SCHMITZ2003). See Table 81.

10.9.2 Overview of clinical findings

There were no extractable efficacy data and therefore it was not possible to assess this treatment.

Table 81: Summary of study characteristics for CBT for comorbid substance use versus medication alone

	CBT for comorbid substance use versus medication alone
No. trials (No. participants)	*1 RCT (46)*
Study ID	SCHMITZ2003
Diagnosis	Bipolar (type not specified) with comorbid substance use disorder
Mean age	35
Bipolar history	Comorbid substance misuse
Outcome measures at start of study	BDI: 23.1 (12.1)
Length of treatment	12 weeks
Length of follow-up	None

10.10 INTERPERSONAL AND SOCIAL RHYTHM THERAPY (IPSRT)

10.10.1 Studies considered for review

There was one study of IPSRT (FRANK1997). This compared IPSRT with ICM. Participants were recruited during an acute episode and randomised to treatment or control. When their illness had stabilised (defined as 4 consecutive weeks with HRSD

<= 7 and Bech-Rafaelsen Mania Scale (BRMS) <= 7), they were randomised to either continue with their acute treatment or switch to the other treatment. The different papers published from this trial give slightly different accounts of how this was done. From earlier papers it appears that participants were randomised to acute treatment and then re-randomised on stabilisation, but the later paper implies that both randomisation procedures were undertaken at the study start, but that the second allocation was not made known until stabilisation. An overview of the study's characteristics is in Table 82.

Table 82: Summary of study characteristics for IPSRT

	IPSRT
No. trials (No. participants)	*1 RCT (82)*
Study ID	FRANK1997
Diagnosis	Bipolar I 100%
Mean age	36
Bipolar history	Age at bipolar onset 20 Median number of previous episodes 20
Outcome measures at start of study	HRSD-17 mean 13.73 (7.68) BRMS mean 13.72 (13.85)
Length of treatment	Unknown
Length of follow-up	2 years

10.10.2   Overview of clinical findings

There were few extractable efficacy data from this trial, so the evidence profile is based on recurrence rates – see Table 83 for a summary. Also, since participants were re-randomised to maintenance treatment, it is not appropriate to calculate effect sizes from groups at the level of acute-maintenance treatment, since this violates the principle of independent data points. Additionally, only those who had stabilised were entered into the maintenance phase. Therefore, acute-phase treatments and maintenance-phase treatments were compared separately regardless of allocation in the other phase of the trial.

On raw recurrence rates at 2 years, based on separate analyses of allocation acute- and maintenance-phase data, and including all those randomised in the analysis based on acute-phase allocation, there is an effect for acute-phase IPSRT.

Table 83: Summary of evidence profile for IPSRT

	IPSRT
Evidence for efficacy (quality)	IPSRT as acute-phase treatment reduces relapse (low)
Evidence for acceptability/ tolerability (quality)	Other than for leaving treatment early, which was inconclusive (low), there are no acceptability/tolerability data

10.11 PSYCHOLOGICAL THERAPY FOR MEDICATION ADHERENCE

10.11.1 Studies considered for review

There was one study of psychological therapy aimed specifically at medication adherence (COCHRAN1984). See Table 84.

Table 84: Summary of study characteristics for psychological therapy for medication adherence

	Medication adherence
No. trials (No. participants)	*1 RCT (38)*
Study ID	COCHRAN1984
Diagnosis	75% bipolar I 15% bipolar II 3/28 cyclothymic disorder
Mean age	33
Bipolar history	Median number previous hospitalisations: 3; median 15.5 months' previous experience with lithium
Outcome measures at start of study	No baseline data available
Length of treatment	6 weeks
Length of follow-up	6 months

10.11.2   Overview of clinical findings

See Table 85 for a summary. All outcomes were inconclusive.

Table 85: Summary of evidence profile for psychological therapy for medication adherence

	Medication adherence
Evidence for efficacy (quality)	Efficacy data are inconclusive (low)
Evidence for acceptability/ tolerability (quality)	Other than for leaving treatment early, which was inconclusive (low), there are no acceptability/tolerability data

10.12   Clinical summary

10.12.1   Psychological treatments aimed at preventing relapses of bipolar disorder

In common with many other treatment interventions for bipolar disorder, there is relatively little research in this area, with only a few promising studies largely undertaken by specialist research groups. Therefore, it is uncertain whether the results generated by these studies, which show some effect of treatment, are generalisable to the wider clinical situation. Although there is a slightly wider base for CBT compared with other therapies, there are problems in the research base, such as population comparability. Overall, there are considerable methodological problems relating to the illness phase during which people are recruited into trials and there are problems with inconsistent outcomes. In addition, there is no evidence for populations such as adolescents and older adults, and no evidence for people in the acute illness phase (in particular, depression, where evidence from unipolar populations indicates that psychological therapy is effective). Future research should focus on which populations are likely to gain benefit from psychological therapy, for example, based on whether patients are more liable to depressed or manic relapses.

10.12.2   Psychological approaches aimed at substance misuse

There is no evidence for psychological therapies in the treatment of bipolar disorder with comorbid substance use disorder.

10.12.3 Psychological approaches aimed at improving adherence

There is one low-quality study where the intervention is specifically aimed at improving medication adherence using basic CBT techniques and on no outcome is there convincing evidence in favour of the treatment. However, there is some evidence from other studies reviewed in this section that psychological therapies in general, rather than specific compliance therapy, improve compliance.

10.13 SUMMARY OF ECONOMIC EVIDENCE

There is evidence suggesting that CBT added to pharmacological treatment is a cost-effective option for the long-term maintenance of patients with bipolar I disorder in the UK.

10.14 PSYCHOLOGICAL TREATMENTS FOR CHILDREN AND ADOLESCENTS

There are no formal evaluations of psychological interventions for children and adolescents with bipolar disorder, despite the fact that broad psychological approaches to their treatment and management are common. In most cases psychologically informed care management services are offered to children with bipolar disorder. This would include a comprehensive multidisciplinary assessment and a range of individual psychological and family interventions. In most cases this also involves significant liaison with school, home (including home visiting where necessary) and primary care. Rarely will formal therapy such as cognitive behavioural or psychodynamic psychotherapy be offered to children with these. The most likely psychological approach is an eclectic one aimed at elaborating and formulating the individual's problems with an attempt at interventions that are perceived as reducing the individual's vulnerability to further episodes. In these circumstances, considerable caution should be exercised before offering formal psychological therapies but it seems likely that the individual structured psychological therapies, for which there is evidence from adults that they are potentially effective, would have application in particular for developmentally advanced adolescents.

Of paramount importance in the management of children with severe mental illness such as bipolar disorder, is the involvement of their families. Again, there is very little evidence to support the use of formal interventions, although a number of detailed intensive interventions aimed at families have been developed (MIKLOWITZ2000, REA2003). Again, with more developmentally advanced adolescents the offer of these structured formal family interventions may be of benefit.

10.15   CLINICAL RECOMMENDATIONS

Recommendations for psychological therapy during an acute depressive episode are included in the relevant section of Chapter 9.

General principles of the management of people with bipolar disorder

10.15.1.1 Healthcare professionals should aim to develop a therapeutic relationship with all patients with bipolar disorder, and advise them on careful and regular self-monitoring of symptoms (including triggers and early warning signs), lifestyle (including sleep hygiene and work patterns) and coping strategies.

Psychological therapy following recovery from an acute episode

10.15.1.2 Individual structured psychological interventions should be considered for people with bipolar disorder who are relatively stable, but may be experience mild to moderate affective symptoms. The therapy should be in addition to prophylactic medication, should normally be at least 16 sessions (over 6 to 9 months) and should:
- include psychoeducation about the illness, and the importance of regular daily routine and sleep and concordance with medication
- include monitoring mood, detection of early warnings and strategies to prevent progression into full-blown episodes
- enhance general coping strategies.

10.15.1.3 Structured psychological interventions should be delivered by people who are competent to do this and have experience of patients with bipolar disorder.

10.15.1.4 Healthcare professionals should consider offering a focused family intervention to people with bipolar disorder in regular contact with their families, if a focus for the intervention can be agreed. The intervention should take place over 6–9 months, and cover psychoeducation about the illness, ways to improve communication and problem solving.

Harmful drug/alcohol use in bipolar disorder

10.15.1.5 For people with bipolar disorder and comorbid harmful drug and/or alcohol use, a psychosocial intervention targeted at the drug and/or alcohol use (for example, psychoeducation and motivational enhancement) should be considered. This should normally be delivered by general mental health services, working with specialist substance use services where appropriate.

Early warnings

10.15.1.6 Healthcare professionals, in collaboration with patients, should develop a plan to identify the symptoms and indicators of a potential exacerbation of the disorder, and how to respond (including both psychosocial and pharmacological interventions)

Personality disorder

10.15.1.7 People with bipolar disorder and comorbid personality disorder should receive the same care as others with bipolar disorder, because the presence of a personality disorder does not preclude the delivery of effective treatments for bipolar disorder.

Special considerations for children and adolescents

10.15.1.8 When planning the care of children and adolescents with bipolar disorder, healthcare professionals should consider:

- stressors and vulnerabilities in their social, educational and family environments, including the quality of interpersonal relationships
- the impact of any comorbidities, such as attention deficit hyperactivity disorder (ADHD) and anxiety disorders
- the impact of the disorder on their social inclusion and education
- their vulnerability to exploitation, for example, as a result of disinhibited behaviour.

10.15.1.9 Parents or carers (and possibly other family members) should be involved in developing care plans so that they can give informed consent, support the psychological goals of treatment, and help to ensure treatment adherence.

10.15.1.10 Children and adolescents should be offered separate individual appointments with a healthcare professional in addition to joint meetings with their family members or carers.

11. LIVING WITH BIPOLAR DISORDER: INTERVENTIONS AND LIFESTYLE ADVICE

11.1   INTRODUCTION

11.1.1   Environmental effects on the onset and course of bipolar disorder

A prevailing view among some psychiatrists and other healthcare professionals has been that bipolar disorder is a genetically inherited disorder and its course is therefore biologically pre-determined. In this view, environmental factors such as life stress plays little if any role in the development and course of bipolar disorder, which might respond to pharmacological treatment but not psychosocial interventions (Post *et al.*, 1986).

However, the benefits of self-help and self-management interventions involving the environment have been reported by service users on the overall course of bipolar disorder. For example, people who had stayed well with bipolar disorder for 2 years reported that their successful strategies for staying well included making lifestyle changes, managing sleep and stress, and identifying triggers (such as life stress) for illness episodes (Russell & Browne, 2005). Furthermore, the prevailing view in the research community is now that both genetic and environmental factors determine the onset and course of bipolar disorder. For instance, a history of child or adolescent physical or sexual abuse is associated with a range of adverse outcomes in service users with bipolar disorder, such as earlier onset of bipolar disorder, increased number of other comorbid physical and mental health problems, alcohol and drug misuse, more frequent rapid cycling of mood, and more suicide attempts (Leverich *et al.*, 2002).

A historically important theory has been that life stress is important in bringing on the first bipolar episodes but life stress becomes less important in subsequent bipolar episodes as progressive biological processes then determine the course of the bipolar disorder (Post *et al.*, 1986). Childbirth provides the best evidence that an environmental factor is a risk factor for the onset of bipolar disorder (Tsuchiya *et al.*, 2003). A major life event, such as death in the family, unemployment, recent marriage or marital breakdown, may be associated with a first admission with bipolar disorder (Kessing *et al.*, 2004a). However, there is conflicting evidence whether life events are important only to early episodes of bipolar disorder, or are important in at least some service users with bipolar disorder, in relation to both the onset and recovery from episodes throughout the service user's life (Hammen & Gitlin, 1997; Johnson & Miller, 1997; Hlastala *et al.*, 2000). The importance of life events to the course of illness is difficult to establish because of methodological problems in dating life events and determining their nature, severity and context (Sclare & Creed, 1990). A life stress for one person may not be a life stress to another person who has a different set of beliefs, past experiences and current social situation. Life stress may also have differing effects on the onset or course of bipolar disorder depending on developmental and demographic factors such as gender and age of onset (Hays *et al.*, 1998; Johnson *et al.*, 2000).

A psychological autopsy study suggests that recent life stress is associated with completed suicide in bipolar disorder, especially if the individual is in a depressive episode. (Isometsa *et al.*, 1995).

Another historically important environmental theory is the role of sleep deprivation in both precipitating and maintaining mania (Wehr *et al.*, 1987). The concept has developed so that disrupted social routine (social rhythms) may precipitate mania (Malkoff-Schwartz *et al.*, 1998), while depression may be precipitated by life stress in the form of stressful life events (Malkoff-Schwartz *et al.*, 2000) or criticism and hostility from the family (Yan *et al.*, 2004). Positive life events such as receiving praise at work have also been linked to the onset of mania (Johnson *et al.*, 2000).

Potentially these concepts may have important implications for the work and lifestyle of service users with bipolar disorder, their carers, families and healthcare professionals. For instance if sleep deprivation, disruption of sleep patterns and social routine bring on mania, then people with bipolar disorder may be advised not to carry out shift work, fly across time zones, and to avoid night flights and early morning travel. Time spent in a family, or even on a ward, when the family or ward atmosphere is stressful, hostile or critical, may be detrimental to the patient with mania or depression and the patient may need to spend time in a different environment or the family may need extra support. Therefore, this chapter will review the evidence relating to whether lifestyle has an impact on the onset of mania or depressive episodes, or suicide attempts.

11.1.2 Lifestyle in relation to overall health and quality of life in bipolar disorder

The effects of lifestyle in people with bipolar disorder are not confined to considerations about the onset of bipolar disorder, the onset and recovery from manic and depressive episodes, and prevention of suicide. While these outcomes tend to be, and probably should remain the most important issues in the mind of many healthcare professionals, there are other important considerations in the minds of people with bipolar disorder and their carers. Issues that are important to people with bipolar disorder include social adjustment and function, quality of life, physical health and appearance, spiritual life, the life of carers and family, issues of personal control over their life, stigma and finances (Osby *et al.*, 2001; Mitchell & Romans, 2003; Morselli *et al.*, 2004). The way a person with bipolar disorder conducts their life can have important implications for these outcomes in addition to their overall mood and recent course of illness. Some of the difficulties in caring for a person with bipolar disorder can be due to a conflict between issues such as personal control of the service user over their treatment and adherence to medication, concern over physical health and appearance and adherence to prophylactic medication associated with weight gain, stigma and receipt of help from mental health services. Persistence from healthcare professionals in an appropriate health setting, coupled with the experience of the service user with bipolar disorder and their carer over time, tends in time to produce a workable and effective management plan.

The quality of life and function of service users with bipolar disorder is comparable to or below the quality of life of other chronic medical illnesses such as multiple sclerosis and diabetes mellitus (Cooke *et al.*, 1996). Symptom-free service users with bipolar disorder may have a better quality of life than clinically stable service users with schizophrenia (Chand *et al.*, 2004) and similar social adjustment to service users with highly recurrent unipolar depressive episodes (Morriss *et al.*, in preparation). Quality of life, function and disability tend to be predicted by the presence of symptoms, especially depressive episodes and depressive symptoms appearing between bipolar episodes, and the number of previous episodes and hospitalisations (Ozer *et al.*, 2002). However, daily stesses, other psychiatric comorbidity, physical health problems, substance misuse, borderline or antisocial personality disorder, oversedation from medication, social isolation and neurocognitive impairment (Judd *et al.*, 2002; Chand *et al.*, 2004; Thompson *et al.*, 2005; Morriss *et al.*, in preparation) all have an important bearing on the quality of life, function and social adjustment of people with bipolar disorder. Service users with bipolar disorder often have a high degree of educational achievement that is not reflected in their occupational functioning (MDF The BiPolar Organisation, 2001; Morselli *et al.*, 2004). There are particular concerns among a large proportion of service users about stigma and the breakdown of relationships with some family members and friends (Morselli *et al.*, 2004).

Additionally, there is some preliminary evidence that the high intake of omega 3 fatty acids in the diet, typically as fish oil, can have short-term benefits symptomatically in people with bipolar disorder. A small RCT trial involving 30 patients with bipolar disorder found that high doses of omega 3 fatty acids delayed acute bipolar relapse over 4 months (Stoll *et al.*, 1999). An RCT of moderate doses of omega 3 fatty acids in 28 patients with unipolar major depression reduced the severity of depressive symptoms over 8 weeks (Su *et al.*, 2003). However, omega 3 fatty acids can cause gastrointestinal symptoms such as nausea and their effectiveness is unknown over the longer-term, so recommendations about dietary change beyond short-term use cannot be made.

There is a growing concern about the physical health of service users with bipolar disorder. In addition to high mortality (expressed as standardised mortality rates) from suicide and possibly accidents, there is increasing evidence of a doubling of the SMR for cardiovascular mortality and increased mortality from pulmonary embolism in people with bipolar disorder (Osby *et al.*, 2001; Angst *et al.*, 2002; Strudsholm *et al.*, 2005). Compared with United States national population data, the prevalence of diabetes mellitus, chronic obstructive airways disease, lower back pain, HIV infection and hepatitis C seem to be raised (Kilbourne *et al.*, 2004; Beyer *et al.*, 2005). HIV infection and hepatitis C may be explained by comorbid intravenous street drug use, while other health problems, particularly diabetes mellitus and ischaemic heart disease, are likely to be related to increased rates of obesity and metabolic syndrome (McElroy *et al.*, 2002; Mackin *et al.*, 2005). There are many possible reasons for increased obesity, diabetes mellitus and cardiovascular disease in bipolar disorder, including poor diet and lack of activity (Elmslie *et al.*, 2001) and weight gain induced by many of the drugs used to manage bipolar disorder, in addition to growing rates of obesity in the general population. There is evidence that attendance at lithium clinics and longer-term use of medication may be associated with reduced mortality from all causes in people with bipolar disorder (Ahrens *et al.*, 1995; Kallner *et al.*, 2000; Angst *et al.*, 2005). These results may be explained by the choice of patients offered longer-term medication, or attendance at clinics and adherence to medication may be associated with greater interest in lifestyle and reduced exposure to adverse lifestyle factors such as substance misuse, or that people who are adequately treated for their bipolar disorder are better able to look after themselves in relation to their physical health.

There is growing concern over the quality of general medical care that service users with bipolar disorder receive. Service users with bipolar disorder over 50 years of age received less general medical care than people with other mental disorders (Cradock-O'Leary *et al.*, 2002) and obtained fewer investigative or operational procedures after myocardial infarction (Druss *et al.*, 2001).

The rise in obesity and growing evidence of increased morbidity and mortality as a result of obesity require a positive approach by people with bipolar disorder and healthcare professionals. Therefore, the evidence for strategies to prevent weight gain and the benefits of exercise have been examined (Menza *et al.*, 2004), including the effectiveness of exercise in terms of improving mood and preventing recurrence of depressive episodes (Babyak *et al.*, 2000).

11.1.3   Topics covered

This chapter covers the following topics:
- lifestyle interventions:
  - the prevention and management of weight gain
  - exercise in the management of bipolar depression
  - psychoeducation and information giving
- managing daily life:
  - sleep patterns
  - social rhythms
  - life events
  - family atmosphere
  - implications for lifestyle and work
- social support.

11.2   THE PREVENTION AND MANAGEMENT OF WEIGHT GAIN

11.2.1   Introduction

Many drugs used in the routine treatment of bipolar disorder are known to cause weight gain, in particular, olanzapine, quetiapine, valproate and lithium. Many patients find weight gain distressing and it can lead to poor adherence to medication regimes. It is therefore important that healthcare professionals not only take a baseline weight measurement at initiation of treatment, but also monitor weight regularly during treatment. It is also important to advise patients on weight management at the outset of treatment and also if patients gain weight during treatment.

Table 86: Databases searched and inclusion/exclusion criteria for the treatment or prevention of medication-induced weight gain

Electronic databases	MEDLINE, EMBASE, PsycINFO, CINAHL from database inception to 27 January 2005
Update searches	September 2005
Study design	RCT, non-RCTs
Patient population	Those with any mental health disorder treated with antipsychotics, anticonvulsants or lithium
Interventions included	Any, including psychosocial and pharmacological
Outcomes	Weight change from baseline (kg), change in BMI from baseline, leaving treatment early for any reason, psychiatric symptom levels

11.2.2   Evidence search

Since there are very few RCTs for the management or prevention of weight gain specifically in people with bipolar disorder, an additional search was undertaken for trials of interventions for, or prevention of, weight gain during treatment with antipsychotics, anticonvulsants and lithium regardless of diagnosis. Databases searched are in Table 86.

Outcomes
Critical outcomes for this review were those measuring weight change, with body mass index (BMI) being considered the most relevant. When considering the clinical significance of mean changes in weight from baseline following treatment, the GDG acknowledged that the importance of weight loss or gain is a personal issue varying from patient to patient. However, for the purposes of assessing the evidence, a change of 2 kg or more was adopted as an initial indicator of potentially useful benefit.

11.2.3   Weight gain prevention

Studies considered for review
Five trials were identified from searches of electronic databases, three of which met the eligibility criteria set by the GDG. Excluded studies with reasons for exclusion can be seen in Appendix 22. See Table 87 for an overview of included studies. Further characteristics of included studies are available in Appendix 22.

Table 87: Summary of study characteristics for weight gain prevention interventions

	Psychosocial interventions	Pharmacological interventions
No. trials (No. participants)	*1 RCT (70)*	*3 RCTs (201)*
Study ID	LITTRELL2003	(1) CAVAZZONI2003 (2) POYUROVSKY2003
Diagnosis	Schizophrenia and related disorders	(1) Schizophrenia and related disorders (2) Schizophrenia and related disorders
Mean age	34	(1) Not given; range 16–65 (2) 30
Intervention	Psychoeducation including nutrition, exercise	(1) Nizatidine 600 mg or 150 mg (two groups) (2) Reboxetine 4 mg
Comparator treatment	Standard care	(1) Placebo (2) Olanzapine 10 mg and placebo
Psychotropic medication	Olanzapine	(1) Olanzapine (2) Olanzapine
Outcome measures at start of study	Mean BMI: psychoeducation 26.26 (3.68); standard care 27.17 (5.79)	(1) Mean weight (kg): nizatidine 600 mg 75.69 (14.33); 150 mg 80.1 (14.21); placebo 77.21 (14.57) (2) Mean BMI: reboxetine 22.76 (3.62); placebo 31.7 (11.8)
Setting	US; community mental health centres	(1) US; in- and outpatients (2) Israel; inpatients receiving hospital meals
Length of treatment	16 weeks	(1) 16 weeks (2) 6 weeks
Length of follow-up	2 months	(1) No follow-up (2) No follow-up

Weight gain prevention review

There is some evidence that nizatidine at 600 mg per day helps prevent weight gain during treatment with olanzapine. However, the weight-gain difference compared with placebo is small. This evidence is from a population with schizophrenia. Although 600 mg is above the dose recommended in the BNF, it is within the licensed dose (summary of product characteristics on www.medicines.org.uk, site visited 3 March 2005).

There is also evidence of the effectiveness of reboxetine (4 mg) in the prevention of weight gain during treatment with olanzapine in people with schizophrenia.

An overview of the results is provided in Table 88, with the full profile in Appendix 23.

Clinical implication

Patients with bipolar disorder who are at high risk of weight gain through starting medication such as olanzapine, and especially those at high risk of adverse consequences of weight gain, for example, several risk factors for metabolic syndrome or existing diabetes or cardiovascular disease, should receive dietary and exercise advice on commencement of medication with the propensity for weight gain.

Table 88: Summary evidence profile for interventions for weight gain prevention

	Psychosocial interventions	**Pharmacological interventions**
Evidence for efficacy (quality)	Psychoeducation is more effective than standard care at preventing weight gain (moderate)	Antidepressants: no more effective at preventing weight gain than placebo (moderate) High or moderate dose nizatidine: unlikely to be a difference compared with placebo (moderate)
Evidence for acceptability/ harm (quality)	Unlikely to be a difference (moderate)	Inconclusive (moderate) Nizatidine unlikely to be a difference compared with placebo (moderate)

11.2.4 Weight gain management

Studies considered for review

Eight trials were identified from searches of electronic databases, four of which met the eligibility criteria set by the GDG. Excluded studies with reasons for exclusion can be seen in Appendix 22. See Table 89 for an overview of included studies. Further characteristics of included studies are available in Appendix 22.

Summary of evidence profile for interventions for weight gain management

Weight gain management clinical summary

There is some evidence that psychosocial interventions such as giving dietary advice are effective in helping people who have gained weight during treatment with psychotropic drugs. These data include patients with bipolar disorder. However, it is not clear from the available studies whether patients should be referred to a dietician or whether healthcare professionals can give adequate dietary advice without referral.

Table 89: Summary of study characteristics for weight gain management interventions

	Psychosocial interventions	Pharmacological interventions
No. trials (No. participants)	*4 (1 RCT, 3 non-RCTs)* *(211)*	*3 RCTs* *(193)*
Study ID	(1) BALL2001 (2) HARMATZ1968 (RCT) (3) HOLT1996 (4) VREELAND2003	(1) BUSTILLO2003 (2) DEBERDT2005 (3) HENDERSON2005
Diagnosis	(1) (2) (4) Schizophrenia and related disorders (3) Bipolar disorder	(1) Schizophrenia and related disorders (2) 55% schizophrenia and related disorders; 45% bipolar** (3) Schizophrenia and related disorders
Description of weight gain	(1) Olanzapine-related weight gain (2) Judged overweight (3) 82% taking one or more psychotropic drugsreported to cause weight gain (4) >= 2.3 kg weight gain within 2 months of starting medication	(1) >=3% increase in baseline weeks weight following 4–8 olanzapine (2) >=5% increase in baseline weight following 9 months' olanzapine (3) BMI > 30
Intervention	(1) Weight Watchers plus exercise	(1) Fluoxetine 60 mg (2) Amantadine 100 mg–300 mg

Continued

Table 89: (*Continued*)

	Psychosocial interventions	Pharmacological interventions
No. trials (No. participants)	*4 (1 RCT, 3 non-RCTs) (211)*	*3 RCTs (193)*
	(2) Behaviour modification or group therapy + 1800 calorie diet (3) Dietary advice (4) Multi-modal programme including nutrition and exercise	(3) Sibutramine + dietary advice
Comparator treatment	Control	(1) Control (2) Placebo (3) Placebo + dietary advice
Medication	(1) Olanzapine (2) Not clear (3) Lithium (4) Atypical antipsychotics	Olanzapine
Length of treatment	(1) 10 weeks (2) 6 weeks (3) 25 weeks (4) 16 weeks	(1) 17 weeks * (2) 8 weeks
Length of follow-up	(1) (3) no follow-up (2) 4 weeks (4) 2 months	No follow-up
Mean age	(1) 43 (2) Not given; range 29–48 (3) 34 (4) 45	(1) 34 (2) 41 (3) 42
Study problems	(2) No extractable data	

Notes: *mean; ** data entered for bipolar group only

There is also evidence that adding sibutramine to existing medication helps reduce weight, although this evidence is from people with schizophrenia and related disorders. In a bipolar population there is a risk that such a strategy may induce mania and therefore using an antidepressant would not be considered first-line treatment for preventing or reducing weight gain.

An overview of the results is provided in Table 90 with the full evidence profile in Appendix 23.

Table 90: Summary evidence profile for interventions for weight gain management

	Psychosocial interventions	**Pharmacological interventions**
Evidence for efficacy (quality)	Both dietary advice and Weight Watchers were more effective than control (moderate)	Amantadine: inconclusive (low) Sibutramine: effective at endpoint but not at 3 months (moderate) Fluoxetine: inconclusive (low)
Evidence for acceptability/ harm (quality)	Data for acceptability and harm are inconclusive (very low)	Amantadine: data for acceptability and harm are inconclusive (low) Sibutramine: evidence of side effects (low) Fluoxetine: data for acceptability and harm are inconclusive (low)

11.2.5 Clinical practice recommendations

11.2.5.1 If a person gains weight during treatment their medication should be reviewed, and the following considered:
- dietary advice and support from primary care and mental health services
- advising regular aerobic exercise
- referral to mental health services for specific programmes to manage weight gain
- referral to a dietitian if the person has complex comorbidities (for example, coeliac disease).

11.2.5.2 Drug treatments such as high-dose antidepressants, sibutramine or topiramate[*] are not recommended to promote weight loss.

11.3 EXERCISE IN THE TREATMENT OF DEPRESSION IN PEOPLE WITH BIPOLAR DISORDER

11.3.1 Introduction

Since depressive symptoms, often below the level of a depressive episode, are present for around one third of the time in people with bipolar disorder (Judd *et al.*, 2002), effective simple treatments for depression can play a useful role in bipolar disorder. There is a growing body of literature primarily from North America examining the effects of exercise in the management of depression. In the past decade 'exercise on prescription' schemes have become popular in primary care in the United Kingdom (Biddle *et al.*, 1994), many of which include depression as a referral criterion. Guidelines for exercise referral schemes have been laid down by the Department of Health (2005a).

Several plausible mechanisms for how exercise affects depression have been proposed. In the developed world, taking regular exercise is seen as a virtue; the patient with depression who takes regular exercise may, as a result, get positive feedback from other people and an increased sense of self-worth. Exercise may act as a diversion from negative thoughts, and the mastery of a new skill may be important (Lepore, 1997; Mynors-Wallis *et al.*, 2000). Social contact may be an important mechanism, and physical activity may have physiological effects such as changes in endorphin and monoamine concentrations (Leith, 1994; Thoren *et al.*, 1990).

11.3.2 Definition

For the purposes of the guideline, exercise was defined as a structured, achievable physical activity characterised by frequency, intensity and duration and used as a treatment for depression. It can be undertaken individually or in a group.

Exercise may be divided into aerobic forms (training of cardio-respiratory capacity) and anaerobic forms (training of muscular strength/endurance and flexibility/co-ordination/relaxation) (American College of Sports Medicine, 1980).

The aerobic forms of exercise, especially jogging or running, have been most frequently investigated. In addition to the type of exercise, the frequency, duration and intensity should be described.

11.3.3 Databases searched and inclusion/exclusion criteria

Since no RCT for the management of bipolar depression was found, the GDG used the review of the use of exercise undertaken for the NICE depression guideline (NCCMH, 2005), updating this with newly published studies. Databases searched are in Table 91.

11.3.4 Studies considered for review

Twenty-three trials were identified from searches of electronic databases, 11 of which met the eligibility criteria set by the GDG. Excluded studies with reasons for exclusion can be seen in Appendix 22. See summary tables below for an overview of included studies. Further characteristics of included studies are available in Appendix 22. Included studies compared exercise with no treatment, psychotherapy, antidepressants, meditation and relaxation, in addition to comparing different forms of exercise. Some studies included only participants with a diagnosis of depression according to DSM criteria (or

Table 91: Databases searched and inclusion/exclusion criteria for clinical effectiveness of exercise in depression

Electronic databases	MEDLINE, EMBASE, PsycINFO, CINAHL from database inception to November 2002 (searches originally undertaken as part of the NICE depression guideline (NCCMH, 2005))
Update searches	February 2004, October 2004 (for RCTs in bipolar patients), January 2005 (for RCTs in depressed patients), March 2005 (for non-RCTs in bipolar patients), September 2005 (for RCTs in bipolar patients)
Study design	RCT; non-RCTs for March 2005 search
Patient population	Major depressive disorder, minor depression, dysthymia, 'depression' however diagnosed
Interventions included	Exercise as defined above
Outcomes	Remission, symptom levels (depression), discontinuation from treatment for any reason
Exclusion criteria	See appendices

equivalent) and some included participants with depression symptoms, most commonly defined as a Beck Depression Inventory (BDI) score of 12 or over.

11.3.5   Exercise versus no exercise

Six studies comparing exercise with no exercise in the treatment of depressive symptoms met inclusion criteria. Two studies included only participants with a diagnosis of depression according to DSM criteria (or equivalent), and four included participants provided they had a BDI score of 12 or over (or equivalent). Summary study characteristics are in Table 92.

Summary of evidence profile for exercise versus no exercise
An overview of the results is provided in Table 93, with the full profile available in Appendix 23.

11.3.6   Exercise versus psychotherapy or antidepressants

Four studies comparing exercise with other treatments for depressive symptoms met inclusion criteria. Three studies compared exercise with psychotherapy (two with a full depression diagnosis). Summary study characteristics are in Table 94.

Table 92: Summary of study characteristics for exercise interventions versus no treatment/waitlist

	Exercise versus no exercise treatment	
	Full depression diagnosis	*Diagnosis based on BDI score =>12 or other*
No. trials (No. participants)	*2 RCTs (112)*	*4 RCTs (188)*
Study ID	(1) DUNN2005 (2) SINGH1997	(1) McCANN1984 (2) McNEIL1991 (3) VEALE1992 (4) WOOLERY2004
Diagnosis	(1) MDD (2) MDD, minor depressive disorder, dysthymia (% of each not given)	(1) (2) (4) BDI score =>12 (3) Clinical Interview Schedule score 2 (opinion of interviewer)
Mean age	(1) 36 (2) 71	(1) Not given but all undergraduates (2) 72 (3) 35.5 (4) 21
Exercise intervention	(1) Treadmill or exercise bike; high dose, 3 times a week** (2) Strengthening exercises	(1) Aerobics (2) Walking (3) Running (4) Yoga
Comparator	(1) Flexibility training (2) Health education	(1) (3) No treatment (2) (4) Waitlist (also has 'social contact' comparison)
Baseline depression scores	(1) HRSD mean: 19.4 (2.3) (2) HRSD mean 12 (1)	(1) BDI 15.35 (2) BDI 15.2 (2.4) to 16.6 (3.1) (3) BDI 22.91 (7.6) and 26.66 (2.6) (4) HRSD 12.77 (4.53) and 12.07 (4.41)
Length of treatment	(1) 12 weeks (2) 10 weeks*	(1) 10 weeks * (2) 6 weeks * (3) 12 weeks (4) 5 weeks *

Continued

Table 92: (*Continued*)

	Exercise versus no exercise treatment	
	Full depression diagnosis	*Diagnosis based on BDI score =>12 or other*
No. trials (No. participants)	*2 RCTs (112)*	*4 RCTs (188)*
Length of follow-up	(1) No follow-up (2) 10 weeks	No follow-up
Problems with study	(1) Poor external validity since participants exercised under close supervision due to the dose-finding nature of the study**	(1) Poor external validity as student sample

*mean

**study included treatment groups for high and low intensity, 3 or 5 times a week (2 × 2 design). The study showed that number of sessions per week made no difference to outcomes (regardless of intensity) and that there was no difference between low intensity and control. Therefore, high intensity 3 times a week was chosen to represent this study in this comparison.

Table 93: Summary evidence profile for exercise versus no exercise

	Exercise
Evidence for efficacy (quality)	Exercise more effective than no exercise for those with depressed symptoms (but no diagnosis of bipolar disorder) particularly for those without a full diagnosis of depression (high)
Evidence for acceptability/harm (quality)	Inconclusive (low)

Summary of evidence profile for exercise versus psychotherapy or antidepressants
An overview of the results is provided in Table 95, with the full evidence profile available in Appendix 23.

Table 94: Summary of study characteristics for exercise versus psychotherapy and antidepressants

	Exercise versus psychotherapy		Exercise versus antidepressants
	Full depression diagnosis	*Diagnosis based on BDI*	*Full depression diagnosis*
No. trials (No. participants)	*2 RCT (102)*	*1 RCT (61)*	*1 RCT (156)*
Study ID	(1) GREIST1979 (2) KLEIN1985	FREMONT1987	HERMAN2002
Diagnosis	(1) Minor depression (2) Major or minor depression	BDI => 9 and =< 30	Major depressive disorder
Mean age	(1) Range 18–30 (2) 30	Range 19–62	57
Exercise intervention	(1) Running (2) Running	Running	Walking/ jogging
Comparators	(1) Time-limited psychotherapy (no details) (2) Group psychotherapy	Cognitive therapy	Sertraline (median peak dose 100 mg) Combination treatment
Baseline depression scores	(1) Not reported (2) SCL-D 2.39 (0.47)	BDI 17 (6.2) to 19 (7.8)	HRSD around 18 (given as bar chart)
Length of treatment	(1) 10 weeks* (2) 12 weeks*	10 weeks	16 weeks
Length of follow-up	(1) No follow-up (2) 9 months	4 months	6 months

* mean

11.3.7 Exercise versus low-intensity exercise and other treatments

Three studies comparing exercise with low-intensity exercise and other treatments in the treatment of depressive symptoms met inclusion criteria. Participants in two had a full depression diagnosis. Summary study characteristics are in Table 96.

Table 95: Summary evidence profile for exercise versus psychotherapy or antidepressants

	Psychotherapy	Antidepressants
Evidence for efficacy (quality)	Unlikely to be a difference between exercise and psychotherapy (low)	Unlikely to be a difference between exercise and antidepressants (or between monotherapy and combination therapy) (moderate)
Evidence for acceptability/ harm (quality)	Data for acceptability/ harm outcomes are inconclusive (low)	Data for acceptability/harm outcomes are inconclusive (low)

Summary of evidence profile for exercise versus low-intensity exercise and other treatments

An overview of the results is provided in Table 97, with the full evidence profile available in Appendix 23.

11.3.8   Clinical summary

There is some evidence that exercise is helpful in reducing depressive symptoms, both in major and minor depression. This evidence could be extrapolated to bipolar patients experiencing a depressed episode, to those beginning to develop a depressed episode, those who have persistent mild depressive symptoms and those trying to prevent depressive symptoms getting worse.

There is the potential for exercise to be both helpful and harmful in mania but there is no research evidence to support either scenario. Exercise may be a healthy way of using up the excess energy in a person with mania and a useful distraction. However, exercise might further arouse the body physiologically, increasing energy, social contact and self-efficacy, exacerbating manic symptoms and potentially increasing further cardiovascular strain.

11.3.9   Clinical practice recommendations

Advice about exercise is included in the general advice recommendation at the end of this chapter.

Table 96: Summary of study characteristics for exercise versus low-intensity exercise and other treatments

	Exercise versus low intensity exercise		**Exercise versus other therapies**
	Full depression diagnosis	*Full depression diagnosis*	*Diagnosis based on BDI score =>12*
No. trials (No. participants)	*1 RCT (24)*	*1 RCT (74)*	*1 RCT (47)*
Study ID	BOSSCHER1993	KLEIN1985	McCANN 1984
Diagnosis	Major or minor depression	Major or minor depression	BDI score =>12
Mean age	34	30	Not given but all undergraduates
Exercise intervention	Running	Running	Aerobics
Comparator	Low-intensity exercise	Meditation	Relaxation
Baseline depression scores	Not given on usable scale	SCL-D 2.39 (0.47)	BDI 15.35
Length of treatment	8 weeks*	12 weeks*	10 weeks*
Length of follow-up	No follow-up	9 months	No follow-up
Problems with trials			(1) poor external validity as student sample

Table 97: Summary evidence profile for exercise versus low-intensity exercise and other treatments

	Exercise versus low-intensity exercise	**Exercise versus other therapies**
Evidence for efficacy (quality)	Exercise (running) is more effective at reducing depression symptoms (full diagnosis) than low-intensity exercise (moderate)	Exercise (running) unlikely to be more or less effective than meditation (full diagnosis), but more effective than relaxation (depressive symptoms) (moderate)
Evidence for acceptability/ harm (quality)	Data for acceptability/ harm outcomes are inconclusive (low)	Data for acceptability/harm outcomes are inconclusive (low)

11.4 PSYCHOEDUCATION AND INFORMATION GIVING

11.4.1 Introduction

Psychoeducation given as a group intervention to people with bipolar disorder or to a family has been demonstrated to reduce bipolar recurrence (Colom *et al.*, 2003a; Colom *et al.*, 2003b; Miklowitz *et al.*, 2003). However, even if psychoeducation were ineffective in reducing bipolar recurrence, people with bipolar disorder and their carers have a need and right to information on the condition. While there are now a variety of websites run by patient and professional organisations, for example MDF The BiPolar Organisation, beyondblue, and the Royal College of Psychiatrists, that will provide general information about the condition, people with bipolar disorder would like to receive information about the condition in relation to their own individual circumstances. The best people to provide this are the healthcare professionals in primary and secondary care who have assessed the patient and their individual circumstances. An important aspect of the therapeutic relationship is the communication between the healthcare professional and patient. Central to this communication is information given about the condition of the patient and the degree to which the healthcare professional meets the patient's needs for information. There is now a growing evidence base that an important determinant of patient adherence to medication is the quality of the relationship between the patient and the healthcare professional identified as responsible for the medication (Day *et al.*, 2005). A key point is that such information giving should take into consideration the person with bipolar disorder and their carer's previous experience of the condition and its treatment through health services. Similarly the burden of carers and the psychological well-being of carers may be reduced by accurate information about bipolar disorder applied to the patient in their care (Morselli, 2000).

Like all health interventions where the aim is to support the patient in managing their condition, the healthcare professional should consider a motivational interviewing approach to information giving. The healthcare professional should provide information about bipolar disorder to demonstrate the reality of the problem, explore what is possible with treatment and examine the pros and cons of treatment in both the short-term and longer term as applied to the person's particular circumstances. Information should be given to the person with bipolar disorder when they are acutely ill but will need to be given again if their symptoms have remitted. The information in the acute phase will be concerned with improving the person's mental state and returning them as close as possible to normal function. Given the high rates of recurrence (Harrow *et al.*, 1990; Tohen *et al.*, 1990; Keller *et al.*, 1993), the information given on remission will focus on staying well, including preventing further relapse, as well as symptomatic and functional improvement. Thus information giving should be regarded as a continuous process. Carers should be included; carers and the person with bipolar disorder can help each other with their information needs.

Psychoeducation programmes may contain sessions on the nature of bipolar disorder, causal and triggering factors, symptoms of mania and depression, course and outcome, using diaries of mood, drug treatments, pregnancy and genetic counselling, risks from treatment withdrawal, alcohol and street drugs, early detection and management of manic and depressive episodes, lifestyle regularity, managing stress and problem solving (Colom *et al.*, 2003a, b). Teaching people with bipolar disorder to recognise the early warning symptoms of mania and depression successfully reduced the number of manic episodes and improved function but did not reduce depressive episodes (Perry *et al.*, 1999). Good coping with mania (Lam & Wong, 1997), such as calming activities, taking time off work and delaying impulsive actions, is encouraged and the person with bipolar disorder advised to seek help from a healthcare professional who may also provide early treatment with medication (Morriss, 2004). Good coping with depression, such as keeping busy to avoid rumination, accomplishing the minimal routine, getting the support of family and friends, and answering unrealistic negative thoughts, have been adopted as part of CBT interventions for early symptoms of relapse (Lam *et al.*, 2003). The recognition and management of early warning symptoms of mania and depression are key features of the self-management training programme of MDF The BiPolar Organisation.

Psychoeducation programmes such as these have been systematically incorporated into care programmes to keep people with bipolar disorder well, along with assessment, care planning and monthly telephone monitoring of symptoms and medication fed back to the treating mental health team (Simon *et al.*, 2005).

However, psychoeducation delivered by healthcare agencies may not provide information on important aspects of social care that can be considerably affected by bipolar disorder, such as work, housing, monetary, legal and insurance matters. Advice on some of these matters can be provided by MDF The BiPolar Organisation, citizen's advice bureaus, job centres and housing agencies and appropriate members of a CMHT.

11.4.2   Clinical practice recommendation

11.4.2.1   Healthcare professionals should establish and maintain collaborative relationships with patients and their families and carers (within the normal bounds of confidentiality), be respectful of the patient's knowledge and experience of the illness, and provide relevant information (including written information) at every stage of assessment, diagnosis and treatment (including the proper use and likely side-effect profile of medication).

11.5 MANAGING DAILY LIFE

11.5.1 Sleep patterns

Concerns over sleep are common among people with bipolar disorder when they are well (Harvey *et al.*, 2005) because sleep disturbance is the most common early symptom of mania and also one of the early symptoms of depression (Jackson *et al.*, 2003). Furthermore, there is some experimental and observational evidence that psychological, interpersonal, environmental and pharmacological factors may precipitate mania though decreased sleep duration (Wehr *et al.*, 1987; Leibenluft *et al.*, 1996). People with bipolar disorder who had no bipolar episodes for two years valued obtaining adequate amounts of sleep and recognising early warning signs of relapse, including sleep disturbance as useful strategies for staying well (Russell & Browne, 2005).

However, sleep disturbance is sometimes a late rather than early symptom of mania and depression (Jackson *et al.*, 2003) and commonly found in people with bipolar disorder who are currently well (Millar *et al.*, 2004; Harvey *et al.*, 2005). Polysomnograph studies show that the sleep disturbance of mania and bipolar depression is very similar to that of unipolar depression, suggesting that the sleep disturbance in bipolar disorder is not unique nor specific to bipolar disorder (Hudson *et al.*, 1992).

Sleep disturbance occurs frequently in everyday life and it is unwise to conclude that sleep disturbance in a person with bipolar disorder will inevitably bring on a manic or depressive episode. Sleep disturbance is too non-specific a symptom to use as an early warning symptom of mania or depression on its own, but it can be useful as one of a number of symptoms and signs that could be used as a relapse signature of impending manic or depressive relapse (Lam & Wong, 1997; Perry *et al.*, 1999). There is enough evidence to suggest that patients with a history of mania precipitated by a period of sleep disturbance should take care over obtaining adequate amounts of sleep (Riemann *et al.*, 2002). Establishing whether sleep disturbance triggers episodes of mania and depression requires meticulous attention to detail concerning the timing and order of symptoms; often sleep disturbance does not trigger an episode of mania or depression but is an early symptom of mania or depression (Sclare & Creed, 1990; Malkoff-Schwartz *et al.*, 1998).

11.5.2 Social rhythms

There is evidence that the daily lifestyle or social rhythm of well people with bipolar disorder is different from people without bipolar disorder (Ashman *et al.*, 1999; Jones *et al.*, 2005). The daily activities do not show as regular a routine pattern from day to day, even when a person with bipolar disorder is well. Often the morning activities of well people with bipolar disorder start later than other people. These activity patterns are unrelated to sleep disturbance. Both a further loss of regularity in the daily pattern of social activities and starting daily activities early in the morning may be associated with the later development of mania (Malkoff-Schwartz *et al.*, 1998; Malkoff-Schwartz *et al.*, 2000). A recently published RCT suggested that increased regularity in the daily routine of activities of people with bipolar disorder may delay the onset of the next bipolar episode (Frank *et al.*, 2005). Avoidance of starting activities too early in the morning may be a useful clinical strategy if there is a personal history of early morning activity preceding the first symptoms of mania.

11.5.3   Life events

As described above, there is a view that life events and life stress may be important precipitants of the first or second episodes of bipolar disorder but subsequently the onset of bipolar disorder is largely unrelated to life stress. The phenomenon is called behavioural sensitisation and has been applied also to highly recurrent unipolar depressive disorders (Post *et al.*, 1986). The evidence for this hypothesis is unclear. There is also some evidence that life stress may have a greater impact on the onset of bipolar depressive episodes than manic episodes (Johnson, 2005). In addition there is evidence of an association between stressful life events and the onset of bipolar depressive episodes in the 3 to 6 months following the life event (Malkoff-Schwartz *et al.*, 1998, 2000; Hlastala *et al.*, 2000). Social support that is non-judgemental and available when it is required may prevent episodes of bipolar depression in the face of life stress but not mania (Johnson *et al.*, 1999). Stressful life events may delay the recovery from depressive episodes (Johnson & Miller, 1997) and decrease the effectiveness of lithium prophylaxis for bipolar disorder (Chand *et al.*, 2004). Life events may also be associated with completed suicide in people with bipolar disorder (Isometsa *et al.*, 1995).

There is quite a lot of evidence that the first admission to hospital with mania is precipitated by a stressful life event (Ambelas, 1987; Kessing *et al.*, 2004a). There is also some preliminary evidence that some types of positive life event may precipitate mania. Some people with bipolar disorder are driven to achieve goals and in some attainment, or the possibility of attainment of these goals, may precipitate mania (Johnson *et al.*, 2000).

11.5.4   Family atmosphere

A series of studies have shown that time spent in a family where there is an adverse family atmosphere is associated with a recurrence of depressive episodes rather than manic episodes in people with bipolar disorder (Miklowitz *et al.*, 1988; Yan *et al.*, 2004). The adverse family atmosphere involves emotional, hostile and critical comments directed to the person with bipolar disorder even when they are not in a bipolar episode. Often the comments concern behaviours attributable to bipolar symptoms. For instance, the person with bipolar disorder may lack motivation to look after themselves or the household because they have not fully recovered from a depressive episode but a family member sees them as slovenly rather than ill. When there is an adverse family atmosphere, the family members perceive the symptoms and behaviours of the person with bipolar disorder to be under the person's direct control and not due to an illness beyond their control (Wendel *et al.*, 2000). The degree to which the person is distressed by the relative's adverse comments predicts more time spent ill in bipolar episodes over the next year (Miklowitz *et al.*, 2005).

RCTs of interventions targeted at educating the family about bipolar disorder and moderating these negative comments about the person with bipolar disorder show evidence for the reduction of these comments and also a reduction in depressive episodes (Miklowitz *et al.*, 2003; Rea *et al.*, 2003). There is no data to determine whether interventions to reduce the time spent with hostile family members would also reduce depressive episodes in bipolar disorder, but findings on similar approaches in families with schizophrenia (Vaughn & Leff, 1976) suggest that such social interventions may be effective.

11.5.5   Implications for the lifestyle and work of people with bipolar disorder

Overall, there is evidence that in some people with bipolar disorder, their pattern of daily life and exposure to stress can have a clinically important impact on the number of bipolar episodes and the proportion of time they are ill. It is unlikely that all the bipolar episodes can be prevented by interventions that modify lifestyle and reduce life stress, even in people who appear susceptible to such factors. The best guide to the importance of lifestyle factors in any given person with bipolar disorder is a careful review of the person's past history of illness, especially in relation to bipolar episodes in the previous 5-year period. The clinician should consider with the patient and carer, who can act as a useful informant, the role of sleep disruption, disruption to the person's daily social routine (especially by activities scheduled for the early morning), seasonal factors, stress from life events and difficulties, positive life situations (especially in relation to goal attainment) and family atmosphere. If any of these factors seem to have preceded a bipolar episode, it is particularly important to establish the timing of this lifestyle factor and the start of any manic or depressive symptoms. There should be evidence that the lifestyle factor definitely preceded the manic or depressive episode.

If lifestyle factors are identified as precipitating one or more manic or depressive episode, then there are implications for the person with bipolar disorder in terms of their lifestyle. There are also a range of interventions that may possibly help the person. The lifestyle factor can be used as an early warning sign that the person may be becoming ill, although over-reliance on just one lifestyle factor should be discouraged. A history of sleep disturbance or disruption of daily routine precipitating a bipolar episode may mean that the person with bipolar disorder should not undertake shift work, should try to avoid night and early morning travelling and lead a more regular life. A history of stressful life events precipitating bipolar episodes suggests strategies to reduce the likelihood of exposure to these life events (such as taking a less stressful job), cognitive therapy strategies to modify pessimism concerning life stress when it happens, family interventions targeted at reducing hostility and criticism, or spending less time with family members who are critical or hostile.

11.5.6 Clinical practice recommendations

11.5.6.1 Patients with bipolar disorder should be given advice (including written information) on:
- the importance of good sleep hygiene and a regular lifestyle
- the risks of shift work, night flying and flying across time zones, and routinely working excessively long hours, particularly for patients with a history of relapse related to poor sleep hygiene or a irregular lifestyle
- ways to monitor their own physical and mental state.

11.5.6.2 People with bipolar disorder should be given additional support after significant life events, such as loss of job or a close bereavement. This should include increased monitoring of mood and general well-being, and encouraging the patient to discuss difficulties with family and friends.

11.6 SOCIAL SUPPORT

11.6.1 Provision of social support

Prospective studies show that good quality social support is associated with a better outcome in bipolar disorder in terms of full recovery, improved depressive symptoms and preventing recurrence of depressive episodes (Johnson *et al.*, 1999; Johnson *et al.*, 2000; Johnson *et al.*, 2003; Cohen *et al.*, 2004). Good quality social support may also reduce the chances of emergency compulsory admission (Webber & Huxley, 2004). In people with depressive episodes, poor-quality social support and poorly integrated social networks are associated with suicidal ideas and suicide attempts (Sokero *et al.*, 2003; Dennis *et al.*, 2005). Therefore, paying attention to helping people with bipolar disorder to obtain good-quality social support and networks of social support that are available at a time of crisis can have an important impact on symptomatic recovery, prevention of recurrence and their safety. Such support should be provided if necessary by health services through CRHTTs, CMHTs, outpatient services or primary care services.

Usually, social support requires an emotionally supportive relationship involving confiding personal information and trust. The social support should be available when it is needed by the person with bipolar disorder. Social support may be provided by one person but a person with bipolar disorder may require a network of social support.

11.6.2 Role of service user groups

Like other mental disorder, people with bipolar disorder may experience isolation because friends, family members, employers and the public at large do not seem to understand their condition and experiences (Morselli *et al.*, 2003; Morselli *et al.*, 2004). Under these circumstances, people with bipolar disorder may feel less isolated and receive valuable information and support from local or national service user groups such as MDF The BiPolar Organisation. Most parts of England and Wales are served by local self-help groups of MDF The BiPolar Organisation and nationally the organisation is able to provide a lot of useful practical advice.

11.6.3 Befriending

There is evidence from a series of studies that providing social support in the sense of befriending (women with depression) confers benefits (Brown & Harris, 1978). In this trial befriending was defined as 'meeting and talking with a depressed woman for a minimum of one hour each week and acting as a friend to her, listening and "being there for her"'. The trained volunteer female befrienders were also encouraged to accompany their 'befriendee' on trips, to broaden their range of activities, to offer practical support with ongoing difficulties and to help create 'freshstart' experiences often found to precede remission in previous work. 'Befriendees' were women with chronic depression in inner London who were interested in being befriended. Women were allowed to be on other treatments such as antidepressants and contact with other healthcare professionals. Befriending was found to have a clinically significant effect upon remission at one year.

11.6.4 Clinical practice recommendations

11.6.4.1 Healthcare professionals should consider offering befriending to people who would benefit from additional social support, particularly those with chronic depressive symptoms. Befriending should be in addition to drug and psychological treatments, and should be by trained volunteers providing, typically, at least weekly contact for between 2 and 6 months.

11.6.4.2 Patients, family and carers should be informed of self-help and support groups and be encouraged to take part in them, particularly at initial diagnosis, and regularly after that. Such groups may provide information on early warning signs, treatment and side effects, and support in time of crisis.

11.7 ADDITIONAL CLINICAL PRACTICE RECOMMENDATION

11.7.1.1 Patients with depressive symptoms should be advised about techniques such as a structured exercise programme, activity scheduling, engaging in both pleasurable and goal-directed activities, ensuring adequate diet and sleep, and seeking appropriate social support, and given increased monitoring and formal support.

12. APPENDICES

Appendices

APPENDIX 1:
SCOPE FOR THE DEVELOPMENT OF
A CLINICAL GUIDELINE ON THE MANAGEMENT
OF BIPOLAR DISORDER

GUIDELINE TITLE

Bipolar disorder: the management of bipolar disorder in adults, children and adolescents, in primary and secondary care

Short title

Bipolar disorder

BACKGROUND

The National Institute for Health and Clinical Excellence ('NICE' or 'the Institute') has commissioned the National Collaborating Centre for Mental Health to develop a clinical guideline on the management of bipolar disorder for use in the NHS in England and Wales. This follows referral of the topic by the Department of Health and Welsh Assembly Government (see below). The guideline will provide recommendations for good practice that are based on best available evidence of clinical and cost effectiveness. The guideline will also incorporate relevant technology appraisal guidance issued by the Institute, for example, *Guidance on the Use of Electroconvulsive Therapy (2003)*. It will update *Olanzapine and Valproate Semisodium in the Treatment of Acute Mania Associated with Bipolar I Disorder (2003)*.

The Institute's clinical guidelines will support the implementation of National Service Frameworks (NSFs) in those aspects of care where a Framework has been published. The statements in each NSF reflect the evidence that was used at the time the Framework was prepared. The clinical guidelines and technology appraisals published by the Institute after an NSF has been issued will have the effect of updating the Framework.

CLINICAL NEED FOR THE GUIDELINE

Bipolar disorder is an episodic, potentially life-long, disabling disorder. Diagnostic features include periods of mania and depression, or hypomania and depression. Bipolar disorder is characterised by periods of abnormally elevated mood or irritability, which may alternate with periods of depressed mood. These episodes are distressing and often interfere with occupational or educational functioning, social activities and relationships.

The lifetime prevalence of bipolar I disorder (depression and mania) is estimated at 0.8% of the adult population, with a range between 0.4% and 1.6%. Bipolar II disorder (depression and hypomania) affects approximately 0.5% of the population. Bipolar II disorder is more common in women; bipolar I disorder appears to be evenly distributed between men and women. The median age of onset is 21 years for both men and women, although the disorder may first appear through to the mid-forties. The peak age at which symptoms first appear is 15–19 years, followed closely by 20–24 years. However, there is often a substantial delay between the onset of the disorder and first contact with treatment services.

Bipolar disorder in children and adolescents can be difficult to diagnose because of the nature of its presentation and complex comorbidities, for example, with attention deficit hyperactivity disorder. As a consequence, epidemiological data is very limited. Onset of bipolar disorder after the age of 60 years is more likely to be associated with identifiable general medical conditions, including stroke or other central nervous system disorders.

The aetiology of the disorder is uncertain but genetic and biological factors are important. The impact of environmental factors is also uncertain but there is growing evidence that environmental and lifestyle features can have an impact on severity and course of illness.

Bipolar disorder is often comorbid with a range of other mental disorders (for example, substance misuse and personality disorders) and this has significant implications for both the course of the disorder and its treatment.

Individuals with bipolar disorder are currently treated in a range of NHS settings, including primary-care services, general mental health services and specialist secondary-care mental health services.

A number of guidelines, consensus statements and local protocols exist. This guideline will review evidence of clinically effective and cost-effective practice, together with current guidelines, and will offer guidance on best practice.

THE GUIDELINE

a) The guideline development process is described in detail in two booklets that are available from the NICE website (see 'Further information'). *The Guideline Development Process – An Overview for Stakeholders, the Public and the NHS* describes how organisations can become involved in the development of a guideline.

b) This document is the scope. It defines exactly what this guideline will (and will not) examine, and what the guideline developers will consider. The scope is based on the referral from the Department of Health and Welsh Assembly Government (see subsequently).

c) The areas that will be addressed by the guideline are described in the following sections.

Population

Groups that will be covered
a) Adults, adolescents and children who meet the standard diagnostic criteria of bipolar disorder.
b) People with bipolar disorder whether they present with mania, hypomania, depression, mixed or rapidly cycling states.
c) People with bipolar disorder and significant comorbidities, such as substance misuse or personality disorder.
d) Consideration will be given to the needs of pregnant women, older people and those with a range of cognitive impairments.

Groups that will not be covered
a) Although the guideline will be of relevance to all people with bipolar disorder, whether or not the condition is accompanied by other illnesses, it will not address separately or specifically the treatment and care of the other physical or psychiatric conditions, except in the presence of bipolar disorder.

Healthcare setting

a) The guideline will cover the care and shared care provided in primary and secondary healthcare services (including prison healthcare services), and that provided by healthcare professionals and others working in healthcare settings who have direct contact with and make decisions concerning the care of patients with bipolar disorder.
b) The guideline will also be relevant to the work of, but will not provide specific recommendations, to non-NHS services, for example:
   - social services
   - voluntary sector
   - education.

However, it will consider the interface between healthcare services and these services.

Clinical management – areas that will be covered

The guideline will cover the following areas of clinical practice and will do so in a way that is sensitive to the cultural, ethnic and religious backgrounds of people with bipolar disorder and their carers:
a) The full range of care routinely made available by the NHS with regard to people with bipolar disorder, both during and between acute episodes of the disorder.
b) Clarification and confirmation of diagnostic criteria currently in use, and therefore the diagnostic factors that trigger the use of this guideline and the assessment methods that might be used in diagnosis.
c) Psychological and psychosocial interventions including type, format, frequency, duration and intensity.

d) Pharmacological treatments including type, dose and duration. When referring to pharmacological treatments, normally guidelines will recommend only within the licensed indications. However, where the evidence clearly supports it, recommendations for use outside the licensed indications may be made in exceptional circumstances. It is the responsibility of prescribers to be aware of circumstances where medication is contraindicated. The guideline will assume that prescribers are familiar with the side-effect profile and contraindications of medication they prescribe for patients with bipolar disorder.

e) Appropriate use of combined pharmacological, psychological and psychosocial interventions.

f) Appropriate use of self-management strategies, for example, self-help methods and interventions to promote medication adherence.

g) Service-level interventions that may affect outcomes for people with bipolar disorder.

h) Electroconvulsive therapy and other relevant physical treatments.

i) Identification and management of suicide risk.

j) The side effects, toxicity and other disbenefits of all treatments.

k) The role of the family and carers in the treatment and support of people with bipolar disorder and the provision of relevant information to them.

Clinical management – areas that will not be covered

a) The guideline will not cover treatments that are not normally available within the NHS.

Audit support within the guideline

The guideline will include review criteria for the audit of the key recommendations.

Status

Scope
This is the scope, which has been through a 5-week period of consultation with stakeholders and has been reviewed by the Institute's independent Guidelines Review Panel.

Guideline
The development of the guideline will begin in March 2004.

FURTHER INFORMATION

Information on the guideline development process is provided in:
- *The Guideline Development Process – An Overview for Stakeholders, the Public and the NHS.*

- *Guideline Development Methods – Information for National Collaborating Centres and Guideline Developers.*

These booklets are available as PDF files from the NICE website (www.nice.org.uk). Information on the progress of the guideline will also be available from the website.

REFERRAL FROM THE DEPARTMENT OF HEALTH AND WELSH ASSEMBLY GOVERNMENT

The Department of Health and Welsh Assembly Government asked the Institute: 'to prepare a clinical guideline for the NHS in England and Wales for the drug and non-drug management of bipolar affective disorder (manic-depressive illness) in all age groups. The guidance will:
- cover the drug and non-drug treatment and management of manic and hypo-manic episodes, depressive episodes, mixed affective states and prophylaxis (maintenance)
- cover patients of all ages
- include consideration of shared care between specialist mental health services and primary care
- examine and incorporate the developing body of evidence on self-management
- build on the appraisal of new drugs for bipolar disorder already included in the NICE work programme.'

APPENDIX 2:
ADVISORS TO THE GUIDELINE
DEVELOPMENT GROUP

SPECIAL ADVISORS

Robert Baldwin
Sophie Frangou
David Osborn
Lucy J Robinson

PARTICIPANTS IN CONSENSUS CONFERENCE ON THE DIAGNOSIS OF BIPOLAR DISORDER IN CHILDREN AND ADOLESCENTS

SPEAKERS

David Coghill
Chris Hollis
Guy Goodwin – Conference Chair
Anthony James
Catrien Reichart
Eric Taylor
Stan Kutcher

INVITED OBSERVERS

Vicky Lawson
Christine Sealey
Cathy Street

REVIEWERS

Ellen Leibenluft
Willem Nolen

SPEAKERS IN CONSENSUS CONFERENCE ON THE PHARMACOLOGICAL MANAGEMENT OF METAL DISORDERS IN PREGNANCY AND LACTATING WOMEN

Elizabeth McDonald
David Chadwick
Peter Haddad
Patricia McElhatton
Patrick O'Brien

RESEARCHERS CONTACTED FOR INFORMATION ON UNPUBLISHED OR SOON-TO-BE PUBLISHED STUDIES

R.A. Kowatch
Mick Power
Thomas Meyer
Jan Scott
Greg Simon

APPENDIX 3:
STAKEHOLDERS WHO RESPONDED TO EARLY
REQUESTS FOR EVIDENCE

AstraZeneca UK Ltd
British National Formulary (BNF)
College of Occupational Therapists
Eli Lilly and Company Ltd
Janssen-Cilag UK Ltd
MDF The BiPolar Organisation
Patient and Public Involvement Programme for NICE
Pfizer Ltd
Rethink
Royal College of Nursing
Royal College of Pathologists
Royal College of Psychiatrists
Royal Pharmaceutical Society of Great Britain
Sanofi-Aventis
UK Psychiatric Pharmacy Group

APPENDIX 4:
STAKEHOLDERS AND EXPERTS WHO
RESPONDED TO THE FIRST CONSULTATION
DRAFT OF THE GUIDELINE

STAKEHOLDERS

Antenatal and Postnatal Mental Health Guideline Development Group
The Association of Clinical Biochemists
AstraZeneca UK Ltd
Bolton, Salford and Trafford Mental Health NHS Trust
Bristol-Myers Squibb Pharmaceuticals Ltd
British Association for Counselling and Psychotherapy
British Association for Psychopharmacology
The British Psychological Society
Cambridgeshire and Peterborough Mental Health Partnership NHS Trust
College of Occupational Therapists
Critical Psychiatry Network
Department of Health
Doctors' Support Network
Eli Lilly and Company Ltd
GlaxoSmithKline UK
Hampshire Partnership NHS Trust
Institute for Psychiatry
Janssen-Cilag UK Ltd
Leeds Mental Health Teaching NHS Trust
MDF The BiPolar Organisation
Mind
North Staffordshire Combined Healthcare NHS Trust
Patient and Public Involvement Programme for NICE
Powys Local Health Board
Royal College of Nursing
Royal College of Pathologists
Royal College of Psychiatrists
Sanofi-Aventis
Social Care Institute for Excellence
Suffolk Mental Health Partnership NHS Trust
Sustain: The alliance for better food and farming
Trafford Primary Care Trusts
UK Council for Psychotherapy

Appendix 4

UK Psychiatric Pharmacy Group
Welsh Assembly Government

EXPERTS

Charles Bowden
Ellen Leibenluft
Willem Nolan

APPENDIX 5:
CLINICAL QUESTIONS

SERVICE TOPIC GROUP

1. In the long-term treatment of people with bipolar disorder are lifestyle interventions aimed at improving lifestyle helpful in reducing relapse?
2. For people who have experienced an episode of bipolar disorder (and are stabilised), does managed care/chronic disease management help to reduce relapse/reduce the severity of present or future episodes?
3. In people who have an episode of bipolar disorder, what social support systems, for example, social support groups, befriending, and so on are effective in reducing relapse/reducing the severity of future episodes?
4. For people who are experiencing an acute and/or recovery phase of bipolar disorder, do specialist services help to reduce the severity of the episodes?
5. In the management of people experiencing an acute illness episode which aspects of the treatment environment improve patient outcomes?
6. For people with bipolar disorder who also misuse drugs or alcohol, does an intervention aimed at this client group improve outcomes?
7. For people with bipolar disorder who are at risk of self-harm (including suicide) or harming others, can specific interventions reduce the risk?
8. a) What is the optimal duration for a person who has recovered from an acute episode of bipolar disorder to maintain contact with specialist services?
   b) What are the respective roles of primary care services and secondary care services in the management of such people?
9. What interventions are effective in improving the experience of families and carers?

PHARMACOLOGY TOPIC GROUP

Acute phase: rapid tranquillisation

1. For people experiencing an acute illness episode (manic/depressed with psychotic features) who have become behaviourally disturbed and for whom rapid tranquillisation is appropriate, which strategies including pharmacological agent/combination of agents are most effective and safe?

Acute phase: manic or mixed episode

2. For people experiencing an acute illness episode (manic and mixed phase)
   a) is any single drug better?
   b) is combination therapy better than monotherapy?

3. For people experiencing an acute illness episode (manic or mixed phase), which combinations of medications are best?

Acute phase: depressed episode

4. For people experiencing an acute illness episode (depressed phase), is any single drug better?
5. For people experiencing an acute illness episode (depressed phase), which combinations are best?

Acute phase in the context of rapid cycling

6. When treating people with rapid cycling in the acute phase (mania or depression) of bipolar disorder, what treatments are effective?

Incomplete response

7. What pharmacological strategies are effective in treating people where there is a lack of, or a limited, response to treatment?

Long-term treatment: recovery (maintenance)

8. In people in whom an acute illness phase has been stabilised, which pharmacological strategies are effective to prevent relapse?
9. How should discontinuation of medication be undertaken?

Long-term treatment: continuation phase in the context of rapid cycling

10. In people with rapid cycling, what pharmacological strategies are effective in ameliorating the pattern of illness?

Acute phase – other physical treatments

11. For people in the acute phase of bipolar disorder (mania/depression), is ECT or transcranial magnetic stimulation effective?

Other

12. What are the best strategies for the management of pregnancy and the perinatal period in bipolar disorder?
13. What physical monitoring is required, by whom and where should it be done?

PSYCHOLOGY TOPIC GROUP

Acute-phase treatment

1. For people experiencing an acute illness episode (hypomania, depression, mixed), which combined psychological and pharmacological strategies are effective?

Long-term treatment

2. Which combined psychological and pharmacological strategies are effective for long-term maintenance?
3. Are psychological treatments alone effective for long-term maintenance?

Other

4. Do psychological approaches aimed at improving adherence to drug therapy work?
5. What psychological strategies are effective in treating people where there is a lack of, or a limited, response to treatment?

APPENDIX 6:

SEARCH STRATEGIES FOR THE IDENTIFICATION OF STUDIES

1   GENERAL SEARCH FILTERS

BIPOLAR DISORDER

a.   *MEDLINE, EMBASE, PsycINFO, CINAHL – OVID interface*
1. exp bipolar disorder/
2. ((bipolar or bi polar) adj5 (disorder$ or depress$)).tw.
3. (hypomania$ or mania$ or manic$).tw.
4. (((cyclothymi$ or rapid or ultradian) adj5 cycl$) or RCBD).tw.
5. or/1-4

b.   *Cochrane Database of Systematic Reviews – Wiley Interscience interface*
#1 MeSH descriptor Bipolar Disorder explode all trees in MeSH products
#2 (bipolar or bi polar) near (disorder* or depress*) in Record Title or (bipolar or bi polar) near (disorder* or depress*) in Abstract or (bipolar or bi polar) near (disorder* or depress*) in Keywords in all products
#3 hypomania* or mania* or manic* in Record Title or hypomania* or mania* or manic* in Abstract or hypomania* or mania* or manic* in Keywords in all products
#4 ((cyclothymi* or rapid or ultradian) near cycl*) or RCBD in Record Title or ((cyclothymi* or rapid or ultradian) near cycl*) or RCBD in Abstract or ((cyclothymi* or rapid or ultradian) near cycl*) or RCBD in Keywords in all products
#5 #1 or #2 or #3 or #4

c.   *Database of Abstracts of Reviews of Effects – Wiley Interscience interface*
#1 MeSH descriptor Bipolar Disorder explode all trees in MeSH products
#2 (bipolar or bi polar) near (disorder* or depress*) in Record Title or (bipolar or bi polar) near (disorder* or depress*) in Abstract or (bipolar or bi polar) near (disorder* or depress*) in Keywords in all products
#3 hypomania* or mania* or manic* in Record Title or hypomania* or mania* or manic* in Abstract or hypomania* or mania* or manic* in Keywords in all products
#4 ((cyclothymi* or rapid or ultradian) near cycl*) or RCBD in Record Title or ((cyclothymi* or rapid or ultradian) near cycl*) or RCBD in Abstract or

((cyclothymi* or rapid or ultradian) near cycl*) or RCBD in Keywords in all products

#5 #1 or #2 or #3 or #4

d.   *Cochrane Central Register of Controlled Trials (CENTRAL) – Wiley Interscience interface*

#1 MeSH descriptor Bipolar Disorder explode all trees in MeSH products

#2 (bipolar or bi polar) near (disorder* or depress*) in Record Title or (bipolar or bi polar) near (disorder* or depress*) in Abstract or (bipolar or bi polar) near (disorder* or depress*) in Keywords in all products

#3 hypomania* or mania* or manic* in Record Title or hypomania* or mania* or manic* in Abstract or hypomania* or mania* or manic* in Keywords in all products

#4 ((cyclothymi* or rapid or ultradian) near cycl*) or RCBD in Record Title or ((cyclothymi* or rapid or ultradian) near cycl*) or RCBD in Abstract or ((cyclothymi* or rapid or ultradian) near cycl*) or RCBD in Keywords in all products

#5 #1 or #2 or #3 or #4

e.   *NHS Economic Evaluation Database (NHS EED) – Wiley Interscience interface*

#1 MeSH descriptor Bipolar Disorder explode all trees in MeSH products

#2 (bipolar or bi polar) near (disorder* or depress*) in Record Title or (bipolar or bi polar) near (disorder* or depress*) in Abstract or (bipolar or bi polar) near (disorder* or depress*) in Keywords in all products

#3 hypomania* or mania* or manic* in Record Title or hypomania* or mania* or manic* in Abstract or hypomania* or mania* or manic* in Keywords in all products

#4 ((cyclothymi* or rapid or ultradian) near 'cycl*) or RCBD in Record Title or ((cyclothymi* or rapid or ultradian) near cycl*) or RCBD in Abstract or ((cyclothymi* or rapid or ultradian) near cycl*) or RCBD in Keywords in all products

#5 #1 or #2 or #3 or #4

f.   *Health Technology Assessment Database (HTA) – Wiley Interscience interface*

#1 MeSH descriptor Bipolar Disorder explode all trees in MeSH products

#2 (bipolar or bi polar) near (disorder* or depress*) in Record Title or (bipolar or bi polar) near (disorder* or depress*) in Abstract or (bipolar or bipolar) near (disorder* or depress*) in Keywords in all products

#3 hypomania* or mania* or manic* in Record Title or hypomania* or mania* or manic* in Abstract or hypomania* or mania* or manic* in Keywords in all products

#4 ((cyclothymi* or rapid or ultradian) near cycl*) or RCBD in Record Title or ((cyclothymi* or rapid or ultradian) near cycl*) or RCBD in Abstract or ((cyclothymi* or rapid or ultradian) near cycl*) or RCBD in Keywords in all products

#5 #1 or #2 or #3 or #4

g.　　　*OHE EED – Clarinet interface*
1. AX =　bipolar or manic* or mania* or hypomania*
2. AX =　(cyclothymi* or rapid or ultradian) and cycl*
3. AX =　rapid cycl* or RCBD
4. CS =　1 or 2 or 3

SERIOUS MENTAL ILLNESS (SMI)

a.　　　*MEDLINE, EMBASE, PsycINFO, CINAHL – OVID interface*
1. exp chronic mental illness/ or exp mental disorders, chronic/ or ((mental disease/ or mental disorders/ or mental patient/) and (chronic disease/ or chronic illness/))
2. ((chronic$ or sever$) and mental$ and (disease$ or disorder$ or ill$)).tw. or SMI$1.ti.
3. exp psychosis/ or exp psychotic disorders/ or exp "schizophrenia and disorders with psychotic features"/
4. (hebephreni$ or oligophreni$ or paranoia or psychiatric$ or psychos$ or psychotic$ or schizo$).mp.
5. exp affective disorders/ or exp affective disorders, psychotic/ or exp bipolar disorder/ or depressive disorder, major/ or depressive psychosis/ or major depression/
6. (((bipolar or bi polar) adj5 (disorder$ or depress$)) or (mania or manic or hypomania) or (((cyclothymi$ or rapid or ultradian) adj5 cycl$) or rapid?cycl$ or RCBD) or ((chronic$ or major or unipolar$) adj depress$)).tw.
7. akathisia, drug-induced/ or dyskinesia, drug-induced/ or exp movement disorders/ or exp neuroleptic malignant syndrome/ or exp "side effects (drug)"/
8. ((tardiv$ and dyskine$) or akathisi$ or acathisi$ or (neuroleptic$ and malignant and syndrome) or (neuroleptic and movement and disorder) or parkinsoni$ or neuroleptic-induc$).tw.
9. (or/1-8) not (parkinson$ and disease).ti.

b.　　　*Cochrane Database of Systematic Reviews – Wiley Interscience interface*
#1 MeSH descriptor Mental Disorders, this term only in MeSH products
#2 ((chronic* or sever*) and mental* and (disease* or disorder* or ill*)) in Record Title or ((chronic* or sever*) and mental* and (disease* or disorder* or ill*)) in Abstract in all products
#3 SMI in Record Title or SMI in Abstract in all products
#4 MeSH descriptor Psychotic Disorders explode all trees in MeSH products
#5 MeSH descriptor Schizophrenia explode all trees in MeSH products
#6 hebephreni* or oligophreni* or paranoi* or psychiatric* or psychotic* or schiz* in Record Title or hebephreni* or oligophreni* or paranoi* or psychiatric* or psychotic* or schiz* in Abstract or hebephreni* or oligophreni* or paranoi* or psychiatric* or psychotic* or schiz* in Keywords in all products

#7 MeSH descriptor Affective Disorders, Psychotic explode all trees in MeSH products

#8 MeSH descriptor Depressive Disorder, Major, this term only in MeSH products

#9 (((bipolar or bi polar) near (disorder* or depress*)) or (mania or manic or hypomania) or (((cyclothymi* or rapid or ultradian) near cycl*) or rapid?cycl* or RCBD) or ((chronic* or major or unipolar*) adj depress*)) in Record Title or (((bipolar or bi polar) near (disorder* or depress*)) or (mania or manic or hypomania) or (((cyclothymi* or rapid or ultradian) near cycl*) or rapid?cycl* or RCBD) or ((chronic* or major or unipolar*) adj depress*)) in Abstract in all products or (((bipolar or bi polar) near (disorder* or depress*)) or (mania or manic or hypomania) or (((cyclothymi* or rapid or ultradian) near cycl*) or rapid?cycl* or RCBD) or ((chronic* or major or unipolar*) adj depress*)) in Keywords in all products

#10 MeSH descriptor Akathisia, Drug-Induced, this term only in MeSH products

#11 MeSH descriptor Dyskinesia, Drug-Induced, this term only in MeSH products

#12 MeSH descriptor Movement Disorders explode all trees in MeSH products

#13 MeSH descriptor Neuroleptic Malignant Syndrome explode all trees in MeSH products

#14 ((tardiv* and dyskine*) or akathisi* or acathisi* or (neuroleptic* and malignant and syndrome) or (neuroleptic and movement and disorder) or parkinsoni* or neuroleptic-induc*) in Record Title or ((tardiv* and dyskine*) or akathisi* or acathisi* or (neuroleptic* and malignant and syndrome) or (neuroleptic and movement and disorder) or parkinsoni* or neuroleptic-induc*) in Abstract in all products or ((tardiv* and dyskine*) or akathisi* or acathisi* or (neuroleptic* and malignant and syndrome) or (neuroleptic and movement and disorder) or parkinsoni* or neuroleptic-induc*) in Keywords in all products

#15 (parkinson* and disease) in Record Title in all products

#16 (#1 OR #2 OR #3 OR #4 OR #5 OR #6 OR #7 OR #8 OR #9 OR #10 OR #11 OR #12 OR #13 OR #14)

#17 (#16 AND NOT #15)

c.   *Database of Abstracts of Reviews of Effects – Wiley Interscience interface*

#1 MeSH descriptor Mental Disorders, this term only in MeSH products

#2 ((chronic* or sever*) and mental* and (disease* or disorder* or ill*)) in Record Title or ((chronic* or sever*) and mental* and (disease* or disorder* or ill*)) in Abstract in all products

#3 SMI in Record Title or SMI in Abstract in all products

#4 MeSH descriptor Psychotic Disorders explode all trees in MeSH products

#5 MeSH descriptor Schizophrenia explode all trees in MeSH products

#6 hebephreni* or oligophreni* or paranoi* or psychiatric* or psychotic* or schiz* in Record Title or hebephreni* or oligophreni* or paranoi* or psychiatric* or psychotic* or schiz* in Abstract or hebephreni* or oligophreni* or paranoi* or psychiatric* or psychotic* or schiz* in Keywords in all products

#7 MeSH descriptor Affective Disorders, Psychotic explode all trees in MeSH products

417

#8 MeSH descriptor Depressive Disorder, Major, this term only in MeSH products

#9 (((bipolar or bi polar) near (disorder* or depress*)) or (mania or manic or hypomania) or (((cyclothymi* or rapid or ultradian) near cycl*) or rapid?cycl* or RCBD) or ((chronic* or major or unipolar*) adj depress*)) in Record Title or (((bipolar or bi polar) near (disorder* or depress*)) or (mania or manic or hypomania) or (((cyclothymi* or rapid or ultradian) near cycl*) or rapid?cycl* or RCBD) or ((chronic* or major or unipolar*) adj depress*)) in Abstract in all products or (((bipolar or bi polar) near (disorder* or depress*)) or (mania or manic or hypomania) or (((cyclothymi* or rapid or ultradian) near cycl*) or rapid?cycl* or RCBD) or ((chronic* or major or unipolar*) adj depress*)) in Keywords in all products

#10 MeSH descriptor Akathisia, Drug-Induced, this term only in MeSH products

#11 MeSH descriptor Dyskinesia, Drug-Induced, this term only in MeSH products

#12 MeSH descriptor Movement Disorders explode all trees in MeSH products

#13 MeSH descriptor Neuroleptic Malignant Syndrome explode all trees in MeSH products

#14 ((tardiv* and dyskine*) or akathisi* or acathisi* or (neuroleptic* and malignant and syndrome) or (neuroleptic and movement and disorder) or parkinsoni* or neuroleptic-induc*) in Record Title or ((tardiv* and dyskine*) or akathisi* or acathisi* or (neuroleptic* and malignant and syndrome) or (neuroleptic and movement and disorder) or parkinsoni* or neuroleptic-induc*) in Abstract in all products or ((tardiv* and dyskine*) or akathisi* or acathisi* or (neuroleptic* and malignant and syndrome) or (neuroleptic and movement and disorder) or parkinsoni* or neuroleptic-induc*) in Keywords in all products

#15 (parkinson* and disease) in Record Title in all products

#16 (#1 OR #2 OR #3 OR #4 OR #5 OR #6 OR #7 OR #8 OR #9 OR #10 OR #11 OR #12 OR #13 OR #14)

#17 (#16 AND NOT #15)

d.   *Cochrane Central Register of Controlled Trials (CENTRAL) – Wiley Interscience interface*

#1 MeSH descriptor Mental Disorders, this term only in MeSH products

#2 ((chronic* or sever*) and mental* and (disease* or disorder* or ill*)) in Record Title or ((chronic* or sever*) and mental* and (disease* or disorder* or ill*)) in Abstract in all products

#3 SMI in Record Title or SMI in Abstract in all products

#4 MeSH descriptor Psychotic Disorders explode all trees in MeSH products

#5 MeSH descriptor Schizophrenia explode all trees in MeSH products

#6 hebephreni* or oligophreni* or paranoi* or psychiatric* or psychotic* or schiz* in Record Title or hebephreni* or oligophreni* or paranoi* or psychiatric* or psychotic* or schiz* in Abstract or hebephreni* or oligophreni* or paranoi* or psychiatric* or psychotic* or schiz* in Keywords in all products

#7 MeSH descriptor Affective Disorders, Psychotic explode all trees in MeSH products

#8 MeSH descriptor Depressive Disorder, Major, this term only in MeSH products

#9 (((bipolar or bi polar) near (disorder* or depress*)) or (mania or manic or hypomania) or ((((cyclothymi* or rapid or ultradian) near cycl*) or rapid?cycl* or RCBD) or ((chronic* or major or unipolar*) adj depress*)) in Record Title or ((((bipolar or bi polar) near (disorder* or depress*)) or (mania or manic or hypomania) or ((((cyclothymi* or rapid or ultradian) near cycl*) or rapid?cycl* or RCBD) or ((chronic* or major or unipolar*) adj depress*)) in Abstract in all products or ((((bipolar or bi polar) near (disorder* or depress*)) or (mania or manic or hypomania) or ((((cyclothymi* or rapid or ultradian) near cycl*) or rapid?cycl* or RCBD) or ((chronic* or major or unipolar*) adj depress*)) in Keywords in all products

#10 MeSH descriptor Akathisia, Drug-Induced, this term only in MeSH products

#11 MeSH descriptor Dyskinesia, Drug-Induced, this term only in MeSH products

#12 MeSH descriptor Movement Disorders explode all trees in MeSH products

#13 MeSH descriptor Neuroleptic Malignant Syndrome explode all trees in MeSH products

#14 ((tardiv* and dyskine*) or akathisi* or acathisi* or (neuroleptic* and malignant and syndrome) or (neuroleptic and movement and disorder) or parkinsoni* or neuroleptic-induc*) in Record Title or ((tardiv* and dyskine*) or akathisi* or acathisi* or (neuroleptic* and malignant and syndrome) or (neuroleptic and movement and disorder) or parkinsoni* or neuroleptic-induc*) in Abstract in all products or ((tardiv* and dyskine*) or akathisi* or acathisi* or (neuroleptic* and malignant and syndrome) or (neuroleptic and movement and disorder) or parkinsoni* or neuroleptic-induc*) in Keywords in all products

#15 (parkinson* and disease) in Record Title in all products

#16 (#1 OR #2 OR #3 OR #4 OR #5 OR #6 OR #7 OR #8 OR #9 OR #10 OR #11 OR #12 OR #13 OR #14)

#17 (#16 AND NOT #15)

e. *NHS Economic Evaluation Database (NHS EED) – Wiley Interscience interface*

#1 MeSH descriptor Mental Disorders, this term only in MeSH products

#2 ((chronic* or sever*) and mental* and (disease* or disorder* or ill*)) in Record Title or ((chronic* or sever*) and mental* and (disease* or disorder* or ill*)) in Abstract in all products

#3 SMI in Record Title or SMI in Abstract in all products

#4 MeSH descriptor Psychotic Disorders explode all trees in MeSH products

#5 MeSH descriptor Schizophrenia explode all trees in MeSH products

#6 hebephreni* or oligophreni* or paranoi* or psychiatric* or psychotic* or schiz* in Record Title or hebephreni* or oligophreni* or paranoi* or psychiatric* or psychotic* or schiz* in Abstract or hebephreni* or oligophreni* or paranoi* or psychiatric* or psychotic* or schiz* in Keywords in all products

#7 MeSH descriptor Affective Disorders, Psychotic explode all trees in MeSH products

#8 MeSH descriptor Depressive Disorder, Major, this term only in MeSH products

#9 (((bipolar or bi polar) near (disorder* or depress*)) or (mania or manic or hypomania) or ((((cyclothymi* or rapid or ultradian) near cycl*) or rapid?cycl* or RCBD) or ((chronic* or major or unipolar*) adj depress*)) in Record Title or (((bipolar or bi polar) near (disorder* or depress*)) or (mania or manic or hypomania) or ((((cyclothymi* or rapid or ultradian) near cycl*) or rapid?cycl* or RCBD) or ((chronic* or major or unipolar*) adj depress*)) in Abstract in all products or ((((bipolar or bi polar) near (disorder* or depress*)) or (mania or manic or hypomania) or (((cyclothymi* or rapid or ultradian) near cycl*) or rapid?cycl* or RCBD) or ((chronic* or major or unipolar*) adj depress*)) in Keywords in all products

#10 MeSH descriptor Akathisia, Drug-Induced, this term only in MeSH products
#11 MeSH descriptor Dyskinesia, Drug-Induced, this term only in MeSH products
#12 MeSH descriptor Movement Disorders explode all trees in MeSH products
#13 MeSH descriptor Neuroleptic Malignant Syndrome explode all trees in MeSH products
#14 ((tardiv* and dyskine*) or akathisi* or acathisi* or (neuroleptic* and malignant and syndrome) or (neuroleptic and movement and disorder) or parkinsoni* or neuroleptic-induc*) in Record Title or ((tardiv* and dyskine*) or akathisi* or acathisi* or (neuroleptic* and malignant and syndrome) or (neuroleptic and movement and disorder) or parkinsoni* or neuroleptic-induc*) in Abstract in all products or ((tardiv* and dyskine*) or akathisi* or acathisi* or (neuroleptic* and malignant and syndrome) or (neuroleptic and movement and disorder) or parkinsoni* or neuroleptic-induc*) in Keywords in all products
#15 (parkinson* and disease) in Record Title in all products
#16 (#1 OR #2 OR #3 OR #4 OR #5 OR #6 OR #7 OR #8 OR #9 OR #10 OR #11 OR #12 OR #13 OR #14)
#17 (#16 AND NOT #15)

f.   *Health Technology Assessment Database (HTA) – Wiley Interscience interface*

#1 MeSH descriptor Mental Disorders, this term only in MeSH products
#2 ((chronic* or sever*) and mental* and (disease* or disorder* or ill*)) in Record Title or ((chronic* or sever*) and mental* and (disease* or disorder* or ill*)) in Abstract in all products
#3 SMI in Record Title or SMI in Abstract in all products
#4 MeSH descriptor Psychotic Disorders explode all trees in MeSH products
#5 MeSH descriptor Schizophrenia explode all trees in MeSH products
#6 hebephreni* or oligophreni* or paranoi* or psychiatric* or psychotic* or schiz* in Record Title or hebephreni* or oligophreni* or paranoi* or psychiatric* or psychotic* or schiz* in Abstract or hebephreni* or oligophreni* or paranoi* or psychiatric* or psychotic* or schiz* in Keywords in all products
#7 MeSH descriptor Affective Disorders, Psychotic explode all trees in MeSH products
#8 MeSH descriptor Depressive Disorder, Major, this term only in MeSH products
#9 (((bipolar or bi polar) near (disorder* or depress*)) or (mania or manic or hypomania) or ((((cyclothymi* or rapid or ultradian) near cycl*) or rapid?cycl* or RCBD) or ((chronic* or major or unipolar*) adj depress*)) in Record Title or (((bipolar or bi polar) near (disorder* or depress*)) or (mania or manic or

hypomania) or (((cyclothymi* or rapid or ultradian) near cycl*) or rapid?cycl* or RCBD) or ((chronic* or major or unipolar*) adj depress*)) in Abstract in all products or (((bipolar or bi polar) near (disorder* or depress*)) or (mania or manic or hypomania) or (((cyclothymi* or rapid or ultradian) near cycl*) or rapid?cycl* or RCBD) or ((chronic* or major or unipolar*) adj depress*)) in Keywords in all products

#10 MeSH descriptor Akathisia, Drug-Induced, this term only in MeSH products

#11 MeSH descriptor Dyskinesia, Drug-Induced, this term only in MeSH products

#12 MeSH descriptor Movement Disorders explode all trees in MeSH products

#13 MeSH descriptor Neuroleptic Malignant Syndrome explode all trees in MeSH products

#14 ((tardiv* and dyskine*) or akathisi* or acathisi* or (neuroleptic* and malignant and syndrome) or (neuroleptic and movement and disorder) or parkinsoni* or neuroleptic-induc*) in Record Title or ((tardiv* and dyskine*) or akathisi* or acathisi* or (neuroleptic* and malignant and syndrome) or (neuroleptic and movement and disorder) or parkinsoni* or neuroleptic-induc*) in Abstract in all products or ((tardiv* and dyskine*) or akathisi* or acathisi* or (neuroleptic* and malignant and syndrome) or (neuroleptic and movement and disorder) or parkinsoni* or neuroleptic-induc*) in Keywords in all products

#15 (parkinson* and disease) in Record Title in all products

#16 (#1 OR #2 OR #3 OR #4 OR #5 OR #6 OR #7 OR #8 OR #9 OR #10 OR #11 OR #12 OR #13 OR #14)

#17 (#16 AND NOT #15)

g.   *OHE EED – Clarinet interface*
1. AX = (chronic* or sever*) and mental* and (disease* or disorder* or ill*)
2. AX = SMI
3. AX = hebephreni* or oligophreni*
4. AX = paranoi* or psychiatric* or psychotic* or schiz*
5. AX = bipolar or manic* or mania* or hypomania*
6. AX = (cyclothymi* or rapid or ultradian) and cycl*
7. AX = rapid cycl* or RCBD or chronic depress* or major depress* or unipolar depress*
8. AX = (tardiv* and dyskine*) or akathisi* or acathisi* or (neuroleptic* and malignant and syndrome)
9. CS = 1 or 2 or 3 or 4 or 5 or 6 or 7 or 8

2.   SYSTEMATIC REVIEW SEARCH FILTERS

a.   *MEDLINE, EMBASE, PsycINFO, CINAHL – OVID interface*
1. exp meta analysis/ or exp systematic review/ or exp literature review/ or exp literature searching/ or exp cochrane library/ or exp review literature/
2. ((systematic or quantitative or methodologic$) adj5 (overview$ or review$)).mp.

3. (metaanaly$ or meta analy$).mp.
4. (research adj (review$ or integration)).mp.
5. reference list$.ab.
6. bibliograph$.ab.
7. published studies.ab.
8. relevant journals.ab.
9. selection criteria.ab.
10. (data adj (extraction or synthesis)).ab.
11. ((handsearch$3 or (hand or manual)) adj search$).tw.
12. ((mantel adj haenszel) or peto or dersimonian or der simonian).tw.
13. (fixed effect$ or random effect$).tw.
14. review$.pt,mp. and (bids or cochrane or index medicus or isi citation or medlars or psyclit or psychlit or scisearch or science citation or web adj1 science).mp.
15. (systematic$ or meta$).pt.
16. or/1-15

3. RCT SEARCH FILTERS

a. MEDLINE, EMBASE, PsycINFO, CINAHL – OVID interface
1. exp clinical trials/ or exp clinical trial/ or exp controlled clinical trials/
2. exp crossover procedure/ or exp cross over studies/ or exp crossover design/
3. exp double blind procedure/ or exp double blind method/ or exp double blind studies/ or exp single blind procedure/ or exp single blind method/ or exp single blind studies/
4. exp random allocation/ or exp randomization/ or exp random assignment/ or exp random sample/ or exp random sampling/
5. exp randomized controlled trials/ or exp randomized controlled trial/
6. (clinical adj2 trial$).tw.
7. (crossover or cross over).tw.
8. (((single$ or doubl$ or trebl$ or tripl$) adj5 (blind$ or mask$ or dummy)) or (singleblind$ or doubleblind$ or trebleblind$)).tw.
9. (placebo$ or random$).mp.
10. (clinical trial$ or clinical control trial or random$).pt,dt.
11. animals/ not (animals/ and human$.mp.)
12. animal$/ not (animal$/ and human$/)
13. (animal not (animal and human)).po.
14. (or/1-10) not (or/11-13)

4. HEALTH ECONOMICS AND QUALITY OF LIFE SEARCH FILTERS

a. MEDLINE, EMBASE, PsycINFO, CINAHL – OVID interface
1. exp "costs and cost analysis"/ or "health care costs"/

2. exp health resource allocation/ or exp health resource utilization/
3. exp economics/ or exp economic aspect/ or exp health economics/
4. exp value of life/
5. (burden adj5 (disease or illness)).tw.
6. (cost$ or economic$ or expenditure$ or price$1 or pricing or pharmacoeconomic$).tw.
7. (budget$ or fiscal or funding or financial or finance$).tw.
8. (resource adj5 (allocation$ or utilit$)).tw.
9. or/1-8
10. (value adj5 money).tw.
11. exp quality of life/
12. (quality$ adj5 (life or survival)).tw.
13. (health status or QOL or well being or wellbeing).tw.
14. or/9-13

5.   SEARCH STRINGS SUPPORTING SPECIFIC REVIEWS

Assertive outreach team (AOT) search filters

Medline, Embase, PsycINFO and CINAHL were searched using the search filter for SMI (see above) combined with:

[and (((case or care) adj5 management) or (care adj5 program$ adj5 approach$) or (assertive adj5 community adj5 treatment) or (training adj5 community adj5 living) or (Madison adj5 model$)).mp. or (cpa or pact or tcl).tw.]

NHS EED and the HTA database were searched using the search filter for SMI (see above) combined with:

[and (((case or care) near management) or (care near program* near approach*) or (assertive near community near treatment) or (training near community near living) or (madison near model*)) in Record Title or (((case or care) near management) or (care near program* near approach*) or (assertive near community near treatment) or (training near community near living) or (madison near model*)) in Abstract or (((case or care) near management) or (care near program* near approach*) or (assertive near community near treatment) or (training near community near living) or (madison near model*)) in Keywords in all products or cpa or pact or tcl in Record Title or cpa or pact or tcl in Abstract in all products]

Case management search filters

Medline, Embase, PsycINFO and CINAHL were searched using the search filter for SMI (see above) combined with:

[and (((case or care) and management) or CPA or care programme approach).mp.]

NHS EED and the HTA database were searched using the search filter for SMI (see above) combined with:

[and ((case or care) and management) or CPA or care programme approach in Record Title or ((case or care) and management) or CPA or care programme approach in Abstract or ((case or care) and management) or CPA or care programme approach in Keywords]

Community and adolescent mental health service (CAMHS) search filters

Medline, Embase, PsycINFO and CINAHL were searched using the search filter for SMI (see above) combined with:

[and ((exp child health care/ or exp child health services/ or exp adolescent health services/ or adolescent/ or adolescence/ or adolescent development/ or child/ or child-hood development/) and (exp mental health service/ or exp mental health services/)) or (camhs or ((child$ or adolescen$) and mental and service$)).tw.]

NHS EED and the HTA database were searched using the search filter for SMI (see above) combined with:

[and ((MeSH descriptor Child Health Services explode all trees in MeSH products or MeSH descriptor Adolescent Health Services explode all trees in MeSH products or MeSH descriptor Adolescent, this term only in MeSH products or MeSH descriptor Adolescent Development explode all trees in MeSH products or MeSH descriptor Child explode all trees in MeSH products) and MeSH descriptor Mental Health Services explode all trees in MeSH products) or (child* or adolescen*) and mental and service* in Record Title or (child* or adolescen*) and mental and service* in Abstract or (child* or adolescen*) and mental and service* in Keywords in all products or camhs in Record Title or camhs in Abstract in all products]

Community mental health team (CMHT) search filter

Medline, Embase, PsycINFO and CINAHL were searched using the search filter for SMI (see above) combined with:

[and exp community mental health centers/ or ((exp community mental health/ or exp community mental health services/ or exp community psychiatry/ or community services/) and (exp institutional management teams/ or exp teams/ or exp teamwork/ or team$.mp.)) or (communit$ adj5 (team$ or center$ or centre$ or treat$) and mental).mp. or cmht.tw.]

NHS EED and the HTA database were searched using the search filter for SMI (see above) combined with:

[and MeSH descriptor Community Mental Health Centers explode all trees in MeSH products or ((MeSH descriptor Community Mental Health Services explode all trees in MeSH Products or MeSH descriptor Community Psychiatry explode all trees in MeSH products) and (MeSH descriptor Institutional Management Teams, this term only in MeSH products or MeSH descriptor Patient Care Team explode all trees in MeSH products or team* in All Fields or team* in Abstract or team* in Keywords in all products)) or (communit* near (team* or center* or centre* or treat*)) in Record Title or (communit* near (team* or center* or centre* or treat*)) in Abstract in all products or cmht in Record Title or cmht in Abstract in all products]

Crisis resolution and home treatment team (CRHTT) search filters

Medline, Embase, PsycINFO and CINAHL were searched using the search filter for SMI (see above) combined with:

[and ((time adj5 limit$) or (hospital$ adj5 (diversion or alternative$)) or ((acute or cris$ or emergenc$ or intensive$ or mobile) adj5 (care$ or interven$ or treat$ or therap$ or management$ or model$ or program$ or team$ or service$ or base$1))).tw. or exp crisis intervention/ or exp crisis theory/ or exp community care/ or exp community mental health/ or exp community mental health nursing/ or exp community mental health services/ or exp community institutional relations/ or exp community programs/ or exp community trials/ or exp community psychiatry/ or exp social psychiatry/ or exp home care services/ or exp home care/ or exp home visiting programs/ or exp mobile health units/ or exp emergency services, psychiatric/ or exp emergency services/ or exp emergency health service/ or exp psychiatric hospital readmission/ or exp partial hospitalization/ or exp preventive health service/]

NHS EED and the HTA database were searched using the search filter for SMI (see above) combined with:

[and (time near limit*) or (hospital* near (diversion or alternative*)) in Record Title or (time near limit*) or (hospital* near (diversion or alternative*)) in Abstract or (time near limit*) or (hospital* near (diversion or alternative*)) in Keywords in all products or (acute or cris* or emergenc* or intensive* or mobile) near (care* or interven* or treat* or therap* or management* or model* or program* or team* or service* or base*) in Record Title or (acute or cris* or emergenc* or intensive* or mobile) near (care* or interven* or treat* or therap* or management* or model* or program* or team* or service* or base*) in Abstract or (acute or cris* or emergenc* or intensive* or mobile) near (care* or interven* or treat* or therap* or management* or model* or program* or team* or service* or base*) in Keywords in all products or MeSH descriptor Crisis Intervention, this term only in MeSH products or MeSH descriptor Community Mental Health Services explode all trees in MeSH products MeSH descriptor Community Psychiatry explode all trees in MeSH products MeSH descriptor Home Care Services explode all trees in MeSH products or MeSH descriptor Mobile Health Units explode all trees in MeSH products or MeSH descriptor Emergency Services, Psychiatric explode all trees in MeSH products]

Day hospital search filters

Medline, Embase, PsycINFO and CINAHL were searched using the search filter for SMI (see above) combined with:

[and ((day adj5 (hosp$ or care$ or treatment$ or cent$ or unit$)) or (partial adj5 hosp$) or dispensary).mp.]

NHS EED and the HTA database were searched using the search filter for SMI (see above) combined with:

[and ((day near (hosp* or care* or treatment* or cent* or unit*)) or (partial near hosp*) or dispensary) in Record Title or ((day near (hosp* or care* or treatment* or cent* or unit*)) or (partial near hosp*) or dispensary) in Abstract or ((day near (hosp* or care* or treatment* or cent* or unit*)) or (partial near hosp*) or dispensary) in Keywords in all products]

Early intervention service (EIS) search filters

Medline, Embase, PsycINFO and CINAHL were searched using the search filter for SMI (see above) combined with:

[and (((risk$ or screen) adj5 schiz$) or ((duration or length) adj5 untreat$) or ((first or initial or primary) adj5 (admission of hospital$ or episod$ or break?down$ or break down$)) or (early adj5 (intervent$ or treat$ or recogni$ or detect$)) or (delay$ adj5 treat$) or (dup or pre?morbid$ or pre morbid$ or prodrom$)).mp.]

NHS EED and the HTA database were searched using the search filter for SMI (see above) combined with:

[and (((risk* or screen) near schiz*) or ((duration or length) near untreat*) or ((first or initial or primary) near (admission of hospital* or episod* or break?down* or break down*)) or (early near (intervent* or treat* or recogni* or detect*)) or (delay* near treat*) or (dup or pre?morbid* or pre morbid* or prodrom*)) in Record Title or (((risk* or screen) near schiz*) or ((duration or length) near untreat*) or ((first or initial or primary) near (admission of hospital* or episod* or break?down* or break down*)) or (early near (intervent* or treat* or recogni* or detect*)) or (delay* near treat*) or (dup or pre?morbid* or pre morbid* or prodrom*)) in Abstract or (((risk* or screen) near schiz*) or ((duration or length) near untreat*) or ((first or initial or primary) near (admission of hospital* or episod* or break?down* or break down*)) or (early near (intervent* or treat* or recogni* or detect*)) or (delay* near treat*) or (dup or pre?morbid* or pre morbid* or prodrom*)) in Keywords in all products]

Inpatient environment search filters

Medline, Embase, PsycINFO and CINAHL were searched using the search filter for SMI (see above) combined with:

[and (exp aggression/ or exp aggressive behavior/ or violence/ or (aggress$ or ((agonistic or attack$ or destruct$ or threaten$) adj5 behav$) or hostil$ or violen$2).tw.) and (hospital patient/ or inpatients/ or (hospitalization/ and patients/) or exp psychiatric hospitalization/ or (hospitali$ patient$ or in?patient$).tw.) or ((hospital patient/ or inpatients/ or (hospitalization/ and patients/) or exp psychiatric hospitalization/ or ((hospitali$ patient$) or in?patient$).tw.) and (health facility environment/ or hospital environment/ or ((hospital department/ or hospital departments/ or hospital units/ or hospitals, psychiatric/ or psychiatric department/ or psychiatric

department, hospital/ or psychiatric hospitals/ or psychiatric units/ or ward/)
and (environment/ or psychosocial environment/ or social environment/ or therapeutic environment/ or work environment/)) or ((health facility$ or hospital$ or (psychiatric adj (department or unit$)) or ward or work$3 or workplace) adj3 (atmosphere$ or environment$)).tw. or (ward atmosphere scale or working environment scale).it,tm.))]

NHS EED and the HTA database were searched using the search filter for SMI (see above) combined with:

[and ((MeSH descriptor Aggression explode all trees in MeSH products or MeSH descriptor Violence explode all trees in MeSH products or aggress* or hostil* or violen* in Record Title or aggress* or hostil* or violen* in Abstract or aggress* or hostil* or violen* in Keywords in all products or (agonistic or attack* or destruct* or threaten*) near behav* in Record Title or (agonistic or attack* or destruct* or threaten*) near behav* in Abstract in all products) and (MeSH descriptor Inpatients explode all trees in MeSH products or (MeSH descriptor Patients explode all trees in MeSH products and MeSH descriptor Hospitalization explode all trees in MeSH products) or (hospitali* near patient*) or in?patient* in Record Title or (hospitali* near patient*) or in?patient* in abstract or (hospitali* near patient*) or in?patient* in Keywords in all products)) or ((MeSH descriptor Inpatients explode all trees in MeSH products or (MeSH descriptor Patients explode all trees in MeSH products and MeSH descriptor Hospitalization explode all trees in MeSH products) or (hospitali* near patient*) or in?patient* in Record Title or (hospitali* near patient*) or in?patient* in abstract or (hospitali* near patient*) or in?patient* in Keywords in all products)) and (MeSH descriptor Health Facility Environment explode all trees in MeSH products or ((MeSH descriptor Hospital Departments explode all trees in MeSH products or MeSH descriptor Hospital Units explode all trees in MeSH products or MeSH descriptor Hospitals, Psychiatric explode all trees in MeSH products or MeSH descriptor Psychiatric Department, Hospital explode all trees in MeSH products or MeSH descriptor Psychiatric Department, Hospital explode all trees in MeSH products) and (MeSH descriptor Environment, this term only in MeSH products or MeSH descriptor Social Environment explode all trees in MeSH products)) or (health facility* or hospital* or (psychiatric near (department or unit*)) or ward or work* or workplace in Record Title or health facility* or hospital* or (psychiatric near (department or unit*)) or ward or work* or workplace in Record Title or health facility* or hospital* or (psychiatric near (department or unit*)) or ward or work* or workplace in Keywords in all products) and (atmosphere* or environment* in Record Title or atmosphere* or environment* in Record Title or atmosphere* or environment* in Keywords in all products))]

Vocational rehabilitation search filters

Medline, Embase, PsycINFO and CINAHL were searched using the search filter for SMI (see above) combined with:

[and ((supp$ adj employ$) or employment or ((psychosocial or psychiatric or occupational or soc$ or work or job) adj rehab$) or sheltered work$ or transitional employ$ or rehabilitation counsel?ing or vocation$ or fountain house$ or fountain-house$ or clubhouse$ or club house$).mp.]

NHS EED and the HTA database were searched using the search filter for SMI (see above) combined with:

[and supp* employ* or employment or ((psychosocial or psychiatric or occupational or soc* or work or job) near rehab*) or sheltered work* or transitional employ* or rehabilitation counselling or vocation* or fountain house* or fountainhouse* or club house* or club house* in Record Title or supp* employ* or employment or ((psychosocial or psychiatric or occupational or soc* or work or job) near rehab*) or sheltered work* or transitional employ* or rehabilitation counselling or vocation* or fountain house* or fountainhouse* or club house* or club house* in Abstract or supp* employ* or employment or ((psychosocial or psychiatric or occupational or soc* or work or job) near rehab*) or sheltered work* or transitional employ* or rehabilitation counselling or vocation* or fountain house* or fountainhouse* or club house* or club house* in Keywords in all products]

Details of additional searches undertaken to support the development of this guideline are available on request.

APPENDIX 7:

CLINICAL STUDY ELIGIBILITY CHECKLIST

TABLE 98: ELIGIBILITY CHECKLIST FOR INCLUDED STUDIES

Exclusion criteria	Code options ✓ × ?
Only concerned with:	
• Primary prevention, unless relapse prevention	
• Care options that could be routinely made available by the NHS	
• Treatments given at less than the therapeutic dose (for pharmacological treatments based on BNF dosages; for psychological treatments)	
Inclusion criteria	
Population	
• Reported results from patients who meet the standard diagnostic criteria of bipolar disorder	
Topic Area	
1. Physical treatments	
1.1. Antipsychotics	
1.2. Antidepressants	
1.3. Anticonvulsants	
1.4. Benzodiazepines	
1.5. Lithium	
1.6. ECT	
1.7. TMS	
2. Psychological	
2.1. Cognitive behavioural therapies	
2.2. Psychoeducation	
2.3. Family therapies	
2.4. Approaches aimed at improving adherence to pharmacotherapy	
2.5. Combined pharmacological and psychological treatments	
3. Service/other treatments and issues	
3.1. Self-help	
3.2. Lifestyle interventions	
3.3. Managed care/chronic disease management	
3.4. Non-statutory support	
3.5. Crisis resolution and home treatment teams	
3.6. Assertive outreach teams	
3.7. Day hospitals	
3.8. Early intervention	
3.9. Vocational rehabilitation	

APPENDIX 8:

RCT METHODOLOGICAL QUALITY CHECKLIST

TABLE 99: QUALITY CHECKLIST FOR AN RCT

Depression Guideline Quality checklist for an RCT		
Report reference ID:		
Checklist completed by:	**Date completed:**	
SECTION 1: INTERNAL VALIDITY		
Evaluation criteria	**How well is this criterion addressed?**	
1.1 Was the assignment of subjects to treatment groups randomised?		
If there is no indication of randomisation, the study should be rejected. *If the description of randomisation is poor, or the process used is not truly random (for example allocation by date, alternating between one group and another) or can otherwise be seen as flawed, the study should be given a lower quality rating.*		
1.2 Was an adequate concealment method used?		
Centralised allocation, computerised allocation systems or the use of coded identical containers would all be regarded as adequate methods of concealment and may be taken as indicators of a well-conducted study. If the method of concealment used is regarded as poor, or relatively easy to subvert, the study must be given a lower quality rating and can be rejected if the concealment method is seen as inadequate.		
SECTION 2: OVERALL ASSESSMENT	**Comments**	**Code**
2.1 Low risk of bias	*Both criteria met*	**A**
Moderate risk of bias	*One or more criteria partly met*	**B**
High risk of bias	*One or more criteria not met*	**C**

APPENDIX 9:

CLINICAL STUDY DATA EXTRACTION FORMS

TABLE 100: STUDY CHARACTERISTICS EXTRACTION FORM

Topic area:		Report reference ID:	
Comparisons:			
Ref list checked		Data entered in Rev Man		Characteristics entered	
Data checked		Reference Manager updated		Excluded	

Randomised?		Blind?	
Age:		Young/elderly (mean age over 65)	
Setting:		In/out/mixed/primary care (80% patients)	
Analysis:		Completer/ITT (continuous data)	
Diagnosis			% Dysthymic
			% Bipolar
Mean baseline			

Trial length
Interventions (dose): 1 2 3
Notes

TABLE 101: RCT DATA EXTRACTION FORM

Data extraction form for a randomised controlled trial											
Completed by:						**Report reference ID:**					

1 TREATMENT GROUP:

Dropouts		Treatment responders		Side effects (total)				
n	*N*	*n*	*N*	*n*	*N*		*n*	*N*

Definition of responders

Post-treatment means	*n*	*Mean*	*SD*	*n*	*Mean*	*SD*	*n*	*Mean*	*SD*	*n*	*Mean*	*SD*

Other data	*n*	*N*		*n*	*N*		*n*	*Mean*	*SD*	*n*	*Mean*	*SD*

2 TREATMENT GROUP:

Dropouts		Treatment responders		Side effects (total)				
n	*N*	*n*	*N*	*n*	*N*		*n*	*N*

Definition of responders

Post-treatment means	*n*	*Mean*	*SD*	*n*	*Mean*	*SD*	*n*	*Mean*	*SD*	*n*	*Mean*	*SD*

Other data	*n*	*N*		*n*	*N*		*n*	*Mean*	*SD*	*n*	*Mean*	*SD*

APPENDIX 10:

FORMULAE FOR CALCULATING STANDARD DEVI-

ATIONS

The following formulae were used to calculate standard deviations (SD) where these were not available in study reports:

(n = sample size of group)

$$SD = \text{standard error} \times \sqrt{n}$$

$$SD = \frac{(\text{upper 95\% confidence interval} - \text{mean})}{1.96} \times \sqrt{n}$$

$$SD = \frac{(\text{mean}_1 - \text{mean}_2)}{\sqrt{F} \left(\frac{\sqrt{1}}{n_1} \right) + \left(\frac{\sqrt{1}}{n_2} \right)}$$

(If F ratio is not given, then $F = t_2$)

APPENDIX 11: OUTCOMES, RATING SCALES AND DIAGNOSTIC SCALES

TABLE 102: OUTCOMES

Outcome	Outcome used for analysis	Definition	Statistic(s)
Efficacy of treatment			
Remission*	Number of participants not achieving remission	For example, Young Mania Rating Scale >12 HRSD-17>7	RR/NNT (NNH)
Symptom level*	Mean change in rating scale score (or endpoint score)	Rating scales – see below	WMD (or SMD)
Relapse	Number of participants relapsing	Recurrence of manic or depressed state during maintenance treatment	RR/NNT (NNH)
Recurrence	Number of participants experiencing a recurrence of symptoms (at particular time points)	Recurrence of manic or depressed state during acute phase treatment	RR/NNT (NNH)
Time to recurrence	Number of days to next episode	Recurrence of symptoms (DSM-IV mania, mixed affective state, hypomania, major depression or all recurrences)	WMD

Time to clinical outcome (hospitalisation/self-harm)	Number of days to clinical outcome	Recurrence of symptoms (DSM-IV mania, mixed affective state, hypomania, major depression or all recurrences)	WMD
Number of adverse clinical outcomes (hospitalisation/ self-harm)	Number of days to clinical outcome	Recurrence of symptoms (DSM-IV mania, mixed affective state, hypomania, major depression or all recurrences)	WMD
Recurrence leading to withdrawal	Number of participants experiencing a recurrence of symptoms leading to withdrawal from the study	Recurrence of manic or depressed state during acute-phase treatment leading to withdrawal from the study	RR/NNT (NNH)
Introduction of additional medication	Number of participants requiring additional medication	Introduction of additional medication during study	RR/NNT (NNH)
Number of days participants fulfil criteria for episodes during time period	Mean number of days per time period	Must be specifically measured in the study	WMD
Number of episodes per time period [for rapid cyclers]	Mean episodes per time period	Recurrence of manic/ depressed phase in rapid cyclers	WMD

Continued

435

Table 102: (Continued)

Outcome	Outcome used for analysis	Definition	Statistic(s)
Acceptability of treatment			
Attrition from the study	Number of people leaving the study early for any reason	Total number leaving regardless of reason	RR/NNT (NNH)
Tolerability of treatment			
Number reporting side effects	Number reporting side effects	Total or by type of side effect	RR/NNH
Leaving treatment early because of adverse events	Number of people leaving the study early because of adverse events	Numbers must be based on those explicitly withdrawn or leaving study due to side effects	RR/NNH
Specific side effects Weight gain Switching	Number of people experiencing specific side effects Weight gain % needing anticholinergic drug Movement disorders – scales Sedation Cognitive function	Numbers experiencing side effects	RR/NNH

Other		
Measure of medication adherence	Number of participants not achieving full adherence	RR/NNT
	Numbers not achieving full adherence according to self-report or physician reported measure	
Quality of life/general functioning	Mean change in rating scale score	WMD/SMD
	See scales below	
Satisfaction		WMD/SMD
Suicide	Number of participants dying by suicide during study period	RR/NNH
Death	Number of participants dying for any reason during study period	RR/NNH

*See list of rating scales, see Table 104

TABLE 103: DIAGNOSTIC TOOLS

Diagnostic tool	Child/adult	Reference
Children's Interview for Psychiatric Syndromes – Child and Parent Forms (ChIPS, P-ChIPS)	Child	Weller, E. B., Weller, R. A., Rooney, M.T., *et al.* (1999) *Children's Interview for Psychiatric Syndromes (ChIPS).* Washington DC: American Psychiatric Press, Inc. Weller, E. B., Weller, R. A., Rooney, M. T., *et al.* (1999) *Children's Interview for Psychiatric Syndromes – Parent Version. (P-ChIPS).* Washington DC: American Psychiatric Press, Inc.
SCID (Structured Clinical Interview for DSM-)	Adult	First, M. B., Spitzer, R. L., Williams, J. B. W., *et al.* (1996) *Structured Clinical Interview for DSM-IV.* New York, NY: Biometric Research, New York State Psychiatric Institute and Columbia University.
WASH-U-KSADS	Child	Geller, B., Zimerman, B., Williams, M., *et al.* (2001) Reliability of the Washington University in St Louis Kiddie Schedule for Affective Disorders and Schizophrenia (WASH-U-KSADS) mania and rapid cycling sections. *Journal of the American Academy of Child & Adolescent Psychiatry, 40,* 450–455. Geller, B., Warner, K., Williams, M., *et al.* (1998) Prepubertal and young adolescent bipolarity versus ADHD: assessment and validity using the WASH-U-KSADS, CBCL and TRF. *Journal of Affective Disorders, 51,* 93–100. Geller, B., Williams, M., Zimerman, B. (1996) *Washington University in St. Louis Kiddie Schedule for Affective Disorders and Schizophrenia (WASH-U-KSADS).* St. Louis, MO: Washington University.

TABLE 104: SELECTED INSTRUMENTS FOR SYMPTOM ASSESSMENT IN BIPOLAR DISORDER

Scale/reference	Administ-ration+	Illness phase**	Items	Information
DEPRESSION				
HRSD (paper copy) Hamilton, M. (1960) A rating scale for depression. *Journal of Neurology and Neurosurgical Psychiatry, 23,* 56–62.	C	D	1. Depressed mood 2. Feelings of guilt 3. Suicide 4. Insomnia early 5. Insomnia middle 6. Insomnia late 7. Work and activities 8. Retardation: psychomotor 9. Agitation 10. Anxiety (psychological) 11. Anxiety somatic 12. Somatic symptoms (gastrointestinal) 13. Somatic symptoms (general) 14. Genital symptoms 15. Hypochondriasis 16. Loss of weight 17. Insight 18. Diurnal variation 19. Depersonalization and derealization 20. Paranoid symptoms 21. Obsessional and compulsive symptoms Original version: first 17 items only	0–4 or 0–2 on each item Max score 50 on 17-item version Remission cut-off 7 0–7 not depressed 8–13 mild 14–18 moderate 19–22 severe 23+ very severe (APA handbook) 3 points

Continued

439

TABLE 104: *(Continued)*

Scale/reference	Administ-ration+	Illness phase**	Items	Information
MADRS (paper copy) Montgomery, S.A. & Asberg, M. (1979) A new depression scale designed to be sensitive to change *British Journal of Psychiatry*, *134*, 382–389.	C	D	1. Apparent sadness 2. Reported sadness 3. Inner tension 4. Reduced sleep 5. Reduced appetite 6. Concentration difficulties 7. Lassitude 8. Inability to feel 9. Pessimistic thoughts 10. Suicidal thoughts	Scored 0,2,4,6 (or 1,3,5) No cut-offs appear to have been set N/A
BDI (paper copy) Beck, A. T., Ward, C. H., Mendelson, M.., *et al.* (1961) An inventory for measuring depression. *Archives of General Psychiatry*, *4*, 561–571.	S	D	1. Mood 2. Pessimism 3. Sense of failure 4. Self-dissatisfaction 5. Guilt 6. Punishment 7. Self-dislike 8. Self-accusations 9. Suicidal ideas 10. Crying 11. Irritability 12. Social withdrawal 13. Indecisiveness 14. Body image change	Scored 0–3 Max score 63 0–9 not depressed 10–16 mild 17–21 moderate 22–29 severe 30+ very severe (APA) 3 points

SADS-C Schedule for Affective Disorders and Schizophrenia, Change Version (SADS-C). New York: New York State Psychiatric Institute.	C	15. Work difficulty 16. Insomnia 17. Fatigability 18. Loss of appetite 19. Weight loss 20. Somatic preoccupation 21. Loss of libido Used in several RCTs	
MANIA			
MAS (paper copy) Bech-Rafaelsen Mania Scale	C	M	1. Elevated mood 2. Increased verbal activity 3. Increased social contact 4. Increased motor activity 5. Sleep disturbances 6. Social activities (distractibility) 7. Hostility, irritable mood 8. Increased sexual activity 9. Increased self-esteem 10. Flight of thoughts 11. Noise level	Time frame: previous 3 days Each item scored – 0–4 Total possible score = 44 5 no mania 6–14 hypomania 15 mild mania 21 moderate mania 29 marked mania 33 severe mania 44 extreme mania

Continued

441

TABLE 104: *(Continued)*

Scale/reference	Administration+	Illness phase**	Items	Information
YMRS (paper copy) Young, R. C., Biggs, J. T., Ziegler, V. E., et al. (1978) A rating scale for mania: reliability, validity and sensitivity. *British Journal of Psychiatry*, 133, 429–435.	C	M	1. Elevated mood 2. Increased motor-activity energy 3. Sexual interest 4. Sleep 5. Irritability 6. Speech (rate and amount) 7. Language-thought disorder 8. Content 9. Disruptive-aggressive behaviour 10. Appearance 11. Insight 15–30 mins to do Telephone use inappropriate	(Based on CGI categories) Time frame: none 0–4 or 0–8 (in 2s) Highest possible score = 60 13 minimal severity 20 mild 26 moderate 38 severe NB: these are averages based on only 20 patients
DEPRESSION & MANIA				
Life Chart Post, R., Roy-Byrne, P., Uhde, T. (1988) Graphic representation of the life course	S	M D	Specifically for bipolar disorder	

of illness in patients with affective disorders. *American Journal of Psychiatry, 145,* 844–848.			
ISS (paper copy) Bauer, M. & Whybrow, P. (1991) Rapid-cycling bipolar disorder: clinical features, treatment, and etiology. *Advances in Neuropsychiatry & Psychopharmacology,* 2, 191.	S	M D P*	1. Today my mood is changeable 2. Today I feel irritable 3. Today I feel like a capable person 4. Today I feel like people are out to get me 5. Today I actually feel great inside 6. Today I feel impulsive 7. Today my thoughts are going fast 8. Today it seems like nothing will ever work out for me 9. Today I feel overactive 10. Today I feel as if the world is against me 11. Today I feel 'sped up' inside 12. Today I feel restless 13. Today I feel argumentative 14. Today I feel energized 15. Today I feel (depressed/normal/manic) Takes 10–15 mins	Time frame: past 24 hours Marked on visual analogue scale (0 not at all/rarely to 100 very much so/much of the time) 4 sub-scales: Activation (impulsive, fast thoughts, overactive, sped up, restless) Well being (capable, great, energized) Perceived conflict (changeable, irritable, argumentative, world against, out to get)

Continued

TABLE 104: *(Continued)*

Scale/reference	Administration+	Illness phase**	Items	Information
				Depression Index (depressed, no work out)
				Plus a single-item Global Bipolar Scale
				Well Being subscale used with the Activation subscale:
				Depression = well being < 125
				Mania/hypomania = Well being >= 125 and Activation >= 200
				Remission = Well being >= 125 and Activation < 200
PSYCHOSIS				
BPRS (paper copy) Overall, J. E. & Gorham, D. R. (1962) The brief psychiatric rating scale. *Psychological Report,* *1*, 799–812.	C	M* D* P	1. Somatic concern 2. Anxiety 3. Emotional withdrawal 4. Conceptual disorganization 5. Guilt feelings 6. Tension 7. Mannerisms and posturing 8. Grandiosity 9. Depressive mood	Time frame: past week 0–7 Highest possible score – 126

			10. Hostility 11. Suspiciousness 12. Hallucinatory behaviour 13. Motor retardation 14. Uncooperativeness 15. Unusual thought content 16. Blunted affect 17. Excitement 18. Disorientation Originally 16 items, but 2 added – 18-item most common Takes 20–30 mins to do	
PSYCHOSIS & MANIA				
CARS-M^ (paper copy) Altman, E., Hedeker, D., Janicak, P., *et al.* (1994) The clinician-administered rating scale for mania (CARS-M): development, reliability, and validity. *Biological*	C	M/P	Clinicians also encouraged to use other info such as nursing and family reports. Includes two sub-scales: mania (items 1–10) and psychotic symptoms and disorganization (items 11–15) Takes 30 mins to do	Time frame: past week 0–5, except one item (insight) which is scored 0–4 Highest score = 74 Remission cutoff – 8 Mania subscale: 0–7 = none or questionable mania

Continued

445

TABLE 104: (*Continued*)

Scale/reference	Administ-ration+	Illness phase**	Items	Information
Psychiatry, *36*, 124–134.				8–15 = mild mania 16–25 = moderate mania >=26 severe No information on second subscale
PANSS (Positive and Negative Symptom Scale)	C	P	Measures severity of psychopathology in adults with schizophrenia, schizoaffective disorder and other psychotic disorders. 3 scales (30 items) 1 Positive scale (for example, delusions, conceptual disorganisation, hallucinatory behaviour) 2 Negative scale (for example, blunted affect, emotional withdrawal, poor rapport) 3 General Psychopathology scales (somatic concern, anxiety, guilt feelings, mannerisms and posturing, motor retardation, uncooperativeness, disorientation, poor impulse control)	Time frame: previous week Individual items scored 1 to 7 Potential range: Positive scale –7 to 49 (50th percentile for people meeting DSM-III schizophrenia = 20) Negative scale –7 to 49 (50th percentile for people meeting DSM-III schizophrenia = 22) General Psychopathology – 16–112 (50th percentile for people meeting DSM-III schizophrenia = 40)

GENERAL FUNCTIONING

Longitudinal Interval Follow-Up Evaluation (LIFE). (paper copy) Keller, M. B., Lavori, P. W., Friedman, B., *et al.* (1987) The Longitudinal Interval Follow-up Evaluation. A comprehensive method for assessing outcome in prospective studies. *Archives of General Psychiatry, 44*, 540–548.	C	General functioning	1. Psychopathology (week-by-week psychiatric status ratings, suicide gestures and attempts, alcohol and other drug misuse) 2. Non-psychiatric medical illness 3. Treatment (week-by-week psychotropic drugs, ECT, psychotherapy) 4. Psychosocial functioning (work, household, student, interpersonal, sexual, satisfaction, recreation, global) 5. Overall severity 6. Narrative account	Can also use Composite scale score to indicate predominance of positive or negative symptoms – range from −42 to +42.
Medical Research Council (MRC) Social Performance Schedule (paper copy)	C	General functioning	8 areas of social activity: 1. Household management 2. Employment	Time frame: past month Each area rated: fair to good (0); serious

TABLE 104: (Continued)

Scale/reference	Administration+	Illness phase**	Items	Information
Hurry, J., Sturt, E., Bebbington, P., et al. (1983) Sociodemographic association with social disablement in a community sample. Social Psychiatry, 18, 113–121.			3. Management of money 4. Childcare 5. Intimate relationship with spouse or close friend 6. Other relationship 7. Social presentation of self 8. Coping with emergencies	problems on occasions but can sometimes manage quite well (1); serious problems most of the time (2); virtually no contribution (3) Overall score = sum of scores adjusted for number of applicable sections, expressed as % of max possible score. Semi-structured interview with obligatory questions, plus probe questions to use if necessary
GAS Global Assessment Scale (also GAF, which is a sub-set)	C	General functioning	Considers overall functioning	>0 = socially disabled Scored 1 to 100 divided into 10 equal ranges.

Notes
*May have some utility, though not the primary focus of the instrument
^In APA Handbook of Psychiatric Measures
**M(ania) D(epression) P(sychosis)
+ C(linician) S(elf-report)

APPENDIX 12:

QUALITY CHECKLIST FOR HEALTH

ECONOMICS STUDIES

FULL ECONOMIC EVALUATIONS

Author: **Date:**

Title:

STUDY DESIGN

	Yes	No	NA
1. The research question is stated	☐	☐	
2. The economic importance of the research question is stated	☐	☐	
3. The viewpoint(s) of the analysis are clearly stated and justified	☐	☐	
4. The rationale for choosing the alternative programmes or interventions compared is stated	☐	☐	
5. The alternatives being compared are clearly described	☐	☐	
6. The form of economic evaluation used is stated	☐	☐	
7. The choice of form of economic evaluation used is justified in relation to the questions addressed	☐	☐	

DATA COLLECTION

	Yes	No	NA
1. The source of effectiveness data used is stated	☐	☐	
2. Details of the design and results of effectiveness study are given (if based on a single study)	☐	☐	☐
3. Details of the method of synthesis or meta-analysis of estimates are given (if based on an overview of a number of effectiveness studies)	☐	☐	☐
4. The primary outcome measure(s) for the economic evaluation are clearly stated	☐	☐	
5. Methods to value health states and other benefits are stated	☐	☐	☐
6. Details of the subjects from whom valuations were obtained are given	☐	☐	☐
7. Indirect costs (if included) are reported separately	☐	☐	☐

449

	Yes	No	NA
8. The relevance of indirect costs to the study question is discussed	☐	☐	☐
9. Quantities of resources are reported separately from their unit costs	☐	☐	
10. Methods for the estimation of quantities and unit costs are described	☐	☐	
11. Currency and price data are recorded	☐	☐	
12. Details of currency of price adjustments for inflation or currency conversion are given	☐	☐	☐
13. Details of any model used are given	☐	☐	☐
14. The choice of model used and the key parameters on which it is based are justified	☐	☐	☐

ANALYSIS AND INTERPRETATION OF RESULTS

	Yes	No	NA
1. Time horizon of costs and benefits is stated	☐	☐	
2. The discount rate(s) is stated	☐	☐	☐
3. The choice of rate(s) is justified	☐	☐	☐
4. An explanation is given if costs or benefits are not discounted	☐	☐	☐
5. Details of statistical tests and confidence intervals are given for stochastic data	☐	☐	☐
6. The approach to sensitivity analysis is given	☐	☐	☐
7. The choice of variables for sensitivity analysis is given	☐	☐	☐
8. The ranges over which the variables are varied are stated	☐		
9. Relevant alternatives are compared	☐	☐	
10. Incremental analysis is reported	☐	☐	☐
11. Major outcomes are presented in a disaggregated as well as aggregated form	☐	☐	
12. The answer to the study question is given	☐	☐	
13. Conclusions follow from the data reported	☐	☐	
14. Conclusions are accompanied by the appropriate caveats	☐	☐	

Validity score Yes/No/NA:

APPENDIX 13:
DATA EXTRACTION FORM FOR HEALTH ECONOMICS STUDIES

Reviewer: Date of review:

Authors: Publication date:

Title:

Country: Language:

Interventions compared:

Patient population:

Setting:

Economic study design:

Perspective of the analysis:

Time frame of the analysis:

Modelling:

Source of data for effect size measures:

Primary outcome measures:

Costs included:

Source of resource use and unit costs:

Currency: Price year:

Discounting (costs/benefits):

Sensitivity analysis:

Effectiveness results:

Cost results:

Cost-effectiveness results:

Authors' conclusions:

Comments – limitations:

APPENDIX 14:

HEALTH ECONOMICS EVIDENCE TABLES

PROVISION OF SERVICES: COMMUNITY MENTAL HEALTH TEAMS

References to included studies

BURNS1991

Burns, T., Beadsmoore, A., Ashok, V. B., *et al.* (1993) A controlled trial of home-based acute psychiatric services. I: clinical and social outcome. *British Journal of Psychiatry*, *163*, 49–54.

Burns, T., Raftery, J., Beadsmoore, A., *et al.* (1993) A controlled trial of home-based acute psychiatric services. II: treatment patterns and costs. *British Journal of Psychiatry*, *163*, 55–61.

GATER1997

Gater, R., Goldberg, D., Jackson, G., *et al.* (1997) The care of patients with chronic schizophrenia: a comparison between two services. *Psychological Medicine*, *27*, 1325–1336.

MERSON1992

Merson, S., Tyrer, P., Carlen, D., *et al.* (1996) The cost of treatment of psychiatric emergencies: a comparison of hospital and community services. *Psychological Medicine*, *26*, 727–734.

Merson, S., Tyrer, P., Onyett, S., *et al.* (1992) Early intervention in psychiatric emergencies: a controlled clinical trial. *Lancet*, *339*, 1311–1314.

TYRER1998

Tyrer, P., Evans, K., Gandhi, N., *et al.* (1998) Randomized controlled trial of two models of care for discharged psychiatric patients. *BMJ*, *316*, 106–109.

TABLE 105: HEALTH ECONOMICS EVIDENCE

Study ID and country	Intervention details	Study population Setting Study design – data source	Study type	Costs: description and values Outcomes: description and values	Results: cost effectiveness	Comments Internal validity (Yes/No/NA) Industry support
BURNS 1991 UK	Intervention: Home-based CMHT Comparator: Standard community care	Patients aged 18–74 years, with severe mental illness, not in treatment during the previous 12 months Community Data source of effect size measures & resource use: RCT; CMHT n = 94 Standard care n = 78	Cost-consequences analysis	Costs: Direct medical costs: inpatient, outpatient, day care, specialist care, GPs Direct non-medical costs: local authority social work Mean treatment cost per patient: CMHT £1,429, control £1,696 Non-significant differences in cost between the groups Outcomes: clinical outcomes, social functioning and patient satisfaction measured using the BPRS, the clinical interview for measuring changes in depression and mixed neurotic disorders, the Social Functioning Schedule (SFS), the Consumer Satisfaction Scale, the Family Burden Scale, the carers' assessment of patients' symptoms and social functioning, and the Carers' Satisfaction Scale	Not applicable	Perspective: health and social services Currency: UK £ Cost year: 1987/1988 Discounting: not needed Time horizon: 1 year Analysis based on intention-to-treat Internal validity: 16/5/14

Continued

453

TABLE 105: (*Continued*)

Study ID and country	Intervention details	Study population Setting Study design – data source	Study type	Costs: description and values Outcomes: description and values	Results: cost effectiveness	Comments Internal validity (Yes/No/NA) Industry support
				Non-significant differences in outcomes between groups		
GATER 1997 UK	Intervention: CMHT

Comparator: Hospital-based care | Patients aged 16–65 years, with chronic schizophrenia (onset of symptoms more than 3 years prior to the study and either symptomatic or on medication over 2 years prior to the study) | Cost-consequences analysis | Costs:
Direct health service costs: CMHT, inpatient, outpatient, day hospital, community nursing, depot clinic, psychology, occupational and industrial therapy
Other direct costs (local authority and other services)
Direct and indirect patient and carer costs: money and time
Benefits: patients' earned income

Mean service cost per patient: CMHT £1,879, hospital £1,634
Mean total (societal) cost per patient: CMHT £4,403, hospital £3,849
Non-significant differences in cost between the groups | Not applicable | Perspective: societal
Currency: UK £
Cost year: not stated
Discounting: not needed
Time horizon: 12 months for costs; 2 years for outcomes
Analysis based on intention-to-treat
Internal validity: 15/8/12 |

	Community versus tertiary care Data source of effect size measures and resource use: clustered RCT; CMHT n = 42 Hospital n = 47	Outcomes: Quality of care, expressed as patients' problems and needs of care, and the extent to which these needs were being met, measured using the MRC Needs for Care Schedule Clinical problems: more met needs (P < 0.001) and fewer unmet needs (P < 0.001) for CMHT compared with hospital Social problems: similar met needs (P was non-significant) and fewer unmet needs (P < 0.05) for CMHT compared with hospital CMHT group significantly more satisfied compared with hospital group	Not applicable	Perspective: health and social services Currency: UK £ Cost year: not stated Discounting: not needed Time horizon: 3 months
MERSON 1992 UK	Intervention: Early intervention by CMHT	Patients aged 16–65 years with a psychiatric disorder other than primary alcohol or drug dependence, presenting as psychiatric	Cost-consequences analysis	Costs: Direct health service costs: CMHT, hospital (inpatient, outpatient, day hospital, clinical psychologist, A&E), primary care (GP, district nurse, practice nurse) Other direct costs: social services (social worker, day centre), custodial services (police custody, policed contact, probation officer)

Continued

TABLE 105: (*Continued*)

Study ID and country	Intervention details	Study population Setting Study design – data source	Study type	Costs: description and values Outcomes: description and values	Results: cost effectiveness	Comments Internal validity (Yes/No/NA) Industry support
	Comparator: Standard hospital psychiatric treatment	emergencies but not requiring mandatory inpatient psychiatric admission Community versus secondary care Data source of effect size measures and resource use: RCT; CMHT n = 48 Hospital n = 52		Mean cost per patient: CMHT £1,161, control £2,501 Median cost per patient: CMHT £938, control £610 Difference in median costs: £237 (95% CI −£51 to +£500) Outcomes: Psychiatric symptoms and signs measured using the Comprehensive Psychopathological Rating Scale (CPRS) and its subscales for depression (MADRS) and anxiety (Brief Anxiety Scale, BAS); social functioning measured using the Social Functioning Questionnaire (SFQ); patient satisfaction Significantly greater improvements in CPRS (p = 0.019) and BAS (0.039) but		Analysis based on treatment completers Internal validity: 16/5/14

	Full results on clinical effectiveness on n = 85		not in MADRS (p = 0.082) for CMHT group compared with control group; non-significant differences in clinical outcomes between groups when substituted values for missing results added (p > 0.05) Non-significant differences in SFQ improvements between groups Significantly greater satisfaction of patients in CMHT group (p < 0.001)	
TYRER 1998 UK	Intervention: CMHT Comparator: Hospital-based care	Patients aged 16–65 years, with severe mental illness (psychosis or severe non-psychotic mood disorder) and at least one previous psychiatric	Cost-consequences analysis	Costs: Direct medical costs: community psychiatric services, primary care, hospital psychiatric and general services, miscellaneous Direct non-medical costs: social services Mean total cost per patient: CMHT £16,765 Hospital £19,125 No statistically significant differences in costs between groups	Not applicable	Perspective: health and social services Currency: UK £ Cost year: not stated Discounting: not needed Time horizon: 1 year analysis based on intention-to-treat

Continued

457

TABLE 105: (*Continued*)

Study ID and country	Intervention details	Study population Setting Study design – data source	Study type	Costs: description and values Outcomes: description and values	Results: cost effectiveness	Comments Internal validity (Yes/No/NA) Industry support
		admission within the previous 3 years Community versus secondary care Data source of effect size measures and resource use: RCT; CMHT n = 82 Hospital n = 73		Outcomes: Ratings of clinical psychopathology, depression, anxiety and social functioning No statistically significant differences in outcomes between groups		Internal validity: 14/7/14

PROVISION OF SERVICES: CASE MANAGEMENT

References to included studies

BURNS1999(UK700)

UK700 Group (2000) Cost-effectiveness of intensive v. standard case management for severe psychotic illness. UK700 case management trial. *British Journal of Psychiatry, 176*, 537–543.

FORD1995

Ford, R., Raftery, J., Ryan, P., *et al.* (1997) Intensive case management for people with serious mental illness – site 2: cost-effectiveness. *Journal of Mental Health, 6*, 191–199.

Ford, R., Ryan, P., Beadsmoore, A., *et al.* (1997) Intensive case management for people with serious mental illness – site 2: clinical and social outcome. *Journal of Mental Health, 6*, 181–190.

FORD2001

Ford, R., Barnes, A., Davies, R., *et al.* (2001) Maintaining contact with people with severe mental illness: 5-year follow-up of assertive outreach. *Social Psychiatry & Psychiatric Epidemiology, 36*, 444–447.

MARSHALL1995

Gray, A.M., Marshall, M., Lockwood, A., *et al.* (1997) Problems in conducting economic evaluations alongside clinical trials. Lessons from a study of case management for people with mental disorders. *British Journal of Psychiatry, 170*, 47–52.

Marshall, M., Lockwood, A., Gath, D. (1995) Social services case-management for long-term mental disorders: a randomised controlled trial. *Lancet, 345*, 409–415.

MUIJEN1994

McCrone, P., Beecham, J. & Knapp, M. (1994) Community psychiatric nurse teams: cost-effectiveness of intensive support versus generic care. *British Journal of Psychiatry, 165*, 218–221.

Muijen, M., Cooney, M., Strathdee, G., *et al.* (1994). Community psychiatric nurse teams: Intensive support versus generic care. *British Journal of Psychiatry, 165*, 211–217.

RUTTER2004

Rutter, D., Tyrer, P. & Emmanuel, J., *et al.* (2004) Internal vs. external care management in severe mental illness: randomized controlled trial and qualitative study. *Journal of Mental Health, 13*, 453–466.

TABLE 106: HEALTH ECONOMICS EVIDENCE

Study ID and country	Intervention details	Study population / Setting / Study design – data source	Study type	Costs: description and values / Outcomes: description and values	Results: cost effectiveness	Comments / Internal validity (Yes/No/NA) / Industry support
BURNS 1999 (UK700) UK	Intervention: ICM; caseload 10–15 Comparator: Standard case management (SCM); caseload 30–35	Patients aged 18–65 years, with psychotic illness of at least 2 years and a history of repeated hospital admissions (at least two, one within the past 2 years). Exclusion criteria: organic brain damage or primary diagnosis of substance misuse Community Data source of effect size measures and resource use: multicentre	Cost-minimisation analysis	Costs: Direct medical: case managers, hospital (inpatient, outpatient, day care, A&E), primary care (GPs, nurses), medication Direct non-medical: accommodation, prison and police custody, social and non-statutory services Total costs per patient (mean, SD): ICM £24,553 (£23,408) SCM £22,704 (£22,000) Difference £1,849 (p = 0.29, 95%CI − £1,605 to £5,304) Non-significant difference between groups Primary outcome: number of days in hospital for psychiatric problems Number of days in hospital per patient (mean, sd): ICM 73.5 (124.2)	ICM and SCM were similar in terms of both costs and benefits	Perspective: all service-providing sectors Currency: UK £ Cost year: 1997/98 Discounting: 6% Time horizon: 24 months Analysis based on intention-to-treat Internal validity: 25/2/8

Study	Intervention / Comparator & patients	Study design / analysis	Outcomes	Costs	Methods
		RCT (four sites); randomisation stratified by centre. Economic analysis n = 667: ICM 335 SCM 332	SCM 73.1 (111.2) Difference 0.4 (p = 0.97, 95% CI −17.4 to 18.1) Non-significant difference between groups. Also: non-significant differences in secondary outcome measures (clinical status, quality of life, unmet needs, social disability, patient satisfaction).		
FORD 1995 UK	Intervention: ICM; maximum case load 15. Comparator: Standard psychiatric services. Patients with psychotic illness and either a recent inpatient admission, impairment in social functioning, problems in compliance with medication / treatment regimes, or problems in receiving necessary multi-agency care. Exclusion criteria: primary diagnosis of learning difficulty,	Cost-consequences analysis	Not applicable	Costs: Direct service costs: psychiatric services (inpatient, outpatient, CPN, other), medical inpatient and outpatient, case management, GPs, other primary care, day services, residential care, social worker, other social services. Total mean costs per patient (95% CI): ICM £21,759 (£16,450 to £27,067); control £8,604 (£5,574 to £11,633) Total median costs per patient: ICM £19,620; control £5,691 Costs in ICM group significantly higher than costs in the control group (p < 0.05)	Perspective: all publicly financed services Currency: UK £ Cost year: 1990/91 Discounting: not necessary Time horizon: 18 months Internal validity: 18/3/14

Continued

TABLE 106: (*Continued*)

Study ID and country	Intervention details	Study population Setting Study design – data source	Study type	Costs: description and values Outcomes: description and values	Results: cost effectiveness	Comments Internal validity (Yes/No/NA) Industry support
		alcohol/drug dependency or organic psychosis Community Data source of effect size measures and resource use: RCT; ICM n = 39 Control n = 38		<u>Outcomes:</u> Clinical symptoms measured using the BPRS; social functioning measured using the Life Skills Profile (LSP); patients' quality of life measured using the Lehman Quality of Life Interview Non-significant differences in outcomes between groups		
FORD 2001 UK	<u>Intervention 1:</u> Team providing intensive case management (caseload maximum 15 clients)	Patients with severe mental illness Community	Cost-consequences analysis	<u>Costs:</u> Direct medical: inpatient care, outpatient care, day care, ICM, CPN Direct non-medical: social worker, residential care	Not applicable	Perspective: health and social services Currency: UK £ Cost year: 1996/1997 Discounting: not

	Data source of effect size measures & resource use:			undertaken Time horizon: 18 months and 5 years Internal validity: 18/5/12
for 5 years (ICM1) Intervention 2: Team providing ICM (caseload maximum 15 clients) for 18 months, then amalgamated with local CPNs, retaining case management culture but with responsibility for more clients (ICM2) Intervention 3: Team providing intensive case management (caseload	multi-site prospective cohort study Follow-up at 18 months: n = 128 ICM1 45 ICM2 47 ICM3 36 Follow-up at 5 years: n = 120 (all live subjects included) ICM1 43 ICM2 47 ICM3 30	Mean annualised costs per patient (mean, SD): At 0–18 months: ICM1: £10,974 (£9,039) ICM2: £13,132 (£11,949) ICM3: £12,654 (£11,549) Non-significant difference between groups At 18 months – 5 years: ICM1: £13,734 (£10,820) ICM2: £11,037 (£13,603) ICM3: £5,742 (£7,007) Significant differences between groups after controlling for severity of mental health problems (p = 0.015) Outcomes: Clinical outcomes measured using the BPRS; social functioning measured using the LSP No significant differences in the mean total BPRS or LSP scores at follow-up, after controlling for baseline differences		

Continued

Study ID and country	Intervention details	Study population Setting Study design – data source	Study type	Costs: description and values Outcomes: description and values	Results: cost effectiveness	Comments Internal validity (Yes/No/NA) Industry support
	maximum 15 clients) for 18 months, then disbanded and patients transferred to other services (ICM3)					
MARSHALL 1995 UK	Intervention: Case management Comparator: Standard care (defined as any care received before the study)	Patients with severe, persistent psychiatric disorder; homeless, or at risk of homelessness, or living in temporary, supported, or poor quality accommodation; coping	Cost-consequences analysis	Costs: Direct medical: general and psychiatric care (hospital, day care, home visits, GPs, occupational therapy, medication) Direct non-medical: local welfare services (day centres, social workers), accommodation, law enforcement agencies, state benefits, supported employment, resources for untoward and non-routine events involving patients Total weekly cost per patient (mean, 95% CI): Case management £249 (£215-£288); control £272 (£224-£329)	Not applicable	Perspective: all service providing sectors Currency: UK £ Cost year: 1993/1994 Discounting: not needed Time horizon: 14 months Analysis based on treatment completers Study sample found to be far too

Study	Intervention	Patients / Design	Type of analysis	Results	Perspective
		badly, experiencing social isolation or causing disturbances; not clines of another case-management service Community Data source of effect size measures & resource use: RCT: Case management n = 40 Control n = 40 Dropout rate: 13.7% (11/80)	Not applicable	No significant difference in costs between groups Outcomes: Need for psychiatric and social care using a modified version of the MRC Needs for Care Schedule; quality of life in terms of employment status, accommodation, subjects' own ratings on the Lehman Quality of Life Interview; social behaviour rated by observers with a standardised behaviour scale (REHAB) and by patients with the Social Integration Questionnaire; severity of psychiatric symptoms using the Manchester Scale No statistically significant differences in outcomes between groups, with the exception of REHAB deviant behaviour score which was significantly better for the case management group	small to detect large differences in costs Internal validity: 17/4/14
MUIJEN 1994 UK	Intervention: Community support team with staff acting as case	Patients aged 18–64 years, with a psychotic	Cost-consequences analysis	Costs: Direct medical: general and mental health care (hospital inpatient + outpatient, day care, healthcare professionals) Direct non-medical: accommodation and	Perspective: all service-providing sectors Currency: UK £

Continued

465

Study ID and country	Intervention details	Study population, Setting Study design – data source	Study type	Costs: description and values, Outcomes: description and values	Results: cost effectiveness	Comments, Internal validity (Yes/No/NA), Industry support
	managers Comparator: Generic CPN care	disorder (schizophrenia or affective psychosis) lasting more than 2 years and at least two hospital admissions in the previous 2 years. Patients with primary organic disorders excluded. Community Data source of effect size measures and resource use: RCT: Community support team n = 41 Control n = 41		living costs, local social care services (day centres, social workers), law and order services (police, court), education services, employment services, voluntary sector services Total weekly cost per patient (mean, SD): Case management £285 (£165) Control £395 (£269) Difference in costs: £110, not statistically significant Driven mainly by a significant difference at 6 months: Case management £277 (£181), control £419 (£355), $p < 0.05$ Outcomes: Clinical outcomes measured using the GAS, the Present State Examination (PSE), and the BPRS; social and behavioural functioning using the Social Adjustment Scale (SAS); patient and carer satisfaction		Cost year: 1992/1993 Discounting: not needed Time horizon: 18 months Analysis based on treatment completers Internal validity: 18/3/14

	Cost data at 18 months: Community Support team 32 Control 29		No statistically significant differences in outcomes between groups			
RUTTER 2004 UK	Intervention: Internal care management, where the case manager (social worker) is part of the multidisciplinary team Comparator: External care management (ECM), where the case manager operates externally to the health-care team	Patients with SMI Integrated care Data source of effect size measures and resource use: RCT: Internal care management n = 13 ECM n = 13	Cost-effectiveness analysis	Costs: Direct medical: hospital, day care, psychiatrists, psychologists, CPNs, GPs, counselling, medication Direct non-medical: social workers, day care, accommodation, criminal justice Total cost per patient (mean, SD): Internal care management £16,792 (£13,011) ECM £15,132 (£12,258) ΔC £1,661 (95%CI −£8,572 to £11,893) Non-significant difference in costs between groups Primary outcome: Number of days spent in hospital Mean number of days spent in hospital per patient: Internal care management 58.3, ECM 42.4 Non-significant difference in outcomes between groups	There were no significant differences in outcomes or costs between internal care management and ECM	Perspective: all service providing sectors Currency: UK £ Cost year: 1999/2000 Discounting: not necessary Time horizon: 6 months Analysis based on intention-to-treat Internal validity: 18/3/14

Δ = difference in cost

Continued

467

PROVISION OF SERVICES: CRISIS RESOLUTION AND HOME TREATMENT TEAMS

References to included studies

JOHNSON2005A

McCrone, P., Johnson, S., Nolan, F., *et al.* Impact of a crisis resolution team on service costs. Unpublished

Johnson, S., Nolan, F., Hoult, J., *et al.* Outcomes of crises before and after introduction of a crisis resolution team. *British Journal of Psychiatry, 187*, 68–75.

MUIJEN1992

Knapp, M., Marks, I.M., Wolstenholme, J., *et al.* (1998) Home-based versus hospital-based care for serious mental illness: controlled cost-effectiveness study over four years. *British Journal of Psychiatry, 172*, 506–512.

Knapp, M., Beecham, J., Koutsogeorgopoulou, V., *et al.* (1994) Service use and costs of home-based versus hospital-based care for people with serious mental illness. *British Journal of Psychiatry, 165*, 195–203.

Marks, I.M., Connolly, J., Muijen, M., *et al.* (1994) Home-based versus hospital-based care for people with serious mental illness. *British Journal of Psychiatry, 165*, 179–194.

Muijen, M., Marks, I.M., Connolly, J., *et al.* (1992) Home based care and standard hospital care for patients with severe mental illness: a randomised controlled trial. *BMJ, 304*, 749–754.

TABLE 107: HEALTH ECONOMICS EVIDENCE

Study ID and country	Intervention details	Study population Setting Study design – data source	Study type	Costs: description and values Outcomes: description and values	Results: cost effectiveness	Comments Internal validity (Yes/No/NA) Industry support
JOHNSON 2005A UK	Intervention: CRHTT Comparator: Standard care following a psychiatric crisis	Patients aged 18–65 years, with SMI presenting to secondary mental health services with a psychiatric crisis Community versus secondary care Data source of effect size measures and resource use: quasi-experimental study	Cost-consequences analysis	Costs: Direct service: CRHTT, inpatient, day care, crisis house, residential care, staff (psychiatrist, other clinician, GP, psychologist, CPN, practice nurse), casualty, social worker, criminal justice system Total cost per patient at 6 months (mean, SD): 6 months: CRHTT £8,094 (£7,268), control £9,746 (£7,962) Non-significant difference in costs after adjusting for patient characteristics Primary outcomes: Admission rate; patient satisfaction using the Client Satisfaction Questionnaire (CSQ-8) Secondary outcomes: Changes in the BPRS, Health of the Nation Outcome Scale (HoNOS),	Not applicable	Perspective: health and social services Currency: UK £ Cost year: 2001 Discounting: not necessary Time horizon: 6 months (some outcomes evaluated at 6 weeks) Analysis based on intention-to-treat Internal validity: 18/3/14

Continued

469

TABLE 107: (Continued)

Study ID and country	Intervention details	Study population Setting Study design – data source	Study type	Costs: description and values Outcomes: description and values	Results: cost effectiveness	Comments Internal validity (Yes/No/NA) Industry support
		CRHTT n = 123 Control n = 77 Service use based on CRHTT n = 116 Control n = 65		Manchester Short Assessment of Quality of Life (MANSA), Life Skills Profile (LSP); adverse events Admission rate: 6 weeks: CRHTT 49%, control 71%; odds ratio 0.38 (95% CI 0.21 – 0.70, p = 0.002) 6 months: CRHTT 60%, control 75%; odds ratio 0.49 (95% CI 0.26 – 0.93, p = 0.029) Patient satisfaction at 6 weeks: significantly higher for CRHTT group (p < 0.0005) Non-significant differences in other outcomes between groups		
MUIJEN 1992, UK	Intervention: Home-based community care (Daily Living	Patients aged 17–64 years, with SMI	Cost-consequences analysis	Costs: Direct medical: DLP, inpatient, outpatient, day care, staff Direct non-medical: accommodation, social services, social	Not applicable	Perspective: societal Currency: UK £ Cost year: 1996/97

Programme, DLP) Comparator: Standard care (inpatient followed by outpatient care)	(schizophrenia or severe affective disorder) facing crisis inpatient admission; exclusion criteria: primary addiction, acute or chronic organic brain syndrome, pregnancy Community versus secondary care Data source of effect size measures and resource use: RCT Phase I (1–20 months); DLP n = 92, control n = 97	benefits, patients' and carers' resources, criminal justice system Indirect: lost employment, informal care Total direct service weekly costs per patient (mean, SD) Months 1–20: DLP £286 (£142), control £522 (£352), p = 0.015 Months 30–34: continuing DLP £164 (£68), DLP-to-control £277 (£214), p = 0.001 Months 35–45: continuing DLP £196 (£75), DLP-to-control £294 (£330), control £272 (£273), non-significant difference Months 1–45: continuing DLP £188 (£123), DLP-to-control £218 (£113), control £287 (£175) DLP versus control p = 0.002 Continuing DLP versus control p = 0.002 Continuing DLP versus DLP-to-control p = 0.328 No evidence of significant differences in indirect costs	Discounting: not undertaken Time horizon: Phase I: 20 months Phase II: 45 months Clinical analysis based on intention-to-treat Cost analysis based on DLP 74, control 70 (1-20 months), continuing DLP 32, DLP-to-control 28, control 70 (30-45 months) Internal validity: 18/5/12

Continued

TABLE 107: *(Continued)*

Study ID and country	Intervention details	Study population Setting Study design – data source	Study type	Costs: description and values Outcomes: description and values	Results: cost effectiveness	Comments Internal validity (Yes/No/NA) Industry support
		Phase II (30–45 months): Re-randomisation of DLP patients who had received at least 18 months of DLP care; Continuing DLP n = 33, DLP-to-control n = 33; Remaining control n = 70		Outcomes: Improvements in GAS, 9th edition of Present State Examination (PSE), BPRS, Social Adjustment Scale (SAS), Daily Living Skills rating (DLS), patients' and carers' satisfaction. DLP improved symptoms and social adjustment slightly but significantly (phase I) and enhanced patients' and carers' satisfaction (both phases).		

PROVISION OF SERVICES: ACUTE DAY HOSPITALS

References to included studies

CREED1997

Creed, F., Mbaya, P., Lancashire, S., *et al.* (1997) Cost effectiveness of day and inpatient psychiatric treatment: results of a randomised controlled trial. *BMJ, 314,* 1381–1385.

TABLE 108: HEALTH ECONOMICS EVIDENCE

Study ID and country	Intervention details	Study population Setting Study design – data source	Study type	Costs: description and values Outcomes: description and values	Results: cost effectiveness	Comments Internal validity (Yes/No/NA) Industry support
CREED 1997 UK	Intervention: Day hospital treatment Comparator: Routine inpatient care	Patients aged 18-65 years with acute psychiatric illness, presenting for hospital admission; exclusion criteria: compulsory admission, mental condition too severe for day treatment, discharge within 5 days, admissions solely for detoxification of drugs and alcohol, diagnosis of organic	Cost-consequences analysis	Costs: Direct service costs: hospital (inpatient, day care), other mental health services, specialists, GPs, CPNs, medication, social workers Direct patient and carer costs: travelling, increased household expenses Indirect costs: earning losses of patients and carers Direct median hospital costs: Day hospital £2,370, inpatient £5,296; ΔC = £1,923, p < 0.001 Other median direct service costs: Day hospital £163, inpatient £180; ΔC = 11, p = 0.63 Total median costs including direct patient & carer direct and indirect costs: Day hospital £2,880, inpatient £5,931; ΔC = £2,165, p = 0.001	Not applicable	Perspective: societal Currency: UK £ Cost year: 1994/1995 Discounting: not needed Time horizon: 12 months Analysis based on intention-to-treat Internal validity: 19/4/12

brain disease, personality disorder, or mania. Tertiary care Data source of effect size measures and resource use: RCT; Day hospital n = 90 Inpatient n = 89	<u>Outcomes:</u> Psychiatric symptoms measured using the CPRS; social role performance, abnormal behaviour and burden on care measured using the Social Behaviour Assessment Schedule; distress experienced by the carer measured using the General Health Questionnaire No statistically significant differences in clinical and social outcomes between groups, except burden on carers being significantly less in day hospital care	

Δ = difference in cost

PROVISION OF SERVICES: ASSERTIVE COMMUNITY TREATMENT/ASSERTIVE OUTREACH TEAMS

References to included studies

HARRISON-READ2002

Harrison-Read, P., Lucas, B., Tyrer, P., *et al.* (2002) Heavy users of acute psychiatric beds: randomized controlled trial of enhanced community management in an outer London borough. *Psychological Medicine, 32*, 403–416.

TABLE 109: HEALTH ECONOMICS EVIDENCE

Study ID and country	Intervention details	Study population Setting Study design – data source	Study type	Costs: description and values / Outcomes: description and values	Results: cost effectiveness	Comments Internal validity (Yes/No/NA) Industry support
HARRISON-READ2002 UK	Intervention: Assertive community treatment (ACT) complementary to standard care Comparator: Standard care alone (local psychiatric services)	Patients aged between 16–64 with severe mental illness, heaviest users of psychiatric inpatient services according to number of hospital admissions and number of bed days (median number of 5 admissions over 6.5 years). Community Source of outcome	Cost-consequences analysis	Costs: Direct medical: mental health services (inpatient, outpatient, day-hospital, community team) Medication costs excluded from the analysis Total costs per patient (mean, SE): Year 0–1 ACT: £8,310 (£12,685) Control: £7,868 (£9,434) ΔC = £441 (95%CI −£2,735 to £3,617) p = 0.78 Year 1–2 ACT: £6,968 (£9,753) Control: £7,316 (£11,361) ΔC = −£347 (95%CI −£3,353 to £2,658) p = 0.82 Non-significant differences in costs between groups	Not applicable	Perspective: NHS Currency: UK £ Cost year: 1995–6 Discounting: not required Time horizon: 2 years Analysis based on intention-to-treat Internal validity: 20/2/13

Continued

Study ID and country	Intervention details	Study population Setting Study design – data source	Study type	Costs: description and values Outcomes: description and values	Results: cost effectiveness	Comments Internal validity (Yes/No/NA) Industry support
		measure and resource use: RCT; ACT n = 97, control n = 96		Outcomes: Improvements in the HoNOS, the Krawiecka Scale (KS), the Camberwell Assessment of Need (CAN), and three subject-rated scales: the SFQ, the Hospital Anxiety and Depression Scale (HADS), and a modified form of the Well-Being Questionnaire (WBQ). Non-significant differences in outcomes between groups		

Δ = difference in cost

PROVISION OF SERVICES: VOCATIONAL REHABILITATION

References to included studies

SCHNEIDER1997

Hallam, A. & Schneider, J. (1999) Sheltered work schemes for people with severe mental health problems: service use and costs. *Journal of Mental Health*, *8*, 171–186.

Schneider, J. & Hallam A. (1997) Specialist work schemes: user satisfaction and costs. *Psychiatric Bulletin*, *21*, 331–333.

TABLE 110: HEALTH ECONOMICS EVIDENCE

Study ID and country	Intervention details	Study population Setting Study design – data source	Study type	Costs: description and values Outcomes: description and values	Results: cost effectiveness	Comments Internal validity (Yes/No/NA) Industry support
SCHNEIDER 1997 UK	Intervention 1: Sheltered workshop for prevocational training (VOC) Intervention 2: Clubhouse approach of prevocational training (CLB)	Patients with severe mental illness Community Data source of effect size measures and resource use: Cross-sectional study VOC n = 16 CLB n = 20	Cost-consequences analysis	Costs: Direct medical: hospital (inpatient, outpatient, A&E), mental health services (psychiatry, psychology, community-based care), GPs, opticians, dentists, medication Direct non-medical: work scheme, social work, day care, accommodation, personal expenditure, miscellaneous (jobcentre, education, legal, sport, holidays, other)	Not applicable	Perspective: health and social care Currency: UK £ Cost year: 1994/1995 Discounting: not relevant Internal validity: 14/7/14

Other work schemes, not reviewed in the guideline, also examined		Total mean weekly costs per subject: VOC £272.93; CLB £307.11 Work schemes' net costs per placement: VOC £3,449; CLB £6,172 <u>Outcomes:</u> Patient satisfaction and size of personal social networks No statistically significant differences in patient satisfaction or size of personal social networks between schemes

Appendix 14

PHARMACOLOGICAL MANAGEMENT: TREATMENT OF ACUTE MANIC EPISODES

References to included studies

BRIDLE2004

Bridle, C., Palmer, S., Bagnall, A.M., *et al.* (2004) A rapid and systematic review and economic evaluation of the clinical and cost-effectiveness of newer drugs for treatment of mania associated with bipolar affective disorder. *Health Technology Assessment, 8,* 1–187.

KECK1996

Keck, P.E. Jr, Nabulsi, A.A., Taylor, J.L., *et al.* (1996) A pharmacoeconomic model of divalproex vs. lithium in the acute and prophylactic treatment of bipolar I disorder. *Journal of Clinical Psychiatry, 57,* 213–222.

REVICKI2005

Revicki D.A., Hirschfeld R.M.A., Ahearn E.P., *et al.* (2005) Effectiveness and medical costs of divalproex versus lithium in the treatment of bipolar disorder: results of a naturalistic clinical trial. *Journal of Affective Disorders, 86,* 183–193.

TOHEN1999A

Namjoshi M.A., Rajamannar G., Jacobs T., *et al.* (2002) Economic, clinical, and quality-of-life outcomes associated with olanzapine treatment in mania: results from a randomized controlled trial. *Journal of Affective Disorders, 69,* 109–118.

Tohen, M., Sanger, T.M., McElroy, S.L., *et al.* (1999) Olanzapine versus placebo in the treatment of acute mania. Olanzapine HGAY Study Group. *American Journal of Psychiatry, 156,* 702–709.

TOHEN2002A

Zhu B., Tunis S.L., Zhao Z., *et al.* (2005) Service utilization and costs of olanzapine versus divalproex treatment for acute mania: results from a randomized, 47-week clinical trial. *Current Medical Research and Opinion, 21,* 555–564.

Tohen, M., Ketter, T.A., Zarate, C.A., *et al.* (2003) Olanzapine versus divalproex sodium for the treatment of acute mania and maintenance of remission: a 47 week study. *American Journal of Psychiatry, 160,* 1263–1271.

Tohen, M., Baker, R.W., Altshuler, L.L., *et al.* (2002) Olanzapine versus divalproex in the treatment of acute mania. *American Journal of Psychiatry, 159,* 1011–1017.

ZAJECKA2002

Revicki, D.A., Paramore, C., Sommerville, K.W., *et al.* (2003) Divalproex sodium versus olanzapine in the treatment of acute mania in bipolar disorder: health-related quality of life and medical cost outcomes. *Journal of Clinical Psychiatry, 64,* 288–294.

Zajecka, J.M., Weisler, R., Sachs, G., *et al.* (2002) A comparison of the efficacy, safety, and tolerability of divalproex sodium and olanzapine in the treatment of bipolar disorder. *Journal of Clinical Psychiatry, 63,* 1148–1155.

TABLE 111: HEALTH ECONOMICS EVIDENCE

Study ID and country	Intervention details	Study population Setting Study design – data source	Study type	Costs: description and values Outcomes: description and values	Results: cost effectiveness	Comments Internal validity (Yes/No/NA) Industry support
BRIDLE 2004, UK	Intervention: Quetiapine 619.2 mg/day Olanzapine 16.2 mg/day Valproate semisodium 1513.5 mg/day Comparator: Lithium 1417 mg/day Haloperidol 10.4 mg/day	Patients with bipolar disorder experiencing an acute manic episode Secondary care Probabilistic model for the evaluation of cost effectiveness Data source of effect size measures: systematic review and meta-analysis (seven studies included)	Cost-effectiveness analysis	Costs: Direct medical: hospitalisation, drug acquisition, specific diagnostic and laboratory tests required for monitoring Costs of adverse events excluded Quetiapine £3,165 Olanzapine £3,161 Valproate semisodium £3,139 Lithium £3,162 Haloperidol £3,047 Primary outcome: Response rate, based on ≥50% improvement in a patient's baseline manic symptoms, derived from an interview-based mania assessment scale (YMRS). Mean response rates (95% CI) Quetiapine 0.47 (0.38–0.55) Olanzapine 0.54 (0.46–0.62) Valproate semisodium 0.45 (0.37–0.54)	Lithium, valproate semisodium and quetiapine dominated by haloperidol ICER of olanzapine compared with haloperidol: £7,179 per additional responder Probabilistic analysis: Probability of agents being cost effective for maximum	Perspective: NHS Currency: UK £ Cost year: 2001–2002 Discounting: not necessary Time horizon: 3 weeks All patients assumed to be hospitalised during the total 3 weeks of time horizon examined Internal validity: 28/1/6 NHS HTA report

Study	Intervention/Comparator	Population/Data source	Analysis	Costs/Effectiveness	Results	Perspective
		Data source of resource use: assumptions, manufacturer submission		Lithium 0.50 (0.39–0.60) Haloperidol 0.52 (0.41–0.62)	willingness-to-pay $\lambda = £20,000$ per additional responder: Olanzapine 0.44 Haloperidol 0.37 Lithium 0.16 Quetiapine 0.02 Valproate semisodium 0.01	
KECK 1996, US	Intervention: Valproate semisodium rapid oral loading, 20 mg/kg/day Comparator: Lithium 900 mg/day,	Patients with bipolar I disorder, with classic mania, mixed mania or rapid cycling Secondary care	Cost-effectiveness analysis	Costs: Direct medical: Initial hospitalisation, drug acquisition, outpatient long-term care and related procedures, laboratory tests, concomitant medication, management of relapses, treatment of side effects Cost per patient:	Valproate semisodium dominated lithium (lithium was more costly and less effective)	Perspective: health service Currency: US $ Cost year: 1994 Discounting: not necessary Time horizon: 1 year of acute and

Continued

485

TABLE 111: (*Continued*)

Study ID and country	Intervention details	Study population Setting Study design – data source	Study type	Costs: description and values Outcomes: description and values	Results: cost effectiveness	Comments Internal validity (Yes/No/NA) Industry support
	titrated according to plasma levels obtained 4–5 days after initiation	Decision-analytic modelling Data source of effect size measures: Systematic review for response rates; other published and unpublished data and expert panel opinion for rest of input parameters Data source of resource use: Cohort study for length of initial hospitalisation;		Valproate semisodium $39,643 Lithium $43,400 Cost per patient with classic mania: Valproate semisodium $33,139 Lithium $31,426 Cost per patient with mixed mania: Valproate semisodium $43,672 Lithium $50,856 Cost per patient with rapid cycling: Valproate semisodium $42,792 Lithium $49,078 Primary outcome: response rate, based on ≥50% symptomatic improvement. Mean response rates: Valproate semisodium 0.59 Lithium 0.49	Results highly sensitive to length of initial hospitalisation: a 30% increase in the length of stay for valproate semisodium or a 37% decrease in the length of stay for lithium led to total costs being equal for the two drugs	long-term treatment following initial hospitalisation for a manic episode Validity score: 20/5/10 Funded by Abbott Laboratories

	Treatment/Comparator		Analysis	Costs/Outcomes		Perspective
REVICKI 2005, US	Treatment: Valproate semisodium added to usual psychiatric care (including other medications); initiated at 15 to 20 mg/kg/day or based on usual psychiatric practice. Comparator: Lithium added to usual psychiatric care (including other medications); dosed up to	expert panel for long-term care resource use. Patients with bipolar I disorder over 18 years of age, hospitalised for an acute manic or mixed episode. Secondary care. Data source of effect size measures and resources used: Multi-centre, open-label RCT (33 US sites) Valproate n = 112 Lithium n = 109	Cost-consequences analysis	Costs: Direct medical: hospitalisation, outpatient psychiatric physician, psychologist and other mental health provider visits, emergency room visits, home health service visits, medication. Mean (SE) total medical costs per patient: Valproate semisodium $28,911 ($3,599) Lithium $30,666 ($7,364), p = 0.693. Outcomes: Number of months without DSM-IV-level manic or depressive symptoms; patient functioning and quality of life measured using the MCS and PCS scores of the	Not applicable	Perspective: health service. Currency: US $ Cost year: 1997 Discounting: not needed. Time horizon: 1 year in total, consisting of an acute phase, extending from hospitalisation to hospital discharge, and a maintenance phase starting following discharge and continued for a total duration of 12 months. Analysis based on intention-to-treat

Continued

TABLE 111: (*Continued*)

Study ID and country	Intervention details	Study population / Setting / Study design – data source	Study type	Costs: description and values / Outcomes: description and values	Results: cost effectiveness	Comments / Internal validity (Yes/No/NA) / Industry support
	1800 mg/day during acute mania, between 900–1200 mg/day for maintenance therapy During acute episodes study drug dosages titrated so as to optimise clinical response	Entering maintenance phase: Valproate semisodium n = 104 Lithium n = 97 Analysis based on: Valproate semisodium n = 86 Lithium n = 86		PCS scores of the SF-36, the Mental Health Index (MHI-17) and a questionnaire on disability days; adverse events and continuation rates Number of months without DSM-IV mania or depression (mean, SD): Valproate semisodium 5.3 (4.6) Lithium 5.4 (4.4), p = 0.814 Non-significant differences in other outcomes between groups		Pragmatic, non-blind trial, under conditions of routine psychiatric practice Clinical, quality of life and medical resource use data collected by telephone interviews Validity score: 18/3/14 Funded by Abbott Laboratories

| TOHEN 1999A US | Treatment: Olanzapine 5–20 mg/day Comparator: Placebo | Patients with bipolar I disorder with a manic or mixed episode. Secondary care. Data source of effect size measures: RCT for a 3-week acute phase n = 70 olanzapine n = 69 placebo Mirror-image study for a 49-week open-label extension (all patients treated with olanzapine) | Cost-consequences analysis | Costs: Direct medical: inpatient stay; outpatient visits to psychiatrists, physicians, psychologists, social workers, case managers; day hospital treatment; emergency room visits; home health care visits; olanzapine. Excluded: costs of adjunctive medication; drug costs prior to trial. Monthly cost per patient (mean ± SD): 49-week phase: $649 ± $399. 12 months prior to trial: $1533 ± $2262 (p < 0.01). Outcomes: Clinical symptoms as measured by the YMRS; HRQOL measured using the SF-36 | Not applicable | Perspective: third party payer. Currency: US $. Cost year: 1995. Discounting: not needed. Over the 49-week period, lithium and fluoxetine allowed to patients with breakthrough symptoms. All patients initially hospitalised for minimum 1 week; no costs measured for acute phase; likely bias in probability of subsequent hospitalisations. Likely recall bias of resource use over 12 months prior to trial |

Continued

TABLE 111: *(Continued)*

Study ID and country	Intervention details	Study population Setting Study design – data source	Study type	Costs: description and values Outcomes: description and values	Results: cost effectiveness	Comments Internal validity (Yes/No/NA) Industry support
		Data source of resource use: Mirror-image study (costs of the 49-week open label phase compared with costs 12 months prior to trial) n = 76		Changes in YMRS scores, acute phase: Olanzapine −10.3 (baseline 28.6) Placebo −4.9 (baseline 27.6) (p = 0.02) Changes in YMRS scores, 49-week phase: all patients −11.8 (baseline 19.3) (p < 0.01) Changes in SF-36 scores: Acute phase: olanzapine +4.0, placebo −1.8 in 'physical functioning' (p = 0.02) 49-week phase: significant decrease in 'vitality'; significant increase in 'bodily pain', 'general health', 'role-emotional', 'social functioning'		Validity score: 18/3/14 Funded by Eli Lilly and Company

| TOHEN 2002A, US | Treatment: Olanzapine 5–20 mg/day Comparator: Valproate semisodium 500–2500 mg/ day | Patients with bipolar I disorder aged 18–75 years, hospitalised for an acute manic or mixed episode and with a YMRS total score of ≥20 at both screening and baseline. Secondary care Data source of effect size measures and resource use: Double-blind, multi-centre RCT (48 US sites) Acute phase (3 weeks): | Cost-consequences analysis | Costs: Direct medical: hospitalisation (full/partial), outpatient psychiatric physician and other mental health provider visits, emergency room visits, home visits by healthcare professionals, medication, laboratory tests Average annual total costs per patient: Olanzapine $14,967, valproate semisodium $15,801 (no statistically significant difference) Outcomes: Clinical improvement based on YMRS and rate of symptom remission (defined as YMRS score ≤12) at 3 weeks (acute phase); median time to remission of manic symptoms; dropout rates between 3–47 weeks Improvement in manic symptoms at 3 weeks: significantly greater for olanzapine | Not applicable | Perspective: healthcare system Currency: US $ Cost year: 1999–2000 Discounting: not required Time horizon: 47 weeks Analysis based on intention to treat No significant differences in demographic or baseline clinical variables between patients who did and patients who did not enter maintenance phase Resource use data collected by patient reports and medical records, where available |

Continued

491

TABLE 111: *(Continued)*

Study ID and country	Intervention details	Study population Setting Study design – data source	Study type	Costs: description and values Outcomes: description and values	Results: cost effectiveness	Comments Internal validity (Yes/No/NA) Industry support
		Olanzapine n = 125 Valproate semisodium n = 126 Maintenance phase (3–47 weeks): n = 147 (59% of acute phase) Olanzapine n = 77 Valproate semisodium n = 70		Rate of symptom remission at 3 weeks: olanzapine 54.4%, valproate semisodium 42.3% (statistically significant) Median time to remission of manic symptoms: olanzapine 14 days, valproate semisodium 62 days (statistically significant) Dropout rates between 3–47 weeks: similar in both groups		Validity score: 17/4/14 Funded by Eli Lilly and Company
ZAJECKA 2002 US	Treatment: Valproate semisodium; initiated at 20 mg/kg/day, could be increased by	Patients with bipolar I disorder between 18–65 years old, experiencing an acute manic episode	Cost-consequences analysis	Costs: Direct medical: hospitalisation and physicians' fee; emergency room; psychiatric, physician, psychologist or other mental health provider visits; home health service visits; medication	Not applicable	Perspective: health service Currency: US $ Cost year: not stated Discounting: not needed Time horizon: 12 weeks

500 mg/day on days 3 and 6 if clinically important symptoms or mania persisted. Max dose allowed: 1000 mg/day Comparator: Olanzapine; initiated at 10 mg/day, could be increased by 5 mg/day on days 3 and 6 if manic symptoms persisted Max dose allowed: 20 mg/day	Secondary care Data source of effect size measures and resources used: Double-blind, multi-centre RCT (21 US sites): Valproate semisodium n = 63 Olanzapine n = 57 Sample size for the economic analysis: Valproate semisodium n = 27 Olanzapine n = 25	Mean (±SD) outpatient costs: Valproate semisodium $541±$327 Olanzapine $1,080±$638 (p = 0.004) Mean (±SD) total medical costs: Valproate semisodium $13,703 ± $8,708 Olanzapine $15,180 ± $16,780 (p = 0.88) Outcomes: Clinical improvement based on MRS and the HRSD; HRQOL based on Q-LES-Q and restricted activity days. Changes in MRS scores at 3 weeks: Valproate semisodium −14.9 (baseline 30.8) Olanzapine −16.6 (baseline 32.3) (p = 0.368) Changes in Q-LES-Q scores (subjective feelings) at 12 weeks Valproate semisodium −4.4 Olanzapine −4.7 (p = 0.95)	Analysis based on intention to treat Initial hospital follow-up: 3 weeks; if no clinical improvement, then discontinuation of drugs Follow-up to 3 weeks: n = 78 (65%) HRQOL and medical resource use data collected by telephone interviews Validity score: 16/5/14 Funded by Abbott Laboratories

PHYSICAL MANAGEMENT: ELECTROCONVULSIVE THERAPY FOR ACUTE EPISODES

References to included studies

KUTCHER1995

Kutcher, S. & Robertson, H.A. (1995) Electroconvulsive therapy in treatment-resistant bipolar youth. *Journal of Child and Adolescent Psychopharmacology*, 5, 167–175.

TABLE 112: HEALTH ECONOMICS EVIDENCE

Study ID and country	Intervention details	Study population Setting Study design – data source	Study type	Costs: description and values Outcomes: description and values	Results: cost effectiveness	Comments Internal validity (Yes/No/NA) Industry support
KUTCHER 1995, Canada	Intervention: ECT (2 sessions per week, brief pulse method) Comparator: Standard pharmacological inpatient care	Adolescents and young adults (ages 16–22) with treatment-resistant acute bipolar episodes (either manic or depressive) Tertiary care Data source of effect size measures and resource use: retrospective comparative study; groups defined by self-selection 22 patients eligible for ECT; 16 agreed	Cost-consequences analysis	Costs: Hospital Resource use estimated: length of hospital stay Average cost per admission: ECT $58,608 Control group $143,264 Outcomes: Improvement in BPRS scores Side effects of ECT Length of hospitalisation BPRS: significant improvement overtime for both groups: ECT group p < 0.0001, control group p = 0.001 ECT group significantly lower BPRS scores at discharge than control group (p < 0.03) Side effects of ECT: generally	Not applicable	Perspective: hospital Currency: Canadian $ Cost year: not reported Discounting: not needed Time horizon: until hospital discharge follow-ing an acute manic or depressive episode Internal validity: 12/9/14

Continued

495

TABLE 112: *(Continued)*

Study ID and country	Intervention details	Study population Setting Study design – data source	Study type	Costs: description and values Outcomes: description and values	Results: cost effectiveness	Comments Internal validity (Yes/No/NA) Industry support
		(ECT group) and 6 denied (control group). Proportion of manic and depressive acute episodes within each group: 1:1		mild, in 28% of the 166 ECT sessions. Length of hospital stay (mean): ECT group 73.8 days, control group 176 days		

PSYCHOLOGICAL MANAGEMENT: COGNITIVE BEHAVIOURAL THERAPY

References to included studies

LAM2003

Lam, D., McCrone, P., Wright, K., *et al.* (2005) Cost-effectiveness of relapse-prevention cognitive therapy for bipolar disorder: 30-month study. *British Journal of Psychiatry*, *186*, 500–506.

Lam, D., Hayward, P., Watkings, E.R., *et al.* (2005) Outcome of a two-year follow-up of a cognitive therapy of relapse prevention in bipolar disorder. *American Journal of Psychiatry*, *162*, 324–329.

Lam, D., Watkings, E.R., Hayward, P., *et al.* (2003) A randomised controlled study of cognitive therapy for relapse prevention for bipolar affective disorder. Outcome of the first year. *Archives of General Psychiatry*, *60*, 145–152.

TABLE 113: HEALTH ECONOMICS EVIDENCE

Study ID and country	Intervention details	Study population Setting Study design – data source	Study type	Costs: description and values Outcomes: description and values	Results: cost effectiveness	Comments Internal validity (Yes/No/NA) Industry support
LAM2003, UK	Intervention: Cognitive behavioural therapy (CBT) added to standard care (CBT: 14 sessions on average for 6 months and two booster sessions for the following 6 months) Comparator: Standard care (mood stabilisers at a recommended	Patients with bipolar I disorder aged 18–70 years under long-term care, without a bipolar episode at the time of the study, who experienced frequent relapses despite the prescription of commonly used mood stabilisers Secondary care Source of both effect size measures and	Cost-effectiveness analysis	Costs: Direct health and social service Hospital care: inpatient (psychiatric and general), outpatient, day hospital, A&E Staff: psychiatrists, GPs, psychologists, social workers, counsellors, other therapists Community mental healthcare, day centres Residential care, support groups Medication Mean cost per patient: 12 months: CBT £4,383 (SD £5,264) Standard care £5,356 (SD £6,599) 30 months:	CBT added to standard care associated with lower costs compared with standard care alone; difference in costs not statistically significant CBT added to standard care significantly more effective than standard care alone Probabilistic analysis – net benefit approach:	Perspective: NHS and social care Currency: UK £ Cost year: 1999/2000 Discounting: not undertaken Resource use based on self report and hospital records Time horizon: 12 and 30 months Internal validity: 23/4/8

level and regular psychiatric outpatient follow-up)	resource use: RCT CBT group: n = 51 Control group: n = 52 Cost data at 30 months: CBT group: n = 43 Control group: n = 40	CBT £10,352 (SD £13,464) Standard care £11,724 (SD £12,061) Primary outcome: Number of days in acute bipolar episodes per patient; benefit expressed as number of days free of bipolar episodes per patient Mean number of days in bipolar episodes per patient: 12 months: CBT 26.6 (SD 46.0); standard care 88.4 (SD 108.9) 30 months: CBT 95.3 (SD 152.1); standard care 201.0 (SD 95.3)	For $\lambda = 0$, probability of CBT being cost effective: 0.85 at 12 months 0.80 at 30 months For $\lambda = £10$, probability of CBT being cost effective: 0.90 at 12 months 0.85 at 30 months *λ = willingness to pay per additional day free of bipolar episodes

APPENDIX 15:
COST ESTIMATES OF MAINTENANCE AND ACUTE TREATMENT OF PATIENTS WITH BIPOLAR I DISORDER UTILISED IN THE ECONOMIC MODEL

Cost element	Cost estimate	Comments
Annual costs of maintenance medication:		Cost estimates include drug acquisition costs and respective monitoring testing costs; costs of first year are higher due to additional monitoring tests required at initiation of treatment
Lithium		
–first year of maintenance treatment	£109	
–following years of maintenance treatment	£96	
Valproate semisodium		
–first year of maintenance treatment	£263	
–following years of maintenance treatment	£249	
Olanzapine		
–first year of maintenance treatment	£1,043	
–following years of maintenance treatment	£1,038	
Costs per acute episode:		Cost estimates include inpatient care or CRHTT management, plus medication for acute treatment; costs of subsequent visits to healthcare professionals are not included. In the case of depression managed with enhanced outpatient care, costs relate to medication only; costs incurred by additional healthcare professional contact are provided separately (see below)
Mania		
–inpatient care	£6,900	
–CRHTT management	£1,389	
weighted mean	£5,798	

Depression	Costs associated with treatment of mania are slightly lower for patients under long-term treatment with olanzapine, as in this sub-cohort acute treatment involves adjustment of olanzapine dosage, and not addition of olanzapine to maintenance medication. Weighted means are calculated based on proportion of patients receiving each type of care
–inpatient care £8,222	
–CRHTT management £1,333	
–enhanced outpatient care £8	
weighted mean £1,095	
Annual costs of healthcare professional contacts:	Cost estimates are higher in the first year of maintenance treatment due to the higher frequency of healthcare professional contact expected at initiation of therapy. For patients experiencing an acute episode, healthcare professional costs depend on the time point at which frequency of contact with healthcare professionals increases, following inpatient care or CRHTT management (the time point is affected by duration of acute care); increased frequency of contact with healthcare professionals has also been assumed in the case of patients receiving enhanced outpatient care for the management of a depressive episode
Patients remaining stable over the year	
–first year of maintenance treatment £1,642	
–following years of maintenance treatment £936	
Patients experiencing a manic episode over the year	
–first year of maintenance treatment £2,179	
–following years of maintenance treatment £1,474	
Patients experiencing a depressive episode over the year	(NB Costs of first year of patients experiencing an episode are slightly higher for patients receiving no maintenance treatment, as acute episodes have been assumed to occur at an earlier time point)
–first year of maintenance treatment £2,224	
–following years of maintenance treatment £1,519	

APPENDIX 16:

ESTIMATION OF ONE-YEAR ABSOLUTE RELAPSE RATES OF MANIC AND DEPRESSIVE EPISODES ASSOCIATED WITH LONG-TERM PLACEBO TREATMENT, FOR USE IN THE ECONOMIC MODEL OF MAINTENANCE PHARMACOLOGICAL TREATMENT OF PATIENTS WITH BIPOLAR I DISORDER

According to Judd and colleagues (2002), who followed patients with bipolar I disorder over 14 years, patients experienced manic or mixed symptoms during 15.2% of the time and depressive symptoms during 31.9% of the time of the follow-up period.

A key assumption used in the economic model was that manic/mixed episodes lasted 9 weeks, while depressive episodes lasted 13 weeks.

Combining the above data:

Number of manic/mixed episodes $\times$ 9 weeks = 15.2% $\times$ total follow-up time (1)

Number of depressive episodes $\times$ 13 weeks = 31.9% $\times$ total follow-up time (2)

By dividing (1)/(2):

$$\frac{\text{Number of manic/mixed episodes} \times 9}{\text{Number of depressive episodes} \times 13} = \frac{15.2}{31.9} \Rightarrow$$

$$\frac{\text{Number of manic/mixed episodes}}{\text{Number of depressive episodes}} = \frac{15.2 \times 13}{31.9 \times 9} \Rightarrow$$

$$\frac{\text{Rate of manic/mixed}}{\text{to depressive episodes}} = \frac{\text{Number of manic/mixed episodes}}{\text{Number of depressive episodes}} = \frac{41}{59} \quad (3)$$

According to meta-analysis of data from BOWDEN2000 and TOHEN2006, the 1-year overall relapse rate for placebo was 0.63, therefore, for 1 year:

Manic/mixed relapse rate for placebo + depressive relapse rate
for placebo = 0.63 (4)

By combining (3) and (4):
  1-year manic/mixed relapse rate = 0.26
  1-year depressive relapse rate = 0.37

APPENDIX 17:

ECONOMIC EVALUATION OF

PHARMACOLOGICAL AGENTS USED FOR

LONG-TERM TREATMENT OF PATIENTS WITH

BIPOLAR I DISORDER. BASE-CASE RESULTS FOR

MALE PATIENTS IN THE FORM OF GRAPHS

Figure 5: Total costs and acute episodes averted relative to no treatment per 1,000 male patients over 5 years associated with each treatment option assessed

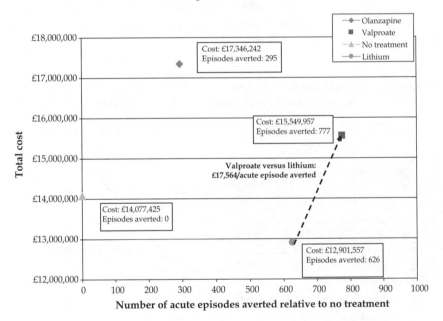

Figure 6: Total costs and days free from episode per 1,000 male patients over 5 years associated with each treatment option assessed

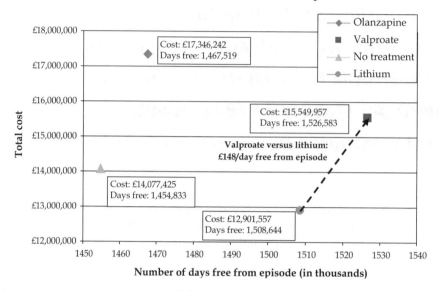

Figure 7: Total costs and QALYs gained per 1,000 male patients over 5 years associated with each treatment option assessed

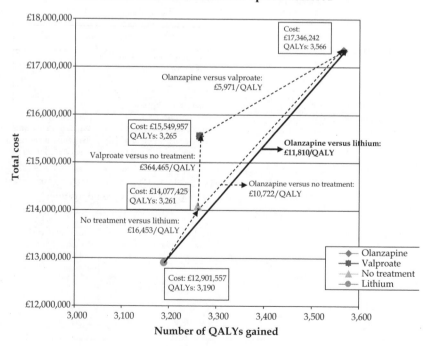

APPENDIX 18:

ECONOMIC EVALUATION OF PHARMACOLOGICAL AGENTS USED FOR LONG-TERM TREATMENT OF PATIENTS WITH BIPOLAR I DISORDER. RESULTS OF SENSITIVITY ANALYSIS

ONE-WAY SENSITIVITY ANALYSIS

Note: treatment options have been ranked from the most to the least effective. Results for valproate semisodium do not apply to female patients with child-bearing potential.

A. EXPLORING UNCERTAINTY CHARACTERISING EFFICACY DATA

TABLE 115: EXCLUSION OF BOWDEN2000 AND CALABRESE2003 FROM META-ANALYSIS

Measure of benefit: number of acute episodes averted relative to no treatment			
Treatment option	**Cost effectiveness: male patients**	**Cost effectiveness: female patients without child-bearing potential**	**Cost effectiveness: female patients with child-bearing potential**
Lithium	**Dominates all treatment options**	**Dominates all treatment options**	**Dominates all treatment options**
Valproate	Dominated by lithium	Dominated by lithium	
Olanzapine	Dominated by lithium and valproate	Dominated by lithium and valproate	Dominated by lithium
No treatment	Dominated by lithium	Dominated by lithium	Dominated by lithium
Measure of benefit: number of days free from acute episode			
Treatment option	**Cost effectiveness: male patients**	**Cost effectiveness: female patients without child-bearing potential**	**Cost effectiveness: female patients with child-bearing potential**
Lithium	**Dominates all treatment options**	**Dominates all treatment options**	**Dominates all treatment options**
Valproate	Dominated by lithium	Dominated by lithium	
Olanzapine	Dominated by lithium and valproate	Dominated by lithium and valproate	Dominated by lithium
No treatment	Dominated by lithium	Dominated by lithium	Dominated by lithium
Measure of benefit: number of QALYs gained			
Treatment option	**Cost effectiveness: male patients**	**Cost effectiveness: female patients without child-bearing potential**	**Cost effectiveness: female patients with child-bearing potential**
Olanzapine	Olanzapine vs lithium: £18,688/QALY	Olanzapine vs lithium: £17,909/QALY	Olanzapine vs lithium: £17,909/QALY
Valproate	Dominated by extended dominance	Dominated by extended dominance	
No treatment	Dominated by extended dominance	Dominated by extended dominance	Dominated by extended dominance
Lithium			

TABLE 116: EXCLUSION OF PRIEN1973 AND STALLONE1973
FROM META-ANALYSIS

Measure of benefit: number of acute episodes averted relative to no treatment			
Treatment option	Cost effectiveness: male patients	Cost effectiveness: female patients without child-bearing potential	Cost effectiveness: female patients with child-bearing potential
Valproate	Valproate versus no treatment: £1,896/episode a verted	Valproate versus no treatment: £1,887/episode averted	
Olanzapine	Dominated by valproate	Dominated by valproate	Olanzapine versus lithium: £27,736/episode averted
Lithium	Dominated by extended dominance	Dominated by extended dominance	Lithium versus no treatment: £3,833/episode averted
No treatment			

Measure of benefit: number of days free from acute episode			
Treatment option	Cost effectiveness: male patients	Cost effectiveness: female patients without child-bearing potential	Cost effectiveness: female patients with child-bearing potential
Valproate	Valproate versus no treatment: £21/day free from episode	Valproate versus no treatment: £20/day free from episode	
Lithium	Dominated by extended dominance	Dominated by extended dominance	Lithium versus no treatment: £47/episode averted
Olanzapine	Dominated by valproate and lithium	Dominated by valproate and lithium	Dominated by lithium
No treatment			

Measure of benefit: number of QALYs gained			
Treatment option	Cost effectiveness: male patients	Cost effectiveness: female patients without child-bearing potential	Cost effectiveness: female patients with child-bearing potential
Olanzapine	Olanzapine versus no treatment: £10,722/QALY	Olanzapine versus no treatment £10,689/QALY	Olanzapine versus no treatment: £10,689/QALY
Valproate	Dominated by extended dominance	Dominated by extended dominance	
No treatment			
Lithium	Dominated by no treatment	Dominated by no treatment	Dominated by no treatment

TABLE 117: DIRECT COMPARISON BETWEEN OLANZAPINE
AND LITHIUM (TOHEN2005)

All measures of benefit	
Treatment option	Cost effectiveness: all patients
Olanzapine	Dominates lithium
Lithium	Dominated by olanzapine

TABLE 118: INTENTION-TO-TREAT ANALYSIS, CONSIDERING PATIENTS DISCONTINUING TREATMENT AS 'GOOD OUTCOMES'

Measure of benefit: number of acute episodes averted relative to no treatment			
Treatment option	**Cost effectiveness: male patients**	**Cost effectiveness: female patients without child-bearing potential**	**Cost effectiveness: female patients with child-bearing potential**
Valproate	**Valproate versus lithium: £3,912/episode averted**	**Valproate versus lithium: £3,894/episode averted**	
Olanzapine	Dominated by valproate	Dominated by valproate	**Olanzapine versus lithium: £15,911/episode averted**
Lithium			
No treatment	Dominated by valproate and lithium	Dominated by valproate and lithium	Dominated by lithium
Measure of benefit: number of days free from acute episode			
Treatment option	**Cost effectiveness: male patients**	**Cost effectiveness: female patients without child-bearing potential**	**Cost effectiveness: female patients with child-bearing potential**
Valproate	**Valproate versus lithium: £45/day free from episode**	**Valproate versus lithium: £37/day free from episode**	
Olanzapine	Dominated by valproate	Dominated by valproate	**Olanzapine versus lithium: £296/day free from episode**
Lithium			
No treatment	Dominated by valproate and lithium	Dominated by valproate and lithium	Dominated by lithium
Measure of benefit: number of QALYs gained			
Treatment option	**Cost effectiveness: male patients**	**Cost effectiveness: female patients without child-bearing potential**	**Cost effectiveness: female patients with child-bearing potential**
Olanzapine	**Olanzapine versus lithium: £7,437/QALY**	**Olanzapine versus lithium: £7,247/QALY**	**Olanzapine versus lithium: £7,247/QALY**
Valproate	Dominated by extended dominance	Dominated by extended dominance	
No treatment	Dominated by valproate	Dominated by valproate	Dominated by extended dominance
Lithium			

B. EXPLORING UNCERTAINTY CHARACTERISING OTHER INPUT PARAMETERS

TABLE 119: CHANGING THE RATE OF MANIC TO DEPRESSIVE EPISODES FOLLOWING NO TREATMENT TO 75:25

Measure of benefit: number of acute episodes averted relative to no treatment			
Treatment option	**Cost effectiveness: male patients**	**Cost effectiveness: female patients without child-bearing potential**	**Cost effectiveness: female patients with child-bearing potential**
Lithium	**Dominates all treatment options**	**Dominates all treatment options**	**Dominates all treatment options**
Olanzapine	Dominated by lithium	Dominated by lithium	Dominated by lithium
Valproate	Dominated by lithium and olanzapine	Dominated by lithium and olanzapine	
No treatment	Dominated by lithium	Dominated by lithium	Dominated by lithium
Measure of benefit: number of days free from acute episode			
Treatment option	**Cost effectiveness: male patients**	**Cost effectiveness: female patients without child-bearing potential**	**Cost effectiveness: female patients with child-bearing potential**
Lithium	**Dominates all treatment options**	**Dominates all treatment options**	**Dominates all treatment options**
Olanzapine	Dominated by lithium	Dominated by lithium	Dominated by lithium
Valproate	Dominated by lithium and olanzapine	Dominated by lithium and olanzapine	
No treatment	Dominated by lithium	Dominated by lithium	Dominated by lithium
Measure of benefit: number of QALYs gained			
Treatment option	**Cost effectiveness: male patients**	**Cost effectiveness: female patients without child-bearing potential**	**Cost effectiveness: female patients with child-bearing potential**
Olanzapine	**Olanzapine versus lithium: £9,175/QALY**	**Olanzapine versus lithium: £8,947/QALY**	**Olanzapine versus lithium: £8,947/QALY**
No treatment	Dominated by extended dominance	Dominated by extended dominance	Dominated by extended dominance
Valproate	Dominated by olanzapine	Dominated by olanzapine	
Lithium			

TABLE 120: CHANGING THE RATE OF MANIC TO DEPRESSIVE
EPISODES FOLLOWING NO TREATMENT TO 25:75

Measure of benefit: number of acute episodes averted relative to no treatment		
Treatment option	**Cost effectiveness: male patients**	**Cost effectiveness: female patients without child-bearing potential**	**Cost effectiveness: female patients with child-bearing potential**
Valproate	**Valproate versus lithium: £2,168/episode averted**	**Valproate versus lithium: £2,210/episode averted**	
Lithium			**Lithium dominates all treatment options**
Olanzapine	Dominated by valproate and lithium	Dominated by valproate and lithium	Dominated by lithium
No treatment	Dominated by lithium	Dominated by lithium	Dominated by lithium
Measure of benefit: number of days free from acute episode		
Treatment option	**Cost effectiveness: male patients**	**Cost effectiveness: female patients without child-bearing potential**	**Cost effectiveness: female patients with child-bearing potential**
Valproate	**Valproate versus lithium: £24/day free from episode**	**Valproate versus no treatment: £22/day free from episode**	
Lithium			**Lithium dominates all treatment options**
No treatment	Dominated by lithium	Dominated by lithium	Dominated by lithium
Olanzapine	Dominated by all treatment options	Dominated by all treatment options	Dominated by all treatment options
Measure of benefit: number of QALYs gained		
Treatment option	**Cost effectiveness: male patients**	**Cost effectiveness: female patients without child-bearing potential**	**Cost effectiveness: female patients with child-bearing potential**
Olanzapine	**Olanzapine versus no treatment: £16,495/QALY**	**Olanzapine versus no treatment: £16,452/QALY**	**Olanzapine versus no treatment: £16,452/QALY**
Valproate	Dominated by extended dominance	Dominated by extended dominance	
No treatment	**No treatment versus lithium: £1,513/QALY**	**No treatment versus lithium: £1,813/QALY**	**No treatment versus lithium: £1,813/QALY**
Lithium			

TABLE 121: INCREASING THE DURATION OF ACUTE
EPISODES BY 25%

Measure of benefit: number of acute episodes averted relative to no treatment			
Treatment option	Cost effectiveness: male patients	Cost effectiveness: female patients without child-bearing potential	Cost effectiveness: female patients with child-bearing potential
Valproate	**Valproate versus lithium: £21,002/episode averted**	**Valproate versus lithium: £19,740/episode averted**	
Lithium			**Lithium dominates all treatment options**
Olanzapine	Dominated by valproate and lithium	Dominated by valproate and lithium	Dominated by lithium
No treatment	Dominated by lithium	Dominated by lithium	Dominated by lithium
Measure of benefit: number of days free from acute episode			
Treatment option	Cost effectiveness: male patients	Cost effectiveness: female patients without child-bearing potential	Cost effectiveness: female patients with child-bearing potential
Valproate	**Valproate versus lithium: £124/day free from episode**	**Valproate versus lithium: £96/day free from episode**	
Lithium			**Lithium dominates all treatment options**
Olanzapine	Dominated by valproate and lithium	Dominated by valproate and lithium	Dominated by lithium
No treatment	Dominated by lithium	Dominated by lithium	Dominated by lithium
Measure of benefit: number of QALYs gained			
Treatment option	Cost effectiveness: male patients	Cost effectiveness: female patients without child-bearing potential	Cost effectiveness: female patients with child-bearing potential
Olanzapine	**Olanzapine versus lithium: £12,307/QALY**	**Olanzapine versus lithium: £11,899/QALY**	**Olanzapine versus lithium: £11,899/QALY**
Valproate	Dominated by extended dominance	Dominated by extended dominance	
No treatment	Dominated by extended dominance	Dominated by extended dominance	Dominated by extended dominance
Lithium			

TABLE 122: REDUCING THE DURATION OF ACUTE
EPISODES BY 25%

Measure of benefit: number of acute episodes averted relative to no treatment			
Treatment option	Cost effectiveness: male patients	Cost effectiveness: female patients without child-bearing potential	Cost effectiveness: female patients with child-bearing potential
Valproate	Valproate versus lithium: £14,065/episode averted	Valproate versus lithium: £13,261/episode averted	
Lithium			Lithium dominates all treatment options
Olanzapine	Dominated by valproate and lithium	Dominated by valproate and lithium	Dominated by lithium
No treatment	Dominated by lithium	Dominated by lithium	Dominated by lithium
Measure of benefit: number of days free from acute episode			
Treatment option	Cost effectiveness: male patients	Cost effectiveness: female patients without child-bearing potential	Cost effectiveness: female patients with child-bearing potential
Valproate	Valproate versus lithium: £206/day free from episode	Valproate versus lithium: £116/day free from episode	
Lithium			Lithium dominates all treatment options
Olanzapine	Dominated by valproate and lithium	Dominated by valproate and lithium	Dominated by lithium
No treatment	Dominated by lithium	Dominated by lithium	Dominated by lithium
Measure of benefit: number of QALYs gained			
Treatment option	Cost effectiveness: male patients	Cost effectiveness: female patients without child-bearing potential	Cost effectiveness: female patients with child-bearing potential
Olanzapine	Olanzapine versus no treatment: £12,812/QALY	Olanzapine versus no treatment: £12,777/QALY	Olanzapine versus no treatment: £12,777/QALY
Valproate	Dominated by extended dominance	Dominated by extended dominance	
No treatment	No treatment versus lithium: £6,060/QALY	No treatment versus lithium: £5,551/QALY	No treatment versus lithium: £5,551/QALY
Lithium			

TABLE 123: REDUCING THE ABSOLUTE RELAPSE RATE OF NO TREATMENT AT 40%

Measure of benefit: number of acute episodes averted relative to no treatment			
Treatment option	Cost effectiveness: male patients	Cost effectiveness: female patients without child-bearing potential	Cost effectiveness: female patients with child-bearing potential
Valproate	Valproate versus lithium: £23,196/episode averted	Valproate versus lithium: £19,639/episode averted	
Lithium	Lithium versus no treatment: £1,580/episode averted	Lithium versus no treatment: £1,524/episode averted	Lithium versus no treatment: £1,524/episode averted
Olanzapine	Dominated by valproate and lithium	Dominated by valproate and lithium	Dominated by lithium
No treatment			
Measure of benefit: number of days free from acute episode			
Treatment option	Cost effectiveness: male patients	Cost effectiveness: female patients without child-bearing potential	Cost effectiveness: female patients with child-bearing potential
Valproate	Valproate versus lithium: £284/day free from episode	Valproate versus lithium: £129/day free from episode	
Lithium	Lithium versus no treatment: £17/day free from episode	Lithium versus no treatment: £20/day free from episode	Lithium versus no treatment: £20/day free from episode
Olanzapine	Dominated by valproate and lithium	Dominated by valproate and lithium	Dominated by lithium
No treatment			
Measure of benefit: number of QALYs gained			
Treatment option	Cost effectiveness: male patients	Cost effectiveness: female patients without child-bearing potential	Cost effectiveness: female patients with child-bearing potential
Olanzapine	Olanzapine versus no treatment: £16,300/QALY	Olanzapine versus no treatment: £16,260/QALY	Olanzapine versus no treatment: £16,260/QALY
No treatment			
Valproate	Dominated by no treatment	Dominated by no treatment	
Lithium	Dominated by no treatment	Dominated by no treatment	Dominated by no treatment

TABLE 124: INCREASING THE ABSOLUTE RELAPSE RATE OF NO TREATMENT AT 86%

Measure of benefit: number of acute episodes averted relative to no treatment			
Treatment option	**Cost effectiveness: male patients**	**Cost effectiveness: female patients without child-bearing potential**	**Cost effectiveness: female patients with child-bearing potential**
Valproate	**Valproate versus lithium: £15,421/episode averted**	**Valproate versus lithium: £15,152/episode averted**	
Lithium			**Dominates all treatment options**
Olanzapine	Dominated by valproate and lithium	Dominated by valproate and lithium	Dominated by lithium
No treatment	Dominated by lithium	Dominated by lithium	Dominated by lithium
Measure of benefit: number of days free from acute episode			
Treatment option	**Cost effectiveness: male patients**	**Cost effectiveness: female patients without child-bearing potential**	**Cost effectiveness: female patients with child-bearing potential**
Valproate	**Valproate versus lithium: £116/day free from episode**	**Valproate versus lithium: £93/day free from episode**	
Lithium			**Dominates all treatment options**
Olanzapine	Dominated by valproate and lithium	Dominated by valproate and lithium	Dominated by lithium
No treatment	Dominated by lithium	Dominated by lithium	Dominated by lithium
Measure of benefit: number of QALYs gained			
Treatment option	**Cost effectiveness: male patients**	**Cost effectiveness: female patients without child-bearing potential**	**Cost effectiveness: female patients with child-bearing potential**
Olanzapine	**Olanzapine versus lithium: £12,733/QALY**	**Olanzapine versus lithium: £12,313/QALY**	**Olanzapine versus lithium: £12,313/QALY**
Valproate	Dominated by extended dominance	Dominated by extended dominance	
No treatment	Dominated by extended dominance	Dominated by extended dominance	Dominated by extended dominance
Lithium			

TABLE 125: EXTENDING THE TIME HORIZON TO 10 YEARS

Measure of benefit: number of acute episodes averted relative to no treatment			
Treatment option	**Cost effectiveness: male patients**	**Cost effectiveness: female patients without child-bearing potential**	**Cost effectiveness: female patients with child-bearing potential**
Valproate	**Valproate versus lithium: £18,772/episode averted**	**Valproate versus lithium: £16,786/episode averted**	
Lithium			**Dominates all treatment options**
Olanzapine	Dominated by valproate and lithium	Dominated by valproate and lithium	Dominated by lithium
No treatment	Dominated by lithium	Dominated by lithium	Dominated by lithium
Measure of benefit: number of days free from acute episode			
Treatment option	**Cost effectiveness: male patients**	**Cost effectiveness: female patients without child-bearing potential**	**Cost effectiveness: female patients with child-bearing potential**
Valproate	**Valproate versus lithium: £279/day free from episode**	**Valproate versus lithium: £113/day free from episode**	
Lithium			**Dominates all treatment options**
Olanzapine	Dominated by valproate and lithium	Dominated by valproate and lithium	Dominated by lithium
No treatment	Dominated by lithium	Dominated by lithium	Dominated by lithium
Measure of benefit: number of QALYs gained			
Treatment option	**Cost effectiveness: male patients**	**Cost effectiveness: female patients without child-bearing potential**	**Cost effectiveness: female patients with child-bearing potential**
Olanzapine	**Olanzapine versus lithium: £12,231/QALY**	**Olanzapine versus lithium: £11,526/QALY**	**Olanzapine versus lithium: £11,526/QALY**
Valproate	Dominated by extended dominance	Dominated by extended dominance	
No treatment	Dominated by extended dominance	Dominated by extended dominance	Dominated by extended dominance
Lithium			

TABLE 126: REDUCING THE AMOUNT AND DURATION OF HEALTHCARE PROFESSIONAL CONTACT BY 25%

Measure of benefit: number of acute episodes averted relative to no treatment			
Treatment option	**Cost effectiveness: male patients**	**Cost effectiveness: female patients without child-bearing potential**	**Cost effectiveness: female patients with child-bearing potential**
Valproate	**Valproate versus lithium: £17,822/episode averted**	**Valproate versus lithium: £16,727/episode averted**	
Lithium			**Dominates all treatment options**
Olanzapine	Dominated by valproate and lithium	Dominated by valproate and lithium	Dominated by lithium
No treatment	Dominated by lithium	Dominated by lithium	Dominated by lithium
Measure of benefit: number of days free from acute episode			
Treatment option	**Cost effectiveness: male patients**	**Cost effectiveness: female patients without child-bearing potential**	**Cost effectiveness: female patients with child-bearing potential**
Valproate	**Valproate versus lithium: £150/day free from episode**	**Valproate versus lithium: £105/day free from episode**	
Lithium			**Dominates all treatment options**
Olanzapine	Dominated by valproate and lithium	Dominated by valproate and lithium	Dominated by lithium
No treatment	Dominated by lithium	Dominated by lithium	Dominated by lithium
Measure of benefit: number of QALYs gained			
Treatment option	**Cost effectiveness: male patients**	**Cost effectiveness: female patients without child-bearing potential**	**Cost effectiveness: female patients with child-bearing potential**
Olanzapine	**Olanzapine versus lithium: £11,710/QALY**	**Olanzapine versus lithium: £11,308/QALY**	**Olanzapine versus lithium: £11,308/QALY**
Valproate	Dominated by extended dominance	Dominated by extended dominance	
No treatment	Dominatedby extended dominance	Dominated by extended dominance	Dominated by extended dominance
Lithium			

PROBABILISTIC SENSITIVITY ANALYSIS

Analysis for men and women with no child-bearing potential

Figure 8: Cost effectiveness acceptability curves: probability of cost effectiveness for each treatment option depending on willingness to pay per additional acute episode averted

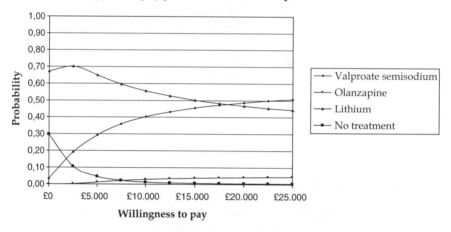

Figure 9: Cost effectiveness acceptability curves: probability of cost effectiveness for each treatment option depending on willingness to pay per additional day free from acute episode

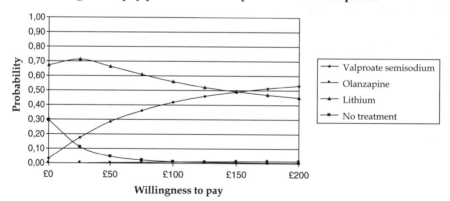

516

Figure 10: Cost effectiveness acceptability curves: probability of cost effectiveness depending on willingness to pay per additional QALY gained

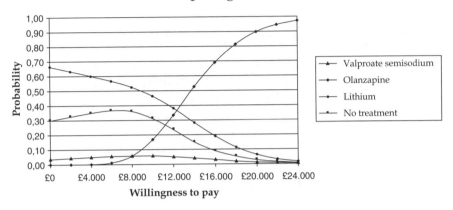

Women of child-bearing potential

Figure 11: Cost effectiveness acceptability curves: probability of cost effectiveness for each treatment option depending on willingness to pay per additional acute episode averted

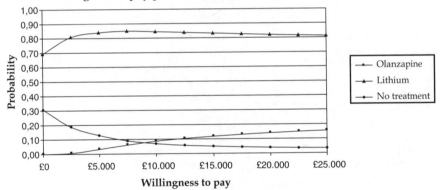

Figure 12: Cost effectiveness acceptability curves: probability of cost effectiveness for each treatment option depending on willingness to pay per additional day free from acute episode

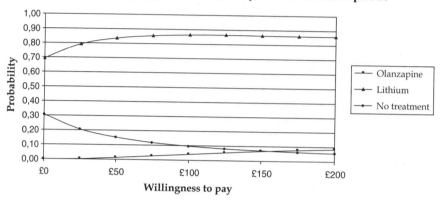

Figure 13: Cost effectiveness acceptability curves: probability of cost effectiveness depending on willingness to pay per additional QALY gained

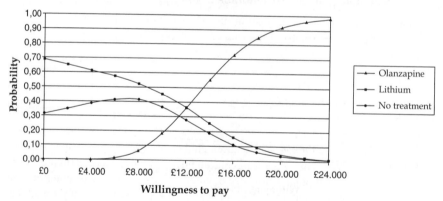

APPENDIX 19:

CONSENSUS CONFERENCE ON THE DIAGNOSIS OF BIPOLAR I DISORDER IN CHILDREN AND ADOLESCENTS

INTRODUCTION

Background

The diagnosis of bipolar I disorder in children and adolescents is an area of considerable difficulty and some controversy. In order to produce appropriate guidance, the GDG held a consensus conference to draw on the expertise of national and international experts in this area. This document provides an overview of relevant issues, together with statements of the conference's position on the diagnosis of bipolar I disorder in children and adolescents, and recommendations to clinicians.

It should be noted that much of the existing published literature in this area is based on work undertaken in the US, where diagnosis of bipolar disorder is more common in prepubertal children than in the UK. An issue for the conference, therefore, was to apply these data to the diagnosis of bipolar disorder in children and adolescents within the UK healthcare system.

Epidemiology and natural course

It has been estimated that around 20% of adults with bipolar disorder experience initial symptoms before the age of 19, although data are based on retrospective studies (Harrington, 1994). This is a significant number of people since estimates of the lifetime prevalence of bipolar I disorder in adults, across a variety of countries and cultures, are between 3% and 6% (Weissman *et al.*, 1996), with the figure for adolescents being estimated at 1% (Lewinson *et al.*, 1995), and a first incidence of 1.4% up to the age of 18 and 0.7% for ages 19 to 23 (see also Kessler *et al.*, 1997 and Weissman *et al.*, 1996). However, other studies estimate much lower rates, including 0.02% in a community sample of 717 (Johnson *et al.*, 2000) and < 0.1% in a community sample of 1420 (Costello *et al.*, 2003). For subsyndromal bipolar disorder (that is, a period of elevated mood or irritability, plus at least one other manic symptom (see Box 3 below), and never having met criteria for bipolar disorder) there is a weighted lifetime prevalence through age 18 of 4.5%.

The Oregon Adolescent Depression Project (OADP; Lewinsohn *et al.*, 1993, 2003), which followed 1,709 adolescents (mean age 16.6 (±1.2) years) until they were 24 years old, measured a point prevalence of bipolar disorder of 0.6% at the start of the study, 0.5% at 1 year, and 0.7% at age 24. It measured point prevalence of subsyndromal bipolar disorder as 1.2%, 0.3% and 0.0% at each time point. There were only three cases of prepubertal bipolar disorder.

The diagnosis of bipolar I disorder in prepubertal children in general, and very young children in particular, is controversial. Indeed, little is known about the longitudinal outcome of so-called child-onset mania (Geller *et al.*, 2001, 2002). However, in a recent study 65.2% recovered in 2 years, with 55.2% of these relapsing after recovery (Geller *et al.*, 2002). The OADP study found that, of the 18 adolescents who started bipolar I disorder in the first year of the study, the mean age of onset of symptoms was 11.8 (range 7–15) (Lewinsohn *et al.*, 1993, 2003).

Clinical and demographic characteristics

A typical adult with bipolar disorder has a discrete episode of mania or major depressive disorder lasting about 2–8 months that is responsive to treatment (Goodwin & Jamison, 1990). However, in children and adolescents presentation tends to be atypical compared with adults.

The OADP study found that in those with early onset (mean 11.8 years) the majority of cases were first depressed rather than manic, with the median duration of the most recent episode being 10.8 months (Lewinsohn *et al.*, 1993, 2003). A high proportion of adolescents with bipolar I disorder in the study had impaired social, family, or school functioning (66.7%, 55.6% and 83.3% respectively). However, of prepubertal children with bipolar disorder around 55% are reported to show a mixed presentation with 77% of these rapid cycling continuously for around 3.6 years (Geller *et al.*, 2001). Unlike in adults with bipolar disorder, rapid cycling does not appear to be more frequent in females (Geller *et al.*, 2002). These data from prepubertal children assumes such diagnoses are in fact valid; while the specialist case series may well have identified relevant psychopathology, there is a danger that the extension of bipolar constructs to describe rather different behaviour in children is unreliable in non-specialist hands.

The manifestations of mania and hypomania are different in children, adolescents and adults since features such as grandiosity and excessive involvement in pleasurable activities vary as a function of age and developmental level. What is pathological in an adult might not be appropriately so described in a child. For example, an adult running into a public meeting giggling might invite speculation about their mental state, whereas this would be unremarkable in a child. Also, the use of stimulants to treat conditions such as ADHD may risk inducing abnormal mood states in children and even precipitating bipolar I disorder in those at risk. This is clearly a risk proportional to the level of prescribing of stimulants, which is high in the USA.

Diagnostic issues

Manic disorders are defined by symptoms best seen in adults. It is difficult to diagnose mood elevation in prepubertal children for several reasons: the child's age and developmental level influence the interpretation of 'symptoms of elation'; there is the potential for significant overlap between the behavioural changes of mania and those of other disorders, notably ADHD and conduct disorder; and there is a low base rate of the severe disorder (Emslie *et al.*, 1994). Therefore, bipolar diagnoses in prepubertal children may be an admixture of a few patients with very early onset bipolar I disorder and others with mood lability and over-activity. However, increasing the sensitivity to bipolar diagnoses in childhood will inevitably reduce the specificity.

The symptoms included in DSM-IV criteria for a manic episode are in Box 3. In DSM-IV symptoms have to be present for the previous week for mania, and for the previous 4 days for hypomania.

Box 3: DSM-IV criteria for a manic episode
(APA, 1994, p. 332)

A. A distinct period of abnormally and persistently elevated, expansive, or irritable mood, lasting at least 1 week (or any duration if hospitalisation is necessary).

B. During the period of mood disturbance, three (or more) of the following symptoms have persisted (four if the mood is only irritable) and have been present to a significant degree:

1. inflated self-esteem or grandiosity
2. decreased need for sleep (e.g. feels rested after only 3 hours of sleep)
3. more talkative than usual or pressure to keep talking
4. flight of ideas or subjective experience that thoughts are racing
5. distractibility (i.e. attention too easily drawn to unimportant or irrelevant external stimuli)
6. increase in goal-directed activity (either socially, at work or school, or sexually) or psychomotor agitation
7. excessive involvement in pleasurable activities that have a high potential for painful consequences (e.g. engaging in unrestrained buying sprees, sexual indiscretions, or foolish business investments)

For childrens the KSADS diagnostic tool (Puig-Antich & Chambers, 1978) was developed to aid research in childhood major depressive disorder. However, this was before there was widespread acceptance of the existence of childhood mania. Therefore, an updated version, WASH-U-KSADS (Geller *et al.*, 1996), which builds on the KSADS was developed. This includes prepubertal-specific mania items, a section on rapid cycling, items for each occurrence of every symptom and syndrome and items to assess ADHD and other DSM-IV diagnoses. It retains separate interviews for parents and children.

In the clinical environment, however, although a diagnostic tool based on DSM-IV exists for use with adult patients (SCID-CV; First *et al.*, 1997), no such tool exists for use with children. Given that the clinical presentation of mania and the early course of the disorder are so different in children compared with adults (see above) and there are additional issues of differential diagnosis (discussed below), it is unlikely that applying adult criteria to children is adequate in making a secure diagnosis in young people.

Diagnosing mania in prepubertal children

Atypical presentation of mania
It is claimed that mania presents differently in children compared with adults (that is, presentation would be considered atypical in adults) and this could lead to underdiagnosis (Reddy & Srinath, 2000). Whilst younger children present with irritability and emotional lability, older children present with euphoria, elation, paranoia, grandiose delusions (*ibid.*). Existing adult criteria require persistence of symptoms and make no allowance for the unstable and variable clinical presentation of mania in children (*ibid.*). As seen above, child-onset illness presents differently to the adult-onset disorder with cycles in which dysphoria, hypomania and agitation are commonly intermixed with cyclical extremes of depression and manic excitement becoming more apparent with the onset of puberty.

Identifying prepubertal manifestations of mania
Developmentally children cannot present with many of the behavioural manifestations of mania seen in late-teenage- and adult-onset mania, such as overspending on credit cards. Also, some manic symptoms are difficult to differentiate from developmentally appropriate behaviours (Reddy & Srinath, 2000). Children can commonly be elated, expansive and grandiose and judging the inappropriateness of its contexts is likely to be difficult.

Diagnosing mania in adolescents

The diagnosis of mania in adolescents broadly follows the principles applied to adults. A number of prospective studies of those at high risk are ongoing in Europe and Canada, looking at the children of bipolar patients and this will partly clarify the typical onsets for the disorder. In preliminary oral reports (6th Stanley Bipolar meeting, Aarhus, September 2004), there was little comorbidity with ADHD. The associations – and common premorbid symptoms – were associated with anxiety, depression, sleep disorder and substance misuse. In some cases, the development of psychopathology showed sequential progression from sleep disorder to depression to a manic episode. In others, symptoms of new disorders developed without any decline in existing symptoms resulting in comorbidity. These children did not show frank manic symptoms before puberty. While they not uncommonly showed prepubertal, psychiatric disorder, there is scepticism as to whether it could have been diagnosed as distinct and bipolar.

Specific issues in differential diagnosis

There are specific symptoms and disorders that can make bipolar disorder difficult to diagnose in prepubertal children and adolescents.

Irritability

Although irritability is reported as the most common symptom of mania, it is not specific to bipolar disorder as it is present in many other child psychiatric disorders, including oppositional defiant disorder, conduct disorder, ADHD, major depressive disorder, autism and Asperger's syndrome. Concurrent elation and irritability was reported in 87.1% of children with bipolar disorder (Geller *et al.*, 2002), which is similar to that in adults with bipolar disorder (Goodwin & Jamison, 1990).

ADHD

There are major issues in the diagnosis of bipolar I disorder in prepubertal children and adolescents relating to ADHD. For example, in one study 88.9% of subjects less than 13 years old with mania also had ADHD (Geller *et al.*, 2003). The comorbidity rate for adolescents has been estimated at 30% (Geller & Luby, 1997). There is uncertainty in distinguishing between the two disorders. In DSM-IV, bipolar disorder and ADHD share three criteria: distractibility, physical restlessness and over-talkativeness. However, an important distinction is that whilst bipolar is episodic, ADHD is not.

In addition to sharing non-mania specific symptoms such as irritable mood, accelerated speech, distractibility and increased energy, bipolar disorder and ADHD share poor judgement symptoms (for example, hypersexuality and daredevil acts). However, ADHD is primarily a disorder of attention and behavioural regulation, with onset before age of 7 years, with between 50% and 80% persisting into adolescence. Although mania is widely diagnosed in the US before the age of 7, some American authorities agree that it is rare before this age (Geller *et al.*, 2003).

Other differential/comorbid disorders diagnosis issues

Schizophrenia

Schizophrenia is a major differential diagnosis for children and adolescents because of the greater perceptual distortions seen in bipolar illness during this time. Differentiation can be helped by a family history of mania, which is more probable for adolescents with bipolar disorder than for those with schizophrenia. In addition, the presence of psychotic features in mania and the fact that psychotic features in young people are mood incongruent can lead to misdiagnosis (Reddy & Srinath, 2000).

Substance misuse

Substance misuse is important during adolescence – for example, laughing fits may be due to marijuana rather than elation, very rapid cycling can be mimicked by amphetamine highs followed by withdrawal 'crashes' and hallucinogens can mimic bipolar perceptual distortions (Geller & Luby, 1997).

Conduct disorder
Conduct disorder co-occurs in 20% of bipolar children and 18% of bipolar adolescents. It may be the initial manifestation of prepubertal-onset bipolar disorder and is related to poor judgement and grandiosity (Geller *et al.*, 2003). Conduct disorder shares some symptoms with bipolar, but classic manic symptoms such as grandiose delusions, flight of ideas, reduced need for sleep and loss of reality testing, are not part of conduct disorder (Reddy and Srinath, 2000). There may be additional problems of diagnosis when mania develops on the background of pre-existing ADHD or conduct disorder (Reddy & Srinath, 2000). However, as with ADHD, an important distinction is that whilst bipolar is episodic, conduct disorder is not.

Sexual abuse
The differential diagnosis of the consequences of sexual abuse is also important because manic hypersexuality is often manifested by bipolar disorder children (Geller & Luby, 1997), whereas sexual abuse in bipolar children is estimated at 1% (Geller *et al.*, 2000). The suggestion has been made that mania should be included in the differential diagnosis of hypersexual behaviours.

Anxiety conditions
Anxiety conditions are frequently comorbid with bipolar. In one estimate, 33% of prepubertal patients and 12% of adolescent patients had the two conditions (Geller *et al.*, 1995).

Personality disorders
The issue of comorbid personality disorders is poorly studied, but is important based on reported inter-episode personality trait impairments in bipolar adults. It has been found that adults with bipolar II disorder and borderline personality disorder had a significantly lower onset age compared with those without borderline personality disorder (Benazzi, 2002). It should be noted that in DSM-IV, a diagnosis of personality disorder should only be rarely made before the age of 18 years (American Psychiatric Association, 1994).

Language disorders
A problem may arise here in differentiating between language disorders and flight of ideas because children/adolescents with language disabilities may exhibit behaviours which mimic thought disorder (Geller & Luby, 1997).

Summary

Diagnosing bipolar disorder reliably in adolescents is a reasonable clinical objective, and outcomes may be improved by early diagnosis and treatment. However, diagnosis is made difficult by a number of factors, including comorbidities and the prominence of behavioural disturbance which may be non-specific for bipolar patients. Its different presentations and early course compared with the disorder in adults are the subjects of current study.

In prepubescent children, bipolar disorder diagnoses are more problematic because of shared symptoms with other conditions seen much more commonly in children, such as ADHD, oppositional defiant disorder and conduct disorder. Anecdotally, many adults with the disorder believe they first experienced symptoms as children or adolescents. Unfortunately, retrospective judgement is potentially misleading. The question, not so far answered, is just how early reliable prospective diagnosis is possible.

METHOD USED TO DEVELOP THE CONSENSUS STATEMENTS

The statement was developed by a multidisciplinary group including academics, healthcare professionals representing all stages in the care of people with bipolar disorder, patients and carers. They were supported by a team of researchers who undertook literature searches, critical appraisal and review, and writing and editing. In order to draw up recommendations about the diagnosis of bipolar I disorder in children and adolescents, a consensus conference was held to which relevant national and international experts were invited. During the day-long conference they gave presentations to the GDG, and commented on the draft position statement. (Invited speakers and additional attendees are in Appendix 2). The updated position statement was sent to additional national and international reviewers for comment before recommendations were drawn up by the GDG. This paper (below) presents these positions statements (one for children and one for adolescents).

POSITION STATEMENTS FOR THE DIAGNOSIS OF BIPOLAR I DISORDER IN CHILDREN AND ADOLESCENTS

GENERAL COMMENT: A NARROW PHENOTYPE – BIPOLAR I DISORDER (CHILDREN AND ADOLESCENTS)

After careful consideration of the evidence, the consensus of the conference was that it is possible to establish a diagnosis of bipolar I disorder in prepubescent children and adolescents. However, the conference took the position that the diagnosis should normally be limited to a narrow phenotype (that is, bipolar I disorder with modified and more restrictive criteria than for adults) and that this is rare in adolescents and very rare in prepubescent children. Although children and adolescents can present with many features suggestive of a diagnosis of bipolar disorder and presentation might be expected to be atypical compared with adults, the conference was not convinced that evidence currently exists to support the everyday clinical use of diagnoses of bipolar II disorder or bipolar disorder not otherwise specified for these age groups. The appropriateness and utility of these diagnoses represent areas of genuine uncertainty, awaiting clarification by prospective developmental studies.

We recognise the value of the use of the diagnoses bipolar II disorder and bipolar disorder not otherwise specified when they are used operationally for research in children (Leibenluft *et al.*, 2003). However, they imply the reliable identification of hypomania or manic symptoms with major depression. We are concerned that the more permissive criteria that define hypomania are unsuitable for children and young people. The lack of specificity of some symptoms, which we will emphasise for mania, must apply *a fortiori* to hypomania. Thus, there is a need for caution in ordinary practice because milder elated states are much more difficult to distinguish from high spirits in younger children, and to accept modified criteria for childhood bipolar disorder will loosen the link with adult conditions. Children with behavioural disturbance and emotional instability may often need clinical assessment and help, but to make a specifically bipolar diagnosis could draw a misleading link to better characterised states in adults. In the absence of treatment trials in children, it may be useful in bipolar I cases to extrapolate treatment options developed for adults to children, but in bipolar II disorder and bipolar disorder not otherwise specified there is little or no adult data in any case, so the potential advantage does not exist. Indeed, there is a balancing risk that medicines may be used inappropriately to treat a bipolar diathesis that does not exist.

POSITION STATEMENT FOR THE DIAGNOSIS OF BIPOLAR I DISORDER IN PREPUBESCENT CHILDREN

The consensus of the conference was that it is possible to establish a diagnosis of bipolar I disorder in prepubescent children. However, the conference took the position that the diagnosis should be limited to a narrow phenotype (that is, bipolar I disorder with modified and more restrictive criteria than for adults) and that this is considered to be rare in prepubescent children. Although children can present with many features suggestive of a diagnosis of bipolar disorder and presentation might be expected to be atypical compared with adults, the conference was not convinced that evidence currently exists to support the use of diagnoses of bipolar II disorder or bipolar disorder not otherwise specified for prepubescent children. The reasons are given in the introduction.

1.   CRITERIA FOR DIAGNOSIS

The conference agreed that it was possible to diagnose bipolar I disorder in prepubertal children on the basis of an episode of mania alone without any depressive episode but that, although irritability is a common symptom, it should not be a key diagnostic criterion. This approach echoes the emphasis on euphoria proposed first by

Geller and colleagues (1998). The conference took the view that irritability is simultaneously too common a symptom in children and too non-specific to be useful. In doing so, the conference took a decision to deviate from the adult criteria and expects that the effect will be to narrow the diagnosis of mania. The *core symptoms* for bipolar I disorder modified from current DSM-IV criteria for prepubescent children are set out in Box 4.

Box 4: Criteria for manic episode
(Adapted from DSM-IV; APA, 1994, p. 332)

A. A distinct period of abnormally and persistently elevated or expansive mood, normally lasting 1 week.

B. During the period of mood disturbance, three (or more) of the following symptoms have persisted and have been present to a significant degree:

1. inflated self-esteem or grandiosity that is developmentally inappropriate and impairing
2. decreased need for sleep (e.g. feels rested after only 3 hours of sleep)
3. more talkative than usual or pressure to keep talking
4. flight of ideas or subjective experience that thoughts are racing
5. distractibility (i.e. attention too easily drawn to unimportant or irrelevant external stimuli)
6. increase in goal-directed activity (either socially, at school, or sexually) or psychomotor agitation
7. excessive involvement in pleasurable activities that have a high potential for painful consequences (e.g. engaging in unrestrained buying sprees, sexual indiscretions)

C. Symptoms do not meet criteria for mixed episode

D. The mood disturbance is sufficiently severe to cause marked impairment in educational functioning or in usual social activities or relationships with others or to necessitate hospitalization to prevent harm to self or others, or there are psychotic features.

E. The symptoms are not due to the direct physiological effects of a substance (e.g. a drug of abuse, a medication, or other treatment) or a general medical condition (e.g. hyperthyroidism or epilepsy)

Note: The status of manic episodes apparently precipitated by antidepressants or stimulants is uncertain. If the episode is self-limiting with medication withdrawal, it should not count towards a Bipolar I diagnosis.

In the case of mania related to antidepressants, a drug of abuse, stimulant drugs or steroids, a higher index of suspicion is warranted if the manic episode is severe and prolonged.

As in adults, criterion D (impairment) is as crucial to the diagnosis as the identification of symptoms. In DSM-IV, this is arguably the most critical distinction between mania and hypomania (Goodwin, 2002). However, DSM-IV criteria do not specify the way in which mania must be present over at least a 7-day period. We accept the recommendation of Leibenluft and colleagues (2003) that euphoria should be present most days, most of the day, and agree that at other times the clinical picture may be dominated by irritability.

The diagnosis of bipolar II or bipolar spectrum disorder in children

As already noticed, hypomania may be identifiable using operational criteria in children but it is unlikely to be reliable because of the developmental background. Hypomania in children would usually have to be diagnosed on the basis of the history in patients presenting with depression. Clinical observation of the elevated mood state would not be possible. Thus, the conference was not convinced that bipolar diagnoses other than bipolar I can be made reliably in children. Furthermore, the majority of children presenting with over-activity will have syndromes usually best subsumed under ADHD and conduct disorder diagnoses. The description of bipolar disorder as often comorbid with these diagnoses begs the question of whether it can reliably be distinguished from them. More often the same symptoms, such as overactivity and irritability, can satisfy the criteria for both diagnoses if the bipolar criteria, in particular, are relaxed. This is especially likely to occur if the requirement for a distinct period of mood change – or episode – is also ignored (Leibenluft *et al.,* 2003). Emotional instability may be present in this age group with or without ADHD or conduct disorder. Rather than make an unreliable distinction for or against bipolarity, it may be better clinical practice to keep an open mind on the question of a bipolar diagnosis, while closely monitoring the patient. It is a pragmatic, if unanswered, question whether 'mood stabilisers' could be helpful in managing emotional symptoms in children. More research in this area is clearly needed.

2.   **DIAGNOSTIC ISSUES**

When establishing a diagnosis of bipolar disorder the following symptoms and pattern of presentation should be considered:

a. *Irritability* – the conference took the position that unlike in adults, in children that of all the mood symptoms, irritability alone was not sufficient to make a diagnosis of bipolar disorder because it is common to many other psychiatric disorders of childhood. For prepubescent children the key symptoms that have most discriminatory validity are elevated mood and grandiosity (Geller *et al.,* 1996, 1998). Therefore, the presence of irritability in the absence of elevation of mood and grandiosity is not sufficient to arrive at a diagnosis of bipolar disorder. This is particularly important in distinguishing bipolar disorder from ADHD (see below). Care should be taken to define pathological elation or grandiosity in terms that are developmentally appropriate, but with this caveat bipolar I disorder should be confidently recognised".

b. *Cycling presentation* – A cycling course of presentation can sometimes be important in distinguishing bipolar disorder from another disorder such as ADHD, which does not follow the episodic, cyclical course typical of bipolar disorder. In determining the required duration of an episode, it was agreed that the arbitrary criteria employed for adults be adopted, that is, a minimum 7 days' duration. Information on the longitudinal nature of the problems will be required to support a diagnosis.

c. *Impairment* – symptomatic episodes should be accompanied by marked impairment of personal, educational or social functioning.

d. *Developmental level* – consideration must also be given to the child's developmental level. While elation (and grandiosity) is the key specifier for mania, it is also problematic because normal children in the pre-school age group particularly, may entertain improbably grandiose ideas, viewed from an adult perspective. For example, a child pretending to be Superman would not be seen alone as evidence of grandiosity, but a child who became convinced he had the special powers of Superman and acted on this by attempting to 'fly' off the top of a high building would. Box 5 gives an additional example.

e. *Learning difficulties* – prepubescent children with learning difficulties and other neurological and neurodevelopmental disorders may present significant diagnostic challenges. The view of the consensus conference was that no particular symptom cluster or clinical profile was associated with this group, but that careful behavioural observation was required to establish a diagnosis. Pervasive developmental disorder and related spectrum diagnoses may also complicate assessment and differential diagnosis in young children.

Box 5: Vignette

A 9-year-old boy is sent repeatedly to the headteacher throughout the school day for disobedient and disruptive behaviour. Among other things, he was interrupting his teacher every few minutes, telling her how to teach the class. The boy tells the headteacher that the school authorities have no power over him as he is the Prime Minister's son. The boy appears happy and laughing and full of energy. His high energy level continues at home where he re-arranges furniture throughout the house until midnight. At 2am he begins making multiple phone calls and then becomes suddenly miserable and tearful, saying his thoughts are interrupting him.

3. DISTINGUISHING BIPOLAR I DISORDER FROM OTHER DISORDERS

An important issue in diagnosing bipolar I disorder in children is to distinguish it from other more common disorders that present with similar symptoms, notably

ADHD, oppositional defiant disorder and conduct disorder. The most common shared symptom is irritability. However, the core symptoms of bipolar disorder must be present for the diagnosis to be made, in particular a child must have had at least one manic episode characterized by elevated mood and meeting full duration criteria. In general, comorbidity should be judged on the basis of an interval of euthymia.

The following is a brief overview of these more common disorders and their distinguishing symptoms.

a. ADHD
    The following symptoms are NOT part of ADHD:
    ● Unusually elated mood
    ● Inappropriate and impairing grandiosity
    ● Cycles of mood (that is, one or more distinct manic episodes)
    However, ADHD may present with emotional instability. When present, it may indicate a dimension of bipolarity recognised in adults as bipolar II or bipolar spectrum disorder.

b. Conduct disorder – there is little overlap in symptomatology between bipolar disorder and conduct disorder, hence the presence of mania cannot be inferred solely on the basis of the behavioural disturbance found in conduct disorder. Nor should conduct disorder be diagnosed on the basis of behaviour arising in a manic interval. In general, comorbidity should be judged on the basis of an interval of euthymia.

c. Depression – although a previous diagnosis of depression is not required to establish a diagnosis of bipolar disorder, a first presentation of a depressive disorder, especially if it is severe or psychotic, may indicate that the individual belongs to a high-risk group for whom major depressive disorder precedes bipolar disorder. Since bipolar I disorder in childhood is rare, this group is small. There is also an increased risk for children who have had an episode of major depression and have a family history of bipolar disorder, although these circumstances should not automatically lead to a diagnosis of bipolar disorder. Such children should be monitored carefully.

d. Substance and alcohol misuse – this can produce symptoms similar to those of a bipolar episode but these should remit after a few days off the substance. When assessing a child for a diagnosis of bipolar disorder a history of drug and alcohol use should be taken.

e. Sexual, emotional and physical abuse – certain symptoms in abused children can mimic symptoms of bipolar disorder but may remit with disclosure and appropriate intervention. These symptoms include disinhibition, hypervigilance and hypersexual symptoms. These behaviours should be assessed with respect to the child's developmental age.

f. Medical conditions including neurological diseases, endocrinopathies, epilepsy, and the use of prescribed medication, as the cause of manic and other symptoms should always be considered.

g. Schizophrenia spectrum disorders – psychotic symptoms are a feature of both bipolar disorder and schizophrenia, although in prepubertal children schizophrenia is considerably rarer than bipolar I disorder in the same age group. Schizophrenia tends to have a different course to bipolar disorder, with a gradual decline in functioning rather than an episodic course. Schizo-affective diagnoses may exceptionally be made, where patients meet operational criteria for both conditions.

h. Severe anxiety disorders with associated irritability may be confused with bipolar I disorder in children.

i. As well as differential diagnoses, potential comorbid diagnoses to be considered include anxiety disorders, panic disorder, PTSD, and disinhibited attachment disorder.

4.   ASSESSMENT METHODS

Assessment should take place in a multidisciplinary team and diagnosis should be made by a clinician with specialist training and expertise in the diagnosis of childhood mental disorders. Full assessment should involve interviews with the parents or carers as well as a direct interview with the child. The assessment should consider seeking to include significant others such as the child's school, social services, or other agencies involved in the care of the child.

In addition to a full clinical interview, a specialist diagnostic instrument may be used such as the WASH-U-KSADS (Geller *et al.*, 1996). In addition, scales completed by parents or carers can be helpful to aid differential diagnosis, including both general scales, such as the Child Behaviour Checklist (Achenbach, 1991) but which however fails to distinguish episodic from continuous symptoms, or the Conners' Abbreviated Rating Scale (Hirschfeld, 2005) and more specific scales, such as the Parent Young Mania Rating Scale (Gracious *et al.*, 2002), and the Parent General Behaviour Inventory (Depue *et al.*, 1989). However, such tools cannot replace a full assessment.

When assessing a child where a diagnosis of bipolar I disorder is being considered, it is essential that the following are taken into account:

Presentation of the problem

A detailed account of the presenting problem from the perspective of the child, parents/carers and significant others, such as teachers, is required.

Personal and developmental history

A personal and developmental history should be obtained which includes:

a. Detailed developmental and neurodevelopmental history, covering the child's full lifespan and including birth history, speech and language development, behaviour problems, attachment behaviour and history of abuse

b. Detailed psychosocial and family history, including any history of trauma and the family psychiatric history
c. History of behavioural changes
d. Previous psychiatric history – for example, depressive episodes, ADHD, psychotic symptoms, and so on.
e. History of risk behaviours, such as suicidal/self-harming behaviour and harm to others
f. Evidence of substance misuse
g. Cultural/ethnic factors relevant to the child's history and presentation of the problem
h. Educational attainment or disruptions in educational attainment

Examination

a. Detailed mental state examination must be conducted based on individual interview with the child
b. Full physical examination to exclude organic causes (epilepsy, brain tumour, thyroid disease, and so on)
c. Neuro-psychiatric/neurological assessment.

5.   COURSE AND PROGNOSIS

There is considerable uncertainty about long-term outcomes for conservatively defined bipolar I disorder in children. It is usually assumed that recovery is more likely if the child is living in a consistently supportive environment, with support also available for the parents and/or carers.

POSITION STATEMENT FOR THE DIAGNOSIS OF BIPOLAR I DISORDER IN ADOLESCENTS

After careful consideration of the evidence the consensus of the conference was that it is possible to establish a diagnosis of bipolar I disorder in adolescents. The conference took the position that the diagnosis, as for children, should be limited to a narrow phenotype – that is, bipolar I disorder with modified and tighter criteria than for adults, again emphasising euphoria in preference to irritability. Depending on their developmental age, adolescents can present with many features of bipolar disorder and the presentation tends to be atypical compared with adults. However, it was recognised that, while bipolar I disorder remains quite rare in adolescents, it becomes an increasingly important diagnosis during late adolescence, and there is no defined boundary between late adolescence and adulthood.

The conference was not convinced that evidence exists to support the use of the diagnoses of bipolar II disorder or bipolar disorder not otherwise specified in most adolescents. However, with increasing maturity, adult diagnoses will obviously assume more relevance in this age group.

Criteria for diagnosis

The conference agreed that it was possible to diagnose bipolar I disorder in adolescents on the basis of an episode of mania alone without any depressive episode but that, although irritability is a common symptom, it should not be a defining diagnostic criterion. The *core symptoms* for bipolar 1 disorder modified from current DSM-IV criteria for adolescents are set out in Box 6.

**Box 6: Criteria for manic episode
(Adapted from DSM-IV; APA, 1994, p. 332)**

A. A distinct period of abnormally and persistently elevated or expansive mood, normally lasting 1 week.

B. During the period of mood disturbance, three (or more) of the following symptoms have persisted and have been present to a significant degree:

    1. inflated self-esteem or grandiosity that is developmentally inappropriate and impairing

    2. decreased need for sleep (e.g. feels rested after only 3 hours of sleep)

    3. more talkative than usual or pressure to keep talking

    4. flight of ideas or subjective experience that thoughts are racing

    5. distractibility (i.e. attention too easily drawn to unimportant or irrelevant external stimuli)

    6. increase in goal-directed activity (either socially, at school, or sexually) or psychomotor agitation

    7. excessive involvement in pleasurable activities that have a high potential for painful consequences (e.g. engaging in unrestrained buying sprees, sexual indiscretions)

C. Symptoms do not meet criteria for mixed episode

D. The mood disturbance is sufficiently severe to cause marked impairment in educational functioning or in usual social activities or relationships with others or to necessitate hospitalization to prevent harm to self or others, or there are psychotic features.

E. The symptoms are not due to the direct physiological effects of a substance (e.g. a drug of abuse, a medication, or other treatment) or a general medical condition (e.g. hyperthyroidism or epilepsy)

Note: The status of manic episodes apparently precipitated by antidepressants or stimulants are uncertain. If the episode is self-limiting with medication withdrawal, it should not count towards a Bipolar I diagnosis.

In the case of mania related to antidepressants, a drug of abuse, stimulant drugs or steroids, a higher index of suspicion is warranted if the manic episode is severe and prolonged.

The diagnosis of bipolar II or bipolar spectrum disorder in adolescents
The conference was not convinced that bipolar diagnoses other than bipolar I can be made reliably in most adolescents. In the less mature, the same considerations apply as for younger children (see above). Thus, hypomania would usually have to be diagnosed on the basis of the history in patients presenting with depression. Clinical observation of the elevated mood state would not be possible. In more mature adolescents, adult diagnoses may be possible. More research in this area is needed together with improved adult data on bipolar II and bipolar spectrum disorders.

DIAGNOSTIC ISSUES

When establishing a diagnosis of bipolar disorder, the following symptoms and pattern of presentation should be considered:

Irritability – the conference took the position that unlike in adults, in adolescents irritability alone (instead of mood elevation) was not sufficient to make a diagnosis of bipolar disorder because it is common to many other psychiatric disorders in this age group. For adolescents, the key symptoms that have most discriminatory validity are elevated mood and grandiosity (Geller *et al.*, 2002). However, the conference took the view that in contrast to prepubertal children, irritability is a clinically important symptom that may suggest the diagnosis: it should be episodic, severe, result in impaired function, be out of character and out of keeping with the context.

a. *Cycling presentation* – A cycling course of presentation can be important in suggesting bipolar disorder and distinguishing it from another disorder such as ADHD, which does not follow an episodic course. In determining the duration of an episode, it was agreed that the criteria for adults are adopted, that is, a minimum 7 days' duration. But this is arbitrary, designed to err on the side of a conservative view of bipolarity in adolescence. Information on the longitudinal nature of the problems will be required to support a diagnosis.

b. *Impairment* – symptomatic episodes should be accompanied by marked impairment of personal, educational or social functioning.

c. *Developmental level* – consideration must also be given to the adolescent's developmental level. For example, an adolescent pretending to be a famous DJ would not be seen alone as evidence of grandiosity, but an adolescent who became convinced he was a famous DJ and acted on this by, for example, trying to book the key slot in his local nightclub, world. Box 7 gives an additional example.

d. *Learning difficulties* – adolescents with learning difficulties and other neurological and neurodevelopmental disorders may present significant diagnostic challenges. The view of the consensus conference was that no particular symptom cluster or clinical profile was associated with this group but that careful and often behavioural observation was required to establish a diagnosis.

Box 7: Vignette

A 15-year-old girl has been irritable and uncharacteristically noisy and demand-ing for the past 10 days. Her schoolwork has deteriorated and her parents report that she is awake and active until the early hours of the morning. She makes frequent visits to the local music shop and is talkative, effusive and over-familiar with the shop owner. She picks up a number of different guitars and attempts to play them. She stops people in the street, telling them she is a famous pop star. She dresses in an uncharacteristically revealing and sexually provocative manner and hugs and kisses young men in the street. At home she talks non-stop about her destiny as a famous pop star. She is active, cheerful and laughing. She jumps from subject to subject and nobody else can get a word in. She is intermittently short tempered and irritable for no apparent reason. At midnight she informs her family that the music shop owner is sexually attracted to her and wants an affair with her. She then becomes distressed, tearful and suicidal about the dilemma of combin-ing this relationship with her career as a pop star.

DISTINGUISHING BIPOLAR DISORDER FROM OTHER DISORDERS

An important issue in diagnosing bipolar I disorder in children is that of distinguish-ing it from other more common disorders that present with similar symptoms, notably ADHD, oppositional defiant disorder and conduct disorder. A common shared symp-tom is irritability. However, ADHD and oppositional defiant disorder will normally have become evident in childhood. Thus, the development of adolescent bipolar I disorder would normally imply the appearance of new relevant symptoms. Specifically, the core symptoms of bipolar disorder must be present for the diagnosis to be made; in particular, a child must have had at least one manic episode, charac-terised by elevated mood and meeting full duration criteria. The diagnosis of other disorders, such as conduct disorder or ADHD, should be made during a time of euthymia.

The following is a brief overview of these more common disorders and their distinguishing symptoms.

a. ADHD

The following symptoms are NOT part of ADHD:
- Unusually elated mood
- Inappropriate and impairing grandiosity
- Cycles of mood

ADHD with emotional instability can look very similar to some adult presenta-tions that would be classified as bipolar not otherwise specified.

b. Oppositional defiant disorder – the essential features are a recurrent picture of nega-tive, defiant and hostile behaviour towards authority, which usually starts before the age of 8 years with a gradual onset. The conflictual nature of relationships and high motor activity seen in children and adolescents with oppositional defiant disorder, along with lability of mood and use of drugs and alcohol, may require careful differentiation from symptoms of bipolar disorder or ADHD with which it may be present comorbidly.

c. Conduct disorder – there is little formal overlap in symptomatology between bipolar disorder and conduct disorder; hence the presence of mania cannot be inferred solely on the basis of the behavioural disturbance found in conduct disorder. Conversely, conduct disorder should not be diagnosed on the basis of behaviour arising in a manic interval. So, in general, comorbidity should be judged on the basis of an interval of euthymia (that is, behavioural disturbance is present).

d. Schizophrenia spectrum disorders – psychotic symptoms are a feature of both bipolar disorder and schizophrenia, although in the adolescent age group, schizophrenia is probably rarer than bipolar disorder. Schizophrenia tends to have a different course to bipolar disorder, with a gradual decline in functioning rather than clear cyclical episodes. Schizoaffective diagnoses may exceptionally be made, where patients meet operational criteria for both conditions. Schizoaffective disorder is distinguished from bipolar disorder by the presence of psychotic symptoms at a time when a mood disorder (mania or depression) is not present.

e. Depression – although a previous diagnosis of depression is not required to establish a diagnosis of bipolar disorder, a first presentation of a depressive disorder, especially if it is severe or psychotic, may indicate that the individual belongs to a high-risk group for whom major depressive disorder precedes bipolar disorder. Since bipolar I disorder in adolescence is rare, this group is small. There is also an increased risk for adolescents who have had an episode of major depression and have a family history of bipolar disorder, although these circumstances should not automatically lead to a diagnosis of bipolar disorder. Such young people should be monitored carefully.

f. Substance and alcohol misuse – this can produce symptoms similar to those of a bipolar episode but these should remit after a few days off the substance. When assessing an adolescent for a diagnosis of bipolar disorder, a history of drug and alcohol use must be taken.

g. Sexual, emotional and physical abuse – certain symptoms in abused adolescents can mimic symptoms of bipolar disorder but may remit with disclosure and appropriate intervention. These include disinhibition, hypervigilance and hypersexual symptoms. These should be assessed within respect to the young person's developmental age.

h. Medical conditions including neurological diseases, endocrinopathies, epilepsy, and the use of prescribed medication as the cause of manic and other symptoms should always be considered.

i. Potential comorbid diagnoses to be considered include anxiety disorders, panic disorder, PTSD, and disinhibited attachment disorder.

6.   ASSESSMENT METHODS

Assessment should take place in a multidisciplinary team and diagnosis should be made by a clinician with specialist training and expertise in the diagnosis of mental disorders in adolescents. Full assessment should involve interviews with the parents or carers as well as a direct interview with the young person. The assessment should consider seeking to include significant others such as the young person's school, social services or other agencies involved in their care.

In addition to a full clinical interview, a specialist diagnostic instrument may be used such as the Schedule for Affective Disorders and Schizophrenia for School-Age Children — Present and Lifetime Version (K-SADS-PL) (Kaufman *et al.*, 1997), WASH-U-KSADS (Geller *et al.*, 1996). In addition, scales completed by the clinician, parents or carers can be helpful to aid differential diagnosis, such as the YMRS (Young *et al.*, 1978), Parent Young Mania Rating Scale (Gracious *et al.*, 2002), and the Parent General Behaviour Inventory (Depue *et al.*, 1989). However, such tools cannot replace a full assessment.

When assessing an adolescent where a diagnosis of bipolar I disorder is being considered, it is essential that the following are taken into account:

Presentation of the problem

A detailed account of the presenting problem from the perspective of the adolescent, parents/carers and significant others, such as a teacher, is required.

Personal and developmental history

A personal and developmental history should be obtained which includes:
a. Detailed developmental and neurodevelopmental history, covering the adolescent's full lifespan and including birth history, speech and language development, behaviour problems, attachment behaviour and history of abuse
b. Detailed psychosocial and family history, including any history of trauma and the family psychiatric history
c. History of behavioural changes
d. Previous psychiatric history – for example, depressive episodes, ADHD, psychotic symptoms
e. History of risk behaviours, such as suicidal/self-harming behaviour and harm to others
f. Evidence of substance misuse
g. Cultural/ethnic factors relevant to the adolescent's history and presentation of the problem
h. Educational attainment or disruptions in educational attainment

Examination

a. Detailed mental state examination must be conducted based on individual interview with the adolescent
b. Full physical examination to exclude organic causes (epilepsy, brain tumour, thyroid disease, and so on)
c. Neuropsychiatric/neurological assessment

7.   COURSE AND PROGNOSIS

It is usually assumed that recovery is more likely if the adolescent is living in a consistently supportive environment, with support also available for the parents and/or carers. There is some uncertainty about long-term outcomes for this group of patients.

CLINICAL PRACTICE RECOMMENDATIONS

Diagnosing bipolar I disorder in prepubescent children

1.1.1.1   When diagnosing bipolar I disorder in prepubescent children the same criteria should be used as in adults except that:
  ● mania must be present
  ● euphoria must be present most days, most of the time (for a period of 7 days)
  ● irritability is not a core diagnostic criterion.
1.1.1.2   Bipolar I disorder should not be diagnosed solely on the basis of a major depressive episode in a child with a family history of bipolar disorder. However, children with a history of depression and a family history of bipolar disorder should be carefully followed up.

Diagnosing bipolar I disorder in adolescents

1.1.1.3   When diagnosing bipolar I disorder in adolescents the same criteria should be used as for adults except that:
  ● mania must be present
  ● euphoria must be present most days, most of the time (for at least 7 days)
  ● irritability can be helpful in making a diagnosis if it is episodic, severe, results in impaired function and is out of keeping or not in character; however, it should not be a core diagnostic criterion.
1.1.1.4   Bipolar I disorder should not be diagnosed solely on the basis of a major depressive episode in an adolescent with a family history of bipolar disorder. However, adolescents with a history of depression and a family history of bipolar disorder should be carefully followed up.

Diagnosing bipolar I disorder in older or developmentally advanced adolescents

1.1.1.5   In older or developmentally advanced adolescents, the criteria for establishing a diagnosis of bipolar I disorder in adults should be used.

Bipolar II disorder in both children and adolescents

1.1.1.6   Bipolar II disorder should not normally be diagnosed in children or adolescents because the diagnostic criteria are not well-enough established for routine use.
1.1.1.7   In older or developmentally advanced adolescents, the criteria for diagnosing bipolar II disorder in adults should be used.

Differential diagnosis for both children and adolescents

1.1.1.8   The presence of clear-cut episodes of unduly elated mood, inappropriate and impairing grandiosity, and cycles of mood should be used to distinguish bipolar I disorder from attention deficit hyperactivity disorder (ADHD) and conduct disorder.
1.1.1.9   The presence of mood cycles should be used to distinguish bipolar disorder from schizophrenia.
1.1.1.10   Before diagnosing bipolar I disorder in a child or adolescent, other possible explanations for the behaviour and symptoms should be considered, including:
   ● sexual, emotional and physical abuse if they show disinhibition, hypervigilance or hypersexuality
   ● the possibility of drug and/or alcohol misuse as a cause of mania-like symptoms; consider a diagnosis of bipolar disorder only after 7 days of abstinence
   ● previously undiagnosed learning difficulties
   ● organic causes such as excited confusional states in children with epilepsy, and akathisia resulting from neuroleptic medication.

Children and adolescents with learning difficulties

1.1.1.11   When diagnosing bipolar I disorder in a child or adolescent with learning difficulties, the same criteria as are applied to children and adolescents without learning difficulties should be used.

Children and adolescents with sub-threshold symptoms of bipolar disorder

1.1.1.12   If it is not possible to make a diagnosis in a child or adolescent with sub-threshold symptoms of bipolar disorder, they should be carefully followed up.

Assessment methods for children and adolescents

1.1.1.13 The diagnosis of bipolar disorder in children and adolescents should be made by a clinician with specialist training in child and adolescent mental health.

1.1.1.14 Assessment should include:
- a detailed mental state examination based on an individual interview with the child
- a medical evaluation to exclude organic causes
- further neuropsychological and neurological evaluation as appropriate
- a detailed account of the presenting problem from the child, parents or carers, and other significant adults such as teachers
- a detailed developmental and neurodevelopmental history, including birth history, speech and language development, behaviour problems, attachment behaviour and any history of abuse.

1.1.1.15 A specialist diagnostic instrument such as the WASH-U-KSADS may be used; scales completed by parents or carers such as the Child Behaviour Checklist, Conners' Abbreviated Rating Scale, Parent Young Mania Rating Scale and Parent General Behaviour Inventory may also be used. These should not replace a full clinical interview.

1.1.1.16 In severely mentally ill children and adolescents with psychotic symptoms, a diagnosis should be attempted as early as practical, and should be subject to regular specialist review.

CONCLUSION

This statement sets out the position on the diagnosis of bipolar disorder in children and adolescents as developed by a consensus conference established for the purpose of developing guidance for the NICE clinical practice guideline on the treatment and management of bipolar disorder in adults, children and adolescents. It makes specific recommendations for a narrow use of the diagnosis of bipolar I disorder and the avoidance of the use of a bipolar II diagnosis in children and adolescents while uncertainty about its reliability remains questionable. It also provides recommendations for the differential diagnosis of bipolar I disorder and the use of various assessment methods.

REFERENCES

Achenbach, T. M., Howell, C. T. & Quay, H. C. (1991) National survey of problems and competencies among four- to sixteen-year-olds: parents' reports for normative and clinical samples. *Monographs of the Society for Research in Child Development, 56,* 1–131.

American Psychiatric Association (1994) *Diagnostic and Statistical Manual of Mental Disorders* (DSM-IV) (4th edn). Washington DC: APA.

Benazzi, F. (2002) Borderline personality disorder comorbidity in early- and late-onset bipolar II disorder. *Canadian Journal of Psychiatry, 47*, 195–196.

Costello, E. J., Mustillo, S. & Erkanli, A. (2003) Prevalence and development of psychiatric disorders in childhood and adolescence. *Archives of General Psychiatry, 60*, 837–844.

Depue, R. A., Krauss, S. & Spoont, M. R. (1989) General behavior inventory identification of unipolar and bipolar affective conditions in a nonclinical university population. *Journal of Abnormal Psychology, 98*, 117–126.

Emslie, G. J., Kennar, B. D. & Kowatch, R. A. (1994) Affective disorders in children: diagnosis and management. *Journal of Child Neurology, 10*, S42–S49.

First, M. B., Spitzer, R. L., Gibbon, M., *et al.* (1997) *Structured Clinical Interview for DMS-IV Axis I Disorders-Clinician Version (SCID-CD)*. Washington DC: APA.

Geller, B., Sun, K., Zimerman, B., *et al.* (1995) Complex and rapid-cycling in bipolar children and adolescents: a preliminary study. *Journal of Affective Disorders, 34*, 259–68.

Geller, B., Williams, M., Zimerman, B., *et al.* (1996) *Washington University in St. Louis Kiddie Schedule for Affective Disorders and Schizophrenia (WASH-U-KSADS)*. St. Louis: Washington University.

Geller, B. & Luby, J. (1997) Child and adolescent bipolar disorder: a review of the past 10 years. *Journal of the American Academy of Child & Adolescent Psychiatry, 36*, 1168–1176.

Geller, B., Williams, M., Zimerman, B., *et al.* (1998) Prepubertal and early adolescent bipolarity differentiate from ADHD by manic symptoms, grandiose delusions, ultra-rapid or ultradian cycling. *Journal of Affective Disorders, 51*, 81–91.

Geller, B., Bolhofner, K., Craney, J. L., *et al.* (2000) Psychosocial functioning in a prepubertal and early adolescent bipolar disorder phenotype. *Journal of the American Academy of Child & Adolescent Psychiatry, 39*, 1543–1548.

Geller, B., Craney, J. L., Bolhofner, K., *et al.* (2001) One-year recovery and relapse rates of children with a prepubertal and early adolescent bipolar disorder phenotype. *American Journal of Psychiatry, 158*, 303–305.

Geller, B., Craney, J. L., Bolhofner, K., *et al.* (2002) Two-year prospective follow-up of children with a prepubertal and early adolescent bipolar disorder phenotype. *American Journal of Psychiatry, 159*, 927–933.

Geller, B., Craney, J. L., Bolhofner, K., *et al.* (2003) Phenomenology and longitudinal course of children with a prepubertal and early adolescent bipolar disorder phenotype. In *Bipolar Disorder in Childhood and Early Adolescence* (eds B. Geller & M. P. Delbello) pp. 25–50. New York & London: Guilford Press.

Goodwin, F. K. & Jamison, K. R. (1990) *Manic-Depressive Illness*. New York: Oxford University Press.

Goodwin, G. (2002) Hypomania: what's in a name? *British Journal of Psychiatry, 181*, 94–95.

Gracious, B. L., Youngstrom, E. A. & Findling, R. L. (2002) Discriminative validity of a parent version of the Young Mania Rating Scale. *Journal of the American Academy of Child & Adolescent Psychiatry, 41*, 1350–1359.

Harrington, R. (1994) Affective disorders. In *Child and Adolescent Psychiatry: Modern Approaches* (eds M. Rutter, E. Taylor & L. Hersov) London: Blackwell.

Hirschfeld, R. M. (2005) Are depression and bipolar disorder the same illness? *American Journal of Psychiatry, 162*, 1241–1242.

Johnson, J. G., Cohen, P. & Brook, J. S. (2000) Associations between bipolar disorder and other psychiatric disorders during adolescence and early adulthood: a community-based longitudinal investigation. *American Journal of Psychiatry, 157*, 1679–1681.

Kaufman, J., Birmaher, B., Brent, D., *et al.* (1997) Schedule for Affective Disorders and Schizophrenia for School-Age Children—Present and Lifetime version (K-SADS-PL): initial reliability and validity data. *Journal of the American Academy of Child & Adolescent Psychiatry, 36*, 980–988.

Kessler, R. C., Rubinow, D. R., Holmes, C., *et al.* (1997) The epidemiology of DSM-III-R bipolar I disorder in a general population survey. *Psychological Medicine, 27*, 1079–1089.

Leibenluft, E., Charney, D. S., Towbin, K. E., *et al.* (2003) Defining clinical phenotypes of juvenile mania. *American Journal of Psychiatry, 160*, 430–437.

Lewinsohn, P. M., Hops, H., Roberts, R. E., *et al.* (1993) Adolescent psychopathology: I. Prevalence and incidence of depression and other DSM-III-R disorders in high school students. *Journal of Abnormal Psychology, 102*, 133–144.

Lewinsohn, P. M., Klein, D. N. & Seeley, J. R. (1995) Bipolar disorders in a community sample of older adolescents: prevalence, phenomenology, comorbidity, and course. *Journal of American Academy of Child and Adolescent Psychiatry, 34*, 454–463.

Lewinsohn, P. M., Seeley, J. R. & Klein, D. N. (2003) Bipolar disorders during adolescence. *Acta Psychiatrica Scandinavica, 418*, 47–50.

Puig-Antich, J. & Chambers, W. (1978) *The Schedule for Affective Disorders and Schizophrenia for School-Age Children* (Kiddie-SADS). New York: New York State Psychiatric Institute.

Reddy, Y. C. & Srinath, S. (2000) Juvenile bipolar disorder. *Acta Psychiatrica Scandinavica, 102*, 162–170.

Tillman, R. & Geller, B. (2005) A brief screening tool for a prepubertal and early adolescent bipolar disorder phenotype. *American Journal of Psychiatry, 162*, 1214–1216.

Weissman, M. M., Bland, R. C. & Canino, G. J. (1996) Cross-national epidemiology of major depression and bipolar disorder. *Journal of the American Medical Association, 276*, 293–299.

Young, R. C., Biggs, J. T., Ziegler, V. E., *et al.* (1978) A rating scale for mania: reliability, validity and sensitivity. *British Journal of Psychiatry, 133*, 429–435.

APPENDIX 20:

CONSENSUS STATEMENT FOR THE PHARMACOLOGICAL MANAGEMENT OF PREGNANT AND LACTATING WOMEN WITH BIPOLAR DISORDER

INTRODUCTION

This statement has been developed from a consensus conference held on 11th July 2005 and attended by members of the NICE GDGs on bipolar disorder and antenatal and postnatal mental health, along with invited experts. It should be read in conjunction with the recommendations for the care of all people with bipolar disorder contained in the main body of the guideline. A full list of the attendees at the conference and the title of their presentations (where appropriate) is given in Appendix 2.

For women with bipolar disorder pregnancy and the immediate post partum period is a time of increased risk. (Jones & Craddock, 2005; O'Hara & Swain, 1996; Robertson *et al.*, 2005). For those currently being treated for a mental disorder, pregnancy may require a review of existing treatment regimes. This is important as there is reasonable evidence that an untreated mental disorder during this period can have a significant and detrimental impact on the physical and mental well-being of the mother, the foetus and the infant. For example, untreated severe depression is associated with an increased rate of obstetric complications, still birth, suicide attempts, postnatal specialist care for the infant, and low birth weight babies (Bonari *et al.*, 2004). In schizophrenia and bipolar disorder there is also an increased rate of suicide and potentially significant exacerbation of the disorder if not treated and poorer obstetric outcomes including increased preterm delivery, low birth weight babies and babies who are small for gestational age (Howard, 2005; Jablensky *et al.*, 2005). Similarly, poor fetal outcomes have been associated with maternal eating disorders during pregnancy (Kouba *et al.*, 2005). There is also emerging evidence that untreated mental disorder in pregnancy may be associated with poorer long-term outcomes to children beyond the immediate postnatal period (Nulman *et al.*, 2002). All of these factors point to the importance of appropriate treatment and management of the mother during pregnancy and the mother and the infant in the postnatal period. In some cases, effective treatment may be non-pharmacological, but for a significant proportion of women with bipolar, pharmacological treatments may be the treatment advocated by a healthcare professional or may be the choice of treatment that the women herself makes. There is good evidence in the treatment of most major mental disorders that pharmacological interventions can have significant benefits in both promoting remission, reducing

543

the severity of symptomatology and maintaining mental well-being (NICE, 2002; 2004a; 2004b; 2004c; 2005a).

It is also established that many pharmacological agents used in the treatment of mental disorder in pregnancy carry some risk of harm, in particular to the fetus, in addition to the base-rate obstetric risk and risks of congenital malformation already faced by mother and foetus (between 2–4% rate of abnormalities in the general population (Brockington, 1996)). However, the magnitude of the risks associated with the pharmacological treatment of mental disorder are not well understood (for example, Patton *et al.*, 2002), nor is their relative risk balanced against the harm of untreated disorder and systems for communicating these to patients are not well understood (Epstein *et al.*, 2004; Scialli, 2005). In significant part, this lack of information arises from the difficulty in conducting appropriate clinical trials with pregnant women. In addition to the risks arising from the potentially teratogenic properties of the drugs, the altered physical state of the mother over the course of a pregnancy means that increased physical monitoring, for example of liver function, blood pressure and blood glucose during pregnancy, the consideration of the impact of analgesic drugs during delivery, the impact of rapidly changing body fluid levels postnatally and the impact on lactation all need to be considered.

THE CONSENSUS STATEMENT

As long as the risk-benefits of the pharmacological treatment of mental disorder in pregnancy are unclear, clinicians and patients are faced with difficult choices in the use of any pharmacological agent for the treatment of bipolar disorder during pregnancy and the postnatal period. The aim of this consensus statement (which is focused only on bipolar disorder and is therefore a summary version of the consensus statement developed for all disorders at the conference) is to synthesis the best available evidence and to provide guidance for clinicians and patients on the appropriate use of pharmacological agents in the treatment of bipolar disorder in pregnancy and the perinatal period. The statement is focused on with an identified range of routinely used drugs. It is also limited in that it takes its evidence base for effectiveness of the drugs considered almost exclusively from trials from which pregnant women are excluded.

The following groups of drugs are considered: antidepressants (including SSRIs, tricyclics, MAOIs and novel antidepressants), mood stabilisers (including the anticonvulsants commonly used in the treatment of bipolar disorders (sodium valproate, lamotrigine and carbamazepine) and lithium carbonate), antipsychotics (including both typical and atypical antipsychotics) and benzodiazepines.

The structure of the consensus statement is also designed to reflect three important factors: the stage of pregnancy (preconception/contraception, first, second and third trimesters, the intrapartum period, the postnatal period and lactation), whether the disorder is pre-existing or a new onset and whether or not the patient is currently being treated.

A number of principles should guide the practice of clinicians treating women with bipolar disorder who are considering pregnancy, are pregnant or are in the postnatal period. They are:

1. Patient history of previous treatment response should guide future treatment decisions.
2. That the lowest dose from within the recommended range (that is, from the BNF) be considered and considerable care be taken before titrating the dose up. This is particularly important where identified risks are potentially dose related.
3. That the monotherapy of a disorder should be the preferred treatment option.
4. That drug interactions with non-psychotropic drugs should be carefully considered.
5. The balance of risks and benefits of treatment during pregnancy (particularly in the first trimester) may raise the threshold before initiating pharmacological treatment compared with non-pregnant women.
6. That changes of medication regime may be considered to reduce the risk of harm but the disadvantages to change of regime should also be considered.
7. That the drug that is known to have the potentially least harmful effects on mother, foetus or infant during the postnatal period should be considered first.
8. That increased medical and psychiatric monitoring, including risk assessment, of women, fetus and infant should be the norm for all women taking psychotropic medication in pregnancy and the postnatal period.
9. That wherever possible, suitable treatment options should be found for women who wish to breastfeed.
10. That the most effective means of communicating the magnitude of risk and benefit to patients, partners and families should be adopted.

RISK ASSOCIATED WITH PHARMACOLOGICAL TREATMENT IN PREGNANCY AND THE POSTNATAL PERIOD

1.   LITHIUM

The primary risk that has been identified with lithium occurs in the first trimester and is associated with an increase in the rate of congenital heart disease. Rates of 0.01% to 0.005% have been found for Ebstein's anomaly compared with 0.0005% in a non-lithium-treated population (Cohen *et al.*, 1994). There is no other consistent evidence of increased congenital abnormalities. However, the use of lithium in the second to third trimester has also been associated with the floppy baby syndrome, potential thyroid abnormalities and nephrogenic diabetes insipidus (Llewellyn *et al.*, 1998). Lithium is present in high concentrations in breast milk and is generally not recommended for breastfeeding.

2.   SODIUM VALPROATE

Sodium valproate is associated with the development of a range of major abnormalities including facial dysmorphias, distal digit hypoplasia and neural tube defects (Homes *et al.,* 2001; Morrow *et al.,* 2006; O'Brien & Gilmour-White, 2005). Data from the UK Epilepsy and Pregnancy Register shows an MMR of 2.4% (0.9 to 6.0) in women with epilepsy who were not taking anti-epileptic drugs, 4% (2.7 to 4.4) for patients on monotherapy and 6.5% (5.0 to 9.4) on polytherapy. The monotherapy MMR for valproate was 5.9% (4.3 to 8.2), significantly higher than the other commonly used mood stabilising drugs (carbamazepine 2.3% (1.4 to 3.7), lamotrigine 2.1% (1.0 to 4.0)). The risk is thought to be greater in those prescribed >1 g valproate per day versus lower doses (Omtzigt *et al.,* 1992). It is important to note that the neural tube closes at day 30 of gestation, which will usually be before a pregnancy has been confirmed. For this reason, prevention is essential In addition, there is evidence that the use of valproate is associated with a significant reduction in cognitive functioning of children born to mothers who used valproate during pregnancy (Adab *et al.,* 2004a, b).

There is strong evidence that folic acid supplements reduce the incidence of neural tube defects (Lumley *et al.,* 2001). As a result, all women planning pregnancy are advised to take 0.4 mg folic acid per day before conception and during the first 12 weeks of pregnancy. Women with a neural tube defect, or a neural tube defect in a previous child, are advised a higher dose of 5 mg per day (BNF). Given the association of valproate and carbamazepine with neural tube defects, and the fact that both drugs interfere with folic acid metabolism, some authorities recommend that women of childbearing potential prescribed these drugs should receive folic acid supplements. However, to date, no study has demonstrated that prescribing folic acid supplements to women taking anticonvulsants during pregnancy reduces the risk of neural tube defects; in fact neural tube defects have been reported in the offspring of such women (for example, Duncan *et al.,* 2001). There is a danger that routine folic acid prescribing in this group may incorrectly imply that getting pregnant is safe and that the risk of neural tube defect posed by the anticonvulsant has been counteracted. Given this and the lack of data, it is unclear whether prescribers should routinely prescribe folic acid to women of child-bearing potential taking valproate and carbamazepine. If a woman receiving either of these drugs presents at less than 12 weeks of pregnancy, it would seem prudent to start folic acid supplementation; though given that the neural tube closes by day 28 after fertilisation, it is debatable whether or not this provides any protection.

3.   CARBAMAZEPINE

Carbamazepine is associated with a higher rate of congenital abnormalities including neural tube defects (prevalence of around 1% compared with rates of 0.1% in the general population), distal digit hypoplasia and craniofacial abnormalities (Artama, 2005), giving an overall MMR of around 2.3% (Canger *et al.,* 1999). In addition, some studies have suggested an increase in minor malformations such as a small nose with a long space between the nose and the upper lip and small fingernails (Wide *et al.*, 2000). There are reported high concentrations in the breast milk.

4.   LAMOTRIGINE

There is no consistent evidence of a significant increase in major malformations in children where women have taken lamotrigine in pregnancy (Tomson *et al.*, 2004) with rates little different in the UK register for women treated with lamotrigine (2.1% (1.0 to 4.0)) than those on no medication (2.4% (0.9 to 6.0)). However, evidence has emerged of a relatively high rate of cleft palate in infants born to women taking lamotrigine during pregnancy with a rate of 8.9 per 1000 (Holmes *et al.*, 2006). Also Morrow and colleagues (2006) also found that whilst the overall rate of malformations in babies of women taking the drug during pregnancy is similar to the background rate (3.2%), there may be a dose-response relationship with the rate rising to 5.4% in those taking more than 200 mg daily, whilst for those on the lowest dose the rate was 1.3%. The Morrow and colleagues (2006) study is based on those taking drugs to control epilepsy. In addition, the summary of product characteristics states: 'Lamotrigine is a weak inhibitor of dihydrofolate reductase. There is a theoretical risk of human fetal malformations when the mother is treated with a folate inhibitor during pregnancy. However, reproductive toxicology studies with lamotrigine in animals at doses in excess of the human therapeutic dosage showed no teratogenic effects.There are insufficient data available on the use of lamotrigine in human pregnancy to evaluate its safety. Lamotrigine should not be used in pregnancy unless, in the opinion of the physician, the potential benefits of treatment to the mother outweigh any possible risks to the developing fetus. Physiological changes during pregnancy may result in decreased lamotrigine levels. These changes in lamotrigine levels can occur from early in pregnancy and progress during pregnancy, then revert quickly after delivery. The dose of lamotrigine should not be increased routinely in pregnancy but should only be adjusted on clinical grounds. To maintain seizure control during pregnancy a dose increase may be needed, although other factors including vomiting should also be considered if seizure control deteriorates. Post-partum a dose decrease may be needed to avoid toxicity. Women on lamotrigine must be monitored closely during pregnancy and post-partum.'

Little is known about the effect of lamotrigine on breastfed infants but given the potential seriousness of the rash associated with lamotrigine, considerable caution should be exercised before advising breastfeeding.

5.   BENZODIAZEPINES

Benzodiazepines may be associated in the first trimester with an increased risk of some malformations, for example, cleft palate (Eros *et al.*, 2002; McElhatton, 1994; Dolovich *et al.*, 1998). Use later in pregnancy may also be associated with floppy baby syndrome and the possibility of withdrawal symptoms and restlessness in neonates (Briggs *et al.*, 2002).

6.   ANTIPSYCHOTICS

There is some indication of a small overall increased risk of malformations associated with the use of antipsychotics (3.5% compared with 1.6%), although it is not clear if this may relate to the underlying illness (information on individual drugs is very limited (Rumeau-Rouquette *et al.*, 1976; Slone *et al.*, 1976). There is little evidence to distinguish between any first- or second-generation antipsychotic, although there is some evidence of a possible link between olanzapine and pre-eclampsia and gestational diabetes (Kirchheiner *et al.*, 2000) and some uncertainty that the accumulation of clozapine in the fetus may increase likelihood of floppy baby syndrome and neonatal seizures. There is concern about the accumulation of antipsychotics in the breast milk and the potential impact on children (Briggs *et al.*, 2002).

7.   ANTIDEPRESSANTS

For antidepressants as an overall group, there is no indication of an increase in major malformations but some suggestion of a potential increased rate of spontaneous abortion (Ericson *et al.*, 1999; Hendrick *et al.*, 2003; Hemels *et al.*, 2005). For SSRIs there is no reported increase in risk over other antidepressants, although there has been a recent warning by the Food and Drug Administration concerning the use of paroxetine in pregnancy. For MAOIs there is limited evidence of an increased risk of congenital malformation while for novel antidepressants there is no evidence of increased risk, although caution is recommended in the use of venlafaxine. There is concern about the potential impact on the baby, including preterm delivery, the possibility of the evidence of serotonergic syndrome or serotonin withdrawal syndrome and the sedating effects of some antidepressants (Kallen, 2004).

RECOMMENDATIONS

General principles of management for women of child-bearing potential and for women with bipolar disorder who are pregnant

1.1.1.1 The absolute and relative risks of problems associated with both treating and not treating the bipolar disorder during pregnancy should be discussed with women.

1.1.1.2 More frequent contact by specialist mental health services (including, where appropriate, specialist perinatal mental health services), working closely with maternity services, should be considered for pregnant women with bipolar disorder, because of the increased risk of relapse during pregnancy and the postnatal period.

1.1.1.3 A written plan for managing a woman's bipolar disorder during the pregnancy, delivery and postnatal period should be developed as soon as possible. This should be developed with the patient and significant others, and shared with her obstetrician, midwife, GP and health visitor. All medical decisions should be recorded in all versions of the patient's notes. Information about her medication should be included in the birth plan and notes for postnatal care.

1.1.1.4   If a pregnant woman with bipolar disorder is stable on an antipsychotic and likely to relapse without medication, she should be maintained on the antipsychotic, and monitored for weight gain and diabetes.

1.1.1.5   The following drugs should not be routinely prescribed for pregnant women with bipolar disorder:

- valproate – because of risk to the fetus and subsequent child development
- carbamazepine – because of its limited efficacy and risk of harm to the fetus
- lithium – because of risk of harm to the fetus, such as cardiac problems
- lamotrigine* – because of the risk of harm to the fetus
- paroxetine – because of the risk of cardiovascular malformations in the fetus
- long-term treatment with benzodiazepines – because of risks during pregnancy and the immediate postnatal period, such as cleft palate and floppy baby syndrome.

Women planning a pregnancy

1.1.1.6   Women with bipolar disorder who are considering pregnancy should normally be advised to discontinue taking valproate, carbamazepine, lithium and lamotrigine*, and alternative propylactic drugs (such as an antipsychotic) should be considered.

1.1.1.7   Women taking antipsychotics who are planning a pregnancy should be advised that the raised prolactin levels associated with some antipsychotics reduce the chances of conception, with the likelihood that this will decrease the possibility of success. If prolactin levels are raised, an alternative drug should be considered.

1.1.1.8   If a woman who needs antimanic medication plans to become pregnant, a low-dose typical or atypical antipsychotic should be considered, because they are of least known risk.

1.1.1.9   If a woman taking lithium plans to become pregnant, the following options should be considered:

- if the patient is well and not at high risk of relapse – gradually stopping lithium
- if the patient is not well or is at high risk of relapse:
  - switching gradually to an antipsychotic, or
  - stopping lithium and restarting it in the second trimester if the woman is not planning to breastfeed and her symptoms have responded better to lithium than to other drugs in the past, or
  - continuing with lithium, after full discussion of the risks, while trying to conceive and throughout the pregnancy, if manic episodes have complicated the woman's previous pregnancies, and her symtoms have responded well to lithium.

1.1.1.10 If a woman remains on lithium during pregnancy, serum lithium levels should be monitored every 4 weeks, then weekly from the 36th week, and less than 24 hours after childbirth. The dose should be adjusted to maintain appropriate serum levels within the therapeutic range. The woman should maintain adequate fluid intake.

1.1.1.11 If a woman planning a pregnancy becomes depressed after stopping prophylactic medication, psychological therapy (CBT) should be offered in preference to an antidepressant because of the risk of switching associated with antidepressants. If an antidepressant is used it should usually be an SSRI (but not paroxetine because of the risk of cardiovascular malformations in the fetus) and the woman should be monitored closely.

Women with an unplanned pregnancy

1.1.1.12 If a woman with bipolar disorder has an unplanned pregnancy:
- the pregnancy should be confirmed as quickly as possible
- the woman should be advised to stop taking valproate, carbamazepine and lamotrigine*
- if the pregnancy is confirmed in the first trimester, and the woman is stable, lithium should be stopped gradually over 4 weeks, and the woman informed that this may not remove the risk of cardiac defects in the fetus
- if the woman remains on lithium during pregnancy serum lithium levels should be checked every 4 weeks, then weekly from the 36th week, and less than 24 hours after childbirth; the dose should be adjusted to keep serum levels within the therapeutic range, and the woman should maintain adequate fluid intake
- an antipsychotic should be offered as prophylactic medication
- offer appropriate screening and counselling about the continuation of the pregnancy, the need for additional monitoring and the risks to the fetus if the woman stays on medication.

1.1.1.13 If a woman with bipolar disorder continues with an unplanned pregnancy, the newborn baby should have a full paediatric assessment and social and medical help should be provided for the mother and child.

Pregnant women experiencing acute mania or depression

Acute mania

1.1.1.14 If a pregnant woman who is not taking medication develops acute mania, an atypical or typical antipsychotic should be considered. The dose should be kept as low as possible and the woman monitored carefully.

1.1.1.15 If a pregnant woman develops acute mania while taking prophylactic medication, prescribers should:
- check the dose of the prophylactic agent and adherence

- increase the dose if the woman is taking an antipsychotic or consider changing to an antipsychotic if she is not
- if there is no response to changes in dose or drug and the patient has severe mania, consider the use of ECT, lithium and, rarely, valproate.

1.1.1.16 If there is no alternative to valproate the women should be informed of the increased risk to the fetus and the child's intellectual development. The lowest possible effective dose should be used and augmenting it with additional antimanic medication (but not carbamazepine*) considered. The maximum dosage should be 1 gram per day, in divided doses and in the slow-release form, with 5 mg/day folic acid.

Depressive symptoms

1.1.1.17 For mild depressive symptoms in pregnant women with bipolar disorder the following should be considered:
- self-help approaches such as guided self-help and computerised CBT
- brief psychological interventions
- antidepressant medication.

1.1.1.18 For moderate to severe depressive symptoms in pregnant women with bipolar disorder the following should be considered:
- psychological treatment (CBT) for moderate depression
- combined medication and structured psychological interventions for severe depression.

1.1.1.19 For moderate to severe depressive symptoms in pregnant women with bipolar disorder, quetiapine* alone, or SSRIs (but not paroxetine) in combination with prophylactic medication should be preferred because SSRIs are less likely to be associated with switching than the tricyclic antidepressants. Monitor closely for signs of switching and stop the SSRI if patients start to develop manic or hypomanic symptoms.

1.1.1.20 Women who are prescribed an antidepressant during pregnancy should be informed of the potential, but predominantly short-lived, adverse effects of antidepressants on the neonate.

Care in the perinatal period

1.1.1.21 Women taking lithium should be delivered in hospital, and be monitored during labour by the obstetric medical team, in addition to usual midwife care. Monitoring should include fluid balance, because of the risk of dehydration and lithium toxicity.

1.1.1.22 After delivery, if a woman with bipolar disorder who is not on medication is at high risk of developing an acute episode, prescribers should consider establishing or reinstating medication as soon as the patient is medically stable (once the fluid balance is established).

1.1.1.23   If a woman maintained on lithium is at high risk of a manic relapse in the immediate postnatal period, augmenting treatment with an antipsychotic should be considered.

1.1.1.24   If a woman with bipolar disorder develops severe manic or psychotic symptoms and behavioural disturbance in the intrapartum period rapid tranquillisation with an antipsychotic should be considered in preference to a benzodiazepine because of the risk of floppy baby syndrome. Treatment should be in collaboration with an anaesthetist.

Breast feeding

1.1.1.25   Women with bipolar disorder who are taking psychotropic medication and wish to breastfeed should:
   ● have advice on the risks and benefits of breastfeeding
   ● be advised not to breastfeed if taking lithium, benzodiazepines or lamotrigine*, and offered a different prophylactic agent that can be used when breastfeeding – an antipsychotic should be the first choice (but not clozapine*)
   ● be prescribed an SSRI if an antidepressant is used (but not fluoxetine or citalopram).

Care of the infant

1.1.1.26   Babies whose mothers took psychotropic drugs during pregnancy should be monitored for adverse drug effects, drug toxicity or withdrawal (for example, floppy baby syndrome, irritability, constant crying, shivering, tremor, restlessness, increased tone, feeding and sleeping difficulties and rarely seizures). If the mother was prescribed antidepressants in the last trimester, such symptoms may be a serotonergic toxicity syndrome rather than withdrawal, and the neonate should be monitored carefully.

REFERENCES

Adab, N., Kini, U. & Vinten, J. (2004a) The longer term outcome of children born to mothers with epilepsy. *Journal of Neurology, Neurosurgery and Psychiatry, 75,* 1575–1583.

Adab, N., Tudur, S.C. & Vinten, J. (2004b) Common antiepileptic drugs in pregnancy in women with epilepsy. *Cochrane Database of Systematic Reviews, 3,* CD004848.

Artama, M., Auvinen, A. & Raudaskoski, T. (2005) Antiepileptic drug use of women with epilepsy and congenital malformations in offspring. *Neurology, 64,* 1874–1878.

Bonari, L., Pinto, N., Ahn, E., *et al.* (2004) Perinatal risks of untreated depression during pregnancy. *Canadian Journal of Psychiatry, 49,* 726–735.

Briggs, G.G., Freeman, R.K. & Yaffe, S.J. (2002) *Drugs in Pregnancy and Lactation: A Reference Guide to Fetal and Neonatal Risk* (6th edn). Philadelphia PA & London: Lippincott Williams & Wilkins.

Brockington, I. F. (1996) *Motherhood and Mental Health*. Oxford: Oxford University Press.

Canger, R., Battino, D., Canevini, M.P., *et al.* (1999) Malformations in offspring of women with epilepsy: a prospective study. *Epilepsia, 40*, 1231–1236.

Cohen, L.S., Friedman, J.M. & Jefferson, J.W. (1994) A re-evaluation of risk of in-utero exposure to lithium. *Journal of the American Medical Association, 271*, 146–150.

Dolovich, L.R., Addis, A. & Vaillancourt, J.M. (1998) Benzodiazepine use in pregnancy and major malformations or oral cleft: meta-analysis of cohort and case-control studies. *BMJ, 317*, 839–843.

Duncan, S., Mercho, S. & Lopes-Cendes, I. (2001) Repeated neural tube defects and valproate monotherapy suggest a pharmacogenetic abnormality. *Epilepsia, 42*, 750–753.

D'Souza, R.E. & Guillebaud, J. (2002) Risks and benefits of oral contraceptive pills. *Best Practice & Research. Clinical Obstetrics & Gynaecology, 16*, 133–154.

Einarson, A., Fatoye, B., Sarkar, M., *et al.* (2001) Pregnancy outcome following gestational exposure to venlafaxine: a multicenter prospective controlled study. *American Journal of Psychiatry, 158*, 1728–1730.

Epstein, R.M., Alper, B.S. & Quill, T.E. (2004) Communicating evidence for participatory decision making. *Journal of the American Medical Association, 291*, 2359–2366.

Ericson, A., Kallen, B. & Wiholm, B. (1999) Delivery outcome after the use of antidepressants in early pregnancy. *European Journal of Clinical Pharmacology, 55*, 503–508.

Eros, E., Czeizel, A.E., Rockenbauer, M., *et al.* (2002) A population-based case-control teratologic study of nitrazepam, medazepam, tofisopam, alprazolum and clonazepam treatment during pregnancy. *European Journal of Obstetrics & Gynecology and Reproductive Biology, 101*, 147–154.

Hemels, M.E., Einarson, A., Koren, G., *et al.* (2005) Antidepressant use during pregnancy and the rates of spontaneous abortions: a meta-analysis. *The Annals of Pharmacotherapy, 39*, 803–809.

Hendrick, V., Smith, L.M., Suri, R., *et al.* (2003) Birth outcomes after prenatal exposure to antidepressant medication. *American Journal of Obstetrics and Gynecology, 188*, 812–815.

Holmes, L.B., Harvey, E.A. & Coull, B.A. (2001) The teratogenicity of anticonvulsant drugs. *New England Journal of Medicine, 244*, 1132–1138.

Holmes, L.B., Wyszynski, D.F., Baldwin, E.J., *et al.* (2006) Increased risks for non-syndromic cleft palate among infants exposed to lamotrigine during pregnancy. *Birth Defects Research Part A: Clinical and Molecular Teratology, 76*, 318.

Howard, L.M. (2005) Fertility and pregnancy in women with psychotic disorders. *European Journal of Obstetrics & Gynecology and Reproductive Biology, 119*, 3–10.

Howard, L.M., Kumar, C., Leese, M., *et al.* (2002) The general fertility rate in women with psychotic disorders. *American Journal of Psychiatry, 159*, 991–997.

Jablensky, A.V., Morgan, V., Zubrick, S.R., *et al.* (2005) Pregnancy, delivery, and neonatal complications in a population cohort of women with schizophrenia and major affective disorders. *American Journal of Psychiatry, 162,* 79–91.

Jones, I. & Craddock, N. (2005) Bipolar disorder and childbirth: the importance of recognising risk. *British Journal of Psychiatry, 186,* 453–454.

Kallen, B. (2004) Neonate characteristics after maternal use of antidepressants in late pregnancy. *Archives of Pediatrics & Adolescent Medicine, 158,* 312–316.

Kirchheiner, J., Berghofer, A. & Bolk-Weischedel, D. (2000) Healthy outcome under olanzapine treatment in a pregnant woman. *Pharmacopsychiatry, 33,* 78–80.

Kouba, S., Hallstrom, T., Lindholm, C., *et al.* (2005) Pregnancy and neonatal outcomes in women with eating disorders. *Obstetrics & Gynecology, 105,* 255–260.

Llewellyn, A., Stowe, Z.N. & Strader, J.R., Jr. (1998) The use of lithium and management of women with bipolar disorder during pregnancy and lactation. *Journal of Clinical Psychiatry, 59,* Suppl 6, 57–65.

Lumley, J., Watson, L., *et al.* (2001) Periconceptional supplementation with folate and/or multivitamins for preventing neural tube defects. *Cochrane Database of Systematic Reviews, 3,* CD001056.

McElhatton, P.R. (1994) The effects of benzodiazepine use during pregnancy and lactation. *Reproductive Toxicology, 8,* 461–475.

Morrow, J.L., Russell, A., Guthrie, E., *et al. (*2006) Malformation risks of anti-epileptic drugs in pregnancy: a prospective study from the UK Epilepsy and Pregnancy Register. *Journal of Neurosurgery and Psychiatry, 77,* 193–198.

NICE (2002) *Schizophrenia: Core Interventions in the Treatment and Management of Schizophrenia in Primary and Secondary Care.* Clinical Guideline No. 1. London: NICE.

NICE (2004a) *Depression: Management of Depression in Primary and Secondary Care.* Clinical Guideline No. 23. London: NICE.

NICE (2004b) *Eating Disorders: Core Interventions in the Treatment and Management of Anorexia Nervosa, Bulimia Nervosa and Related Eating Disorders.* Clinical Guideline No. 9. London: NICE.

NICE (2004c) *Anxiety: Management of Anxiety (Panic Disorder, With or Without Agoraphobia, and Generalised Anxiety Disorder) in Adults in Primary, Secondary and Community Care.* Clinical Guideline No. 22. London: NICE.

NICE (2005a) *Post-Traumatic Stress Disorder: The Management of PTSD in Adults and Children in Primary and Secondary Care.* Clinical Guideline No. 26. London: NICE.

Nulman, I., Rovet, J., Stewart, D.E., *et al.* (2002) Child development following exposure to tricyclic antidepressants or fluoxetine throughout fetal life: a prospective, controlled study. *American Journal of Psychiatry, 159,* 1889–1895.

O'Brien, M.D. & Gilmour-White, S.K. (2005) Management of epilepsy in women. *Postgraduate Medical Journal, 81,* 278–285.

O'Hara, M.W. & Swain, A.M. (1996) Rates and risk of postpartum depression: a meta-analysis. *International Review of Psychiatry, 8,* 37–54.

Oinonen, K.A. & Mazmanian, D. (2002) To what extent do oral contraceptives influence mood and affect? *Journal of Affective Disorders, 70,* 229–240.

Omtzigt, J.G., Los, F.J. & Grobbee, D.E. (1992) The risk of spina bifida aperta after first-trimester exposure to valproate in a prenatal cohort. *Neurology, 42,* Suppl 5, 119–125.

Patton, S.W., Misri, S., Corral, M.R., *et al.* (2002) Antipsychotic medication during pregnancy and lactation in women with schizophrenia: evaluating the risk. *Canadian Journal of Psychiatry, 47,* 959–965.

Robertson, E., Jones, I., Haque, S., *et al.* (2005) Risk of puerperal and non-puerperal recurrence of illness following bipolar affective puerperal (post-partum) psychosis. *British Journal of Psychiatry, 186,* 258–259.

Rumeau-Rouquette, C., Breart, G. & Deniel, M. (1976) The concept of risk in perinatology. Results of epidemiologic surveys (author's transl). *Revue d'epidémiologie et de santé publique, 24,* 253–276.

Scialli, A.R. (2005) *Counseling. Reprotox in a Nutshell.* http://reprotox.org/docs/nutshell01_05.pdf [accessed July 2005].

Slone, D., Siskind, V. & Heinonen, O.P. (1976) Antenatal exposure to the phenothiazines in relation to congenital malformations, perinatal mortality rate, birth weight, and intelligence quotient score. *American Journal of Obstetrics and Gynecology, 128,* 486–488.

Tomson, T., Perucca, E. & Battino, D. (2004) Navigating toward fetal and maternal health: the challenge of treating epilepsy in pregnancy. *Epilepsia, 45,* 1171–1175.

Wide, K., Winbladh, B., Tomson, T., *et al.* (2000) Psychomotor development and minor anomalies in children exposed to antiepileptic drugs in utero: a prospective population-based study. *Developmental Medicine and Child Neurology, 42,* 87–92.

APPENDIX 21: SCHEDULE FOR PHYSICAL MONITORING

Test or measurement	Monitoring for all patients		Monitoring for specific drugs				
	Initial health check	Annual check up	Antipsychotics	Lithium	Valproate*	Carbamazepine	
Thyroid function	✓	✓[a]		At start and every 6 months; more often if evidence of deterioration			
Liver function	✓				At start and at 6 months	At start and at 6 months	
Renal function	✓			At start and every 6 months; more often if there is evidence of deterioration or the patient starts taking drugs such as ACE inhibitors, diuretics or NSAIDs		Urea and electrolytes every 6 months.	

Test			Only if clinically indicated	At start and once during first 6 months		At start and at 6 months
Full blood count	✓					At start and at 6 months
Blood (plasma) glucose	✓		At start and at 3 months (and at 1 month if taking olanzapine); more often if there is evidence of elevated levels			
Lipid profile	✓	Over 40s only	At start and at 3 months; more often if evidence of elevated levels			
Blood pressure	✓	✓				
Prolactin	Children and adolescents only		Risperidone only at start and if symptoms of raised prolactin develop			
ECG	If indicated by history or clinical picture		At start if there are risk factors for or existing cardiovascular disease	At start if there are risk factors for or existing cardiovascular disease		

Continued

	Monitoring for all patients		Monitoring for specific drugs				
Test or measurement	Initial health check	Annual check up	Antipsychotics	Lithium	Valproate*	Carbamazepine
Weight and height	✓	✓ [b]	At start and every 3 months for first year; more often if the patient gains weight rapidly	At start and when needed if the patient gains weight rapidly	At start and at 6 months if the patient gains weight rapidly	At start and at 6 months if the patient gains weight rapidly
Drug screening and chest X-ray	If suggested by the history or clinical picture					
EEG, MRI and CT scans	If organic aetiology or comorbidity is suspected					
Smoking/ alcohol	✓	✓				

		1 week after initiation and 1 week after every dose change, until levels stable, then every 3 months	Only if there is evidence of ineffectiveness, poor adherence or toxicity	–	Every 6 months[c]
Serum levels of drug					

For patients on lamotrigine*; do an annual health check, but no special monitoring tests are needed.

[a] every 6 months for people with rapid-cycling bipolar disorder, plus thyroid antibody levels if clinically indicated, for example, by the thyroid function tests

[b] For children and adolescents, monthly for 6 months, then every 6 months

[c] Note therapeutic and toxic levels of carbamazepine are close

ACE = angiotensin-converting enzyme

NSAID = non-steroidal anti-inflammatory drug

13.　REFERENCES

For reasons of space, full references of studies included in systematic reviews, that is, those which appear in the summary of study characteristics tables in the evidence chapters (recognisable from their study ID of author name in capitals plus year of publication), are listed with the relevant full study characteristics table in Appendix 22, and do not appear in this chapter.

Adab, N., Kini, U., Vinten, J., *et al.* (2004a) The longer term outcome of children born to mothers with epilepsy. *Journal of Neurology, Neurosurgery and Psychiatry, 75,* 1575–1583.

Adab, N., Tudur, S.C., Vinten, J., *et al.* (2004b) Common antiepileptic drugs in pregnancy in women with epilepsy. *Cochrane Database of Systematic Reviews, 3,* CD004848.

AGREE Collaboration (2003) Development and validation of an international appraisal instrument for assessing the quality of clinical practice guidelines: the AGREE project. *Quality and Safety in Health Care, 12,* 18–23.

Ahrens, B. & Muller-Oerlinghausen, B. (2001) Does lithium exert an independent antisuicidal effect? *Pharmacopsychiatry, 34,* 132–136.

Ahrens, B., Grof, P., Moller, H.J., *et al.* (1995) Extended survival of patients on long-term lithium treatment. *Canadian Journal of Psychiatry, 40,* 241–246.

Akiskal, H.S., Walker, P., Puzantian, V.R., *et al.* (1983) Bipolar outcome in the course of depressive illness. Phenomenologic, familial and pharmocologic factors. *Journal of Affective Disorders, 5,* 115–128.

Akiskal, H.S., Maser, J.D., Zeller, P.J., *et al.* (1995) Switching from 'unipolar' to bipolar II. An 11-year prospective study of clinical and temperamental predictors in 559 patients. *Archives of General Psychiatry, 52,* 114–123.

Akiskal, H.S., Bourgeois, M.L., Angst, J., *et al.* (2000) Re-evaluating the prevalence of and diagnostic composition within the broad clinical spectrum of bipolar disorders. *Journal of Affective Disorders, 59,* Supp. 1, S5–S30.

Allison, D.B., Mentore, J.L., Heo, M., *et al.* (1999) Antipsychotic-induced weight gain: a comprehensive research synthesis. *American Journal of Psychiatry, 156,* 1686–1696.

Altman, E.G., Hedeker, D., Peterson, J.L., *et al.* (1997) The Altman Self-Rating Mania Scale. *Biological Psychiatry, 42,* 948–955.

Altshuler, L.L. (1995) T2 hyperintensities in bipolar disorder: magnetic resonance imaging comparison and literature meta-analysis. *American Journal of Psychiatry, 152,* 1139–1144.

Altshuler, L., Suppes, T., Black, D., *et al.* (2004) Impact of antidepressant discontinuation after acute bipolar depression remission on rates of depressive relapse at 1-year follow-up. *American Journal of Psychiatry, 160,* 1252–1262.

Ambelas, A. (1987) Life events and mania. A special relationship? *British Journal of Psychiatry, 150,* 235–240.

American Academy of Pediatrics Committee on Drugs (2000) Use of psychoactive medication during pregnancy and possible effects on the fetus and newborn. *Pediatrics*, *105*, 880–887.

American College of Sports Medicine (1980) *Guidelines for Graded Exercise Testing and Exercise Prescription*. American College of Sports Medicine.

American College of Sports Medicine (2005) *Guidelines for Exercise Testing and Prescription*. Philadelphia, PA: Lippincott Williams & Wilkins.

American Psychiatric Association (1994) *Diagnostic and Statistical Manual of Mental Disorders* (DSM-IV) (4th edn). Washington DC: APA.

Anderson, I.M., Haddad, P.M. & Chaudhry, I. (2004) Changes in pharmacological treatment for bipolar disorder over time in Manchester: a comparison with Lloyd *et al.* (2003). *Journal of Psychopharmacology*, *18*, 441–444.

Angst, F., Stassen, H.H., Clayton, P.J., *et al.* (2002) Mortality of patients with mood disorders: follow-up over 34–38 years. *Journal of Affective Disorders*, *68*, 167–181.

Angst, J. (1966) *Zur Aetiologie und Nosologie Endogener Depressiver Psychosen: eine Genetische Soziologische und Klinische Studie*. Berlin: Springer.

Angst, J. (1998) The emerging epidemiology of hypomania and bipolar II disorder. *Journal of Affective Disorders*, *50*, 143–151.

Angst, J., Gamma, A., Benazzi, F., *et al.* (2003) Toward a re-definition of subthreshold bipolarity: epidemiology and proposed criteria for bipolar-II, minor bipolar disorders and hypomania. *Journal of Affective Disorders*, *73*, 133–146.

Angst, J., Angst, F., Gerber-Werder, R., *et al.* (2005) Suicide in 406 mood-disorder patients with and without long-term medication: a 40 to 44 years' follow-up. *Archives of Suicide Research*, *9*, 279–300.

Arnold, L.M., McElroy, S.L. & Keck, P.E., Jr. (2000) The role of gender in mixed mania. *Comprehensive Psychiatry*, *41*, 83–87.

Ashman, S.B., Monk, T.H., Kupfer, D.J., *et al.* (1999) Relationship between social rhythms and mood in patients with rapid cycling bipolar disorder. *Psychiatry Research*, *86*, 1–8.

Atakan, Z. & Davies, T. (1997) ABC of mental health. Mental health emergencies. *BMJ*, *7096*, 1740–1742.

Babyak, M., Blumenthal, J.A., Herman, S., *et al.* (2000) Exercise treatment for major depression: maintenance of therapeutic benefit at 10 months. *Psychosomatic Medicine*, *62*, 633–638.

Baldassano, C.F. (2005) Assessment tools for screening and monitoring bipolar disorder. *Bipolar Disorders*, *7*, Suppl 1, 8–15.

Baldassano, C.F., Marangell, L.B., Gyulai, L., *et al.* (2005) Gender differences in bipolar disorder: retrospective data from the first 500 STEP-BD participants. *Bipolar Disorders*, *7*, 465–470.

Baldessarini, R.J. & Tondo, L. (2003) Suicide risk and treatments for patients with bipolar disorder. *Journal of the American Medical Association*, *290*, 1517–1519.

Baldessarini, R.J., Tondo, L., Floris, G., *et al.* (1997) Reduced morbidity after gradual discontinuation of lithium treatment for bipolar I and II disorders: a replication study. *American Journal of Psychiatry*, *154*, 551–553.

References

Baldessarini, R.J., Tondo, L. & Hennen, J. (2003a) Lithium treatment and suicide risk in major affective disorders: update and new findings. *Journal of Clinical Psychiatry*, *64*, Suppl 5, 44–52.

Baldessarini, R.J., Tondo, L. & Hennen, J. (2003b) Treatment-latency and previous episodes: relationships to pretreatment morbidity and response to maintenance treatment in bipolar I and II disorders. *Bipolar Disorders*, *48*, 491–496.

Ball, J.R., Mitchell, P.B., Corry, J.C., *et al.* (2006) A randomized controlled trial of cognitive therapy for bipolar disorder: focus on long-term change. *Journal of Clinical Psychology*, in press.

Bauer, M.S. (2001) The collaborative practice model for bipolar disorder: design and implementation in a multi-site randomized controlled trial. *Bipolar Disorders*, *3*, 233–244.

Bauer, M.S. & Mitchner, L. (2004) What is a 'mood stabilizer'? An evidence-based response. *American Journal of Psychiatry*, *161*, 3–18.

Bauer, M.S., Calabrese, J., Dunner, D.L., *et al.* (1994) Multisite data reanalysis of the validity of rapid cycling as a course modifier for bipolar disorder in DSM-IV. *American Journal of Psychiatry*, *151*, 506–515.

Bauer, M.S., McBride, L., Shea, N., *et al.* (1997) Impact of an easy-access VA clinic-based program for patients with bipolar disorder. *Psychiatric Services*, *48*, 491–496.

Bauer, M.S., Williford, W.O., Dawson, E.E., *et al.* (2001) Principles of effectiveness trials and their implementation in VA Cooperative Study #430: 'Reducing the efficacy-effectiveness gap in bipolar disorder'. *Journal of Affective Disorders*, *67*, 61–78.

Bauer, M.S., Simon, G.E., Ludman, E., *et al.* (2005) 'Bipolarity' in bipolar disorder: distribution of manic and depressive symptoms in a treated population. *British Journal of Psychiatry*, *187*, 87–88.

Bearden, C.E., Hoffman, K.M. & Cannon, T.D. (2005) The neuropsychology and neuroanatomy of bipolar affective disorder: a critical review. *Bipolar Disorders*, *3*, 106–150.

Begley, C.E., Annegers, J.F., Swann, A.C., *et al.* (2001) The lifetime cost of bipolar disorder in the US: an estimate for new cases in 1998. *Pharmacoeconomics*, *19*, 483–495.

Bendz, H. & Aurell, M. (1992) Drug-induced diabetes insipidus: incidence, prevention and management. *Drug Safety*, *21*, 449–456.

Bennett, D. & Freeman, H. (1991) Principles and prospect. In *Community Psychiatry* (eds D. Bennett & H. Freeman), pp. 1–39. Edinburgh: Churchill Livingstone.

Bentall, R. (2004) *Madness Explained: Psychosis and Human Nature*. London: Penguin.

Bentall, R.P., Kinderman, P. & Manson, K. (2006) Self-discrepancies in bipolar disorder: a comparison of manic, depressed, remitted and normal participants. *British Journal of Clinical Psychology*, in press.

Berlin, J.A. (2001) Does blinding of readers affect the results of meta-analyses? *Lancet*, *350*, 185–186.

Bey, D.R., Chapman, R.E. & Tornquist, K.L. (1972) A lithium clinic. *American Journal of Psychiatry*, *48*, 491–496.

Beyer, J., Kuchibhatla, M., Gersing, K., *et al.* (2005) Medical comorbidity in a bipolar outpatient clinical population. *Neuropsychopharmacology*, *30*, 401–404.

Biddle, S., Fox, K. & Edmund, L. (1994) *Physical Activity in Primary Care in England*. London: Health Education Authority.

Biederman, J., Mick, E., Faraone, S.V., *et al.* (2000) Pediatric mania: a developmental subtype of bipolar disorder? *Biological Psychiatry, 48*, 458–466.

Birnbaum, H.G., Shi, L., Dial, E., *et al.* (2003) Economic consequences of not recognizing bipolar disorder patients: a cross-sectional descriptive analysis. *Journal of Clinical Psychiatry, 64*, 1201–1209.

Blanco, C., Laje, G., Olfson, M., *et al.* (2002) Trends in the treatment of bipolar disorder by outpatient psychiatrists. *American Journal of Psychiatry, 159*, 1005–1010.

Boerlin, H.L., Gitlin, M.J., Zoellner, L.A., *et al.* (1998) Bipolar depression and antidepressant-induced mania: a naturalistic study. *Journal of Clinical Psychiatry, 59*, 374–379.

Bonari, L., Pinto, N., Ahn, E., *et al.* (2004) Perinatal risks of untreated depression during pregnancy. *Canadian Journal of Psychiatry, 49*, 726–735.

Bottlender, R., Rudolf, D., Strauss, A., *et al.* (2001) Mood-stabilisers reduce the risk of developing antidepressant-induced maniform states in acute treatment of bipolar I depressed patients. *Journal of Affective Disorders, 63*, 79–83.

Bouras, N., Tufnell, G., Brough, D.I., *et al.* (1986) Model for the integration of community psychiatry and primary care. *Journal of the Royal College of General Practice, 36*, 62–66.

Bowden, C.L., Brugger, A.M., Swann, A.C., *et al.* (1994) Efficacy of divalproex vs lithium and placebo in the treatment of mania. The Depakote Mania Study Group. *Journal of the American Medical Association, 271*, 918–924.

Briscoe, J.J., Harrington, R.C. & Prendergast, M. (1995) Development of mania in close association with tricyclic antidepressant administration in children. A report of two cases. *European Child & Adolescent Psychiatry, 4*, 280–283.

British Medical Association & Royal Pharmaceutical Society of Great Britain (March 2006) British National Formulary 51. London: British Medical Association & Royal Pharmaceutical Society of Great Britain.

Broadstock, M. (2001) *The Effectiveness and Safety of Drug Treatment for Urgent Sedation in Psychiatric Emergencies. A Critical Appraisal of the Literature*. New Zealand Health Technology Appraisal Report, 4.

Brockington, I.F. (1996) Puerperal psychosis. In *Motherhood and Mental Health* (ed I.F. Brockington) pp. 200–284. Oxford: Oxford University Press.

Brodersen, A., Licht, R.W. & Vestergaard, P. (2000) Sixteen-year mortality in patients with affective disorder commenced on lithium. *British Journal of Psychiatry, 176*, 429–433.

Brown, G. & Harris, T. (1978) *The Social Origins of Depression: A Study of Psychiatric Disorder in Women*. London: Tavistock Publications.

Brown, G.R., McBride, L., Bauer, M.S., *et al.* (2006) Impact of childhood abuse on the course of bipolar disorder: a replication study in U.S. veterans. *Journal of Affective Disorders*, in press.

Bryant-Comstock, L., Stender, M. & Devercelli, G. (2002) Health care utilization and costs among privately insured patients with bipolar I disorder. *Bipolar Disorders, 4*, 398–405.

Chaudron, L.H. & Pies, R.W. (2003) The relationship between postpartum psychosis and bipolar disorder: a review. *Journal of Clinical Psychiatry, 64,* 1284–1292.

Calabrese, J.R., Rapport, D.J. & Kimmel, S.E. (1999) Controlled trials in bipolar I depression: focus on switch rates and efficacy. *European Neuropsychopharmacology, 9,* S109–S112.

Calabrese, J.R., Suppes, T., Bowden, C.L., *et al.* (2000) A double-blind, placebo-controlled, prophylaxis study of lamotrigine in rapid-cycling bipolar disorder. Lamictal 614 Study Group. *Journal of Clinical Psychiatry, 61,* 841–850.

Calabrese, J., Shelton, M.D., Bowden, C.L., *et al.* (2001) Bipolar rapid cycling: focus on depression as its hallmark. *Journal of Clinical Psychiatry, 62,* 34–41.

Calabrese, J., Shelton, M.D., Rapport, D.L., *et al.* (2002) Long-term treatment of bipolar disorder with lamotrigine. *Journal of Clinical Psychiatry, 63,* 18–22.

Casey, D.E., Daniel, D.G., Wassef, A.A., *et al.* (2003) Effect of divalproex combined with olanzapine or risperidone in patients with an acute exacerbation of schizophrenia. *Neuropsychopharmacology, 28,* 182–192.

Cassidy, F. & Carroll, B.J. (2001) Frequencies of signs and symptoms in mixed and pure episodes of mania: implications for the study of manic episodes. *Progress in Neuropsychopharmacology and Biological Psychiatry, 25,* 659–665.

Cassidy, F., Forest, K. & Murray, E. (1998) A factor analysis of the signs and symptoms of mania. *Archives of General Psychiatry, 55,* 27–32.

Chand, P.K., Mattoo, S.K. & Sharan, P. (2004) Quality of life and its correlates in patients with bipolar disorder stabilized on lithium prophylaxis. *Psychiatry and Clinical Neurosciences, 58,* 311–318.

Cipriani, A., Pretty, H., Hawton, K., *et al.* (2005) Lithium in the prevention of suicidal behavior and all-cause mortality in patients with mood disorders: a systematic review of randomized trials. *American Journal of Psychiatry, 162,* 1805–1819.

Clement, S., Singh, S.P. & Burns, T. (2003) Status of bipolar disorder research. Bibliometric study. *British Journal of Psychiatry, 182,* 148–152.

Cochran, S.D. (1984) Preventing medical non-compliance in the outpatient treatment of bipolar affective disorders. *Journal of Consulting and Clinical Psychology, 52,* 873–878.

Cochrane Collaboration (2004) *Review Manager (Rev Man),* Version 4.2.7 for Windows. Oxford: The Cochrane Collaboration.

Cohen, A.N., Hammen, C., Henry, R.M., *et al.* (2004) Effects of stress and social support on recurrence in bipolar disorder. *Journal of Affective Disorders, 82,* 143–147.

Cohen, L.S., Friedman, J.M. & Jefferson, J.W. (1994) A re-evaluation of risk of in-utero exposure to lithium. *Journal of the American Medical Association, 271,* 150.

Coid, J. (1994) Failure in community care: psychiatry's dilemma. *BMJ, 308,* 805–806.

Colom, F., Vieta, E., Martinez-Aran, A., *et al.* (2003a) A randomized trial on the efficacy of group psychoeducation in the prophylaxis of recurrences in bipolar patients whose disease is in remission. *Archives of General Psychiatry, 60,* 402–407.

Colom, F., Vieta, E., Reinares, M., *et al.* (2003b) Psychoeducation efficacy in bipolar disorders: beyond compliance enhancement. *Journal of Clinical Psychiatry, 64*, 1.

Conus, P. & McGorry, P.D. (2002) First-episode mania: a neglected priority for early intervention. *Australia and New Zealand Journal of Psychiatry, 36*, 158–172.

Cooke, R.G., Robb, J.C., Young, L.T., *et al.* (1996) Well-being and functioning in patients with bipolar disorder assessed using the MOS 20-ITEM short form (SF-20). *Journal of Affective Disorders, 39*, 93–97.

Cookson, J.C., Katona, C. & Taylor, D. (2002) *Use of Drugs in Psychiatry: the Evidence from Psychopharmacology* (5th edn). London: Gaskell.

Cooper, S.A. & Collacott, R.A. (1993) Mania and Down's syndrome. *British Journal of Psychiatry, 162*, 739–743.

Coryell, W., Solomon, D., Turvey, C., *et al.* (2003) The long-term course of rapid-cycling bipolar disorder. *Archives of General Psychiatry, 60*, 914–920.

Courtney, M.E., Acomb, J.A. & Lovatt, V. (1995) A pharmacy-controlled lithium clinic. *Psychiatric Bulletin, 19*, 1–17.

Craddock, N. & Jones, I. (1999) Genetics of bipolar disorder. *Journal of Medical Genetics, 36*, 585–594.

Craddock, N. & Jones, I. (2001) Molecular genetics of bipolar disorder. *British Journal of Psychiatry*, Suppl 41, S128–S133.

Craddock, N., O'Donovan, M.C. & Owen, M.J. (2005) The genetics of schizophrenia and bipolar disorder: dissecting psychosis. *Journal of Medical Genetics, 42*, 193–204.

Cradock-O'Leary, J., Young, A.S., Yano, E.M., *et al.* (2002) Use of general medical services by VA patients with psychiatric disorders. *Psychiatric Services, 53*, 874–878.

Creed, F., Black, D., Anthony, P., *et al.* (1990) Randomised controlled trial of day patient versus inpatient psychiatric treatment. *BMJ, 300*, 1033–1037.

Creed, F., Mbaya, P., Lancashire, S., *et al.* (1997) Cost effectiveness of day and inpatient psychiatric treatment: results of a randomised controlled trial. *BMJ, 314*, 1381–1385.

Crowther, R., Marshall, M., Bond, G., *et al.* (2001) Vocational rehabilitation for people with severe mental illness. *Cochrane Database of Systematic Reviews, 2*, CD003080.

Cunnane, J.G. (1994) Drug management of disturbed behaviour by psychiatrists. *Psychiatric Bulletin, 18*, 138–139.

Curtis, L. & Netten, A. (2005) *Unit Costs of Health and Social Care 2005.* Canterbury: PSSRU.

Das, A.K., Olfson, M., Gameroff, M.J., *et al.* (2005) Screening for bipolar disorder in a primary care practice. *Journal of the American Medical Association, 293*, 956–963.

Das Gupta, R. & Guest, J.F. (2002) Annual cost of bipolar disorder to UK society. *British Journal of Psychiatry, 180*, 227–233.

Davison, G.C. (2000) Stepped care: doing more with less? *Journal of Consulting and Clinical Psychology, 68*, 580–585.

Day, J.C., Bentall, R.P., Roberts, C., *et al.* (2005) Attitudes toward antipsychotic medication: the impact of clinical variables and relationships with health professionals. *Archives of General Psychiatry, 62*, 717–724.

Deeks, J.J. (2002) Issues in the selection of a summary statistic for meta-analysis of clinical trials with binary outcomes. *Statistics in Medicine*, *21*, 1575–1600.

Deltito, J., Martin, L., Riefkohl, J., *et al.* (2001) Do patients with borderline personality disorder belong to the bipolar spectrum? *Journal of Affective Disorders*, *67*, 221–228.

Denicoff, K.D., Leverich, G.S., Nolen, W.A., *et al.* (2000) Validation of the prospective NIMH-Life-Chart Method (NIMH-LCM-p) for longitudinal assessment of bipolar illness. *Psychological Medicine*, *30*, 1391–1397.

Dennis, M., Wakefield, P., Molloy, C., *et al.* (2005) Self-harm in older people with depression: comparison of social factors, life events and symptoms. *British Journal of Psychiatry*, *186*, 538–539.

Department of Health (1983) *Mental Health Act* 1983. London: DHSS.

Department of Health (1989) *Children Act* 1989. London: HMSO.

Department of Health (1990) *Caring for People. The CPA for People with a Mental Illness Referred to Specialist Mental Health Services*. Joint Health/Social Services Circular. C(90)23/LASSL(90)11.

Department of Health (1999a) *The NHS Plan: A Plan for Investment, a Plan for Reform*. London: Department of Health.

Department of Health (1999b) *National Service Framework for Mental Health*. London: Department of Health.

Department of Health (2000) *The NHS Plan. A Plan for Investment, a Plan for Reform*. London: Department of Health.

Department of Health (2001) *The Expert Patient: A New Approach to Chronic Disease Management for the 21st Century*. London: Department of Health.

Department of Health (2002) *National Service Framework for Mental Health: Modern Standards and Service Models*. London: Department of Health.

Department of Health (2004a) *Hospital Episode Statistics. England: Financial Year 2003–2004*. London: Department of Health.

Department of Health (2004b) *Children Act 2004*. London: HMSO.

Department of Health (2004c) *Child and Adolescent Mental Health – National Service Framework for Children, Young People and Maternity Services*. London: Department of Health.

Department of Health (2005) *Exercise Referral Systems: A National Quality Assurance Framework*. London: Department of Health.

Department of Health (2006) *NHS Reference Costs 2005*. London: Department of Health.

Department of Health & National Institute for Mental Health in England (2003) *Fast-Forwarding Primary Care Mental Health. Graduate Primary Care Mental Health Workers — Best Practice Guidance*. London: Department of Health.

Depp, C.A., Lindamer, L.A., Folsom, D.P., *et al.* (2005) Differences in clinical features and mental health service use in bipolar disorder across the lifespan. *American Journal of Psychiatry*, *13*, 290–298.

Depue, R.A., Krauss, S.P. & Spoont, M.R. (1987) A two-dimensional threshold model of seasonal bipolar affective disorder. In *Psychopathology: An Interactionist Perspective* (eds D. Magnusson & A. Ohman). New York: Academic Press.

DerSimonian, R. & Laird, N. (1986) Meta-analysis in clinical trials. *Controlled Clinical Trials*, *7*, 177–188.

de Zelicourt, M., Dardennes, R., Verdoux, H., *et al.* (2003) Frequency of hospitalisations and inpatient care costs of manic episodes in patients with bipolar I disorder in France. *Pharmacoeconomics*, *21*, 1081–1090.

Dick, P., Ince, A. & Barlow, M. (1985) Day treatment: suitability and referral procedure. *British Journal of Psychiatry*, *147*, 250–253.

Dore, G. & Romans, S.E. (2001) Impact of bipolar affective disorder on family and partners. *Journal of Affective Disorders*, *67*, 147–158.

Dowell, D.A. & Ciarlo, J.A. (1983) Overview of the Community Mental Health Centers Program from an evaluation perspective. *Community Mental Health Journal*, *19*, 95–128.

Drummond, M.F. & Jefferson, T.O. (1996) Guidelines for authors and peer reviewers of economic submissions to the BMJ. *BMJ*, *313*, 275–283.

Druss, B.G., Bradford, W.D., Rosenheck, R.A., *et al.* (2001) Quality of medical care and excess mortality in older patients with mental disorders. *Archives of General Psychiatry*, *58*, 565–572.

D'Souza, R.E. & Guillebaud, J. (2002) Risks and benefits of oral contraceptive pills. *Best Practice & Research. Clinical Obstetrics & Gynaecology*, *16*, 133–154.

Duncan, S., Mercho, S. & Lopes-Cendes, I. (2001) Repeated neural tube defects and valproate monotherapy suggest a pharmacogenetic abnormality. *Epilepsia*, *42*, 750–753.

Dunner, D.L., Fleiss, J.L. & Fieve, R.R. (1976) Lithium carbonate prophylaxis failure. *British Journal of Psychiatry*, *129*, 40–44.

Eccles, M. & Mason, J. (2001) How to develop cost-conscious guidelines. *Health Technology Assessment*, *5*, 1–69.

Eccles, M., Freemantle, N. & Mason, J. (1998) North of England evidence based guideline development project: methods of developing guidelines for efficient drug use in primary care. *BMJ*, *316*, 1232–1235.

Ellenberg, J., Salamon, I. & Meaney, C. (1980) A lithium clinic in a community mental health center. *Hospital and Community Psychiatry*, *31*, 834–836.

Ellicott, A., Hammen, C., Gitlin, M., *et al.* (1990) Life events and the course of bipolar disorder. *American Journal of Psychiatry*, *147*, 1194–1198.

Elmslie, J.L., Mann, J.I., Silverstone, J.T., *et al.* (2001) Determinants of overweight and obesity in patients with bipolar disorder. *Journal of Clinical Psychiatry*, *62*, 486–491.

Epstein, R.M., Alper, B.S. & Quill, T.E. (2004) Communicating evidence for participatory decision making. *Journal of the American Medical Association*, *291*, 2359–2366.

Faedda, G.L., Tondo, L., Baldessarini, R.J., *et al.* (1993) Outcome after rapid vs gradual discontinuation of lithium treatment in bipolar disorders. *Archives of General Psychiatry*, *50*, 448–455.

Faravelli, C., Guerrini Degl'Innocenti, B., Aiazzi, L., *et al.* (1990) Epidemiology of mood disorders: a community survey in Florence. *Journal of Affective Disorders*, *20*, 135–141.

Fenton, M., Coutinho, E.S. & Campbell, C. (2000) Zuclopenthixol acetate in the treatment of acute schizophrenia and similar serious mental illnesses. *Cochrane Database of Systematic Reviews*, CD000525.

Fenton, W.S., Mosher, L.R., Herrell, J.M., *et al.* (1998) Randomized trial of general hospital and residential alternative care for patients with severe and persistent mental illness. *American Journal of Psychiatry, 155,* 516–522.

Ferrier, I.N. & Thompson, J.M. (2003) Cognitive impairment in bipolar affective disorder: implications for the bipolar diathesis. *British Journal of Psychiatry, 180,* 293–295.

Fieve, R.R. (1975) The lithium clinic: a new model for the delivery of psychiatric services. *American Journal of Psychiatry, 132,* 1018–1022.

Frank, E. (1999) Interpersonal and social rhythm therapy prevents depressive symptomatology in bipolar I patients. *Bipolar Disorders*, Suppl 1, 13.

Frank, E., Kupfer, D.J., Thase, M.E., *et al.* (2005) Two-year outcomes for interpersonal and social rhythm therapy in individuals with bipolar I disorder. *Archives of General Psychiatry, 62,* 996–1004.

Franks, S. (1995) Polycystic ovary syndrome. *New England Journal of Medicine, 333,* 853–861.

Gaily, E., Kantola-Sorsa, E. & Granstrom, M.L. (1988) Intelligence of children of epileptic mothers. *Journal of Pediatrics, 113,* 677–684.

Garety, P.A. & Jolley, S. (2000) Early intervention in psychosis. *Psychiatric Bulletin, 24,* 321–323.

Garno, J.L., Goldberg, J.F. & Ramirez, P.M. (2005) Impact of childhood abuse on the clinical course of bipolar disorder. *British Journal of Psychiatry, 186,* 121–125.

Ghaemi, S.N., Lenox, M.S. & Baldessarini, R.J. (2001) Effectiveness and safety of long-term antidepressant treatment in bipolar disorder. *Journal of Clinical Psychiatry, 62,* 569.

Ghaemi, S.N., Hsu, D.J., Soldani, F., *et al.* (2003) Antidepressants in bipolar disorder: the case for caution. *Bipolar Disorders, 5,* 421–433.

Ghaemi, S.N., El-Mallakh, R.S., Baldassano, C.F., *et al.* (2005) A randomized clinical trial of efficacy and safety of long-term antidepressant use in bipolar disorder. *Bipolar Disorders, 7,* 59.

Gijsman, H.J., Geddes, J.R., Rendell, J.M., *et al.* (2004) Antidepressants for bipolar depression: a systematic review of randomized controlled trials. *American Journal of Psychiatry, 161,* 1537–1547.

Gitlin, M.J. & Jamison, K.R. (1984) Lithium clinics: theory and practice. *Hospital and Community Psychiatry, 35,* 363–368.

Gitlin, M.J., Swendsen, J., Heller, T.L., *et al.* (1995) Relapse and impairment in bipolar disorder. *American Journal of Psychiatry, 152,* 1635–1640.

Goetzel, R.Z., Ozminowski, R.J., Meneades, L., *et al.* (2000) Pharmaceuticals – cost or investment? An employer's perspective. *Journal of Occupational and Environmental Medicine, 42,* 338–351.

Goetzel, R.Z., Hawkins, K., Ozminkowski, R.J. *et al.* (2003) The health and productivity cost burden of the 'top 10' physical and mental health conditions affecting six large U.S. employers in 1999. *Journal of Occupational and Environmental Medicine*, *45*, 5–14.

Goldberg, J.F. & Garno, J.L. (2005) Development of posttraumatic stress disorder in adult bipolar patients with histories of severe childhood abuse. *Journal of Psychiatric Research*, *39*, 595–601.

Goldberg, J.F. & Truman, C.J. (2003) Antidepressant-induced mania: an overview of current controversies. *Bipolar Disorders*, *5*, 407–420.

Goldberg, J.F., Harrow, M. & Whiteside, J.E. (2001) Risk for bipolar illness in patients initially hospitalized for unipolar depression. *American Journal of Psychiatry*, *158*, 1265–1270.

Goldney, R.D., Fisher, L.J., Grande, E.D., *et al.* (2005) Bipolar I and II disorders in a random and representative Australian population. *Australia and New Zealand Journal of Psychiatry*, *39*, 726–729.

Goodwin, F.K. (1994) Recurrence of mania after lithium withdrawal. Implications for the use of lithium in the treatment of bipolar affective disorder. *British Journal of Psychiatry*, *164*, 149–152.

Goodwin, F.K. (2002) Rationale for long-term treatment of bipolar disorder and evidence for long-term lithium treatment. *Journal of Clinical Psychiatry*, *63*, 5–12.

Goodwin, F.K. & Jamison, K.R. (1990) *Manic-Depressive Illness*. New York: Oxford University Press.

Goodwin, F.K., Murphy, D.L. & Bunney, W.E. (1969) Lithium-carbonate treatment in depression and mania. *Archives of General Psychiatry*, *36*, 840–844.

Goodwin, F.K., Fireman, B., Simon, G.E., *et al.* (2003) Suicide risk in bipolar disorder during treatment with lithium and divalproex. *Journal of the American Medical Association*, *290*, 1473.

Gowers, S., Clarke, J., Alldis, M., *et al.* (2001) Inpatient admission of adolescents with mental disorder. *Clinical Child Psychology and Psychiatry*, *6*, 537–544.

Grade Working Group (2004) Grading quality of evidence and strength of recommendations. *BMJ*, *328*, 1490–1497.

Greenhalgh, J., Knight, C., Hind, D., *et al.* (2005) Clinical and cost-effectiveness of electroconvulsive therapy for depressive illness, schizophrenia, catatonia and mania: systematic reviews and economic modelling studies. *Health Technology Assessment*, *9*, 1–156.

Guberman, A.H., Besag, F.M., Brodie, M.J., *et al.* (1999) Lamotrigine-associated rash: risk/benefit considerations in adults and children. *Epilepsia*, *40*, 985–991.

Haddad, P.M. (2001) Antidepressant discontinuation syndromes: clinical relevance, diagnosis and management. *Drug Safety*, *24*, 183.

Haddad, P. & Wieck, A. (2004) Antipsychotic-induced hyperprolactinaemia: mechanisms, clinical features and management. *Drugs*, *64*, 2291–2314.

Haddad, P., Pal, B.R., Clarke, P., *et al.* (2005) Neonatal symptoms following maternal paroxetine treatment: serotonin toxicity or paroxetine discontinuation syndrome? *Journal of Psychopharmacology*, in press.

Hakkaart-van Roijen, L., Hoeijenbos, M.B., Regeer, E.J., *et al.* (2004) The societal costs and quality of life of patients suffering from bipolar disorder in the Netherlands. *Acta Psychiatrica Scandinavica*, *110*, 383–392.

References

Hammen, C. & Gitlin, M. (1997) Stress reactivity in bipolar patients and its relation to prior history of disorder. *American Journal of Psychiatry*, *154*, 856–857.

Hammen, C., Gitlin, M. & Altshuler, L. (2000) Predictors of work adjustment in bipolar I patients: a naturalistic longitudinal follow-up. *Journal of Consulting and Clinical Psychology*, *68*, 220–225.

Harrington, R.C., Bredenkamp, D., Groothues, C.R. M., *et al.* (1994) Adult outcomes of childhood and adolescent depression. III. Links with suicidal behaviours. *Journal of Child Psychology and Psychiatry*, *35*, 1309–1319.

Harrow, M., Goldberg, J.F., Grossman, L.S., *et al.* (1990) Outcome in manic disorders. A naturalistic follow-up study. *Archives of General Psychiatry*, *47*, 665–671.

Harvey, A.G., Schmidt, D.A., Scarna, A., *et al.* (2005) Sleep-related functioning in euthymic patients with bipolar disorder, patients with insomnia, and subjects without sleep problems. *American Journal of Psychiatry*, *162*, 50–57.

Hatfield, B., Huxley, P. & Mohamad, H. (1992) Accommodation and employment: a survey into the circumstances and expressed needs of users of mental health services in a northern town. *British Journal of Social Work*, *22*, 73.

Hawton, K., Sutton, L., Haw, C., *et al.* (2005) Suicide and attempted suicide in bipolar disorder: a systematic review of risk factors. *Journal of Clinical Psychiatry*, *66*, 693–704.

Hays, J.C., Krishnan, K.R., George, L.K., *et al.* (1998) Age of first onset of bipolar disorder: demographic, family history, and psychosocial correlates. *Depression and Anxiety*, *7*, 76–82.

Healy, D. (2002) *The Creation of Psychopharmacology*. London: Harvard University Press.

Henderson, C., Flood, C., Leese, M., *et al.* (2004) Effect of joint crisis plans on use of compulsory treatment in psychiatry: single blind randomised controlled trial. *BMJ*, *329*, 136.

Henry, C., Sorbara, F., Lacoste, J., *et al.* (2001) Antidepressant-induced mania in bipolar patients: identification of risk factors. *Journal of Clinical Psychiatry*, *62*, 249–255.

Herz, M.I., Endicott, J., Spitzer, R.L., *et al.* (1971) Day versus in-patient hospitalization: a controlled study. *American Journal of Psychiatry*, *10*, 1382.

Hickie, I.B. (2000) Building a 'National Coalition for People with Depression'. *Australas Psychiatry*, *8*, 125–131.

Higgins, J.P.T. & Thompson, S.G. (2002) Quantifying heterogeneity in a meta-analysis. *Statistics in Medicine*, *21*, 1539–1558.

Highet, N.J., McNair, B.G., Thompson, M., *et al.* (2004) Experience with treatment services for people with bipolar disorder. *Medical Journal of Australia*, *181*, S47–S51.

Hill, R.G., Shepard, G. & Hardy, P. (1998) In sickness and in health: the experiences of friends and relatives caring for people with manic depression. *Journal of Mental Health*, *7*, 611–620.

Hirschfeld, R.M., Williams, J.B., Spitzer, R.L., *et al.* (2000) Development and validation of a screening instrument for bipolar spectrum disorder: the Mood Disorder Questionnaire. *American Journal of Psychiatry*, *157*, 1873–1875.

Hirschfeld, R.M., Holzer, C., Calabrese, J.R., *et al.* (2003a) Validity of the mood disorder questionnaire: a general population study. *American Journal of Psychiatry*, *160*, 178–180.

Hirschfeld, R.M., Lewis, L. & Vornik, L.A. (2003b) Perceptions and impact of bipolar disorder: how far have we really come? Results of the national depressive and manic-depressive association 2000 survey of individuals with bipolar disorder. *Journal of Clinical Psychiatry*, *64*, 161–174.

Hlastala, S.A., Frank, E., Kowalski, J., *et al.* (2000) Stressful life events, bipolar disorder, and the 'kindling model.' *Journal of Abnormal Psychology*, *109*, 786.

Holmes, L.B., Harvey, E.A. & Coull, B.A. (2001) The teratogenicity of anticonvulsant drugs. *New England Journal of Medicine*, *244*, 1132–1138.

Hoult, J., Reynolds, I., Charbonneau-Powis, M., *et al.* (1983) Psychiatric hospital versus community treatment: the results of a randomised trial. *Australia and New Zealand Journal of Psychiatry*, *17*, 160–167.

Howard, L.M. (2005) Fertility and pregnancy in women with psychotic disorders. *European Journal of Obstetrics & Gynecology and Reproductive Biology*, *119*, 3–10.

Howard, L.M., Kumar, C., Leese, M., *et al.* (2002) The general fertility rate in women with psychotic disorders. American Journal of Psychiatry, 159, 991–997.

Hu, T.W. & Rush, A.J. (1995) Depressive disorders: treatment patterns and costs of treatment in the private sector of the United States. Social Psychiatry & Psychiatric Epidemiology, 30, 224–230.

Hudson, J.I., Lipinski, J.F., Keck, P.E. Jr., *et al.* (1992) Polysomnographic characteristics of young manic patients. Comparison with unipolar depressed patients and normal control subjects. Archives of General Psychiatry, 49, 378–383.

Hunt, N., Bruce-Jones, W. & Silverstone, T. (1992) Life events and relapse in bipolar affective disorder. Journal of Affective Disorders, 25, 13–20.

IRIS (2002) Initiative to Reduce the Impact of Schizophrenia. http://www.iris-initiative.org.uk

Isaac, M.N. (1996) Trends in the development of psychiatric services in India. *Psychiatric Bulletin*, *20*, 43–45.

Isometsa, E., Heikkinen, M., Henriksson, M., *et al.* (1995) Recent life events and completed suicide in bipolar affective disorder. A comparison with major depressive suicides. *Journal of Affective Disorders*, *33*, 99–106.

Jablensky, A.V., Morgan, V., Zubrick, S.R., *et al.* (2005) Pregnancy, delivery, and neonatal complications in a population cohort of women with schizophrenia and major affective disorders. *American Journal of Psychiatry*, *162*, 79–91.

Jackson, A., Cavanagh, J. & Scott, J. (2003) A systematic review of manic and depressive prodromes. *Journal of Affective Disorders*, *74*, 209–217.

Jadad, A.R., Moore, R.A. & Carroll, D. (1996) Assessing the quality of reports of randomised clinical trials: is blinding necessary? *Controlled Clinical Trials*, *17*, 1–12.

Jamison, K. (2000) Suicide and bipolar disorder. *Journal of Clinical Psychiatry*, *61*, 47–51.

Jick, H., Kaye, J.A. & Jick, S.S. (2004) Antidepressants and the risk of suicidal behaviors. *Journal of the American Medical Association*, *292*, 338–343.

References

Johannessen, J.O., Larsen, T.K., McGlashan, T.H., *et al.*. (2000) Early intervention in psychosis: the TIPS project, a multi-centre study in Scandinavia. In *Psychosis: Psychological Approaches and their Effectiveness. Putting Psychotherapists at the Centre of Treatment* (ed B. Martindale). London: Gaskell.

Johnson, J.G., Cohen, P. & Brooks, J.S. (2000) Associations between bipolar disorder and other psychiatric disorders during adolescence and early adulthood: a community-based longitudinal investigation. *American Journal of Psychiatry, 157,* 1679–1681.

Johnson, L., Lundstrom, O., Aberg-Wistedt, A., *et al.* (2003) Social support in bipolar disorder: its relevance to remission and relapse. *Bipolar Disorders, 5,* 129–137.

Johnson, S.L. (2005) Life events in bipolar disorder: towards more specific models. Clinical Psychology Review, in press.

Johnson, S.L. & Miller, I. (1997) Negative life events and time to recovery from episodes of bipolar disorder. Journal of Abnormal Psychology, 106, 449–457.

Johnson, S.L., Meyer, B., Winett, C.A., *et al.* (2000) Social support and self-esteem predict changes in bipolar depression but not mania. *Journal of Abnormal Psychology, 108,* 558–566.

Johnson, S.L., Sandrow, D., Meyer, B., *et al.* (2000) Increases in manic symptoms after life events involving goal attainment. *Journal of Abnormal Psychology, 109,* 721–727.

Johnson, S.L., Winett, C.A., Meyer, B., *et al.* (1999) Social support and the course of bipolar disorder. *Journal of Abnormal Psychology, 108,* 558–566.

Jones, I. & Craddock, N. (1996) Familiarity of the puerperal trigger in bipolar disorder: results of a family study. *American Journal of Psychiatry,* 158, 913–917.

Jones, I. & Craddock, N. (2005) Bipolar disorder and childbirth: the importance of recognising risk. *British Journal of Psychiatry, 186,* 453–454.

Jones, S.H., Hare, D.J. & Evershed, K. (2005) Actigraphic assessment of circadian activity and sleep patterns in bipolar disorder. *Bipolar Disorders,* 7, 176–186.

Joy, C.B., Adams, C.E. & Rice, K. (2002) Crisis intervention for people with severe mental illnesses. *Cochrane Database of Systematic Reviews, 1,* CD001087.

Joy, C.B., Adams, C.E. & Rice, K. (2004) Crisis intervention for people with severe mental illnesses. *The Cochrane Database of Systematic Reviews, 4,* CD001087.

Judd, L., Akiskal, H.S., Schettler, P., *et al.* (2002) The long-term natural history of the weekly symptomatic status of bipolar I disorder. *Archives of General Psychiatry, 59,* 530–537.

Judd, L., Akiskal, H.S., Schettler, P., *et al.* (2003) A prospective investigation of the natural history of the long-term weekly symptomatic status of bipolar II disorder. *Archives of General Psychiatry, 60,* 261–269.

Kallert, T.W., Glockner, M., Priebe, S., *et al.* (2004) A comparison of psychiatric day hospitals in five European countries: implications of their diversity for day hospital research. *Social Psychiatry and Psychiatric Epidemiology, 39,* 788.

Kallner, G., Lindelius, R., Petterson, U., *et al.* (2000) Mortality in 497 patients with affective disorders attending a lithium clinic or after having left it. *Pharmacopsychiatry, 33,* 8–13.

Katon, W., von Korff, M., Lin, E., *et al.* (1995) Collaborative management to achieve treatment guidelines. Impact on depression in primary care. *Journal of the American Medical Association, 273*, 1026–1031.

Katon, W., Robinson, P., von Korff, M., *et al.* (1996) A multifaceted intervention to improve treatment of depression in primary care. *Archives of General Psychiatry, 53*, 924–932.

Katon, W., von Korff, M., Lin, E., *et al.* (1999) Stepped collaborative care for primary care patients with persistent symptoms of depression: a randomized trial. *Archives of General Psychiatry, 56*, 1109–1115.

Kay, J.H., Altshuler, L.L., Ventura, J., *et al.* (1999) Prevalence of axis II comorbidity in bipolar patients with and without alcohol use disorders. *Annals of Clinical Psychiatry, 11*, 187–195.

Keller, M.B., Lavori, P.B., Coryell, W., *et al.* (1993) Bipolar I: a five year prospective follow-up. *Journal of Nervous and Mental Disease, 181*, 238–245.

Kendrick, T. (2000) Depression management clinics in general practice? Some aspects lend themselves to the mini-clinic approach. *BMJ, 320*, 527–528.

Kennedy, N., Boydell, J., van Os, J., *et al.* (2004) Ethnic differences in first clinical presentation of bipolar disorder: results from an epidemiological study. *Journal of Affective Disorders, 83*, 161–168.

Kent, L.S.W. & Laidlaw, J.D.D. (1995) Suspected congenital sertraline dependence. *British Journal of Psychiatry, 167*, 412–413.

Kerr, I.B. & Taylor, D. (1997) Mental health emergencies. Caution is needed with rapid tranquillisation protocol. *BMJ, 315*, 885.

Kessing, L.V. (2005) Diagnostic stability in bipolar disorder in clinical practise as according to ICD-10. *Journal of Affective Disorders, 85*, 293–299.

Kessing, L.V., Agerbo, E. & Mortensen, P.B. (2004a) Major stressful life events and other risk factors for first admission with mania. *Bipolar Disorders, 6*, 122–129.

Kessing, L.V., Hansen, M.G., Andersen, P.K., *et al.* (2004b) The predictive effect of episodes on the risk of recurrence in depressive and bipolar disorders – a life-long perspective. *Acta Psychiatrica Scandinavica, 109*, 339–344.

Kessing, L.V., Soudergard, L. & Kvist, K. (2005) Suicide risk in patients treated with lithium. *Archives of General Psychiatry, 62*, 860–866.

Kessler, R.C., Rubinow, D.R., Holmes, C., *et al.* (1997) The epidemiology of DSM-III-R bipolar I disorder in a general population survey. *Psychological Medicine 27*, 1079–1089.

Kilbourne, A.M., Cornelius, J.R., Han, X., *et al.* (2004) Burden of general medical conditions among individuals with bipolar disorder. *Bipolar Disorders, 6*, 368–373.

Kilbourne, A.M., Bauer, M.S., Williford, W.O., *et al.* (2005) Clinical, psychosocial and treatment difference in minority patients with bipolar disorder. *Bipolar Disorders, 7*, 89–97.

Kim, E.Y. & Miklowitz, D.J. (2004) Expressed emotion as a predictor of outcome among bipolar patients undergoing family therapy. *Journal of Affective Disorders, 82*, 343–352.

Kinon, B.J., Basson, B.R., Gilmore, J.A., *et al.* (2001) Long-term olanzapine treatment: weight change and weight-related health factors in schizophrenia. *Journal of Clinical Psychiatry, 62*, 92–100.

References

Kleinman, N.L., Brook, R.A., Rajagopalan, K., *et al.* (2005) Lost time, absence costs, and reduced productivity output for employees with bipolar disorder. *Journal of Occupational and Environmental Medicine, 47,* 1117–1124.

Kouba, S., Hallstrom, T., Lindholm, C., *et al.* (2005) Pregnancy and neonatal outcomes in women with eating disorders. *Obstetrics & Gynecology, 105,* 255–260.

Kramlinger, K.G. & Post, R. (1996) Ultra-rapid and ultradian cycling in bipolar affective illness. *British Journal of Psychiatry, 168,* 314–323.

Kris, E.B. (1965) Day hospitals. *Current Therapeutic Research, 7,* 323.

Krishnan, K.R. (2005) Psychiatric and medical comorbidities of bipolar disorder. *Psychosomatic Medicine, 67,* 1–8.

Kupfer, D.J., Frank, E., Grocochinsky, V.J., *et al.* (2002) Demographic and clinical characteristics of individuals in a bipolar case registry. *Journal of Clinical Psychiatry, 63,* 120–125.

Kupfer, D.J., Frank, E., Grocochinsky, V.J., *et al.* (2005) African-American participants in a bipolar disorder registry: clinical and treatment characteristics. *Bipolar Disorders, 7,* 82–88.

Kupka, R.W., Luckenbaugh, D.A., Post, R., *et al.* (2003) Rapid and non-rapid cycling bipolar disorder: a comparative study using daily prospective mood ratings in 539 outpatients. *Bipolar Disorders, 5,* 62.

Kupka, R.W., Luckenbaugh, D.A., Post, R.M., *et al.* (2005) Comparison of rapid-cycling and non-rapid-cycling bipolar disorder based on prospective mood ratings in 539 outpatients. *American Journal of Psychiatry, 162,* 1273–1280.

Kusumakar, V. (2002) Antidepressants and antipsychotics in the long-term treatment of bipolar disorder. *Psychopharmacology Bulletin, 26,* 409–427.

Laine, K., Heikkinen, T., Ekblad, U., *et al.* (2003) Effects of exposure to selective serotonin reuptake inhibitors during pregnancy on serotonergic symptoms in newborns and cord blood monoamine and prolactin concentrations. *Archives of General Psychiatry, 60,* 720–726.

Lam, D.H. (2002) Psychotherapy for bipolar affective disorder. *Current Medical Literature, 13,* 1–4.

Lam, D. & Wong, G. (1997) Prodromes, coping strategies, insight and social functioning in bipolar affective disorders. *Psychological Medicine, 27,* 1091–1100.

Lam, D. & Wong, G. (2005) Prodromes, coping strategies and psychological intervention in bipolar disorders. *Clinical Psychology Review, 25,* 1028–1042.

Lam, D.H., Bright, J., Jones, S., *et al.* (2000) Cognitive therapy for bipolar illness: a pilot study of relapse prevention. *Cognitive Therapy & Research, 24,* 503–520.

Lam, D., Wong, G. & Sham, P. (2001) Prodromes, coping strategies and course of illness in bipolar affective disorders – a naturalistic study. Psychological Medicine, 31, 1397–1402.

Lam, D.H., Watkins, E.R., Hayward, P., *et al.* (2003) A randomized controlled study of cognitive therapy for relapse prevention for bipolar affective disorder: outcome of the first year. *Archives of General Psychiatry, 60,* 145–152.

Lambert, D., Middle, F., Hamshere, M.L., *et al.* (2005) Stage 2 of the Wellcome Trust UK-Irish bipolar affective disorder sibling-pair genome screen: evidence for linkage on chromosomes 6q16-q21, 4q12-q21, 9p21, 10p14-p12 and 18q22. *Molecular Psychiatry*, *10*, 831–841.

Lammer, E.J., Sever, L.E. & Oakley, G.P. (1987) Teratogen update: valproic acid. *Teratology*, *35*, 465–473.

Leff, J., Fisher, M. & Bertelsen, A. (1976) A cross national epidemiological study of mania. *British Journal of Psychiatry*, *129*, 428–437.

Leff, J. (2001) *The Unbalanced Mind*. New York: Columbia University Press.

Lehman, A.F., Goldberg, R., Dixon, L.B., *et al.* (2002) Improving employment outcomes for persons with severe mental illnesses. *Archives of General Psychiatry*, 59, 165–172.

Leibenluft, E., Albert, P.S., Rosenthal, N.E., *et al.* (1996) Relationship between sleep and mood in patients with rapid-cycling bipolar disorder. *Psychiatric Research*, *63*, 161–168.

Leith, L.M. (1994) *Foundations of Exercise and Mental Health*. Morgantown: Fitness Information Technology.

Lembke, A., Miklowitz, D.J., Otto, M.W., *et al.* (2004) Psychosocial service utilization by patients with bipolar disorders: data from the first 500 participants in the systematic treatment enhancement program. *Journal of Psychiatric Research*, *10*, 81–87.

Lepore, S.J. (1997) Expressive writing moderates the relation between intrusive thoughts and depressive symptoms. *Journal of Personality and Social Psychology*, *73*, 1030–1037.

Leverich, G.S., McElroy, S.L., Suppes, T., *et al.* (2002) Early physical and sexual abuse associated with an adverse course of bipolar illness. *Biological Psychiatry*, *51*, 288–297.

Lewinsohn, P.M., Hops, H., Roberts, R.E., *et al.* (1993) Adolescent psychopathology: I. Prevalence and incidence of depression and other DSM-III-R disorders in high school students. *Journal of Abnormal Psychology*, *102*, 133–144.

Lewinsohn, P.M., Klein, D.N. & Seeley, J.R. (1995) Bipolar disorders in a community sample of older adolescents: prevalence, phenomenology, comorbidity, and course. *Journal of American Academy of Child and Adolescent Psychiatry*, *34*, 454–463.

Lewinsohn, P.M., Seeley, J.R. & Klein, D.N. (2003) Bipolar disorders during adolescence. *Acta Psychiatrica Scandinavica*, *418*, 47–50.

Lieberman, J.A., Stroup, T.S., Mcevoy, J.P., *et al.* (2005) Effectiveness of antipsychotic drugs in patients with chronic schizophrenia. *New England Journal of Medicine*, *353*, 1209–1223.

Li, J., McCombs, J.S. & Stimmel, G. (2002) Cost of treating bipolar disorder in the California Medicaid (Medi-Cal) program. *Journal of Affective Disorders*, *71*, 131–139.

Lindhout, D. & Schmidt, D. (1986) In-utero exposure to valproate and neural tube defects. *Lancet*, 14, 1392–1393.

Lloyd, A.J., Harrison, C.L., Ferrier, I.N., *et al.* (2003) The pharmacological treatment of bipolar affective disorder: practice is improving but could still be better. *Journal of Psychopharmacology*, *17*, 230–233.

Lloyd, T., Kennedy, N., Fearon, P., *et al.* (2005) Incidence of bipolar affective disorder in three UK cities: results from the AESOP study. *British Journal of Psychiatry*, *186*, 126–131.

References

Loebel, A.D., Lieberman, J.A., Alvir, J.M., *et al.* (1992) Duration of psychosis and outcome in first-episode schizophrenia. *American Journal of Psychiatry, 149,* 1183–1188.

Lumley, J., Watson, L., *et al.* (2001) Periconceptional supplementation with folate and/or multivitamins for preventing neural tube defects. *Cochrane Database of Systematic Reviews, 3,* CD001056.

Lyon, H.M., Startup, M. & Bentall, R.P. (1999) Social cognition and the manic defense: attributions, selective attention, and self-schema in bipolar affective disorder. *Journal of Abnormal Psychology, 108,* 273–282.

Mackin, P. & Young, A.H. (2004) Rapid cycling bipolar disorder: historical overview and focus on emerging treatments. *Bipolar Disorders, 6,* 523–529.

Mackin, P. & Young, A.H. (2005) Bipolar disorders. In Core Psychiatry (eds P. Wright, J. Stern, M. Phelan). Edinburgh: Elsevier Saunders.

Mackin, P., Watkinson, H.M. & Young, A.H. (2005) Prevalence of obesity, glucose homeostasis disorders and metabolic syndrome in psychiatric patients taking typical or atypical antipsychotic drugs: a cross-sectional study. *Diabetologia, 48,* 215–221.

Macritchie, K. & Young, A.H. (2004) Adverse syndromes associated with lithium. In Adverse Syndromes and Psychiatric Drugs: A Clinical Guide (eds P. Haddad, S. Dursun & B. Deakin). Oxford: Oxford University Press.

Magg, R. (1963) Treatment of manic illness with lithium carbonate. *British Journal of Psychiatry, 109,* 56–65.

Maj, M., Maliano, L., Pirozzi, R., *et al.* (1994) Validity of rapid cycling as a course specifier for bipolar disorder. *American Journal of Psychiatry, 151,* 1015–1019.

Maj, M., Pirozzi, R., Formicola, A.M., *et al.* (1999) Reliability and validity of four alternative definitions of rapid-cycling bipolar disorder. *American Journal of Psychiatry, 156,* 1421–1424.

Malkoff-Schwartz, S., Frank, E., Anderson, B., *et al.* (1998) Stressful life events and social rhythm disruption in the onset of manic and depressive bipolar episodes: a preliminary investigation. *Archives of General Psychiatry, 55,* 702–707.

Malkoff-Schwartz, S., Frank, E., Anderson, B.P., *et al.* (2000) Social rhythm disruption and stressful life events in the onset of bipolar and unipolar episodes. *Psychological Medicine, 30,* 1005–1016.

Manic Depression Fellowship (2001) *Users Survey of Experiences of Health Services.* London: Manic Depression Fellowship.

Manning, J.S., Haykal, R.F., Connor, P.D., *et al.* (1997) On the nature of depressive and anxious states in a family practice setting: the high prevalence of bipolar II and related disorders in a cohort followed longitudinally. *Comprehensive Psychiatry, 38,* 102–108.

Mannion, L., Sloan, D. & Connolly, L. (1997) Rapid tranquillisation: are we getting it right? *Psychiatric Bulletin, 20,* 411–413.

Mantere, O., Suominen, K., Leppamaki, S., *et al.* (2004) The clinical characteristics of DSM-IV bipolar I and II disorders: baseline findings from the Jorvi Bipolar Study (JoBS). *Bipolar Disorders, 6,* 395–405.

Marshall, M. & Lockwood, A. (1998) Assertive community treatment for people with severe mental disorders. *The Cochrane Database of Systematic Reviews*, 2, CD001089.

Marshall, M. & Lockwood, A. (2003) Early Intervention for psychosis. *Cochrane Database of Systematic Reviews*, 2, CD004718.

Marshall, M., Crowther, R., Almaraz-Serrano, A., *et al.* (2001) Systematic reviews of the effectiveness of day care for people with severe mental disorders: (1) acute day hospital versus admission; (2) vocational rehabilitation; (3) day hospital versus outpatient care. *Health Technology Assessment*, 5, 1–75.

Marshall, M., Gray, A., Lockwood, A., *et al.* (2002) Case management for people with severe mental disorders. *Cochrane Database of Systematic Reviews*, 4, CD000050.

Martin, A., Young, C., Leckman, J.F., *et al.* (2004) Age effects on antidepressant-induced manic conversion. *Archives of Pediatrics & Adolescent Medicine*, 158, 773–780.

Martinez, C., Rietbrock, S., Wise, L., *et al.* (2005) Antidepressant treatment and the risk of fatal and non-fatal self harm in first episode depression: nested case-control study. *BMJ*, 330, 389.

Masterton, G., Warner, M. & Roxburgh, B. (1988) Supervising lithium. A comparison of a lithium clinic, psychiatric out-patient clinics, and general practice. *British Journal of Psychiatry*, 152, 535–538.

Matza, L.S., Rajagopalan, K.S., Thompson, C.L., *et al.* (2005) Misdiagnosed patients with bipolar disorder: comorbidities, treatment patterns, and direct treatment costs. *Journal of Clinical Psychiatry*, 66, 1432–1440.

Mbaya, P., Creed, F. & Tomenson, B. (1998) The different uses of day hospitals. *Acta Psychiatrica Scandinavica*, 98, 283–287.

McDonald, C., Bullmore, E.T., Sham, P.C., *et al.* (2004) Association of genetic risks for schizophrenia and bipolar disorder with specific and generic brain structural endophenotypes. *Archives of General Psychiatry*, 61, 974–984.

McElroy, S.L., Altshuler, L.L., Suppes, T., *et al.* (2001) Axis I psychiatric comorbidity and its relationship to historical illness variables in 288 patients with bipolar disorder. *American Journal of Psychiatry*, 158, 420–426.

McElroy, S.L., Frye, M.A., Suppes, T., *et al.* (2002) Correlates of overweight and obesity in 644 patients with bipolar disorder. *Journal of Clinical Psychiatry*, 63, 207–213.

McGorry, P.D., Edwards, J., Mihalopoulos, C., *et al.* (1996) EPPIC: an evolving system of early detection and optimal management. *Schizophrenia Bulletin*, 22, 305–326.

McGorry, P.D., Yung, A.R., Phillips, L.J., *et al.* (2002) Randomized controlled trial of interventions designed to reduce the risk of progression to first-episode psychosis in a clinical sample with subthreshold symptoms. *Archives of General Psychiatry*, 59, 921–928.

McGrew, J.H. & Bond, G.R. (1995) Critical ingredients of assertive community treatment: judgments of the experts. *Journal of Mental Health Administration*, 22, 113–125.

McGrew, J.H., Bond, G.R., Dietzen, L., *et al.* (1994) Measuring the fidelity of implementation of a mental health program model. *Journal of Consulting and Clinical Psychology*, 62, 670–678.

References

McGuffin, P. & Katz, R. (1989) The genetics of depression and manic-depressive disorder. *British Journal of Psychiatry, 155*, 294–304.

McGuffin, P., Rijsdijk, F., Andrew, M., *et al.* (2003) The heritability of bipolar affective disorder and the genetic relationship to unipolar depression. *Archives of General Psychiatry, 60*, 497–502.

McIntyre, R.S., Mancini, D.C. & McCann, S. (2003) Valproate, bipolar disorder and polycystic ovarian syndrome. *Bipolar Disorders, 5*, 28–35.

McQueen, M.B., Devlin, B., Faraone, S.V., *et al.* (2005) Combined analysis from eleven linkage studies of bipolar disorder provides strong evidence of susceptibility loci on chromosomes 6q and 8q. *American Journal of Human Genetics, 77*, 582–595.

Manic Depression Fellowship (2004) Membership survey: 'Making your views count' (part one). *Pendulum: The Journal of the Manic Depression Fellowship, 20*, 12–13.

Mendelson, W.B. (1992) Clinical distinctions between long-acting and short-acting benzodiazepines. *Journal of Clinical Psychiatry, 53*, Suppl 4, 7–9.

Menza, M., Vreeland, B., Minsky, S., *et al.* (2004) Managing atypical antipsychotic-associated weight gain: 12-month data on a multimodal weight control program. *Journal of Clinical Psychiatry, 65*, 471–477.

Merson, S., Tyrer, P., Onyett, S., *et al.* (1992) Early intervention in psychiatric emergencies: a controlled clinical trial. *Lancet, 339*, 1311–1314.

Messenheimer, J., Mullens, E.L., Gorgi, L., *et al.* (1998) Safety review of adult clinical trial experience with lamotrigine. *Drug Safety, 18*, 281–96.

MHRA (2004) *Report of the Committee on Safety of Medicine's Expert Working Group on the Safety of Selective Serotonin Reuptake Inhibitor Antidepressants.* www.mhra.gov.uk

Michaelis, B.H., Goldberg, J.F., Davis, G.P., *et al.* (2004) Dimensions of impulsivity and aggression associated with suicide attempts among bipolar patients: a preliminary study. *Suicide and Life Threatening Behavior, 34*, 172–176.

Mikkonen, K., Vainionpaa, L. & Pakarinen, A.J. (2004) Long-term reproductive endocrine health in young women with epilepsy during puberty. *Neurology, 10*, 445–450.

Miklowitz, D.J., Goldstein, M.J., Nuechterlein, K.H., *et al.* (1988) Family factors and the course of bipolar affective disorder. *Archives of General Psychiatry, 45*, 225–231.

Miklowitz, D.J., Simoneau, T.L., George, E.L., *et al.* (2000) Family-focused treatment of bipolar disorder: 1-year effects of a psychoeducational program in conjunction with pharmacotherapy. *Biological Psychiatry, 48*, 582–592.

Miklowitz, D.J., George, E.L., Richards, J.A., *et al.* (2003) A randomized study of family-focused psychoeducation and pharmacotherapy in the outpatient management of bipolar disorder. *Archives of General Psychiatry, 60*, 904–912.

Miklowitz, D.J., Wisniewski, S.R., Miyahara, S., *et al.* (2005) Perceived criticism from family members as a predictor of the one-year course of bipolar disorder. *Psychiatry Research, 136*, 101–111.

Millar, A., Espie, C.A. & Scott, J. (2004) The sleep of remitted bipolar outpatients: a controlled naturalistic study using actigraphy. *Journal of Affective Disorders, 80*, 145–153.

Mitchell, L. & Romans, S. (2003) Spiritual beliefs in bipolar affective disorder: their relevance for illness management. Journal of Affective Disorders, 75, 247–257.

Mitchell, P.B. & Malhi, G.S. (2004) Bipolar depression: phenomenological overview and clinical characteristics. *Bipolar Disorders, 6,* 530–539.

Moller, H.J. & Grunze, H. (2000) Have some guidelines for the treatment of acute bipolar depression gone too far in the restriction of antidepressants? *European Archives of Psychiatry and Clinical Neuroscience, 250,* 57–68.

Molnar, G., Feeney, M.G. & Fava, G.A. (1988) Duration and symptoms of bipolar prodromes. *American Journal of Psychiatry, 145,* 1576–1578.

Moore, P.B., Shepherd, D.J., Eccleston, D., *et al.* (2001) Cerebral white matter lesions in bipolar affective disorder: relationship to outcome. *British Journal of Psychiatry, 178,* 172–176.

Morriss, R.K. (2003) Problems of initial management. In *Managing Acute Mania* (ed R.K. Morriss). London: Science Press.

Morriss, R. (2004) The early warning symptom intervention for patients with bipolar disorder. *Advances in Psychiatric Treatment, 10,* 18–26.

Morriss, R., Marshall, M. & Harris, A. (2002) Bipolar affective disorder – left out in the cold. *BMJ, 324,* 61–62.

Morriss, R., Scott, J., Paykel, E., *et al.* (2005) The role of mood and other clinical factors on social adjustment based on reported behaviour in recently ill patients with bipolar affective disorder. Submitted.

Morrow, J.L., Russell, A. & Guthrie, E. (2006) Malformation risks of anti-epileptic drugs in pregnancy: a prospective study from the UK Epilepsy and Pregnancy Register. *Journal of Neruosurgery and Psychiatry, 77,* 193–198.

Morselli, P.L. (2000) Present and future role of Mental Illness Advocacy Associations in the management of the mentally ill: realities, needs and hopes at the edge of the third millennium. *Bipolar Disorders, 2,* 294–300.

Morselli, P.L., Elgie, R. & GAMIAN-Europe (2003) GAMIAN-Europe/BEAM survey I: global analysis of a patient questionnaire circulated to 3450 members of 12 European advocacy groups operating in the field of mood disorders. *Bipolar Disorder, 5,* 265–278.

Morselli, P.L., Elgie, R. & Cesana, B.M. (2004) GAMIAN-Europe/BEAM survey II: cross-national analysis of unemployment, family history, treatment satisfaction and impact of the bipolar disorder on lifestyle. *Bipolar Disorders, 6,* 487–497.

Mueser, K.T., Clark, R.E., Haines, M., *et al.* (2001) The Hartford study of supported employment for persons with severe mental illness. *Journal of Consulting and Clinical Psychology, 72,* 479–490.

Muller, B. (2002) Bipolar disorder. *Lancet, 359,* 241–247.

Muller-Oerlinghausen, B., Felber, W. & Berghofer, A. (2005) The impact of lithium long-term medication on suicidal behaviour and mortality of bipolar patients. *Archives of Suicide Research, 9,* 307–319.

Murray, C.J.L. & Lopez, A.D. eds (1996) *The Global Burden of Disease: a Comprehensive Assessment of Mortality and Disability from Diseases, Injuries, and Risk Factors in 1990 and Projected to 2020.* Cambridge, Mass: Harvard School of Public Health on behalf of the World Health Organization and the World Bank.

Mynors-Wallis, L.M., Gath, D.H. & Baker, F. (2000) Randomised controlled trial and cost analysis of problems solving treatment for emotional disorders given by community nurses in primary care. *BMJ, 320,* 26–30.

NCCMH (2002) *Schizophrenia: Core Interventions in The Treatment and Management of Schizophrenia in Primary and Secondary Care.* London: Gaskell and the British Psychological Society.

NCCMH (2005) *Depression: Management of Depression in Primary and Secondary Care.* London: Gaskell & The British Psychological Society.

Nemeroff, C.B. (2000) An ever-increasing pharmacopoeia for the management of patients with bipolar disorder. *Journal of Clinical Psychiatry, 61,* Suppl 13, 19–25.

NEPP (2002) *National Early Psychosis Project.* http://www.earlypsychosis.org

NHS Health Advisory Service (1995) *Child and Adolescent Mental Health Services: Together We Stand: The Commissioning, Role and Management of Child and Adolescent Mental Health Services.* London: HMSO.

NHS Executive (1996) *Clinical Guidelines: Using Clinical Guidelines to Improve Patient Care Within the NHS.* NHS Executive.

NICE (2002) *Schizophrenia: Core Interventions in the Treatment and Management of Schizophrenia in Primary and Secondary Care.* Clinical Guideline No. 1. London: NICE.

NICE (2003) *Guidance on the Use of Electroconvulsive Therapy.* Technology Appraisal, 59. London: NICE.

NICE (2004a) *Depression: Management of Depression in Primary and Secondary Care,* Clinical Guideline No. 23. London: NICE.

NICE (2004b) *Eating Disorders: Core Interventions in the Treatment and Management of Anorexia Nervosa, Bulimia Nervosa and Related Eating Disorders.* Clinical Guideline No. 9. London NICE.

NICE (2004c) Anxiety: Management of Anxiety (Panic Disorder, With or Without Agoraphobia, and Generalised Anxiety Disorder) in Adults in Primary, Secondary and Community Care. Clinical Guideline No. 22. London: NICE.

NICE (2005a) *Post-Traumatic Stress Disorder: The Management of PTSD in Adults and Children in Primary and Secondary Care.* Clinical Guideline No. 26. London: NICE.

NICE (2005b) *Long-Acting Reversible Contraception.* Clinical Guideline No. 30. London: NICE.

NICE (2006) *Guide to the Methods of Technology Appraisal.* London: NICE.

Nierenberg, A.A., Burt, T., Matthews, J., *et al.* (1999) Mania associated with St. John's wort. *Biological Psychiatry, 46,* 1707–1708.

Nolan, P., Murray, E. & Dallender, J. (1999) Practice nurses' perceptions of services for clients with psychological problems in primary care. *International Journal of Nursing Studies, 36,* 97–104.

Nulman, I., Rovet, J., Stewart, D.E., *et al.* (2002) Child development following exposure to tricyclic antidepressants or fluoxetine throughout fetal life: a prospective, controlled study. *American Journal of Psychiatry, 159,* 1889–1895.

O'Brien, M.D. & Gilmour-White, S.K. (2005) Management of epilepsy in women. *Postgraduate Medical Journal, 81,* 278–285.

Office for National Statistics, General Register Office for Scotland & Northern Ireland Statistics and Research Agency (2002) *Death Rates from Suicide: by*

Gender and Age, 1974–2000: Social Trends 32. http://www.statistics.gov.uk/ statbase/ssdataset.asp?vlnk 5 5228&Pos 5 1&ColRank 5 1&Rank 5 192

Ogilvie, A.D., Morant, N. & Goodwin, G.M. (2005) The burden of informal caregivers of people with bipolar disorder. *Bipolar Disorder, 7*, 25–32.

O'Hara, M.W. & Swain, A.M. (1996) Rates and risk of postpartum depression: a meta-analysis. *International Review of Psychiatry, 8*, 37–54.

O'Herlihy, A., Worrall, A., Lelliott, P., *et al.* (2003) Distribution and characteristics of in-patient child and adolescent mental health services in England and Wales. *British Journal of Psychiatry, 183*, 547–551.

Oinonen, K.A. & Mazmanian, D. (2002) To what extent do oral contraceptives influence mood and affect? *Journal of Affective Disorders, 70*, 229–240.

Olié, J.P. & Lévy, E. (2002) Manic episodes: the direct cost of a three-month period following hospitalisation. *European Psychiatry, 17*, 278–286.

Omtzigt, J.G., Nau, H., Los, F.J., *et al.* (1992) The disposition of valproate and its metabolites in the late first trimester and early second trimester of pregnancy in maternal serum, urine, and amniotic fluid: effect of dose, co-medication, and the presence of spina bifida. *European Journal of Clinical Pharmacology, 43*, 381–388.

Osby, U., Brandt, L., Correia, N., *et al.* (2001) Excess mortality in bipolar and unipolar disorder in Sweden. *Archives of General Psychiatry, 58*, 844–850.

Osser, D.N. & Sigadel, R. (2001) Short-term in-patient pharmacotherapy of schizophrenia. *Harvard Review of Psychiatry, 9*, 89–104.

Otto, M.W., Perlman, C.A., Wernicke, R., *et al.* (2004) Posttraumatic stress disorder in patients with bipolar disorder: a review of prevalence, correlates, and treatment strategies. *Bipolar Disorders, 6*, 470–479.

Ozer, S., Ulusahin, A., Batur, S., *et al.* (2002) Outcome measures of interepisode bipolar patients in a Turkish sample. *Social Psychiatry and Psychiatric Epidemiology, 37*, 31–37.

Palmer, A. & Scott, J. (2003) Self-management and the expert patient. In *Mood Disorders: A Handbook of Science and Practice* (ed M. Power). London: Wiley.

Papageorgiou, A., King, M., Janmohamed, A., *et al.* (2002) Advance directives for patients compulsorily admitted to hospital with serious mental illness. Randomised controlled trial. *British Journal of Psychiatry, 181*, 513–519.

Patton, S.W., Misri, S., Corral, M.R., *et al.* (2002) Antipsychotic medication during pregnancy and lactation in women with schizophrenia: evaluating the risk. *Canadian Journal of Psychiatry, 47*, 959–965.

Paykel, E.S., Abbott, R., Morriss, R., *et al.* (2005) Subsyndromal and syndromal symptoms in the longitudinal course of bipolar disorder. *British Journal of Psychiatry*, in press.

Peele, P.B., Scholle, S.H., Kelleher, K.J., *et al.* (1998) Datapoints: costs of employee behavioral health care by diagnosis. *Psychiatric Services, 49*, 1549.

Peele, P.B., Xu, Y. & Kupfer, D.J. (2003) Insurance expenditures on bipolar disorder: clinical and parity implications. *American Journal of Psychiatry, 160*, 1286–1290.

Peet, M. (1994) Induction of mania with selective serotonin re-uptake inhibitors and tricyclic antidepressants. *British Journal of Psychiatry, 164*, 549–550.

Peet, M. & Harvey, N.S. (1991) Lithium maintenance: 1. A standard education programme for patients. *British Journal of Psychiatry, 158,* 197–200.

Perlick, D., Clarkin, J.F., Sirey, J., *et al.* (1999) Burden experienced by care-givers of persons with bipolar affective disorder. *British Journal of Psychiatry, 175,* 56–62.

Perlick, D.A., Hohenstein, J.M., Clarkin, J.F., *et al.* (2005) Use of mental health and primary care services by caregivers of patients with bipolar disorder: a preliminary study. *Bipolar Disorders, 7,* 126–135.

Perris, C. (1966) A study of bipolar (manic-depressive) and unipolar recurrent depressive psychoses. *Acta Psychiatrica Scandinavica, 194,* 9–14.

Perry, A., Tarrier, N., Morriss, R., *et al.* (1999) Randomised controlled trial of efficacy of teaching patients with bipolar disorder to identify early symptoms of relapse and obtain treatment. *BMJ, 318,* 149–153.

Perugi, G., Toni, C., Frare, F., *et al.* (2002) Obsessive-compulsive-bipolar comorbidity: a systematic exploration of clinical features and treatment outcome. *Journal of Clinical Psychiatry, 63,* 1129–1134.

Pierides, M. (1994) Mental health services in Cyprus. *Psychiatric Bulletin, 18,* 427.

Pilowsky, L.S., Ring, H., Shine, P.J., *et al.* (1992) Rapid tranquillisation: a survey of emergency prescribing in a general psychiatric hospital. *British Journal of Psychiatry, 160,* 831–835.

Pini, S., de Queiroz, V., Pagnin, D., *et al.* (2005) Prevalence and burden of bipolar disorders in European countries. *European Neuropsychopharmacology,* 425–434.

Post, R.M., Rubinow, D.R. & Ballenger, J.C. (1986) Conditioning and sensitisation in the longitudinal course of affective illness. *British Journal of Psychiatry, 149,* 191–201.

Post, R., Denicoff, K. & Leverich, G. (2003) Morbidity in 258 bipolar outpatients followed for 1 year with daily prospective ratings on the NIMH life chart method. *Journal of Clinical Psychiatry, 64,* 680–690.

Potash, J.B., Kane, H.S., Chiu, Y.F., *et al.* (2000) Attempted suicide and alcoholism in bipolar disorder: clinical and familial relationships. *American Journal of Psychiatry, 157,* 2048–2050.

Power, P., Elkins, K., Adlard, S., *et al.* (1998) Analysis of the initial treatment phase in first-episode psychosis. *British Journal of Psychiatry,* Suppl 172, 71–76.

Prien, R.F. & Potter, W.Z. (1990) NIMH workshop report on treatment of bipolar disorder. *Psychopharmacology Bulletin, 26,* 409–427.

Quanbeck, C.D., Stone, D.C., Scott, C.L. *et al.* (2004) Clinical and legal correlates of inmates with bipolar disorder at time of criminal arrest. *Journal of Clinical Psychiatry, 65,* 198–203.

Rasgon, N.L. (2004) The relationship between polycystic ovary syndrome and antiepileptic drugs: a review of the evidence. *Journal of Clinical Psychopharmacology, 24,* 322–334.

Rasgon, N.L., Altshuler, L. & Fairbanks, L. (2005) Reproductive function and risk for PCOS in women treated for bipolar disorder. *Bipolar Disorder, 7,* 246–259.

Rea, M.M., Tompson, M.C., Miklowitz, D.J., *et al.* (2003) Family-focused treatment versus individual treatment for bipolar disorder: results of a randomized clinical trial. *Journal of Consulting and Clinical Psychology, 71,* 482–492.

Reilly, J.G., Ayis, S.A., Ferrier, I.N. *et al.* (2000) QTc-interval abnormalities and psychotropic drug therapy in psychiatric patients. *Lancet, 355*, 1048–1052.

Reilly-Harrington, N.A., Alloy, L.B., Fresco, D.M., *et al.* (1999) Cognitive styles and life events interact to predict bipolar and unipolar symptomatology. *Journal of Abnormal Psychology, 108*, 567–578.

Revicki, D.A., Hanlon, J., Martin, S., *et al.* (2005) Patient-based utilities for bipolar disorder-related health states. *Journal of Affective Disorders, 87*, 203–210.

Revicki, D.A. & Wood, M. (1998) Patient-assigned health state utilities for depression-related outcomes: differences by depression severity and antidepressant medications. *Journal of Affective Disorders, 48*, 25–36.

Riemann, D., Voderholzer, U. & Berger, M. (2002) Sleep and sleep-wake manipulations in bipolar depression. *Neuropsychobiology, 45*, Suppl 1, 7–12.

Rihmer, Z., Barsi, J., Arato, M., *et al.* (1990) Suicide in subtypes of primary major depression. *Journal of Affective Disorders, 18*, 221–225.

Rihmer, Z. & Kiss, K. (2002) Bipolar disorders and suicidal behaviour. *Bipolar Disorders, 4*, 21–25.

Robertson, E., Jones, I., Haque, S., *et al.* (2005) Risk of puerperal and non-puerperal recurrence of illness following bipolar affective puerperal (post-partum) psychosis. *British Journal of Psychiatry, 186*, 258–259.

Robinson, L.J. & Ferrier, I.N. (2006) Evolution of cognitive impairment in bipolar disorder: a systematic review of cross-sectional evidence. *Bipolar Disorders, 8*, 103–116.

Royal College of Psychiatrists (1997) *The Association Between Antipsychotic Drugs and Sudden Death. Council Report 57.* London: Royal College of Psychiatrists.

Royal College of Psychiatrists (1998) *Management of Imminent Violence: Clinical Practice Guidelines to Support Mental Health Services. Occasional Paper OP41.* London: Royal College of Psychiatrists.

Runge, C. & Grunze, H. (2004) Annual costs of bipolar disorders in Germany. *Der Nervenarzt, 75*, 896–903.

Russell, S.J. & Browne, J.L. (2005) Staying well with bipolar disorder. *Australia and New Zealand Journal of Psychiatry, 39*, 187–193.

Rybakowski, J.K. & Twanrdowska, K. (1999) The dexamethasone/corticotropin-releasing hormone test in depression in bipolar and unipolar affective illness. *Journal of Psychiatric Research, 33*, 363–370.

Sabers, A., Ohman, I., Christensen, J., *et al.* (2003) Oral contraceptives reduce lamotrigine plasma levels. *Neurology, 61*, 570–571.

Sachs, G.S., Grossman, F., Ghaemi, S.N., *et al.* (2002) Combination of a mood stabilizer with risperidone or haloperidol for treatment of acute mania: a double-blind, placebo-controlled comparison of efficacy and safety. *American Journal of Psychiatry, 159*, 1146–1154.

Sanderson, K., Andrews, G., Corry, J., *et al.* (2003) Reducing the burden of affective disorders: is evidence-based health care affordable? *Journal of Affective Disorders, 77*, 109–125.

Scharer, L.O., Hartweg, V., Hoern, M., *et al.* (2002) Electronic diary for bipolar patients. *Neuropsychobiology, 46*, Suppl 1, 10–12.

Schneck, C.D., Miklowitz, D.J., Calabrese, J., *et al.* (2004) Phenomenology of rapid-cycling bipolar disorder: data from the first 500 participants in the systematic treatment enhancement program. *American Journal of Psychiatry, 161,* 1902–1908.

Schou, M., Juel-Nielsen, N., Stromgren, E., *et al.* (1954) The treatment of manic psychoses by the administration of lithium salts. *Journal of Neurosurgery and Psychiatry, 17,* 250–260.

Schulberg, H.C., Block, M.R., Madonia, M.J., *et al.* (1996) Treating major depression in primary care practice. Eight-month clinical outcomes. *Archives of General Psychiatry, 53,* 913–919.

Scialli, A.R. (2005) *Counseling. Reprotox in a nutshell.* http://www.reprotox.org/Pdfs/632627483150351677.pdf [July 2005].

Sclare, P. & Creed, F. (1990) Life events and the onset of mania. *British Journal of Psychiatry, 156,* 514.

Schmider, J., Lammers, C.H., Gotthardt, U., *et al.* (1995) Combined dexamethasone/corticotropin-releasing hormone test in acute and remitted manic patients, in acute depression, and in normal controls: I. *Biological Psychiatry, 38,* 797–802.

Scott, J., Garland, A. & Moorhead, S. (2001) A pilot study of cognitive therapy in bipolar disorders. *Psychological Medicine, 31,* 459–467.

Scott, J., Paykel, E. & Morriss, R. (2006) Cognitive behaviour therapy for severe and current bipolar disorders: a randomised controlled trial. *British Journal of Psychiatry, 188,* 313–320.

Shapiro, S., Hartz, S.C., Siskind, V., *et al.* (1976) Anticonvulsants and parental epilepsy in the development of birth defects. *Lancet, 1,* 272–275.

Shepherd, G. & Hill, R.G. (1996) Manic depression: do people receive adequate support? *Nursing Times, 92,* 42–44.

Shepherd, G., Murray, A. & Muijen, M. (1994) *Relative Values: The Different Views of Users, Family Carers and Professionals on Services for People with Schizophrenia in the Community.* London: Sainsbury Centre for Mental Health.

Shi, L., Thiebaud, P. & McCombs, J.S. (2004) The impact of unrecognized bipolar disorders for patients treated for depression with antidepressants in the fee-for-services California Medicaid (Medi-Cal) program. *Journal of Affective Disorders, 82,* 373–383.

Simon, G.E. & Unützer, J. (1999) Health care utilization and costs among patients treated for bipolar disorder in an insured population. *Psychiatric Services, 50,* 1303–1308.

Simon, G.E., von Korff, M., Rutter, C., *et al.* (2000) Randomised trial of monitoring, feedback, and management of care by telephone to improve treatment of depression in primary care. *BMJ, 320,* 550–554.

Simon, G.E., Ludman, E., Unutzer, J., *et al.* (2002) Design and implementation of a randomized trial evaluating systematic care for bipolar disorder. *Bipolar Disorders, 4,* 226–236.

Simon, G.E., Ludman, E.J., Unutzer, J., *et al.* (2005) Randomized trial of a population-based care program for people with bipolar disorder. *Psychological Medicine, 35,* 13–24.

Simpson, D. & Anderson, I. (1996) Rapid tranquillisation: a questionnaire survey of practice. *Psychiatric Bulletin, 20,* 149–152.

Slade, M., Rosen, A. & Shankar, R. (1995) Multidisciplinary mental health teams. *International Journal of Social Psychiatry, 41,* 180–189.

Sledge, W.H., Tebes, J., Wolff, N., *et al.* (1996) Day hospital/crisis respite care versus inpatient care, part II: service utilization and costs. *American Journal of Psychiatry, 153,* 1074–1083.

Smith, D.J., Harrison, N., Muir, W., *et al.* (2005) The high prevalence of bipolar spectrum disorders in young adults with recurrent depression: toward an innovative diagnostic framework. *Journal of Affective Disorders, 84,* 167–178.

Smith, J.A. & Tarrier, N. (1992) Prodromal symptoms in manic depressive psychosis. *Social Psychiatry & Psychiatric Epidemiology, 27,* 245–248.

Sokero, T.P., Melartin, T.K., Rytsala, H.J., *et al.* (2003) Suicidal ideation and attempts among psychiatric patients with major depressive disorder. *Journal of Clinical Psychiatry, 64,* 1094–1100.

Spina, E., Pisani, F. & Perucca, E. (1996) Clinically significant pharmacokinetic drug interactions with carbamazepine: an update. *Clinical Pharmacokinetics, 31,* 198–214.

Sproule, B.A., Hardy, B.G. & Shulman, K.I. (2000) Differential pharmacokinetics of lithium in elderly patients. *Drugs and Aging, 16,* 165–177.

Stein, L.I. & Test, M.A. (1980) Alternative to mental hospital treatment. I. Conceptual model, treatment program, and clinical evaluation. *Archives of General Psychiatry, 37,* 392–397.

Stender, M., Bryant-Comstock, L. & Phillips, S. (2002) Medical resource use among patients treated for bipolar disorder: a retrospective, cross-sectional, descriptive analysis. *Clinical Therapeutics, 24,* 1668–1676.

Stokes, P.E., Shamoian, C.A., Stoll, P.M., *et al.* (1971) Efficacy of lithium as acute treatment of manic-depressive illness. *Lancet, 26,* 1319–1325.

Stoll, A.L., Severus, W.E. & Freeman, M.P. (1999) Omega 3 fatty acids in bipolar disorder: a preliminary double-blind, placebo-controlled trial. *Archives of General Psychiatry, 56,* 407–412.

Storosum, J.G., *et al.* (2004) How real are patients in placebo-controlled studies of acute manic episode? *European Neuropsychopharmacology, 14,* 319–323.

Strober, M. & Carlson, G. (1982) Bipolar illness in adolescents with major depression: clinical, genetic, and psychopharmacologic predictors in a three- to four-year prospective follow-up investigation. *Archives of General Psychiatry, 39,* 549–555.

Strudsholm, U., Johannessen, L., Foldager, L., *et al* (2005) Increased risk for pulmonary embolism in patients with bipolar disorder. *Bipolar Disorders, 7,* 77–81.

Su, K.P., Huang, S.Y., Chiu, C.C., *et al.* (2003) Omega-3 fatty acids in major depressive disorder. A preliminary double-blind, placebo-controlled trial. *European Neuropsychopharmacology, 13,* 267–271.

Subramaniam, M., Chong, S. & Pek, E. (2003) Diabetes mellitus and impaired glucose tolerance in patients with schizophrenia. *Canadian Journal of Psychiatry, 48,* 345–347.

Suppes, T., Rush, A.J., Dennehy, E.B., *et al.* (2003) Texas Medication Algorithm Project, phase 3 (TMAP-3): clinical results for patients with a history of mania. *Journal of Clinical Psychiatry*, *64*, 370–382.

Swann, A.C., Dougherty, D.M., Pazzaglia, P.J., *et al.* (2004) Impulsivity: a link between bipolar disorder and substance abuse. *Bipolar Disorders*, *6*, 204–212.

Szadoczky, E., Papp, Z., Vitrai, J., *et al.* (1998) The prevalence of major depressive and bipolar disorders in Hungary. Results from a national epidemiologic survey. *Journal of Affective Disorders*, *50*, 153–162.

ten Have, M., Vollebergh, W., Bijl, R., *et al.* (2002) Bipolar disorder in the general population in the Netherlands (prevalence, consequences and care utilisation): results from the Netherlands Mental Health Survey and Incidence Study (NEMESIS). *Journal of Affective Disorders*, *68*, 203–213.

Thies-Flechtner, K., Muller-Oelinghausen, B. & Seibert, W. (1996) Effect of prophylactic treatment on suicide risk in patients with major affective disorders. Data from a randomized prospective trial. *Pharmacopsychiatry*, *29*, 103–107.

Thompson, J.M., Gallagher, P., Hughes, J.H., *et al.* (2005) Neurocognitive impairment in euthymic patients with bipolar affective disorder. *British Journal of Psychiatry*, *186*, 32–40.

Thompson, K.N., Conus, P.O., Ward, J.L., *et al.* (2003) The initial prodrome to bipolar affective disorder: prospective case studies. *Journal of Affective Disorders*, *77*, 79–85.

Thompson, K.S., Griffith, E.E. & Leaf, P.J. (1990) A historical review of the Madison model of community care. *Hospital and Community Psychiatry*, *41*, 625–634.

Thoren, P., Floras, J.S. & Hoffmann, P. (1990) Endorphins and exercise: physiological mechanisms and clinical implications. *Medical Science, Sports and Exercise*, *22*, 417–428.

Tohen, M., Waternaux, C.M. & Tsuang, M.T. (1990) Outcome in mania. A 4-year prospective follow-up of 75 patients utilizing survival analysis. *Archives of General Psychiatry*, *47*, 1106–1111.

Tohen, M., Shulman, K.I. & Satlin, A. (1994) First-episode mania in late life. *American Journal of Psychiatry*, *151*, 130–132.

Tohen, M., Ketter, T.A., Zarate, C., *et al.* (2003) Olanzapine versus divalproex sodium for the treatment of acute mania and maintenance of remission: a 47-week study. *American Journal of Psychiatry*, *160*, 1263–1271.

Tondo, L., Hennen, J. & Baldessarini, R.J. (2001) Lower suicide risk with long-term lithium treatment in major affective illness: a meta-analysis. *Acta Psychiatrica Scandinavica*, *104*, 136–172.

Tsevat, J., Keck, P.E., Hornung, R.W., *et al.* (2000) Health values of patients with bipolar disorder. *Quality of Life Research*, *9*, 579–586.

Tsuchiya, K.J., Byrne, M. & Mortensen, P.B. (2003) Risk factors in relation to an emergence of bipolar disorder: a systematic review. *Bipolar Disorders*, *5*, 231–242.

Turley, B., Bates, G.W., Edwards, J., *et al.* (1992) MCMI-II personality disorders in recent-onset bipolar disorders. *Journal of Clinical Psychology*, *48*, 320–329.

Tyrer, P., Coid, J., Simmonds, S., *et al.* (2002) *Community mental health teams (CMHTs) for people with severe mental illnesses and disordered personality Cochrane Database of Systematic Reviews*, *2*, CD000270.

van Gent, E.M. & Zwart, F.M. (1991) Psychoeducation of partners of bipolar-manic patients. *Journal of Affective Disorders*, *21*, 15–18.

van Os, J., Takei, N., Castle, D.J., *et al.* (1996) The incidence of mania: time trends in relation to gender and ethnicity. *Social Psychiatry & Psychiatric Epidemiology*, *31*, 129–136.

Vanstraelen, M. & Tyrer, S.P. (1999) Rapid cycling bipolar affective disorder in people with intellectual disability: a systematic review. *Journal of Intellectual Disability Research*, *43*, 349–359.

Vaughn, C.E. & Leff, J.P. (1976) The influence of family and social factors on the course of psychiatric illness. A comparison of schizophrenic and depressed neurotic patients. *British Journal of Psychiatry*, *129*, 125–137.

Viguera, A.C., Nonacs, R., Cohen, L.S., *et al.* (2000) Risk of recurrence of bipolar disorder in pregnant and nonpregnant women after discontinuing lithium maintenance. *American Journal of Psychiatry*, *158*, 1741–1742.

Vinten, J., Adab, N., Kini, U., *et al.* (2005) Neuropsychological effects of exposure to anticonvulsant medication in utero. *Neurology*, *64*, 949–954.

von Korff, M. & Goldberg, D. (2001) Improving outcomes in depression. *BMJ*, *323*, 948–949.

von Korff, M., Katon, W., Bush, T., *et al.* (1998) Treatment costs, cost offset, and cost-effectiveness of collaborative management of depression. *Psychosomatic Medicine*, *60*, 143–149.

Wagner, E.H. (2000) The role of patient care teams in chronic disease management. *BMJ*, *320*, 569–572.

Wagner, E.H., Austin, B.T. & von Korff, M. (1996) Organizing care for patients with chronic illness. *Millbank Quarterly*, *74*, 544.

Ward, E., King, M., Lloyd, M., *et al.* (2000) Randomised controlled trial of non-directive counselling, cognitive-behaviour therapy, and usual general practitioner care for patients with depression. I: clinical effectiveness. *BMJ*, *321*, 1383–1388.

Watson, S., Gallagher, P., Ritchie, J.C., *et al.* (2004) Hypothalamic-pituitary-adrenal axis function in patients with bipolar disorder. *British Journal of Psychiatry*, *184*, 496–502.

Webber, M. & Huxley, P. (2004) Social exclusion and risk of emergency compulsory admission. A case-control study. *Social Psychiatry & Psychiatric Epidemiology*, *39*, 1000–1009.

Wehr, T.A., Sack, D.A. & Rosenthal, N.E. (1987) Sleep reduction as a final common pathway in the genesis of mania. *American Journal of Psychiatry*, *144*, 201–204.

Wehr, T.A., Sack, D.A., Rosenthal, N.E., *et al.* (1988) Rapid cycling affective disorder: contributing factors and treatment responses in 51 patients. *American Journal of Psychiatry*, *145*, 179–184.

Weinstein, N.D. (1982) Unrealistic optimism about susceptibility to health problems. *Journal of Behavioural Medicine*, *5*, 441–460.

Weissman, M.M., Bland, R.C. & Canino, G.J. (1996) Cross-national epidemiology of major depression and bipolar disorder. *Journal of the American Medical Association*, *276*, 293–299.

Weissman, M.M. & Myers, J.K. (1978) Affective disorders in a US urban community: the use of research diagnostic criteria in an epidemiological survey. *Archives of General Psychiatry, 35*, 1304–1311.

Wells, K.B., Sherbourne, C., Schoenbaum, M., *et al.* (2000) Impact of disseminating quality improvement programs for depression in managed primary care: a randomized controlled trial. *Journal of the American Medical Association, 283*, 212–220.

Wendel, J.S., Miklowitz, D.J., Richards, J.A., *et al.* (2000) Expressed emotion and attributions in the relatives of bipolar patients: an analysis of problem-solving interactions. *Journal of Abnormal Psychology, 109*, 792–796.

White, P., Chant, D., Edwards, N., *et al.* (2005) Prevalence of intellectual disability and comorbid mental illness in an Australian community sample. *Australia and New Zealand Journal of Psychiatry, 39*, 395–400.

Wicki, W. & Angst, J. (1991) The Zurich Study X: Hypomania in a 28- to 30-year-old cohort. *European Archives of Psychiatry and Clinical Neuroscience, 240*, 348.

Wiersma, D., Kluiter, H., Nienhuis, F. *et al.* (1989) *Day-treatment with Community Care as an Alternative to Standard Hospitalization: An Experiment in The Netherlands.* Groningen; Netherlands: Department of Social Psychiatry, University of Groningen.

Winters, K.C. & Neale, J.M. (1985) Mania and low self-esteem. *Journal of Abnormal Psychology, 94*, 282–290.

World Health Organization (1992) *The ICD-10 Classification of Mental and Behavioural Disorders: Clinical Descriptions and Diagnostic Guidelines.* Geneva: World Health Organization.

Wyatt, R.J. & Henter, I. (1995) An economic evaluation of manic-depressive illness – 1991. *Social Psychiatry & Psychiatric Epidemiology, 30*, 213–219.

Yan, L.J., Hammen, C., Cohen, A.N., *et al.* (2004) Expressed emotion versus relationship quality variables in the prediction of recurrence in bipolar patients. *Journal of Affective Disorders, 83*, 199–206.

Yanos, P.T., Primavera, L.H. & Knight, E.L. (2001) Consumer-run service participation, recovery of social functioning, and the mediating role of psychological factors. *Psychiatric Services, 52*, 493–500.

Young, R.C. & Klerman, G.L. (1992) Mania in late life: focus on age at onset. *American Journal of Psychiatry, 149*, 867–876.

Zablotsky, B., Ghaemi, S.N., El-Mallakh, R.S., *et al.* (2005) Do antidepressants improve remission in bipolar patients? *Bipolar Disorders, 7*, 114.

Zajecka, J., Weisler, R. & Sachs, G. (2002) A comparison of the efficacy, safety, and tolerability of divalproex sodium and olanzapine in the treatment of bipolar disorder. *Journal of Clinical Psychiatry, 63*, 1148–1155.

Zawadski, J.K. & Dunaif, A. (1992) Diagnostic criteria for polycystic hyperandrogenism ovary syndrome: towards a rational approach. In *Polycystic Ovary Syndrome* (eds A. Dunaif, J.R. Givens, F.P. Haseltine). Oxford: Blackwell Scientific.

14.   ABBREVIATIONS

ACT	assertive community treatment
ADHD	attention deficit hyperactivity disorder
AOT	assertive outreach team
APA	American Psychiatric Association
BAS	Brief Anxiety Scale
BDI	Beck Depression Inventory
BMI	body mass index
BPRS	Brief Psychiatric Rating Scale
BRMS	Bech-Rafaelsen Mania Scale
CAMHS	child and adolescent mental health services
CARS-M	Clinician-Administered Rating Scale for Mania
CAST	computer-assisted cognitive strategy training
CBT	cognitive behavioural therapy
CDRS-R	Children's Depression Rating Scale Revised
CEAC	cost-effectiveness acceptability curves
CI	confidence interval
CINAHL	Cumulative Index to Nursing and Allied Health Literature
CLB	Clubhouse approach of prevocational training
CM	case management
CMHT	community mental health team
CPA	care programme approach
CPN	community psychiatric nurse
CPRS	Comprehensive Psychopathological Rating Scale
CRHTT	crisis resolution and home treatment team
DALY	disability adjusted life year
DLP	Daily Living Programme
DLS	Daily Skills Programme
DSM	Diagnostic and Statistical Manual of Mental Disorders (versions III-R and IV)
DUP	duration of untreated psychosis
ECM	external care management
ECT	electroconvulsive therapy
EIS	early intervention services
EMBASE	Excerpta Medica Database
EPS	extrapyramidal symptoms

GAS	Global Assessment Scale (GAF; Global Assessment of Functioning)
GDG	guideline development group
GP	general practitioner
GRP	guideline review panel
HRSD	Hamilton Rating Scale for Depression
HCHS	hospital and community health services
HoNOS	Health of the Nation Outcome Scale
HPA	hypothalamic pituitary adrenal
HPT	hypothalamic pituitary thyroid
HRQOL	health-related quality of life
HTA	Health Technology Assessment
ICD	International Classification of Diseases (10th edition)
ICER	incremental cost-effectiveness ratio
ICM	Intensive case management
IM	Intramuscular
IPD-SBAS	Individual Patient Data-Social Behaviour Assessment Scale
IPSRT	Interpersonal and social rhythm therapy
ISS	Internal State Scale
K-SADS-PL	Schedule for Affective Disorders and Schizophrenia for School-Age Children – Present and Lifetime Version
LEO	Lambeth Early Onset Service
LOCF	Last observation carried forward
LSP	Life Skills Profile
MADRS	Montgomery Asberg Depression Rating Scale
MCS	mental component summary
MDD	Major depressive disorder
MDF	Manic Depression Fellowship (now known as MDF The BiPolar Organisation)
MEDLINE	Compiled by the US National Library of Medicine and published on the web by Community of Science, MEDLINE is a source of life sciences and biomedical bibliographic information
MHRA	Medicines and Healthcare Products Regulatory Agency
MMR	major malformation rate
MRC	Medical Research Council
MRS	Mania Rating Scale
N	number of participants
NCCMH	National Collaborating Centre for Mental Health

NEPP	National Early Psychosis Project
NHS	National Health Service
NHS EED	National Health Service Economic Evaluation Database
NICE	National Institute for Health and Clinical Excellence
NIMH	National Institute for Mental Health
NNT	number needed to treat (B-benefit; H-harm)
NSF	National Service Framework
OADP	Oregon Adolescent Depression Project
OECD	Organisation for Economic Co-operation and Development
OHE HEED	Office of Health Economics, Health Economics Evaluation Database
OP	Outpatient
OT	Occupational therapist
PANSS (-EC)	Positive and Negative Symptom Scale (-Excited Component)
PCS	physical component summary
PSE	Present State Examination
PsycINFO	An abstract (not full text) database of psychological literature from the 1800s to the present
PTSD	post-traumatic stress disorder
Q-LES-Q	Quality of Life Enjoyment and Satisfaction Questionnaire
QT, QTc	the interval between Q and T waves in the electrocardiogram
RCT	randomised controlled trial
REHAB	Rehabilitation Evaluation Hall and Baker
RR	relative risk
SADS	Schedule for Affective Disorders and Schizophrenia (C-Change Version)
SCID	Structured Clinical Interview for DSM
SCL-D	Symptom Checklist-Depression
SCM	standard case management
SD	standard deviation
SE	standard error
SFQ	Social Functioning Questionnaire
SF-36	Medical Outcomes Study 36-item Short-Form Health Survey
SHO	senior house officer
SMD	standardised mean difference
SMI	severe mental illness
SMR	standardised mortality ratio

SSRI	selective serotonin reuptake inhibitor
STEP-BD	Systematic Treatment Enhancement Program for Bipolar Disorder
SUM (D, M)	Subscales of the Clinical Monitoring Form (D: depression; M: mania)
TAU	treatment as usual
TCA	tricyclic antidepressants
TMS	transmagnetic stimulation
TSSN	training on self-management skills for negative symptoms
VOC	sheltered workshop for prevocational training
WASH-U-KSADS	Washington University in St. Louis Kiddie Schedule for Affective Disorders and Schizophrenia
WLC	Waitlist control
WMD	Weighted mean difference
WTP	willingness to pay
YMRS	Young Mania Rating Scale